THE BO
OF PREF

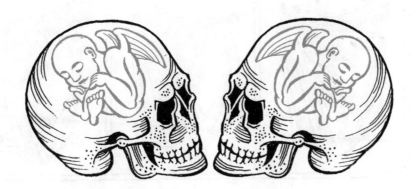

ENGLAND

IRELAND

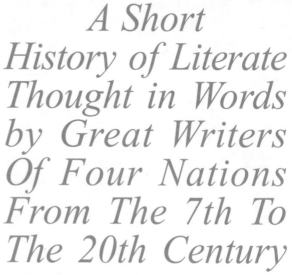

A Short History of Literate Thought in Words by Great Writers Of Four Nations From The 7th To The 20th Century

LONDON AND
NEW YORK 2002

THE BOOK
of
PREFACES

Edited & Glossed
by Alasdair Gray
Mainly
BLOOMSBURY
PUBLISHING

United States

SCOTLAND

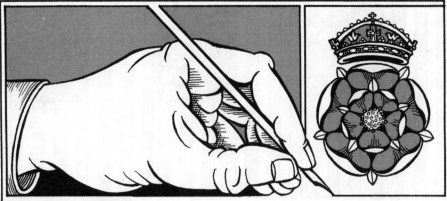

First published in the United Kingdom 2000 by
Bloomsbury Publishing, 38 Soho Square, London W1D 3HB
This paperback edition published in 2002

Set by Joe Murray of EM-DEE Productions, Glasgow

Printed by The Bath Press

A CIP catalogue record for this book is available from
the British Library

International Standard Book Number – 0-7475-5912-0
10 9 8 7 6 5 4 3 2 1

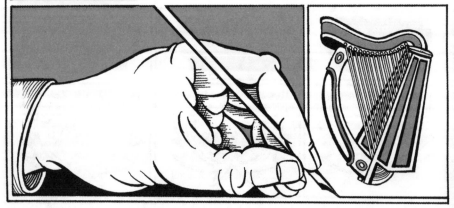

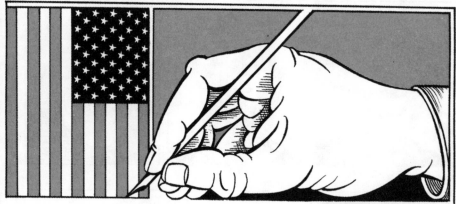

TO
PHILIP
HOBSBAUM
POET, CRITIC AND
SERVANT OF
SERVANTS
OF ART
$^0O^0$

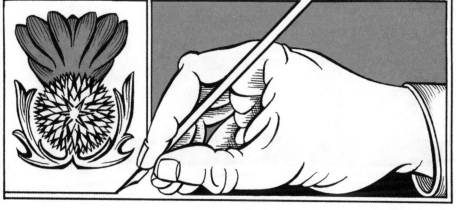

Alasdair Gray:
designer & editor.

Scott Pearson:
researcher & word processor.

Liz Calder:
publisher.

Joe Murray:
typesetter.

William Smellie,
who conceived this book.

Jan Dalton:
typesetter's manager.

Morag McAlpine:
editor's manager.

Julie Cuzin:
typist.

Colin Beattie:
sponsor.

AN EDITOR'S ADVERTISEMENT

Reviews are a kind of childhood illness afflicting more or less all newborn books. Sometimes the healthiest die of them while the weak survive unhurt. Several don't catch them at all. Efforts are often made to render them harmless with the lucky charm of a preface ... this doesn't always work.
– GEORG LICHTENBERG'S APHORISMS

"EVERY PREFACE," SAYS WILLIAM SMELLIE at the start of his preface to *The Philosophy of Natural History* published in Edinburgh in 1790, "Every preface, besides occasional and explanatory remarks, should contain not only the general design of the work, but the motives and circumstances which led the author to write on that particular subject. If this plan had been universally observed, a collection of prefaces would have exhibited a short, but curious and useful history both of literature and authors."

This plan was never universally observed but it has been widely observed. Saint John starts his life of Jesus with a preface on the nature of speech and godhead. Five of Shakespeare's plays have prologues spoken straight to the audience. Few great writers have not placed before one of their books a verbal doorstep to help readers leave the ground they usually walk on and allow them a glimpse of the interior. Prefaces are advertisements and challenges. They usually indicate the kind of reader the book was written to please, the kind of satisfaction it aims to give.

By preface I mean any beginning entitled PREFACE, PROLOGUE, PROHEME, INTRODUCTION, INTRODUCTORY, APOLOGY, DESIGN, FOREWORD or ADVERTISEMENT, and a few opening lines or paragraphs which are not labelled but prepare the reader for the following without being essential to it. I also include some dedicatory epistles that make a political statement (Coverdale to Henry VIII) or give a specimen of the author's style (Sterne to

William Pitt). In a few cases I give more than one preface per author; where one is too short to show an author's genius I add the start of what follows. With prefaces to Biblical translations I give the first verses of Genesis and preface to Saint John's Gospel for comparison. The prefaces are ranged chronologically to display sometimes gradual, sometimes quick changes in English literature since its start in Northumbria. The flow is stopped in 1920 by costs of using work still in copyright. The letter **C** beside the date of a work means *circa* – around that time – the exact date of writing or printing being unknown.

I list four pleasures I hope you find in this book, the nastiest first.

SEEING GREAT WRITERS IN A HUFF

Prefaces to first editions usually try to forestall criticism, those to later editions often counterblast it. Some authors resort to unfair tactics. The conservative monk or nun who wrote *The Cloud of Unknowing*, the sturdy corrupt journalist who wrote *Moll Flanders* are centuries apart, but both hint that their books will be abused or misunderstood by the vicious. The commonest defensive tactic is the lofty intimation, the second commonest is its counterpart, the poor mouth. Both show intelligences uneasy about their social standing – a very British disease. Sir Thomas More says he only publishes to stop enemies misquoting private correspondence. Wordsworth is even loftier: "Readers accustomed to the gaudiness and inane phraseology of many modern writers, if they persist in reading this book to its conclusion, will perhaps frequently have to struggle with feelings of strangeness and awkwardness." He enjoyed constructing that sentence but our amusement is partly at his expense. American writers are better at critic-deflecting irony because they treat readers as equals: see Twain's Notice to *Huckleberry Finn*. For a poor mouth defence see the start of Spenser's *Faerie Queene* and Burns' Dedication to the Caledonian Gentry. Charlotte Brontë's preface to her second novel, *Shirley*, is in a class of its own, making such bitter fun of a snob who reviewed *Jane Eyre* that her genteel publisher would not print it.

THE BIOGRAPHICAL SNIPPET

Some prefaces blend declarations of faith with a personal experience, so we discover Shelley writing and sunbathing on a platform of green turf high among the ruins of the baths of Caracalla, George Bernard Shaw gallantly repelling a London prostitute. Such gossipy details make us feel at home in earlier times: sometimes more at home then than we feel in our own time.

THE PLEASURE OF THE ESSAY

Preface essays vary as greatly as their authors and often report on the state their civilization has reached, sometimes (like Pope and Walt Whitman) with satisfaction, sometimes (like King Alfred and Karl Marx) without. An essayist's remarks, of course, only please when they confirm our settled opinions. As a Scottish socialist who thinks home rule a necessary step toward making a humane democracy I like Shelley's statement in 1820 that "If England were divided into forty republics, each equal in population and extent to Athens . . . under institutions not more perfect than those of Athens, each would produce philosophers and poets equal to those who (if we except Shakspeare) have never been surpassed"; also Mandeville's remark a century earlier that small peaceful, self-supporting states are the best homes of happiness. Those who find such statements comic, unconvincing or irrelevant will find plenty of remarks to support their own prejudices.

THE PLEASURE OF HEARING WRITERS CONVERSE

Many writers use prefaces to say what they love and hate in each other. Thus, Gavin Douglas before his translation of Virgil's *Aeneid* tells why he likes that poem, scorns Caxton for using it as a cheap source of badly told stories, and gently criticizes Chaucer. Thus Shelley, before *Prometheus Unbound*, uses Plato and Bacon (who argued that societies can be improved) against Malthus and Paley (who argued that they cannot). It is refreshing to read how makers find great allies in the past to help them tackle the present. It helps us to see that literature is a conversation across boundaries of nation, century and language.

THE PLEASURE OF HISTORY

Great literature is the most important part of history. We forget this because we are inclined to see great works as worlds of their own rather than phases of the world shared by everyone. No wonder! At first sight the differences in style between Chaucer, Shakespeare,

Dickens and today's newspaper are so great that it is easier to think each describes a separate planet instead of our own world at different times and places. It is very hard to imagine a passage of history in any solidity and fluidity for more than a few years, even when we have lived through it. But we may get some experience of a civilization over several centuries from extracts which let us see, on adjacent pages, language changing from decade to decade in words of authors who usually know they are changing it. The taste, rhythm and meaning of a statement is the taste, rhythm and meaning of life when it was uttered.

But I want this book to be popular as well as scholarly, and here lies a problem. Most of us were taught just one way to spell the words we use, taught that other spellings are wrong or unreadable. To many an original page of Chaucer or Shakespeare therefore seems a gloomy exam they need extra teaching to pass, when the knack of understanding it can be picked up in an afternoon by anyone who thinks of it as an interesting puzzle, a pleasant wordgame. *Storys to rede are delitabill, Suppos that thai be nocht bot fabill* invites us into a great region of our language and history, and with a little thought is as easy to follow as the speech of Nigger Jim in *Huckleberry Finn*. But it takes time to see that, so I aim to seduce the general reader with the five following ploys.

EDITORIAL ESSAYS

English vernacular literature began and flourished with help from the first English rulers but was split into three periods (now called Early, Middle and Modern) by rulers who deliberately rejected it. An essay at the start sketches the history which at last let Caedmon dictate the first written English poem; later essays fill and explain two big gaps. Since Elizabethan times only British drama has been interrupted by government censorship so I have broken the flow of other writing into periods suggested by events that influenced it, prefacing each with a short essay on the event. If the language of an essay seems extra splendid, pompous or glib it may have been taken without acknowledgement from Thomas Carlyle, Thomas Babington Macaulay or an earlier book of my own. This warning also applies to marginal glosses.

TRANSLATIONS

All poetic prologues before 1500 and one after it have a modern version beside them to explain obsolete words. As prose loses less than poetry in translation I have saved space by modernising most prose prefaces before 1530 *without* giving the original.

CUTTING BITS OUT

Some prefaces were too long to print completely and too important to omit; so I shortened them but show where cuts are made by a line of these: *OOOOOOOOOOOOOOOOOOOOOOOOOOOOOOOOOOOOOOOOOOOOOOOOOOOOOOOO*

ROMAN TYPE THROUGHOUT

English was first written by Irish monks who enlarged the Roman alphabet with two letters not now used. The first introductory essay tells how these have been modernized.

MARGINAL GLOSSES

Each preface has notes in small type about its book, author, language and events shaping these. If the small type strains your eyes please use a magnifying glass. It will also help to read telephone directories. I wished – yes, and contracted with my publisher – to write every gloss myself, but could not finish them before the third millennium AD without help from a host of good writers working without pay. Their parts of the book are listed in an index at the end.

William Smellie said authors' prefaces should contain the motives and circumstances which led them to make their books. I leave that explanation to the postscript. Meanwhile, since nobody reads a book like this from start to finish, I advise you to tackle it like a reviewer. Go first to the author and period you like best, then fish for tasty bits in other places. I hope you find them.

GLOSS—*Noun*— a marginal commentary.

GLOSS—*Verb*— to veil in specious language.

TABLE OF

CONTENTS

TABLE OF
in principio

BETWEEN TWO REVOLUTIONS

CONTENTS

THE ESTABLISHMENT

TABLE OF *in principio*

THE DISTURBED ESTABLISHMENT

CONTENTS

LIBERAL ENGLISH

CONTENTS
in principio

ON WHAT LED TO ENGLISH LITERATURE

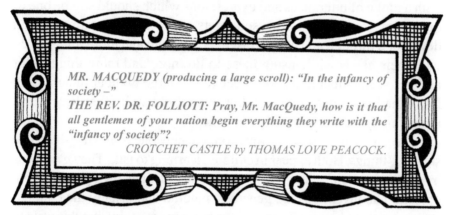

> MR. MACQUEDY (producing a large scroll): "In the infancy of society –"
> THE REV. DR. FOLLIOTT: Pray, Mr. MacQuedy, how is it that all gentlemen of your nation begin everything they write with the "infancy of society"?
> CROTCHET CASTLE by THOMAS LOVE PEACOCK.

BABIES EMBARRASS MASTERFUL MEN who find it queer that once they too could only wail, suck and excrete. When one year old we totter through a bewildering world on unsteady legs while small birds of the same age have already flown, mated, built nests and begun feeding their own children. What unique ability in the following years enables us to handle the world in so many surprising ways? Some say the strength and cleverness to fight in gangs for what we want, even against our own kind. We would have nothing worth fighting for if that was true. Our unique ability is to imagine and make new things through sharing. Conversation, not selfish belligerence, explains us best. It supplies and shapes all our thoughts yet we think little of it because all vocal creatures use it. Birds start singing before dawn to stir each other into briskness for the day ahead, then keep up a quieter texture of noise till sunset, announcing their position and territory with calls which tell when they are congregating toward food or dispersing from a danger. Cats meowl in chorus to declare their separate identities, sexual readiness and united cattishness. For the same reasons our ancestors the tree-rodents must have scolded and chattered a lot.

Though bigger than squirrels they were as alert, inquisitive, and varied in their diet, eating nuts, snails, berries, eggs, carrion, fruit and lice. Conscious choice ("Shall I part my hair behind? Do I dare to eat a peach?") began with this variety of edibles and increased when we came to scramble on the ground. Like pigs we grubbed up roots, like foxes grabbed fresh meat, but we grubbed and grabbed with forepaws, not snouts and teeth. Our comparatively flat faces were free to play with a range of utterances and expressions which should still be one of our great freedoms. Some scientists think the big human brain developed through ape people discovering more and more things to do with their hands while using these to do more and more things. Our ability to remember and choose between a large number of actions at last wiped from our nerves all but one inbred skill other beasts use, replacing the rest by a wholly new one.

The surviving instinct is imitation; the new one is making shareable signs for things. Both appear in children learning to talk. They get words by imitating their elders but invent names of their own for favourite objects. The inventions are generally ignored and usually the children stop using them because imitated words are more useful, but this private gibberish shows intelligence, not folly. At the same age children without dolls take a handy object and treat it as they want to be treated or as they wish to treat others. They make it a sign of life and hold communion with it. By shaping sounds and handling objects, by attaching memories and hopes to them, we learn to converse with ourselves and others. Conversing with ourself is thinking when done consciously, dreaming when not. Conversing with others enlarges both faculties.

In every age and society good conversation is informed by intelligent reading. Roughly a quarter million years ago folk like us began moving through the world, reading appearances of land, water, air with the intelligence of scholars mastering the contents of a profound book. Differences in the call of a bird and shape of a tree hinted at the presence of beasts to be hunted or avoided. Patterns and colours of stars, clouds and herbage foretold good or bad weather, showed when shifting camp was wise or dangerous. A constant need to interpret and explain gave the smallest and most isolated tribes descriptive vocabularies as intricate as those of Greece or Rome, languages as different as the lands they lived upon. From a genesis in Africa such tribes moved to Asia, peopling the Chinese plains so thoroughly later migrants went north and west and south, all living by methods which could change in a lifetime if surroundings changed. Speech and close reading were arts that made every other art possible.

At least once in human history the Arctic ice cap expanded south, changing the weather, sea levels, coastlines, nature of plants and animals. Elephants, rhinoceroses, ground sloths and other vast creatures survived by evolving thick pelts in ways Charles Darwin described. People survived by hunting such creatures, sometimes to extinction, and using their parts for food, covering and utensils. Social adaptation did not wholly replace Darwinian adaptation. People grew fatter and paler in the north, leaner and darker in the south. The unmigratory Chinese evolved extra inches of gut to get more nourishment from their rice. Where food was abundant the average human height became six feet or more. Exhaustion of the food supply or growing too many for it made us dwarfish, or caused warfare and more migration: but for a quarter million years we have kept the same pattern of brain and skeleton by changing our minds, tools, clothes and societies. Our biological conservatism has been prolonged by continual social reform prompted by questions no human brain can avoid or finally answer, questions all children must brood upon as soon as they start thinking.

Who am I? How did I come here?
What should I do? Where am I going?

All ways of life – skills, arts, faiths, traditions, customs, laws, politics, sciences – answer these questions. History is a summary of replies to them. Prehistoric replies have been deduced by seeing how the earliest Egyptian and Greek legends agree with those of folk living prehistorically.
Who am I?
One of YOUR family, YOUR tribe.
How did I come here?
The ground gave birth to the ancestors of you and every creature after a sexual union with the sky. All couplings and births re-enact that union, all seasons of growth repeat that birth.
What should I do?
Support your family and tribe by actions which revive them and the ground and creatures you live upon.
Where am I going?
Into the timeless state of ancestors who talk to us in dreams, traditions and legends.

I have simplified these answers. Some communities, seeing no connection between fucking and birth, thought a female sun, moon and earth had generated everything. Australian aborigines and at least one African nation thought a single father-god made everything single-handed; but male and female communion was the most widespread explanation of origins. Even today highly educated folk believe life was caused by extra-terrestrial radiations inducing fertility in a moist solution of earthly chemicals. And in every age people feel the finality of death is lessened by having children or doing deeds that get them remembered.

Greek and Roman historians thought primitive people happier than themselves, who lived in an age of iron weapons and warfare. Later historians thought the lives of uncivilized folk nasty, brutish and short because, lacking the discipline of strong governments, they must always be fighting each other. Neither view wholly convinces nowadays. In the first ninety-eight per cent of human history – roughly a quarter million years minus the equally rough six thousand when cities got built – the biggest communities were extended families, the biggest governments were elders of tribal federations meeting to settle local disputes or choose a leader in time of war. Wars were short and infrequent since plunder did not produce enough essential food. In very infertile places families lived so far apart that warfare and governments were equally impossible. Fewer were born in that unimaginably long time than in the first quarter of the twentieth century yet they mastered fire, domesticated animals, and by 4000 B.C. had settlements where grain and vines were cultivated. Though too small to be called cities such settlements invented arts making cities possible – fine stonework, carpentry, weaving, pottery and metalwork.

Great corporate achievements like the pyramid of Gizeh and a carriage that took three men to the moon and back seem astonishingly wasteful when compared with the first efficient axe or plough, yet we can sympathize with nineteenth-century scientists who first glimpsed the vast aeons of human existence and dismissed most of them as prehistoric savagery. Modern folk also want simple answers to "How did I come here?" and nobody can try to imagine over two hundred thousand centuries of human life – at least a million generations of nameless folk as intelligent and important as we are – without weariness and despair. It was easier to think them unimportant because they left no writing. Complex vocal signs are the only language small communities need. Only when big ones jostle to produce great properties and class divisions are complex written signs invented.

On a landmass split into three continents by the Mediterranean Sea
many kinds of producer and maker began exchanging goods in markets,
and markets attract thieves as surely as larders attract mice and rats.
Plato thought the first city was created when hunters on horseback invaded
farmlands and made a stronghold from which to regularly plunder them.
This may not have happened everywhere. In Italy farmers protected their
produce in small walled towns, but by 3000 B.C. twenty cities of at least
ten thousand people existed in Asia and north Africa. Though as different
from each other as New York from Beijing or Rome they all stood on
rivers amid a rich geometry of fields. All contained an underclass of
slaves and craftsmen, a ruling class of professional soldiers and clerks, a
king entitled Son of Heaven or Lord of Lords. Reigning dynasties had
been founded by a conquering general whose senior officers usually kept
his offspring in the job because when bosses fight among themselves
underlings grow uncontrollable.

But the extent and stability of these empires also depended on a
caste of writers who were civil service and priesthood. They supervised
the gathering of wheat, barley or rice into stores that were the first
national treasuries and banks: holy places because stored nourishment
was stored life. A measure of grain could nourish a family for a month.
From such a city tracks radiated into wildernesses beyond the power
of the city, tracks that were the first trade routes. They were beaten by
nomads bringing produce, ores and captured enemies to exchange for
grain and other goods. The clergy managed weights, measures, tolls,
taxes and answered essential questions on behalf of everyone.

Who am I?

A servant of this great empire.

How did I come here?

*Your ancestors were created to serve this great empire by heavenly
gods who made the empire while putting heaven and earth in order.*

What should I do?

*Obey the orders of the son of heaven who rules this great empire on
behalf of eternal landlords in the sky.*

Where am I going?

*Into death for the empire, or into children who replace you in the glory
of this great empire.*

Some priests, writers and teachers in British and Japanese empires
gave similar answers until soon after World War II. Rulers who were

called sons of heaven probably believed it. Even Napoleon and Hitler thought themselves elevated by a star or supernatural intuition rather than people who found them useful.

When social grabbing and shoving dominate architecture it builds Babylon, Nineveh, Norman castles, Victorian factories, tower blocks, car parks and shopping centres: structures designed to take in as much as possible at guarded entrances and elsewhere show forbidding surfaces. Many cities have looked better than that. Borges describes how one appeared to a nomad it attracted:

He sees something he has never seen, or has not seen . . . in such plenitude. He sees the day and cypresses and marble. He sees a whole that is complex and yet without disorder; he sees a city, an organism composed of statues, temples, gardens, dwellings, stairways, urns, capitals, of regular and open spaces. None of these artifacts impresses him (I know) as beautiful; they move him as we might be moved today by a complex machine of whose purpose we are ignorant but in whose design we intuit an immortal intelligence.

The intelligence which makes a city attractive is knowledge and craftsmanship working for the good of the majority; in the variety of convenient goods and luxuries which are suggested, made and shared when many people converse. Knowledge dies if not widely shared. Early cities had libraries of law tables, religious and medical treatises, historical and astronomical records, maps, poems, stories and tax registers: all destroyed when the small class who could write and read was defeated by conquerors of a different speech. The Aryans who plundered the earliest Indian civilizations and destroyed their writings existed without writing for a thousand years. The literatures of ancient Babylon, Crete, Carthage and Etruria now exist as a few indecipherable inscriptions. Lengthy Egyptian and Assyrian texts survive but for fifteen centuries nobody could read them. Only China was so densely peopled, had such tightly organized communities, that every conqueror before the Euro-American invasion of 1839 could only govern it by learning the speech and writing of the conquered – which made them Chinese.

Not all learning in the shattered city libraries was lost. Every phonetic alphabet the world uses was adapted from the scripts of Sumeria, Assyria and Egypt by travellers and seafarers who had learnt to read lists and contracts by trading there. These mobile people also wrote agreements which are the best human laws, undiscussable dictates which are the worst, songs and epics about heroes and prophets who had made their nations. These writings became so widespread that city libraries were not needed to preserve them. Literate folk heard the dead talk to them through books and sometimes talked back. The words of Isaiah and Jesus were put beside those of Moses, the words of Aristophanes and Plato beside Homer, so later readers heard their ancestors converse across centuries. National literatures also began conversing. Oriental Buddhism happened when some Indian texts reached scholars in China, inspiring them with hunger for more. Before the nineteenth century barriers of desert and perplexingly different script stopped Indian and Chinese literature informing European readers, but intercourse between, intercourse *with* Hebrew, Greek and Roman writings changed people's thinking in every European land, then every other civilization.

Scholars once thought the oldest Jewish and Greek books had been written around 1200 B.C., soon after the exodus from Egypt and Trojan war they describe. Modern scholars think they were edited into their present form between 600 and 500 B.C., though chanted, sung and partly written in earlier times. I will discuss the writings of these peoples separately under the headings of their most famous cities, mentioning books that inspired English writing.

JERUSALEM

The Hebrew bible is a collection of legends, law-codes, histories, hymns, novellas, political diatribes, prophecies and proverbs unified by the earliest accounts of the most influential character in literature – the one and only invisible God. It says he made mankind out of clay, like a potter, but a century or two before Christ was born editors prefaced these books with a poem saying he made the whole universe like a poet, out of words –

Then God said *let there be light* **and there was LIGHT.**
No other folk have given such authority to speech reflected in writing. Others also thought important knowledge came from the spirit world through the mouths of priests and witch-doctors. The Jews preserved these messages through centuries, so it is possible to read God's words changing as his chosen people grow from a family of Bedouin shepherds into a nation among other nations. In two comic chapters of Genesis the only God connives with a cunning trader who tricks foreigners out of wealth by pretending his wife is his sister. When the Israelites escape

from Egypt God talks to them like a Pharaoh making a treaty with a weak neighbour, promising unlimited protection in return for unlimited obedience. When helping them conquer Palestine he orders the killing of helpless women, children and cattle, smiting the invaders with plague when they disobey. Later he refrains from destroying the city of the Jews' greatest enemy because "it contains a multitude of people, above a hundred thousand who know not their right hand from their left, and also much cattle". When the Jews get Palestinian kingdoms with Jerusalem as their holy city he becomes the voice of social justice, saying that worshipping him will not save them from foreign enemies if greedy kings and rich men take land from the poor. This voice lets nobody rest in the simple formula that God rewards virtue with worldly success. When the Persian empire does destroy Jerusalem and scatter the Jewish people the prophet Isaiah praises God for it – says that only when his people learn through misery to obey him in justice, mercy and humility will God send a Messiah to restore Israel. And throughout these writings, even among the queerest tales in Genesis, are statements that the Jews must keep God's words alive for the good of people everywhere. The prophet Micah says the Messiah will bring peace to the world by bringing all people to follow God's word. After Solomon's temple was destroyed in 586 B.C. an orthodox Jew would have answered the big questions thus.

Who am I?

A man made in God's image, and a Jew.

How did I come here?

God made all people wanderers when he drove them out of Eden for disobedience; made a pact with your own ancestors when he gave them the Ten Commandments while leading them out of Egypt; gave them the promised land of Palestine and Holy City of Jerusalem, sent them again into exile: perhaps because they broke the pact by further disobedience: perhaps for reasons we do not yet know.

What should I do?

Trust God whatever happens. Obey the Ten Commandments and other laws in the Holy Books; maintain and educate a family that keeps God's Word alive among nations who do not know it.

Where am I going?

Only God knows, but if your descendants keep God's Word he will one day restore them to Jerusalem.

By this faith Jews survived conquest and dispersal by Babylon, Persia, Greece, Egypt and later empires until Ibsen called Jews the aristocracy of nations because (he said) they needed no homeland or government. This was not quite true. Their homeland and government were their scriptures. Devotion to these gave them more cohesion, education and intelligence than can exist in nations whose governments discourage education because they want obedient underlings, not ones who think for themselves.

ATHENS

The tiny settlements of the earliest Greeks resembled those of the Vikings in their oared sailing ships and piratical war codes. They grew into city-states on so many Mediterranean islands, coasts and narrow valleys that not even Alexander's empire could bring them under one government. Though often at war with each other all spoke the language of the *Iliad* and *Odyssey*; Homer united them more than any political federation because his epic poems showed folk like themselves fighting, scheming, slaughtering cattle, pruning hedges, laundering sheets and arguing strongly with their kings and immortal gods. Their many kinds of government (landed aristocracies, military castes, popular dictatorships, electoral democracies) were small enough to be influenced by single voices, so discussion ruled them as much as force. This, plus curiosity about other people, gave the Greeks astonishing intellectual freedom. Socrates (for example) paid tribute to the several gods of his state, sometimes spoke of one God who was superior to all, obeyed the small god or daemon of his own intuition, and while insisting on his ignorance questioned the reasons given for everything.

Hebrew literature shows one great idea adapting to many ages and places. Greek literature shows a multitude of ideas, equally valid but often in conflict. These produce the tragedy and comedy of Greek drama, the fair-mindedness of history books which explain their enemies' viewpoint, the balance of Plato's dialogues and scope of Aristotle's lectures. If an educated Athenian of 400 B.C. had questioned himself, one who could vote because he was neither slave, woman nor descended from immigrants, he might have said this.

Who am I?

A Greek who talks the language of Homer; a citizen of the world's foremost democracy.

How did I come here?

Ancient stories say different things: that the one and only First Mother was made pregnant by the wind her dancing raised, or that chaos and darkness laid an egg from which earth and immortal gods were hatched. The first gods were Titans and giants, a crude lot conquered by the family of Zeus, the gods of our cities. Yet a Titan called Prometheus is supposed to have made the first people from clay and water then given them fire, which hitherto only gods had enjoyed. Aeschylus describes Prometheus as a sort of revolutionary hero. Democritus, a great joker, explained everything by the atomic hypothesis. He said chaos was a flux of atoms so unstable that they combined in every possible way until a time HAD to come (for time is endless) when they formed our universe. That means the supreme God is chance – fate – destiny. City folk have always suspected that; only farmers think each year can be made to repeat the last. Anaxagoras tried to get rid of fate by saying mind was a natural property of atoms – that they united into plants and animals as inevitably we unite in tribes and cities. He even said freak births were nature's way of making new species. For that we condemned him to death as an atheist. Reason is one of the gods' greatest gifts but nothing should be overdone.

What should I do?

Not like Diogenes! He says men are no better than dogs and proves it by living in a barrel, feeding on scraps and cursing all political systems. I live as happily as I can. That needs health and wealth so I bathe and exercise often in the public gymnasium, eat and drink well (though never too much) and mind my business. But no business can prosper if the state does not, so I attend parliament, listen closely to debates and vote on major issues. If the majority vote for war and the rota orders men of my constituency oversea I collect weapons and rations and am ready to embark in an hour, even though I voted for peace. Athens will only stay richer than envious rivals if Athenians act together, however much we argue before casting our votes. Luckily the few and the many, the snobs and the proles know that as well as I do.

Where am I going?

The soul may be immortal but whoever heard of a happy ghost? My funeral rites should gain me eternal rest, even if I do die in battle. I can't foretell the future of my city. No state like the Athenian democracy has existed before; that's why Pericles called us schoolmasters of the world. Pessimists say that, compared with Egypt and Sparta, we're too changeable to last. But the steady Egyptians and Spartans lead miserable lives! The first are obsessed with dying, the second with killing. Half the wealth of Egypt is put into tombs and Spartan boys are taught that death in battle is better than retreat. We Athenians are more flexible, yet we beat Spartans as often as they beat us. If chance IS the supreme god then Athens, like Troy, will be conquered one day but we will leave as famous a name. What better can any nation do?

Athens was conquered by the Macedonians in 338 B.C. and fifty years later the east Mediterranean was ruled by descendants of Alexander's generals. The Greek language grew so widespread that a group of rabbis translated the Hebrew scriptures into Greek so that Grecian Jews could read them. This made easy the later addition of Christian gospels, also written in Jewish-Greek dialect, but most Greek and Jewish scholars shared cities as foxes and hedgehogs share forests. Greeks snapped up useful ideas anywhere. Jews cultivated a carefully protected tradition. Greeks saw life as a possibly tragic struggle with the political present. Jews saw it as a stage in a hard journey from a better but remote past to a better, maybe equally remote future. Only the furnace of imperial Rome forged such different wisdoms together, making something new.

ROME

Rome began as a small republic of belligerent farmers. Rich landowners managed the senate and officered the army while allowing plebeians just enough representation to give the state unity in a crisis. The crisis lasted until Rome led a federation of Italian towns that conquered every coast round the Mediterranean. Nations east of Italy were accustomed to imperial rule and here the Roman army taxed and took tolls by policing towns, roads and shipping lanes. In western Europe roads and towns hardly existed so the army built them. It could only prevail in territories that became sources of revenue so commanders made permanent bases on boggy streams which at first sight did not look like trade routes. That is how Paris and London were founded. The Celts of France, Spain and Britain probably viewed Roman incomers like native Americans viewing the first Europeans. They could not be defeated in fight but there was room to avoid them: until native plantations and hunting grounds were inside a network of roads linking fortresses and garrison towns. Then garrison commanders offered local tribes the benefits of Roman rule in return for regular supplies of local produce, and ordered local chieftains to supply labour to repair roads and dig mines, and enclosed fertile ground to make estates for Roman officials. Tribes who resisted were conquered and men, women, children sold through slave markets on the Mediterranean coast: thus resistance was also turned into revenue.

The Romans extended and adminstered their empire by writing laws and reports in clear, curt, pithy Latin, but those who needed ideas along with big estates stocked their libraries with Greek literature because for centuries great poetry and philosophy were as beyond Latin authors as the art of making bronze statues was beyond Roman craftsmen. As the republic ended in conspiracies and civil war the best account of Mediterranean civilization was still Homer's, the best thing Rome had done was preserve and propagate the work of the Greeks. Educated Romans knew this.

Twenty-seven years before Christ was born Caesar Augustus became first Roman emperor with the help of Maecenas, a Roman banker. After defeating his civil-war rivals Augustus (I quote the *Oxford Classical Dictionary*) "assured freedom of trade and wealth to the upper classes", and, "gave peace, as long as it was consistent with the interests of the empire and the myth of his glory". As smart a publicist as Louis XIV or Napoleon, he wanted writers to glorify his empire too, but the most popular was Ovid who described the love affairs of men and gods, sometimes from a comic standpoint. Augustus banished him to Russia after finding a Roman poet who, like the Greek Hesiod, had made verse about peaceful farming. Encouraged and funded by the most powerful men in the new empire Virgil, who hated war, wrote an epic to rival Homer and justify Rome's conquests.

Like all deep thinkers on human history Virgil was more disturbed by the sufferings of the defeated than dazzled by splendid winners. He did not describe the empire growing from a small thatch-roofed republic to a marble-surfaced, world-bullying capital. His story describes the struggles of a Trojan refugee, Aeneas, who escapes from Troy while the Greeks loot and burn it. Aeneas leads his son and a few survivors round several Mediterranean coasts, suffering hardship and abandoning the woman he loves before reaching Italy and fighting to found the state which will become Rome. Homer's heroes are moved by greed for fame, sex and wealth. Virgil's Aeneas is modest, careful, steady and guided like Moses by one idea: to get a home for his people. During that struggle the gods encourage him with a vision of the future when his greatest descendant, Caesar Augustus, will make a peaceful home for all mankind by becoming emperor of Europe, Asia and Africa. Virgil died before completing this epic and after ordering his secretaries to burn it. He has been called a perfectionist who did not want to be remembered by something incomplete. The obvious reason is his loss of faith in conquest, in Caesarism. Caesar Augustus preserved and published the *Aeneid* because it answered four questions exactly as he wished.

Who am I?

A citizen of the world's greatest empire.

How did I come here?

Through efforts of heroic ancestors who made this empire by conquest of Europe, Africa, Asia.

What should I do?

Be brave, steady, patient. Despise death while defending Roman law and empire. Let others sing sweeter songs and make more beautiful statues – your business is war and taxation, which preserve civilized order and peace.

Where am I going?

To a contented death if you have taught your children to preserve and inherit Roman order.

These answers could inspire folk who prospered with Rome but not slaves, women and Jews. Slaves were defined as property by Roman law, so it was no crime for owners to kill them and Roman games made their torture and massacre a spectator sport. This was supposed to strengthen the state by teaching children not to fear death. Motherhood was violated by a law saying children were also property. Masterful men who only wanted one or two heirs had unwanted babies, mostly girls, left in public places to die or be picked up by anybody with a use for one. The babies of slaves were valued even less. While wars filled the slave market with male and female adults it was cheaper to buy one than pay to have it reared from infancy. Slaves and women were practically powerless but the Jews had their homeland again under the rule of King Herod. He had rebuilt Solomon's temple so thought himself the Messiah foretold by the prophets. Most of his subjects disagreed. He kept killing those he suspected of plotting against him, including wife and son. The land was policed by a Roman army since Herod was a client of Augustus Caesar, who the Roman senate had proclaimed a god. This, with human blood sport and infanticide, broke most of the Ten Commandments. It made the Roman Empire an open blasphemy for Jews who wanted a true Messiah. Many orthodox families who bore a son – many an intelligent son hearing the scriptures recited – must have wondered if he was the chosen redeemer and shudderingly prayed he was not. Jews often regarded God as small children regard an alarming father. One of the Psalms attributed to David begs God to stop tormenting his people with terrible commands.

CHRISTIANITY

Soon after A.D. 50 Latin writers reported that a Jewish religion had spread like a plague even to Rome, moving lowly folk to abandon their ancestral gods, split with their families and undermine the State. They held love-feasts (it was claimed) where they drank blood and enjoyed promiscuous sex. What made them dangerous were their answers to the big questions, and success in teaching them to others.

Who am I?

A Christian made in God's image, as all people are.

How did I come here?

From God, who made the world and everyone in it because he loves them, and from Adam and Eve who brought sin and suffering into the world because they disobeyed him.

What should I do?

Believe first the word of God which he gave through Moses and the prophets of Israel: obey the Ten Commandments, love God with all your heart and mind and soul, and your neighbour as yourself. Believe also Jesus who is God's word made flesh and was killed by Roman law and rose from the dead because God's word is stronger than death. Jesus says: Forgive those who sin against you and God will forgive your sins. Bless them who curse you, love those who hate you, don't resist evil. If you have wealth, give it to the poor. By helping others you increase Christ's kingdom; by hurting others (children especially) you injure him.

Where am I going?

To the kingdom of heaven where Christ will bring all who believe and obey him, for he will return on the last day to judge mankind when the dead are resurrected.

The first Christian priests were folk who had heard of Jesus and were spreading news of his life and teaching. The earliest services were a sharing of bread and wine in memory of his last supper. All we now know of him is in four short Greek Gospels written or edited into their present state about fifty years after his crucifixion. They do not perfectly agree. In one he says Those who are not against us are for us, in another, Those who are not for us are against us. At least two accounts of his resurrection contradict each other. His terrible last words on the cross, **My God my God why have you forsaken me?** show the totally defeated that he was one of them, but have led some to doubt that he made the universe. But the Gospels agree in showing one who preached a wholly selfless life in words from Hebrew scripture, whose deeds were based on its prophecies, who angered established teachers, priests and rulers by the size of his following.

Nobody doubted that Christianity was a Jewish faith before A.D. 70 when a Judean rising against Rome was bloodily crushed, Jerusalem and Solomon's temple destroyed yet again. A majority of Christians now lived outside Judea. To help them evade anti-semitic law an addition was made to the Gospels. It said Pontius Pilate, governor of Judea, asked a Jewish mob for permission to release Christ in accordance with a Jewish custom of pardoning a criminal on the feast of the Passover, and the mob got Christ crucified by demanding the release of a robber instead. But Jews never celebrated Godly festivals by releasing folk who had broken the Ten Commandments, nor did Roman governors consult local mobs as if they were juries. Shifting blame for Christ's death from Roman rule to Jewish crowd made Christians and Jews obnoxious to each other. It also made Christianity more agreeable to Roman rulers. When Caesar Constantine moved the seat of imperial government from Rome to Constantinople in A.D. 331 the new capital was dedicated to the Virgin Mary. Christianity was the official imperial religion. Christian bigots then destroyed their neighbours' synagogues and temples, sometimes urged to it by bishops quarrelling with each other about the nature of the God who had told them to love their enemies. But infanticide was reduced, gladiatorial games banned, and in churches the owners and slaves received communion as equals.

Nietzsche thought Christianity the invention of cunning slaves who made a virtue of being poor and powerless. Gibbon, seeing the power of imperial rule weaken as the churches multiplied, blamed Christianity for its decline and fall. But the fall of the Roman Empire has been exaggerated. Christianity and foreign invasion changed it into the several states that became modern Europe. If civilizations live by language, knowledge and art then Jerusalem, Athens and Rome are living still. In east Europe the empire belonged to those who ruled and worshipped God in Greek, in the west the main language was Latin. The great early Christian authors (Saints Paul, Jerome and Augustine) worked in Palestine and north Africa where Greek, Latin and Hebrew mingled. Paul's letters show how scattered congregations were drawn into one church. Jerome, using Latin, turned Hebrew and Greek scripture into one Bible. Augustine's *City of God* revived a Hebrew legend that the rabbis who edited Genesis had omitted. It said that in a previous universe God had been served by lesser gods who rebelled against him so were sent to hell. God then made humanity to take their place in heaven, with the world where the loyalty of each would first be tested. He let the devils in hell become the false gods of the pagans. From this origin Augustine used the Bible, Greek philosophy and Roman history to show humanity as two vast processions marching through the ages, one led heavenward by the church, one hellward without. Maybe Christ's answers to the main questions did not need this elaboration, but it was used to propagate them. For at least seventeen centuries Christians fought over church government and points of doctrine, but men of every Christian sect accepted Augustine's overall framework. It gave them dignity.

Women were less well served. Hebrew *and* Greek traditions described male gods making men in their own image, with women as afterthoughts who brought evil into the world. Only Greek Sappho left lasting songs about the joy and sorrow of womanly love. Only Euripides wrote tragedy about the oppression of women by glory-seeking warriors. Official Christianity condemned warlike fame but still deprived women of respect. It said God's Word had refused to become flesh in the dirty vessel of a naturally pleased womb, so women without the priestlike strength to love God alone should submit to breeding Christians in a posture of stoical passivity. Between Aristophanes' *Lysistrata* and Chaucer's *Wife of Bath* very few women with freedom of choice appear in literature. All are saints or harlots.

In the fourth century A.D. the Chinese empire expanded beyond its Great Wall, displacing fierce nomads who invaded Europe from the north. The Greek part of the empire held firm and advised the western provinces to start ruling and defending themselves, but years of dependence had made them incapable. The new conquerors had no central government or monetary economy. From a chaos of warrior landlords grew feudal Europe: a collection of states ruled by knights, dukes, counts and kings, whose wealth was the men they commanded. The millennium between A.D. 400 and 1400 was once called **The Dark Ages** as if a foggy valley separated the sunny heights of pagan Rome from the bright slopes of Renaissance Italy; but these ages seemed as bright as ours to most who dwelled in them. There is continuous information about every province Rome lost except Britain because elsewhere Christian priests remained active where the legions retreated. The strength of literate thought, or God's word, or both, is shown in how fast belligerent invaders got christened. Chieftains who had worshipped Thor and Wodin in the German forests conquered Paris and Toledo, Arles and Ravenna, yet their children became kings who adored the relics of martyrs, discussed the Holy Trinity with archbishops and gave monastic lands to abbots. The new military rulers did not know how to read, write or talk easily in the language of the natives. The Christian church was an organization that helped them with all these things. The church had bishops and priests in every town and most settlements. Monasteries became almost the only homes of literature. The few kings who tried ruling in spite of the church were soon replaced by better Christians everywhere, except Britain.

BRITAIN

In Virgil's first pastoral poem a small farmer robbed of his land by the government laments that he and those like him must now disperse:

To Scythia, bone-dry Africa, the chalky spate of the Oxus,
Even to Britain, that place cut off at the very world's end.

Britain is now the home of nearly fifty-six million people (56,000,000!) over nine-tenths of them in dense urban clusters. Of the remaining land nearly half is very fertile and supports mixtures of arable and cattle farming. The rest is mountain, hill, moorland and downs where very few folk live because it is used for sheep farms, military projects, cheap forestry and the sports of the wealthy. When Julius Caesar invaded Britain it housed less than a million who dwelt mainly in high valleys, bays and islands round the coast and on moorlands and downs where the prehistoric stone monuments and earth-works stand. Land now occupied by our cities and agriculture was mostly swampy forest because good soil near slow wide rivers can only be cultivated when banks are made firm and the ground drained. Outside the uplands farming had to be in clearings. The legions subdued Britain up to Pictland, though their hold on Wales and the north was slight and they did not touch Ireland. They built towns supported by villa farming and linked by roads piercing the deciduous jungle. General Constantine was opposing the Picts in A.D. 306 when his father died and the troops proclaimed him Caesar. It was he who, without being christened, made Christianity the imperial religion and moved the capital east from Rome to Constantinople. Two and a half centuries later a historian and diplomat there wrote a geography book saying an area of Britain is under so thick a layer of snakes that none can stand there, some air so poisonous none can breathe it. He said Britain was a home of the dead because boatmen on the French coast ferried ghosts by night across the narrow channel to the British shore. Like the planet Mars in the early twentieth century, Britain had become a place of which anything could be imagined. The English had come.

THE ENGLISH

The press of populations westward had moved Danish and German tribes across the sea in ships. Their skill in woodcraft is proved by those ships, in metalwork by their weapons. In Roman Britain they found woodlands like those they had left. Though gladly grabbing the lands of Roman villas they shunned towns, identifying these with slavery. Many little quarrelsome kingdoms were founded, six with the names and territories of modern English counties.

The completeness of their conquest is astonishing. The Britons these English drove into Cornwall and Wales, Galloway and Strathclyde were descendants of a race that had built Stonehenge and stoutly resisted Rome. The whites who conquered the American red folk let rivers, towns, counties, whole states in the U.S.A. keep Indian names. But in England hardly a Celtic name survives. In A.D. 314 British bishops attended a synod of the Roman church in France. By the end of the next century all England was pagan and even days were named after Norse gods. The North Sea became a German sea with German tribes and kingdoms on its coasts from Norway down to France in the east, from Kent up to Edinburgh in the west. But the Germans in mainland Europe were being informed by the language and faith of those they conquered. In the land of the English Roman and Christian thought vanished as completely as the art of building with stone and brick.

But though the North sea had become a German Mediterranean, the Irish sea was still Celtic with kingdoms of Ireland on its west shores, Scottish islands and peninsula to the north, Strathclyde, Cumbria, Wales and Cornwall on the east and south. The vitality of Christianity is proved by how it throve among Gaels who neither Romans nor English had conquered. Monasteries were founded where monks copied Jerome's Bible and other Latin classics while writing chronicles and poems in Gaelic as well as Latin. For two or three centuries before the Viking invasions this Celtic Mediterranean was safe for scholarship. The cathedral island of Iona became its spiritual capital. Two seas and stormy new pagan kingdoms separated this Celtic church from the Roman one, which had little time for peaceful scholarship. Islam was taking Africa and Spain away from it; and in north Europe the priesthood helping to civilize the fierce Gothic monarchies was for a while semi-barbarized by them. The bishop of Rome and heads of the Greek church in Constantinople disagreed about the Holy Trinity. It is no wonder that Irish–Scottish clergy got a high reputation round the old Mediterranean. They founded monasteries in Burgundy and Switzerland. Their Christian scholarship from the far side of a pagan wilderness encouraged the idea of Britain as a dank dangerous forested place lit by supernatural gleams. The English inhabitants also had this view of life when they learned to write it. Reader, after another four paragraphs and a prayer you will reach the start of this anthology.

In the seventh century Northumbria became the biggest and most stable English kingdom, holding back Picts north of the Forth and Mercians south of the Humber, while driving the Welsh of Cumbria further into the west: yet in less than fifty years it was Christianized by monks from Iona. At Jarrow, Wearmouth and the Holy Isle of Lindisfarne they and their pupils made gospel books in a style sometimes called Hiberno–Saxon, meaning Irish–English. The initials of words were surrounded or filled with richly interwoven Celtic scrolls and spirals, skilfully inlaid with gold and the jewelled colours the Anglo-Saxons used in their finest metal ornaments. Remember a piece of music, or a building, or machine, or anything which gave you delight along with astonishment that people could make it. Pages of the book of Kells and the Lindisfarne gospel are as good as that. Until the ninth century such books, with church ornaments of metal and ivory, were Britain's only notable export – the continental clergy wanted them. And at Whitby in a monastery with a Gaelic name (Streaneshalch) the new Christian learning stirred two very different people into making the first English literature.

Hilda's uncle Edwin was a pagan king whose conquest of Gaelic Dun Eiden turned it into Saxon Edinburgh. He got baptized five years before he died and Hilda, then thirteen, was baptized with him. She became an abbess and saint after ruling the double monastery for nuns and monks at Whitby. It was there she heard that a local herdsman wanted to be a poet though he had not composed anything. An angel in a dream had ordered him to sing about "the beginning of things", but he knew too little to start. Hilda tested the man's talent by getting priests to tell him the Christian creation story and to write down what he made of it. His verses were good. He never learned to write but was enrolled in the monastery where he dictated more poems.

Any talent which gives a good new thing to others is a miracle, but commentators have thought it extra miraculous that England's first known poet was an illiterate herd. They forgot three things.

ONE

Poetry is a kind of speech, not a kind of writing. For over half a million years poets learned to make it by hearing it sung or recited, then by repeating it with the changes and additions they preferred. In a very few places, three or four thousand years ago, writing approached poetry as a humble secretary, able to record an especially good poem so that later folk could not change or lose it. The vulgar notion that a poet must be a writer arrived when a lot of wealthy literate folk decided nothing good could be made without the help of their expensive educations, except by a miracle. In Hilda's day even emperors could not write. Nobody expected it of a poet.

TWO

After hearing and repeating poems until the rhythms and the vocabularies are in their nerves, poets need long uninterrupted spells of talking to themselves. Herding once allowed this. From Theocritus in ancient Greece to James Hogg twenty centuries later, the link between herding and poetry was so famous a literary cliché that even writers forgot it had been a fact.

THREE

The miracle was a clever strong ruler using her learning and advantages to free a poet in the serf class. Most patrons who want poetry seek it where Augustus and Maecenas searched – in a social class close to their own. With more like Hilda literature would not now contain such huge silences and absences about most people's lives. She really was a saint.

So now English literature can start. A monk who got learning from the Irish Scots is taking dictation from a herdsman singing to him in a Northumbrian dialect of Anglo-Saxon. He sings a Jewish creation story transmitted to him through at least three other languages by a Graeco–Roman–Celtic–Christian church. The verse forms and vocabularies in the poet's nerves were learned from pagan German warrior chants, the climate is north British so his Genesis poem is fiercer, more spooky and colder than the version most of us know in the translation authorized by James the sixth and first in 1611. The monk writing this down uses an alphabet close to our own, a Roman adaptation of a Greek adaptation of a Semitic adaptation of an Egyptian adaptation of signs first used beside the Euphrates river in the city of Sumer, later called Babylon, four thousand years before Christ.

The Anglo-Saxon alphabet had two letters we do not now use: one for the soft noise which starts *thud* and ends *bath*, one for the lightly buzzing noise which starts *the*, ends *breathe* and *wreathe*. Bede, King Alfred and Geoffrey Chaucer wrote these letters, but after 1474 they were pushed out by the coming of movable type from Germany through France: countries whose alphabets had not been enlarged. I apologize for replacing both thorn and hook by th. This compromise will not stop you getting some taste of the language the poet and the monk used if you murmur aloud

Christ's best known prayer in Anglo-Saxon. The more familiar Tudor English version will help understanding. Note that in 650 the c is always hard, and a final e is pronounced, so *rice* sounds like *ricki*.

CHRIST'S PRAYER: c. 650	CHRIST'S PRAYER: c. 1550
Faeder ure,	*Our father*
Thu the eart on heofonum,	*Whyche art in heaven,*
Si thin nama gehalgod.	*Halowed be thy name.*
Tobecume thin rice.	*Thy Kyngdome come.*
Gewurthe thin willa on eorthan	*Thy wyll be doen in yearth, as it*
swa swa on heofonum.	*is in heaven.*
Urne gedaeghwamlican hlaf	*Geve us this daye our dayly*
syle us to daeg.	*breade.*
And forgyf us ure gyltas swa	*And forgeve us our trespaces, as*
swa we forgyfath urum	*wee forgeve them that trespasse*
gyltendum.	*agaynst us.*
And ne gelaed thu us on	*And leade us not into*
costnunge	*temptacion.*
Ac alys us of yfele. Sothlice.	*But deliver us from evill.*
	Amen.

All these old English words contain sounds of words we still use in similar ways, apart from *rice* (realm, or *reich* in German) and *sothlice* (truth-like or truly). *Gewurthe* means, worth be given: the unwieldy-looking *gedaeghwamlican* has daily inside it: *hlaf* means loaf: *gyltas*, guilt: *gyltendum*, guilty-doers-to: *costnunge*, a bad or costly choice: *alys*, release. Spoken in northern accents Christ's prayer in Anglo-Saxon sounds oddly familiar. Some Scottish and Northumbrian folk
still say "oor faither" and "thoo art".
Read on, please.

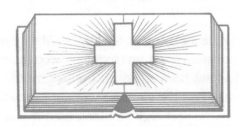

675c

GENESIS
Attributed to CAEDMON
WHITBY, NORTHUMBRIA

Here God is a strong, perfectly generous Anglo-Saxon king wanting nobles he has created to enjoy his gifts & glory. The row of 000000000s shows omitted lines which say how God's chief angel led others away to the heavenly north in a plot to take God's place. God builds Hell, & when the rebels attack throws them in. (Pagan Picts & Vikings raided Christian England from the north.)

WE are mighty right   that to the sky-warden,
mankind's king,   we lift up our words
with minds of love!   He is greatest wealth,
chieftain of all   the high creation,
lord almighty.   None ever formed him
or protected   nor now end come
to eternal rightness   but he be a king-ship
over the heavenly seats.   The highest throne
truthfast and strongformed   sunbosomed he held,
then were seated   wide on all side
through the realm of god   splendours born of
the ghostly word.   Having gleam and song
and appointed order   angel legions
berthed in bliss.   Was their glory mighty!

0000000000000000000000000000000000000000000000000000000

God now makes the world, not (as the Bible says) with light on day 1, sea & sky on day 2, land & herb on day 3 et cetera, enriching it all with goodness till it is fit for his last & best work, MAN – with woman as a kind after-thought. This God, with revenge in mind, first makes earth ugly as hell. Caedmon's tutors thought Satan's revolt explained why God had made the universe, but they only knew the Bible's Genesis from 2nd or 3rd-hand reports. Copying out a whole version of the Bible was a huge task. Abbey libraries would possess a 10 Commandments, Psalms & at least one

Then considered   our commander,
mind conceiving   how he the grand creation's
noble chairs   again get filled,
by the sunbright seat   with a better race
than who boastfully scorned   the rejected chief
high in the heaven.   Forthwith holy god
under heaven's hand   (that mighty kingdom)
willed him that earth   and upper sky
and wide water   get set by his word
in a world created   the bad to repay,
they that withheld   from shelter given.
Nor was there yet   unless darkly cold
creature bespoken,   but this wide ground
stood deep and dim,   sternly framed,
idle and useless.   On that turned his eye
the strong king   and the place beheld
soundless,   seeing dark that work
as middle night   black under heaven
blind and waste   until this creation
through word got worth   from the glorious king.

THE GENESIS POEM
Attributed to CAEDMON
ABBEY of STREANESHALCH

c675

*U*S is riht micel   thaet we rodera weard
  wereda wuldorcining,   wordum herigen
modum lufien!   He is maegna sped,
heafod ealra   heahgesceafta,
frea aelmihtig.   Naes him fruma aefre,
or geworden,   ne nu ende cymth
ecean drihtnes,   ac he bith a rice
ofer heofenstolas.   Heagum thrymmum
sothfaest and swithfeorm   sweglbosmas heold,
tha waeron gesette   wide and side
thurh geweald godes   wuldres bearnum
gasta weardum.   Haefdon gleam and dream
and heora ordfruman,   engla threatas,
beorhte blisse.   Waes heora blaed micel!

OOOOOOOOOOOOOOOOOOOOOOOOOOOOOOOOOOOOOOOOOOOOOOOOOOOO

Tha theahtode   theoden ure
modgethonce,   hu he tha maeran gesceaft
ethelstatholas   eft gesette,
swegltorhtan seld,   selran werode
tha hie gielpsceathan   ofgifen haefdon,
 heah on heofenum.   Fortham halig god
under roderas feng,   ricum mihtum,
wolde thaet him eorthe   and uproder
and sid waeter   geseted wurde
woruldgesceafte   on wrathra gield,
thara the forhealdene   of hleo sende.
Ne waes her tha giet   nymthe heolstersceado
wiht geworden,   ac thes wida grund
stod deop and dim,   drihtne fremde,
idel and unnyt.   On thone eagum wlat
stithfrihth cining,   and tha stowe beheold
dreama lease,   geseah deorc gesweorc
semian sinnihte   sweart under roderum,
wonn and weste,   oththaet theos woruldgesceaft
thurh word gewearth   wuldorcyninges.

Here first   eternal order,
helmet of all things,   heaven and earth,
sky-ceiling reared   and this roomy land
over-arched   strong and mighty
from the almighty.   Earth was still yet
of grass ungreen;   spearman's weather
black as night,   height and width
dark in all ways.   Then was the glory-bright
heavenward ghost   over the waves born,
mightily sped.   Creator of angel-troops,
life bringer,   light forth coming
over the plain ground.   Soon was fulfilled
high king's behest;   of him was holy light
over the wastes,   as so the maker bade.

731

*A free man was known by his weapon, a slave by not having one – his master was all that protected him. Priests, having promised Christ never to shed blood, went weaponless too. They named themselves Christ's slaves, a proud humility since a slave of the **King of Kings** could give his master's commands to a lesser ruler: exactly what happens here.*

Bede sends the first history of England to Northumbria's King Ceolwulf, telling him that God has made him king in order to teach his people wisdom & goodness.

THE CHURCH HISTORY OF THE ENGLISH
THE VENERABLE BEDE
JARROW ABBEY

PRAEFATIO: I, Bede, Christ's slave and mass-priest, send greetings to well-loved king Ceolwulf. And I send that story, which I newly wrote about the Angles and Saxons, for yourself to read and consider, and also in more places to get written and learned; and I trust your eagerness, for you are swift to mind and think on men of the old days' words and deeds, and most of all the famous worthies of our people. For in this is written either good tales about good men, so they that hear rehearse them, or evil stories of evil men, so they that hear flee that and shun it. For it is good goodness to praise and evilness not to requite that this be added to the hearer. If making it will not, how else will he learn? For your benefit and your people I wrote this; for God chose you to be king, to benefit your people with learning. And that there will be less doubt whether this is truth, I say how the story came to me.

My first helper and teacher was the allworthy

Her aerest gesceop   ece drihten,
helm eallwihta   heofon and eorthan,
rodor araerde,   and this rume land g
estathelode   strangum mihtum
frea aelmihtig.   Folde waes tha gyta
graes ungrene;   garsecg theahte
sweart synnihte,   side and wide,
wonne waegas.   Tha waes wuldortorht
heofonweardes gast   ofer holm boren
miclum spedum.   Metod engla heht,
lifes brytta,   leoht forth cuman
ofer rumne grund.   Rathe waes gefylled
heahcininges haes;   him waes halig leoht
ofer westenne,   swa se wyrhta bebead.

Caedmon reshuffled Biblical creation, but otherwise the story in his poem is orthodox Catholic & Protestant theology. Dante took it for granted. Milton retold it 1000 years later, still with rebel angels attacking from the heavenly north, for Scots armies had helped conquer a king, before attacking, & being smashed by, the commonwealth ruling instead of him.

---

abbot Albinus, who had travelled and read widely, and was the best learned man in England. Chiefly he told me what holy Theodorus taught, bishop of Canterbury, and holy abbot Adrianus, with whom he mainly studied. All that he knew about the men of Kent and those on the lands nearby, all he had got from writings or from sayings of older men, or from the missionaries of pope St. Gregory, he gave me all that was mindworthy, through Nothhelm the faithful mass-priest of London – sending him to me, or sending me his writings.

    From the start of these books till the time the English embraced Christ's faith, is what old men say; then up to our own time most is learned from missionaries of good pope St. Gregory, written under the kings who were rulers then, through the sayings of Nothhelm. They told me much about the bishops and kings which were in the times when Essex and Wessex and East Anglia and Northumbria received the gift of Christ's faith.

    Through Albinus I was chiefly urged to begin this work, and also through Daniel the allworthy

*Then Bede (like a good scholar in any period) names those who gave information that made his writing possible. These abbots, bishops, priests were the only civilized intelligences joining nations hardly ever at peace since their rulers were kings whose main job was warfare. Bede's book shows the origins of these states & the Christian church too. Pious yet sceptical, he introduces reports of miracles with, **It is said that** – a form he uses when not wholly sure. Fair-minded, he records the good work of Celtic clergy who, unlike the English, had not acknowledged the rule of Rome.*

Westsaxon bishop, who is yet now living. Much he said to me about Sussex and Wessex; and about Wight, that island, he sent me writings. And through Cedde, the allworthy Mercian bishop, and Ceaddan of the folk of Mercia and Eastsaxony; and about the bishop's life and death we have learned from the brothers of the monastery he himself founded, and is called Lastingham.

Of things in East Anglia, some word we got from the writings of older men or their sayings: some we have gained from the lore of the venerable abbot Isse.

In Lindsey news of Christ's faith was gained through words of the allworthy bishop Cyneberht,

---

760c
THE DREAM OF THE CROSS
Attributed to BISHOP CYNEWULF
LINDISFARNE, NORTHUMBRIA

*H*O THERE! The best of dreams   I will tell
    that met me   in the middle night
when talkative men   lie still.
It seemed that I saw   a marvellous tree
aloft in the sky,   and branched with light
beaming brightly.   All that beacon was
begotten in gold,   in rubies standing
fairly and fixed,   with five gems likewise
up on that axlespan.

            Behold there all angel bands
brighten through time and space:
                there was no sin-stained gallows
but those who behold   are holy ghosts
men upon mold   and all this great creation.

and through writings from him and other learned and renowned people. Of things known about the faith of Christ in Northumbria up to the present day, I do not use the authority of one person, but the words of many truthful witnesses, who knew and remembered the events: and things known and remembered by myself I have not left unwritten. The deeds and life of the holy father Cuthbert I took from writings I found among the brothers of the church at Lindisfarne, with details I ascertained from other truthful people.

And I now humbly beg the reader and ask him that
if he hear or read things which are different
from this, that he will not blame me.

*Soon after Ceolwulf received this book his opponents forced him to become a slave of God. Then they made war on Britons, Picts & each other, causing famine & plague. But round the Baltic sea lived more people than the land they called the **Womb of Nations** fed. They had splashed out to make dukedoms in France & Italy, Scots earldoms, Russian principalities, English kingdoms. Fertile Britain still attracted these Norse invaders.*

THE DREME OF THE RODE
Attributed to BISHOP CYNEWULF
LINDISFARNE, NORTHUMBRIA

c760

*H*WAET, ic swefna cyst   secgan wylle,
hwaet me gemaette   to midre nihte,
syththan reordberend   reste wunedon.
Thuhte me thaet ic gesawe   syllicre treow
on lyft laedan   leohte bewunden,
beama beorhtost.   Eall thaet beacen waes
begoten mid golde;   gimmas stodon
faegere aet foldan sceatum,   swylce thaer fife waeron
uppe on tham eaxlgespanne.

          Beheoldon thaer engel dryhtnes ealle
faegere thurh forthgesceaft:

              ne waes thaer huru fracodes gealga,
ac hine thaer beheoldon   halige gastas,
men ofer moldan,   and eall theos maere gesceaft.

*Odin or Wotan, hero-god of Vikings, was said to have won a new lease of life by wounding & hanging himself on the world tree. (Their name for the gallows was **Odin's horse**.) This made it easier for them to see Jesus as an even greater hero-god who leased eternal life for all his followers by being nailed to the cross-tree, holy-rood or crucifix.*

800c

BEOWULF
ANON
NORTHUMBRIA or MERCIA

Viking raids resumed. Pirates, blackmailers & unchristian looters of monasteries, the invaders' speech & ancestry was near to that of the English, who were so disunited that some kings paid raiders to help them fight neighbours.

This poem was surely sung in hall or camp where English & Danes were mixed. The first words show the Viking spirit. The heroic origin of kingship is told by a poet who wants us to revel in it.

Schooled by hard knocks, a smart orphan becomes chief of a leaderless settlement, forms a gang for its defence & raids other settlements. His son too gets followers by leading raids, sharing loot fairly & winning enough support to inherit his dad's job.

*H*O THERE! We Spear-Danes   in days long gone,
a kingly people   well skilled in glory,
had strong men   who framed them bravely.
Oft Scyld Scefing   mid threatening foes
from many men's households   took mead benches
most from the nobles.   He who was found
an outcast orphan   (that woe was made good)
waxed under heaven   growing in worth
until the peoples   who dwelt about him
over the whale-roads   had to obey him,
giving him gold: that was good kinging!

Then his bairn was   afterward born
a lad in the king's house   sent by God
to defend the folk.   God knew they suffered
cruel pains   when lacking a leader
a long while.   So the Life-Ruler
and world's Well-Doer   forgave worldly fame.
Beowulf was brilliant – his glory wide sprang –
Scyld's son   in all of the Scandian lands.
So should a young lad   do good work,
give rich gifts   when his father's bairn,
then as he ages   all his comrades
willingly at his side   when war come,
fight for his folk.   By generous deeds
through every homeland   a man shall thrive.

800c

THE EARTH TRAMPER
ANON
NORTHUMBRIA or MERCIA

In a world governed by warbands, raids & battle at least half the survivors experience defeat.

*O*FTEN he, the homeless,   must call
on merciful God,   while he heartsick
goes the waterways,   long at the oar
churning with hands   that rime-cold sea,
the exile's road: doom bitter and fixed."

BEOWULF
ANON
NORTHUMBRIA or MERCIA
c800

*H*WAET, we Gar-Dena   in geardagum
       theodcyninga   thrym gefrunon
hu tha aethelingas   ellen fremedon.
Oft Scyld Scefing   sceathena threatum
monegum maegthum   meodosetla ofteah;
egsode eorlas.   Syth-than aerest wearth
feasceaft funden,   (he thaes frofre gebad)
weox under wolcnum   weorthmyndum thah,
oththaet him aeghwylc   thara ymbsittendra
ofer hronrade   hyran scolde,
gomban gyldan: thaet waes god cyning!

Thaem eafera waes   aefter cenned
geong in geardum   thone God sende
folce to frofre.   Fyrenthearfe ongeat,
thaet hie aer drugon   aldorlease
lange hwile.   Him thaes Liffrea,
wuldres Wealdend   woroldare forgeaf;
Beowulf waes breme – blaed wide sprang –
Scyldes eafera   Scedelandum in
Swa sceal geong guma   gode gewyrcean
fromum feohgiftum   on faeder bearme
thaet hine on ylde   eft gewunigen
wilgesithas   thonne wig cume,
leode gelaesten.   Lofdaedum sceal
in maegtha gehwaere   man getheon.

The main story tells how a Danish warband frees a Swedish king from nocturnal demons born of Cain, the first murderer in the Bible; but the only religious idea is that God can make good the bad luck of brave men.

SCYLD SCEFING
In days before written history every nation had a heroic ancestor. Romans had Romulus, Athenians Theseus, Scandinavians Scyld Scefing. He was more than a warmonger. Swedes said he brought them the wheat from which came their first crops, bread & beer.

Had fighting been the Vikings' one skill they would never have gained so much. By farming, fishing & trading in small communities on barren coasts, they learned to combine independent courage with trust & co-operation .

EARDSTAPA
ANON
NORTHUMBRIA or MERCIA
c800

*O*FT him anhaga   are gebideth
       metudes miltse,   theah the he modcearig
geond lagulade   longe sceolde
hreran mid hondum   hrimcealde sae,
wadan wraeclastas: wyrd bith ful araed."

Here is how life tastes to the homeless & leaderless single survivor of a defeated warband.

*Seeking work which is
not mere serfdom, one
whose only talent is
warfare travels round
northern coasts as an
oarsman or on foot. He
may have to tramp till
he dies, for there are
many men like him. His
misery is increased by
a need to hide it. Like
the hero in* **Death of a
Salesman** *he can only
get work while seeming
cheerful without. That
is* **the warrior's code**.

*So says the earth-tramper   mindful of toil,
grief of slaughter   dear kinsfolk felled.
"Often shall I   lonely at daybreak,
lament my cares.   Not now to the living, to none
may I show my thoughts   daring
to openly speak.   I now truly know
the warrior's code,   that noble custom
of locking his heart,   binding it fast,
held hard shut   let him think what he will.
no care-worn heart   withstands its weird.
No troubled mind   can draw help to it.
Who seeks respect   and is dreary often
deep in his breast-coffin   binds that fast."*

890c

POPE GREGORY'S PASTORAL CARE
KING ALFRED'S TRANSLATION
WINCHESTER, CAPITAL OF WESSEX

*In 865 a big Viking
army landed; smashed
England's east &
central kingdoms;
made the rest buy
peace with money.
Alfred of Wessex was
the one king not to
submit, though often
hiding in woods & fens.
The Viking army was
strengthened by ad-
dition of new raiders,
weakened when its men
took to farming or
trading on English soil.
(They knew more
tramps than rich
heroes are made by
endless warfare.) In
878 Alfred's army so
beat the Danes that
they left Wessex alone.
Success in war was
then thought a king's
only duty, but Alfred
disagreed.*

KING ALFRED greets bishop * * * * with loving and friendly words, and I would have you know it comes often to my mind, what wise men there were once throughout England, both the godly kind and the worldly kind; and how happy the times were then throughout England; and how the kings wielding power in those days served the people of God and his messengers, and how they held their peace, and their decencies, and their power at home, and also enlarged them; and how they did well in war and in wisdom and learning; and how the holy men were eager both in teaching and learning, and in all the services they owed to God; and how foreigners came here to our land, and how we must now send abroad for these, if we would have them. So clean were these swept from England that there were few on this side of the Humber who could understand the divine service in English, or write a word out of Latin into English; and I think there were not many beyond the Humber either. So few there were that I cannot

Swa cwaeth eardstapa,   *earfetha gemyndig*
wrathra waelsleahta,   *winemaega hryre:*
"Oft ic sceolde ana,   *uhtna gehwylce,*
mine ceare cwithan.   *Nis nu cwicra nan*
the ic him modsefan   *minne durre*
sweotule asecgan.   *Ic to sothe wat*
thaet bith in eorle   *indryhten theaw*
thaet he his ferthlocan   *faeste binde,*
healde his hordcofan,   *hycge swa he wille.*
Ne maeg werig mod   *wyrde withstondan,*
ne se hreo hyge   *helpe gefremman.*
Forthon domgeorne   *dreorigne oft*
in hyra breostcofan   *bindath faeste."*

*This begins a poem as grand as **Ecclesiastes** in evoking a world of change & loss. It is also more bitter.*

*   **Ecclesiastes** says it is good to do the work that is in you & cling to the wife of your bosom. This tramp has neither.*

*   Wyrde is both root of the modern word and Scottish weird, meaning fate or inevitable end.*

---

remember a single one south of the Thames when I took power. God almighty be thanked that we now have any teachers among us. Therefore I order you to do that what I believe you will, that you leave worldly things as often as you may, and spread the wisdom God gave you wherever you can make it steadfast. Think how we would be punished in this world, if we neither loved learning ourselves or let other men love it: that we had the name of Christian only, and few of the virtues. When I call this to mind I mind also how I once saw, before it was all plundered and burned, how the kirks through all England stood filled with treasure and books, and also a great many of God's servants, and they had very little knowledge of the books, for they could not grasp anything in them for they were not written in their language. Which was to say, "Our elders, who once held these places, loved wisdom and through that begot wealth and left it to us. Here we might see their way, but we cannot go after them, and for that we have now forgone both wealth and wisdom, for we would not bend our minds to follow in their footsteps." When I mind all this I wonder

Abbot Bede told a king to educate his people. Here King Alfred tells bishops how to teach their priests. Asterisks show where names of those who got copies were inscribed.

*   Alfred's homeguard army & navy defended the kingdom in shifts so wars did not stop essential work. Towns were now strongholds for goods & cattle in event of a raid. Folk living far from towns were helped to turn neolithic forts & Roman camps into strongholds which grew into villages & burghs.*

*   But the king had ordered all these things by word-of-mouth. He knew that if written orders, laws & agreements were not understood in Wessex it would not last.*

Unlike most of his people Alfred read and wrote his own tongue. He could not read Latin & thus, like England, was shut out of a world of knowledge. Northumbria & the east coast was owned by library-destroying pagans who had again split British Christians from Christian Europe & deprived English kingdoms of literate clergy. Alfred persuaded into his court every good teacher he could: a Welsh bishop, Mercian & French priests. They made a school in his palace of the kind he asks his bishops to make in this preface – where all pupils learn to write their own speech before Latin is taught to potential priests. Here sons of nobles & lesser folk learned to read laws they should come to obey or enforce. But Alfred (though putting together an English lawcode headed by the 10 commandments) got them other books to read.

At 38 years he mastered Latin & started both to translate, & employ others to translate, good books into his native tongue. These were copied & sent to cathedral & monastery libraries.

again and again that the good and wise who were all through England, and were fully learned in all the books, that none of them had thought to translate. But I soon answered myself and said: "They never thought that men would ever be so reckless and learning so fallen; through that belief they forsook the task, and wished there were more wisdom in our land through the knowledge of other languages." Then I was reminded how wisdom was first founded in Hebrew, and after, when the Greeks had learned it, they turned all of it into their own language, and all other books also. And afterward the Latin folk did the same when they learned how to, and they turned all they knew through wise understanding into their own language. And also all other Christians have turned some of it into their own language. Therefore I think it better – if you think so – that we too should take some books, that are needful to the wisdom of all men, that we turn them into the language known to our own kind, and you do what may be done with God's help, if we have the stillness; that all the youth of the English free men who have wealth to apply themselves to it, work at learning while they are not yet able for other work, and that first they all know the English writing and reading: learning may then be further given in the Latin language to those who are willing to learn further, and willing to rise higher. When I was reminded how far knowledge of the Latin language had fallen in England, and yet how many could read what was written in English, then I began in the middle of various and many other businesses of this kingdom, to turn that book that is named in Latin *Pastoralis* and in English the *Herdsman's Book*, sometimes word by word, sometimes meaning for meaning, as I had learned from Plegmund my archbishop, and Asser my bishop, and from Grimbold my mass-priest, and John my mass-priest.

When I had gained this learning, then as far as I understood it, and as meaningfully and rightly as I could, I turned it into English; and to all the bishops' seats in my kingdom will it be sent; and in each there is a book-mark worth fifty moncessa. And I bid you in God's name that no man take the mark from the book, nor the book from the cathedral: it is unknown how long such learned bishops will be seen, which now, through God, are soon nearly everywhere; therefore I want this always to stay where it is, unless the bishop wants to take it with him or lend it, so that another be written from it.

This message Augustine over the salt sea southward brought to the islanders, as he was earlier commanded by order of his captain the pope of Rome. These right teachings Gregory gathered through his bright wisdom, his hoard of skilful thoughts. For the greatest of all mankind grew to be heavenly warden, best of Romans, wisest man and most widely famed. Since then King Alfred turned every word of me into English, and sent me to his writers south and north; ordered copies to be brought him, that he might send them to his bishops, for some needed it, as the Latin speech was almost unknown to them.

Among them were –
POPE GREGORY'S PASTORAL CARE which taught priests how to do their job & read the Bible.
THE PSALMS OF DAVID The Church's favourite Old Testament wisdom, & singable poetry.
BOETHIUS' CONSOLATIONS For nearly 1000 years Europe's most admired work of philosophy.
OROSIUS' HISTORIES from the Creation of the World to the Creation of Christ's Kingdom.
BEDE'S HISTORY OF THE ENGLISH CHURCH How Christ's Kingdom grew in Britain.
By importing this good work King Alfred strengthened English as Chaucer, Tyndal, Shakespeare did later.

GENESIS
AELFRIC THE MONK
CERNE ABBAS WESSEX

c990

[INCIPIT PREFATIO GENESIS ANGLICE]

AELFRIC the monk greets Aethelward the earl humbly. You bade me, dear sir, that I should change from Latin into English the book of Genesis, when it seemed to me a heavy task to do this, though you said I need translate no more of the book than up to Isaac, Abraham's son, for then you would have some other man translate the book from Isaac to the end.

Now I thought, dear sir, that that work would

In 1870 Alfred's scheme to have all free men's sons taught letters was at last tried in Britain, but by 990 sons of noblemen had been taught them. A taste for books roused a hunger for more, making this book.

greatly endanger me before other men also undertook it, since I would be in dread that some foolish man read this book until, reading wrongly, he change the meaning and start to live now under the new law of Christ, like the dear old patriarchs, in their time, lived under the old law that was Moses' law. I used to wish that a certain mass priest, who was my teacher in past times, had owned the book of Genesis, so that he by a little Latin could have understood, then explained from it, why the patriarch Jacob had four wives, two sisters and his two handmaidens. Full truly he said (though he knew not why, nor do I know) how mighty the split betwixt the Old and New Testament! In the beginning of this world brother took sister to wife and sometimes a father begat upon his own daughter, and many had more wives in addition, and no man could start wiving but on his siblings. If we will now live after Christ came, as men lived before Moses and under Moses' law, no man will stay a Christian, or have further worth, nor will any Christian man have blessing.

When unlearned priests have a little understanding of the Latin Bible they soon come to think they are splendid teachers, but they do not read the ghostly, the spiritual meaning of it, and how the old law was a signal pointing toward later things, when the New Testament, after Christ's humanity, fulfilled these things; for the Old Testament pointed toward Christ, and by his choosing. They talk also about Peter, why they are not allowed to have a wife just as Peter the apostle had, and they do not wish to hear or know that the blessed Peter lived according to Moses' law, until the Christ came to his time of manhood and began to preach his holy gospel, and chose Peter earliest to follow him: then Peter at once forsook his wife, and all the twelve apostles (they that had wives) forsook everywhere wives and property, and followed Christ's teaching into the new law and cleanliness, that himself created. Since priests have sworn to teach unlearned folk, it is fitting that they read the old law with ghostly understanding, and what Christ himself taught, and his apostles in their New Testament, that they may make folk wiser in Godly living, and set examples of Godly work.

We say also as foreword to this book, that it is hard, deep, ghostly to understand, and we have written no more than the naked tale it tells. Then think them ignorant who are locked out of the meaning of this simple narrative – for it is very far from simple. This book is called Genesis, which means The Book of Nature, for it is the first and foremost book and speaks of everything born, but does not speak of the angels' creation. It begins thus: In principio creavit Deus coelum et terram; that is in English, "In the beginning God created heaven and earth." It was truly so done, God almighty wrought in the beginning that which he had willed: creation. But in its holiest meaning that beginning is Christ, for he himself said to the Jews, "I am the beginning, who speaks to you." Through this beginning God the Father wrought heaven and earth, for then he formed all creation through that Son, he that forever went forth from him, the wisdom of the wise Father. Placed in the book after the former verse: Et spiritus Dei ferebatur super aquas; that is in English, "God's ghost fared over the waters." God's ghost is the Holy Ghost, by which the father gives life to all the creation that he formed through the Son, and so the Holy Ghost travels into man's heart, giving our sins forgiveness, first through water on our whole bodies, and after through repentance, and if we forsake the forgiveness that is the Holy Ghost's gift, then this sin will be unpardoned through all eternity. Often is the holy threeness revealed in this book, as is in the word when God says, "Let us make man in our likeness." Since he said, "Let US make" his trinity is signified; since he said, "in our likeness" his true oneness is signified. He did not speak in the plural, "in our likenesses", but in the singular, "in our likeness". Later came three angels to Abraham and he spoke to them all just as they to him. How cried out Abel's blood to God if all man's misdeeds do not denounce him to God in words? By these little things men may understand how deep this book is in holy meanings. Who yet since these words of light has written so!

Afterward Joseph, who was sold to Egypt's land and rescued the folk there from their great hunger, foretells Christ who was sold for us, and killed too, and rescued us from everlasting hungry hellish torture. That shining tent, which Moses wrought with wonderful craft in the waste desert, just as God's self ordered him, foretells God's agony by which himself created through his apostles manifold treasures and generous virtues. To this work the folk brought gold and silver and precious gemstones and manifold ornaments; some also brought goats' hair, for so the law commanded them. That gold foretells the faith and good conscience that we should offer to God; that silver foretells godly speech and holy learning we should bring to God's work; the gemstones foretell the various gifts of godly men; the goats' hair points toward the strong penitence of men, their sorrow for sins. Men also offered many kinds of livestock in sacrifice before this tent. Very much is here signified, for they were commanded that the beasts offered should always be whole, even to their tails; for this shows that God wills that we continually do well to the end of our lives, then let our ending be offered him with our other work.

Now the aforesaid book on many levels is so closely packed with very deep and holy meanings, and these so ordered and arranged as God's self dictated to the writer Moses, that we dare write no more in English than the Latin has, nor change the word order, except where it is proved that Latin and English do not have the same order of words: always we should translate to show the Latin in English, after arranging it so that the English has the same

AELFRIC'S GENESIS IN MODERN ENGLISH

In the beginning created God heaven and earth.
The earth truly was idle and empty, and the dark was over that aimless breadth, and God's ghost was faring over waters.
God quoth then: Be there light, and light was wrought.
God saw that it good was, and he divided light from the dark.
And named the light day, and the dark night, then there was evening and morning, one day.
God quoth then after: Be there now fastness amidst that water
and divide the water from that water.
And God wrought the fastness,
and divided the waters that were under the fastness,
from them that were above the fastness: it was then so done.
And God named the fastness heaven, and was then the evening and morning another day.
God then truly quoth: Be gathered the waters that be under the heaven and appear dryness. It was so then done.
And God called the dryness earth and the waters gathered he named sea. God saw then that it good was.

sense; otherwise it will be very confusing to read, as the Latin in no way is.

It is known there were some mistaken men who would throw out the old law, and some who would have the old law and throw out the new, as the Jews do; but Christ's self and his apostles taught us to hold the old spiritually with the new truly as a whole work. God made us two eyes and two ears, two nostrils, two lips, two hands and two feet, and he would also have two testaments in the world, the old and the new; because he himself is so honourable that he will have none not to get instruction, nor no man so poor that God cannot ask him, "Why do you so?" We should mend our wills to his commanding, and may not fit his commands to our desires.

I say now that I do not dare and do not wish to change another book from Latin into English; and I bid thee, dear earl, no longer bid me do this, lest I be unfaithful if I do. God's eternal mercy be with you. I now urge in God's name, that whoever will rewrite this book, that he copy it out correctly, since I have no control; and if he bring error through untrue writings then it will be his fault, not mine. Much evil does the bad writer, if he will not correct his writings.

AELFRIC'S GENESIS IN ANGLO-SAXON

On angynne gesceop God heofonan & eorthan.
Seo eorthe sothlice waes idel & aemti, & theostra waeron ofer thaere nywelnysse bradnysse; & Godes gast waes geferod ofer waeteru.
God cwaeth tha: Gewurthe leoht, & leoht waearth geworht. God geseah tha thaet hit god waes, & he todaelde thaet leoht fram tham thystrum.
& het thaet leoht daeg & tha thystru niht: tha waes geworden aefen & merigen an daeg.
God cwaeth tha eft: Gewurthe nu faestnys tomiddes tham waeterum & totwaeme tha waeteru fram tham waeterum.
& God geworhte tha faestnysse,
& totwaemde tha waeteru, tha waeron under thaere faestnysse,
fram tham the waeron bufan thaere faestnysse: hit waes tha swa gedon.
& God het tha faestnysse heofonan, & waes tha geworden aefen & mergen other daeg.
God tha sothlice cwaeth: Beon gegaderode tha waeteru the synd under thaere heofonan & aeteowige drignys. Hit waes tha swa gedon.
& God gecygde tha drignysse eorthan & thaera waetera gegaderunga he het sae. God geseah tha thaet hit god waes.

1066

This book was part of Alfred's plan to help the English know they were one nation. It was a year by year diary of events in south Britain since the Romans came. Made from spoken & written sources by Alfred's clergy, maybe with Alfred's help, copies were sent to abbeys & cathedrals so that events could be added & the diary reach into the future. In disjointed but often urgent prose that becomes verse, the chronicles tell how after Alfred's day the English found unity, were forced into the Danish empire of King Knut, regained home-rule when that ended & at last were defeated by Normans. 7 copies still exist, with 3 differences made by the different politics & location of scribes. In 1066 or soon after 6 of them ended. In Peterborough additions were made to a copy that stutters to a halt in 1154, after great lamentions on the cruelty of England's new baronial rulers.

ANGLO-SAXON CHRONICLE
ANON: WINCHESTER, CANTERBURY, PETERBOROUGH ETC.

THE MAIN British island is 800 miles long and 200 miles broad. And within the island are five nations; English, Welsh (or British), Scots, Picts and Latins. The earliest people were the Britains who came from Armorica and first peopled the south part. Then it happened that the Picts came south from Russia with a few long ships, and landing first on the northern coast of Ireland, told the Scots who lived there that they meant to settle. The Scots would not allow this, "But," said the the Scots, "we'll give you advice. There is an island to the east where you can live if you wish, and we'll help you take it from anyone who resists." So the Picts entered the north of this land and, as we said, southward the Britons had it. And the Picts got wives from the Scots, on condition that they chose their kings always on the female side, which they have done ever since. After some years a number of Scots left Ireland for Britain and settled in part of the north. Their leader was called Riada, so they are called Dalriadans.

Sixty winters before Christ was born Caius Julius, emperor of the Romans, came to Britain with 80 ships. Here he was first beaten in a terrible fight, losing a great part of his army. Then he let the rest of it remain through the winter, went south to Gaul, gathered six hundred ships and returned with them to Britain. When they charged each other Caesar's tribune, Labienus was slain. Then the Welsh took sharp stakes, and hammered them with big clubs into the water of a ford in the river called Thames. This stopped the Romans crossing that ford. Then the Britons fled to the depths of the woods and Caesar, after much fighting, gained the chief towns and returned to Gaul.

THE WASTING
OF OLD ENGLISH
SPEECH AND HOW
A NEW WAS GOT

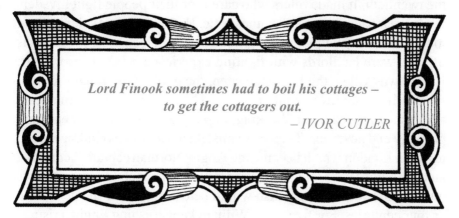

Lord Finook sometimes had to boil his cottages –
to get the cottagers out.

– IVOR CUTLER

W ILLIAM, BOSS OF NORMANDY, belonged to the fourth
or fifth generation of those Scandinavian pirates who had forced
themselves as a military aristocracy upon much of England, France and
Italy. Being closely related their strongest chiefs always had
genealogical excuses for claiming a neighbour's territory, and at land-
grabbing nobody beat boss William. He was strong, brave, clever,
patient, greedy, violent and revengeful – a nasty man, but those who
fought for him and survived were sure of victory and loot. Like some
others of Viking blood he felt entitled to the English throne. Hearing
that the English national assembly of wise men had elected Harold, an
Englishman, to the job, William prepared to invade. First he persuaded
his barons to follow him, for the feudal code gave him no right to
order them overseas against unthreatening Christians, and conquest
would be hard. For twelve years Harold had ruled England peacefully
and well as the previous king's chief minister, which was why the
leaders of England's mingled Celtic, Saxon and Danish communities
had crowned him. William told the Norman barons that he could double
their estates in France by the addition of English ones. They believed
him. In a Europe with hardly any international money system he raised

a lot of money, and built a fleet, and hired mercenary troops from French neighbours who might otherwise have attacked Normandy when he left.

In 1066 the army of another warrior who wanted England landed in the north, and while Harold was defeating it William invaded the south and began laying waste. Turning a peopled, productive land into wilderness was as common a military tactic in the eleventh century as the twentieth. It made rulers who cared for their people fight invaders while the invaders were still enthusiastic. Harold's private soldiers were mostly farmers and ploughmen, not trained mercenaries. Most of his officers were landlords with fighting experience, not a warrior class. Harold was killed, the English beaten, the nobles who fought for him fled. William set fire to south London. The remaining southern nobles and bishops proclaimed him king, hoping he would leave them their property and positions. They were mistaken. He began building a great tower in London which became the Anglo-Norman capital. Across the land his barons used forced labour to build steep mounds with fortresses on top from which the English would be controlled for the next three or four centuries. For five years William kept crushing English risings in the south, the east, the west (where they were aided by their old enemies the Welsh) but especially in the north, where they were helped by Scots and Danes. In the north he bribed the Danes to leave, then burned towns and villages, killing resisters or driving them over the Scottish border. He carefully destroyed homes, harvests, cattle and farming tools, making a famine to kill all survivors. The north never troubled him again. Half a century later the sixty miles northward of York was still unpeopled desert. Official gossip has ever since called him William the Conqueror.

They should have called him the Waster. Even in peacetime he laid waste, getting a hunting park the size of a small county by clearing from it people, farms and religious settlements. His five years of spectacular violence at last forced peace on the land whose peace he had destroyed, but he could only keep England now by making permanent the army used to grab it. He did so by a vast confiscation of productive soil. The defeat of widespread English resistance had killed or driven abroad all the big native landlords and many small ones. He evicted others, letting the most servile keep a small part of their estate in return for giving him the rest and a promise to serve him always.

William could now give his poorest mercenary land with a village on it, his biggest supporters and nearest relations estates of a hundred manors and more. He kept the biggest estates, and where he lacked troops to overawe the natives he evicted the natives and made a game reserve. His strongest supporters (potential rivals) each had to be rewarded with several big estates, but he made sure they were far apart: some on the dangerous borders of Wales and Scotland, some in the counties near London. This meant they could not swiftly unite their troops against him. To efficiently locate and tax his subjects he made an itinerant bureaucracy name, number, measure and record every estate, property and owner. All England was now under the martial law of a widespread army he could mobilize any time.

In those days the bishop of Rome, another Gregory, invited Christian kings to do him honour as their earthly overlord. The German emperor did so but William refused, rejecting it as a novelty without precedent. He replaced nearly every English bishop and abbot with a Norman French clergyman who paid him the same homage as his barons did, communicated only through him with the papacy, made no big decisions without his consent. Having made himself as complete a master of church and state as did the eighth Henry five centuries later, William spent most of his remaining years in Normandy from where he wasted towns and countryside in warfare with the king of France.

Primo Levi says there is no violence against people without violence against language. Douglas, in a small book called *The Norman Conquest and British Historians*, says, "Perhaps the two greatest achievements of mediaeval England were Anglo-Saxon vernacular literature and Anglo-Norman executive administration." Perhaps. The second achievement destroyed the first. The livelihood of the English now depended on them understanding the orders of confident foreign despots who, like all that sort, acted as if the natives were mostly fools or villains. "Do you think I'm an Englishman?" was a Norman French way of saying, "Do you think I'm a fool?" *Villain* was originally Norman French for a villager who tilled the soil: the most essential kind of worker, but despicable from the viewpoint of a military aristocrat. So in the new language the English made by blending the words of their masters with their own, *villainous* means *criminal*. William ordered the church grammar schools to start teaching in French. By the twelfth century the invaders had persuaded the English priests, merchants and small gentry that their history and literature were best forgotten, their language was a speech of the ignorant. The last purely English bishop had been deposed because "he was a superannuated English idiot who spoke no French".

England was now half of an empire split in two by a channel of the sea, an empire whose military landlords fought to add Wales, Ireland and Scotland to their northern estates, all France to their southern ones. Their attacks on Wales united that land in a resistance which, successful at first, inspired Welsh bards to make poetry still recited and enjoyed by Welsh readers. The first Spanish epic, *El Cid*, was from the twelfth century, when singers and fabulists also made the first literature of Mediterranean France. A century later Dante wrote *The Divine Comedy*, a Christian epic as great as Homer's and Virgil's. In three hundred years of Welsh, Spanish, French and Italian vernacular excellence a few poignant sentences in old English lament for lost learning, describe a scholar's tearful joy that a book by Bede still exists. Part of the lament (modernized!) says –

> *Such as these taught our people in English,*
> *Not dark was their light and it fairly glowed.*
> *Now the lore is forgotten, our folk forlorn,*
> *Now other language is laid on our folk*
> *And most of the teachers are lost, the folk with them.*

The Anglo-French meanwhile wrote laws, state annals and hunting manuals. Their imaginative writing (anti-clerical satire and fabulous Arthurian history) was got from the Celts of Wales and Brittany.

Which does not mean intelligent life ended in England for three hundred years. No kings who came after William could be so absolute. The church got partly free of them, then the barons. Wasted ground was resettled. People, trades and towns increased as they would have done had the Normans been repelled. Prospering tradesmen and merchants could pay high taxes, so kings protected them from the barons and big towns won free of military landlords. Some farmers got partly free too, paying rent in coin instead of labour. The king, church, towns, landlords were now linked by codes and contracts which made understanding these a full-time job. The colleges in the towns added law to their curriculums and, while still training priests besides lawyers, got the name of UNIVERSITIES. Though founded by clergy they became self-governing states protected by the king. Then trade, crusades and pilgrimages brought Islamic writing to Europe. It contained developments in Arabic science with translations of work by Aristotle and other Greek thinkers lost to the west. The universities spread word of them. Translation, commentary, subtle ideas now seemed adventurous things, repulsive only to the conservative and timid. Western universities expanded like boom towns on the American frontier. Life there was quarrelsome, democratic, sometimes murderous; but the coarsely gowned and often barefoot fellows who jostled sons of nobility in the lecture halls were seeking knowledge, not gold. Oxford housed students from England, Scotland, Wales, Normandy and Gascony. Roger Bacon, Duns Scotus, William of Ockham taught in Oxford: wise thinkers who lectured and wrote in Latin. With equally wise French and Italian thinkers they joined ancient science and Christian theology until all questions about the material and spiritual universe had clear answers: answers supported by such logical arguments and ancient authorities that only ignorant pagans or heretics could dispute them. In this system the world was both static centre of the universe and the only vicious part, for it contained hell. Adam's sin had given Satan everything on earth not devoted to God, so the best people were nuns and monks who lived only to pray. The social system was explained thus: the peasants worked for all; the clergy prayed for all; the nobles fought for all.

By the fourteenth century the French people had more nobility than they could bear. The nobles thought battles a traditional, legal way to get fame and property, a natural extension of combats which were their education in childhood and sports in peacetime. They were proud of their politeness to fallen enemies of their own rank. Unhorsed in fights that killed many foot soldiers, protected by armour a dagger could hardly pierce, a captured knight might soon be dining with his captor and his captor's wife in a castle like his own, suffering only some bruises and a rueful awareness of the large ransom his estate would pay for his release. But the cost was mostly paid by his peasants, and plunder was a legal right of the higher nobility when their supplies ran short. In France, Europe's most fertile and cultivated land, the tillers of it suffered more and more hunger. Alas, only nobles had the technology to destroy nobles. A full set of armour was then the equivalent of a twentieth-century tank. From a wholly French view the most superfluous nobles were obviously the Anglo-French.

Warfare started which at last drove these from their French estates and made them wholly English, but for over a hundred years they could not believe it because they kept winning battles. Mainland Britain was a safe place to retreat to, a good recruiting ground to attack from. Their English estates could not yield enough men to fight a war for five generations, so they raised regiments from the free townsmen and free farmers by offering pay, loot, and ransoms of captured French. They urged them to use the longbow, a new invention which enabled strong men to shoot arrows through armour. Middle-class tradesmen and yeomen could handle it, being muscular as peasants and well fed as gentry. Noble commanders spoke to them in English, as if such soldiers were almost their equals. For centuries the nobles (like German and Russian nobles before Napoleon's wars) had spoken French to show their superiority: a bad tactic when ordering Englishmen to kill Frenchmen in France. The middle-class troops and their longbows were effective. England's kings and barons kept regaining nominal lordship of French land which paid them little or nothing. Their footsoldiers got coins, a loot of fine clothing, ornaments, household goods, and a new confidence in their speech. Froissart, historian of that time, was astonished by the arrogance low-ranking English showed to Frenchmen of every rank. When these soldiers returned to their trades and small properties in England they also spoke more directly to their rulers. Then a worse disease than warfare made every social rank talk straight to each other.

There were perhaps four million English when the Black Death reached them in 1349. By the end of the century epidemics had killed between a third and half. People of every rank died, but the loss of a third of the labourers wrought biggest changes – their work fed the rest. They too discovered some freedom of choice, for despite government efforts to keep down wages, employers who could afford to bid high for labour did so. The building of great cathedrals and palaces stopped. Chronicles filled with laments for the terrible greed of the poor, a sign of social improvement where wealth is unequally shared. Debate grew widespread, everywhere people arguing what was due to them as nobility, Christians, citizens, householders, Englishmen, spokesmen for a trade, craft, closed shop or open union. All sorts of English were about to enter the public house of a new literate speech.

This speech was no longer the speech of Caedmon and Alfred.

The English no longer (like folk in other lands) made words for complex things by linking short ones, so that guilt-doing became gyltendum, the-world-shaping became woruldgesceafte. Three centuries of national and local bossing in French had ground the Anglo-Saxon-Danish word-hoard down small and kept it small, leaving curt little words which did, and still do, most of the hard work in English: *a the and for or but me she he you it that those these them what when?* and verbs showing tense by changing their start, middle or end like *is – was / see – saw / think – thought / keep – kept*; and verbs which were useful nouns and vice versa, like *work love milk stick*; and adjectives which could be nouns, like *fat good salt red kind*; even *light*, a word which toils discreetly and well as noun, adjective and verb. But such words no longer connected and supported large combinations of themselves. The large words had been mostly got from the French of landlords, clergy, lawyers and schoolteachers, had different spellings from the short words and different pronunciations: even though the native English spoke them with flatter mouths than the French.

Thus, since the fourteenth century English vocabulary has looked like a garden of turf and herbs in which grow flowers of greater height from another climate. Looking back through a sentence (this sentence) for words of French origin I immediately see *immediately*, *origin* and *sentence*. If I hated French things I could replace *immediately* by *at once* and gain terseness, but to replace origin I would need to turn *words of French origin* into *words got long ago from the French*, which is wordier, or *words of French birth,* which is too earthy for modern discussion of speech. And there is now no easily understood group of English words from the Anglo-Saxon which could mean sentence. Not all French Latinate words are longer than Anglo-Saxon equivalents: *centre – middle, comprehension – understanding* are equal lengths, but the first of each pair seems politer, grander, the result of dearer educations. Walter Scott pointed out that slaughter converted Saxon pigs (or swine) into French pork. Of course! Haute Cuisine had raised it to the landlord's table. The ease with which English words can be split into polite = rich and homely = poor is (apart from the English political constitution) the legacy of the Norman conquest most open to abuse. Snobs have always found it easy to pretend that the king or queen's English is theirs, that poorer people cannot think deeply or talk with authority because their homely speech ties them to *common* objects and feelings. England's best writing proves that false. "Dust to dust and ashes to ashes", spoken over a grave, means more than "the transience of human existence". The translators of the Bible into English deliberately used an English so plain that the grandest words are Hebrew and Latin names. Chaucer, Shakespeare, Thomas Hardy used and also invented big words, but only to add force or grandeur to common speech they mostly depended on.

But the new English of Chaucer's century was not exactly ours. This shows the main verbal differences:

Whan that Averyll with his shoures soote
The droghte of March hath perced to the roote,

WHAN (*when*) rhymes more with swan than with can.

SHOURES (*showers*). The first four letters rhyme with *hour*, the last two with *yes*, but with the *s* said more lightly.

SOOTE (*sweet*) should be pronounced delicately and Frenchly with protruded lips, the final *e* said very short, so that it sounds very different from *sooty*.

DROGHTE (*drought*). The *gh* is pronounced like the last two letters of *Bach* or a highland *loch*: the final *e* as in soote, but shorter still, as the rhythm leaves less room for it.

PERCED (*pierced*). The first four letters sound like the first four in *Percy*, the last two like the last two in *bedded*.

ROOTE (*root*) rhymes with soote.

This English had an almost Italianate lilt and flow from sounding the short *e* at the end of many words that have dropped it, and at the end of words like *inspired* where we no longer pronounce it, and in the use of *es* for a plural ending. The lilt was ballasted by that harsh *gh* which is still a conspicuous part of English spelling, though now only pronounced by some lowland Scots.

Please read on.

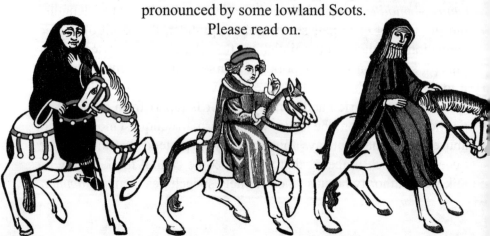

ENGLISH REMADE

1330c

The Yorkshire dialect of this preface was easy to modernize, being the earliest good prose in middle English. Richard Rolle of Hampole studied at Oxford, mastered Latin, but decided philosophy was not Christian, for it was based on the thoughts of Greeks who had never known Jesus. He returned at the age of 19 to his father's house, made his clothes look as much like a hermit's as possible, ran away to become one. Like very holy folk in every faith he felt God's love is best enjoyed by those who truly want nobody & nothing else. Such saints have created holy orders but cannot always enter them. The father of a friend saved Richard from hunger, decided he was sane, supported him as a hermit. His books in Latin & English were read by many who thought God's love made most earthly establishments look silly or corrupt. He taught other recluses, by incantation, not by untrustworthy logic.

THE LATIN PSALTER OR PSALMS OF DAVID
Preface by Translator RICHARD ROLLE
of HAMPOLE near DONCASTER

GREAT abundance of ghostly comfort and joy in God comes in the hearts of them that says or sings devoutly the psalms in love of Jesu Christ. They drop sweetness in man's soul, and healing delights in their thoughts, and kindle their wills with the fire of love, making them hot and burning within, and fair and lovely in Christ's eyes. And them that last in their devotion he raises them to contemplative life, and oft sees them into the sound and mirth of heaven. The singing of psalms chases fiends, excites angels to our help, it does away sin, it pleases God, it informs perfectness, it does away pain and anger of soul and makes peace between body and soul, it brings desire of heaven and despite of earthly things. Truly this shining book is a chosen song before Christ, also a lamp lighting our life, healing of a sick heart, honey of a bitter soul, dignity of ghostly persons, tongue of private virtues; the which holds the proud to meekness and kings to bow down to poor men, fostering bairns with kindliness. In them is so much beauty of understanding and medicine of words that this book is called garden enclosed, well uncovered, paradise full of apples. Now, with wholesome learning, driven and stormy souls it brings into clear and peaceful life, now admonishing to prevent sin with tears, now heightening joy of righteous men, now menacing hell to the wicked. This song that gladdens hearts and teaches the soul is made for a singing voice; that with angels whom we may not hear we may mingle loving words, so that rightly he should think himself alien from very life who has no delight in this gift of wonderful sweetness, which is not soured through the corruptions of this world, but is ay lasting in the dignity of it, gaining in grace of purest softness. All earthly delight vanishes and at last wastes to nought, but this, the longer it lasts the more it is, and becomes most at a man's death, when love is perfectest.

THE CLOUD OF UNKNOWING: *a treatise containing many high points of Divine Contemplation, in which a Soul is Oned with God* ANON: ENGLAND

c1360

IN THE NAME OF THE FATHER, AND OF THE SON, AND OF THE HOLY GHOST. AMEN.

I charge thee and I beseech thee, with as much power and virtue as the bond of charity is sufficient to suffer, whatsoever thou be that this book shall have in possession, whether by property, or by keeping, or by bearing as messenger, or else by borrowing, that inasmuch as in thee is by will and advisement, thou neither read it, write it, nor speak it, nor yet suffer it to be read, written, or spoken by any other or to any other, unless it be by such a one or to such a one as hath (in thy supposing) in a true will and by a whole intent purposed him to be a perfect follower of Christ. And that not only in active living, but also in the sovereignest point of contemplative living the which is possible by grace to be come to in this present life by a perfect soul yet abiding in this deadly body. And he should be such a one as doth all that in him is, and (in thy supposing) hath done long time before, for to able him to contemplative living, by the virtuous means of active living. For else it accordeth nothing to him.

And over this I charge thee and I beseech thee, by the authority of charity, if any such shall read it, write it, or speak it, or else hear it read or spoken, that thou charge them, as I do thee, for to take them time to read it, speak it, write it, or hear it, all over. For peradventure there is some matter therein, in the beginning or in the middle, the which is hanging and not fully declared where it standeth; and if it be not there, it is soon after, or else in the end. Wherefore, if a man saw one matter and not another, peradventure he might lightly be let into error. And therefore, for eschewing of this error both in thyself and in all others, I pray thee for charity do as I tell thee.

Fleshly janglers, open praisers and blamers of themselves or of any other, runners and tattlers of tales, and all manner of pinchers, cared I never that they saw this book. For mine intent was never to write such thing unto them.

A monk, nun or hermit is going to tell those who feel capable of it how to turn their backs on the bad job of the world & find an inner way to eternal truth & comfort. The author believes the best thing people can do is live in pure contemplation of God. But in abbeys & hermitages plagues are killing more people than in the world outside, which suggests those who most profess God have most annoyed him. There is good reason to think so, for outright schism & simony are rending the church, while those who want to reform it are suspected of heresy.

*This prologue has the form of a prayer, but uses the careful clauses of an Anglo-French legal contract: it is trying to exclude all **curiously learned** readers who might quote the book in a public debate. By **curiously learned** the writer means those who read books out of curiosity, not from a wish to become better people. The curiously learned are linked with the ignorant, for* *though both kinds may be **full good men in active living**, both sorts are equally removed from the greatest good, who is God.*

And therefore I would that they meddled not therewith; neither they nor any of their curiously learned or ignorant men. Yea, though they be full good men in active living, yet this matter accordeth nothing to them. But not so to those men, the which although they stand in activity by outward form of living, nevertheless yet by inward stirring under the privy spirit of God – whose dooms be hid – be full graciously disposed: not continually, as is proper to true contemplatives, but now and then, to be partakers in the highest point of this contemplative act. If such men might see it, they should by the grace of God be greatly comforted thereby.

This book is distinguished in seventy chapters and five. Of the which chapters the last chapter of all teacheth some certain tokens by the which a soul may verily prove whether he be called by God to be a worker in this work or not.

THE VOYAGES OF SIR JOHN MANDEVILLE
JEAN de BOURGOGNE or À LA BARBE
ENGLISHED BY ANON

1360c

The last prologue was an author's anxious, but closely reasoned, prayer for a special kind of Christian reader. This beginning sounds far more confidently pious. It uses the style of a sermon: the form of vernacular speech which carried most authority for at least 16 centuries. It tells us why we should fight a crusade. The scholarship & reasoning are poor. Nowhere in the Greek, Hebrew or Latin scriptures did Jesus ever say, "I am

FOR as much as the land beyond the sea, that holy land called the land of promise or behest, passing all other lands it is the most excellent, worthy and sovereign lady; for in this land our lord Jhesu Crist enclosed himself in the flesh and blood of the blessed and glorious virgin Marie, and became man to work miracles and teach Cristian faith unto his children. And here it liked him to suffer many reprovings and scorns for us. And he that was kyng of heaven of air of earth of sea and of all things that be contained in them, would be called kyng of that land only when he said: REX SUM JUDEORUM: that is to say: I am kyng of the Jews. And that land he chose as the best and most virtuous, for it is the heart and midst of all the world. Witness the philosopher that sayeth: VERTUS RERUM IN MEDIO CONSISTIT: that is to say: the virtue of things is in the middle. And he that was kyng of glory and of joy, who deserved not evil for he thought none evil, chose in that land to suffer death for to buy and deliver us from pains of hell and death without end, which were ordained to us for the sins of our first father Adam and for our own sins also. For he that will publish a thing to make it openly known will make it to be cried and pronounced in the middle part of a town so that the thing proclaimed may stretch evenly to all sides. Right so, he that formed all the world would suffer death for us at Jerusalem, the midmost centre of the world, to that end and intent that his passion and death be published equally to all parts of the world.

Dear God, how he loved us sinners! No more precious possession nor greater ransom be put for us than his blessed body, precious blood and holy life. Well may that land be called delightful and fruitful which was be-bled and moisted with the precious blood of our lord Jhesu Crist. Wherefore every good Cristian man of power and means should take all pains to conquer our right heritage and chase out all the unbelieving men. For we be called Cristians after Crist our father. And if we be true children of Crist we ought to claim the heritage our father left us and take it out of heathen men's hands. But now pride, greed and envy have so inflamed the hearts of lords of the world that they are more busy to disinherit their neighbours than to challenge or conquer their right heritage before said. And the common people that would put their bodies and possessions out to conquer our heritage may not do it without the lords. For an assembly of people without a chieftain or a chief lord is as a flock of sheep without a shepherd which wanders and disperses and knows not where to go. Would to God that all worldly lords were at good accord with the common people, would take this holy voyage over the sea, then I swear that in a little time our right heritage should be put in the hands of the right heirs of Jhesu Crist.

Because it is a long time past since there was a general passage or voyage over the sea, and many men desire to hear of the holy land and have thereof great solace and comfort, I, John Mandeville, knight (however unworthy) who was born in England, in the town of Saint Albion's, and crossed the sea in the year of our lord Jhesu Crist one

King of the Jews", & if he had, it would be no reason for the natives of Christian Europe to conquer the Muslim & Jewish natives of Palestine: the author is simply telling his readers what he knew they liked to hear.

The original author was French: perhaps a doctor in Liège called Jean de Bourgogne. He pretended to be an old English knight describing the world-wide travels of his youth & manhood. With this excuse he strung together every amusing or fantastic anecdote he could steal from other writings on legend, religion, travel & history, not letting evidence, consistency, likelihood & truth hinder him in the slightest. His book thus became a fantastic & popular encyclopaedia of everywhere. It was fast translated into English & several other tongues, & copied & printed for over 300 years. The blend of a little fact with much popular fiction suggested that the world was as marvellous yet God-controlled as the readers wanted. Bunyan's description of The Valley of The

*Shadow came partly from a valley in Asia in the **Voyages of Mandeville**.*

Prose was the tool of clergy, lawyers & merchants keen to omit no detail from their accounts, & who wanted the dignity of ritual. This led to long slow sentences with many clauses hooked to the main nouns & verbs; so before roughly 1650 most stories could be told more swiftly & simply in verse. The metrical version is not great poetry, but sounds more like easy speech than the original prose. The writer is cheerfully sure his version is better.

millennium three centuries and twenty four, on the day of Saint Michael, and until now have been a long time oversea and have seen and gone through many divers lands and many provinces Persia Syria Arabia Egypt the high and the low through Amazonia India the less and the more and throughout kingdoms and isles, and have passed through Germany the little and the great through Turkey Tartary many other isles where dwell many divers people of divers manners and laws and shapes of men. Of which lands and isles I shall speak more plainly hereafter. And especially for them that purpose to visit Jerusalem and the holy places thereabout. And I shall tell the way, for I have often ridden that way with good company of many lords, God be thanked.

And ye should understand that I have put this book out of Latin into French, and translated it again out of French into English that every man of my nation may understand it. But lords and knights who read but little Latin and have been beyond the sea know if I speak truth or not. And if I err in the writing they may change and amend it. For things long passed from a man's mind or sight turn soon into forgetting because of the frailties of mankind.

1370c

MAWNDEVILE'S VOIAGES
IN RHYMED METRE
BY ANON

HERE BIGINNITH THE BOKE
OF MAWNDEVILE

Almighty God in trinity	*ALMYGHTI GOD in trenite*
One God and persons three	*Oo God and persoones thre*
Father and son and holy ghost	*Fadir and sone and holi gooste*
Blessèd God of might the most	*Blessid god of myghtis moste*
Now speed us at our tale's beginning	*Nowe spede us atte oure begynnynge*
And save all this fair gathering	*And save alle this faire gaderinge*
And grant us grace so benign	*And graunte us grace so binynne*
To live out of debt and deadly sin	*To live out of dette and deedeli synne*
And teach us the right way	*And teche us the right way*
Unto that bliss that lasteth ay. Amen.	*Unto that blisse that lasteth ay. Amen.*

Nowe lordis and ladies leve and dere	Now lords and ladies, true and dear,
Yif ye wolle of wondris here	If ye will of wonders hear
A litille stounde yif ye wolle dwelle	Stand a while: if you remain
Of grete mervailis I mai you telle	Of great marvels I will explain.
Som time in Engelonde was a knyght	Some time in England lived a knight,
A fers man boothe stronge and wyght	A forceful man of strength and weight,
He was a man of noble fame	Also a man of noble fame –
Sir john maundevile was his name	Sir John Mandeville was his name
And in seinte Albones he was born	And in Saint Albeyn's he was born,
And his auncestres hym biforn	And his ancestors him beforn,
And yitte in Engelonde wete ye wele	And still in England, know ye well,
Of his kynne there liven ful fele	Many of his kindred dwell.
A worthi sowdioure forsothe was he	A worthy soldier in truth was he
And wel travailid biyonde the see	And well travelled beyond the sea
In many a dyvers kinges londe	In many a different king's land
As affter ye shal undirstonde	(As after you will understand)
For he was out of this londe here	For he was out of this land here
Holiche foure and thirti yere	Wholly four and thirty year,
And ever he travailid without wene	And ever he travelled without stay
The wondres of this worlde to sene	The wonders of this world to see,
And al that he sawe he undirtoke	And all he saw or undertook
And ever he wrote it in a boke	Ever he wrote it in a book
And al that men hym tolde thereto	And all that men told him thereto
He wrote it in a boke also	He wrote within a book also.
But in that boke is moch thinge	But in that book, without a doubt,
That nedeth naught in this talkinge	Is much we need not talk about,
And therefor seth hit nedeth naught	And therefore since we need it nought
As I have herde men sein offt	(As I have often heard and thought)
Be it in geste othir in songe	Be it in story or in song
And it be made overlonge	And extended overlong
Hit maketh men werie and lothe to here	It makes men weary, loth to hear it all,
Though hit be never so good matere	However good the tale's material,
And therefor this litille tretis	And therefore this little treatise
Out of that boke drawe it ys	Drawn out of that book it is
That of alle merveilis tellys	And only of the marvels tells
That he sawe and some thinge elles	That he saw – with something else.
A thousand and thre hundrid also	A thousand and three hundred also

And two and twenty put thereto

Was Christ's date Anno Domini

When out of this land journeyed he,

And even on Michaelmas day

That worthy knight took his way.

At Dover that is a town in Kent

The gentle Knight to ship he went.

They draw up sail and forth proceed.

Now Christ in heaven give us speed!

To whom he made his prayer

As David says in his psalter:

Point, O Lord, toward thy way.

Lead upon it. Save me, pray,

According to your own mercy.

Between this and the country of Rome

Often times men go and come

That can well tell and nothing miss

Of all they know and how it is;

But in truth they know not all

And therefore here I shall you tell

Of how that city was first begun

And how the course of things had run

So as to make that great city

Chief of all Christianity

And also head of Holy Kirk.

THERE will I first begin to work

As says a wise clerk in his verse,

The which I shall to you rehearse:

Rome, heading the world, rules the world.

He says that city was chief found

For Empire of all this world round.

Listen and ye shall know

What chronicles have to show.

From the time that God the world began

Until the time they founded Rome

Was four thousand and four hundred year

And two and twenti put thereto

Was cristis date veremente

When he out of this londe went

And even on migelmasse day

That worthi knyght toke his way

Atte dover that is a toune in kent

The gentil knyght to shippe he went

Thei drowe up saile and forth thei yede

Nowe criste of heven be oure spede,

To whom he made his praiere

As david saith in his sautere.

Vias tuas domine demonstra michi

Et semitas tuas edoce me. Salvum me fac

Secundum misericordiam tuam.

Bitwene this and the cuntre of Rome

Offten times men gone and come

That conne wel tel withouten mys

Of al that thei knowen and howe it is

But forsothe thei knowen not alle

And therefor I you telle here shalle

Ere that cite was first bigonne

And howe the cours is forth ironne

And for cause that same cite

Is chief of alle cristiante

And also hede of holi church

There wol I beginne frist to worch

As seith a wise clerk in his vers

The which I shal to you rehers.

Roma capud mundi tenet imperium mundi.

He seith that cite was chieff founde

Empire of alle this worlde rounde

Lesteneth and ye shalle weten

Howe in croniclis it is written

Fro the time that god the worlde bigan

Til that Rome was makid than

Was iiii. m. and cccc. yere

And iiii. and fiffti ferre ne nere
And fro the fundacioun of that toun
Unto cristis incarnacioun
Were vii. hundrid yere and fiffti also
Beth written in the croniclis and no mo
So that bifore er Rome bigan
As I you rede and telle can
With moch sorowe and litel ioy
Was the grete sege of troy

The grettest sege forsothe was hit
That was ever accountid yit
For it endurid seven yere
Or that cite taken were
A noble kinge ser Eneas
Captaine and lorde thereof he was
He had two sones of grete renoun
That were princis of that toun
And remus and romulus
Tho two bretheren were callid iwys
But whan that noble cite sholde
Taken ben and up iyolde,
Thoo twoo bretheren as I you say
Bi nyghte in shippe scaped away
And othir seven kingis moo
Escaped awaie with hem alsoo.
And brute that al this lande wan
That same time fro troie cam
But herkeneth nowe and ye shal here
These kingis names what thei were

And four and fifty, not less nor more;
And from the foundation of that town
Until Christ's incarnation
Were seven hundred years and fifty also
Is written in the chronicles and no mo
That earlier than Rome began
(For so I read, and so tell can)
With much sorrow and little joy
Was the great siege of Troy.

The greatest siege in truth was it
That ever was recounted yet,
For it endurèd seven year
Before that city taken were.
A noble king, Sir Aeneas,
Captain and lord thereof he was.
He had two sons of great renown
That were princes of that town,
Remus and Romulus, those two
Brethren were called, I know,
But when that noble city should
Taken been, and made to yield,
Those two brethren, I you say,
By night in ship escaped away
And seven other kings mo
Escaped away with them also.
Brutus, that all of Britain won,
That same time from Troy he came!
But hearken now and ye shall hear
These kings' names and who they were.

1375c

SIR GAWAIN AND THE GREEN KNIGHT
ANON
NORTHERN ENGLAND

*S*INCE the siege and assault was ceasèd at Troy,
   The burgh broken and burned to brands and ashes
(The tyke that the trammels of treason there wrought
Was tried for his treachery, the truest on earth).
It was Aeneas the Able and his high kind
Who since depressed provinces and patrons became
Wellnigh of all the wealth in the West Isles;
For rich Romulus to Rome riches he swipes,
With great bobbaunce that burgh he builds upon first
And names with his own name as now it hath;
Ticius in Tuscany township founds,
Langbeard in Lombardy lifts up homes
And far over the French flood Felix Brutus,
On many banks full broad Britain he builds
           with his winnings
      Where war and wreck and wonder
      By times have waxed therein,
      And oft both bliss and blunder
      Have had their innings.

And when Britain was built by this baron rich,
Bold brethren therein, that brawling loved,
Through much wild warfare wrought great wrong.
More fearfulness befell in these fields
Than in any other that I know since that time.
But of all that here built, of British kings,
Aye was Arthur the courtliest, as I have heard tell.
So an earthly adventure I aim to show,
An eerie adventure some men have beheld,
An outrageous adventure of Arthur's wonders.
If ye listen this lay but one little while,
I shall tell it straight as I in town heard,
               with tongue,
      As is stated and stocked,
      In swift tale and strong,
      With leal letters locked
      As this land hath known long.

This poem uses the same lore as the doggerel above, but puts it to the service of social & historical truth. The sacking of Troy truly was part of a westward movement of wealth & conquest that slowly filled Europe before it broke into Britain &, after filling that, 400 years later crossed to the Americas & Pacific before recoiling on Africa & Asia where it began. Like Virgil the Gawain poet makes the founder of his nation a refugee Trojan prince, but casts doubt on the virtues of such princes. They caused much grief but King Arthur (he has heard) was best of them. With the rhythm of an eagle flapping its wings before taking to the sky our poet promises to amaze us. He then describes an England like a harsh wilderness where joy & polite life occupy a few far-apart castles – unlike his own England where wealth was being made by wool exports. Then comes a tale of how Arthur's most heroic Christian knight almost

SIR GAWAYN AND THE GRENE KNIGHT
ANON
CHESHIRE c1375

*S*ITHEN the sege & the assaut watz sesed at troye
the borgh brittened & brent to brondez & askez
the tulk that the trammes of tresoun ther wroght
watz tried for his tricherie the trewest on erthe
hit watz ennias the athel & his high kynde
that sithen depreced provinces & patrounes bicome
welneghe of al the wele in the west iles
fro riche romulus to rome ricchis hym swythe
with gret bobbaunce that burghe he biges upon fyrst
& nevenes hit his aune nome as hit now hat
ticius to tuskan & teldes bigynnes
langaberde in lumbardie lyftes up homes
& fer over the french flod felix brutus
on mony bonkkes ful brode bretayn he settez
          with wynne
      where werre & wrake & wonder
      bi sythez hatz wont therinne
      & oft bothe blysse & blunder
      ful skete hatz skyfted synne
ande quen this bretayn watz bigged by this burn rych
bolde bredden therinne baret that lofden
in mony turned tyme tene that wroghten
mo ferlyes on this folde han fallen here oft
then in any other that i wot syn that ilk tyme
bot of alle that here bult of bretaygne kynges
ay watz arthur the hendest as i haf herde telle
forthi an aunter in erde i attle to schawe
that a selly in sight summe men hit holden
& an outtrage awenture of arthurez wonderez
if ye wyl lysten this laye bot on littel quile
i schal telle hit as tit as i in toun herd
          with tonge
      as hit is stad & stoken
      in stori stif & stronge
      with lel letteres loken
      in londe so hatz ben longe

fails a test set by the weird but genial god of a more ancient faith. It ends by urging the best people not to be proud of themselves.

This great poem is in a northern dialect & uses the alliterative line which did not die with the Saxon kings. Some southerners thought it sounded like the barking of dogs. Chaucer quotes one who called it **rum, ram, ruf**. *Alan Garner, whose people were craftsmen in Alderley Edge, says the dialect is still common there & near Macclesfield where it is thought the poem was written. The author may have made 2 other fine, openly Christian poems,* **Cleanness & Pearl.** **Athel** *had come to mean a prince born of princes, but originally meant someone made noble by his deeds or abilities, so I translate it* **able. Swythe** *means* **sways** *or* **moves,** *so* **swipe** *may derive from it.* **Bobbaunce** *means* **proud, pompous, boastful,** *but is too good a word to replace by 1 of these.*

1375c

THE BRUCE
JOHN BARBOUR
ARCHDEACON of ABERDEEN

HERE BEGINS THE BOOK COMPOSED BY MASTER JOHN BARBOUR, ARCHDEACON OF ABERDEEN: ON THE HISTORY, WARS AND VIRTUES OF LORD ROBERT THE BRUCE, BRILLIANT KING OF SCOTS, AND ON THE CONQUEST OF THE SCOTTISH KINGDOM THROUGH HIM, AND THE LORD JAMES DOUGLAS.

Before Irish & North Americans began cultivating their own form of English in the 17th century only Lowland Scots wrote it outside England. Like other folk the Scots had legends about the making of their nation but did not need them after 1314, for then they had remade it themselves.

Some years earlier Edward I created at Westminster a strong parliament, high court of law & civil service to tax & manage England while he added Wales, Scotland & France to it. He invaded Scotland thrice with big armies, putting his own governors & troops in the towns & castles. They were resisted by an alliance of small lairds & chiefs backed by the Scots clergy. William Wallace, leader of the Scots commons, was caught & killed by the English after victories that proved they could be

*S*TORIES *to read are delightable,*
Suppose that they be nocht but fable:
Then should stories that truthful were,
Be they said in good manner,
Give double pleasure in hearing.
The first pleasure is the telling,
The other in the truthfulness
Which shows the thing right as it was:
And true things that are likand
To man's hearing are pleasand.
Therefore I would set my will
(Give that my wit suffice theretill)
To put in writ a truthfast story,
That it last ay in memory,
And that no length of time it rot,
Or let it wholly be forgot.
For auld stories that men reads,
Represent to them deeds
Of stalwart fold that lively are,
Right as if they in presence were.
And certain is it, we would prize
Who in their time were weighty, wise,
And led their life in great trouble
And oft in hard dirt of battle,
Won right great prize of chivalry
And voided were of cowardy
As was King Robert of Scotland,
That hardy was of heart and hand;
And good Sir James of Douglas,

THE BRUIS
JOHN BARBOUR c1375
ABERDONE: SCOTLAND

INCIPIT LIBER COMPOSITUS PER MAGISTRUM IOHANNEM BARBER, ARCHIDIACONUM ABYRDONENSEM: DE GESTIS, BELLIS, ET VIRTUTIBUS DOMINI ROBERTI DE BRWYSS, REGIS SCOCIE ILLUSTRISSIMI, ET DE CONQUESTU REGNI SCOCIE PER EUNDEM, ET DE DOMINO IACOBO DE DOUGLAS.

*S*TORYS to rede ar delitabill
suppos that thai be nocht bot fabill
than suld storys that suthfast wer
and thai war said on gud maner
hawe doubill plesance in heryng
the fyrst plesance is the carpyng
and the tothir the suthfastnes
that schawys the thing rycht as it wes
and suth thyngis that are likand
tyll mannys heryng ar plesand.
tharfor i wald fayne set my will
giff my wyt mycht suffice thartill
to put in wryt a suthfast story
that it lest ay furth in memory
swa that na tyme of lenth it let
na ger it haly be forget
for auld storys that men redys
representis to thaim the dedys
of stalwart folk that lywyt ar
rycht as thai than in presence war
and certis thai suld weill hawe prys
that in thar tyme war wycht and wys
and led thar lyff in gret trawaill
and oft in hard stour off bataill
wan gret price off chewalry
and war woydyt off cowardy
as wes king robert off scotland,
that hardy wes off hart and hand
and gud schyr james off douglas

beaten. Scots nobles, Robert Bruce among them, had sided with Edward because they had property in England they feared to lose; but Bruce had a claim to the Scots crown. Realising he might now win a kingdom, he murdered his nearest rival for it then led an 8 year guerilla war that brought him victory at Bannockburn.

King Robert II gave John Barbour a pension for writing this poem of over 13,500 lines glorifying his grandpa, Robert I. Barbour was a priest & diplomat who studied at Oxford & Paris universities. He wrote a Scots speech enriched (as was Chaucer's speech) with many French words. He avoids mentioning Wallace by dealing only with the heroic part of Bruce's life, but it does not hide that he killed a rival Scot in church. It allows him

*That of his time, so worthy was,
That for his price and his bounty
In far lands renownit was he.
On them I think this book to do:
Now God give grace that I may so
Treat and it bring to such ending
That I say nocht but truthful thing!*

1377c

THE VISION OF PETER PLOUGHMAN
WILLIAM LANGLAND
LONDON: ENGLAND

*I*N a summer season when soft was the sun
*I wrapped me in wool as I a sheep were;
Garbed like a hermit, of unholy works,
Walking wide in this world, wonders to hear.
And on a May morning on Malvern hills
Magic befell me, of Fairy methought.
Farwandered and weary, went I to rest
Under a broad bank by a burn side,
And as I lay and leaned and looked on the water
I slumbered into a sleeping, it swayed so merry.*

*A marvellous dream I met in my swoon,
That I was in a wilderness, knowing not where,
And beheld in the East, as high as the sun,
A tower on a tall mound splendidly built,
A deep dale beneath, a dungeon therein,
With deep ditches and dark and dreadful of sight.
A fair field full of folk found I there between,
All manner of men, the mean and the rich,
Working and wandering as the world urges.
Some put them to plough, plying full sorely,
In setting and sowing sweating full hard,
Winning what wasters with gluttony destroyeth.*

Some put them to pride,
                                    *right proudly apparelled,
In courtly appparels coming disguised.*

that in his tyme sa worthy
was that off hys price & hys bounte
in fer landis renownyt wes he
off thaim I thynk this buk to ma
now god gyff grace that I may swa
tret it and bring it till endyng
that I say nocht bot suthfast thing

Barbour is both father of Scots poetry AND history, as very little of either survives from earlier times.

THE VISION OF PIERS PLOWMAN
WILLIAM LANGLAND
ENGLAND

c1377

*I*N a somer seson · whan soft was the sonne
I shope me in shroudes · as I a shepe were
In habite as an heremite · unholy of workes
Went wyde in this world · wondres to here
Ac on a May mornynge · on Malverne hulles
Me byfel a ferly · of fairy me thoughte
I was wery forwandred · and went me to reste
Under a brode banke · bi a bornes side
And as I lay and lened · and loked in the wateres
I slombred in a slepyng · it sweyved so merye

Thanne gan I to meten · a merveilouse swevene
That I was in a wildernesse · wist I never where
As I bihelde in to the est · an hiegh to the sonne
I seigh a toure on a toft · trielich ymaked
A depe dale binethe · a dongeon there Inne
With depe dyches & derke · and dredful of sight
A faire felde ful of folke · fonde I there bytwene
Of alle maner of men · the mene and the riche
Worchyng and wandryng · as the worlde asketh
Some put hem to the plow · pleyed ful selde
In settyng and in sowyng · swonken ful harde
And wonnen that wastours · with glotonye destruyeth

And some putten hem to pruyde ·
                    apparailed hem there after
In contenaunce of clothyng · comen disgised

All we know of Langland is what this poem later says. Of poor country folk, he went to an abbey-school near Malvern, but lack of cash ended the schooling before he could be a priest. With his psalter & prayerbook he tramps the London streets, hiring himself to those who want prayers or dirges chanted for the dead. He is tall, thin & religious ideas so craze him that at times he does not see the friendly greetings of rich lawyers & well-dressed ladies. His wife Kit laments that age reduces his sexual vigour. This man is a humorist, & truthful.

Like most Christians Langland thought hermits who lead strict lives earn God's mercy for the whole community.

In prayers and penancy put them many,
For love of our lord living right strictly
In hope for to have the heavenly bliss,
And as hermits and anchorites held to their cells,
Coveting nought in the country about
Nor in lecherous living their lusts to please.

And some chose to bargain, to better their trade,
And it seems to our sight that such men thrive.

He hints that those who thrive by their business deals should not be richer than others.

And some make mirth as minstrels can,
Getting gold with glee and guiltlessly, yes.
But jesters and jugglers, Judas's children,
Feigning folly and mimicking madness
Have wit at will to work if they would.
What Paul preaches of them I dare not prove here,
But a wicked windbag is Lucifer's arse.

Tramps and beggars strode about
Their bellies and bags with bread full crammed;
Cadging for food, brawling for beer,
In gluttony, God knows, going to bed,
And rising up ribald, the rankest of knaves.

Langland is hottest against the strolling beggars & religious parasites because (as he says later) he fears he is one of them.

Sleep and sorry sloth soweth they ever.

Pilgrims and palmers, pledged all together
To seek Saint James and the saints at Rome,
Went forth on the highway with many wise tales
And had leave to be liars all their life after.
I saw some that said they had sought out saints –
Each tale that they told their tongue tampered to lie
More than to say truth, it seemed by their speech.

Hermits in heaps, wielding hooked staves,
Wended to Walsingham, their wenches behind them.

Religious beggars spill out of the fair field & now surround us like a crowd on a highway.

Great lubbers and long that loth were to sweat
Had clapped on copes to be known from others,
Hired hermits' hoods, ease for to have.
I found there friars, all the four orders

In prayers and penance · putten hem manye
Al for love of owre lorde · lyveden ful streyte
In hope forto have · heveneriche blisse
As ancres and heremites · that holden hem in here selles
And coveiten nought in contre · to kairen aboute
For no likerous liflode · her lykam to plese

And somme chosen chaffare · they cheven the bettere
As it semeth to owre syght · that suche men thryveth
And somme murthes to make · as mynstralles conneth
And geten gold with here glee · synneles I leve
Ac japers & jangelers · Judas chylderen
Feynen hem fantasies · and foles hem maketh
And han here witte at will · to worche yif thei sholde
That Poule precheth of hem · I nel nought preve it here
Qui turpiloquium loquitur · is luciferes hyne

Bidders and beggeres · fast aboute yede
With her bely and her bagge · of bred ful ycrammed
Fayteden for here fode · foughten atte ale
In glotonye god it wote · gon hii to bedde
And risen with ribaudye · tho roberdes knaves
Slepe and sori sleuthe · seweth hem evre

Pilgrymes and palmers · plighted hem togidere
To seke seynt James · and seyntes in rome
Thei went forth in here wey · with many wise tales
And hadden leve to lye · al here lyf after
I seigh somme that seiden · thei had ysought seyntes
To eche a tale that thei tolde · here tonge was tempred to lye
More than to sey soth · it semed bi here speche

Heremites on an heep · With hoked staves
Wenten to Walsyngham · and here wenches after
Grete lobyes and longe · that loth were to swynke
Clotheden hem in copis · to ben knowen fram othere
And shopen hem heremites · here ese to have
I fonde there Freris · alle the foure ordres

EXPLANATION OF
LANGLAND'S JOB
Egyptians had sought eternal life by being mummified, Greeks by deeds that made them remembered. Jesus said eternal life was got by loving God & other folk & being wholly harmless & generous & forgiving. Since only saints could always be so pure the church taught that most Christians would enter heaven after a spell of pain in purgatory. The pain could be shortened by paying full clergy (who were given most) & lay clergy (like Langland) to hold services for the dead. Langland says he often carried off his wages in the bag of his belly. Like Bertolt Brecht he knew the food supply makes all else possible. In this poem the ploughman who produces the nation's corn is likened to Saint Peter, the commoner on whom Christ was said to build his church. Later he is shown to be Christ himself, the host who lets his body be broken so that others feed & live.

All sorts of clergy are using religion mainly to get cash out of rich & poor. Langland says something horrid must come of it.

Preaching to people for profit of belly,
Glossing the gospel as pleased them best
And for greed of rich copes, construed as they would.
Many such masters dress as they like –
Money and merchandise march well together.
Since charity turned shopman who chiefly shrives lords
Many marvels have fallen within a few years.
Unless church and priesthood hold better together
The worst mischief on earth is mounting up fast.

This lad will be shown more fully when we meet him in Chaucer's prologue.

There preached a pardoner as he a priest were;
Brought forth a bull with Bishop's seals,
Said he himself might absolve them all
Of falsehood, fasting and broken oaths.

Low men believed him and liked his speech,
Came up kneeling to kiss his bull.
With that blinding brief he blears their sight,
That rag-roll gets for him rings and brooches.
Thus ye give your gold to gorge great gluttons
And lend it to liars who lechery hunteth.

Cutting off ears was a punishment for thieves.

Were the Bishop blessèd and worth both his ears
He would not give his gold to deceive the people.
It is not by the Bishop this boy preaches;
Parish priest and the pardoner part the silver
The poor of the parish would have did they not.

Parsons and parish priests pled to the Bishop
That their parish was poor since the pestilence came,

Since the Black Death hit the bishop lets parish priests go to London where they earn more serving the rich or working as the king's accountants.

They sought leave and licence in London to dwell,
Singing for simony, since silver is sweet.

Bishops and bachelors, both masters and doctors,
That have care under Crist, and tonsure in token
And sign that they should be shriving parishioners
Preaching well, praying well and the poor feeding,
Leg it to London in Lent and in other times.
Some serve the king and connive as accountants

Preched the peple · for profit of hem selven
Glosed the gospel · as hem good lyked
For coveitise of copis · construed it as thei wolde
Many of this maistres Freris · mowe clothen hem at lykyng
For here money and marchandise · marchen togideres
For sith charite hath be chapman · and chief to shryve lordes
Many ferlis han fallen · in a fewe yeris
But holychirche and hii · holde better togideres
The moste mychief on molde · is mountyng wel faste

There preched a Pardonere · as he a prest were
Broughte forth a bulle · with bishopes seles
And seide that hym self myghte · assoilen hem alle
Of falshed of fastyng · of vowes ybroken

Lewed men leved hym wel · and lyked his wordes
Comen up knelyng · to kissen his bulles
He bonched hem with his brevet · & blered here eyes
And raughte with his ragman · rynges and broches
Thus they geven here golde · glotones to kepe
And leveth such loseles · that lecherye haunten
Were the bischop yblissed · and worth bothe his eres
His seel shulde nought be sent · to deceyve the peple
Ac it is naught by the bischop · that the boy precheth
For the parisch prest and the pardonere · parten the silver
That the poraille of the parisch · sholde have yif thei nere

Persones and parisch prestes · pleyned hem to the bischop
That here parisshes were pore · sith the pestilence tyme
To have a lycence and a leve · at London to dwelle
And syngen there for symonye · for silver is swete

Bischopes and bachelers · bothe maistres and doctours
That han cure under criste · and crounyng in tokne
And signe that thei sholden · shryven here paroschienes
Prechen and prey for hem · and the pore fede
Liggen in London · in lenten an elles
Somme serven the kyng · and his silver tellen

Langland's faith that God is found in the common life divides him from other mystics of his age, who wanted to withdraw from that. The author of **The Cloud** of unknowing praises 3 classes of Christian: **Do Wells** who obey the 10 commandments & attend church; **Do Betters** who have leisure to contemplate God privately; **Do Bests** who are able to contemplate God all the time. Langland's **Do Wells** also obey Jehovah's negative orders. His **Do Betters** add to this by loving their enemies as Jesus ordered. In all the early copies of **Piers Plowman, Do Best** is a strong active priest (maybe based on Wyclif) who can keep the damned out of hell & pull down high-living wickedness. In copies made after the peasant's revolt he is none but Jesus who must be sought beside Piers Plowman who feeds us all.

In exchequer and chancery claiming his debts
From wardens and wardcourts, widows and orphans.

And some serve as servants to lords and to ladies,
Instead of the Stewards, sitting and judging.
Their mass and their matins and much of their prayers
Are said undevoutly; I fear at the last
That Crist in his Council will curse full many.

A glance toward
Rome & a hint that its
cardinals may not be
very virtuous. (The
church was then split
between a French &
Italian pope, both
elected by cardinals
who changed their
minds after crowning
the 1st choice.)

I perceived of the power that Saint Peter held
To damn or redeem us, as the book telleth,
That he left it with love as our lord commanded
Among four virtues, the Cardinals called:
Prudence and temperance, courage and justice
Which close and which open the gates of Crist's kingdom,
Bind and unbind, and heaven's bliss show.
But the Roman Cardinals caught that name,
And presumed they had power a pope to make
To have power that Peter had – doubt I it never –
For to love and to learning the election belongeth;
I can but I cannot of that court speak more.

A staggering satire on
politics in most ages.
*For **king** read Prime*
Minister or President.
*For the **knighthood***
read heads of the
money market. For
clerics *read civil*
service & publicity
agencies.

Then came there a king, his knighthood leading;
Might of the commons made him to reign.
Then came common sense whom clerics created
To counsel the king and the commonwealth save.
The king and knighthood and clergy decide
That the common people should fend for themselves.

The commons contrive, with common sense, crafts
And for profit of all people Plowmen ordain
To till and to toil as true life asketh.
The king and the people and common sense too
Made law and obedience that each know his own.
Then leapt up a lunatic, a lean thing withal,
And kneeled to the king, and clericlike says,

This lean lunatic is the
poet who seems to
urge some sort of
reform.

"Crist keep ye, sir king, as well as thy kingdom,
Let ye lead the land so that loyalty loves ye,
And your righteous rule be rewarded in heaven."

In cheker and in chancerye · chalengen his dettes
Of wardes and wardmotes · weyves and streyves

And some serven as servantz · lordes and ladyes
And in stede of stuwardes · sytten and demen
Here messe and here matynes · and many of here oures
Arn don undevoutlych · drede is at the laste
Lest crist in consistorie · acorse ful manye
I parceyved of the power · that Peter had to kepe
To bynde and to unbynde · as the boke telleth
How he it left with love · as owre lorde hight
Amonges foure vertues · the best of alle vertues
That cardinales ben called · & closyng yatis
There crist is in kyngdome · to close and to shutte
And to opne it to hem · and hevene blisse shewe
Ac of the cardinales atte Courte · that caught of that name
And power presumed in hem · a Pope to make
To han that power that peter hadde · inpugnen I nelle
For in love and letterure · the eleccioun bilongeth
For thi I can and can naughte · of courte speke more

Thanne come there a kyng · knyghthod hym ladde
Might of the comunes · made hym to regne
And thanne cam kynde wytte · and clerkes he made
For to conseille the kyng · and the comune save
The kyng and knyghthode · and clergye bothe
Casten that the comune · shulde hem self fynde

The comune contreved · of kynde witte craftes
And for profit of alle the poeple · plowmen ordeygned
To tilie and travaile · as trewe lyf asketh
The kynge and the comune · and kynde witte the thridde
Shope lawe & lewte · eche man to knowe his owne
Thanne loked up a lunatik · a lene thing with alle
And knelyng to the kyng · clergealy he seyde
Crist kepe the sire kyng · and thi kyngriche
And leve the lede thi londe · so leute the lovye
And for thi rightful rewlyng · be rewarded in hevene

See how smartly Langland widens his field. After a short look at Rome he looks back at the corrupt English throng as a new king leads his knights into it. They debate how to rule all these people & reach the usual conclusion — don't try.

Then high in the air an Angel of heaven
Stooped low to speak Latin, lest ignorant men
Jangle and judge, to feel themselves just, who should
suffer and serve: forthwith said the Angel,
"Ye are king, ye are prince; but could become neither.
It is a king's duty to rule by Crist's law.
To do this the better, be just and be pious!
Nude justice by you should be clothed in religion.
Strip judgement bare of its merciful garments
And you too shall be judged by bare justice alone.
If you sow mercy then mercy you'll win."

This angel talks against reform like a papal legate or bishop. Using Latin to keep the debate private he says the church can depose kings, so the king must be kind to corrupt clergy if he wants church support.

This angered a Goliard, a glutton of words
Who to the Angel responded (in Latin):
"Since a king can be only a king when he's ruling
He can't be a king if he don't enforce laws!"
Then all of the folk started shouting in Latin
To the king's council, construe it who will:
"The King's orders and laws are the same thing to us!"

An intellectual loudmouth objects & soon everyone joins the debate. Latin is no longer an exclusive upper-class property.

With that there ran in a huge rout of rats
And small mice among them, more than a thousand
Come to a Council for the common profit.
For a cat of the court came when he liked,
Overleaping them lightly, laughing at them the while,
And played with them perilously, and pawed them about.
"For dread of these dangers we hardly dare look!
If we grouch at his game he will grieve us all,
Scratching and clawing us, in his clutch holding us,
Till we loathe our life ere he let us pass.
If we with some wit his will could withstand
We might be lofty lords living at ease."

As in a cartoon film the king, angel & shouting people are swept away by a cataract of rats & mice who set up their own parliament. The rats are big landlords, the mice middle-class MPs for country & town. The cat of the court is John of Gaunt, ruler of England, since the king is senile & his son is a child.

Then a rat of renown, most ready of tongue,
Suggested a sovereign salvation for all.
"I have seen sage men in the city of London
Wearing bright chains about their necks
With well-crafted collars, yet unleashed they wander

This rat was de la Mare, speaker of the House of Commons & braver than he is shown here.

And sithen in the eyre an hiegh · An angel of hevene
Lowed to speke in latyn · for lewed men ne coude
Jangle ne jugge · that justifie hem shulde
But suffren & serven · for thi seyde the angel
Sum Rex sum Princeps · neutrum fortasse deinceps
O qui iura regis · Christi specialia regis
Hoc quod agas melius · iustus es esto pius
Nudum ius a te · vestiri vult pietate
Qualia vis metere · talia grana sere
Si ius nudatur · nudo de iure metatur
Si seritur pietas · de pietate metas

Thanne greved hym a Goliardeys · a glotoun of wordes
And to the angel an heigh · answeres after
Dum rex a regere · dicatur nomen habere
Nomen habet sine re · nisi studet iura tenere
And thanne gan alle the comune · crye in vers of latin
To the kynges conseille · construe ho so wolde
Precepta Regis · sunt nobis vincula legis

With that ran there a route · of ratones at ones
And smale mys with hem · mo then a thousande
And comen to a conseille · for here comune profit
For a cat of a courte · cam whan hym lyked
And overlepe hem lyghtlich vand laughte hem at his wille
And pleyde with hem perilouslych · and possed aboute
For doute of dyverse dredes · we dar noughte wel loke
And yif we grucche of his gamen · he wil greve us alle
Cracche us or clowe us · and in his cloches holde
That us lotheth the lyf · or he lete us passe
Myghte we with any witte · his wille withstonde
We myghte be lordes aloft · and lyven at owre ese

A raton of renon · most renable of tonge
Seide for a sovereygne · help to hym selve
I have ysein segges quod he · in the cite of london
Beren bighes ful brighte · abouten here nekkes
And some colers of crafty werk · uncoupled thei wenden

Most church people saw themselves as potential angels; their critics as Goliath's people – Goliards for short. In religious dramas Goliath was nearly as popular as Satan or Herod. Unfrocked clerics who lived by their wits, students on the tramp in search of learning were called Goliards. These met in pubs & sang, sometimes in Latin, songs that said sex, booze & money were the best things in a world ruled by greed & luck. Critics of the social order from a low place in it were called Goliards. Their enemies said they had more words than sense. From a book of Goliard songs in the library of a German abbey Carl Orff made **Carmina Burana***.*

Town concillors wore chains round their necks like the collars of hunting dogs. The lowest serfs had iron collars riveted on; serf-criminals with bells attached to them. This made stealthy movement impossible.

In warrens and wastes, wherever they wish,
And otherwhiles elsewhere, as I have heard tell.
Were a bell on their chains, by Jhesu, me thinketh
Men might know where they went, and leave them room!
And so," quoth the rat, "right reason shows
We should buy a bell of bright brass or silver,
Knit to a collar for our common profit,
Hang it on the cat's neck, then hear when he moves,
Raiding or resting or roaming to play.
If he longs to be licking then look that we move
And appear in his presence while he likes to play
And if he be wrathful, beware, shun his way."

The whole rout of rats to this reason assented,
But the bell being bought, and hanged on the chain,
No rat in that rout, for the whole
                              realm of France,
Dare bind that bell about the cat's neck,
Or reach round his throat all England to win.
They knew themselves cowards, their council feeble;
Held their labour lost and all their long study.

The bell discussed here is an act of parliament to limit royal power.

Then a mouse of much merit and sense, me thought,
Strode forth sternly, stood before them,
And to the rabble of rats rehearsed these words.
"Though we killed the cat, there would then come another
To catch us and our kind,
                         though we crept under benches.
I counsel the commons to let the cat be,
And be never so bold to show him that bell.
For I heard my sire say, seven years since:
When the cat is a kitten the court is right wretched,
As witnesseth holy writ where you may read:
Woe to the land which hath too young a king et cetera,
For fear of rodents no rank could then rest.
While he catches rabbits
                              he craves not our carcase,

*This sensible mouse is heard in every age, advising us to leave our bosses alone because they get worse if you try to replace them. He says that the cat only **toys** with noble English rats & middle-class mice, since the rodents he prefers to **eat** are the French rabbits. Let us lie low while he gets on with it!*

Bothe in wareine & in waste · where hem leve lyketh
And otherwhile thei aren elles where · as I here telle
Were there a belle on here beigh · bi Ihesu as me thynketh
Men myghte wite where thei went · and awei renne
And right so quod that ratoun · reson me sheweth
To bugge a belle of brasse · or of brighte sylver
And knitten on a colere · for owre comune profit
And hangen it up on the cattes hals · thanne here we mowen
Where he ritt or rest · or renneth to playe
And yif him list for to laike · thenne loke we mowen
And peren in his presence · ther while hym plaie liketh
And yif him wrattheth be ywar · and his weye shonye

Alle this route of ratones · to this reson thei assented
Ac tho the belle was ybought · and on the beighe hanged
There ne was ratoun in alle the route · for alle
                              the rewme of Fraunce
That dorst have ybounden the belle · aboute the cattis nekke
Ne hangen it aboute the cattes hals · al Engelonde to wynne
And helden hem unhardy · and here conseille feble
And leten here laboure lost · & alle here longe studye

A mous that moche good · couthe as me thoughte
Stroke forth sternly · and stode biforn hem alle
And to the route of ratones · reherced these wordes
Though we culled the catte · yut sholde ther come another
To cracchy us and al owre kynde ·
                    though we croupe under benches
For thi I conseille alle the comune · to lat the catte worthe
And be we never so bolde · the belle hym to shewe
For I herde my sire seyn · is sevene yere ypassed
There the catte is a kitoun · the courte is ful elyng
That witnisseth holiwrite · who so wil it rede
Ve terre ubi puer rex est &c
For may no renke there rest have · for ratones bi nyghte
The while he caccheth conynges ·
                    he coveiteth nought owre caroyne

In 1378 Gaunt, allied with London bankers & monopolists, asked the Commons for money to resume war in France. The high cost of labour made most MPs object to this. They discussed a bill to take power from the crown, but thought it safer to vote the money in return for a promise to limit monopolies & mend some other church and state abuses. The promise was given, & the money voted by a parliament nicknamed the GOOD. When sure of the money the royal party broke its promise, jailed the speaker of the Commons & burned all the GOOD parliament's records.

While he feeds on such venison, never defame him.
Better a little loss than a long sorrow.
This mischief among us may let us miss worse,
And many men's malt we mice would destroy

But the wise mouse is also a radical critic. He says that fear of the cat stops the rodents fighting each other & eating all the produce of MEN, on whom they depend. At which dangerous point Langland asks some joker to explain his dream – Langland dare not.

While rats like you chewed their clothes to rag –
Were it not that the court cat overleaps you.
If you rats had your way
                    you could not rule yourselves.
As for me," said the mouse, "I see so far ahead
That no cat and no kitten by me shall be grieved.
I paid nothing toward this collar,
And if I had I would keep my mouth shut
And suffer the cat to slay who he likes,
Going coupled or single to catch what he can.
The wise ones among us will guard well our own."
What this dream means, ye men that be merry,
Divine it! I dare not, by dear God in heaven.

Then hoved in a hundred in hoods of silk,
Lawyers it seemed that served at the bar,
Pleaded for pennies and pounds the law,
Nor for love of our lord unlocked their lips once.

The rodent parliament is swept away by a herd of greedy lawyers. Again we are jostled by a crowd in what now seems a busy street market, loud with the shouts of vendors.

You may sooner draw mist from the Malvern hills
Than a murmur from their mouths ere money be shown.

Barons and Burgesses and Bondsmen also,
I saw in this assembly as you shall hear after;
Bakers and Brewers and Butchers many,
Woollen Websters and Weavers of linen,
Tailors and Tinkers, Tax-takers in markets,
Masons, Miners and many more crafts;
Of all kinds of labourers loped forth some,
Such as dykers and delvers who do their jobs ill
And drive through the dear day singing
                    "God save sweet Emma!"
Cooks and their knaves cry "Hot pies! Hot!
Good geese and grease! Come dine! Come dine!"

But fet hym al with venesoun · defame we hym nevere
For better is a litel losse · than a longe sorwe
The mase amonge us alle · though we mysse a schrewe
For many mannus malt · we mys wolde destruye
And also ye route of ratones · rende mennes clothes
Nere that cat of that courte · that can yow overlepe
For had ye rattes yowre wille ·
                                  ye couthe nought reule yowre selve
I sey for me quod the mous · I se so mykel after
Shal never the cat ne the kitoun · bi my conseille be greved
Ne carpyng of this coler · that costed me nevre
And though it had coste me catel · biknowen it I nolde
But suffre as hym self wolde · to do as hym liketh
Coupled & uncoupled · to cacche what thei mowe
For thi uche a wise wighte I warne · wite wel his owne
What this meteles bemeneth · ye men that be merye
Devine ye for I ne dar · bi dere god in hevene

Yit hoved there an hondreth · in houves of selke
Serjauntz it semed · that serveden atte barre
Plededen for penyes · and poundes the lawe
And nought for love of owre lorde · unlese here lippes onis
Thow myghtest better mete the myste · on malverne hulles
Than gete a momme of here mouthe · but money were shewed

Barones an burgeis · and bonde men als
I seigh in this assemble · as ye shul here after
Baxsteres & brewesteres · and bocheres manye
Wollewebsteres · and weveres of lynnen
Taillours and tynkeres · & tolleres in marketes
Masons and mynours · and many other craftes
Of alkin libbyng laboreres · lopen forth somme
As dykers & delveres · that doth here dedes ille
And dryven forth the dere day ·
                                  with Dieu vous save Dame Emme
Cokes and here knaves · crieden hote pies hote
Gode gris a gees · gowe dyne gowe

John Richard Green calls Langland **gaunt poet of the poor**, says what makes this poem great is its **deep undertone of sadness**, for it shows a world where only the vicious thrive. This ignores the energy & freedom of the old English verse lines rhyming at the start of words instead of ends, & the energy & comedy of the **quick cutting** (as film makers call it) from scene to scene. Langland steers our vision with the skill of Chaplin or Buñuel.

Taverners with them were telling the same:
"White wine of Alsace! Red wine of Gascony!
Rhenish or Rochelle to wash down your roast!"
All this I saw sleeping, and seven times more.

1385c

THE CANTERBURY TALES
PROLOGUE by GEOFFREY CHAUCER
LONDON, ENGLAND

HERE BEGINS THE BOOK OF THE TALES OF CANTERBURY.

Chaucer's 1st sentence is a whole verse of 9 rhymed couplets. Their rhythm is not the Mandeville rhymer's jog-trot couplets, not the martial stride of Barbour's. Chaucer's lines are nearly as long as the lines of the Gawain poet and Langland, so like them each line holds 2 well-balanced phrases. In a long rhyming couplet the 2nd line usually sounds so final that Shakespeare mainly used them singly to conclude scenes & sonnets. Poets in the Age of Reason liked to sound conclusive so wrote big poems in couplets that now strike most of us as monotonous. But Chaucer's rhymes aid, not interrupt, a varied and sparkling speech through an 18 line sentence that never runs out of breath or sense, though it takes us far into a social spring holiday in Chaucer's modern England.

*W*HEN that April with his shourès sootè
     The drocht of March hath piercèd to the rootè,
And bathèd every vein in such liquour
Of which virtue engendered is the flower;
When Zephirus eke with his sweetè breath
Inspirèd hath in every holt and heath
The tender crops, and the young sun
Hath in the Ram his half course run,
And the small fowls make melody
That sleep all night with open eye
(So nature pricks in their courages)
Then people long to go on pilgrimages,
And palmers for to seek out foreign strands,
To holy places, couched in sundry lands;
And specially from every shirès end
Of Engeland to Caunterbury they wend,
The holy blissful martyr for to seek
That them have helped, in times when they were sick.

Befell that in that season on a day
In Southwark at the Tabard as I lay
Ready to wend upon my pilgrimage
To Canterbury with full devout courage,
At nicht was come into that hostelry
Well nine and twenty in a company
Of sundry folk, by accident they fall
In fellowship, and pilgrims were they alle,
That toward Canterbury would them ridè.
The chambers and the stables were full widè

Taverners un til hem · tolde the same
White wyn of Oseye · and red wyn of Gascoigne
Of the Ryne and of the Rochel · the roste to defye
Al this seigh I slepyng · and sevene sythes more

THE CAUNTERBURY TALES
PROLOGUE by GEOFFREY CHAUCER
LONDON, ENGELOND

c1385

HERE BYGYNNETH THE BOOK OF THE TALES OF CAUNTERBURY.

W HAN that Averyll with his shoures soote
     The droghte of March / hath perced to the roote
And bathed every veyne in swich lycour
Of which vertu engendred is the flour
Whan zephirus eek with his sweete breeth
Inspired hath in every holt and heeth
The tendre croppes / and the yonge sonne
Hath in the Ram / his half cours yronne
And smale foweles / maken melodye
That slepen al the nyght with open Iye
So priketh hem nature / in hir corages
Thanne longen folk to goon on pilgrymages
And Palmeres for to seeken straunge strondes
To ferne halwes / kouthe in sondry londes
And specially / from every shyres ende
Of Engelond / to Caunterbury they wende
The holy blisful martir / for to seke
That hem hath holpen whan that they weere seeke

Bifel that in that sesoun on a day
In Southwerk at the Tabard / as I lay
Redy to weenden / on my pilgrymage
To Caunterbury / with ful devout corage
At nyght was come / in to that hostelrye
Wel .xxix. in a compaignye
Of sondry folk / by aventure yfalle
In felaweshipe / and pilgrymes weere they alle
That toward Caunterbury wolden ryde
The chambres and the stables / weeren wyde

Chaucer seems to do it easily because his rhythm rides mainly on buoyant vowels inside his lines. For his voice is more southern as well as more northern than the British queen's accent today. He uses the speech of a court which spoke French as readily as English, and worshipped God in Latin services chanted with a more Italian lilt than was heard in England after she split with Rome.

On the left pages I hint at Chaucer's lilt by some signs over vowels we now neglect. I suggest the northern sharpness by putting ch for the neglected gh, as most of us can read how it used to sound at the end of loch and Bach. All translations hint at the original by a more or less cranky blending of sense and sound. The crankiness of my version should turn you to the original quite quickly. The describing voice of the

1st verse arrives bodily in the 2nd among some folk in a south London inn. He seems a modest likeable man – a good inquirer and listener. He says nothing about himself but is soon so friendly with 29 strangers that he can tell us all about them, their trades, looks, clothes and natures. The party contains folk from every class in England around 1380 except royalty and landless labourers. Said Dryden of Chaucer in 1700:

He has taken into the Compass of his Canterbury Tales the various Manners and Humours (as we now call them) of the whole English Nation, in his Age. Not a single character has escap'd him.

Blake, in 1809, went further:

**The characters of Chaucer's Pilgrims are the characters which compose all ages & nations ... for we see the same characters repeated again and again, in animals, vegetables, minerals, & in men...
As Newton numbered the stars, & Linnaeus numbered the plants, so Chaucer numbered the classes of men.**

Chaucer depicts folk with a relish suggesting his world is

And well we were there easèd at the best;
And shortly, when the sunnè was to restè,
So had I spoken with them everyone,
That I was of their fellowship anon,
And started forward early for to rise,
To take our way there, as I you devise.

But natheless, while I have time and place
Ere that I further in this story pace,
Me thinketh it accordant with reason
To tellè you all the condition
Of each of them, so as it seemed to me,
And which they weren, and of what degree,
And eke in what array that they were in,
And at a knicht then will I first begin.

A KNICHT there was, and that a worthy man,
That from the time that he first began
To riden out, he lovèd chivalry,
Truth and honour, freedom and courtesy.
Full worthy was he in his lord's war.
And thereto had he ridden, none more far,
As well in Christendom as heathenessè,
And ever honoured for his worthinessè.
At Alexandria he was when it was won.
Full oft at table he the board begun
Abovè all nations in Prussia;
In Latvia had he raided, and in Russia
No Christian man so oft of his degree.
In Granada, at the siege had he be
Of Algeciras, and ridden in Belmarye,
At Anatolia and at Satalye
When they were won; through the Great Middle Sea
With many a noble army had he be.
At mortal battles had he been fifteen.
And fouchten for our fath at Tramyssene
In listès thrice, and ay slain his foe.
This worthy knicht had sometime foucht also

And wel we weeren esed / at the beste
And shortly whan the sonne was to reste
So hadde I spoken with hem everichoon
That I was of hir felaweshipe anoon
And maade forward / erly for to ryse
To take oure wey / ther as I yow devyse

But nathelees / while I have tyme and space
Er that I ferther / in this tale pace
Me thynketh it acordant to resoun
To telle yow / al the condicioun
Of eech of hem / so as it seemed me
And whiche they weere / and of what degree
And eek in what array / that they weere Inne
And at a knyght thanne wol I first bigynne

A KNYGHT ther was / and that a worthy man
That fro the tyme / that he first bigan
To ryden out he loved chivalrye
Trouthe and honour / fredom and curteisye
Ful worthy was he / in his lordes werre
And ther to hadde he ryden / no man ferre
As wel in cristendom / as hethenesse
And evere honured / for his worthynesse
At Alisaundre he was / whan it was wonne
Ful ofte tyme / he hadde the bord bigonne
Aboven alle nacions / in Pruce
In lettow / hadde he reysed / and in Ruce
No cristen man so ofte / of his degree
In Gernade at the seege eek hadde he be
At Algizir / and ryden in Belmarye
At lyeys was he / and at Satalye
Whan they weere wonne / and in the grete see
At many a noble armee / hadde he bee
At mortal batailles / hadde he been fiftene
And foghten for oure feyth / at Tramyssene
In lystes thryes / and ay slayn his foo
This ilke worthy knyght hadde been also

good, that (quoting Dryden again) **Here is God's plenty.** *The* **Tales***, like* **Piers Plowman***, first show us the country in a lovely season and then, through the person of the poet, show the human state of England. At first sight the Englands of Chaucer and Langland differ as much as their accents. Langland deals with folk in mobs: his priests, plowmen, nobles etc. jostle, toil, dispute in field, court and highway. Chaucer approaches them politely, one at a time. They are on holiday, at ease, ready to talk about themselves to friendly, admiring Mr. Chaucer who passes the news straight to us.*

The knight (for example) explains that he loves chivalry, truth, freedom etc. and has been fighting abroad in wars arranged by his feudal overlord. Nobody has gone further than he in warfare, none of his rank have won more honour by it. He has fought with Christians against Christians, with Christians against heathens, for a heathen against heathens; he has been in 15 battles and 3 tournaments, & has always killed his enemy. He has always been well paid for it or won rich booty, for though a bonny fighter he's a wise man too, with manners as meek as a young girl's. He's never said a bad word to anyone in his life. A perfect gentleman!

There is mischief here, the kind of mischief we meet later when Chaucer presents a great chef who confects tasty sweets and soups, is a master of roasting, stewing, baking, has a wet ulcer on his knee and makes excellent blancmange. Chaucer's admiration can plant a sting as deep as Langland's open satire, a sting so fine that readers miss it. James Winny, in a fine modern essay on this prologue, says the knight (with the poor parson and plough-man) is one of the 3 ideally good people among the pilgrims. None have read this prologue more closely than Blake who wrote: The Knight is a true Hero, a good, great, and wise man; his whole-length portrait on horseback, as written by Chaucer, cannot be surpassed. He has spent his life in the field; has ever been a conqueror, and is that species of character which in every age stands as the guardian of man against the oppressor.

*Under a Saracen of Araby
Against another heathen in Turkey,
And every time he gained a sovereign prize;
And though that he was worthy, he was wise,
And of his port as meek as is a maid.
And never yet no villainy had said
In all his life unto no sort of wight.
He was a very perfect, gentle knight.
But for to tellen you of his array,
His horse was goodè, but he was not gay.
His undercoat it was of fustian
And all bismottered was his habergeon,
For he was lately come from his voyage,
And straightway went to do his pilgrimage.*

*With him there was his sonnè, a young SQUIRE,
A lover and a lusty bachelor,
With locks as curly as if laid in press.
Of twenty year of age he was, I guess.
Of his stature he was of even lengthè
And wonderly active, and of greatè strengthè.
And he had raided with the cavalry
In Flanders and Artoise and Picardy,
And born him well, though in so little space
In hope to standen in his lady's grace.
Embroidered was he, as it were a meadè
All full of freshè flowers, white and reedè.
Singing he was or whistling all the day;
He was as fresh as is the month of May.
Short was his gown, with sleevès long and wide.
Well could he sit on horse and fairly ride,
And he could songès make and well endite,
And joust, and dance, and weel portray or write.
So hot he loved that ere the dawn grew pale
He slept no more than did the nichtingale.
Courteous he was, lowly and serviceable,
And carved before his father at the table.
A YEOMAN had he (and no servants mo*

Somtyme / with the lord of Palatye
Agayn another hethen in Turkye
And evere moore / he hadde a sovereyn prys
And thogh that he weere worthy / he was wys
And of his poort as meke / as is a mayde
He nevere yet no vileynye he sayde
In al his lyf unto no manere wight
He was a verray parfit gentil knyght
But for to tellen yow / of his array
Hise hors weere goode / but he ne was nat gay
Of ffustian / he wered a gypon
Al bismotered / with his haubergeon
For he was laate / comen from his viage
And wente / for to doon his pilgrymage

With hym / ther was his sone a yong SQUYER
A lovere / and a lusty Bachiler
With lokkes crulle / as they weere leyd in presse
Of .xx. yeer / he was of age I gesse
Of his stature / he was of evene lengthe
And wonderly delyvere / and of greet strengthe
And he hadde been som tyme / in chyvachye
In Flaundres / in Artoys / and Picardye
And born hym wel / as in so litel space
In hope / to stonden / in his lady grace
Embrouded was he / as it weere a meede
Al ful of fresshe floures / white and reede
Syngynge he was / or floytynge al the day
He was as fressh / as is the Monthe of May
Short was his gowne / with sleves / longe & wyde
Wel koude he sitte on hors / and faire ryde
He koude songes wel make / and endite
Juste and eek daunce / and wel portreye and write
So hoote he loved / that by nyghtertale
He slepte namoore / than dooth a nyghtyngale
Curteys he was / lowely / and servysable
And carf biforn his fader / at the table
A YEMAN he hadde / and servantz namo

*This seems more like Sir Galahad than an absentee landowner enriched by killing foreigners. The poem does not say the knight guarded men against oppressors, only that he fought **in his lordes werre**, and one of the wars mentioned (the raid on Latvia) was a homicidal attack on civilians because they were not Christians. I think, even as a fighter, this knight sounds too good to be true. Can he have boasted a little to guileless, admiring Mr. Chaucer? Maybe not. Like the pirate Byron describes he may indeed be **the mildest mannered man / That ever cut a throat or scuttled ship**. Whether we like or suspect or detest this officer and gent, Blake is right to see him as a type who has lived, will perhaps live as long as mankind. Chaucer, using a form of himself as bait, has caught the type alive. Langland and Dante, Proust and Joyce put sharp self-portraits into their books to let us see and hear them openly shift the action. Chaucer's self-portrait is a mild social surface, a nearly static detail of scenery behind which someone else runs the show. The voice of this ventri-loquist sounds every-*

where. Blake and I can't agree where he stands. Who WAS Chaucer?

Legal records prove Chaucer was born to a dynasty of London wine merchants circa 1342 when ENGLISH ROYALTY SEEK LOYAL LADS FROM PROFESSIONAL CLASS TO GATHER REVENUE & KEEP ACCOUNTS ETC. NO CLERGY SHOULD APPLY. (For nearly 200 years church & state, king & pope had disagreed about power and revenue. Ask Thomas à Becket.) Between 1357 and his death in 1400 Chaucer was:

Page to royal princess then soldier in France. (Captured by enemy. Ransom paid by King Edward.)

Valet of the King's Household.

Diplomat in Genoa, Pisa, Florence.

Controller of the port of London.

Secret agent in Flanders.

Diplomat in France. (Negotiated a peace treaty.)

Controller of wool and customs, London.

Carried king's cash. (Twice robbed.)

Collected king's debts.

Member of Parliament for Kent.

Clerk of works.

At that time, for it pleased him to ride so)
And he was clad in coat and hood of green.
A sheaf of peacock arrows, bright and keen
Under his belt he bare right thriftily,
Well could he dress his tackle yeomanly
(His arrows droopèd noucht with feathers low)
And in his hand he bore a michty bow.
A nut head had he, with a brown visage.
Of woodcraft weel he kenned the usèage.
Upon his arm he bore a gay bracer,
And by his side a sword and buckeler,
And on the other side a gay dagger
Sheathed well and sharp as point of spear;
A Christopher on his breast of silver sheen.
A horn he bore, the baldrick was of green;
A forester was he, surely as I guess.

There also was a nun, a PRIORESS,
That of her smiling was full simple and coy;
Her greatest oath was but by Saintè Loy
And she was called Madame Eglantyne.
Full well she sung the servicè divine,
Entunèd in her nose full seemely,
And French she spoke both fair and primly
After the school of Stratford atte Bowè,
For French of Paris was to her unknowè.
At table so well taught was she withalle
She let no morsel from her lippès falle
Nor wet her fingers in her saucè deep.
Well could she carry a morsel and well keep
That no drop never fell upon her breast.
In courtesy she strove to be the best
Her over lippè wipèd she so clean
That on her cup no spot was ever seen
Of grease, when she drunken had her draught.
Full pleasingly after her meal she coughed,
And certainly she was a splendid sport,
And full pleasant, and amiable of port,

At that tyme / for hym liste ryde so
And he was clad / in coote and hood of greene
A sheef of Pecok arwes / bright and keene
Under his belt he bar ful thriftily
Wel koude he dresse his takel yemanly
His arwes drowped noght with fetheres lowe
And in his hand / he bar a myghty bowe
A not heed hadde he / with a broun visage
Of wodecraft / koude he wel al the usage
Up on his arm / he bar a gay bracer
And by his syde / a swerd and a Bokeler
And on that oother syde / a gay daggere
Harneysed wel / and sharpe / as poynt of spere
A Cristofre on his brest of silver sheene
An horn he bar / the bawdryk was of greene
A Forster was he / soothly as I gesse

Ther was also / a Nonne a PRIORESSE
That of hir smylyng was ful symple and coy
Hir gretteste ooth / was but by Seint Loy
And she was clepyd / madame Eglentyne
Ful wel she soong the servyce dyvyne
Entuned in hir nose / ful semely
And frenssh she spak ful faire and fetisly
After the scole / of Stratford at the Bowe
For frenssh of Parys / was to hire unknowe
At mete / wel ytaught was she with alle
She leet no morsel / from hir lyppes falle
Ne wette hir fyngres / in hir sauce deepe
Wel koude she carye a morsel / and wel keepe
That no drope / fille up on hire brist
In curteisye / was set muchel hir list
Hir over lyppe / wyped she so cleene
That in hir coppe / ther was no ferthyng seene
Of grece / whan she dronken hadde hir draghte
Ful semely / after hir mete she raghte
And sikerly / she was of greet desport
And ful plesaunt and amyable of port

(Saw to repairing Thames embankment, bridges, sewers, the Tower of London, various royal palaces, and erection of the grandstand for a noble tournament.)

Head keeper of royal forest.

So Chaucer lived in the middle of state business, not at the dangerous top or hard-pressed foot. True, his wife's sister married John of Gaunt, the cat of the court who toyed with the bourgeois mice in Langland's poem. Gaunt ruled nearly all England when King Edward went senile. But Chaucer's sister-in-law was not great gentry, had been nurse of Gaunt's children by 2 earlier wives – the 2nd died of plague. Chaucer got pensions from King Edward, King Richard & King Henry, though Henry (Gaunt's son) deposed Richard and had him murdered. This civil servant whose career can be followed in royal account books fits the self-portrait in the **Tales**: an agreeable listener who only knows what others tell him. This is the safest surface if you are working for autocrats.

But Chaucer was about 45 when he began the **Tales**, and

And tried of counterfeit a courtly cheer,
And to be always stately of mannèr,
And to be held in proper reverence,
But let me tell you of her conscience.
She was so charitable and so piteous
She would weep, if that she saw a mouse
Caught in a trap, if it were dead or bled;
And smallè houndès had she that she fed
With roasted meat, or milk and fine white bread,
And sore she wept if one of them were dead,
Or if men smote it with a yardstick smart;
And all was conscience and a tender heart.
Full seemly her wimple pinchèd was,
Her nose well formed, her een as grey as glass,
Her mouth full small, and also soft and red,
And sikerly she had a fair forehead;
Almost a hand-span broad it was, I own;
And certainly she was not undergrown.
Her cloak was neat, as I was well aware.
Of small coral about her arm she bare
A pair of prayer-beads, gauded all with green,
And thereon hung a brooch of golden sheen,
On which there first was wrought a crownèd A,
And after Amor vincit omnia.

Another NUN beside her haddè she,
That was her chapelain, and priestès three.

A MONK there was, surpassing all the rest,
A grain inspector, who loved hunting best.
A manly man, to be an abbot able.
Full many a dainty horse had he in stable,
And when he rode, men might his bridle hear
Jingling in a whistling wind as clear
And eek as loud as did the chapel bell
Wherein this lord was keeper of the cell.
The rule of Saint Maurice or Benedict,
Because that it was old and somewhat strict,

And peyned hire / to countrefete chiere
Of Court and been estatlich of manere
And to been holden / digne of reverence
But for to speken / of hir conscience
She was so charitable / and so pitous
She wolde wepe / if that she sawe a Mous
Caught in a trappe / if it weere deed / or bledde
Of smale houndes / hadde she / that she fedde
With rosted flessh / or mylk / and wastel breed
But soore wepte she / if oon of hem weere deed
Or if men smoot it / with a yerde smerte
And al was conscience / and tendre herte
Ful semely / hir wympel pynched was
Hir nose tretez / hir eyen / greye as glas
Hir mouth ful smal / and ther to / softe and reed
But sikerly / she hadde a fair forheed
It was almoost a spanne brood I trowe
For hardily / she was nat undergrowe
Ful fetys was hir cloke / as I was war
Of smal Coral / aboute hir arm she bar
A peyre of bedes / gauded al with greene
And ther on heeng a brooch of gold ful sheene
On which / was first writen / a crowned A.
And after / amor vincit omnia.

Another NONNE / with hire hadde she
That was hire Chapeleyne / and preestes thre.

A MONK ther was / a fair for the maystrye
An outrydere / that lovede venerye
A manly man / to been an Abbot able
Ful many a deyntee hors / hadde he in stable
And whanne he rood / men myghte his brydel heere
Gyngle in a whistlynge wynd / as cleere
And eek as loude / as dooth the Chapel belle
There as this lord / is kepere of the selle
The rule of seint Maure / or of seint Beneyt
By cause that it was oold / and som deel streyt

poem sorrowing for the death of John of Gaunt's 2nd wife. In a later preface he said that he shut his accounts book at the end of the day's work & hurried home to sit dumb as a stone over another book, setting his wits to turn other writers' love stories into poems and songs until his head was fuddled, his looks dazed. Elsewhere he said that he was no lover, but love used him as her secretary, as he had put into English the great romances she caused. In at least four allegorical poems using stories and images from Latin, French and Italian romance, he had described himself as a book-worm using other folk's ideas. He had decanted into English speech:

DE CONSOLATIONE
   PHILOSOPHIAE
The author, Boethius, had been a Roman senator jailed on a charge of plotting to restore Italian liberty. Before execution he used Plato, Seneca, & Christianity to calm his mind in a work which for at least 1000 years was the best-known book of philosophy in Europe: in some lands the only one. King Alfred translated it into the

English of his day, so
did Chaucer.
ROMAN DE LA ROSE
In polite circles this
was the most famous of
French poems. The first
half described a loved
woman religiously, as a
private garden which
ennobled the man who
humbly & politely
sought to pluck her
innermost rose. The
writer, de Lorris, died
before showing how
the rose got plucked,
and the poem was
completed by de Meun,
a cynical free-thinker
with scientific tastes.
The whole work thus
summed up nearly all
that could be said
about sexual love.
FILOSTRATO
This Italian love story,
realistic & modern
though set in Trojan
times, was written by
Boccaccio, Chaucer's
great contemporary.
While translating it
Chaucer's imagination
enlarged & deepened
characters & story till
*it became **Troilus and***
***Criseyde**, the first*
psychological novel in
English.
Chaucer was now
at the height of his
powers, but all his
other work had been
CONVENTIONAL: the
feelings of polite, rich
people shown through
allegorical dreams
based on other men's
work. Yet this author
with the huge appetite

Inclined this monk to let such old things pass
And to take after the newè world the pace.
He gave not for that text a pullèd hen
That sayeth that hunters be not holy men,
Nor that a monk, when he is order-less,
Is like unto a fish that's waterless –
That is to say, a monk out of the cloister.
A text like that he held not worth an oyster,
And I said his opinion was good.
Why should he study,
                    making himself mad
Over a book in cloister alway to pourè,
Or toiling with his handès, and labourè
As Austen bid? How shall the world be served?
Let Austen have his toil for him reserved!
Therefore he was a galloper aright:
Greyhounds he had as swift as fowl in flight;
Of spurring and of hunting for the hare
Was all his lust, for no cost would he spare.
I saw his sleeves had cuffs about the hand
Of costly fur, the finest in the land;
And, for to fasten his hood under his chin,
He had of gold ywrought a curious pin;
A love-knot in the greater end there was.
His heid was bald, and shone like any glass,
And eek his face, as if with oil anoint.
He was a lord full fat and in good point:
His eyes were large, and rolling in his head,
Gleamed like a fire below a cooking pot.
His boots souple, his horse in great estate.
Now certainly he was a fine prelate,
He was not pale as a forsaken ghost.
A fat swan loved he best of any roast.
His palfrey was as brown as is a berry.

A FRIAR there was, a wanton and a merry,
A mendicant and very proper man.
In all the orders four is none that can

This ilke Monk / leet oolde thynges pace
And heeld / after the newe world the space
He yaf noght of that text a pulled hen
That seith / that hunterys been none holy men
Ne that a Monk. whan he is recchelees
Is likned / til a fissh / that is waterlees
This is to seyn / a Monk out of his Cloystre
But thilke text heeld he nat worth an Oystre
And I seyde / his opynyon was good
What sholde he studie /
           and make hym selven wood
Up on a book in Cloystre alwey to poure
Or swynke with his handes / and laboure
As Austyn bit. how shal the world be served
Lat Austyn heve his swynk. to hym reserved
Ther fore / he was a prykasour aryght
Grehoundes he hadde / as swift as fowel in flyght
Of prikyng and of huntyng for the haare
Was al his lust. for no cost wolde he spaare
I saugh his sleves / purfiled at the hond
With grys / and that the fyneste of a lond
And for to festne his hood / under his chyn
He hadde / of gold / wroght a ful curious pyn
A love knotte / in the gretter ende ther was
His heed was balled / that shoon as any glas
And eek his face / as he hadde been enoynt
He was a lord ful fat and in good poynt
Hise eyen steepe / and rollynge in his heed
That stemed / as a fourneys of a leed
Hise bootes souple / his hors / in greet estaat
Now certeynly / he was a fair prelat
He was nat paale / as is a forpyned goost
A fat swan / loved he / best of any roost
His palfrey / was as broun as any berye

A FRERE ther was / a wantowne and a merye
A lymytour / a ful solempne man
In alle the ordres foure / is noon that kan

for books had been soldier, merchant and judge, knew all the powerful people in London & many on the Continent, got beaten & robbed when carrying the King's money, dealt personally with ship's captains & common workmen, was once released by a lady from a charge of **raptu**, *which means either rape or kidnapping. He must have known Wyclif, who John of Gaunt also patronised. He certainly knew "The Lollard Knights" who upheld Wyclif's plans to reform the church. He lived through the Peasants' Revolt which the Lollards were accused of starting. What a lot Chaucer knew which had NOT got into his work before he wrote the* **Canterbury Tales**! *And before he started the earliest popular versions of* **Piers Plowman** *were circulating in a London whose reading public was less than a few thousand.*

In Chaucer's Europe the greatest modern book (Chaucer had quoted from it) was Dante's poem blending all that Christian Europe knew of hell, purgatory, heaven, science, history & politics. He called it **The Divine Comedy**. *Six centuries later*

Balzac wrote **The Human Comedy**, a vast portrait of France which is less spiritually lofty but wonderfully broad. Both Dante and Balzac had encylopaedic minds which wanted to put all they knew in a single work. So had Chaucer but before he saw how to do it he was middle-aged. I think Langland showed him the way. **The Human Comedy** would be a good name for **The Canterbury Tales**. Chaucer had many stories from France & Italy, many comic English tales which could go in a book. An old way of linking many stories is to put them in the mouth of a fictional teller – see **The Arabian Nights**. Boccaccio in **The Decameron** had put several tales in the mouths of some rich people, entertaining each other in a pleasant place while hiding from the plague. To say **Decameron** + **Piers Plowman** = **Canterbury Tales** is too simple.

It was a unique mental leap to imagine telling his best tales in the voices of all the kinds of folk he knew. A pilgrimage was the best possible setting, but I think Langland's street scenes showed him the way. All the people in **Piers**

Command so much of gossip and fair language.
He had made full many a marriage
Of youngè women at his owen cost.
Unto his order he was a noble post.
Full well beloved and familiar was he
With farmers over all in his countree,
And eek with worthy women of the town;
For he had power of confessioun –
As said himself – more than a curate,
For of his order he was licentiate.
Full sweetly heardè he confession
And pleasant was his absolution:
He was an easy man to give penance,
Thereby he thought to have a good pittance.
For unto a poor order having given
Is signè that a man is well yshriven;
When men paid cash, he boldly dared to vaunt,
He knew that they were truly penitent;
For many a man so hard is of his heart
He may not weep, however sore he smart.
Therefore instead of weeping and of prayers,
He should give silver unto the poorè freres.
His pocket was ay full of little knives
And pretty pins to give to pretty wives,
And certainly he struck a merry note:
Well could he sing and strum upon the lute,
At riddling he always bare the prize.
His neck was white as is the fleur-de-lys;
And yet he strong was as a champion.
He knew the taverns well in every toun,
And every publican and their bartenders
Far better than the lepers or the beggars.
It did not suit a worthy man like he,
A member of a worthy faculty,
To be acquainted with a sickly leper.
It is not honest. It makes nothing better
For to be dealing with suchlike canaille,
Instead of the rich, and sellers of victual.

So muche of daliaunce / and fair langage
He hadde maked / ful many a mariage
Of yonge wommen / at his owene cost
Un to his ordre / he was a noble post
Ful wel biloved / and famylier was hee
With Frankeleyns / over al in his contree
And eek with worthy wommen / of the toun
For he hadde / power of confessioun
As seyde him self / moore than a curaat
For of his ordre / he was licenciaat
Ful swetely / herde he confessioun
And plesant. was his absolucioun
He was an esy man / to yeve penaunce
Ther as he wiste / to have a good pitaunce
For un to a poure ordre / for to yeve
Is signe / that a man / is wel yshryve
For if he yaf he dorste make avaunt
He wiste / that a man was repentaunt
For many a man / so hard is of his herte
He may nat weepe / thogh that he soore smerte
Ther fore / in stede of wepynge / and preyeres
Men moote yeve silver / to the poure freres
His typet was ay farsed ful of knyves
And pynnes / for to yeven faire wyves
And certeynly / he hadde a murye noote
Wel koude he synge / and pleyen on a roote
Of yeddynges / he bar outrely the prys
His nekke whit was / as the flour delys
Ther to he stroong was / as a Champioun
He knew the tavernes wel in every town
And every hostiler / and Tappestere
Bet / than a lazer / or a beggestere
For un to swich a worthy man / as he
Acorded nat / as by his facultee
To have / with syke lazers aqueyntaunce
It is nat honeste / it may noght avaunce
For to deelen / with no swich poraille
But al with riche / and sellerys of vitaille

Plowman's crowded prologue are in this one, but shown singly, in close-up.

The prologue has a party of 58 who agree to tell 2 tales each. Only 24 were written. The last is a long prose sermon on penitence by the poor parson; he tells us to win heavenly joy by the pains of spiritual & bodily poverty. Then Chaucer says goodbye to his readers, begging them & Jesus to forgive him for writings full of worldly vanities which he would now retract, especially his tales. He hopes his translations of pious & moral work will move Lord Jesus & his blessed mother to let him live long enough to save his soul. From Virgil to Tolstoy many writers have wished undone books their readers most love, but Chaucer's retraction may be less simple. It & the sermon ending the tales would make them more welcome to clergy upset by his tales about their own sins. The retraction also lists the titles of every poem Chaucer rejects. They are still read. It names just one of the several pious works he recommends. All but that one are now forgotten. He was as subtle as Shakespeare.

And over all, as profit did arise,
Courteous he was, and humble of service.
There was no man nowhere so virtuous.
He was the bestè beggar in his house;
And paid rent to it for the district granted,
None of his brethren poaching
    where he hunted.
For though a widow haddè nocht a shoe,
So pleasant was his In principio
That he would have a farthing ere he went.
His takings were far bigger than his rent.
And rage he could,
    bark like an angry whelp.
With debt collecting he could greatly help
For then he was not like a cloisterer,
With threadbare cope, as is a poor scholar,
But he was like a lawyer or a pope.
Of double worsted was his semicope,
That rounded like casting round a bell.
He lispèd somewhat, for he thought it well
To make his English sweet upon his tongue;
While he was strumming,
    after he had sung
His eyen twinkled in his heid aricht
As do the stars upon a frosty nicht. This
worthy mendicant was clepèd Hubberd.

A MERCHANT was there with a forkèd beard
In two-toned greatcoat, high on horse he sat;
Upon his heid a Flemish beaver hat,
His buckled boots were polished shiningly.
Opinions, which he spake right solemnly,
Touched always on the increase of his gains.
He would the sea were kept by any pains
Free twixt the Holland ports and Orewell.
Well could he in exchangè sharès sell.
This worthy man so well employed his wit
That no one ever knew he was in debt,

And over al / ther as profit sholde aryse
Curteys he was / and lowely of servyse
Ther was no man / nowheer / so vertuous
He was the beste beggere / of his hous
And yaf a certeyn ferme / for the graunt
Noon of his bretheren /
    cam ther in his haunt
For thogh a wydwe / hadde noght a sho
So plesant was his In principio
Yet wolde he have a ferthyng er he wente
His purchaas / was wel bettre than his rente
And rage he koude /
    as it weere right a whelpe
In lovedayes / koude he muchel helpe
For ther / he was nat lyk a Cloystrer
With a threedbare cope / as is a poure scoler
But he was lyk a maister / or a Pope
Of double worstede / was his semycope
And rounded as a belle / out of the presse
Somwhat he lypsed / for his wantownesse
To make his englyssh / sweete up on his tonge
And in his harpyng /
    whan that he hadde songe
Hise eyen twynkled / in his heed aryght
As doon the sterres / in the frosty nyght
This worthy lymytour / was cleped Huberd

A MARCHANT was ther / with a forked berd
In Motlee / and hye on hors he sat
Up on his heed / a Flaundryssh Bevere hat
His bootes clasped / faire and fetisly
Hise resons / he spak ful solempnely
Sownyng alway / thencrees of his wynnyng
He woolde / the see weere kept for any thyng
Bitwixen Myddelburgh / and Orewelle
Wel koude he / in eschaunge / sheeldes selle
This worthy man / ful wel his wit bisette
Ther wiste no wight. that he was in dette

So estaatly was he / of his governaunce
With his bargaynes /
       and with his chevysaunce
For soothe / he was a worthy man with alle
But sooth to seyn / I noot how men hym calle

So statesmanlike was he in management
Both with his bargains
       and his investment.
He was indeed a man of worthy fame
But, truth to tell, I never learned his name.

A CLERC ther was / of Oxenford also
That un to logyk. hadde longe ygo
As leene was his hors / as is a rake
And he was noght right fat I undertake
But looked holwe / and ther to sobrely
Ful threedbaare /
       was his overeste Courtepy
For he hadde / geten hym yet no benefice
Ne was so worldly / for to have office
For hym was levere / have at his beddes heed
Twenty bookes / clad / in blak / or reed
Of Aristotle / and his Philosophye
Than robes riche / or Fithele / or gay Sautrye
But al be / that he was a Philosophre
Yet hadde he / but litel gold in Cofre
But al that he myghte / of his frendes hente
On bookes / and on lernynge / he it spente
And bisily / gan for the soules preye
Of hem / that yaf hym / wher with to scoleye
Of studye /
       took he moost cure and moost heede
Noght oo word spak he /
       moore than was neede
And that was spoke / in forme / and reverence
And short and quyk and ful of heigh sentence
Sownynge in moral vertu / was his speche
And gladly wolde he lerne / and gladly teche

A CLERK there was, of Oxenford also,
That unto logic gave him long ago.
As leanè was his horse as is a rake,
And he was not richt fat I undertake,
But lookèd hollow, and very sober.
Full threadbare
       was the coat that did him cover,
For he had got him yet no benefice,
Nor was so worldly to have gained office.
For he would rather have at his bed's head
Twenty bookès, clad in black or red,
Of Aristotle and his philosophy,
Than robès rich, or fiddle, or gay psaltèry.
Albeit that he was philosopher
Yet had he but little gold in coffer;
For all the money that his friends could send,
On bookès and on learning he would spend,
And busily then for the soulès pray
Of them that gave him wherewith to study.
Of study took he most care
       and most heed.
Not one word spake he
       more than there was need,
And that was said with form and reverence,
And short and quick and high significance.
Sounding of moral virtue was his speech,
And gladly would he learn, and gladly teach.

A SERGEAUNT OF LAWE / waar / and wys
That often / hadde been at the Parvys
Ther was also / ful ryche of excellence
Discreet he was / and of greet reverence

A LAWYER was there, one of the wisest sort
That often had been at the Inns of Court,
And was also full rich of excellence.
Discreet he was, and of great reverence –

Or so he seemed,	*He seemed swich /*
his wordès were so wise.	*hise wordes weeren so Wyse*
Justice he was full often in assize,	*Justice he was / ful often in Assise*
By patent and by plain commission.	*By patente / and by pleyn commissioun*
Out of his science and his high renown	*For his science / and for his heigh renoun*
Of fees and robes he had got many a one.	*Of fees and robes / hadde he many oon*
Such a conveyancer was nowhere none:	*So greet a purchasour / was nowher noon*
All was fee simple to him, and in fact,	*Al was fee symple / to hym / in effect*
What he conveyanced could not be attacked.	*His purchasyng myghte nat been infect*
Nowhere so busy a man as he there goes,	*Nowher so bisy a man as he / ther nas*
And yet he seemèd busier than he was.	*And yet he seemed / bisyer than he was*
The judgements passed on every case and crime	*In termes / hadde he caas / and doomes alle*
He knew from now back to King William's time,	*That from tyme of kyng william / weere falle*
And so did write, and make a thing of it,	*Ther to / he koude endite / and make a thyng*
That no man living could defy his writ;	*Ther koude no wight pynchen at his writyng*
And every statute he could say by rote.	*And every statut. koude he pleyn by roote*
His garment was a plainly woven coat	*He rood but hoomly / in a medlee coote*
Girt by a belt with metal strips inlaid.	*Girt with a ceynt of sylk. with barres smale*
Of his appearance no more need be said.	*Of his array / telle I no lenger tale*
A FRANKLIN was there in the company.	*A FRANKELEYN / was in his compaignye*
White was his beard as is the day-eye-sy;	*Whit was his berd / as is the dayesye*
Of his complexion he was sanguine.	*Of his complexcion / he was sangwyn*
Well lovèd he his morning sop in wine;	*Wel loved he by the morwe / a sope in wyn*
To living in delight he ever won,	*To lyven in delyt was evere his wone*
For he was Epicurus' owen son,	*For he was / Epicurus owene sone*
That firmly held that bodily delight	*That heeld opynyon / that pleyn delit*
Was of all happiness the very height.	*Was verray / felicitee parfit*
A householder, and that a great, was he;	*An housholdere / and that a greet was hee*
The patron saint of hosts in his countree.	*Seint Julyan he was / in his contree*
His bread and ale were of the finest kind,	*His breed / his ale / was alweys after oon*
A better envied man you'd nowhere find.	*A bettre envyned man / was nevere noon*
Withoutè bake meat never was his house,	*With outen bake mete / was nevere his hous*
Fresh fish and flesh,	*Of fressh fissh / and flessh /*
and that so plenteous	*and that so plentevous*
It snowèd in his house of meat and drink,	*It snewed in his hous / of mete and drynke*
And of all dainties that men couldè think.	*Of alle deyntees / that men koude bithynke*
After the sundry seasons of the year	*After / the sondry sesons / of the yeer*

So chaunged he / his mete / and his soper
Ful many a fat partrych / hadde he in Muwe
And many a breem / and many a luce in Stuwe
Wo was his Cook / but if his Sauce weere
Poynaunt and sharpe / and redy al his geere
His table dormaunt in his halle alway
Stood redy covered / al the longe day
At sessions / ther was he / lord and sire
Full ofte tyme / he was knyght of the Shire
An Anlaas / and a Gipser / al of Sylk
Heeng at his girdel / whit as morne mylk
A Shirreve hadde he been / and a Countour
Was nowheer / swich a worthy vavasour

So changèd he his meat and his suppèr.
Full many a fat partridge had he in mew,
And many a bream, and many a pike in stew.
Woe to his cook unless his sauces were
Poignant and sharp, and all ready his gear.
A steady table in the hall allway
Stood ready covered all the longè day.
At legal sessions was he Lord and Sire,
In parliament would represent his shire.
A sheath knife and a purse made all of silk
Hung at his girdle, white as morning milk.
A sheriff had he been, and auditor.
Was nowhere such a worthy landholder.

AN HABERDASSHERE / and a CARPENTER
A WEBBE / a DYERE / and a TAPYCER
And they weere clothed alle / in oo lyveree
Of a solempne / and a greet fraternytee
Ful fressh and newe / hir geere apyked was
Hir knyves weere chaped /
        noght with bras
But al with silver / wroght ful clene and wel
Hir girdles / and hir pouches / everydel
Wel seemed eech of hem / a fair Burgeys
To sitten in a yeldehalle / on a deys
Everych / for the wisdom / that he kan
Was shaply / for to been an Alderman
For catel / hadde they ynogh / and rente
And eek hir wyves / wolde it wel assente
And ellis certeyn / they weere to blame
It is ful fair / to been yclepyd madame
And goon to vigilies / al bifore
And have a Mantel / realliche ybore

A HABERDASHER and a CARPENTER,
A WEAVER, CARPET-MAKER and DYER –
And they were clothed all in one livery,
Of a solemn and great fraternity.
Full fresh and new their gear appointed was:
Their knives and sheaths were mounted
        not with brass
But all with silver, wrought with thorough art
Their girdles and their pouches, every part.
Well seemèd each of them a fair burgess
To sit within a guild-hall or a dais.
Every one, for the wisdom that he span,
Well fitted was to be an alderman:
For property he had enough, and rent,
A fact to which his wife could well assent,
And if not, he was certainly to blame.
It is a fine thing to be called "madame",
And enter kirk the common folk before,
And have your mantle royally ybore.

A COOK they hadde with hem / for the nones
To boille the chiknes / with the Marybones
And poudre marchaunt. tart and / Galyngale
Wel koude he knowe / a draghte of london ale

A COOK they haddè with them for the nones
To boil the chicken with the marrow bones
And sugartarts, and ginger galingale.
Well did he know a draught of London ale,

Well could he roast, and seethe,
    and broil, and fry,
Simmer a stew, and also bake a pie;
But great harm was it, so it seemed to me,
That on his shin a scabby sore had he.
As for blancmange,
    that made he with the best.
	He koude rooste / and seethe /
	    and broille / & frye
	Maken Mortreux / and wel bake a pye
	But greet harm was it as it thoughte me
	That on his Shyne / a Mormal hadde he
	or Blankmanger /
	    that maade he with the beste

A SHIPMAN was there, homing from the west;
He came from Dartmouth, as I understood,
And rode a farmer's nag as best he could,
In gown of woollen hanging to his knee.
A dagger dangling on a cord had he
About his neck, under his arm adown.
The summer heat
    had made his hue all brown,
And certainly he was a good fellow.
Full many a draught of winè did he draw
Out of Bordeaux,
    while the exciseman slept.
A tender conscience he never kept.
If that he fought, and had the higher hand,
By water he sent them home to every land.
But of his craft: in reckoning his tide,
His currents and the dangers them beside,
Reading the compass, moons
    and harbourage,
There was none such from Hull unto Carthage.
Hardy he was, wisely he undertook.
By many a tempest
    had his beard been shook.
He knew each port and harbour as they were,
From Jutland to the Cape of Finisterre,
And every creek in Britain and in Spain.
His bark ycleped was the Madelaine.
	A SHIPMAN was ther / wonyng fer by weste
	For aught I woot he was of Dertemouthe
	He rood up on a Rouncy / as he kouthe
	In a gowne of faldyng to the knee
	A daggere hangynge on a laas / hadde he
	Aboute his nekke / under his arm adown
	The hoote Somer /
	    hadde maad his hewe al broun
	And certeynly / he was a good felawe
	Ful many a draghte of wyn / hadde he drawe
	Fro Burdeuxward /
	    whil that the Chapman sleepe
	Of nyce conscience / took he no keepe
	If that he faght and hadde the hyer hond
	By watre he sente hem hoom / to every lond
	But of his craft to rekene wel his tydes
	His stremys / and his daungers hym bisydes
	His herberwe and his moone /
	    his lodmenage
	Ther was noon swich / from hulle to Cartage
	Hardy he was / and wys to undertake
	With many a tempest
	    hadde his beerd been shake
	He knew alle the havenes / as they weere
	Fro Gootlond / to the cape of Fynysteere
	And every cryke / in Britaigne / and in Spaigne
	His barge / yclepyd was the Mawdelayne

With us there was a DOCTOR OF MEDICINE; In all this world there was none like him	With us / ther was / a DOCTOUR OF PHISYK In al this world / ne was ther noon hym lyk

To speken of Phisyk and of Surgerye	Could speak of physic and of surgery,
For he was grounded / in Astronomye	For he was grounded in astrology.
He kepte his pacient a ful greet deel	He kept his patients going a great deal
In houres / by his magyk natureel	Of hours by his magic natural.
Wel koude he fortunen / the ascendent	He knew when lucky planets were ascendant
Of hise ymages / for his pacient	For images made of the patient.
He knew the cause / of every maladye	He knew the cause of every malady,
Weere it of hoot or coold / or moyste / or drye	Whether of heat, or cold, or moist, or dry,
And where it engendred /	Where they were generated,
and of what humour	and of what humour.
He was a verray / parfit practisour	He was a very perfect practitioner:
The cause yknowe / and of his harm the roote	The causes known, and of each harm the seeds,
Anoon he yaf / the sike man his boote	Anon he gives the sick man what he needs.
Ful redy hadde he / his Apothecaryes	Full ready had he his apothecaries
To senden hym / his drogges / and his letuaryes	To send him drugs and other remedies.
For eech of hem / maade oother for to wynne	Each helped the other out with what they won –
Hir frendshipe / was noght newe to bigynne	Their friendship had not recently begun.
Wel knew he / the oolde Esculapyus	Well knew he the old Aesculapius,
And Discorides / and eek Rusus	Dioscorides, and also Rufus,
Olde ypocras / Haly / and Galyen	Hippocrates, Hali and Galen,
Serapion / Razis / and Avycen	Serapion, Rhazes and Avicenna,
Averroys / Damascien / and Constantyn	Averroes, Damascenus and Constantine,
Bernard / and Gatesden / and Gilbertyn	Bernard, and Gattesden, and Gilbertine.
Of his diete / mesurable was hee	Of his dietè, very strict was he
For it was / of no superfluytee	That it contain no superfluitee
But of greet norissynge / and digestible	But all nourishing and digestible.
His studye / was but litel on the Bible	His study was but little on the Bible.
In sangwyn and in Pers / he clad was al	Well clad was he in crimson and dark blue
Lyned with Taffata / and with Sendal	With taffeta and silken lining too;
And yet he was / but esy of dispence	And yet he was not reckless with expenses
He kepte / that he wan in pestilence	And kept what he had won in pestilences,
For gold in Phisyk. is a Cordial	For gold in physic is a cordial,
Ther fore / he loved gold in special	Therefore he lovèd gold in special.
A good WYF was ther / OF bisyde BATHE	A good WIFE was there, OF beside BATH,
But she was som del deef and that was scathe	And though it was a pity, somewhat deaf.
Of clooth makynge / she hadde swich an haunt	Of cloth making she had a business
She passed hem / of Ipres / and of Gaunt	Surpassing those of Ghent and of Ypres.

In all the parish wife nor was there none
That to the offering before her had gone,
And if they did, certain so wrath was she
That she was out of allè charitee.
Her shawls they were of finely woven ground,
I dare swear
     that they weighed a full ten pound
That on a Sunday were upon her head.
Her stockings were of fine scarlet red,
Full trimly tied,
    the shoes supple and new.
Bold was her face, and fair, and red of hue.
She was a worthy woman all her life:
At church door had she married husbands five,
Excluding other company in youth –
Of which there is no need to speak, in truth.
Thrice had she pilgrimmed to Jerusalem,
And passed across many a strangè stream;
At Rome she haddè been, and at Boulogne,
Galicia at Saint James, and at Cologne.
She knew a deal of wandering by the way.
Gap-toothèd was she, truthfully to say.
Upon an ambler easily she sat,
And wimpled well, and on her head a hat
As broad as is a buckler or a targe,
A saddle-skirt about her hipès large,
And on her feet a pair of spurrès sharp.
In fellowship
    well could she laugh and carp.
The remedies for love she knew through chance,
For she had known the art of that old dance.

A good man was there of religion
And was a poor PARSON OF A TOWN,
But rich he was of holy thought and work.
He was also a learnèd man, a clerk,
That Christès gospel truly wouldè preach.
His parish folk devoutly would he teach.

In al the parysshe / wyf ne was ther noon
That to the offrynge / bifore hire sholde goon
And if ther dide / certeyn / so wrooth was shee
That she was / out of alle charitee
Hir Coverchiefes / ful fyne weere of grownd
I dorste swere /
     they weyeden. ten pownd
That on a Sonday / weeren up on hir heed
Hir hosen weeren / of fyn Scarlet reed
Ful streyte yteyd / and shoes /
    ful moyste & newe
Boold was hir face / and fair and reed of hewe
She was a worthy womman / al hir lyve
Housbondes at chirche dore / she hadde fyve
With outen oother compaignye / in yowthe
But ther of / nedeth noght to speke as nowthe
And thries / hadde she been at Jerusalem
She hadde passed / many a straunge strem
At Rome she hadde been / and at Boloyne
In Galyce at Seint Jame / and at Coloyne
She koude muchel / of wandrynge by the weye
Gattothed was she / soothly for to seye
Up on an Amblere / esily she sat
Ywympled wel / and on hir heed an hat
As brood as is / a Bokeler / or a Targe
A foot mantel / aboute hir hypes large
And on hir feet a peyre of spores sharpe
In felaweshipe /
    wel koude she laughe and carpe
Of remedies of love / she knew par chaunce
For she koude of that art the olde daunce

A good man / was ther / of Religioun
And was a poure PERSON / OF A TOUN
But riche he was / of holy thoght and werk
He was also / a lerned man a Clerk
That Cristes gospel / trewely wolde preche
His parisshens / devoutly wolde he teche

Benygne he was / and wonder diligent	Benign he was, wondrously diligent,
And in adversitee / ful pacient	And in adversity full patient.
And swich he was proeved /	And such he always proved.
ofte sythes	When times did worsen
Ful looth weere hym / to cursen for his tythes	Full loth was he to get his tithes by cursing,
But rather wolde he yeven / out of doute	But rather would he give, without a doubt
Un to his poure parisshens aboute	Unto his poor parishioners about,
Of his offrynge / and eek of his substaunce	Out of his offerings and his income too.
He koude in litel thyng have suffisaunce	To live, he made a very little do.
Wyd was his parisshe /	Wide was his parish
and houses fer a sonder	houses far asunder.
But he ne lafte noght for reyn ne thonder	None he neglected; neither rain or thunder,
In siknesse / nor in meschief to visite	Sickness or mischance kept him from the door
The ferreste in his parisshe / muche and lyte	Of the farthest in his parish, rich or poor,
Up on his feet and in his hond a staf	Upon his feet, and in his hand a staff.
This noble ensample / to his sheep he yaf	This fine example to his sheep he gave
That first he wroghte /	That first he worked,
and afterward he taughte	and afterwards he taught.
Out of the gospel / he tho wordes caughte	Out of the gospel he the words had caught,
And this figure / he added eek ther to	And this figure he added there unto:
That if gold ruste / what sholde Iren do	That if gold rust, what shall iron do?
For if a preest be foul / in whom we truste	For if a priest be foul, in whom we trust,
No wonder is / a lewed man to ruste	No wonder that a lowly man should rust;
And shame it is / if a preest take keepe	And shame it is, if a priest take keep,
A shiten shepherde / and a clene sheepe	A shitten shepherd and a cleanè sheep.
Wel oghte a preest ensample for to yive	Well ought a priest example for to give
By his clennesse /	By his cleanness,
how that his sheep sholde lyve	how that his sheep should live.
He sette noght. his benefice to hyre	He did not let his benefice for hire,
And leet his sheep / encombred in the Myre	And leave his sheep encumbered in the mire,
And ran to London / un to Seinte Poules	And run to London unto Saintè Paul's
To seeken hym / a Chauntrye for soules	To seek himself a chauntery for souls,
Or with a breetherede / to been withhoolde	Or with a brotherhood to be withhold;
But dwelte at hoom / and kepte wel his foolde	But dwelt at home, and keepèd well his fold
So that the wolf ne maade it noght myscarye	So that the wolf could not make it miscarry.
He was a sheepherde / and noght a Mercenarye	He was a shepherd and nocht a mercenary.
And thogh he hooly weere / and vertuous	And though he holy were and virtuous,
He was noght to synful men despitous	He was to sinful men not despiteous,

English	Original
Nor in his speech threatening or condescending	Ne of his speche / daungerous / ne digne
But in his teaching kind and unpretending.	But in his techyng discreet and benygne
Drawing the folk to heavenly fairness	To drawen folk to hevene / with fairnesse
By good example was his business.	By good ensample / this was his bisynesse
But if there were a fellow obstinate,	But it weere / any persone obstynaat
No matter who, of high or low estate,	What so he weere / of heigh / or lowe estaat
Him would he snub right sharply for that cause.	Hym wolde he snybben / sharply for the nonys
A better priest I trow there nowhere was.	A bettre preest I trowe ther nowher noon ys
He waited after no pomp or reverence,	He wayted / after no pompe / and reverence
Nor makèd him a spicèd conscience,	Ne maked hym / a spyced conscience
But Christès lore and his apostles twelve	But Cristes loore / and hise Apostles twelve
He taught, but first he followed it himselve.	He taughte / but first he folwed it hym selve
With him there was a PLOUGHMAN,	With hym ther was a PLOWMAN /
was his brother,	was his broother
That had of dungload carted many a fother;	That hadde ylad of donge / ful many a Foother
An honest toiler and a good was he,	A trewe swynkere / and a good was he
Living in peace and perfect charitee.	Lyvynge in pees / and parfit charitee
God loved he best with all his whole heart	God loved he best with al his hoole herte
At allè times, however grieved or hurt,	At alle tymes / thogh him gamed / or smerte
And then his neighbour, truly as himselve.	And thanne his Neighebore / right as hym selve
And he would thresh, and thereto dyke and delve	He wolde thresshe / and ther to / dyke and delve
For Christès sake, for every poor wight,	For Cristes sake / with every poure wight
Withouten hire, if it lay in his might.	With outen hyre / if it laye in his myght
His tithès payèd he full fair and well,	His tythes payde he / ful faire and wel
Both with his worldly goods and proper toil.	Bothe of his propre swynk and his catel
In sleeveless coat he rode upon a mare.	In a Tabard he rood / up on a Mere
There was also a REEVE, and a MILLER,	Ther was also / a Reve / and a Millere
A SUMMONER and a PARDONER also,	A Somonour / and a Pardoner also
A MANCIPLE and myself – there were nae mo.	A Maunciple / and my self ther weere namo
The MILLER was a stout lad for the nones.	The MILLERE / was a stout carl / for the nones
Full big he was of brawn and also bones,	Ful byg he was / of brawen / and eek of bones
Well showing over all he'd overcome.	That proeved wel / for over al ther he cam
At wrestling he was sure to win the ram.	At wrastlynge / he wolde have alwey the Ram
He was short-shouldered, broad, a thickset lout.	He was short shuldred / brood / a thikke knarre
No door he could not heave from hinges out	Ther was no dore / that he noolde heve of harre

Or breke it at a rennynge / with his heed	*Or break it at a running with his head.*
His beerd / as any sowe / or fox / was reed	*His beard, like any fox or sow was red,*
And ther to brood / as thogh it weere a spaade	*And thereto broad, as though it were a spade.*
Up on the cope right of his nose he haade	*Upon the summit of his nose he had*
A werte / and ther on stood / a tuft of heerys	*A wart, and thereon stood a tuft of hairs*
Reede / as the bristles / of a Sowes eerys	*Red as the bristles on a sowès ears.*
Hise nosethirles / blake weere and wyde	*His nostrils blackè were and very wide,*
A swerd and a bokeler / baar he by his syde	*A sword and buckler had he by his side.*
His mouth as greet was / as a greet fourneys	*His mouth as great was as a great furnace.*
He was a Janglere / a Golyardeys	*He was a jangler and a goliardays*
And that was moost /	*And sunk full deep*
of synne and harlotryes	*in sin and harlotrice.*
Wel koude he stelen corn / and tollen thryes	*Well could he steal the corn and tax it thrice;*
And yet he hadde / a thombe of gold pardee	*And yet he had a thumb of gold, pardee.*
A whit coote / and a blew hood wered hee	*A white coat and a blue hood wearèd he.*
A Baggepipe / wel koude he / blowe and sown	*A baggypipe well could he blow and sound,*
And ther with al / he broghte us out of towne	*And therewithall he brocht us out of town.*

A gentil MAUNCIPLE / was ther/ of a Temple	*A gentle MANCIPLE of the Inner Temple*
Of which / Achatours myghte take exemple	*Of which all purchasers might take example*
For to been wyse / in byynge of vitaille	*He was so wise in buying of victuale*
For wheither that he payde / or took by taille	*By credit or by paying on the nail.*
Algate he wayted so / in his achaat	*He balanced all the books so well and true*
That he was ay biforn / and in good staat	*He ay had cash in hand, and plenty too.*
Now is nat that of god / a ful greet grace	*Now is it not of God a full fair grace*
That swich a lewed mannes wit shal pace	*That such a low man's ignorance outpace*
The wysdom / of an heepe / of lerned men	*The wisdom of a heap of learnèd men?*
Of Maistres hadde he mo / than thryes ten	*Of masters had he more that three times ten,*
That weeren of lawe / expert and curious	*That were of law expert and curious,*
Of whiche / ther weere a dozeyne /in that hous	*Of which there were a dozen in that house*
Worthy / to been stywardes / of rente / and lond	*Worthy to be stewards in rent and land*
Of any lord / that is in Engelond	*Of any lord that is in Engeland,*
To make hym lyve / by his propre good	*Helping him live upon the goods he had*
In honour dettelees / but if he weere wood	*In honour debtless (if he were not mad),*
Or lyve as scarsly / as hym lyst desire	*Or live as meanly as he might desire,*
And able / for to helpen al a Shire	*While governing a borough or a shire*
In any caas / that myghte falle or happe	*In any accident that might befall:*
And yet this Maunciple / sette hir aller cappe	*The Manciple made dunces of them all.*

The REEVE was a lank choleric man
His beard was shaved as cleanly as he can;
His hair about his ears was closely cropped;
His scalp was in a priestès tonsure docked.
Full longè were his leggès and full lean,
Like to a staff, there was no calf yseen.
Well could he keep a garner and a bin;
There was no auditor
   could on him win.
Well knew he by the drought and by the rain
The yielding of his seed and of his grain.
His lordès sheep, his oxen, his dairy,
His swine, his horse, his store and his poultry
Were wholly in this Reevès governing.
By covenant to give the reckoning,
Since that his lord was aged twenty years.
There was no man could charge him with arrears.
Of bailiff, herdsman, peasant labourer all
He knew the tricks of trade and what they stole;
They were adread of him as of the death.
His homestead was full fair upon a heath,
With greenè trees yshadowed was his place.
He could far better than his lord purchase.
Full rich he was astored prively.
His lord well could he pleasen subtly,
To steer and bend him to his owen good,
And have a thank,
   and yet a coat and hood.
In youth he haddè learned a good mystery;
He was a builder, skilled in carpentry.
This Reeve sat upon a full good stot
That was all dappled grey, and clepèd Scot.
A long and dark blue overcoat he had
And by his side he bore a rusty blade.
Of Norfolk was this Reeve of which I tell
Beside a town men clepen Baldeswell.
His coat was tucked up like a friar about
And ever he rode hinderest of our rout.

The REVE / was a sclendre coleryk man
His beerd was shave / as neigh as ever he kan
His heer was by his eerys / ful rownd yshorn
His tope was dokked / lyk a preest byforn
Ful longe weere hise legges / and ful leene
Ylik a staf. ther was no calf yseene
Wel koude he keepe / a Gerner and a Bynne
Ther was noon Auditour /
   koude on hym wynne
Wel wiste he / by the droghte and by the reyn
The yeldynge / of his seed / and of his greyn
His lordes sheepe / his neet / his dayerye
His swyn / his hors / his stoor / and his pultrye
Was hoolly / in this Reves governynge
And by his covenant. yaf the rekenynge
Syn that his loord / was twenty yeer of age
Ther koude no man / brynge hym in arrerage
Ther nas Baillyf. hierde / nor oother hyne
That he ne knew / his sleyghte / and his covyne
They weere adrad of hym / as of the deeth
His wonyng was ful faire up on an heeth
With greene trees / shadwed was his place
He koude bettre / than his lord purchace
Ful riche / he was astoored pryvely
His lord / wel koude he plesen subtilly
To yeve / and leene hym / of his owene good
And have a thank /
   and yet a coote and hood
In youthe / he lerned hadde / a good Mister
He was a wel good wrighte / a Carpenter
This Reve sat up on a wel good Stot
That was a Pomely gray / and highte Scot
A long Surcote of Pers / up on he haade
And by his syde / he baar a rusty blaade
Of Northfolk was this Reve / of which I telle
Bisyde a town / men clepyn Baldeswelle
Tukked he was / as is a ffrere aboute
And evere he rood / the hyndreste of oure route

A SOMONOUR / was ther with us / in that place	*A SUMMONER was with us in that place*
That hadde / a fyr-reed Cherubynnes face	*That had a fire-red cherubinès face*
For Sawceflewm he was / with eyen narwe	*Inflamed with eczema, with eyen narrow.*
And hoot he was / and lecherous as a Sparwe	*As hot he was and lecherous as a sparrow*
With scaled browes blake / and pyled berd	*With scabby eyebrows and a moulting beard.*
Of his visage / children weere aferd	*Of his visage the children were afeared.*
Ther nas quyk silver / lytarge / ne Brymstoon	*No quick-silver, blood-letting, no brimstone,*
Borace / Ceruce / ne Oille of Tartre noon	*Boracic, white-lead, oil of tartar none,*
Ne oynement. that wolde clense and byte	*No ointment that he tried could cleanse and bite*
That hym myghte helpen / of his whelkes whyte	*And rid him of his scabs, entirely white,*
Nor of the knobbes / sittynge on his chekes	*Nor the carbuncles sitting on his cheeks.*
Wel loved he garlek oynons and eek lekes	*Well loved he garlic, onions, even leeks,*
And for to drynke strong wyn / reed as blood	*And for to drink strong wine as red as blood;*
Thanne wolde he speke / and crye as he were wood	*Then would he talk and shout as he were mad.*
And whan that he / wel dronken hadde the wyn	*And after he well drunken had the wine*
Thanne wolde he speke no word but Latyn	*Then would he utter no word but Latin.*
A fewe termes hadde he / two / or thre	*Several phrases had he, two or three,*
That he hadde lerned / out of som decree	*That he had learnèd out of some decree –*
No wonder is / he herde it al the day	*No wonder, that! He heard it all the day,*
And eek ye knowe wel / how that a Jay	*And ye all know how well a parrot may*
Kan clepen watte / as wel as kan the Pope	*Cry "Pretty Pol!" as clearly as the pope;*
But who so koude / in oother thyng hym grope	*But who will deeper in his learning grope*
Thanne hadde he spent al his philosophie	*Had reached the end of his philosophy;*
Ay Questio quid iuris wolde he crye	*Then "Questio quid juris" would he cry.*
He was a gentil harlot and a kynde	*He was a gentle harlot and a kind,*
A bettre felawe / sholde men noght fynde	*And better company might no man find.*
He wolde suffre / for a quart of wyn	*He would allow, for just a quart of wine,*
A good felawe / to have his concubyn	*A good fellow to have his concubine*
A twelf monthe / and excusen hym at the fulle	*A twelve month, and excuse him to the full,*
Ful pryvely / a fynch eek koude he pulle	*For he had chickens of his own to pull.*
And if he foond owher / a good felawe	*If he found such another good fellow,*
He wolde techen hym / to have noon awe	*He would so teach him that he had no awe*
In swich caas / of the Ercedeknes curs	*In such a case, of the archdeacon's curse,*
But if a mannes soule / were in his purs	*Unless the fellow's soul was in his purse,*
For in his purs / he sholde ypunysshed be	*For in his purse he should ypunished be.*
Purs is the Ercedeknes helle / seyde he	*"Purse is the Archdeacon's hell," said he.*
But wel I woot he lyed right in dede	*But well I know how much he lied indeed,*
Of cursyng oghte ech gilty man drede	*For cursing every guilty man should dread.*

Curses can slay as much as shriving saves.
The bishop's court can put us in our graves.
Like to a herd of milch-cows did he guide
All the young women of the countryside.
He knew their secrets, they did what he said.
A garland had he set upon his head
Big as an inn-sign fixed upon a stake.
A buckler had he made him of a cake.

With him there rode a gentle PARDONER
From Charing Cross, his friend and his compeer
Straight from the court of Rome
       arrived had he.
Full loud he sang "Come hither, love, to me!"
The Summoner's base harmony chimed in.
No trumpeter makes half so great a din.
This Pardoner had hair yellow as wax,
And smooth it hung, as doth a hank of flax;
In narrow strings hung down these locks he had,
And thereupon his shoulders overspread,
And thinly there the hairs lay, one by one:
But hood, for handsomeness, weared he none,
But kept inside his baggage all the while.
He thought he rode all in the newest style.
Dishevelled, save a cap, he rode all bare,
Such glaring eyes he had as hath a hare.
A holy medal had he on the cap.
His wallet lay before him on his lap,
Brimful of pardons, come from Rome all hot.
A voice he had as shrill as hath a goat.
No beard had he, no beard would ever have,
But smooth his face as it were lately shave.
I trow he was a gelding or a mare.
But of his craft! From Berwick down to Ware,
There never has been such a Pardoner yet.
He had a pillow-case in his wallèt
He said was made out of Our Lady's veil.
He said he had a gusset of the sail

For curs wol sle / right as assoillyng savyth
And also / war hym of a significavit /
In daunger hadde he / at his owene gyse
The yonge gerles / of the diocise
And knew hir conseil / and was al hir reed
A gerland / hadde he set up on his heed
As greet. as it were / for an Ale stake
A bokeler / hadde he maad hym of a cake

With hym ther rood / a gentil PARDONER
Of Rouncyval / his freend / and his comper
That streight was comen /
       fro the Court of Rome
Ful loude he soong com hyder love to me
This Somonour baar to hym / a styf burdoun
Was nevere trompe / of half so greet a soun
This Pardoner / hadde heer / as yelow as wex
But smothe it heeng as dooth a stryke of flex
By ounces / henge his lokkes that he hadde
And ther with / he his shuldres overspradde
But thynne it lay / by colpons oon and oon
But hood for Jolitee / wered he noon
For it was trussed up / in his walet
Hym thoughte / he rood al of the newe Jet
Dischevele save his cappe / he rood al bare
Swiche glarynge eyen / hadde he as an hare
A vernycle / hadde he sowed / up on his cappe
His walet biforn hym / in his lappe
Bretful of pardon / comen from Rome al hoot
A voys he hadde / as smal / as hath a Goot
No berd hadde he / ne nevere sholde have
As smothe it was / as it were late yshave
I trowe he were a geldyng or a Mare
But of his craft. fro Berwyk in to Ware
Ne was ther / swich another Pardoner
For in his Male / he hadde a pilwe beer
Which that he seyde / was oure lady veyl
He seyde he hadde / a gobet of the seyl

That seint Peter hadde / whan that he wente	Saint Peter had employed in Galilee
Up on the see / til Jhesu Crist hym hente	Till Jhesu stopped him drowning in the sea.
He hadde a cros of laton / ful of stones	He had a cross of tin stuck full of stones,
And in a glas / he hadde pigges bones	And in a glass he had a piggès bones.
But with thise relykes / whan that he foond	But with these relics, when that he had found
A poure person / dwellyng up on lond	A poor folk's parson on his parish ground
Up on a day / he gat hym moore moneye	He got more money on a single day
Than that the person gat / in Monthes tweye	Than the poor parson got in monthès tway;
And thus / with feyned flaterye and Japes	And thus with feigning flattery and japes
He made the person / and the peple his apes	He made the parson and the folk his apes.
But trewely / to tellen at the laste	But truthfully to tell it at the last,
He was in chirche / a noble Ecclesiaste	He was in kirk a noble ecclesiast.
Wel koude he / rede a lesson / and a Storie	Well could he read a lesson or a story,
But alderbest he soong an Offertorie	But best of all he sang an offertory,
For wel he wiste / whan that soong was songe	For well he knew that when the song was sung
He moste preche / and wel affyle hys tonge	He must then preach and finely tune his tongue
To wynne silver / as he ful wel koude	To winning silver, as he right well could,
Ther fore he soong the muryerly and loude	Therefore he sang both merrily and loud.
Now have I toold yow / soothly in a clause	Now have I told you truly, in a clause,
The staat / tharray / the nombre / and eek the cause	The state, the garments, number and the cause
Why that assembled was this compaignye	Why so assembled was this company
In Southwerk. at this gentil hostelrye	In Southwark, at this gentle hostelry
That highte the tabard / faste by the belle	We call the Tabard, fast beside the Bell.
But now is tyme / to yow for to telle	But now the time has come for me to tell
How that we baren us / that ilke nyght	How we maintained ourselves that very night
Whan we weere / in that hostelrye alyght	When we did in that hostelry alight;
And after wol I telle / of oure viage	And after I will speak of our voyage,
And al the remenant of oure pilgrymage	And all the remnant of our pilgrimage.
But first I pray yow / of youre curteisye	But first I pray you, of your courtesy,
That ye narette it / noght my vileynye	Not to accuse me of rank villainy
Though that I pleynly speke / in this matere	That I speak plainly in this mattèr,
To telle yow / hir wordes / and hir cheere	And tell you all their words and all their cheer,
Ne thogh I speke / hir wordes proprely	In speech not always worded properly.
For this ye knowen / also wel as I	For this ye know also as well as I:
Who so shal telle a tale / after a man	Who tells a tale as spoken by a man
He moot reherce / as neigh as evere he kan	He must repeat as nearly as he can

Every word, if it be in his charge,
Though speak he never so rudely and so large;
Or else he must tell you a tale untrue
And falsify the form in language new.
Change a man's words and,
    though he is your brother,
You may as well say one word as another.
Christ spake himself full broad in holy writ,
And well ye ken no villainy is it.
Eek Plato say, for whoso can him read,
The word must be the co-sign to the deed.
Also I pray that you forgive it me,
If folk are not in order and degree
Within this tale, as in the world they stand.
I am too ignorant, you understand.

Great cheer to us our Host made, every one,
And soon the supper set for us anon.
He served us with victual of the best;
Strong was the wine, we drank it up with zest.
A fitting man OUR HOSTE was withal
For major domo in a banquet hall.
A large man was he, with protruding een
(No finer burgher was in Cheapside seen)
Bold of his speech, and wise, and well-read, who
Of manhood lacked nothing pertaining to;
And with it all he was a merry man;
And after supper playfully began
To speak of mirth among some other things,
And after we had paid our reckonings,
Thus he began: "Now lordings, truthfully,
Ye've been to me right welcome, heartily.
For by my truth, and if I do not lie,
I never had so blithe a company
Within my hostel as I here have now.
Fain would I do you mirth if I knew how,
And of a jest I suddenly have thought
To give you ease, and it shall cost ye nought.

Everich a word / if it be in his charge
Al speke he / never so rudeliche and large
Or ellis / he moot telle his tale untrewe
Or feyne thyng or fynde wordes newe
He may noght spare /
    althogh he weere his brother
He moot as wel / seye o word as another
Crist spak hym self ful brode in holy writ
And wel ye woot no vileynye is it
Ek Plato seith / who so kan hym rede
The wordes / mote be cosyn / to the dede
Also I prey yow / to foryeve it me
Al have I nat set folk / in hir degree
Here in this tale / as that they sholde stonde
My wit is short ye may wel understonde

Greet cheere / made oure hoost us everichon
And to the souper / sette he us anon
He served us / with vitaille / at the beste
Strong was the wyn / and wel to drynke us leste
A semely man / OURE HOOST was with alle
For to been / a Marchal in an halle
A large man he was / with eyen stepe
A fairer burgeys / was ther noon in Chepe
Boold of his speche / and wys / and wel ytaught
And of manhode / hym lakked right naught
Eke ther to / he was right a murye man
And after souper / pleyen he bigan
And spak of murthe / amonges othere thynges
Whan that we hadde maad oure rekenynges
And seyde thus / now lordes trewely
Ye been to me / right wel come hertely
For by my trouthe / if that I shal nat lye
I seigh noght this yeer / so mury a compaignye
At ones in this herberwe / as is now
Fayn wolde I doon yow myrthe / wiste I how
And of a myrthe / I am right now bithoght
To doon yow ese / and it shal coste noght

Ye goon to Caunterbury / god yow spede
The blisful Martir / quyte yow youre mede
And wel I woot as ye goon by the weye
Ye shapen yow / to talen and to pleye
For trewely / confort / ne murthe is noon
To ryde by the weye / domb as a stoon
And ther fore / wol I maken yow desport
As I seyde erst and doon yow som confort
And if yow liketh alle / by oon assent
For to stonden / at my Juggement
And for to werken / as I shal yow seye
Tomorwe / whan ye ryden by the weye
Now by my fader soule / that is deed
But ye be murye / I wol yeve yow myn heed
Hoold up youre hondes /
       with outen moore speche

Oure conseil / was nat longe for to seche
Us thoughte / it was nat worth / to make it wys
And graunted hym / with outen moore avys
And bade hym seye / his voirdit as hym leste
Lordynges quod he / now herkneth for the beste
But taketh it noght I pray yow in desdeyn
This is the poynt to speken short and pleyn
That ech of yow / to shorte with oure weye
In this viage / shal tellen tales tweye
To Caunterburyward / I mene it so
And homward / he shal tellen othere two
Of aventures / that whilom have bifalle
And which of yow / that bereth hym best of alle
That is to seyn / that telleth in this cas
Tales of best sentence / and moost solas
Shal have a Souper / at oure aller cost
Here in this place / sittynge by this post
Whan that we come agayn / fro Caunterbury
And for to make yow / the moore mury
I wol my self goodly with yow ryde
Right at myn owene cost and be youre gyde

You go to Caunterbury – God you speed.
The blissful martyr send you all you need!
And well I ken as ye go by the way
You will contrive to tell tales and to play,
For truthfully, comfort nor mirth is none
To ride along the way as dumb as stone.
Therefore it shall be me who makes you sport
As I have said, and do you some comfort,
And if it pleases all by one assent,
To put yourselves under my judgèment
And then to work together as I say,
Tomorrow as you ride along the way,
Now, by my father's soul that now is dead,
Be ye not merry, I will give you my head!
Hold up your hands,
       withouten further speech."

The answer did not take us long to reach.
We thought the matter was not worth debating
And granted him, without deliberating
The right to give his verdict as he chose.
"Lordings," quoth he, "now listen very close,
And take it not, I pray you, in disdain.
This is the point, to speak it short and plain
That each of you, to speed us on our way,
Shall on the journey tell us stories tway
When Caunterbury-ward, I mean it so,
And homeward he shall tell another two,
Tales of adventure in the bygone past,
And he of you who tells his story best
That is to say, that telleth in each case,
In the best style, what gives the most solace,
Shall have a supper at the others' cost
Here at this table, sitting by this post,
When that we come again from Caunterbury.
And for to make the company more merry
Myself also will goodly with you ride,
Right at my own expense, and be your guide.

And whoso will my judgèment gainsay,
Shall pay for all we spend upon the way.
And if ye will agree that this be so,
Tell me at once, without wordès mo,
And I will early prepare myself therefor."

This thing we granted, and our oathès swore
With full glad heart, and prayed him also
That he would vouchsafe for to do so,
That he would now become our governor,
And of our tales the judge and the reporter.
And set a supper at a certain price
And willingly were ruled by his device
In high and low, and thus by one assent,
We all accorded to his judgement.
And thereupon the wine was fetched anon,
We drank, and so to rest went everyone
Withouten any longer tarrying.

Next morning, when the day began to spring
Up rose our Host, and was our only cock,
And gathered us together in a flock,
And forward riding at an easy pace,
Until we reached Saint Thomas' watering place,
Halted his horse. The company stood still,
Then said he, "Lordings, hearken if you will.
Ye know what you agreed, and if I find
Morning and Even-song of the same mind
Let us now see who first shall tell the tale.
And never may I drink of wine or ale
If whoso rebel against my judgement
Don't pay for all that by the way is spent.
Now draw your cut, before we further win.
He which shall draw the shortest
        shall begin.
Sir Knicht!" quoth he, "my master and my lord,
Now draw your cut, for that is my accord.
Come near," quoth he, "my lady Prioress,

And who so wole / my Juggement with seye
Shal paye / al that we spende by the weye
And if ye vouche sauf / that it be so
Tel me anoon / with outen wordes mo
And I wol erly / shape me ther fore

This thyng was graunted / and oure othes swore
With ful glad herte / and preyden hym also
That he wolde vouche sauf / for to do so
And that he wolde been / oure governour
And of oure tales / Juge and reportour
And sette a souper / at a certeyn prys
And we wol ruled been / at his devys
In heigh and logh / and thus by oon assent
We been acorded / to his Juggement
And ther up on / the wyn was fet anoon
We dronken / and to reste wente echon
With outen / any lenger taryynge

A morwe / whan that day bigan to sprynge
Up roos oure hoost and was oure aller cok
And gadred us / togydres in a flok
And forth we ryden / a litel moore than pas
Un to the wateryng of Seint Thomas
And there oure hoost bigan his hors areste
And seyde / lordes / herkneth if yow leste
Ye woot youre forward / and it yow recorde
If evensong / and morwesong acorde
Lat se now / who shal telle the firste tale
As evere mote I drynke wyn / or Ale
Who so be rebel / to my Juggement
Shal paye / for al / that by the wey is spent
Now draweth cut er that we ferrer twynne
He which that hath the shorteste /
        shal bigynne
Sire knyght quod he / my mayster and my lord
Now draweth cut for that is myn acord
Cometh neer quod he / my lady Prioresse

And ye sire Clerc. lat be your shamefastnesse	*And ye, sir Clerk, let be your shamefastness,*
Ne studieth noght ley hond to / every man	*Nor study nocht! Lay hand to, every man!"*
Anoon to drawen / every wight bigan	*Anon to draw them every wight began*
And shortly / for to tellen / as it was	*And shortly for to tell it as it was,*
Were it by aventure / or sort or cas	*By accident, or fate, or other cause,*
The sothe is this / the Cut fil to the knyght	*The truth is, that the cut fell to the Knight,*
Of which ful blithe and glad was every wight	*Of which full blithe and glad was every wight,*
And telle he moste his tale / as was resoun	*And tell he must his tale, as he has said*
By forward / and by composicioun	*In his foreword, and as we had agreed*
As ye han herd / what nedeth wordes mo	*As ye have heard; what words are neede*
And whan this goode man /	*mo? And when this good man*
sawgh that it was so	*saw that it was so,*
As he / that wys was / and obedient	*And as he was wise and obedient*
To kepe his forward / by his free assent	*To keep his foreword by his free assent*
He seyde / syn I shal bigynne the game	*He said, "Since I shall begin the game,*
What wel come be the Cut in goddes name	*What! Welcome be the cut, in Goddès name!*
Now lat us ryde / and herkneth what I seye	*Now let us ride, and hearken what I say."*
And with that word / we ryden forth oure weye	*And with that word we rode forth on our way,*
And he bigan / with right a murye cheere	*And he began with a right merry cheer*
His tale anoon / and seyde as ye may heere	*His tale anon, and said as ye may hear.*

TRACTATUS DE CONCLUSIONIBUS ASTROLABII
GEOFFREY CHAUCER
ENGLAND

c1390

LITELL LOWYS my sone I have perceived well by certeyne evidences thine abilite to lerne sciencez touchinge noumbres & proporciouns & as wel considere I thy bisi preyere in special to lerne the tretis of the astrelabie. than for as mechel as a philosofre seith he wrappeth him in his frend that condescendith to the rihtful preiers of his frend / therfor have I geven the a suffisaunt astralabie as for owre orizonte compowned after the latitude of Oxenford / upon which by mediacion of this litel tretis I purpose to teche the a certein nombre of conclusions apertenyng to the same instrument. I seye a certein of conclusiouns for thre causes. the furste cause is this truste wel that alle the conclusiouns that han ben fownde or elles possibli miyhten be fownde in

Just as Troilus and Criseyde has been called the first psychological novel in English, this has been called the first English scientific treatise. It shows 14th-century English prose at its best.

The astrolabe was then the most modern of scientific tools. Islamic mathematicians had invented it. The Crusades had brought it to Europe.

By giving little Lewis one along with these instructions Chaucer acts like a modern dad who gives his son a computer & manual. It used the postions of sun, moon & stars to calculate time of day, day of the year & to navigate ships – a very advanced work for a small child! This preface is more than it seems. Aimed at any who read English it states, as if to a child, that as the lore of the astrolabe was written in Greek, Arabic, Hebrew, Latin (but especially Latin, since the lore of other languages had been put into Latin) then these truths can also be said in English since God wants the truth taught in every language. This argument applies to the Bible. In teaching his son a very useful science Chaucer is also taking the radical side in a public debate thus doing 2 very different jobs while seeming to do only 1. If God has a mind it works like this. Age-of-Reason critics called it wit.

so noble an instrument as an astralabie ben unknowe perfitly to any mortal man in this regioun as I suppose. another cause is this that sothly in any tretis of the astrelabie that I have seyn there ben some conclusions that wole nat in alle thinges performen hir byhestes & some of hem ben to harde to thy tendre age of .x. yer to conseyve. this tretis divided in 5 parties wole I shewe the under ful lihte rewles & naked wordes in englissh for latyn ne kanstow yit but smal my lite sone. but natheles suffise to the thise trewe conclusiouns in englissh as wel as suffisith to thise noble clerkes grekes thise same conclusiouns in grek & to arabiens in arabik & to Jewes in Ebrew & to the latyn folk in latyn / whiche latyn folk han hem furst owt of othre diverse langages & writen in hir owne tonge that is to sein in latyn. & god wot that in alle thise langages & in many mo han thise conclusiouns ben suffisantly lerned & tawht / & yit by diverse rewles ryht as diverse pathes leden diverse folk the rihte wey to Roome. Now wol I prey mekly every discret persone that redith or herith this litel tretis to have my rewde endytyng for excused & my superfluite of wordes for two causes. the firste cause is for that curios enditing & hard sentence is ful hevy atones for swich a child to lerne. & the seconde cause is this, that sothly me semeth betre to writen unto a childe twies a good sentence than he forget it ones. And lowis yif so be that I shewe the in my lihte Englissh as trewe conclusiouns touching this matere & nawht only as trewe but as many & as subtil conclusiouns as ben shewed in latyn in ani commune tretis of the astrelabie / kon me the more thank and preye god save the kyng that is lord of this langage & alle that him feyth bereth & obeieth everech in his degree the more and the lasse. but considere wel that I ne usurpe nat to have fownde this werk of my labour or of myn engin. I nam but a lewd compilatour of the labour of olde Astrologens and have hit translated in myn englissh only for thi doctrine & with this swerd shal I slen envie.

THE LOLLARD BIBLE: Chapter 15 of the Prologue
JOHN WYCLIF: MASTER of BALLIOL COLLEGE
OXFORD UNIVERSITY

c1395

FOR as much as Christ sayeth that the gospel shall be preached in all the world, and David sayeth of the apostles and their preaching, *the sound of them went out into each land, and the words of them went out to the ends of the world, and then David sayeth, the Lord shall tell in the scriptures of the people and of these princes that were in it, that is, shall tell it in church, and as Jerome sayeth about that verse, holy writ belongs to all people, for it is made that all people should know it*, and the princes of the church, that were therein, be the apostles, that had authority to write holy writ, for confirming of the Holy Ghost, and faith of Christian men, and this dignity hath no man after them, be they never so holy, never so learned, as Jerome witnesseth. Also Christ sayeth of the Jews that cried Osanna to him in the temple, that though they were still stones they shall cry, and by stones he signified heathen men, that worshipped stones for their gods. And we English men be come of heathen men, therefore we are signified by these stones, that should cry holy writ; and as Jews, interpreted knowingly, signifieth clergy, that should know God by repenting of sins, and by hearing God's voice, so our ignorant men looking to the corner stone Christ, must be meant by stones, stones firm and abiding in the foundation; for though covetous clergy be maddened by simony, and heresy, and many other sins, and despise and stop holy writ as much as they may, yet the common people cry after holy writ, to read it, and keep it, with great cost and peril of their life. For these reasons and others, with common charity to save all men in our realm, which God would have saved, a simple creature hath translated the Bible out of Latin into English.

First, this simple creature had much trouble, along with many different fellows and helpers, to gather many old Bibles, and other teachers and commentaries, and make one Latin Bible somewhat true; and then to study it beside the

This is from the 2nd complete Bible in English made out of St Jerome's Latin Bible by a team of clergy. It was later called The Lollard Bible by priests & statesmen keen to destroy it. The chief editor was John Wyclif, son of a Yorkshire squire. He was also a priest – an agent of the crown – Oxford's last great philosopher – England's champion against the pope – defender of the people's rights – an inciter to revolt – a damned heretic whose corpse was dug up, burnt & its remains flung in a river. This came about through a great national & international debate about property. All things came from God, but should the right to own them be finally decided by kings or popes?

Most Christians agreed that the Church was a multi-national company founded by Jesus to save their souls by prayers & preaching. It ran nearly all schools, charities & hospitals that then existed; its pulpits were the main broadcasting services; it owned vast estates, had its own law courts,

& clerical lawyers who thought earthly kings were mainly a police-force to defend the church with its property & people under their overlord, the pope. Most clergy accepted this idea, & so did most rulers who needed papal help. In 1213 King John (not a popular king) got the church's help by swearing that the pope was his overlord. Later English kings rejected papal rent demands because (as William the Waster had said) it was not customary for feudal bosses to pay a priesthood for land they or their ancestors had won in battle. But in France & Italy feudal law-codes had not displaced Roman law, so lawyers there serving earthly rulers used subtler reasons.

They argued from history that God had made possible Christ's spiritual empire (the church) by making the Roman empire first. Christ had accepted Roman law when he answered a question on taxation saying, "Give to Caesar what is Caesar's & to God what is God's." Kings were the heirs of Caesar, so supreme in worldly affairs as was the pope in matters of faith. They should pay the church for the

new, the text beside the glosses, together with all the teachers he might get, especially Lire on the Old Testament, that helped full much this work; and thirdly to counsel with old grammarians and old divines, of hard words, and hard sentences, how they might best be understood and translated; and fourthly to translate as clearly as he could to the sentence, and to have many good fellows and cunning at the correcting of the translation.

The first thing to know is, that the best translating out of Latin into English, is to translate the whole sentence, and not just word by word, so that the sentence be as open, or opener, in English as in Latin, and not go far from the letter; and if the letter may not be saved in the translating, let the sentence ever be whole and open, for the words ought to serve the intent of the sentence, or else they be superfluous or false.

In translating into English, many solutions can make the sentence open, as an ablative absolute case may be resolved into these three words, with suitable verb, *while, because, if*; as thus, *the master reading, I stand,* may be translated, *while the master reads, I stand,* or *if the master reads, I stand,* or *because the master reads, etc.*; and sometime it will accord well with the sentence to use *when,* or *afterward*; thus, *when the master read, I stood,* or *after the master read, I stood*; and sometime it may well be resolved into a verb of the same tense with the word *and* in English, thus, *arescentibus hominibus prae timore*, that is, *and men shall wax dry for dread.* Also a participle of a present tense, or preterit, of active or passive voice, may be resolved into a verb of the same tense with a copulative conjunction, as thus, *dicens*, that is, *saying*, may become *and sayeth* or *that sayeth*; and this will, in many cases, make the sentence open, when to English it word by word would be dark and doubtful. Also when rightful understanding is hindered by relation, I resolve it openly, thus, where *Dominum formidabunt adversarii eius* should be Englished thus by the letter: *the Lord his adversaries should dread,* I English it: *the adversaries of the Lord should dread him.*

At the beginning I purposed, with God's help, to make the sentence as true and open in English as it is in Latin, or more true and open than it is in Latin; and I pray, for charity and for common profit of Christian souls, that if any wise man may find any default of the truth of the translation, let him set in the true sentence and meaning of holy writ, but let him examine truly his Latin Bible, for no doubt he shall find many Bibles in Latin that are false, if he examine many of the new; and the common Latin Bibles have more need to be corrected, as many as I have seen in my life, than hath the English Bible late translated; and where the Hebrew, by witness of Jerome, of Lire, and other expositors, discordeth from our Latin Bibles, I have set in the margin, by way of a gloss, what the Hebrew hath, and how it is understood in some places; and I did this most in the Psalms, that of all our books discordeth most from Hebrew; for the church readeth not the Psalms by the last translation of Jerome out of Hebrew into Latin, but another translation of other men, that had much less cunning and holiness than Jerome had, as may be proved by the proper originals of Jerome, which he glossed. And where I have translated as openly or openlier in English as in Latin, let wise men judge, that know well both languages, and know well the sentence of holy scripture. And where I have done this, or not done it, never doubt, that they who consider well the sentence of holy writ and the English together, and will toil with God's grace upon it, may make the Bible as true and open, yea, and openlier in English than it is in Latin. And a simple man has no doubt, that with God's grace and great toil, men may expound the Bible in English more openly and shortly than the old great doctors have expounded it in Latin, and much sharper and better grounded than many recent commentators and expounders have done. But God, of his great mercy, give us grace to live well, and to say the truth in a fitting manner, and acceptable to God and his peoples, and to spill not our time, be it short be it long at God's ordinance.

But some, that seem wise and holy, say thus, if men

spiritual aid earthly rulers needed; they should defend the people & property of the church as they defended their own; after which they owed the pope nothing. This argument pleased most European rulers, also Catholics like Dante who thought the pope's earthly power bad for both church & state. It no longer pleased rulers of England led by John of Gaunt.

The rise in workers' wages, the halt in the plunder of France had made these great lords poorer. They envied the rich estates of the church but neither Roman law or Anglo-Norman custom gave reasons for seizing them. They looked to the English universities for such reasons, since Cambridge & Oxford were schools for priests under royal protection. John Wyclif, a popular teacher, had lectured at both. He had advised the Commons on cure of clerical abuses, & as crown diplomat had opposed papal rule. In 1378 the College of Cardinals split the church by electing an antipope. French & Italian popes excommunicated each other, & in the next six years Wyclif's teaching grew as radical as Luther's 150 years later.

In the eyes of God (said Wyclif) the only reason for owning something was the right use of it – any other use was evil, & should be corrected. If the church used its property in ungodly ways then it was lawful for Lords & Commons to remove it. God's word could only be read in the Bible. Not the pope but the Bible should rule the church because all rites not given in it were frauds. If the Bible was widely read folk would see that prayers for the dead, indulgences, pardons, worship of saints, shrines, relics & the miracle that turns the mass bread into Christ's flesh & blood were frauds. These very popular rites were main sources of clerical income. Wyclif attacked them in Latin books & English pamphlets. Pamphlets – letters to the public to change the public mind – are broadcast when reading is common & rulers too divided to settle things by force. Wyclif's were the first in English history. But Milton, Swift & Tom Paine's pamphlets were printed. Each copy of Wyclif's was hand-written, which shows the strength of his support in courts & colleges. So does the

now were as holy as Jerome was, they might translate out of Latin into English, as he did out of Hebrew and Greek into Latin, but we should not translate now, they think, for want of holiness and cunning. Though this argument seems substantial, it hath no good ground, nor reason, nor charity, for this argument is more against Saint Jerome, and against the first translators, and against holy church, than against simple men that now translate into English; for Saint Jerome was not as holy as the apostles and the evangelists, whose books he translated into Latin, nor had he so high gifts of the Holy Ghost as they had; and much more the first translators were not so holy as Moses and the prophets, especially David, nor had they so great gifts of God. Furthermore holy church approveth, not only the true translation of mere Christian men, but also of open heretics, that did away many mysteries of Jesu Christ by guileful translation, as Jerome witnesseth in a prologue on Job, and in the prologue of Daniel. Much more let the church of England approve the true and whole translation of simple men, that would for no good on earth, by their knowledge and power, put away the least truth, yea, the least letter or title of holy writ, that beareth substance or value. And dispute they not of the holiness of men now living in this deadly life, for they judge not thereon, as that is reserved only to God's judgement. If they know any notable default by the translators, or a want in them, let them blame the default with charity and mercy, and let them never damn a thing that is allowed by God's law, such as wearing of a good cloth for a time, or riding on a horse for a great journey, when they know not why it is done; for such things may be done by simple men, with as great charity and virtue, as some that hold themselves great and wise, can ride in a gilt saddle, or use cushions and beds and clothes of gold and silk, with other vanities of the world. God grant pity, mercy and charity, and put away such foolish judgement, that be against reason and charity.

Yet worldly clergy ask loudly what spirit maketh idiots brave enough to translate the Bible into English, since the

THE LOLLARD BIBLE **131**

four great evangelists durst never do this? This argument is so stupid that it needeth no answer, none but stillness or courteous scorn, for these great evangelists were not Englishmen, nor conversant with Englishmen, nor could they use the language of England, but they never ceased till they had holy writ in their mother tongue, of their own people. For Jerome, that was born a Latin man, translated the Bible into Latin; and Augustine, and many more Latins expounded the Bible, in Latin, to Latin men among which they dwelled, and Latin was the common tongue to their people about Rome and beyond, as English is to our people, and yet to this day the common people in Italy speaketh Latin corrupt, as true men say that have been in Italy; and the number of translators out of Greek into Latin passes knowing, as Augustine witnesseth in the 4th book of *Christian Teaching*, and sayeth thus, "The translators out of Hebrew into Greek may be numbered, but Latin translators, or they that translated into Latin, may not be numbered in any manner." For in the first times of faith, each man, as a Greek book came to him, and he seemed to himself to have some cunning in Greek and Latin, had the courage to translate; and this thing helped more than hindered understanding, if readers were not negligent, because the beholding of many books hath showed often, or clarified, some darker sentences. This sayeth Augustine. Therefore Grosseteste sayeth, that diverse men translate, and that diverse translations be in church, for where one said darkly, another might say openly.

Lord God! Since the beginning of faith so many men translated into Latin, and to the great profit of Latin men, let one simple creature of God translate into English, for profit of English men; for if worldy clerics search well their chronicles and books, they shall find that Bede translated the Bible, and expounded much in Saxon, that was the English or common language of this land, in his time; and not only Bede, but also King Alfred, that founded Oxenford University, translated in his last days the beginning of the Psalms into Saxon, and would more, if he had lived longer.

making of 2 whole English Bibles.

The 1st, mainly edited by Nicholas Hereford, was hard to read for it kept the word order of Jerome's Latin original. This preface is from the 2nd Bible revised from the 1st by John Purvey, Wyclif's secretary. The statement that a sentence in one tongue needs a different word order in another occurs in prefaces to many translations. They repeat what St. Jerome wrote around A.D. 400 in the preface to **his** Bible translation. The need is as old as translation itself, so even Jerome was echoing earlier writers.

These Bibles were not widely feared at first. Many bishops thought they would **help** ignorant clergy. Nicholas Hereford was called to Rome, tried for heresy & acquitted. But the more hotly Wyclif's ideas were condemned in the sermons of priest & friar the more radical he grew. He started an order called **simple preachers** who knew scriptures but had sworn no vows to bishop or abbot. They came from the poorer sort of student – Will Langland was maybe one. Like Franciscans they preached in *markets & highways, grew popular with trades & country folk, & from then on Wyclif began to lose the favour of the great. They had wanted him to get the support of landed gentry & burghers in the House of Commons, but those who worked with their hands were now saying that if God meant things to belong to those who used them rightly, why should land not belong to those who cultivated it? And what made heirs of folk who took land by force think they had a right to Church land? Wyclif replied that God let the Devil rule the earth so that good might come of it. "Then why", said some, "did Jesus teach us to ask God* **Thy will be done on earth as it is in heaven?** *Should we not try to get it done now?"*

Then came a rehearsal for the movement led by Luther much later. Wyclif was summoned to Rome, then the only place where folk could be tried & killed for heresy. He gave ill health as a reason for not going, & died soon after.

Also French men, Beemers and Bretons have the Bible, and other books of devotion and exposition, translated in their mother tongue; why English men should not have the same in their mother tongue I cannot think, but for the falseness and negligence of clergy, or because our people are not worthy to have so great grace and gift of God, in punishment of their old sins. God for his mercy amend these evil causes and make our people to have, and con, and keep truly holy writ, to life and death!

But in translating words equivocal, that is, that have many significations under the one letter, may easily be peril, for Augustine sayeth in the 4th book of *Christian Teaching*, that if equivocal words be not translated into the sense understood by the author, it is error; as in that part of the Psalm, *the feet of them be swift to shed blood*, the Greek word is equally *sharp* and *swift*, and he that translated *sharp feet* erred, and a book that hath s*harp feet* is false, and must be amended. Therefore a translator hath great need to study well the sentence, both before and after, and look that such equivoke words accord with the sentence. And he hath need to live a clean life, and be full devout in prayers, and have not his wit occupied about worldly things, that the Holy Spirit, author of wisdom, and cunning, and truth, dress him in his work, and suffer him not for to err. Also this word *ex* sometime signifieth *of*, and sometime *by*; and *enim* signifieth commonly *forsooth*, *truly*, and, as Jerome sayeth, it signifieth *because, forwhy*; and *secundum* is taken for *after*, as many men say, and commonly for *by* or *upon*, thus *by your word*, or *upon your word*. Many such adverbs, conjunctions, and prepositions be set down one for another, and at the free choice of the author sometime; and now should be taken as it accord best to the sentence. By this manner, with good living and great toil, men must come to true and clear understanding of holy writ, seem it never so hard at the beginning. God grant us all grace to con well, and keep well holy writ, and suffer joyfully some pain for it at the last!

Amen.

THE LOLLARD BIBLE:
HERE BIGYNNETH GENESIS

IN THE BIGYNNYNG god made of nought: hevene and erthe / Forsothe the erthe was idel: and voide · & derknessis weren on the face of depthe · And the spiryt of the lord was borun on the watris / And god seide / light be maad / And light was maad / & god seigh the light · that it was good: & he departide the light fro derknessis / And he clepide the light dai: & the derknessis nyght / & the eventid and morwetid was maad: o daie / And god seide / the firmament be maad in the myddis of watris / & departe watris fro watris / & god made the firmament · and departide the watris that weren undur the firmament: fro these watris that weren on the firmament / and it was don so / And god clepide the firmament hevene / & the eventid & morwetid was maad: the secounde dai / forsothe god seide / the watris that ben undur hevene · be gaderid in to o place: & a drie place appere / & it was doon so / And god clepide the drie place erthe: & he clepide the gadryngis togidere of watris: the sees / And god seigh that it was good: & seide / the erthe brynge forth greene eerbe · & makynge seed: & appil tre makynge fruyt bi his kynde · whos seed be in it silf: on erthe / And it was doon so / And the erthe broughte forth greene erbe · & makynge seed bi his kynde: & a tre makynge fruyt · & ech havynge seed: by his kynde / And god seigh that it was good: & the eventid and morwetid was maad: the thridde dai / forsothe god seide / Lightis be maad in the firmament of hevene . & departe tho the dai & night: & be tho in to signes · & tymes · & daies · & yeeris · shyne tho in the firmament of hevene: and lightne tho the erthe / and it was doon so / & god made twei grete lightis · the gretter light: that it schulde be bifore to the dai: & the lesse light: that it schulde be bifore to the night · & god made sterris / and settide tho in the firmament of hevene: that tho schulden schyne on erthe · & that tho schulden be bifore to the dai & nyght: & schulden departe light & derknesse / And god seigh · that it was good: & the eventid and the morwetid was maad: the fourthe dai / Also god seide / the watris brynge forth · a crepynge beeste of lyvynge soule · & a brid fleynge above erthe: undur the firmament of hevene / And god made of nought · grete whallis · & ech lyvynge soule & movable · whiche the watris han brought forth: in to her kyndis · and god made of nought · ech volatile bi his kynde · and god seigh that it was good: & blesside hem · and seide / Wexe ye & be ye multiplied · and fille ye the watris of the see · & briddis be multiplied on erthe / And the eventid & the morwetid was maad: the fyvethe dai / And god seide / the erthe brynge forth a lyvynge soul in his kynde: werk beestis · and crepynge beestis · & unresonable beestis of erthe · bi her kyndis / and it was don so /

And god made unresonable beestis of erthe: bi her kyndes· & werk
beestis · & ech crepynge beeste of erthe in his kynde / & god seigh that
it was good: & seide / Make we man to oure ymage & liknesse · & be
he sovereyn to the fischis of the see · & to the volatilis of hevene · & to
unresonable beestis of erthe / & to ech creature · & to ech crepynge
beest . which is moved in erthe / And god made of nought a man: to his
ymage and liknesse/ god made of nought a man: to the ymage of god /
god made of nought hem · male and female / & god blesside hem &
seide / Encreesse ye and be ye multiplied. & fille ye the erthe. & make
ye it suget: And be ye lordis to fischis of the see: & to volatilis of
hevene: And to alle lyvynge beestis: that ben moved on erthe.

THE GOSPEL OF JON

IN THE BIGYNNYNG was the word & the word was
at god: & god was the word / this was in the bigynnynge at god / alle
thingis ben made bi him/ and with outen hym was maad no thing / that
thing that was maad: in him was liif / & liif was the light of men / &
the light schinyth in derknessis & derknessis conprehendiden not it / a
man was sent fro god to whom the name was Jon / this cam in to
witnessynge: that he schuld bere witnessynge of the light / that alle
men schulden bileve bi him · he was not the light but that he schulde
bere witnessynge of the light / ther was a very light · whiche lighteneth
eche man that cometh in to this world / he was in the world · & the
world was maad bi him: & the world knewe him not / he cam in to his
owne thingis: & hise receyivden him not / but hou many ever receyveden
him he yaf hem power to be maad the sones of god · to hem that bileven
in his name / the whiche not of bloodis · neither of wil of flesche ·
neither of the wil of man . but been borne of god / & the word was
maad man & dwellid amonge us / & we han seen the glory of him: as the
glory of the oon bigeten sone of the fadir /
ful of grace & of truthe.

HOW CLASS WAR DULLED ENGLISH LITERATURE
(BUT NOT EVERYWHERE)

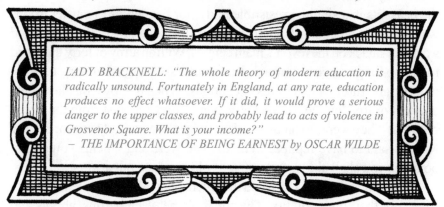

> LADY BRACKNELL: *"The whole theory of modern education is radically unsound. Fortunately in England, at any rate, education produces no effect whatsoever. If it did, it would prove a serious danger to the upper classes, and probably lead to acts of violence in Grosvenor Square. What is your income?"*
> – THE IMPORTANCE OF BEING EARNEST by OSCAR WILDE

AND THEN THE ENGLISH WARLORDS sought riches by renewing the French war and to pay for it invented a wholly new tax: a poll tax on every person in the realm, even labourers and tradesmen who had hitherto only been taxed by their landlords and churches. Through the spring of that year labourers, farmers, tradesmen from country and city planned a great revolt. There had been peasants' revolts before this in France and Germany, revolts caused by famines which drove the starving poor to attack the homes of the wealthy. Such revolts had never been carefully planned and had no long-term aim: except, perhaps, to build the kingdom of heaven on earth by dragging down the mighty from their seats. But the English peasants were not starving and did not expect to build the kingdom of heaven, though some of the poor preachers helped their organization. The majority did not even want to pull down the mighty: they wanted an end to some forms of taxation which benefited none but the wealthy, and an end to land slavery (villeinage), which some landlords were strengthening or reimposing, because they would not or could not pay wages which kept their labourers. When the peasant forces marched to London King Richard, his nobles and army were overwhelmingly outnumbered. The king – a brave, clever lad of fifteen – heard the leaders' demands with an air of sympathetic understanding, then did what he would have done had he been a fool and a coward. He signed legal documents granting the peasantry and small townsmen of his realm all the tax reliefs and freedoms they demanded. They returned to their homes with these charters, happy to have reformed the realm while leaving it intact.

But the big owners of Britain still had the military organization given to them by William the Waster. It took months of careful planning to unite the peasants in a single, irresistible body: for the nobles to muster troops was as easy as breathing. Church, nobility and monarchy swiftly organized a counter-attack on the revolt's main centres. With an army of forty thousand men, the king marched through Kent and Essex spreading terror by the number and ruthlessness of his executions. When met by a display of the charters of freedom he had recently signed, and a protest from the Essex men that "they were, so far as freedom went, the equals of their lords", the King is said to have replied, "Villeins you were and villeins you are. In bondage you shall abide, and not your old bondage but a worse."

When the revolt was crushed the rulers blamed the Simple Preachers for it, not their own poll tax. The squabble between barons, abbots and bishops stopped at once. The military landlords had tried to reform the church with public support got through clever university men, and had been faced with a demand to reform THEMSELVES! What government could bear it? The rulers of England would want no more clever university men, no more skilled public arguers and certainly no more pamphlets. The simple preachers were banned by act of parliament. Those arrested for breaking the ban quoted Wyclif's Bible in their defence, so that Bible was also banned to all who had not a bishop's permission for one. The court put the church in charge of universities. The Archbishop of Canterbury drove Wyclif's followers out and ordered the burning of his papers. The Commons debated a bill forbidding schools and colleges to teach labourers' children. They rejected it, despite which the number of students at Oxford shrank to a third of the number in Wyclif's time. Lectures grew so dull that foreign students stopped enrolling.

Widespread dullness could not be enforced suddenly but it was enforced steadily. Convicted preachers of reform had the muscles of their tongues cut so that they lolled uselessly, hence the name LOLLARD for anyone, anything that suggested reform. *Piers Plowman* got banned for being Lollard. A small group of north country M.P.s were nicknamed the Lollard Knights. Despite their protests parliament passed an act in 1400 allowing the church to burn Lollards in England without trying them in Rome. In 1417 the church got a single pope again. He declared Wyclif a heretic, so the corpse was exhumed, burnt etc. The intellectual state of fifteenth-century England is shown in the career of Reginald Pecock, a clever Welshman who became bishop of Chichester and wrote many books defending orthodox faith and showing the errors of Lollardy, while quoting copiously from the Wyclif Bible. The Archbishop of Canterbury found him guilty of heresy for writing on profound questions in English, and setting reason and nature above scripture. Pecock confessed he had been dreadfully wrong so only his books were burned. Meanwhile, with the church triumphant at home, the English warlords presided over splendidly useless slaughters of the French.

But twenty-five years later met an obstruction. The divine imagination took pity on the French people and spoke to their poorest and roughest soldiers through a peasant girl. She gave them such courage that, despite their treacherous nobility, they drove the English back to England. The English nobles had now nobody to fight but each other, so they did. Some historians think the civil war between the families of York and Lancaster did not touch the productive part of Britain: that cultivation of crops and exchanges of trade were unharmed by royal murders, beheadings, and the battlefields at Saint Albans Northampton Wakefield Towton Barnet Tewkesbury and Bosworth. However, the separation of government from commonsense work could not last for ever. The civil wars ended in a king who fixed his throne on a solid gold foundation. Like his predecessors Henry VII got a large grant of money from parliament by promising to fight the French, but instead used troops to overawe potential rivals at home. He did not battle and behead other military landlords, he fined them. He protected trade, extorted coin from those it profited, grew so wealthy he was able to dispense with parliament and rule the land directly through his servants. Throughout all this the merchants and professional people took the course indicated by Langland's moderate mouse and made money quickly and quietly, chiefly through the wool and cloth trade.

The ending of free speech by organized force did not damage new English literature as fatally as Norman conquest had damaged the old. Chaucer's poetry was still popular and legal. So were sword and sorcery romances, love tales and moral tales of a kind Chaucer wrote beautifully but also parodied. For over a century after his death the best new writing in south Britain was by Catholic mystics or for street theatre. Over 120 years passed between the banning of the first vernacular bible and printing of the next, in which time the best English poetry was written by Scots.

War with another nation is a great uniter of social classes, and between Bannockburn in 1314 and a Protestant reformation in 1560 Scotland and England were almost always at war. The northern nation's population was then (as now) less than an eighth of the southern, but neither side could win. England's richest land and most productive people were mainly in the south, which the small Scottish armies never reached. Scots people and wealth were also mainly in the south, so large English armies invaded there again and again, but could not defeat folk who burned their own crops, retreated into wildernesses and lived rough till the invaders left. Trade was ruined, towns stopped growing but free speech flourished. A French visitor (Froissart) thought it remarkable that if a knight rode his horse over a Scots grainfield an angry peasant ran up and cursed him. No peasants dared to do that in rich lands where the nobility had hundreds of workers so could have one flogged or hung without loss of income. Scots lairds were so poor they needed ALL their peasants and grain crops. Greater freedom of speech was inevitable. Outside the Lothians and Fife the main Scots language was still Gaelic, so the king's court was bilingual with a poet laureate for each tongue. The Scots king's English dialect was closer to old Northumbrian than to south British dialects and, like the English court, was also enriched by contact with Latin and French. Writers there, as elsewhere, were clergy, nobility, or dependent on them, but proved a poor land may have a rich literature.

In this century – the fifteenth after Jesus was born – papermaking came to England. Europeans had learned it from Arabs who learned it from Chinese captured at the siege of Samarkand in 751. Paper was cheaper than sheep or goatskin so speeded the criminal trade in extracts from Wyclif's Bible. A church spy reported that a farmer had given a cartload of hay for some pages of that. When this paper was united with print, intellectual explosions would happen.

A SCOTS FLOWERING

BETWEEN TWO BIBLES

1435c

THE KINGIS QUAIR
KING JAMES I OF SCOTLAND
TOWER OF LONDON

The firths & mountain chains defending Scots against invaders were also barriers between local landlords & their king. If he was a child or weakling they could feud, murder & steal without arrest. In 1406 King Robert III was a sick old man who let the Duke of Albany rule for him. The Duke had a claim to the throne. The king's eldest son mysteriously died in his care. King Robert sent his 2nd son, James, by sea to France for education in a safer land. The ship was captured by merchant pirates from Yarmouth. They gave the 11-year-old boy to Henry IV of England who welcomed this useful hostage. King Robert died a few days later. In the name of the imprisoned James the Albany family ruled Scotland for another 18 years.

In the Tower of London, Windsor Castle & other great houses James grew to be an agile sportsman, a fine musician & poet. He was taken abroad in a diplomatic ploy to break the Scots French alliance. It failed, but he was able to see how Henry IV, V & VI ruled what a historian calls **the most intensely governed country in Europe**. Meanwhile Scotland remained **one of the least intensely governed**.

When most despairing (this poem says) James saw & fell in love with a bonny lady. She gave him hope. She & his situation joined 3 strands of learning then known to every scholar: ASTROLOGY that described the sky as a clock

HEIREFTER FOLLOWIS THE QUAIR MAID BE KING JAMES OF SCOTLAND THE FIRST CALLIT THE KINGIS QUAIR AND MAID QUHEN HIS MAJESTIE WES IN ENGLAND.

HEIGH In the hevynnis figure circulere
The rody sterres twynklyt as the fyre
And In Aquary Cinthia the clere
Rynsid hir tressis like the goldin wyre
That late tofore in fair and fresche atyre
Through capricorn heved hir hornis bright
North northward approchit the myd-nyght

Quhen as I lay In bed allone waking
New partit out of slepe a lyte tofore
Fell me to mynd of many diverse thing
Off this and that can I noght say quharfore
Bot slepe for craft in erth myght I no more
For quhich as tho coude I no better wyle
Bot toke a boke to rede apon a quhile

Off quhich the name is clepit properly
Boece / eftere him that was the compiloure
Schewing the counsele of philosophye
Compilit by that noble senatoure
Off rome /
            quhilom that was the warldis floure
And from estate by fortune a quhile
Forjugit was to povert / in exile

And there to here this worthy
                              lord and clerk
His metir suete full of moralitee
His flourit pen so fair he set awerk
Discryving first of his prosperitee
And out of that his infelicitee
And than how he in his poetly report
In philosophy can him to confort

For quhich thoght I in purpose at my boke
To borowe a slepe at thilke tyme began
Or ever I stent my best was more to loke
Upon the writing of this noble man
That in him self the full recover wan
Off his infortune poverti and distresse
And in tham set his verray sekernesse

And so the vertew of his youth before
Was In his age the ground of his delytis
Fortune the bak him turnyt and therefore
He makith Joye and confort that he quitis
Off theire unsekir warldis appetitis
And so aworth he takith his penance
And of his vertew maid It suffisance

With mony a noble resoun as him likit
Enditing in his faire latyne tong
So full of fruyte and rethorikly pykit
Quhich to declare my scole is over yong
Therefore I lat him pas and in my tong
Procede I will agayn to my sentence
Off my mater / and leve all Incidence

The long nyght beholding as I saide
Myn eyen gan to smert for studying
My buke I schet / and at my hede It laide
And doun I lay bot ony tarying
This matere newe In my mynd rolling
This is to seyne how that eche estate
As fortune lykith / thame will translate

For sothe It is that on hir tolter quhele
Every wight cleverith In his stage
And failyng foting oft quhen hir lest rele
Sum up / sum doun Is non estate nor age
Ensured more the prynce than the page
So uncouthly his werdes sche devidith
Namly In youth that seildin ought providith

whose stars & planets had names of ancient gods: Cynthia or the moon who ruled changes of fortune, Venus who ruled love etc. The One True God let such lesser gods rule people's lives to test & train them. BOETHIUS (the Roman statesman writing in jail) who said trouble could be made good if welcomed as God's discipline, since the universe was turned by Fortune who always put down the high & raised the low. LOVE ROMANCES that put a real lady in place of Fortune & said a patient, faithful, obedient lover must at last win her.

Near the end of this preface our poet hears a bell strike the hour of morning prayer: it sounds like a voice urging **Say on, man, what thee befell!** What befell was this. The Scots parliament agreed to pay a huge ransom for his release, but the Tudor king required that he strengthen ties with England by marrying an English noblewoman. If the poem tells the truth this let him marry Joan Beaufort, the woman he already loved. From the lowest point of fortune's wheel he was whirled up to freedom, kingship & sexual union. Love & wise action, Venus & Minerva became one, moving him to write something new in literature: a love story ending happily in marriage.

Earlier writers, priests & poets, thought this could not be done. They knew husbands & wives could become friends, but true love depended on free will & weddings were property *deals between families who allowed the bride no choice. Since the wedding of James & Joan was also a state treaty some modern critics think that not even the groom had a choice – that the poem uses events from his life to prop up a fancy ending. But in 13 married years this wilful man seems to have been faithful to his wife when such faith was not looked for in husbands & certainly not in kings.*

POSTSCRIPT

With no police, hardly any army & an exchequer in debt to England James brought a system of statute law to his land & built up the power of parliament. The Scots had no single capital so he held parliament in many towns & punished those in the area who broke laws or did not obey him. He seized land from the biggest offenders after beheading them & their nearest male relatives. The Albanies' heads fell first. James was stabbed to death on a visit to Perth, but his son lived long enough to go on with the same frequently bloody job. Long before that happened the war with England had been resumed. The king's ransom was never paid.

Among thir thoughtis rolling to and fro
Fell me to mynd of my fortune and ure
In tender youth how sche was first my fo
And eft my frende / and how I gat recure
Off my distresse and all myn aventure
I gan ourehayle / that langer slepe ne rest
Ne myght I nat / so were my wittis wrest

For wakit and forwalowit thus musing
Wery forlyin I lestnyt sodaynlye
And sone I herd the bell to matyns ryng
And up I rase no langer wald I lye
Bot now how trowe ye suich a fantasye
Fell me to mynd / that ay me thoght the bell
Said to me / tell on man quhat the befell

Thoght I tho to my self quhat may this be
This is myn awin ymagynacioun
It is no lyf that spekis unto me
It is a bell or that impressioun
Off my thoght / causith this Illusioun
That dooth me think so nycely in this wise
And so befell as I shall you devise

Determyt furth therewith in myn entent
Sen I thus have ymagynit of this soun
And in my tyme more Ink and paper spent
To lyte effect I tuke conclusioun
Sum new thing to write I set me doun
And furthwith all my pen In hand I tuke
And maid a ✠ / and thus begouth my buke

1436

Margery Kempe was as wilful as Chaucer's wife of Bath. She wished to be a saint & mystic when such women were usually daughters of nobles & lived as

THE BOOK OF MARGERY KEMPE PROYM by MARGERY KEMPE LYNN, NORFOLK

H ERE begins a short treatise and a comfortable for sinful wretches, wherein they may have great solace and comfort and understand the high & unspeakable mercy of our sovereign Saviour Christ Jhesu, whose name be worshipped and magnified without end, because now, in our days, to us unworthy folk, he deigns to exercise his nobility and goodness. All the works of our Saviour be for our example & instruction, and what grace he works in any creature is our profit, if lack of charity be not our hindrance.

And therefore, by leave of our merciful Lord Christ Jhesu, to the magnifying of his holy name, Jhesu, this little treatise shall deal in part of his wonderful works, how mercifully, how benignly & how charitably he moved and steered a sinful scoundrel into his love, which sinful scoundrel was in will and purpose stirred by the Holy Ghost to follow our Saviour, making great promises to fast, with many other deeds of penance. And ever she was turned back by temptation (like reed-stalk which bows with every wind & never is stable until no wind blows) until the time our merciful Lord Christ Jhesu having pity and compassion on the creature he had made, turned her health into sickness, prosperity into adversity, respectability into condemnation, & love into hatred. Thus all things turning upside down, this creature which many years had ever been unstable was perfectly drawn and steered to enter the way of high perfection, which perfect way Christ our Saviour in his proper person exemplified. Sadly he trod it & rightly he went before.

Then this creature, who through this treatise shall show part of the mercy of Jesus, was touched by the hand of our Lord with great bodily sickness, whereby she lost reason & her wits a long time till our Lord by grace restored her again, as shall be more fully told afterward.

*nuns or recluses. Mrs. Kempe, a mayor's daughter & proud of it, had managed her own brewery & bore her husband 14 children. Saints sometimes wrote their spiritual life stories. Though unable to read or write Mrs. Kempe did not rest till she got a priest to write hers. Other mystics got visions by dying to themselves – losing what Freud calls the ego – so said nothing or little about other folk. Mrs. Kempe tells how her faith caused quarrels with husband, towns-people, fellow pilgrims, priests & bishops. A vision of hellish devils drove her so mad that she was tied up to prevent suicide, but healing came with a vision of Jesus sitting on her bedside: a handsome man who wore a lovely purple robe and who said kindly **Daughter why have you forsaken me? I never forsook you**. Later the Virgin Mary took her back in time to help at Christ's birth. Having flaunted in rich gowns against her husband's wish she took a vow of chastity & wore robes of white. Being moved to cry out, weep & praise God aloud during church service she was at times arrested & once nearly lynched as a Lollard, but when tried for it always proved her orthodoxy. On pilgrimage to shrines in the Holy Land, Italy, Spain, Germany, & many parts of England the help of Jesus, Mary, kindly priests & humble people constantly got her out of trouble.*

The full text of her book was preserved by an old Catholic family, the Butler-Bowdons, who made a version in 1936 which has greatly assisted this translation.

Her worldly goods, which were plentiful & abundant at that time, were shortly after barren and bare. Then was pomp and pride cast down and laid aside. They who before had respected her then full sharply reproved; her kindred & they who had been her friends were now her worst enemies.

Then she, considering this wonderful change, sought succour under the wings of her ghostly mother, Holy Church; went & bowed before her father confessor, accusing herself of her misdeeds, & then did great bodily penance. And soon our merciful Lord granted this creature plentiful tears of contrition day by day, so often that some men said she could weep when she wished & slandered the work of God. She was so used to being slandered & reproved, chidden and rebuked by the world for grace & virtue with which she was inspired through the strength of the Holy Ghost that she found solace and comfort in suffering any disease for the love of God & grace that God wrought in her. For the more slander she suffered, the more she increased in holy meditation & of wonderful speech and dalliance which our Lord spake and held within her soul, teaching how she would be despised for his love, and have patience, putting all her trust, & love, and affection, in him only. She knew and understood many secret & hidden things that befell after by inspiration of the Holy Ghost. And often, while she was kept with such holy speech and dalliance, she so wept and sobbed that many men greatly wondered, for they little knew how at home our Lord was in her soul. She herself could never tell the grace she felt, it was so heavenly, so high above her reason and her bodily wits, and her body so feeble in the presence of grace that she might never express it with her word like she felt it in her soul.

Then had this creature much dread of illusions and deceits from her ghostly enemies. Then she went at the Holy Ghost's bidding to many respected clergymen, archbishops & bishops, doctors of divinity and bachelors also. She spoke also with many hermits, and showed them her manner of living & such grace as the Holy Ghost of his goodness worked in her mind and soul, as her wit managed to express it. And all she showed her secrets to said she was greatly bound to love our Lord for the grace he showed her, & counselled her to follow her movings & stirrings, & trustingly believe they were of the Holy Ghost & of no evil spirit. Some of these worthy and respected clergy said they would answer to God that this creature was inspired by the Holy Ghost, and told her she should make a book of her feelings and revelations. Some offered to write her feelings with their own hands, & she would not consent in no way, for she was commanded in her soul that she should not write so soon, and it was twenty years and more from the time this creature had her first feelings and revelations before she did any writing.

Afterward, when it pleased our Lord, he commanded & charged her that she get written down her feelings & revelations and way of life that his goodness might be known to all the world. Then had the creature no writer who would do what she wished or give credence to her feelings, until a time when a man living in Germany (an Englishman by birth & since wedded in Germany where he had both wife & child) knowing well this creature & her desire & moved I believe by the Holy Ghost, came to England with his wife and goods & dwelled with the foresaid creature till he had written as much as she would tell him for the time they were together. And after that he died.

There was a priest which this creature had great affection to, so she communed with him of this matter and she brought him the book to read. The book was so vilely written that he made little sense thereof, for it was neither good English or German nor were the letters shaped or formed as other letters be. Therefore the priest believed no man could read it, unless by special grace. Nevertheless, he promised her that if he could read it he would copy it out & write it legibly with good will. Then there was so much evil talk about this creature & her weeping that the priest dared not from cowardice speak with her, except seldom, nor would write as he had promised, so he avoided and deferred the writing of this book for at least four years and more, despite the creature crying often on him for it. Then he advised her to go to a good man who had been much conversant with him who wrote the first book, for he had sometimes read letters written by the other man from Germany. And so she went to that good man, praying him to write out this book & never tell anyone as long as she lived, offering him a great sum for his labour. And this good man wrote but a leaf, yet it was little to the purpose, for he could not do well with it, the book was so badly set out and unreasonably written.

Then the priest was vexed in his conscience, for he had promised to write out this book, if he could manage to read it, & had not done his part as well as he might do, and begged this creature to get him the book again if she could do so without offence. Then she got the book again and brought it to the priest with right glad cheer, begging him to do his best, and she would pray to God for him, & purchase grace for him to read and write it also. The priest, trusting to her prayers, began to read this book and it was much more easy (he thought) than it was before, & so he read it over to this creature, every word, she helping him sometimes with any difficulty.

This book is not written in order, everything coming after each other as they did, but like the matter came to the creature's mind when it was being written, for the events were so long before the writing that she had forgotten the time and order when they befell. And therefore she dictated nothing but what she knew right well for very truth.

When the priest began first to write in this book his eyesight was so poor that he could not see to make his letters or mend his pen. All other things he could see sufficiently. He set a pair of spectacles on his nose, & all was worse than it was before. He complained to the creature of his disease. She said his enemy envied his good deed and would block him if he might & bade him do as well as God would give him grace and leave off. When he came again to his book he could see as well, he thought, as ever he did before by daylight and by candlelight too, & this is why, when he had written a whole book, he added a leaf thereto, and then he wrote this proym to express more things openly than does the next following, that was written earlier than this.

Anno domini 1436.

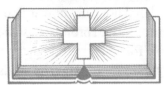

c1450

THE SHEARMEN AND TAILORS' PAGEANT
ANONYMOUS
COVENTRY, WARWICKSHIRE
[ISAYE]

The popular plays that Shakespeare wrote best started as church theatre long before King Alfred. Sunday services used most of the fine arts. Verses were recited & sung by a priest & his helpers

THE Sofferent thatt seithe evere seycrette,
He save you all and make you parfett and stronge,
And geve us grace with his marce forto mete!
For now in grett mesere mankynd ys bownd,
The sarpent hathe gevin us soo mortall a wonde
That no creature ys abull us forto reyles
Tyll thye right uncion of Juda dothe seyse.

Then schall moche myrthe and joi incresse;
And the right rote in Isaraell sprynge,
Thatt schall bryng forthe the greyne off whollenes;
And owt of danger he schall us bryng
Into thatt reygeon where he ys kyng
Wyche abowe all othur far dothe abownde
And thatt cruell Sathan he schall confownde.

Wherefore I cum here apon this grownde
To comforde eyvere creature off birthe;
For I, Isaye the profet, hathe fownde
Many swete matters whereof we ma make myrth
On this same wyse;
For, thogh that Adam be demid to deythe
With all his childur, asse Abell and Scythe,
Yett Ecce virgo consepeet,
Loo, where a reymede schall ryse!

Beholde, a mayde schall conseyve a childe
And gett us more grace then eyver men had,
And hir meydinhod nothing defylid.
Sche ys deputyd to beare the Sun, Almyghte God.
Loo! sufferentis, now ma you be glad,
For of this meydin all we ma be fayne;
For Adam, that now lyis in sorrois full sade,
Hir gloreose birth schall reydeme hym ageyn
From bondage and thrall.

Now be myrre eyvere mon
For this dede bryffly in Isaraell schalbe done,
And before the Fathur in trone,
Thatt schall glade us all.

More of this matter fayne wolde I meve,
But lengur tyme I have not here for to dwell.
That Lorde that ys marcefull
                              his marce soo in us ma preve
For to sawe owre sollis from the darknes of hell;

wearing ornate robes before painted screens & sculpture. On major holy days like Easter & Christmas the service was enriched by mimes of the Bible event then celebrated. Priests wrote & directed, but came to draw more & more on the talents & labour of their parish or town. Then towns grew so big that they held many parishes, each dominated by the trade most followed there. That is how York, Coventry & other cities had trade unions of tailors, goldsmiths, butchers etc. with their own church or chapel. All were keen to act their own pageants.

*Pageant is a word from **pagina**, Latin for plank, & was a raised stage for actors. The pressure of building between cathedral & city wall made the parish churches too narrow for big shows, so the trades put up their stages outside, agreeing that on major holy days each one would act a different scene of Bible history from Creation to Resurrection. Folk in the wool trade played the shepherds who 1st told of **Christ's Nativity**. The Bakers' Guild claimed the right to perform **The Last Supper**. In the biggest towns these*

And to his blys
He us bryng,
Asse he ys
Bothe lord and kyng,
And schalbe eyverlastyng,
In secula seculorum, amen!

THE CRUCIFIXION, ANON, WAKEFIELD, YORKSHIRE

In York 12 open places were chosen where audiences might see every group play in turn. Oxen or horses pulled each group from place to place in a big wheeled box decked like a modern carnival float. When it halted the actors sprang up a ladder to act their part on top. But outside the cities pageants were acted in single fields & market places without help of machines.

*A crowd under an open sky needs a loud voice to tell it a play is starting, & cannot attend long to grave mysteries without comic relief. The prologue to the Coventry **Shearmen & Tailors' Nativity Play** is in the glad but solemn voice of Isaiah who foretold Christ's coming. He is followed by shepherds who, before angels lead them to the new-born Jesus, moan about their low wages, agree that working men cannot afford wives who have a baby or 2 every year, & toss a Scots sheep stealer in a blanket. **The York Crucifixion** shows Jesus being tortured to death in grim detail yet the prologue is roared out by the comic villain **Pilate**. He whirls a sword about like a violent madman, promising death by torture to all who won't attend to the play.*

[PILATE]

PEASSE I byd evereich wight!
Stand as styll as stone in wall,
Whyls ye ar present in my sight,
That none of you clatter ne call;
For if ye do, youre dede is dight,
I warne it you both greatt and small,
With this brand burnyshyd so bright,
Therfor in peasse loke ye be all.

What! peasse in the dwillys name!
Harlottys and dustardys all bedene!
On galus ye be maide full tame,
Thefys and mychers keyn!
Will ye not peasse when I bid you?
By Mahownys bloode, if ye me teyn,
I shall ordan sone for you,
Paynes that never ere was seyn,
And that anone!
Be ye so bold beggars, I warn you,
Full boldly shall I bett you,
To hell the dwill shall draw you,
Body, bak and bone.

I am a lord that mekill is of myght,
Prynce of all Jury, Sir Pilate I hight,
Next Kyng Herode grettyst of all;
Bowys to my byddyng both greatt and small,
Or els be ye shentt;
Therfor stere youre tonges, I warn you all,
And unto us take tent.

WALLACE
HARY THE MINSTREL
LOWLANDS OF SCOTLAND

1477

IHESU SALVATOR TU SIS MIHI AUXILATOR
AD FINEM DIGNUM LIBRUM PERDUC
ATQUE BENIGNUM.

MAY THOU, CHRIST SAVIOUR, BE MY
HELPER. AND BRING THIS BOOK TO A
WORTHY AND FAVOURABLE END

*O*UR antecessowris that we suld of reide
  And hald in mynde,
      thar nobille worthi deid
We lat ourslide throw werray sleuthfulnes,
And castis ws evir till uthir besynes.
Till honour Ennymyis is our haile entent,
It has beyne seyne in thir tymys bywent,
Our ald Ennemys cummyn of Saxonys blud,
That nevyr yeit to Scotland wald do gud
Bot evir on fors and contrar haile thar will,
Quhow gret kyndnes
      thar has beyne kyth thaim till.
It is weyle knawyne on mony divers syde,
How thai haff wrocht in-to thar mychty pryde
To hald Scotlande at wndyr evirmar,
Bot god abuff has maid thar mycht to par.
Yhit we suld thynk one our bearis befor.
Of thir parablys as now I say no mor.
We reide of ane rycht famous of renowne,
Of worthi blude that ryngis in this regioune,
And hensfurth I will my proces hald
Of Wilyham Wallas yhe haf hard beyne tald

The annals of Scots nobles are quiet about Wallace. He was not one of them. Their bravest men had been shamed by his deeds, which were kept alive in tales told by low-bred folk he had led: thus he became a hero of legend like Samson & Romulus. This account of him – the first Scots poem in 10-syllable-line heroic couplets – was mostly made of these legends 170 years after Wallace was executed. It was 1 of the earliest books to be printed in Scotland around 1508, & got reprinted 23 times before the union of parliaments in 1707. In 1722 a version in modernized Scots became 2nd only to the Bible as the most commonly owned book north of the Tweed. Burns said that as a boy **the story of Wallace poured a Scottish prejudice in my veins which will boil along there till the flood-gates of life shut in eternal rest.** *Byron, Keats & Wordsworth admired it too. Later novels about Wallace were based on it, & a 1996 Hollywood film that shows a love affair between Wallace & the English queen. One Scots historian complained of this. Another said Scots historians have been almost as quiet about Wallace as the nobility, & legendary history is better than none.*

1484

In Europe the art of printing type was invented by John Gutenberg of Mainz. From his press in 1456 came the 1st known printed & bound text, a Jerome Bible. Printing caused the same stir as word processors & the internet 5 centuries later. German printers set up presses in Rome, Venice, Paris & other great cities. The church used them to mass-produce Latin Bible, mass books, psalters & documents that forgave the buyer's sins when properly blessed & signed. Law codes & Latin grammars were wanted by colleges, the Greek & Roman classics by scholars; rulers wanted pro-clamations. Some princes of church & state spent big sums to get their printed books as lovely as the finest that could be made by hand. The best types & layouts printers now use were devised for these nobles. They were ignored by a middle-aged Englishman who first printed books for those who just read for amusement.

Caxton was chief

THE CANTERBURY TALES
Proheme by WILLIAM CAXTON
WESTMINSTER ABBEY, LONDON

GRETE thankes laude and honour / ought to be gyven unto the clerkes / poetes / and historiographs that have wreton many noble bokes of wysedom of the lyves / passions / & myracles of holy sayntes of hystoryes / of noble and famous Actes / and faittes / And of the cronycles sith the begynnyng of the creacion of the world / unto thys present tyme / by whyche we ben dayly enformed / and have knowleche of many thynges / of whom we shold not have knowen / yf they had not left to us theyr monumentis wreton.

Emong whom and inespecial to fore alle other we ought to gyve a synguler laude unto that noble & grete philosopher Gefferey chaucer the whiche for his ornate wrytyng in our tongue may wel have the name of a laureate poete / For to fore that he by hys labour enbelysshyd / ornated / and made faire our englisshe / in thys Royame was had rude speche & Incongrue / as yet it appiereth by olde bookes / whyche at thys day ought not to have place ne be compared emong ne to hys beauteuous volumes / and aournate writynges / of whom he made many bokes and treatyces of many a noble historye as wel in metre as in ryme and prose / and them so craftly made/ that he comprehended hys maters in short / quyck and hye sentences / eschewyng prolyxyte/ castyng away the chaf of superfluyte / and shewyng the pyked grayn of sentence / utteryd by crafty and sugred eloquence / of whom emonge all other of hys bokes / I purpose temprynte by the grace of god the book of the tales of cauntyrburye / in whiche I fynde many a noble hystorye / of every astate and degre / Fyrst rehercyng the condicions / and tharraye of eche of them as properly as possyble is to be sayd / And after theyr tales whyche ben of noblesse /

wysedom / gentylesse / Myrthe / and also of veray holynesse and vertue / wherin he fynysshyth thys sayd booke / whyche book I have dylygently oversen and duly examyned to thende that it be made acordyng unto his owen makyng.

For I fynde many of the sayd bookes / whyche wryters have abrydgyd it and many thynges left out / And in somme place have sette certayn versys / that he never made ne sette in hys booke / of whyche bookes so incorrecte was one brought to me vi yere passyd / whyche I supposed had ben veray true & correcte / And accordyng to the same I dyde do enprynte a certayn nombre of them / whyche anon were sold to many and dyverse gentyl men of whome one gentylman cam to me / and said that this book was not accordyng in many places unto the book that Gefferey chaucer had made / To whom I answerd that I had made it accordyng to my copye / and by me was nothyng added ne mynusshyd / Thenne he sayd he knewe a book whyche hys fader had and moche lovyd / that was very trewe / and accordyng unto hys owen first book by hym made / and sayd more yf I wold enprynte it agayn he wold gete me the same book for a copye / how be it he wyst wel / that hys fader wold not gladly departe fro it / To whom I said / in caas that he coude gete me suche a book trewe and correcte / yet I wold ones endevoyre me to enprynte it agayn / for to satysfye thauctour / where as to fore by ygnouraunce I erryd in hurtyng and dyffamyng his book in dyverce places in settyng in somme thynges that he never sayd ne made / and levyng out many thynges that he made whyche ben requysite to be sette in it / And thus we fyll at accord.

And he ful gentylly gate of hys fader the said book / and delyverd it to me / by whiche I have corrected my book / as here after alle alonge by thayde of almyghty god shal folowe / whom I

*agent of the London Merchant Adventurers in Bruges & an agent of the Crown. His main business was with cloth but Bruges had then – after Venice – Europe's biggest book market. Before he retired from the cloth trade Caxton learned the printing trade & in 1476 set up his press in part of Westminster Abbey beside the royal court. At a bad time for original writing he printed all he thought would sell: tales of Troy, lives of saints, philosophy made easy, manuals on chess, sports & cloth dyeing, acts of parliament & indulgences for sale by the church. Many books were translated from works he had picked up abroad, but he printed popular English work starting with Chaucer's **Cant-erbury Tales** from a poor copy. This proheme tells how he came to correct it.*

His books were clumsily designed in gothic type but easy to read. Like nearly all printers then he still punctuated with slant strokes or dots. By the century's end Aldo Manutius, printer in Venice, was using fine Roman & Italic type with the period & comma.

humbly beseche to gyve me grace and ayde to achyeve / and accomplysshe / to hys laude honour and glorye / and that alle ye that shal in thys book rede or heere / wyll of your charyte emong your dedes of mercy / remembre the sowle of the sayd Gefferey chaucer first auctour / and maker of thys book / And also that alle we that shal see and rede therin / may so take and understonde the good and vertuous tales / that it may so prouffyte / unto the helthe of our sowles / that after thys short and transitorye lyf we may come to everlastyng lyf in heven. Amen.

1484

*Sir Thomas was a soldier in France, an MP for Warwickshire, fought on both sides in the York-Lancaster wars, was likely jailed as a result. This book may have been written in prison. He took 5 or 6 of the best Arthurian tales in French poetry & worked them into one continuous prose romance in English. It inspired Spenser, Milton, Walter Scott, Tennyson & endless versions & parodies in novel, play, opera & film. This is partly because (as Roger Ascham said) the main theme is **open manslaughter and adultery**. The other reason is its chivalry.*

This Christian code of unselfish good manners had been invented by & for knights in 11th-century France. It was

LE MORTE D'ARTHUR
SIR THOMAS MALORY
Proheme by CAXTON: LONDON

AFTER that I had accomplysshed and fynysshed dyvers hystoryes as wel of contemplacyon as of other hystoryal and worldly actes of grete conquerors & prynces / And also certeyn bookes of ensaumples and doctryne / Many noble and dyvers gentylmen of thys royame of Englond camen and demaunded me many and oftymes / wherfore that I have not do made & enprynte the noble hystorye of the saynt greal / and of the moost renomed crysten Kyng / Fyrst and chyef of the thre best crysten and worthy / kyng Arthur / whyche ought moost to be remembred emonge us englysshe men tofore al other crysten kynges.

For it is notoyrly knowen thorugh the unyversal world / that there been ix worthy & the best that ever were / That is to wete thre paynyms / thre Jewes and thre crysten men / As for the paynyms they were tofore the Incarnacyon of Cryst / whiche were named / the fyrst Hector of Troye / of whome thystorye is comen bothe in balade and in prose / The second Alysaunder the grete / & the thyrd Julyus Cezar Emperour of Rome of whome thystoryes ben wel kno and had / And as for the thre Jewes whyche also were tofore thyncarnacyon of our lord of whome the fyrst was Duc Josue whyche brought the

chyldren of Israhel in to the londe of byheste / The
second Davyd kyng of Jherusalem / & the thyrd
Judas Machabeus of these thre the byble reherceth
al theyr noble hystoryes & actes / And sythe the
sayd Incarnacyon have ben thre noble crysten men
stalled and admytted thorugh the unyversal world in
to the nombre of the ix beste & worthy / of whome
was fyrst the noble Arthur / whos noble actes I purpose
to wryte in thys present book here folowyng / The
second was Charlemayn or Charles the grete / of
whom thystorye is had in many places bothe in
frensshe and englysshe / and the thyrd and last was
Godefray of boloyn / of whos Actes & lyf I made a
book unto thexcellent prynce and kyng of noble
memorye kynge Edward the fourth / the sayd noble
Jentylmen Instantly requyred me temprynte
thystorye of the sayd noble kyng and conquerour
kyng Arthur / and of his knyghtes wyth thystorye of
the saynt greal / and of the deth and endyng of the
sayd Arthur / Affermyng that I ought rather tenprynte
his actes and noble feates / than of godefroye of

too ideal for much daily use so French poets set tales of chivalry in King Arthur's day: a golden age made out of legends that folk in Brittany shared with the Cornish & Welsh. Tudor kings, having Welsh blood in their veins, welcomed King Arthur as one of their ancestors. Caxton tells us in this proheme how their subjects stifled doubts about it.

It was Caxton who divided Malory's text into chapters, gave them headings, & rewrote sections to remove elements of the old alliterative style. Malory died 15 years before his book was printed.

boloyne / or ony of the other eyght / consyderyng that he was a man
borne wythin this royame and kyng and Emperour of the same / And that
there ben in frensshe dyvers and many noble volumes of his actes / and
also of his knyghtes.

    To whome I answerd / that dyvers men holde oppynyon / that there
was no suche Arthur / and that alle suche bookes as been maad of hym /
ben but fayned and fables / by cause that somme cronycles make of
hym no mencyon ne remembre hym noo thynge ne of his knyghtes /
wher to they answerd / and one in specyal sayd / that in hym that shold
say or thynke / that there was never suche a kyng callyd Arthur / myght
wel be aretted grete folye and blyndenesse / For he sayd that there were
many evydences of the contrarye / Fyrst ye may see his sepulture in the
monasterye of Glastyngburye / And also in polycronycon in the v book
the syxte chappytre / and in the seventh book the xxiii chappytre /
where his bodye was buryed and after founden and translated in to the
sayd monasterye / ye shall se also in thystorye of bochas in his book de
casu principum / parte of his noble actes / and also of his falle / Also

galfrydus in his brutysshe book recounteth his lyf / and in dyvers places of Englond / many remembraunces ben yet of hym and shall remayne perpetuelly / and also of his knyghtes / Fyrst in the abbey of westmestre at saynt Edwardes shryne remayneth the prynte of his seal in reed waxe closed in beryll / In whych is wryton Patricius Arthurus / Britannie / Gallie / Germanie / dacie / Imperator / Item in the castel of dover ye may see Gauwayns skulle / & Cradoks mantel. At wynchester the ronnde table / in other places Launcelottes swerde and many other thynges / Thenne al these thynges consydered there can no man resonably gaynsaye butt here was a kyng of thys lande named Arthur / For in al places crysten and hethen he is reputed and taken for one of the ix worthy / And the fyrst of the thre Crysten men / And also he is more spoken of beyonde the see moo bookes made of his noble actes than there be in englond as wel in duche ytalyen spanysshe and grekysshe as in frensshe / And yet of record remayne in wytnesse of hym in wales in the toune of Camelot the grete stones & mervayllous werkys of yron lyeng under the grounde & ryal vautes which dyvers now lyvyng hath seen / wherfor it is a mervayl why he is nomore renomed in his owne contreye / sauf onelye it accordeth to the word of god / whyche sayth that no man is accept for a prophete in his owne contreye.

Thenne al these thynges forsayd aledged I coude not wel denye / but that there was suche a noble kyng named Arthur / and reputed one of the ix worthy & fyrst & chyef of the crysten men / & many noble volumes be made of hym & of his noble knyghtes in frensshe which I have seen & redde beyonde the see / which been not had in our maternal tongue / but in walsshe ben many & also in frensshe / & somme in englysshe but nowher nygh alle / wherfore suche as have late ben drawen oute bryefly in to englysshe / I have after the symple connynge that god hath sente to me / under the favour and correctyon of al noble lordes and gentylmen enprysed to enprynte a book of the noble hystoryes of the sayd kynge Arthur / and of certeyn of his knyghtes after a copye unto me delyverd / whyche copye Syr Thomas Malorye dyd take oute of certayn bookes of frensshe and reduced it in to Englysshe.

And I accordyng to my copye have doon sette it in enprynte / to the entente that noble men may see and lerne the noble actes of chivalrye / the Jentyl and vertuous dedes that somme knyghtes used in tho dayes / by whyche they came to honour / and how they that were vycious were punysshed and ofte put to shame and rebuke / humbly besechyng al

noble lordes and ladyes and al other estates of what estate or degre they been of / that shal see and rede in this sayd book and werke / that they take the good and honest actes in their remembraunce / and to folowe the same / wherin they shalle fynde many joyous and playsaunt hystoryes / and noble & renomed actes of humanyte / gentylnesse and chyvalryes / For herein may be seen noble chivalrye / Curtosye / Humanyte frendlynesse / hardynesse / love / frendshypp / Cowardyse / Murdre / hate / vertue / and synne / Doo after the good and leve the evyll / and it shal brynge you to good fame and renommee / And for to passe the tyme thys book shal be plesaunte to rede in / but for to gyve fayth and beleve that al is trewe that is conteyned herin / ye be at your liberte but al is wryton for our doctryne / and for to beware that we falle not to vyce ne synne / but texcersyse and folowe vertu / by whyche we may come and atteyne to good fame and renomme in thys lyf / and after thys shorte and transytorye lyfe to come unto everlastyng blysse in heven / the whyche he graunte us that reygneth in heven the blessyd
Trynyte Amen /

THE BOKE OF ENEYDOS: WILLIAM CAXTON
Prologue to His Own Book, Modern Spelling
WESTMINSTER ABBEY, LONDON

1490

AFTER diverse works made, translated and achieved, having no work in hand, I sitting in my study where lay many different pamphlets and books, there happened to my hand a little book in French, which was late translated out of the Latin by some noble clerk in France, which book is named Eneydos made in Latin by that noble poet and great clerk Virgil, which book I glanced over and read therein. How after the general destruction of the great Troy, Aeneas departed bearing his old father Anchises on his shoulders, his little son Iolus on his hand, his wife with many other people following, and how he shipped and departed with all the history of his adventures before he achieved the conquest of Italy, all of which will be shown in the present book.

In that book I had great pleasure because of the

In most nations the professional folk know the speech of their rulers & their underlings. Caxton's press was beside the king's court & the chief abbey of England. His customers were aristocracy & clergy, yet he says there is no widely accepted English dialect & speech has changed in his lifetime. There were at least 3 causes. 1. The Royal families were from Yorkshire or Lancashire & usually warring in France when not fighting each other at home so set no *steady example. 2. Lawyers heard cases in English but still argued them in a French now spoken nowhere else on earth. 3. Literate folk, to avoid charges of heresy, used Latin when they spoke or wrote of **profound matters**. All this caused so great a slippage in south British dialect that Chaucer's poetry, though widely read, was mainly spoken as he had spoken it in the north. To Scots poets he was a living voice; in the south he was the best writer to copy. And as Caxton deplored the chaos of late 15th-century vernacular his printed books helped to fix spelling that still reflects it & will give toil & trouble to teacher & pupil for centuries to come, if reading continues.*

fair and honest expressions and words in French. I had never seen the like before, or none so pleasant or well ordered, and it seemed to me noblemen should be required to read it as much for the eloquence as for the history. How right, that for many hundreds of years the said Eneydos, with other works, was made and learned daily in schools! especially in Italy where the said Virgil had made the history in metre.

And when I had viewed the said book, I deliberated and decided to translate it into English, and forthwith took a pen and ink and wrote a leaf or two, and looked over it again to correct it. And when I saw the elegant and strange expressions in it I feared it would not please some gentlemen who recently blamed me, saying that in my translations were curious expressions which common people could not understand. They desired me to use old and homely terms in my translations. Wanting to satisfy every man, to do as they wished I took an old book and read therein, and the English was so rude and broad that I could not understand it. Also my Lord Abbot of Westminster had lately shown me certain documents written in old English, for me to put into English used nowadays, and it was so much more like German than English that I could not make it understood.

Certainly our language now varies greatly from that used and spoken when I was born. We Englishmen are born under the domination of the moon which is never steadfast, ever wavering, waxes one season and wanes and decreases another. That common English spoken in one shire varies from another. In my lifetime it happened that some merchants took ship in the Thames, in order to sail into Zeeland, but for lack of wind they tarried at the foreland, and went ashore to refresh themselves. And one of them named Sheffield, a mercer, came to a house and asked for food, and specially asked for eggs. The good wife answered that she could speak no French. The merchant was angry for he also could speak no French, but wanted eggs, and she understood him not. At last another said he wanted eyren and the good wife understood him well. So what should a man in these days now write: eggs or eyren?

Diversity and change of language make it hard to please every man. In these days every man that has any reputation in his country will utter his communications and business in such styles and terms that few men shall understand them. And some honest and great clerks have desired me to write the most erudite expressions I could find. And thus between plain rude and curiously erudite I stand abashed.

But in my judgment the common terms in daily use are easier to understand than the old and ancient English, and as this present book is not meant to be laboriously read by a rude outlandish man, but by an educated and noble gentleman with feeling and understanding for feats of arms in love and chivalry, therefore in a mean between both over rude and over elegant I have translated this said book into our English, in such terms as shall be understood by God's grace according to my copy. And if any man stops reading it, finding terms he cannot understand, let him learn and read Virgil or the letters of Ovid, and there he will easily see and understand all – if he has a good teacher. For this book is not for every rude and uneducated man, but for clergy and true gentlemen that understand good manners and polite learning.

Then I pray all who shall read this little book to excuse my translation of it. I acknowledge myself ignorant of skill to undertake so high and noble a work. But I pray master John Skelton, lately created poet laureate of the university of Oxenford to oversee and correct this said book, and adjust and explain where it would be found at fault by them who will acquire it. He, I know, is sufficient to explain and put in English every difficulty therein, for he has translated the epistles of Tully, and the book of Diodorus Syculus, and other works of Latin into English, not in rude and old language but craftily into polished and ornate terms, being one who has read Virgil, Ovid, Tully and all the other noble poets and orators unkown to me. And also he has read the IX muses and understands their musical sciences, and to whom each science is appropriate. I suppose he has drunk from the well of Helicon! So I pray him and others to correct, add or lessen where he or they find fault. I have but followed my copy of the book in French as closely as I could.

This book I now present unto my coming natural and sovereign lord

Arthur, by the grace of God, Prince of Wales, Duke of Cornwall and Earl of Chester: first begotten son and heir to our most dread natural and sovereign lord and most Christian King Henry VII, by the grace of God king of England and of France and lord of Ireland, beseeching his noble grace to receive it with thanks from me his most humble subject and servant. And I shall pray unto almighty God for his prosperous increase in virtue, wisdom and humanity, that he may be equal with the most renowned of all his noble progenitors; and so live in this present
life that after this transitory life he and we all may come
to everlasting life in heaven. Amen.

1495c

*Dunbar strolls out after midnight. He calls it **the merriest of nights**, for in Scotland the air is then pleasantest & the sky never quite dark. Beside a green lawn with gay flowerbeds hedged to a huge height with hawthorn trees, the glad song of a bird on a branch & scent of flowers draw him through the dusk toward sounds of mirth. Beneath a holly tree he pushed into the hedge &, hidden by leaves, spies through the prickles 3 gay ladies in an arbour. They wear garlands of fresh flowers on golden hair combed artfully down over their shoulders, & green gowns of the finest fabric. Their sweet faces have the beauty of newly opened lilies. A table*

THE TRETIS OF THE TUA MARIIT WEMEN AND THE WEDO: WILLIAM DUNBAR: THE COURT OF THE SCOTS KING

*A*pon the Midsummer evin, mirriest of nichtis,
I muvit furth allane, neir as midnicht wes past,
Besyd ane gudlie grein garth, full of gay flouris,
Hegeit, of ane huge hicht, with hawthorne treis;
Quhairon ane bird, on ane bransche,
                              so birst out hir notis
That never ane blythfullar bird
                              was on the beuche harde:
Quhat throw the sugarat sound of hir sang glaid,
And throw the savour sanative of the sueit flouris,
I drew in derne to the dyk to dirkin efter mirthis;
The dew donkit the daill and dynnit the feulis;
I hard, under ane holyn hevinlie grein hewit,
Ane hie speiche, at my hand,
                              with hautand wourdis;
With that in haist to the hege so hard I in thrang
That I was heildit with hawthorne
                              and with heynd leveis:
Throw pykis of the plet thorne I presandlie luikit,
Gif ony persoun wald approche
                              within that plesand garding.
I saw thre gay ladeis sit in ane grene arbeir,
All grathit in to garlandis of fresche gudlie flouris;
So glitterit as the gold wer thair glorious gilt tressis,

Quhill all the gressis did gleme of the glaid hewis;
Kemmit was thair cleir hair, and curiouslie sched
Attour thair schulderis doun schyre, schyning full bricht;
With curches, cassin thair abone,
                              of kirsp cleir and thin:
Thair mantillis grein was as the gress
                         that grew in May sessoun,
Fetrit with thair quhyt fingaris
                    about thair fair sydis:
Off ferliful fyne favour was thair faceis meik,
All full of flurist fairheid, as flouris in June;
Quhyt, seimlie, and soft, as the sweit lillies
New upspred upon spray, as new spynist rose;
Arrayit ryallie about with mony rich vardour,
That nature full nobillie annamalit with flouris
Off alkin hewis under hevin, that ony heynd knew,
Fragrant, all full of fresche odour fynest of smell.
Ane cumlie tabil coverit wes befoir tha cleir ladeis,
With ryalle cowpis apon rawis full of ryche wynis.
And of thir fair wlonkes, tua weddit war with lordis,
Ane wes ane wedow, I wis, wantoun of laitis.
And, as thai talk at the tabill of many taill sindry,
Thay wauchtit at the wicht wyne
                         and waris out wourdis;
And syne thai spak more spedelie,
                    and sparit no matiris.

before them has cups
full of rich wines. Two
of these lovelies are
wedded to lords, one
is a wanton widow.
They weigh into the
strong wine & spill
out words, holding
back nothing. The
widow asks the young
ones what fun they find
in marriage? Is it good
to be tied to someone
they can only escape
through death?

Like delicate hors
d'oeuvres before a
slab of smoking pork
is flung on the table
this precedes a bawdy
debate on marriage. It
appalled Victorian
readers who (unlike
earlier Christians)
thought marriage a
holy sacrament. The
ladies curse it as a
slavery only made
bearable by deceit,
men being sexually
useless if not changed
once a year etc.

THE TESTAMENT OF CRESSEID
ROBERT HENRYSON
DUNFERMLINE, SCOTLAND

*A*NE doolie sessoun to ane cairfull dyte
Suld correspond, and be equivalent.
Richt sa it wes quhen I began to wryte
This tragedie, the wedder richt fervent
Quhen Aries in middis of the Lent
Schouris of Haill can fra the North discend
That scantlie fra the cauld I micht defend.

c1495

A doleful season & a
sorry song should fit
each other, says
Henryson. He starts
this poem in Lent
when good Christians
fast on a diet of fish.
It is also halfway
through April, month
of Aries the Ram, a

time (said Chaucer) of sweet showers & birdsong, soft winds, tender crops & folk setting out on pilgrimage. But the Scots poet lives 5 degrees of latitude nearer the Arctic Pole. He stands in a cold chapel gazing through a window at Venus, the evening star & goddess of love. She shines in a sky swept clear of cloud by such frosty winds that the poet, without praying to her, is forced by cold to the fireside in his chamber. He had meant to beg her to let him love again as he had loved when young. Knowing how old folk need more outer heat as their inner heat fails (for he has studied medicine as well as love) he mends his fire, pulls his robe tightly round him, takes a warming drink & sits down to read Chaucer's **Troilus & Criseyde**. This love story ends sadly, though not tragically, with the heroine coupled to another man. After reading it Henryson takes a book that says how Cressida fared afterward. He tells us the story in that book – it is his own. Henryson was master of the grammar school in Dunfermline

Yit nevertheles within myne Oratur
I stude, quhen Titan had his bemis bricht
Withdrawin doun, and sylit under cure
And fair Venus the bewtie of the nicht
Uprais, and set unto the west full richt
Hir golden face in oppositioun
Of God Phebus direct discending doun.
Throw out the glas hir bemis brast sa fair
That I micht se on everie syde me by
The Northin wind had purifyit the Air
And sched the mistie cloudis fra the sky,
The froist freisit the blastis bitterly
Fra Pole Artick come quhisling loud and schill,
And causit me remufe aganis my will.

For I traistit that Venus luifis Quene
To quhome sum tyme I hecht obedience,
My faidit hart of lufe scho wald mak grene,
And therupon, with humbill reverence,
I thocht to pray hir hie Magnificence,
Bot for greit cald as than I lattit was
And in my Chalmer to the fyre can pas.
Thocht lufe be hait, yit in ane man of age
It kendillis nocht sa sone as in youtheid,
Of quhome the blude is flowing in ane rage,
And in the auld the curage doif and deid:
Of quhilk the fyre outward is best remeid
To help be Phisike quhair that nature faillit
I am expert, for baith I have assailit.

I mend the fyre and beikit me about
Than tuik ane drink my spreitis to comfort
And armit me weill fra the cauld thairout.
To cut the winter nicht and mak it schort
I tuik ane Quair and left all uther sport,
Writtin be worthie Chaucer glorious
Of fair Creiseid, and worthie Troylus.
And thair I fand efter that Diomeid

Ressavit had that Lady bricht of hew,
How Troilus neir out of wit abraid,
And weipit soir with visage paill of hew,
For quhilk wanhope his teiris can renew
Quhill Esperus rejoisit him agane
Thus quhyle in Joy he levit quhyle in pane.
Of hir behest he had greit comforting
Traisting to Troy that scho suld mak retour,
Quhilk he desyrit maist of eirdly thing
Forquhy scho was his only Paramour.
Bot quhen he saw passit baith day and hour
Of hir ganecome, than sorrow can oppres
His wofull hart in cair and hevines.

Of his distres me neidis nocht reheirs,
For worthie Chauceir in the samin buik
In gudelie termis and in Joly veirs
Compylit hes his cairis, quha will luik.
To brek my sleip ane uther quair I tuik,
In quhilk I fand the fatall destenie
Of fair Cresseid, that endit wretchitlie.

Quha wait gif all that Chauceir wrait was trew
Nor I wait nocht gif this narratioun
Be authoreist or fenyeit of the new
Be sum Poeit, throw his Inventioun
Maid to report the Lamentatioun
And wofull end of this lustie Creisseid,
And quhat distres scho thoillit, and quhat deid.

*Abbey, doctor, public notary & humane poet. His sequel has Cressida thrown out by her 2nd man. She curses Venus & Cupid for bringing her to grief, so the gods curse her back for her blasphemy. She ends as a begging leper housed in a public hospital for these outcasts. Before 1600 Dunfermline, like many towns, had such a place outside its walls & Henryson sometimes worked there. His poem does not gloat on the punishment of a faithless woman: the poetry is in his pity. The London book-trade printed it as a sequel to Chaucer's in 1532, 1561, 1598, while Anglifying the spelling. The best text was printed in Edinburgh, 1593. Henryson's **Moral Fables** was another popular work, as rich in humour as in pity.*

ENEADOS c1513
GAVIN DOUGLAS
SAINT GILES, EDINBURGH

Heyr begynnys the proloug of Virgyll prynce of Latyn poetis in hys twelf bukis of Eneados compilit and translatit furth of Latyn in our Scottis langage by ane right nobill and wirschipfull clerk Master Gawyn Dowglas provest of Sanct Gylys Kyrk in Edinburgh and person of Lyntoun in Louthiane quhilk eftyr was bischop of Dunkeld.

Laud, honour, praisings
    and thanks infinite
To thee and thy sweet
    ornate fresh indite
Most reverend Virgil!
    Latin poets' prince,
Gem of invention, flood of eloquence,
Thou peerless pearl, patron of poetry,
Rose, registrar, palm, law-giver and glory,
Chosen carbuncle,
    chief flower and cedar tree,
Lantern, pole star,
    mirror and A per se.
Master of masters,
    sweet shower and springing well!
Wide, where all are,
    is rung thy heavenly bell –
I mean thy crafted work's intricate sense
So quick and joyful and of rich sentence
Pleasant and perfect, felt in all degree,
As if the thing they say was there to see;
In every volume which you choose to write
Surmounting far all other ways to indite
Like as the rose
    in June with her sweet smell
The marigold or daisy doth excel.
Why should I then
    with dull forehead and vain,
With rude invention,
    barren empty brain,
With bad, harsh speech
    and low, barbarous tongue
Presume to write
    where thy sweet bell is rung?
Or counterfeit the precious words so dear?
No, no, not so,
    but kneel when I them hear.

INCIPIT PROLOGUS IN VIRGILII ENEADOS

*L*AWD, honour, praysyngis,
    thankis infynyte
To the and thy dulce
    ornat fresch endyte,
Maist reverend Virgill,
    of Latyn poetis prynce,
Gem of engyne and flude of eloquens,
Thow peirless perle, patroun of poetry,
Royss, regester, palm, lawrer and glory,
Chosyn charbukkill,
    cheif flour and cedyr tre,
Lantarn, laid stern,
    myrrour and A per se,
Maister of masteris,
    sweit sours and spryngand well
Wyde quhar our all
    rung is thyne hevynly bell –
I meyn thy crafty warkis curyus
Sa quyk, lusty and maist sentencyus,
Plesand, perfyte and feilabill in all degre,
As quha the mater beheld tofor thar e,
In every volume quhilk the lyst do wryte
Surmontyng fer all other maner endyte,
Lyke as the royss
    in June with hir sweit smell
The maryguld or dasy doith excell.
Quhy suld I than
    with dull forhed and vayn,
With rude engyne
    and barrand emptyve brayn,
With bad, harsk spech
    and lewit barbour tong
Presume to write
    quhar thy sweit bell is rung
Or contyrfate sa precyus wordys deir?
Na, na, noth swa,
    but kneill quhen I thame heir.

For quhat compair
          betwix mydday and nycht?
Or quhat compair
          betwix myrknes and lycht?
Or quhat compar is
          betwix blak and quhyte?
Far grettar difference
          betwix my blunt endyte
And thy scharp sugurate sang Virgiliane,
Sa wysly wrocht
          with nevir a word invane.
My waverand wyt,
          my cunnyng febill at all,
My mynd mysty,
          thir may nocht myss a fall –
Stra for thys ignorant blabryng imperfyte
Besyde thy polyst termys redymyte.
And netheless
          with support and correctioun,
For naturall lufe and frendely affectioun
Quhilkis I beir to thy warkis and endyte –
All thocht God wait
          tharin I knaw full lyte –
And that thy facund sentence
          mycht be song
In our langage alsweill as Latyn tong –
Alsweill? na, na, impossibill war, per de –
Yit with thy leif, Virgile, to follow the,
I wald into my rurall wlgar gross
Wryte sum savoryng of thyne Eneados.
But sair I dreid forto disteyn the quyte
Throu my corruppit cadens imperfyte –
Disteyn the? nay forsuyth,
          that may I nocht,
Weill may I schaw
          my burral bustuus thocht
Bot thy wark sall endur in lawd and glory
But spot or falt condyng etern memory.

For why compare
          between midday and night?
Or why between
          the darkness and the light?
Or what comparison
          'twixt black and white?
Far greater difference
          between my blunt indite
And thy sweet piercing song Virgilian,
So wisely wrought
          with never a word in vain.
My wavering wits,
          my learning feeble with all,
My mind misty,
          that may not miss a fall –
Strays to this ignorant blabbering, defective
Beside thy polished terms so curative.
Yet even so,
          with help and with correction,
From natural love and friendliest affection
I bear for all the works that you indite
(Although God knows
          my learning is too light)
So that thy fruitful sentences
          be sung
In our language as well as Latin tongue –
As well? No, no, impossible for me –
Yet by your leave, Virgil, to follow thee,
I would in my rude vulgar language gross
Write something tasting of thy Eneados.
But sore I dread to give you some offence
Through my imperfect
          and corrupt cadence –
Offend thee? No, in truth, that may I not!
If I expose my burly, bustling thought
Thy work shall still endure
          in praise and glory,
No stain on thy eternal memory.

Though I offend, undamaged is thy fame.
Thine are the thanks
    and mine shall be the shame.

Thocht I offend, onwemmyt is thy fame;
Thyne is the thank
    and myne salbe the schame.

oooooooooooooooooooooooooooooooooooooooooooooooooooooooooooooooooooo

DOUGLAS EXPLAINS VIRGIL'S IMPORTANCE TO THE BRITISH READER THEN TELLS HOW TO READ HIS TRANSLATION.

oooooooooooooooooooooooooooooooooooooooooooooooooooooooooooooooooooo

Now by your leave, good sirs, I first advise
View my work well before you criticize.
Read more than once.
    Consider. Give it thought.
Not in a blink sly poetry is caught,
And yet in truth I took much busy pain,
All that I could, to make it broad and plain,
Keeping no southern, but our language,
Speaking it as I learned it when a page
But not so pure all southern I refuse.
A few words I pronounce
    as neighbour does.
Just as in Latin are some words of Greek
So I was bound to use (or else not speak)
Some bastard Latin,
    French or English voice
Where Scots fell short –
    I had not other choice.
Not that our tongue in useful terms is scant
But I abundancy of language want
Where Virgil's colourful propriety,
To keep the sentence like it, constrained me,
Or else to make
    my verses short sometime,
Or more capacious, to complete my rhyme.
Therefore, good friends,
    for pastime or in jest,
Avoid, please, putting each word to the test.
That worthy clerk
    called Laurence of the Vale,
Patron of Latin scholars without fail,

Fyrst I protest, beaw schirris,
    be your leif,
Beis weill avisit my wark or yhe repreif,
Consider it warly, reid oftar than anys;
Weill at a blenk sle poetry nocht tayn is,
And yit forsuyth I set my bissy pane
As that I couth to mak it braid and plane,
Kepand na sudron bot our awyn langage,
And spekis as I lernyt quhen I was page.
Nor yit sa cleyn all sudron I refuss,
Bot sum word I pronunce
    as nyghtbouris doys.
Lyke as in Latyn beyn Grew termys sum,
So me behufyt quhilum or than be dum
Sum bastard Latyn,
    French or Inglys oyss
Quhar scant was Scottis –
    I had nane other choys.
Nocht for our tong is in the selwyn skant
Bot for that I the fowth of langage want
Quhar as the cullour of his properte
To kepe the sentens tharto constrenyt me,
Or than to mak
    my sayng schort sum tyme,
Mair compendyus, or to lykly my ryme.
Tharfor, gude frendis,
    for a gymp or a bourd,
I pray you note me nocht at every word.
The worthy clerk
    hecht Lawrens of the Vaill,
Amang Latynys a gret patron sans faill,

Grantis quhen twelf yheris	Admits he,
he had beyn diligent	after twelve years diligent
To study Virgill, skant knew quhat he ment.	To study Virgil, scarce knew what he meant.
Than thou or I, my frend, quhen we best weyn	Then you or I, my friend, when we best would
To have Virgile red, understand and seyn,	Have Virgil seen, and read, and understood,
The rycht sentens perchance is fer to seik.	The rightful sense may still be far to seek.
This wark twelf yheris	This work, although
first was in makyng eyk	it took twelve years to make,
And nocht correct	Was not corrected
quhen the poet gan decess;	at the poet's decease,
Thus for small faltis,	So for small faults,
my wyss frend, hald thy pess.	my wise friend, hold thy peace.
Adherdand to my protestatioun,	Adherent am I to that protestation
Thocht Wilyame Caxtoun,	Though William Caxton,
of Inglis natioun,	of the English nation,
In proyss hes prent	In prose did print
ane buke of Inglys gross,	a book of English gross,
Clepand it Virgill in Eneadoss,	Calling IT Virgil, his Eneados,
Quhilk that he says	Which he says
of Franch he dyd translait,	out of French he did transpose!
It hass na thing ado tharwith, God wait,	It has NO thing to do with it, God knows,
Ne na mair lyke than the devill	No more like it than
and Sanct Austyne,	devil and Saint Augustine.
Have he na thank tharfor,	Don't thank him for it –
bot loyss hys pyne,	let him lose his pain
So schamefully that story dyd pervert.	Who shamefully that story did pervert.
I red his wark with harmys at my hart,	I read his work with harm to my heart.
That syk a buke but sentens or engyne	That such a book, no sense, no manner fine,
Suldbe intitillit eftir the poet dyvyne;	Should be entitled from the poet divine!
Hys ornate goldyn versis mair than gilt	His ornate golden verses more than gilt –
I spittit for dispyte to se swa spilt.	I spat from spite to see so badly spilt!

OOOOOOOOOOOOOOOOOOOOOOOOOOOOOOOOOOOOOOOOOOOOOOOOOOOOOOOOOOOOOOOOOOOOOOO

AFTER REBUKING CAXTON FOR WHAT HE LEFT OUT OF HIS PROSE
VERSION OF VIRGIL'S *AENEID* DOUGLAS PRAISES CHAUCER AS
SUPREME POET IN ENGLISH BUT REGRETS HE ADDED TO VIRGIL'S
ACCOUNT OF DIDO A DENUNCIATION OF AENEAS
FOR DESERTING HER.

OOOOOOOOOOOOOOOOOOOOOOOOOOOOOOOOOOOOOOOOOOOOOOOOOOOOOOOOOOOOOOOOOOOOOOO

But certainly I must, in reason's name,
Excuse Chaucer from every kind of blame.
In loving of their ladies lily white
He set on Virgil and Aeneas this slight
Because he was (God knows)
     all women's friend.
No more of that,
     but gentle reader, send
With all my faults, this last offence away.
Thou prince of poets, I for mercy pray,
I mean thou King of Kings, Eternal Lord,
Thou be my muse,
     pole star and guiding word,
Forgive my trespass, all I do amiss
Through prayer of thy Mother,
     Queen of Bliss.
United Godhead, ever in concordance,
In persons three, equal, of one substance,
On thee I call, and Mary, Virgin mild –
The muse and other pagan goddess wild
Can only do me harm –
     I know they must.
In Christ and heaven's Queen
     is all my trust.
Thou, Virgin Mother and Maiden,
     be my muse,
That never yet a sinless wish refuse
To those who seek devoutly for supply.
Although my song to your high majesty
Is not attuned,
     yet stoop to what I write
For the sweet liquor of thy breasts so white
Fostered that Prince,
     that heavenly Orpheus,
Ground of all good, our saviour, Jesus.
But once again, and lower to descend,
Forgive me Virgil if I thee offend.
Pardon thy scholar, suffer him to rhyme

Bot sikkyrly of resson me behufis
Excuss Chauser fra all maner repruffis
In lovyng of thir ladeis lylly quhite
He set on Virgill and Eneas this wyte,
For he was evir (God wait)
     all womanis frend.
I say na mair, but
     gentil redaris heynd,
Lat all my faltis with this offens pass by.
Thou prynce of poetis, I the mercy cry,
I meyn thou Kyng of Kyngis, Lord Etern,
Thou be my muse,
     my gydar and laid stern,
Remittyng my trespass and every myss
Throu prayer of thy Moder,
     Queyn of Blyss.
Afald godhed, ay lestyng but discrepans,
In personys thre, equale, of a substans,
On the I call, and Mary Virgyn myld –
Calliope nor payane goddis wild
May do to me na thing bot harm,
     I weyn;
In Criste is all my traste,
     and hevynnys queyn.
Thou, Virgyn Moder and Madyn,
     be my muse,
That nevir yit na synfull lyst refuss
Quhilk the besocht devotly for supple.
Albeit my sang to thy hie majeste
Accordis nocht,
     yit condiscend to my write,
For the sweit liqour of thy pappis quhite
Fosterit that Prynce,
     that hevynly Orpheus,
Grond of all gude, our Salvyour Jhesus.
Bot forthirmor, and lawar to discend
Forgeif me, Virgill, gif I the offend.
Pardon thy scolar, suffir hym to ryme

Sen thou was bot	*Since you were but*
ane mortal man sum syme.	*a mortal man some time.*
In cace I faill, have me not at disdenye,	*In case I fail, don't hold me in disdain,*
Thocht I be lewit,	*Though low*
my leill hart can nocht fenye,	*my loyal heart can never fain.*
I sall the follow;	*I shall thee follow,*
suld I tharfor have blame,	*should I thence have blame?*
Quha can do bettir,	*Who can do better,*
sa furth in Goddis name.	*say forth, in God's name!*

ooooooooooooooooooooooooooooooooooooooooooooooooooooooooooooooooo

DOUGLAS SAYS HE IS OPEN TO CORRECTION, FORBIDS OTHERS TO MEDDLE WITH HIS RHYMES, THEN SAYS OF VIRGIL –

ooooooooooooooooooooooooooooooooooooooooooooooooooooooooooooooooo

All thocht he stant in Latyne	*Although in perfect Latin*
maist perfyte	*Virgil sung*
Yyt stude he nevir in our tung endyte	*He never was well written in our tongue*
Less than it be by me	*Unless it is by me,*
now at this tyme.	*now, at this time.*
Gyf I have falyeit,	*If I have failed,*
baldly reprufe my ryme.	*boldly reprove my rhyme.*
Bot first, I pray you,	*But first, I pray you,*
grape the mater clean,	*grip the matter clean,*
Reproche me nocht	*Reproach me not*
quhill wark be ourseyn.	*while the work's overseen.*
Beis not our studyus	*Don't search my eyes*
to spy a moyt in mine e,	*to spy a speck in me*
That in your awyn	*Who in your own*
a ferry boyt can nocht see,	*a ferry-boat can't see.*
And do to me as yhe wald be done to.	*And do to me as you would be done to.*
Now hark, schirris, thar is na mair ado;	*Now listen sirs, there is no more ado.*
Quha list attend,	*Who wants, attend.*
gevis audiens and draw neir,	*Give audience and draw near.*
Me thocht Virgill begouth	*I think Virgil began*
on this maner:	*in this manner:*
I the ilk umquhile	*I that before upon*
that in the small ait reid	*the small oat reed*
Tonyt my sang,	*Entuned my song,*
syne fra the woddis yeid	*then from the woods proceed*

And fields about instructed to obey
The needy farmer's
> *busy husbandry,*
And useful work made
> *for the ploughman's skill*
now horrible
> *stern deeds of Martial will.*
The battles and the man I will describe.

And feildis about taucht to be obesand
(Thocht he war gredy)
> *to the bissy husband,*
Ane thankfull wark maid
> *for the plewchmanis art,*
Bot now the horribill
> *stern dedys of Mart,*
The batalys and the man I will discryve.

This is the first English version of the Aeneid by a scholar who was as good a poet. It was completed in 1513 by the Provost of St. Giles Cathedral, Edinburgh. In the same year James IV lost an army at Flodden, like the 3 Stuarts before him dying a violent death & leaving an infant son on the throne. Douglas was brought into politics by his nephew who married the widowed queen. He was denounced as a traitor by a ruling Scots faction while on a mission to Henry VIII; he died in London of a plague. His book was printed there in 1553 without the prayer to the Virgin Mary, as England had then gone Protestant.

Ezra Pound said that in describing bad weather this version outdid the original. It gives all the details of Virgil's epic though they seem more 15th century than classical.

THE CONTENTIS OF EVERY BUKE FOLLOWYING

*T*he **first** contenys quhou the prynce Ene
> *And Troianys war dryve onto Cartage cite.*
*The **secund** buke schawis the finale ennoy,*
> *The gret myscheif and subversion of Troy.*
*The **thryd** tellith quhou fra Troys cite*
> *The Troianys careit war throu owt the see.*
*The **fred** rehersis of fair Queyn Dido*
> *The dowbill woundis and the mortale wo.*
*The **fyft** contenys funerale gemys glaid*
> *And how the fyre the navy dyd invaid.*
*Into the **saxt** buke syne doith Virgill tell*
> *Quhou that Eneas went and visseit hell.*
*The **sevynt** Ene bryngis to hys grond fatale,*
> *And how Italianys Troianys schup to assale.*
*Ontill Eneas gevis the **auchten** buke*
> *Baith falloschip and armour, quha list luke.*
*Dawnus son Turnus in the **nyte**, tak tent,*
> *Segis New Troy, Eneas tho absent.*
*The **tent** declaris by the cost atanys*
> *The batale betwix Tuscanys and Rutulanys.*
*In the **ellevynt** Rutulyanys beyn ourset*
> *By the decess of Camylla downebet.*
*The **twelft** makis end of all the weir, but dowt,*
> *Throu the slauchtir of Turnus, stern and stowt.*
The last, ekit to Virgillis nowmyr evyn
> *By Mapheus, convoys Ene to hevyn.*

EVERYMAN
ANON c1515
LONDON

HERE BEGYNNETH A TREATYSE HOW THE HYE FADER OF HEVEN
SENDETH DETHE TO SOMON EVERY CREATURE TO COME AND
GYVE A COUNTE OF THEYR LYVES IN THIS WORLDE AND IS IN
MANER OF A MORALL PLAYE.

[MESSENGER]

I PRAY you all gyve your audyence
And here this mater with reverence
By fygure a morall playe
The somonyng of everyman called it is
That of our lyves and endynge shewes
How transytory we be all daye
This matter is wonderous precyous
But the intente of it / is more gracyous
And swete to bere awaye
The story sayth man in the begynnynge
Loke well & take good heed to the endynge
Be you never so gay
Ye thynke synne in the begynnynge full swete
Whiche in the ende causeth thy soule to wepe
Whan the body lyeth in claye
Here shall you se how felawshyp and jolyte
Bothe strengthe / pleasure / and beaute
Wyll vade from the as floure in maye
For ye shall here / how our heven kynge
Calleth everyman to a generall rekenynge
Gyve audyens and here what he wyll saye

[GOD SPEKETH]

I perceyve here in my majestye
How that all creatures / be to me unkynde
Lyvynge without drede / in worldely prosperyte
Of ghostly syght / the people be so blynde
Drowned in synne / they know me not for ther god
In worldely ryches is all theyr mynde
They fere not my ryghtwysenes, / that sharpe rod
My lawe that I shewed / whan I for them dyed

The coming of print brought to light more sorts of play than the pageants of church & trade. Strolling actors clowned & danced & sang at markets & inn yards, did turns between the courses of banquets, hired rooms or fields to stage bigger shows. Around 1500 the best of the new plays showed vices & virtues contending for souls. The vices were usually played as imps out of hell, & allowed for lively black comedy.

There are no devils in **Everyman**, the best of moral plays. The worst folk in it are good middle-class citizens on who **Everyman**, our hero, has always relied: **Friendship**, **Family** & **Property**. When **Death** summons him to meet **God** they all desert him, **Friendship** with apologies, **Family** with excuses, **Property** with scorn. Only his **Good Deeds** wants to accompany him but is too weak to move, having been sinfully neglected.

A guide called **Knowledge** leads our hero to the priest, **Repentance** who helps clean him of sin. **Good Deeds** has now the strength to rise & go with **Everyman** into the grave. **Everyman** enters it without fear, as his **Good Deeds** will now bring him safely to **God**. This quiet, happy ending was on the Roman Catholic side of a quarrel that now tore apart Europe, several nations & many families.

Based on a Dutch play, **Elckerlijc**, this version was printed about 1520 when Martin Luther won fame by declaring that good deeds & priest-aided repentance didn't save souls from Hell: only perfect faith that God gave to very few folk who he had chosen before the world was made. St. Augustine had said this 1100 years before. Later saints had not denied but usually ignored it. To deny was to doubt God's total power & total foresight, but Jesus (they thought) had mainly urged God's loving mercy. God's mercy was now being cheapened by new machinery. Bishops had once sold it in hand-written letters of

They forget clene / & sheddynge of my blod so redde
I hanged bytwene two theves / it caunot be denyed
To get them lyfe I suffrede to be deed
I heled theyr fete / with thornes hurt was my heed
I coulde do no more than I dyde truely
And nowe I se the people do clene forsake me
They use the seven deedly synnes dampnable,
As pryde / coveytyse / wrath / and lechery
Now in the worlde be made commendable
And thus they leve of aungeles the hevenly company
Everyman lyveth so after his owne pleasure
And yet of theyr lyfe they be not sure
I se the more that I them forbere
The worse they are from yere to yere
All that lyveth apperyth faste
Therefore I wyll in all the haste
Have a rekenynge of every mannes persone
For and I leve the people thus alone
In theyr lyfe and wycked tempestes
Verely they wyll becume moche worst than bestes
For now one wolde by envy another up ete
Charytye they all do clene forgete
I hoped well that everyman
In my glorye shulde make his mansyon
And therto I had them all electe
But now I se that lyke traytours dejecte
They thanke me not for the pleasure that
                              I to them ment
Nor yet for theyr beynge that I them have lent
I profered the people great multytude of mercy
And fewe there be that asketh it hertely
They be so cumbred with worldly ryches
That nedes on them I must do justyce
On everyman lyvynge without fere
Where art thou deth thou myghty messengere

[DETH]

Almyghty god I am here at your wyll
Your commaundement to fulfyll

[GOD]

Go thou to everyman
And shew hym in my name
A pylgrymage / he must on hym take
Which he in no wyse may escape
And that he brynge with hym a sure rekenynge
Without delay or ony taryenge.

[DETH]

Lorde I wyll in the worlde go ren over all
And truely out serche bothe great and small
Everyman I wyll beset that lyveth beestly
Out of goddes lawes / and dredeth not foly
He that loveth ryches I wyll stryke with my darte
His syght to blynde / and from heven depart
Excepte that almes dedes be his good frende
In hell for to dwell / worlde without ende

indulgence. By 1520 these were mass-produced in the pope's print works & sold by travelling salesmen, so Luther's defiance of the papacy shocked half north Europe with the force of a mighty truth.

Everyman shows the old Catholic faith at its best, helping goodness go beyond the kind of society & commerce that make the successfully selfish dominant & admired.

MAGNYFYCENCE
JOHN SKELTON
LONDON & DISS   c1516

These be the names of the players:

FELYCYTE	COUNTERFET COUNTENANCE	DYSPARE
LYBERTE	CRAFTY CONVEYAUNCE	MYSCHEFE
MEASURE	CLOKYD COLUSYON	
	COURTLY ABUYSON	GOOD HOPE
MAGNYFYCENCE	FOLY	REDRESSE
	ADVERSYTE	CYRCUMSPECCYON
FANSY	POVERTE	PERSEVERAUNCE

STAGE 1. PROSPERITY
[ENTER FELYCYTE]

Al thyngys contryvyd by mannys Reason,
    The world envyronnyd of Hygh and Low Estate,
Be it erly or late Welth hath a season.
        Welth is of Wysdome the very trewe probate,
        A fole is he with Welth that fallyth at debate.
            But men nowe a dayes so unhappely be vryd
            That nothynge than Welth may worse be enduryd,

To tell you the cayse me semeth it no nede.
 The amense therof is far to call agáyne,
For when men by Welth they have lytyll drede
  Of that may come after, experyence trewe and playne
  Howe after a drought there fallyth a showre of rayne
   And after a hete oft cometh a stormy colde.
   A man may have Welth but not as he wolde

Ay to contynewe and styll to endure.
 But yf Prudence be proved with Sad Cyrcumspeccyon
Welthe myght be wonne and made to the lure
  Yf Noblenesse were aquayntyd with Sober Dyreccyon.
  But Wyll hath Reason so under subjeccyon
   And so dysordereth this worlde over all
   That Welthe and Felicite is passynge small.

But where wonnys Welthe and a man wolde wyt?
 For Welthfull Felicite truly is my name.
   [ENTER LYBERTE WHO SPEAKS]
Mary, Welthe and I was apoynted to mete
  And eyther I am dysseyved or ye be the same.

Henry VIII was crowned at the age of 18 in 1509 when his father's savings made him the wealthiest king in Europe. John Skelton, Henry's former tutor, was then 49, rector of a rich parish & poet laureate to both English universities. His best work came later when he lost the parish by marrying or keeping a concubine (the crime is uncertain) & lost his former pupil's protection by mocking Cardinal Wolsey.

Skelton made the unstable English speech serve him by using it talkatively in several verse forms. One of them had the short, quick, droll lines & rhymes enjoyed by children & rude folk, so centuries of critics thought him rudely childish. His sharpest satire on bad government pretends to be nonsense prattled in many languages & dialects by a parrot. It complains of a dirty monstrous grub grown from an egg laid by a flesh-fly: Wolsey was a stout man whose father had been a butcher. This did not bring the safety enjoyed by Will Summers, Henry's licensed jester. In 1529 Skelton died hiding from Wolsey's anger in the sanctuary of Westminster.

*His moral play is almost the only one written to correct the morals of a ruling king. **Wealthy Felicity**, **Liberty** & **Measure** serve **Magnificence**, a prince who finds **Measure** (who would now be called good judgement) too limiting & replaces him with an amusing chap called **Fancy**. This admits to the prince's court 4 villains whose names, modernized, are **Hypocrisy**, **Fraud**, **Conspiracy** & **Corruption**. While **Folly** distracts the prince these steal his property & betray him to **Poverty**, **Despair** & **Mischief**. Only **Good hope** saves him from suicide, then sober virtues help restore his estate.*

*The play was written in 1516 when Henry had replaced his dad's cautious ministers with the cardinal's men & was wasting his dad's huge fortune in vain displays & wars that gained him nothing. But he was no fool. He evaded poverty & despair by seizing other fortunes, starting with Wolsey's. **Magnyfycence** got printed when Wolsey fell in 1530. It then seemed to be about **him**.*

A NEW WORLD

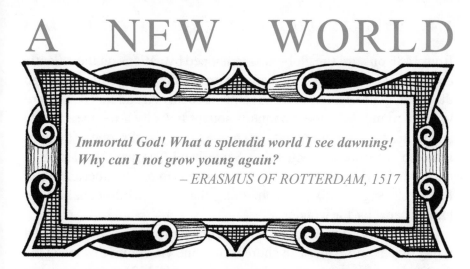

Immortal God! What a splendid world I see dawning!
Why can I not grow young again?
                    — ERASMUS OF ROTTERDAM, 1517

PETRARCH, POET LAUREATE OF ITALY, climbed a mountain, viewed the outspread world with delight, then noticed his delight was natural and therefore sinful: Saint Augustine had said the only good things on earth were church services that brought believers to heaven. Yet a notion that people might enjoy the world without being damned had already revived in Italy. Saint Francis said the sun and moon, fire and water, animals and birds were our brothers and sisters whose company could be innocently enjoyed. Closely cultivated fields, guilds of fine craftsmen, ruling families who preferred trade to warfare had given Italian republics the most comfortable houses, most beautiful civic architecture, best educated citizens in Europe. When seeking precedents for themselves these citizens looked past imperial Rome (whose monuments surrounded them) to the poetry and philosophy of Greece, whose small states had been as variously creative as their own. This interest spread to other nations. After 1453 it was boosted by Greek scholars fleeing west from Turks who had captured Constantinople.

Italian merchants brought timber, hides and wool from north-west Europe, silk, spices and precious metal from Tartary and Arabia, but for fifteen centuries saw nothing that contradicted Greek and Roman geography which said the world was mostly covered by ocean with all Europe, Asia and Africa grouped round the Mediterranean. Christian maps showed Jerusalem in the centre of these continents so that Jesus, on resurrection day, would be seen by everyone on earth when he appeared in the sky above the city where he died. It therefore was pointless and dangerous to sail very far in the Atlantic, since the ocean round the equator must boil as fiercely as it froze at the poles. But from 1486 onward the globe was remapped by nations on the Atlantic coast who also wanted trade with the orient. Portugese sailors crossed the equator unboiled, saw Africa continue south of it and sailed eastward to India round the Cape. Spaniards sought India by a westward route and found two vast continents unknown to the Greeks, one with cities intricate as Venice and richer than Samarkand. The news thrilled more than greedy adventurers. The first Europeans to reach America (Scott Fitzgerald suggested) saw something that for a while equalled the human capacity for wonder.

In 1497 Giovanni Caboto, Italian captain of an English ship, raised a flag on a North American shore. From one viewpoint this made the continent a possession of the English crown. In 1524 another Italian, Giovanni Verrazano, did the same from a French ship for the French Crown. A century passed before both kingdoms had colonies there, less than two before they fought for possession of the whole shebang.

Meanwhile scholars were also making discoveries. Greek texts, Christ's Gospels among them, had previously come west in Latin translations with commentaries building them into the complex systems of the Roman church. Presses now issued original texts which showed the Greeks had questioned all systems they or others had invented. In 1516 Erasmus of Rotterdam published the New Testament in Greek, with notes indicating how several catholic doctrines and institutions were not based on anything Christ or Saint Paul were quoted as saying. In this and other books Erasmus argued so sensibly, gently and wittily for reform that many devout Catholics agreed with him, even in Rome, where cardinals had been bribing themselves into the papacy for over a century. It seemed that in time all Christians might agree in a simpler forms of worship and a less corrupt, more charitable church.

In 1521 Martin Luther published the first German Bible. He had translated it from texts printed by Erasmus, but Luther's marginal notes called the pope an Antichrist who for centuries had led Christians to hell with Latin masses, clerical celibacy, purgatory, prayers for the dead, miraculous images, doctrines that implied freedom of will and much more that true Christians should at once reject. Erasmus was horrified.

In the next three years German peasants who claimed to be Lutheran revolted against their overlords.
Luther was horrified.

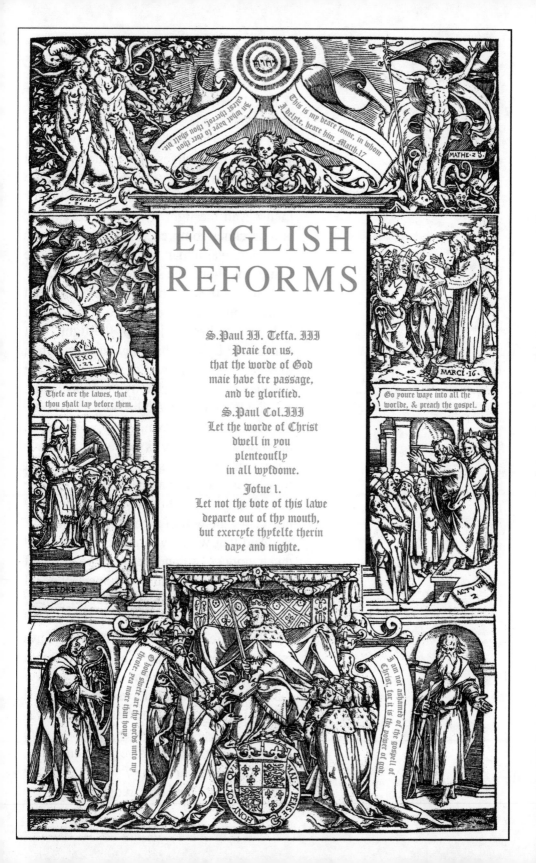

ENGLISH REFORMS

S. Paul II. Tessa. III
Praie for us,
that the worde of God
maie have fre passage,
and be glorified.

S. Paul Col. III
Let the worde of Christ
dwell in you
plenteously
in all wysdome.

Josue 1.
Let not the bote of this lawe
departe out of thy mouth,
but exercyse thyselfe therin
daye and nighte.

This is my deare sonne, in whom
I delyte, heare him. Matth. 17

An whosoever hape of to ever thou
cattest thereof, thou shalt die.

Thefe are the lawes, that
thou shalt lay before them.

Go youre waye into all the
worlde, & preach the gospel.

O how swete are thy wordes unto my
throte; yea more than hony.

I am not ashamed of the gospell of
Christ; for it is the power of god.

1526

THE GOSPELL OF S. JHON
TRANSLATED by WILLIAM TYNDAL
PRINTED at WORMS on the RHYNE

By translating the Bible into his Saxony dialect Luther proved that German could describe great matters as well as Latin, so all later German literature grew from it. English law had stunted England's much earlier growth of good writing. None know how it would have shaped with free use & improvement of Wyclif's Bible, so modern English dates from Tyndal breaking the law with a new Bible. He was a priest **well known, before he went over the sea, for a man of right good living, studious & well learned in scriptures** *. . .* **very well liked, & did great good with preaching** *said Sir Thomas More, his fair-minded enemy. Tyndal, hating the ignorance of most clergy, began translating when many powerful folk liked the idea. Luther's protest changed their mind, some for good reasons, some not. Henry VIII needed papal aid to become the 1st English Holy Roman Emperor. He denounced Luther & his Bible in a book saying the gospels were too precious for commoners. Tyndal went to Germany & for 12 years dodged Henry's agents from city to city, printing his English gospels under false names, one the name of Luther's printer. He also used Luther's belligerent glosses, so some thought all he translated was from Luther's German. He certainly studied every ancient & modern Bible translation he could find: they all strengthened his grasp of the original Greek published by Erasmus.* **Tyndal's honesty, sincerity, simple directness, his modest music** *(says Isaacs)* **have given an authority to his wording that have imposed on all later versions.**

IN THE BEGYNNYNGE was that worde / and that worde was with god: and god was thatt worde. The same was in the begynnynge wyth god. All thynges were made by it / and with out it / was made noo thinge: that made was. In it was lyfe / And lyfe was the light of men / And the light shyneth in darcknes / and darcknes comprehended it not.

There was a man sent from god / whose name was Jhon. The same cam as a witnes / to beare witnes of the light / that all men through him myght beleve. He was nott that light: but to beare witnes of the light. That was a true light / which lighteneth all men that come into the worlde. He was in the worlde / and the worlde by him was made: and the worlde knewe hym not.

He cam into his awne / and his received him not. unto as meny as received him / gave he power to be the sonnes of god: in that they beleved on his name: which were borne not of bloude nor of the will of the flesshe / nor yet of the will of men: but of god.

And that worde was made flesshe / and dwelt amonge us / and we sawe the glory off yt / as the glory off the only begotten sonne off the father / which worde was full of grace / and verite.

Jhon bare witnes off hym sayinge: Thys is he of whome I spake / he that commeth after me / was before me be cause he was yer than I. And of his fulnes have all we received / even favour for favour. For the lawe was geven by Moses / but favour and verite cam by Jesus Christ. No man sawe god at eny tyme. The only begotten sonne / which is in the fathers bosum / hath declared hym.

DIALOGUE CONCERNING HERESIES
SIR THOMAS MORE
LONDON
1529

A dyaloge of syr Thomas More knyghte: one of the counsayll of our soverayne lorde the kyng & chauncellour of hys duchy of Lancaster. Wherin be treatyd dyvers maters / as of the veneration & worshyp of ymagys & relyques / prayng to sayntys / & goyng on pylgrymage. Wyth many othere thyngys touchyng the pestylent sect of Luther & Tyndale / by the tone bygone in Saxony / & by the tother laboryd to be brought in to Englond.

THE FURST BOKE: INTRODUCTORY
ONE BUSYNES BEGETTETH ANOTHER

I T IS an old saying that one business begets and brings forth another, which I found very true myself, because one business provoked a second, and the second now makes a third.

For a right respected friend of mine sent me a discreet sure friend of his, with certain beliefs to be declared to me touching many matters which are certain and undoubted, but which nonetheless ignorant people have recently questioned in ways set forth in the first chapter of this book, so I need not rehearse them here. I at first thought it enough to tell the messenger my mind by mouth, thinking that when our communication ended I would need no further business with it. But after the messenger departed, and I felt my stomach well eased because my labour was done, thinking a little on the business I found it far from that point, and little more than begun.

For when I considered the matter discussed, and how many great things had been treated by the messenger and me, I mistrusted not his good will, and very well trusted his wit and learning in reporting our communication: yet finding our discussion had been so diverse and so long and sometimes so intricate that myself could not without effort call it orderly to mind, methought I had not done well to trust his memory only: especially since

More, son of a judge, studied at an Oxford that again promoted learning. He lived 4 years as a Carthusian monk, praying, fasting, scourging himself; then turned lawyer; married; became MP, Wolsey's helper, & Chancellor of England after Wolsey fell. Erasmus, More's friend, reported how happily this scholar & politician played at home with his children & their pets. He gave his daughters as good an education as his own: helped found the 1st English school to teach Greek: called it **the wooden horse in which are concealed armed Greeks for the destruction of bar-** *barous Troy. By Troy he meant ignorant clergy. He & Erasmus believed that if the words & deeds of Jesus were learned before Latin theology the clergy might be led to live by their vows of poverty, & Christian charity might increase everywhere.*

some parts needed to be attentively read rather than hurriedly heard and passed over. And I also considered that, though I did not suspect the messenger, and in faith do not, I am myself so little distrusting that he could easily show himself like nobody I would think bad. Yet as no man can look into another's breast it is well done to expect the best, but not much amiss to provide for the worst, since then (if a man happen to be worse than we take him for) our good opinion of him will do us no harm. This was why I decided to send our communication to my said friend in writing: so if his messenger for any sinister preference for the wrong side purposely mangled the matter, his master should not only know the truth, but know to beware of the messenger.

Now when after this deliberation I had written all the matter down and sent it to my friend, I thought all finished and my mind was set at rest. But that rest rested not long. For soon after it was showed me, that copies have been made of all my letters to others, and one of them carried over the sea. When I remembered what a shrewd set of apostates are assembled there, part of them run out of religion and all run out of the true faith, I thought great peril might arise if some of that company (which are confederated and conspired together in the sowing and setting forth of Luther's pestilent heresies in this realm) should maliciously change my words to the worse and put in print my book framed after their fantasies: which, when I afterward denounced them and showed the difference, might make me seem, because of the colour of the cause I support, to have amended my own version upon sight of theirs. To prevent which I am now driven, as I say, to this third business of publishing and putting my book in print, whereby their enterprise (if they intend such) shall (I trust) be prevented and frustrate.

This I have not done all on my own, but after consulting more than one: whose advice and counsel for wisdom and learning I asked, and at my request read the book before I put it forth. For though Saint Peter bids us be ready to give an account and show the reasons for our faith and hope to every man, yet to make and put forth any book (wherein are treated such things as touch our faith) I would not presume to do unless those more learned than I thought it profitable or at least harmless. To their examination and judgement I more studiously submitted this work for two reasons among several others. One, because the allegations of the messenger about the wrong party were laid out so boldly, that I stood half in doubt whether it were suitable to repeat anything so roughly and unreverently spoken against God's holy saints and their memories. The other was certain tales and merry words he mingled with his matter, and some such of my own occasionally fell into the communication. In which I saw no harm, but feared lest to serious men they seem too light and playful for the weight and gravity of such earnest matter. On these two points I had seen examples of right holy men who, in their books answering the objections of heretics in their time, have not held back from repeating the very evil words of the writings they refuted, these being sometimes of a manner and sort that a good man would hardly bear, and have also let a merry word into a right earnest work: of which two things I could gather a great deal out of many godly men's books.

Yet in my own work I determined I would allow and defend nothing that the judgement of other virtuous and well-read men disliked. And after several such had read and advised on it, I found as often happens, something that one wise and learned man wanted out, two of like wisdom and learning wanted in, neither side lacking good and probable reasons. Since it was chosen for my judges, it being hard for any man to say which surpassed the others in erudition, wit or prudence, I could do no more than lean to the majority: which I have followed by leaving nothing in this book but what two advised me to let stand, against one that urged me to the contrary.

And this much I thought necessary to advertise all you that shall happen to read this rude simple work, praying for your patience and pardon, whom God of his especial grace grant as much profit in the reading, as my poor heart hath meant and intended you in the making.

1530

THE PENTATEUCH
WILLIAM TYNDAL
ANTWERP

*Tyndal annoyed the catholic orthodoxy by translating the Greek word **Ecclesia** into **Congregation** instead of **Church**. When he translated the Hebrew Bible he made many compound words & phrases now taken for granted: **scapegoat, passover, the Lord's annointed, to fall by the sword** etc, but English was being enlarged by Tyndal's enemies too. More used Latinate words like **obstruction** & **fact**, Greekisms like **paradox** & **monosyllable**. Debate in print taught every reader useful new words, but the most educated writers used earthy phrases for direct reports, comedy & rage: **whoring after strange Gods** & **bare as a bird's arse** etc. Over a century passed before teachers forbade short Anglo-Saxon words for parts of the body, sex, & shit, & dictionaries defined **fornicate** but not **fuck**, & a dinner party where everyone laughed when Doctor Johnson said a woman had a **bottom** of common-sense. (He revised the remark by saying she was **fundamentally** sensible).*

THE FYRST BOKE OF MOSES
CALLED GENESIS

How heaven & erth / the lyght / the fyrmament / the sonne / the mone / the sterres / and all beastes / foules & fysshes in the see were made by the worde of God. And how man also was creat.

THE FYRST CHAPTER

IN THE BEGINNYNG God created heaven and erth. The erth was voyde and emptye / and darcknesse was upon the depe / & the spirite of God moved upon the water.

Than God sayde: let there be lyght: & there was lyght. And God sawe the lyght that it was good: & devyded the lyght from the darcknesse / & called the lyght the daye / & the darknesse the nyght: and so of the evenyng & mornyng was made the fyrst daye.

And God sayde: let there be a fyrmament betwene the waters / & let it devyde the waters asonder. Than God made the fyrmament / & parted the waters whych were under the fyrmament / from the waters that were above the fyrmament: And it was so. And God called the fyrmament Heaven. And so of the evenynge and mornyng was made the seconde daye.

And God sayde: let the waters that are under heaven gather them selves unto one place / that the drye lande may appere. And it came so to passe. And God calle the drye lande the erth / & the gatheryng togyther of waters called he the see. And God sawe that it was good.

And God sayde: let the erth brynge forth herbe & grasse that sowe seed / & frutefull trees / that bere frute every one in hys kynde / havyng their seed in them selves upon the erth. And it came so to passe. And the erth brought forth herbe & grasse soweng seed every one in hys kynde / & trees berynge frute / & havynge their seed in them selves / every one in hys kinde. And God Sawe that it was good / & then of the evening & mornyng was made the thyrde daye.

Than sayde God: let there be lightes in the fyrmament of heaven / to devyde the daye from the nyght/ that they may be unto sygnes/ seasons / dayes & yeares. And let them be lyghtes in the fyrmament of heaven / to shyne upon the erth: And so it was. And God made two greate lyghtes: A greater lyghte to rule the daye / & a lesse lyght to rule the nyght: & he made sterres also. And God put them in the fyrmament of heaven to shyne upon the erth / and to rule the daye and the nyght; & to devyde the lyght from darcknesse. And God sawe that it was good: and so of the evenynge and mornynge was made the fourth daye.

And God sayde: let the water brynge forth creatures that move and have lyfe / & foules for to flee over the erth under the fyrmament of heaven. And God created greate whalles & all maner of creatures that lyve & move / which the waters brought forth in their kyndes / & all maner of federed foules in their kyndes. And God saw that it was good: & God blessed them sayinge: Growe & multyplye & fyll the waters of the sees: and let the foules multyplye upon the erth. And so of the evenynge and mornynge was made the fyfth daye.

And God sayde: let the erth brynge forth lyvynge creatures in their kyndes: catell and wormes & beastes of the erth in their kyndes / & so it came to passe. And God made the beastes of the erth in their kyndes / and catell in their kyndes / & all maner wormes of the erth in their kyndes: & God sawe that it was good.

And God sayde: let us make man in oure symylytude & after oure lycknesse: that he may have rule over the fysh of the see / and over the foules of the ayre / & over catell / & over all the erth / and over all wormes that crepe on the erth. And God created man after hys lycknesse / after the lycknesse of God created he hym: male & female created he them.

And God blessed them / & God sayde unto them: Growe and multyplye & fyll the erth / & subdue it / & have domynion over the
fyshes of the see / and over the foulesof theayre
& over all the beastes that move
on the erth.

1531

BOECE'S CHRONICLES OF SCOTLAND
Translated by JOHN BELLENDEN
EDINBURGH

THE PREFACE OF MAISTER JOHNNE BELLANTYNE, DIRECT UNTO THE RICHT HIE, RYCHT EXCELLENNT, RICHT NOBILL AND POTENT PRINCE, JAMES THE FYFTE OF THAT NAME, KYNG OF SCOTTIS.

Boece (Latin Boethius, modern Boyce) was born in Dundee, became student then professor of philosophy in Paris, friend of Erasmus & 1st principal of Aberdeen University. He wrote this at a bad time. Scotland's army was smashed, her south ravaged by Henry VIII's troops, her king a child swapped between greedy nobles. Boece wrote in Latin. His book, printed in 1527, won international fame by showing Scotland was a more ancient kingdom than France & England. His history was based (he said) upon the archives of Inchcolmkill Abbey & an earlier chronicle written by Veremundus. They gave the Stuarts, who were short of noble ancestors, one called Banquo. This 1531 translation gave Holinshed stories for his British history book. Shakespeare used one in the tragedy of Macbeth. Later historians found that the Inchcolmkill archives & Veremundus & Banquo were equally imaginary. Boece, pretending to be a historian, had written a patriotic romance.

ERASMUS Roterodamus schawis, maist nobill Prince, na thing in moir admiracioun to the pepill than werkis of kingis, for thair lyvis has sa public sycht that every pepill has the samyn in mouth, to thair commendacioun or repreif; and thairfor na thing bene sa fructifull to repress the common errouris of pepill as cleyn lyfe of princis. For the maneris of privat estatis nocht bene sa patent as of publik personis; throu quhilk the life of princes impellis thair subdittis to imitacioun of thair werkis, wourthy and unworthy, quhilkis finalie cumis to licht be impulsioun of fortoun, that na thing sufferis to be hid. And sen na thing is that the pepill followis with moir imitacioun, or kepis in moir recent memorie, than werkis of nobill men, of reassoun thair besynes suld be moir respondent to vertew than of ony uther estatis, quhen moir triumphant glorye and preeminence bene randrit to publik than privatt personis.

Amang all princelie behavingis and werkis of nobill men I fynd no thing moir fructuous, or moir respondent to knychtly besynes, then reding of historiis; for nobill men sall nocht fynd onlie in thame marciall dedis, bot als mony documentis concernyng thair fayme, thair honour, and perpetuall memory, seand every stait apprisit eftir thair merittis and demerittis. Attoure, the froute of history bene sa necessair that, but it, the wailyeand dedis of forsy campionis suddandly evanis. Be contrar, the effect thairof causis thai thingis quhilkis ar mony yeris goyne appere als recent in oure memory as thai war instantlie done. Thairfor sayid Marcus Cicero, "He that is ignorant of sik thingis as bene done afoir his tyme, for lak of experience, is bot ane barn." For thir reassonis, maist nobill Prince, I, that bene thi native and humyll servitour sen thi first infance, be impulsioun of luff and vehement affeccioun quhilk I bere unto the samyn, has translatit "The History of Scotland" sen the first begynnyng therof in vulgair langage; and thocht the charge was importabill throw tedious laboure and feire of this huge volume, quhilk has impeschitt my febill ingyne, havand na crafty witt nor pregnant eloquence to decoir the samyn, yite I am constranit for schort tyme to bring this my translacioun to licht, nakit of perfeccioun and rethory, siklike as implume birdis to flicht.

Nochtheles, I lawlie beseik Thi Magnificence to accept my labouris with sik benevolus wult as thai bene dedicatt to Thi Grace; in quhilkis ar contenit nocht only the nobill feetis of thi wailyeannt anticessouris, bot als be quhat industry and wisedome this realme bene governit thir xviii & lx yeris, quhilk was nevir subdewitt to uncouth empire, bot onlye to the native princis thairof, howbeit the samyn has sustenit grete affliccioun be Romanis, Inglis & Danys, be sindry chancis of fortoun. Thi Hienes sall fynd in this present history mony grave sentence, na less plesand than proffittabill, quhairthrow Thi Hienes may haif sikkir experience to knaw how this realme salbe governit in justice, and quhat personis ar necessair to bere autorite or office within this realme, and sall fynd how illustir princis bene degeneratt fra vertew, becaus thai wer accumpaniit with avaricious pepill and vayn flattoraris, moir sett for conquess of gudis than princelie reverence; throcht quhais corruppit counsale thi nobill anticessouris sum tymes wer abusit, and brocht to sik miserie that thai tynt nocht onlye thair lyiff and triumphand dominioun, bot remanis in memory to thair lamentabill regraitt.

I doute nocht, maist nobill Prince, bot on the samyn maner are now mony personis depending on Thie Hienes, moir affekkit to thair singular proffitt than to the privatt or commoun wele, havand thair perpetuall besynes gevin to na thing sa mekill as perticulare avantage; quhilk thing was occasioun to thi nobill eldaris, quhen thai declynit fra vertew throw parcialite of suspicious personis, as mair cleirly sall appere in reding of this volume.

0000000000000000000000
00000000000
0000

1534

THE NEW TESTAMENT
WILLIAM TYNDAL UNTO THE READER
ANTWERP

HERE THOU hast (moost deare reader) the new Testament or covenaunt made wyth us of God in Christes bloude. Which I have looked over agayne (now at the last) with all dylygence, and compared it unto the Greke, and have weded oute of it many fautes, which lacke of helpe at the begynninge and oversyght, dyd sowe therin. If ought seme chaunged, or not all to gether agreynge with the Greke, let the fynder of the faute consider the Hebrue Phrase or maner of speche lefte in the Greke wordes. Whose preterperfectence and presenttence is ofte both one, and the futuretence is the optative mode also, and the futuretence is ofte the imperatyve mode in the actyve voyce, and in the passyve ever. Lykewyse person for person, nombre for nombre, and an interrogacion for a condicionall, and soche lyke is with the Hebrues a comen usage.

I have also in manye places set lyght in the mergent to understonde the text by. If anye man fynde fautes ether with the translacion or ought besyde (which is easyer for manye to do, then so well to have translated it them selves of their awne pregnant wyttes, at the begynnynge withoute forensample) to the same it shalbe law full to translate it themselves and to put what they lust therto. If I shall perceave ether by my selfe or by the informacion of other, that ought be escaped me, or myght be more playnlye translated, I will shortlye after, cause it to be mended. Howbeit in manye places, me thynketh it better to put a declaracyon in the margent, then to runne to farre from the text. And in manye places, where the text semeth at the fyrst choppe harde to be understonde, yet the circumstances before and after, and often readinge together, maketh it playne ynough etc.

Moreover, because the kyngedome of heaven, which is the scripture and worde of God, maye be so locked up, that he which readeth or heareth it, cannot understonde it: as Christ testifieth how that the Scribes and Pharises had so shut it up. Mat. xxiii. and had taken awaye the keye of knowledge. Luke. xi. that their Jewes which thought them selves within, were yet so locked out, and are to this daye that they can understonde no sentence of the scripture unto their salvacion, though they can reherse the textes every where and dispute thereof as sottelye as the popyshe doctoures of dunces darcke learninge, which with their sophistrye, sarved us, as the Pharises dyd the Jewes. Therfore (that I myght be founde faythfull to my father and lorde in distributinge unto my brethren and felowes of one fayth, their due and necessarye fode: so dressinge it and ceasoninge it, that the weake stomackes maye receave it also, and be the better for it) I thoughte it my dutye (most deare reader) to warne the before, and to shew the the right waye in, and to geve the true keye to open it with all, and to arme the agaynst false Prophetes and malicious ypocrytes, whose perpetuall stodye is to leven the scripture with gloses, and there to locke it up where it shuld save thy soule, and to make us shote at a wronge marke, to put oure trust in those thinges that proffit their belyes onlye and slee oure soules.

The ryght waye: ye and the onlye waye to understonde the scripture unto oure salvacion, is, that we ernestlye and above all thinge, serche for the profession of oure baptyme or covenauntes made betwene God and us. As for an ensample: Christ sayth Mat. v. Happie are the mercifull, for they shall obtayne mercie. Loo, Here God hath made a covenaunt with us, to be mercifull unto us, yf we wilbe mercifull one to another: so that the man which sheweth mercie unto his neyboure, maye be bolde to trust in God for mercie at all nedes. And contrarye wyse, judgement without mercie, shalbe to him that sheweth not mercye. Jaco ii. So now, yf he that sheweth no mercie, trust in God for mercie, his fayth is carnall and worldlye, and but vayne presumpcion. For God hath promysed mercie onlye to the mercifull. And therfore the mercilesse have no Godes worde that they shall have mercie: but contrarye wyse, that they shall have judgement without mercie. And Mat. vi. If ye shall forgeve men their fautes, youre hevenly father shall forgeve you: but and yf ye shall not forgeve men their fautes, no more shall youre father forgeve you youre fautes. Here also by the vertue and strength of this covenaunt wher with God of his mercie hath bounde him selfe to us unworthie, maye he that forgeveth his neyboure, be bolde when he returneth and amendeth to beleve and trust in god for remission of what soever he hath done amysse. And contrarye wyse, he that will not forgeve, cannot but dispeare of forgevenes in the ende, and feare judgement without mercie.

The generall covenaunt wherin all other are comprehended and included, is this. If we meke oure selves to god, to kepe all his lawes, after the ensample of Christ: then God hath bounde him selfe unto us to kepe and make good all the mercies promysed in Christ, thorowout all the scripture.

All the wholelawe which was geven to utter oure corrupt nature, is comprehended in the ten commaundementes. And the ten commaundementes are comprehended in these two: love God and thy neyboure. And he that loveth his neyboure in God and Christ, fulfilleth these two, and consequentlye the ten, and finally all the other. Now if we love oure neyboures in God and Christ: that is to wete, if we be lovinge, kynde and mercifull to them, because God hath created them unto his lykenes, and Christ hath redemed them and bought them with his bloude, then maye we be bolde to trust in God thorow Christ and his deservinge, for all mercie. For God hath promysed and bounde him selfe to us: to shew us all mercie, and to be a father almighty to us, so that we shall not nede to feare the power of all oure adversaryes.

Now yf anye man that submitteth not him selfe to kepe the commaundementes, do thinke that he hath anye fayth in God: the same mannes fayth is vayne, worldlye, damnable, develishe and playne presumpcion, as it is above sayde, and is no fayth that can justifie or be accepted before God. And that is it that James meaneth in his Pistle. For how can a man beleve sayth Paul, without a preacher. Ro. x. Now reade all the scripture and se where God sent anye to preache mercye to anye, save unto them onlye that repent and turne to god with all their hartes, to kepe his commaundementes. Unto the disobedient that will not turne, is threatened wrath, vengeaunce and damnacion, accordinge to all the terrible curses and fearfull ensamples of the Byble."

OOOOOOOOOOOOOOOOOOOOOOOOOOOOOOOOOOOOOOOOOOOOOOOOOOOOOOOOOOOO

TYNDAL THEN DENOUNCES THE PAPACY AT GREAT LENGTH
BEFORE INSERTING THIS FRANTIC POSTSCRIPT.

OOOOOOOOOOOOOOOOOOOOOOOOOOOOOOOOOOOOOOOOOOOOOOOOOOOOOOOOOOOO

WILLIAM TYNDAL

YET ONCE MORE TO THE CHRISTEN READER.

THOU shalt understonde moost dere reader, when I had taken in hande to looke over the new testament agayne and to compare it with the greke, and to mende whatsoever I coulde fynde amysse and had almost fynesshed the laboure: George Joye secretly toke in hand to correct it also by what occasyon his conscyence knoweth: and prevented me, in so moche, that his correccyon was prynted in great nombre, yer myne beganne. When it was spyed and worde brought me, though it semed to dyvers other that George Joye had not used the offyce of an honest man, seinge he knew that I was in correctynge it my selfe: nether dyd walke after the rules of the love and softenes which christ, and his desciples teache us, how that we shuld do nothynge of stryfe to move debate, or of vayne glorie or of covetousnes. Yet I toke the thinge in worth as I have done dyvers other in tyme past, as one that have moare experyence of the nature and dysposicion of the mannes complexion, and supposed that a lytle spyse of covetousnes and vayne glorie (two blynde gydes) had bene the onlye cause that moved him so to do, aboute which thynges I stryve with no man: and so folowed after and corrected forth and caused this to be prynted, without surmyse or lokynge on his correctyon.

But when the pryntynge of myne was almost fynesshed, one brought me a copie and shewed me so manye places, insoche wyse altered that I was astonyed and wondered not a lytle what furye had dryven him to make soche chaunge and to call it a diligent correction. For thorow oute Mat. Mark and Luke perpetually: and ofte in the actees, and sometyme in John and also in the hebrues, where he fyndeth this worde *Resurreccion*, he chaungeth it into the *lyfe after this lyfe*, or *verielyfe*, and soche lyke, as one that abhored the name of the resurrecion.

If that chaunge, to turne resurreccion into *lyfe after this lyfe*, be a dylygent correccion, then must my translacion be fautie in those places, and saynt Jeromes, and all the translatours that ever I heard of in what tonge so ever it be, from the apostles unto this his dylygent correccyon (as he calleth it) which whither it be so or no, I permyt it to other mennes judgementes.

But of this I chalenge George Joye, that he dyd not put his awne name therto and call it rather his awnetranslacion: and that he playeth boo pepe, and in some of his bookes putteth in his name and tytle, and in some kepeth it oute. It is lawfull for who will translate and shew his mynde, though a thousand had translated before him. But is it not lawfull (thynketh me) ner yet expedyent for the edifienge of the unitie of the fayth of christ, that whosoever will, shall by his awne auctorite, take another mannes translacion and put oute and in and chaunge at pleasure, and call it a correccion.

Moreover, ye shall understonde that George Joye hath had of a longe tyme marvelouse ymaginacions aboute this worde resurreccion, that it shuld be taken for the state of the soules after their departinge from their bodyes, and hath also (though he hath been reasoned with therof and desyred to cease) yet sowen his doctryne by secret lettres on that syde the see, and caused great division amonge the brethren. In so moche that John Fryth beynge in preson in the toure of London, a lytle before his death, wrote that we shuld warne him and desyer him to cease, and wolde have then wrytten agaynst him, had I not withstonde him. Therto I have been sence informed that no small nomber thorow his curiosite, utterly denye the resurreccion of the flesshe and bodye, affirminge that the soule when she is departed, is the spirituall bodye of the resurreccion, and other resurreccion shall there none be. And I have talked with some of them my selfe, so doted in that folye, that it were as good perswade a post, as to plucke that madnes oute of their braynes. And of this all is George Joyes unquyet curiosite the hole occasion, whether he be of the sayde faccion also, or not, to that let him answer him selfe.

OOOOOOOOOOOOOOOOOOOOOOOOOOOOOOOOOOOOOOOOOOOOOOOOOOOOOOOOOOOOO

A PASSAGE OMITTED IN WHICH TYNDAL DECLARES THAT THE SCRIPTURES ASSERT THE RESURRECTION OF THE BODY, AND THAT HE BELIEVES IN IT.

OOOOOOOOOOOOOOOOOOOOOOOOOOOOOOOOOOOOOOOOOOOOOOOOOOOOOOOOOOOOO

Tyndal kept improving his translations with each new printing, so an associate could easily make last-minute changes. Joye could not accept both ideas of immortality in the gospels: that on the last day corpses come alive to let the good enjoy heaven on earth, & at death good souls go straight to heaven. Theologians said both ideas were true but the explanation was too elaborate for most understandings. Joye, loving the idea of going straight to heaven, tried to abolish the 1st idea by changing the word for it. The Protestant search for a simple faith led to many such disagreements.

Wherfore I beseche George Joye, ye and all other to, for to translate the scripture for them selves, whether oute of Greke, Latyn or Hebrue. Or (if they wyll nedes) as the foxe when he hath pyssed in the grayes hole chalengeth it for his awne, so let them take my translacions and laboures, and chaunge and alter, and correcte and corrupte at their pleasures, and call it their awne translacions, and put to their awne names, and not to playe boo pepe after George Joyes maner. Which whether he have done faythfully and truly, with soche reverence and feare as becommeth the worde of God, and with soche love and mekenes and affeccion to unite and circumspexcion that the ungodlye have no occasion to rayle on the verite, as becommeth the servauntes of Christ. I referre it to the judgementes of them that knowe and love the trouth. For this, I protest that I provoke not Joye ner any other man (but am provoked and that after the spytfullest maner of provokinge) to do sore agaynst my will and with sorow of harte that I now do. But I nether can ner will soffre of anye man, that he shall goo take my translacion and correct it without name, and make soche chaungynge as I my selfe durst not do, as I hope to have my parte in Christ, though the hole worlde shuld be geven me for my laboure. Vale.

THE BIBLE IN ENGLISH
MILES COVERDALE
COLOGNE or MARBURG 1535

UNTO THE MOST VICTORIOUS PRYNCE AND OURE MOST GRACYOUS SOVERAIGNE LORDE, KYNGE HENRY THE EYGHT, KYNGE OF ENGLONDE AND OF FRAUNCE, LORDE OF IRLONDE. &C. DEFENDOUR OF THE FAYTH, AND UNDER GOD THE CHEFE AND SUPPREME HEADE OF THE CHURCH OF ENGLONDE.

The ryght & just administracyon of the lawes that God gave unto Moses and unto Josua: the testimonye of faythfulnes that God gave of David: the plenteous abundaunce of wysdome that God gave unto Salomon: the lucky and prosperous age with the multiplicacyon of sede whiche God gave unto Abraham and Sara his wyfe, be geven unto you most gracyous Prynce, with your dearest just wyfe, and most vertuous Pryncesse, Quene Anne,

Amen.

CAIPHAS beynge bysshope of that yeare, lyke a blynde prophete (not understandyng what he sayd) prophecied, that it was better to put Christ unto death, then that all the people shulde perysshe: he meanyng, that Christ was an heretike, a deceaver of the people, & a destroyer of the lawe, and that it was better therfore to put Christ unto death, than to suffre hym for to lyve, and to deceave the people. &c. where in very dede Christ was the true prophete, the true Messias, and the onely true Saviour of the worlde, sent of his heavenly father to suffre the moste cruell, most shamefull, and most necessary death for our redempcyon: accordyng to the meanynge of the prophecie truely understonde.

Even after the same maner the blynde bysshoppe

In 1531 Henry VIII got the legal right to divorce his wives by bullying & bribing parliament to make him pope of England's church. He did not wish to change the state religion in other ways, but since his strongest supporters were Protestants he pleased them by allowing this Bible. Tyndal's friend, Coverdale, produced it by removing marginal polemics, replacing Congregation with Church, & making other changes so that Tyndal's English was less shockingly modern. He also wrote this dedication. It pretends to justify the title a pope had given Henry after that king wrote a book denouncing Martin Luther & all Bibles in the vernacular.

of Rome, (that blynde Baalam I saye) not understondynge what he dyd, gave unto your grace this tytle: *Defendour of the fayth*, onely bycause your hyghnes suffred your bysshoppes to burne Gods worde the rote of fayth, and to persecute the lovers and mynisters of the same. where in very dede the blynde bysshoppe (though he knewe not what he dyd) prophecied, that by the ryghteous admynistracyon and contynuall diligence of youre grace, the fayth shulde so be defended, that Gods worde the mother of Fayth with the frutes therof, shulde have his fre course thorowe out all Christendome, but specyally in your realme.

ooooooooooooooooooooooooooooooooooooooooooooooooooooooo

COVERDALE CONDEMNS THE JEWS & PAPACY FOR PRESERVING GOD'S WORD WITHOUT KNOWING ITS MEANING, & ENDS BY HAILING HENRY VIII AS *MY NATURAL SOVEREIGN LIEGE LORD & CHEFE HEADE OF THE CHURCH OF ENGLELONDE, A TRUE DEFENDER & MAYNTEYNER OF GODS LAWES*, A MOSES DELIVERING HIS PEOPLE FROM *THE CRUELL HANDES OF OUR SPIRITUALL PHARAO*, ONE TO WHOM THE ENGLISH BE A THOUSAND TIMES MORE GRATEFUL THAN THE JEWS WERE TO DAVID, *FOR SUBDUYINGE OF GREAT GOLIATH.*

ooooooooooooooooooooooooooooooooooooooooooooooooooooooo

1540

THE THRIE ESTAITIS OF SCOTLAND
SIR DAVID LYNDSAY
EDINBURGH

IN COMMENDATION OF VERTUE AND VITUPERATION OF VICE.
[HERALD]

Lyndsay, like Skelton, tutored a prince who became his king. James V was 17 months when his dad died, 17 years when he seized power from nobles who had misruled in his name. He violently curbed them (it could not be done gently) while seeking support from commoners. Lyndsay was his herald, diplomat, poet. This satire

*T*HE *fader foundar of faith and felicitie*
   That your fassone formit to his similitude
And his sone your salviour scheild in necessitie
That bocht yow frome bailis ransonit on the rude
replegeing his prissonaris with his pretious blude
The haly gaist governour and grundar of grace
Of wisdome and weilfair baith fontane and flude
Save yow all that I se Seisit in this place
      And scheild yow fra syn
And with his spreit yow Enspyre
Till I haif schawin my desyre

Scilence soveranis I requyre
*   For now I begyn*

Pepill tak tent to me and hald yow coy
Heir am I sent to yow ane messingeir
frome ane nobill and richt redowttit roy
The quhilk hes bene absent this mony ane yeir
Humanitie *gif ye his Name wald speir*
Quha bad me schaw to yow but variance
That he Intendis Amang yow to compeir
With ane triumphant awfull ordinance
With croun and swerd and sceptour in his hand
Temperit with mercy quhen penitence Appeiris
Howbeid that he hes bene langtyme sleipand
Quhairthrow misrewill hes rung thir mony yeiris
And Innocentis bene brocht upoun thair beiris
be fals reportaris of this natioun
Thocht yung oppressouris at the Elderis leiris
Be now weill seur of reformatioun

So no misdoaris be so bawld
As to remane In to this Hawld
For quhy be him that Iudas sawld
*   Thay will be heich hangit*
Faithfull folk now may sing
for quhy it is the bidding
Off my soverane the king
*   That na man be wrangit*
Thocht he ane quhyle was in his flowris
be governit be trumpouris
And sumtyme to lufe parramowris
*   Hald him excusit*
*For quhen he meitis with **correctioun***
*With **verety** and **discretioun***
Thay will be baneist of the toun
*   Quhilk hes him abusit*

And heir be oppin proclamatioun
I warne in Name of his magnificence
The thre Estaitis of this Natioun

upon Scotland & its rulers was 1st acted on a hillside by Coupar in Fife with most of the town as audience, the 20 year-old king & his court among it. Nothing like this had been staged since Aristophanes mocked Athenian democrats. This comedy also mixes bawdy fun & moral rage while mocking the vices of the powerful. James's guardians, it seems, had paid women to distract him from their own conduct, & in his short busy reign, although twice wed to French princesses, he had many bastards.

Bad servants get young **King Humanity** to embrace **Sensuality**, a whore. It lets them admit more vices who corrupt clergy, gentry & burghers, the nation's middle class. The vices disguised as virtues imprison real virtues. **Flattery**, dressed as a friar **Devotion**, has **Verity** (truth) arrested for heresy – she uses a vernacular **New Testament**. Because **Sensuality** now rules all 3 estates only a shoemaker & tailor welcome **Chastity**: they prefer booze to sex. Their infuriated wives expel her. Behind the farce we see a nation managed by shameless parasites. It is saved by **Divine Correction**, an angel *who rebukes the king & orders him to summon* **The 3 Estates** *who march in backward, led by their vices. A church spokesman says they've gone backward for years & enjoy it.* **Correction** *orders all who have been wronged to tell the king. From the audience a ragged man jumps on stage: John Commonwealth. He tells how the classes employed to serve the nation help only themselves. Lyndsay (says J. Keay)* **brings 1st ruler then ruled from guilty chaos into moral order.** *His verse is informed by ideas from Langland, Skelton & Erasmus, & while not beautiful is strong & pithy. Says his court jester:* **The king? What kind of man is that? Is yon him in the golden hat?**

James V died of cholera when 30, having given his folk a lasting Court of Session. He left (like his ancestors) an infant heir for nobles to fight over: Mary, Queen of Scots.

that thay compeir with detfull diligence
And till his grace mak thair obedience
And first I warne the **spritualitie**
And see the **burges** *spair nocht for expence*
Bot speid thame heir with **temporalitie**
Als I beseik yow famous awditouris
Convenit in to this congregatioun
To be patient the space of certane howris
Till ye haif hard Our schort narratioun
And als we mak yow supplicatioun
That noman tak our wordis in disdane
Howbeid ye heir be lamentatioun
The **commoun weill** *richt petously complane*

Richt so the verteous lady **veretye**
Will mak ane peteous lamentatioun
And for the trewth scho will Imprissonit bee
And banissit a tyme owt of the toun
And **chestety** *will mak hir narratioun*
How scho can get na lugeing in this land
Till that the hevinly knycht **correctioun**
Meit with our **king** *and* **commoun** *hand till hand*

Prudent pepill I pray yow all
Tak noman greif in speciall
For we sall speik in generall
*   For pastyme and for play*
Thairfoir till our rymes be rung
And our mistonit songis be sung
Lat every man keip weill his tung
*   And every woman tway*

1540

Cranmer was timid yet ambitious, a clerical lawyer so willing to help Henry VIII get all he wanted that he was made Archbishop of

THE GREAT BIBLE
THOMAS CRANMER
LONDON

A PROLOGUE OR PREFACE MADE BY THE MOOST REVERENDE FATHER IN GOD, THOMAS ARCHBYSHOP OF CANTURBURY, METROPOLYTAN AND PRYMATE OF ENGLANDE.

FOR two sondrye sortes of people it semeth moche necessary that somthynge be sayde in the entrye of thys booke, by the waye of a preface or prologue: wherby herafter it maye be both better accepted of them, which hitherto coulde not well beare it: & also the better used of them, which hertofore have mysused it. For truly, some there are that be to slowe, and nede the spurre: some other seme to quycke, and nede more of the brydell. Some loose theyr game by shorte shotynge, some by over shotynge. Some walke to moche on the lefte hande, some to moche on the ryght. In the former sorte be all they that refuse to reade, or to heare redde the scripture in theyr vulgar tonges, moch worse they that also let, or discourage the other from the readynge or hearynge therof. In the latter sorte be they, which by theyr inordinate readyng, undiscrete speakyng, contentious disputyng, or otherwyse, by theyr licencyous lyvinge, slaunder and hynder the worde of God, mooste of all other, wherof they wolde seme to be greatest furtherers. These two sortes albeit they be moost farre unlyke the one to the other, yet they both deserve in effecte lyke reproche. Neyther can I well tell whyther of them I may judge the more offender, hym that doth obstinately refuse so godlye and goodly knowledge: or hym that so ungodly and so ungoodly doth abuse the same: And as touchynge the former I wolde marvayle moche that any man shulde be so madde, as to refuse in darcknes, lyght: in honger, foode: in colde, fyer: for the worde of God is lyght: *Lucerna pedibus meis, verbum tuum.* Foode: *Non in solo pane vivit homo, sed in omni verbo dei.* Fyer: *Ignem veni mittere in terram, et quid volo, nisi ut ardeat?* I wolde marvayle (I saye at this) save that I consyder, howe moche custome and usage maye do. So that yf there were a people as some wryte, *de Cymeriis*, which never sawe the sunne, by reason that they be situated farre towarde the north pole, and be enclosed and overshadowed with hygh mountaynes:

Canterbury before he knew it, & after 1531 ordered the killing of Protestants who denied the mass & Catholics who stayed true to the pope. Thomas More went to his death as cheerily as Socrates drank the hemlock. Cranmer worked with Cromwell, Henry's new chief minister, who in 4 years enriched the king by abolishing the abbeys & selling their land cheap. This ended church social welfare (over 100 hospitals shut in a year) when it was needed, as folk were being evicted by landlords turning their farms into sheep runs. Noble Catholics in the north led a great revolt. Henry's army quelled them, backed by newly enriched Protestant gentry. To make sure of their support Henry let Cranmer make an English Bible for use in church; a thing till now illegal, since it would change the services. To minimise that, most of the English bishops asked Cranmer to base this Bible upon the Vulgate & keep all controversial words in Latin. But Cranmer was 1 of Henry's new men, so far less Catholic than they. He put most of it in clear English like Tyndal or Coverdale's. England's church swung further from Rome.

it is credyble and like ynough, that yf, by the power and will of God, the mountaynes shulde synke downe, and geve place, that the lyght of the sunne might have enteraunce to them: at the fyrst, some of them wolde be offended therwith. And the olde proverbe affermeth, that after tyllage of corne was fyrst founde: many delyted more to feade of maste and acornes, wherwith they had ben accustomed, then to eate breed made of good corne. Soche is the nature of custome that it causeth us to beare all thynges well and easelye, wherwith we have bene accustomed, and to be offended with all thynges therunto contrary. And therfore, I can well thynke them worthy pardon, which at the comyng abroade of scripture doubted and drewe backe. But such as wyll persyste styll in theyr wylfulness, I muste nedes judge, not onely foolyshe frowarde and obstinate: but also pevysshe, perverse and indurate. And yet, yf the matter shulde be tryed by custome, we myght also allege custome for the readynge of the scripture in the vulgare tonge, and prescribe the more auncient custome. For it is not moche above one hundreth yeare agoo, sens scripture hath not bene accustomed to be redde in the vulgar tonge within this realme, and many hundred yeares before that, it was translated and redd in the Saxones tonge, which at that tyme was oure mothers tonge. Wherof there remayneth yet divers copyes found lately in olde abbeis, of soch antique maners of writynge and speaking, that fewe men nowe ben able to reade and understande them. And when this language waxed olde and out of comen usage, because folke shulde not lacke the frute of readyng, it was agayne translated in the newer language. Wherof yet also many copies remayne and be dayly founde. But nowe to lett passe custome, and to weye as wyse men ever shulde, the thyng in hys awne nature. Let us here discusse what it avayleth scripture to be had and redde of the lay and vulgare people. And to this question I entende here to saye nothyng: but that was spoken and wrytten by the noble doctoure and moost morall divine saynt John Chrisostome, in hys thyrde sermon de Lazaro: albeit, I wyl be somthynge shorter, and gether the matter into feawer wordes and lesse rowme then he doth there: because I wolde not be tedyous.

ooooooooooooooooooooooooooooooooooooooooooooooooooooooooooooo

CRANMER QUOTES A FOURTH-CENTURY FATHER OF THE CHURCH ON THE NEED TO KNOW THE SCRIPTURES THEN SAYS HOW ALL GOOD THINGS, EVEN *FYER, WATER, MEATES, DRYNKES, METALS OF GOLDE, SYLVER, IRON AND STELE*, CAN BE BADLY USED, SO READERS SHOULD TRY TO UNDERSTAND THE BIBLE WITHOUT ARGUING .

HE ENDS BY SAYING – *GOD SAVE THE KING.*

THE LABORIOUSE JOURNEY AND SERCHE
FOR ENGLANDES ANTIQUITEES
JOHN LELAND: LONDON

1546

GEVEN OF HYM AS A NEWE YEARES GYFTE TO KING HENRY THE VIII. IN THE XXXVII YEARE OF HIS RAYGNE. TO MY SOVERAIGNE LIEGE KING HENRY THE EIGHT.

WHERE AS it pleasid yowr Highnes apon very juste considerations to encorage me, by the autorite of yowr moste gratius commission yn the xxv. yere of yowr prosperus regne, to peruse and diligently to serche al the libraries of monasteries and collegies of this yowre noble reaulme, to the intente that the monumentes of auncient writers as welle of other nations, as of this yowr owne province mighte be brought owte of deadely darkenes to lyvely lighte, and to receyve like thankes of the posterite, as they hoped for at such tyme as they emploied their long and greate studies to the publique wealthe; yea and farthermore that the holy Scripture of God might bothe be sincerely taughte and lernid, al maner of superstition and craftely coloured doctrine of a rowte of the Romaine bishopes totally expellid oute of this your moste catholique reaulme: I think it now no lesse then my very dewty brevely to declare to your Majeste what frute hath spronge of my laborius yourney and costely enterprise, booth rootid apon yowr infinite goodnes and liberalite, qualites righte highly to be estemid yn al princes, and most especially yn yow as naturally yowr owne welle knowen proprietes.

Firste I have conservid many good autors, the which other wise had beene like to have perischid to no smaul incommodite of good letters, of the whiche parte remayne yn the moste magnificent libraries of yowr royal Palacis. Parte also remayne yn my custodye. Wherby I truste right shortely so to describe your moste noble reaulme, and to publische the Majeste and the excellent actes of yowr

In 1533 Henry VIII gave Leland, his chaplain & librarian, a licence to search English abbeys, colleges & cathedrals for manuscripts, relics & records of national importance. After 1536 the job got too big for him. Abbeys were abolished & churches reformed by gentry who grabbed what they liked. Relics & statues were stripped of rich ornament & burned or flung in rivers. Ancient libraries (even Oxford's) were sold cheap by men who pretended all such books were Roman propaganda. Groceries were wrapped in Latin histories & philosophy: tailors lined suits of clothes with mediaeval & Anglo-Saxon parchment. For 10 years one civil servant saved what he could from a host of wreckers the king had also licensed. This written report on what he had found & his task of preserving it was partly a cry for help. In 1550 he went mad. In 1602 Oxford got a new library which acquired what he had saved.

progenitors (hitherto sore obscurid booth for lak of enprinting of such workes as lay secretely yn corners, and also bycause men of eloquence hath not enterprisid to set them forthe yn a florisching style, yn sum tymes paste not communely usid in England of wryters, otherwise welle lernid, and now yn such estimation that except truethe be delicately clothid yn purpure her written verites can scant finde a reader;) that al the worlde shaul evidently perceyve that no particular region may justely be more extollid then yours for trewe nobilitie and vertues at al pointes renoumed. Farthermore parte of the examplaries curiousely sought by me, and fortunately founde in sundry places of this yowr dominion, hath beene enprinted yn Germany, and now be yn the pressis chiefly of Frobenius that not al only the Germanes, but also the Italians them self, that counte, as the Grekes did ful arrogantely, al other nations to be barbarus and onletterid saving their owne, shaul have a directe occasion openly of force to say that *Britannia prima fuit parens, altrix,* (addo hoc etiam & jure quodam optimo) *conservatrix* cum virorum magnorum, tum maxime ingeniorum.

And that profite hath rysen by the aforesaide journey in bringging ful many thinges to lighte as concerning the usurpid autorite of the Bishop of Rome and his complices, to the manifeste and violente derogation of kingely dignite, I referre my self moste humbly to your moste prudente, lernid and highe jugement to discerne my diligence.

OOOOOOOOOOOOOOOOOOOOOOOOOOOOOOOOOOOOOOOOOOOOOOOOOOOOOOOOOOOOOO

1549

The BOOKE of COMMON PRAYER, Sacramentes & other Rites & Ceremonies of the Churche of England: **THOMAS CRANMER: LONDON**

[THE PREFACE]

Archbishop Cranmer obeyed his employer till the day before he died. He hid his wife when Henry wanted celibate clergy; saw to 4 of his king's divorces & 5 of his weddings; made a Bible in English for use by all when Henry wooed Protestants; denied it to women & labourers when Henry heard they seriously argued over it. In 1544

THERE was never any thing by the wit of man so well devised, or so surely established, which (in continuance of time) hath not been corrupted: as (emong other thinges) it may plainly appere by the common prayers in the Churche, commonlye called divine service: the firste originall and grounde whereof, if a manne woulde searche out by the auncient fathers, he shall finde that the same was not ordeyned, but of a good purpose, and for a great advancement of godlines: For they so ordred the matter, that all the whole Bible (or the greatest parte thereof) should be read over once in the yeare, intendying thereby, that the Cleargie, and specially suche as were Ministers of the congregacion, should (by often readying and meditacion of Gods worde) be stirred up to godlines themselfes, and be more able also to exhorte other by wholsome doctrine, and to confute them that were adversaries to the trueth. And further, that the people (by daily hearying of holy scripture read in the Churche) should continuallye profite more and more in the knowledge of God, and bee the more inflamed with the love of his true religion. But these many yeares passed this Godly and decent ordre of the auncient fathers, hath bee so altered, broken, and neglected, by planting in uncertein stories, Legendes, Respondes, Verses, vaine repeticions, Commemoracions, and Synodalles, that commonly when any boke of the Bible was begon: before three or foure Chapiters were read out, all the rest were unread. And in this sorte the boke of Esaie was begon in Advent, and the booke of Genesis in Septuagesima: but they were onely begon, and never read thorow. After a like sorte wer other bokes of holy scripture used. And moreover, whereas s. Paule would have suche language spoken to the people in the churche, as they mighte understande and have profite by hearyng the same; the service in this Churche of England (these many yeares) hath been read in Latin to the people, whiche they understoode not; so that they have heard with theyr eares onely; and their hartes, spirite, and minde, have not been edified thereby. And furthermore, notwithstandyng that the auncient fathers had devided the psalmes into seven porcions, whereof every one was called a nocturne, now of late tyme a fewe of them have been dailye sayed (and ofte repeated) and the rest utterly omitted. Moreover the nombre and hardnes of the rules called the pie, and the manifolde

Henry, upset for the 1st time by ill health & useless war, wished all England to sing & pray together for unity & victory; Cranmer Englished an old familiar chant in Latin, removed prayers to saints, added ones for the king & victory, & thus moved England toward a Protestant church service.

Henry died in 1547 leaving a son of 10. The council ruling for him wanted more church property. They thought a more Puritan church would let them take it, so created a Calvinist bishop, 2 similar professors of theology at Oxford & Cambridge, & ordered Cranmer to provide an English church service. In trying to please as many folk as possible he made a prayer book more Catholic than his commissioners wanted. Using a Roman breviary revised by a Spanish cardinal he restored the Church of England service to what he thought was its true Catholic state before corruption set in. From Protestant German & Greek Orthodox litany he also borrowed, & though a timid man his English was strong & clear. Changes made in later years were too small to injure a service book that is still mostly Cranmer's words.

chaunginges of the service, was the cause, that to turne the boke onlye, was so hard and intricate a matter, that many times, there was more busines to fynd out what should be read, then to read it when it was founde out.

These inconveniences therfore considered: here is set furth suche an ordre, whereby the same shalbe redressed. And for a readines in this matter, here is drawen out a Kalendar for that purpose, whiche is plaine and easy to be understanded, wherin (so muche as maie be) the readying of holy scripture is so set furthe, that all thynges shall bee doen in ordre, without breakyng one piece therof from another. For this cause be cut of Anthemes, Respondes, Invitatories, and suche like thynges, as did breake the continuall course of the readying of the scripture. Yet because there is no remedy, but that of necessitie there must be some rules: therfore certein rules are here set furth, whiche as they be few in nombre; so they be plain and easy to be understanded. So that here you have an ordre for praier (as touchyng the readying of holy scripture) muche agreable to the mynde and purpose of the olde fathers, and a greate deale more profitable and commodious, than that whiche of late was used. It is more profitable, because here are left out many thynges, whereof some be untrue, some uncertein, some vain and supersticious: and is ordeyned nothyng to be read, but the very pure worde of God, the holy scriptures, or that whiche is evidently grounded upon the same; and that in suche a language and ordre, as is moste easy and plain for the understandying, bothe of the readers and hearers. It is also more commodious, bothe for the shortnes thereof, and for the plaines of the ordre, and for that the rules be fewe and easy. Furthermore by this ordre, the curates shal nede none other bookes for their publique service, but this boke and the Bible: by the meanes whereof, the people shall not be at so great charge for bookes, as in tyme past they have been.

And where heretofore, there hath been great diversitie in saying and synging in churches within this realme: some folowyng Salsbury use, some Herford use, some the use of Bangor, some of Yorke, and some of Lincolne: Now from hencefurth, all the whole realme shall have but one use. And if any would judge this waye more painfull, because that all thynges must be read upon the boke, whereas before, by the reason of so often repeticion, they could saye many thinges by heart: if those men will waye their labor, with the profite in knowlege, whiche dayely they shal obtein by readyng upon the boke, they will not refuse the payn, in consideracion of the greate profite that shall ensue thereof.

And forsomuche as nothyng can, almoste, be so plainly set furth, but doubtes maie rise in the use and practisyng of the same: to appease all suche diversitie (if any arise), and for the resolucion of all doubtes, concernyng the manner how to understande, do, and execute the thynges conteygned in this booke: the parties that so doubt, or diversly take any thyng, shall alwaye resorte to the Bishop of the Diocese, who by his discrecion shall take ordre for the quietyng and appeasyng of the same: so that the same ordre be not contrary to any thyng conteigned in this boke.

Though it be appointed in the afore written preface, that al thinges shalbe read and song in the churche, in the Englishe tongue, to thende that the congregacion maie be therby edified: yet it is not meant, but when men saye Matins and Evensong privatelye, they maye saie the same in any language that they themselves do understande. Neither that anye man shalbe bound to the saying of them, but suche as from tyme to tyme, in Cathedrall and Collegiate Churches, Parishe Churches, and Chapelles to the same annexed, shall serve the congregacion.

***SONGES & SONETTES by the Right Honourable Lorde Henry Howard late Earle of Surrey & Others. Edited by* RICHARD TOTTEL: LONDON**

1557

[THE PRINTER TO THE READER]

THAT to have wel written in verse, yea & in small parcelles, deserveth great praise, the workes of divers Latines, Italians, and other, doe prove sufficiently. That our tong is able in that kynde to do as praiseworthely as the rest, the honorable stile of the noble earle of Surrey, and the weightinesse of the depewitted sir Thomas Wyat the elders verse, with severall graces in sondry good Englishe writers, doe show abundantly. It resteth nowe (gentle reder) that thou thinke it not evill doon, to publish, to the honor of the Englishe tong, and for profit of the studious of Englishe eloquence, those workes which the ungentle horders up of such treasure have

*Courtiers of Henry VIII privately exchanged many forms of verse. Love of Italian gave the lines polite sweet smoothness, & after Tottel published them that was what poets aimed at for centuries. Wyatt's love sonnets, Surrey's **Aeneid** did most good. Surrey drew sense & ease from the Douglas **Eneados**, went beyond it, dropped end-rhyme & invented the blank verse used later by the greatest English playwrights.*

heretofore envied thee. And for this point (good reader) thine own profit and pleasure, in these presently, and in moe hereafter, shal answere for my defence. If parhappes some mislike the statelinesse of stile removed from the rude skill of common eares: I aske help of the learned to defend their learned frendes, the authors of this work: And I exhort the unlearned, by reding to learne to be more skilfull, and to purge that swinelike grossenesse, that maketh the swete majerome not to smell to their delight.

1560

CONFESSION OF FAITH AND DOCTRINE
Belevit and professit be the Protestantis of Scotland
JOHN KNOX: EDINBURGH

THE ESTAITIS OF SCOTLAND WITH THE INHABITANTS OF THE SAME PROFESSAND CHRIST JESUS HIS HALY EVANGEL, TO THEIR NATURAL COUNTRYMEN, AND UNTO ALL UTHER REALMES PROFESSAND THE SAME LORD JESUS WITH THEM, WISH GRACE, MERCIE AND PEACE FRA GOD THE FATHER OF OUR LORD JESUS CHRIST, WITH THE SPIRIT OF RICHTEOUS JUDGEMENT, FOR SALVATIOUN.

England's Protestant monarchs ruled their church with the same system of archbishop & bishop that kept other lands Catholic. Scotland never had an archbishop because its geology, poverty & bad roads stopped any 1 bishop dominating the rest. From 1542 to 80 Scotland was kingless too. English & French troops skirmished in her. The parliament was shifty cliques of lords bribed by both foreign governments. In those years many Scottish Protestants turned to Calvinism, a religion invented for Swiss whose land was also subdivided by

L ANG have we thristed, dear Brethren, to have notified to the Warld the Sum of that Doctrine quhilk we professe, and for the quhilk we have susteined Infamie and Danger: Bot sik hes bene the Rage of Sathan againis us, and againis *Christ Jesus* his eternal Veritie latlie now againe born amangst us, that to this daie na Time hes been graunted unto us to cleir our Consciences, as maist gladlie we wald have done. For how we have been tossit heirtofoir, the maist part of *Europe*, as we suppose, dois understand.

But seing that of the infinit Gudnes of our God (quha never sufferis his afflickit utterlie to be confoundit) abone Expectation we have obteined sum Rest and Libertie, we culd not bot set furth this brefe and plaine Confessioun of sik Doctrine as is proponed unto us, and as we beleeve and professe; partlie for Satisfactioun of our Brethren quhais hartis, we nathing doubt, have been and yit ar woundit be the despichtful rayling of sik as yit have not learned to speke well: And partlie for stapping the mouthis of impudent blasphemers, quha bauldlie damne that quhilk they have nouther heard nor yit understude.

Not that we judge that the cankred malice of sik is abill to be cured be this our simple confession; na, we knaw that the sweet savoure of the evangel is and sal be deathe to the sonnes of perditioun. Bot we have chief respect to our weak and infirme brethren, to quham we wald communicate the bottom of our hartes, leist that they be troubiled or carried awaie be diversity of rumoris, quhilk Sathan spredis abroad againist us to the defeating of this our maist godlie interprize: Protestand that gif onie man will note in this our confessioun onie Artickle or sentence repugnand to Gods halie word, that it wald pleis him of his gentleness and for christian charities sake to admonish us of the same in writing; and we upon our honoures and fidelitie, be Gods grace do promise unto him satisfactioun fra the mouth of God, that is, fra his haly scriptures, or else reformation of that quhilk he sal prove to be amisse. For God we take to recorde in our consciences, that fra our heartis we abhorre all sectis of heresie and all teachers of erronious doctrine: and that with all humilitie we imbrace the purity of *Christs Gospell*, quhilk is the onelie fude of our sauls, and therefoir sa precious unto us, that we ar determined to suffer the extremest of warldlie daunger, rather than that we will suffer our selves to be defraudit of the sam. For heirof we ar maist certainlie perswadit, that quhasumever denieis Christ Jesus, or is aschamit of him in the presence of men, sal be denyit befoir the Father, and befoir his haly Angels. And therefoir be the assistance of the michtie Spirit of the same our Lord Jesus Christ, we firmelie purpose to abide to the end in the confessioun of this our faith, as be Artickles followis.

mountains & poor in soil. This faith used only 1 level of priest & was led locally by popular preachers.

*John Knox led Scotland's Calvinists. Commoners liked his strong faith, rhetoric & defiance of those in power. Folk who had grabbed church goods supported him because religions with bishops would demand some of them back. Even Queen Elizabeth of England, who disliked Calvinism & Knox, supported him since she feared Mary, Queen of Scots & her Catholic allies more. So with that support & in this **Confession**, Knox gave Scotland a presbyterian kirk. To make sure it would bring the Bible to all, in 1560 he printed too a plan of education to unite kirk & state. All clergy would be headmasters of local schools that taught children from every social class equally well. Grants would help capable sons of the poor to university. All would be funded by a tax on what had been church lands. **No rich people supported this idea!** Knox damned the Protestant Scots lords as viler than the abbots they had robbed. For centuries the kirk he founded was the poorest in Britain & a busy disturber of her governments.*

1563

ACTES AND MONUMENTES OF CHRISTIAN MARTYRS
JOHN FOXE: LONDON

*Many were amazed by England's obedience to her monarch's shifting religions. In 1530 she seemed as Catholic as Spain. Henry's doings provoked only 1 swiftly crushed revolt. Under Edward VI priests in the act of traditional old rituals were insulted by Puritans with an impunity that would have made Queen Mary Tudor's restoring of Catholic services a relief to most folk, if she had not married Philip of Spain & begun burning clergy who had agreed with her half-brother & dad. Disease, not rebellion, ended her short reign. Then came Elizabeth, who **had** to be Protestant because the pope said Anne Boleyn, her mum, had not been her dad's legal wife. So England went protestant again.*

Foxe studied at Oxford, taught sons of Protestant nobles, & in Mary's reign fled to Germany with others who feared her. There he lived by correcting printers' proofs, & in 1554 published a Latin version of this book at Stuttgart. Elizabeth became queen in 1558. Foxe came home & was welcomed by folk in

CHRIST our Saviour in the Gospell of S. Mathew, Cap. 16. hearing the confession of Simon Peter, who first of all other openlye acknowledged him to be the sonne of God, and perceaving the secret hand of his father therin, aunswered agayne and alludyng to his name, called him a Rocke, upon which Rocke he would buylde his Church so strong, that the gates of Hell should not prevaile against it.&c. In which wordes three things are to be noted: First, that Christ will have a Churche in this world. Secondly that the same Church should mightely be impugned, not onely by the world, but also by the uttermost strength & powers of all hell. And thirdly, that the same Church notwith-standyng the uttermost of the devill & all his malice should continue. Which Prophesie of Christ, we see wonderfully to be verified. In somuch that the whole course of the Churche to this day, may seeme nothyng els but a verifying of the sayd Prophesie. First that Christ hath set up a Church needeth no declaration. Secondly, what force, what sides and sortes of men, of Princes, Kynges, Monarches, Governours, and rulers of this world, with their subjectes publikely & privately, with all their strength & cunnyng have bent them selves against this Church. And thirdly, how the sayd Church all this notwithstandyng hath yet endured & holden his own. What stormes & tempestes it hath overpast, wonderous it is to behold. For the most evident declaration wherof, I have addressed this present history, entendyng, by the favorable ayde of Christ our Lord, not so much to delight the eares of my countrey in readyng of newes, as most especially to profite the harts of the godly in perusing antiquities of auncient tymes, to the ende, that the wonderfull workes of God first in his Church might appeare to his glory. Also that the continuaunce and proccedings of the Church from tyme to tyme beyng set forth in these Actes and Monumentes, more knowledge and experience may redound therby to the profite of the Reader, and edification of Christian faith.

For the better accomplishyng wherof, so to prosecute the matter, as may best serve to the profite of the Reader, I have thought good first, begynnyng from the tyme of the primitive Church, & so continuyng (by the Lordes grace) to these latter yeares, to runne over the whole state and course of the Church in generall, in such order as digesting the whole tractation of this history, into five sundry diversities of tymes:

First, I will entreat of the suffring tyme of the Church which continued from the Apostles age about 300. yeres.

Secondly, of the florishyng time of the Church, which lasted other 300. yeares.

Thirdly, of the declinyng or backeslidyng tyme of the Church, which comprehendeth other 300. yeares, untill the loosing out of Sathan, which was about the thousand yeare after the ceasing of persecution. During which space of tyme, the Church, although in ambition & pride, it was much altered from the simple sinceritie of the Primitive tyme, yet in outward profession of doctrine and religion, it was somethyng tollerable, & had some face of a Church: notwithstanding some corruption of doctrine, with superstition and hypocrisie was then also crept in. And yet in comparison of that as followed after, it might seeme (as I sayd) somethyng sufferable.

Fourthly, foloweth the tyme of Antichrist, and loosing of Sathan, or desolation of the Church, whose full swyng conteineth the space of 400. yeares. In which tyme, both doctrine and sinceritie of life, was utterly almost extinguished, namely, in the chiefe heades and rulers of this west church, through the meanes of the Romaune Byshops, especially countyng from Gregory the vii. called *Hildebrand, Innocentius* the iii. and Friers which with him crept in, til the tyme of *John Wickliffe*, & *John Husse*, duryng 400. yeres.

*power, 1 of whom was an ex-pupil. Foxe refused a good job in the re-reformed English church (the priests' dresses struck him as too Roman) but he accepted a sinecure & rewrote in English his history of Christianity, bringing it up to date with the folk burned under Mary. It shows snow-white Christians defeating soot-black enemies by bravely dying for their faith. As in most propaganda, no honest enemies, few ignoble allies of the writer's party appear. Foxe's **Book of Martyrs** gave Protestants in Britain what Saints Augustine & Aquinas gave Catholics everywhere; an account of how **their** church was built on foundations laid by Jesus & his apostles. This preface says how Foxe divided over 1500 years into a dramatic & satisfying shape. The Christians martyred by Roman Caesars at the start were balanced by Protestants the Roman church martyred just before the end when godly English and Scots Protestant churches had finally triumphed. The British Protestant temper was shaped by the Bible & this book. Episcopalians, Presbyterians & dissenting evangelists used it.*

Fiftly and lastly, after this tyme of Antichrist, raigning in the Church of God by violence and tyranny, followeth the reformation & purgyng of the church of God, wherein Antichrist begynneth to be revealed, and to appeare in his coulors, and his Antichristian doctrine to be detected, the number of his Church decreasing, and the number of the true Church increasing. The durance of which tyme hath continued hetherto about the space of 280. yeres, and how long shall continue more, thc Lord and governour of all tymes, he onely knoweth.

For in these five diversities & alterations of tymes, I suppose the whole course of the Church may well be comprised. The which Church, because it is universall, and sparsedly through all countreys dilated, therfore in this history standing upon such a generall argument I shall not be bound to any one certaine nation, more then an other: yet notwithstandyng keepyng mine argument aforesayd, I have purposed principally to tary upon such historicall actes and recordes, as most apertaine to this my country of England and Scotland.

1565

Ovidius Nasos METAMORPHOSIS The Fyrst 4 Bookes translated into English meter by **ARTHUR GOLDING GENT.: LONDON**

I WOULD not wish the simple sort offended for too bee,
When in this booke the heathen names of feynèd Godds they see.
The trewe and everliving God the Paynims did not knowe:
Which causèd them the name of Godds on creatures too bestowe.
For nature beeing once corrupt and knowledge blynded quyght
By Adams fall, those little seedes and sparkes of heavenly lyght
That did as yit remayne in man, endevering foorth too burst
And wanting grace and powre too growe too that they were at furst,
Too superstition did decline: and drave the fearefull mynd,
Straunge woorshippes of the living God in creatures for too fynd.
The which by custome taking roote, and growing so too strength,
Through Sathans help possest the hartes of all the world at length.
Some woorshipt all the hoste of heaven:
                              some deadmens ghostes & bones:
Sum wicked feends: sum woormes & fowles,
                              herbes, fishes, trees & stones.
The fyre, the ayre, the sea, the land, and every ronning brooke,
Eche queachie grove, eche cragged cliffe
                              the name of Godhead tooke.

The nyght and day, the fleeting howres, the seasons of the yeere,
And every straunge and monstruous thing,
                    for Godds mistaken weere.
There was no vertue, no nor vice: there was no gift of mynd
Or bodye, but some God thertoo or Goddesse was assignde.
But as there is no Christen man that can surmyse in mynd
That theis or other such are Goddes which are no Goddes by kynd:
So would too God there were not now of christen men profest,
That worshipt in theyr deedes theis Godds
                    whose names they doo detest.
Whoose lawes wee keepe his thralles wee bee,
                    and he our God indeede.
So long is Christ our God as wee in Christen lyfe proceede.
But if wee yeeld too fleshlye lust, too lucre, or too wrath,
Or if that Envy, Gluttony, or Pryde the maystry hath,
Or any other kynd of sinne the thing the which wee serve
Too be accounted for our God most justly dooth deserve.
Then must wee thinke the learned men that did theis names frequent,
Some further things and purposes by those devises ment.
By Jove and Juno understand all states of princely port:
By Ops and Saturne auncient folke that are of elder sort:
By Phoebus yoong and lusty brutes of hand and courage stout:
By Mars the valeant men of warre that love too feight it out.
By Pallas and the famous troupe of all the Muses nyne,
Such folke as in the sciences and vertuous artes doo shyne.
By Mercurie the suttle sort that use too filch and lye,
With theeves, and Merchants whoo too gayne
                    theyr travell do applye.
By Bacchus all the meaner trades and handycraftes are ment:
By Venus such as of the fleshe too filthie lust are bent,
By Neptune such as keepe the sea: by Phebe maydens chast,
And Pilgrims such as wandringly theyr tyme in travell waste.
By Pluto such as delve in mynes, and Ghostes of persones dead:
By Vulcane smythes and such as woorke in yron, tynne or lead.
By Hecat witches, Conjurers, and Necromancers reede,
With all such vayne and devlish artes as superstition breede.
Fowre kynd of things in this his worke the Poet dooth conteyne.
That nothing under heaven dooth ay in stedfast state remayne.

And next that nothing perisheth: but that eche substance takes
Another shape than that it had. Of theis twoo points he makes
The proof by shewing through his woorke the wonderfull exchaunge
Of Goddes, men, beasts, and elements,
                                    too sundry shapes right straunge,
Beginning with creation of the world, and man of slyme,
And so proceeding with the turnes that happened till his tyme.

OOOOOOOOOOOOOOOOOOOOOOOOOOOOOOOOOOOOOOOOOOOOOOOOOOOOOOOOOOOOO

*Lovers of duty & authority thought Virgil the greatest Latin poet. Lovers of fun & games preferred Ovid, whose poetry was too full of sex & magic to promote life as a hard task. Most Christians were taught life **should** be a hard task, so this preface says that Ovid's wild tales of extinct gods hold deep truths. The most notable is, all things turn into others but more surprisingly than ensured by fortune's wheel. Golding's jog-trot couplets spread classical myths that only scholars had hitherto enjoyed. His English, harsh & informative, inspired greater poets, Shakespeare included. Golding was friend of Sir Philip Sydney whose **Defence of Poesy** told England that her lasting glory needed great new writing as much as wealth & victories. Many wanted all 3. Translation & trade brought to Britain both new ideas & goods.*

OOOOOOOOOOOOOOOOOOOOOOOOOOOOOOOOOOOOOOOOOOOOOOOOOOOOOOOOOOOOO

1570

THE SCHOLEMASTER
ROGER ASCHAM
LONDON

[A PRÆFACE TO THE READER]

Though a Protestant, Ascham was prudent enough to become the Latin secretary to Queen Mary & Queen Elizabeth. Like many Renaissance scholars he thought sport as essential as reading & and was one of those who made it a great part of English public schooling. He also wrote a fine treatise on archery. These long sentences, built from carefully punctuated short phrases, show as much of his nature as the talk he reports.

WHEN the great plage was at London, the yeare 1563. the Quenes Majestie Queene *Elizabeth*, lay at her Castle of Windsore: Where, upon the 10. day of December, it fortuned, that in *Sir William Cicells* chamber, hir Highnesse Principall Secretarie, there dined togither these personages, M. Secretarie him selfe, Syr *William Peter*, Syr *J. Mason*, *D. Wotton*, Syr *Richard Sackville* Treasurer of the Exchecker, Syr *Walter Mildmaye* Chauncellor of the Exchecker, M. *Haddon* Master of Requestes, M. *John Astely* Master of the Jewell house, M. *Bernard Hampton*, M. *Nicasius*, and *I*. Of which number, the most part were of hir Majesties most honourable privie Counsell, and the reast serving hir in verie good place. I was glad than, and do rejoice yet to remember, that my chance was so happie, to be there that day, in the companie of so manie wise & good men togither, as hardly than could have beene piked out againe, out of all England beside.

M. Secretarie hath this accustomed maner, though his head be never so full of most weightie affaires of the Realme, yet, at diner time he doth seeme to lay them alwaies aside: and findeth ever fitte occasion to taulke pleasantlie of other matters, but most gladlie of some matter of learning: wherein, he will curteslie heare the minde of the meanest at his Table.

Not long after our sitting doune, I have strange newes brought me, sayth M. Secretarie, this morning, that diverse Scholers of Eaton, be runne awaie from the Schole, for feare of beating. Whereupon, M. Secretarie tooke occasion. to wishe, that some more discretion were in many Scholemasters, in using correction, than commonlie there is. Who many times, punishe rather, the weakenes of nature, than the fault of the Scholer. Whereby, many Scholers, that might else prove well, be driven to hate learning, before they knowe, what learning meaneth: and so, are made willing to forsake their booke, and be glad to be put to any other kinde of living.

M. *Peter*, as one somewhat severe of nature, said plainlie, that the Rodde onelie, was the sworde, that must keepe, the Schole in obedience, and the Scholer in good order. M. *Wotton*, à man milde of nature, with soft voice, and fewe wordes, inclined to M. Secretaries judgement, and said, in mine opinion, the Scholehouse should be in deede, as it is called by name, the house of playe and pleasure, and not of feare and bondage: and as I do remember, so saith *Socrates* in one place of *Plato*. And therefore, if à Rodde carie the feare of à Sworde, it is no marvell, if those that be fearefull of nature, chose rather to forsake the Plaie, than to stand alwaies within the feare of à Sworde in à fonde mans handling. M. *Mason*, after his maner, was verie merie with both parties, pleasantlie playing, both, with the shrewde touches of many courste boyes, and with the small discretion of many leude Scholemasters. M. *Haddon* was fullie of M. *Peters* opinion, and said, that the best Scholemaster of our time, was the greatest beater, and named the Person. Though, quoth I, it was his good fortune, to send from his Schole, unto the Universitie, one of the best Scholers in deede of all our time, yet wise men do thinke, that that came so to passe, rather, by the great towardnes of the Scholer, than by the great beating of the Master: and whether this be true or no, you your selfe are best witnes. I said somewhat farder in the matter, how, and whie, yong children, were soner allured by love, than driven by beating, to atteyne good learning: wherein I was the bolder to say my minde, bicause M. Secretarie curteslie provoked me thereunto: or else, in such à companie, and namelie in his præsence, my wonte is, to be more willing, to use mine eares, than to occupie my tonge.

Syr *Walter Mildmaye*, M. *Astley* and the rest, said verie litle: onelie Syr *Rich. Sackvill*, said nothing at all. After dinner I went up to read with the Queenes Majestie. We red than togither in the Greke tongue, as I well remember, that noble Oration of *Demosthenes* against *Æschines*, for his false dealing in his Ambassage to king *Philip* of Macedonie. Syr *Rich. Sackvile* came up sone after: and finding me in hir Majesties privie chamber, he tooke me by the hand, & carying me to à windoe, said, M. *Ascham*, I would not for à good deale of monie, have bene, this daie, absent from diner. Where, though I said nothing, yet I gave as good eare, and do consider as well the taulke, that passed, as any one did there. M. Secretarie said very wisely, and most truely, that many yong wittes be driven to hate learninge, before they know what learninge is. I can be good witnes to this my selfe: For à fond Scholemaster, before I was fullie fourtene yeare olde, drave me so, with feare of beting, from all love of learninge, as nowe, when I know, what difference it is, to have learninge, and to have litle, or none at all, I feele it my greatest greife, and finde it my greatest hurte, that ever came to me, that it was my so ill chance, to light upon so lewde à Scholemaster. But seing it is but in vain, to lament thinges paste, and also wisdome to looke to thinges to cum, surely, God willinge, if God lend me life, I will make this my mishap, some occasion of good hap, to litle *Robert Sackvile* my sonnes sonne. For whose bringinge up, I would gladlie, if it so please you, use speciallie your good advice. I heare saie, you have à sonne, moch of his age: we wil deale thus togither. Point you out à Scholemaster, who by your order, shall teache my sonne and yours, and for all the rest, I will provide, yea though they three do cost me à couple of hundred poundes by yeare: and beside, you shall finde me as fast à Frend to you and yours, as perchance any you have. Which promise, the worthie Jentleman surely kept with me, untill his dying daie.

We had than farther taulke togither, of bringing up of children: of the nature, of quicke, and hard wittes: of the right choice of à good witte: of Feare, and love in teachinge children. We passed from children and came to yonge men, namely, Jentlemen: we taulked of their to moch libertie, to live as they lust: of their letting louse to sone, to over moch experience of ill, contrarie to the good order of many good olde common welthes of the Persians and Grekes: of witte gathered, and good fortune gotten, by some, onely by experience, without learning. And lastlie, he required of me verie earnestlie, to shewe, what I thought of the common goinge of Englishe men into Italie. But, sayth he, bicause this place, and this tyme, will not suffer so long taulke, as these good matters require, therefore I pray you, at my request, and at your leysure, put in some order of writing, the cheife pointes of this our taulke, concerning the right order of teachinge, and honestie of living, for the good bringing up of children & yong men. And surelie, beside contentinge me, you shall both please and profit verie many others.

PLUTARKE'S LIVES OF THE NOBLE GRECIANS AND ROMANES 1579
Englished By THOMAS NORTH: LONDON

COMPARED TOGETHER BY THAT GRAVE LEARNED PHILOSOPHER AND HISTORIOGRAPHER PLUTARKE OF CHÆRONEA, TRANSLATED OUT OF GREEKE INTO FRENCH BY JAMES AMYOT, BISHOP OF AUXERRE, ONE OF THE KINGS PRIVY COUNSEL, AND OUT OF FRENCH INTO ENGLISHE BY THOMAS NORTH – TO THE READER –

THE profit of stories, and the prayse of the Author, are sufficiently declared by Amiot, in his Epistle to the Reader: So that I shall not neede to make many wordes thereof. And in deede if you will supply the defects of this translation, with your own diligence and good understanding: you shall not neede to trust him, you may prove your selves, that there is no prophane studye better then Plutarke. All other learning is private, fitter for Universities then cities, fuller of contemplacion than experience, more commendable in the students them selves, than profitable unto others. Whereas stories are fit for every place, reache to all persons, serve for all tymes, teache the living, revive the dead, so farre excelling all other bookes, as it is better to see learning in noble mens lives, than to reade it in Philosophers writings. Nowe for the Author, I will not denye but love may deceive me, for I must needes love him with whome I have taken so much payne: but I beleve I might be bold to affirme, that he hath written the profitablest story of all Authors. For all other were fayne to take their matter, as the fortune of the contries whereof they

*North wrote this when profound matters were freely written about in English, & authors & tranlators had invented new words to discuss fine ideas. Sir Thomas Elyot (for example) gave us **dictionary**, **sincerity**, **mediocrity**, **democracy**, **society** ending in **ie, ye**, or **ey**. In Orwell's **1984** an evil society destroys ideas by banning words for them. Between 1525 & 1625 over 11,000 words still in use were made by Englishing Greek, Latin, French & Italian words. These did not swamp wise writers who cruelly mocked verbal pretension. They gave exactness to North's bold, easy accounts of republican politics.*

wrote fell out: But this man being excellent in wit, learning, and experience, hath chosen the speciall actes of the best persons, of the famosest nations of the world. But I will leave the judgement to your selves. My onely purpose is to desire you to excuse the faults of my translation, with your owne gentlenes, and with the opinion of my diligence and good entent. And so I wishe you all the profit of the booke. Fare ye well.

The foure and twenty day of Ianuary. 1579. THOMAS NORTH.

1587
THE HISTORIE OF ENGLAND
RAPHAEL HOLINSHED
LONDON

FROM THE TIME ENGLAND WAS FIRST INHABITED, UNTILL THE TIME THAT IT WAS LAST CONQUERED: WHEREIN THE SUNDRIE ALTERATIONS OF THE STATE UNDER FORREN PEOPLE IS DECLARED ; AND OTHER MANIFOLD OBSERVATIONS.

1588
THE NEW FOUND LAND OF VIRGINIA
THOMAS HARIOT
LONDON

These 2 titles end a chapter showing knowledge available to British readers in the last years of the 16th century. Their Bible, with its intricate prehistory, answered 4 questions on page 32 in ways that satisfied both wise & ignorant. Foxe brought Christian history up to date for Protestants. Holinshed brought politics up to date, showing centuries of British warfare end in peace under Tudor monarchs: the theme of Shakespeare's history plays. This last book is part of Sir Walter Raleigh's campaign to make England's empire as big as Spain's by adding North America (like Ireland) through colonising it.

A BRIEFE AND TRUE REPORT OF THE COMMODITIES THERE FOUND AND TO BE RAYSED, AS WELL MARCHANTABLE, AS OTHERS FOR VICTUALL, BUILDING AND OTHER NECESSARIE USES FOR THOSE THAT ARE AND SHALBE THE PLANTERS THERE; AND OF THE NATURE AND MANNERS OF THE NATURALL INHABITANTS: DISCOVERED BY THE ENGLISH COLONY THERE SEATED BY SIR RICHARD GREINVILE KNIGHT IN THE YEERE 1585, WHICH REMAINED UNDER THE GOVERNMENT OF RAFE LANE ESQUIER, ONE OF HER MAJESTIES ESQUIERS, DURING THE SPACE OF TWELVE MONTHES: AT THE SPECIALL CHARGE AND DIRECTION OF THE HONOURABLE SIR WALTER RALEIGH, LORD WARDEN OF THE STANNERIES; WHO THEREIN HATH BEENE FAVOURED AND AUTHORISED BY HER MAJESTIE AND HER LETTERS PATENTS.

THE ARMADA INTERLUDE

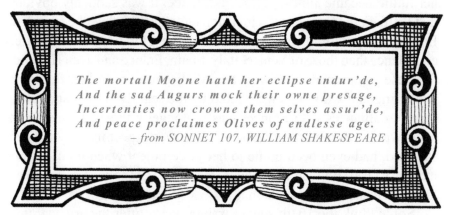

> *The mortall Moone hath her eclipse indur'de,*
> *And the sad Augurs mock their owne presage,*
> *Incertenties now crowne them selves assur'de,*
> *And peace proclaimes Olives of endlesse age.*
>   *– from SONNET 107, WILLIAM SHAKESPEARE*

THE MORTALL MOONE WAS THE BIGGEST FLEET in the world, moving eastward along the Channel in roughly crescent formation during the last eleven days of July, 1588. It contained one hundred and thirty ships, half of them sea-castles carrying an army of over seventeen thousand soldiers, all blessed by the Pope and paid for by Spain. This was the Catholic crusade against England which a generation of worried Protestants there (*sad Augurs*) had been dreading. For thirty years their queen and her counsellors had lied, plotted and prevaricated to prevent it. Elizabeth's power seemed very small compared with King Philip's. England's only empire now was over the Irish, who often gave their English landlords more pain than profit. Spain was the first European state to control an empire bigger than Rome's, an empire on which the sun never set – when daylight faded on Philip's Spanish and Flemish possessions it was brightening his colonies in Mexico, Chile, Brazil and the Argentine. But war was now inevitable between these unequal empires. English ships equipped by merchant bankers in London and Bristol had broken the Spanish monopoly of American trade and plundered Spanish shipping. Queen Elizabeth had apologized to King Philip for the piracy while welcoming the pirates among her courtiers. They were applauded as heroes by the English people, were good for English business, and increased the royal revenues.

For eleven days the Armada sought a position from which to attack, but efficient squadrons of the small English and Dutch vessels outmanoeuvred it until bad winds and a storm broke it up so completely that it could never come together again. England's *incertenties* about her future became almost perfect assurance. It was suddenly obvious that William the Conqueror's invasion tactic would never be repeated. English ships could now trade round the globe with far greater confidence than those of Venice, Italy, Spain, France and even Holland, for these continental states were always disputing over their frontiers, while England's frontiers were fixed by the sea. Even Scotland (once prone to alliances with France) was no longer a threat. Jamie Stuart hated warfare as much as Elizabeth Tudor, was expecting her job when she died, had even been polite to her government when it cut off his mother's head. English Protestants, and many Catholics too, believed that *peace* had at last proclaimed *Olives of endlesse age.*

Some think the 107th sonnet written years after the armada; that the crooked moon is the old virgin queen whose flatterers kept likening her to the chaste moon goddess; and sad augurs were pessimists who thought her death would cause turmoils like those after earlier reigns; that peace proclaims olives of endless age because the 6th Jamie Stuart settled on her throne without bloodshed. Both explanations show that Shakespeare, like Chaucer, can accommodate several meanings in the same words. The sonnet ends thus –

> *Now with the drops of this most balmie time,*
> *My love lookes fresh, and death to me subscribes,*
> *Since spight of him Ile live in this poore rime,*
> *While he insults ore dull and speachlesse tribes.*
> *And thou in this shalt finde thy monumente,*
> *When tyrants crests and tombs of brasse are spent.*

– so the prospering social climate cheered Shakespeare's lover and inspired the poet, either in 1588 or 1603.

We can imagine peace as a winged female soaring in the sky with a herald's trumpet in one hand and a garland of olive leaves in the other. She holds it above a map of the British archipelago, which is engraved with small galleons sailing into all the south British ports, bringing slaves from Africa, silk from India, sugar, tobacco and gold from the Americas. In the century before, citizens of Italian republics had felt they were at the start of a great new era. For a short while scholars like Erasmus and More had felt it. So, in a more savage way, did Luther, Calvin and Knox. The feeling was now widespread in England.

A Great Flowering

1589

THE PRINCIPALL NAVIGATIONS, VOIAGES and DISCOVERIES of the ENGLISH NATION
RICHARD HAKLUYT: LONDON

[TO THE FAVOURABLE READER]

*In 1852 when Britain's empire was the biggest on earth J.A. Froude called this the **prose epic** of the modern English nation. In Hakluyt's childhood most atlases & globes were imaginative works with blank spaces & errors he lusted to fill & correct. He came to teach geography at Oxford & gathered factual reports from English sea captains, a new kind of men who, as profit directed, traded, plundered, explored, enslaved or colonised in small ships along every Atlantic & Pacific coast. Their chiefs (Drake, Raleigh, Hawkins) were courtiers too & he made this guide book to the world with their own findings. Longitude could not then be exactly measured but by comparing the times of voyages Hakluyt helped to make maps seamen could trust. England's queen & politicians were then secretly investing in merchant adventure. They made Hakluyt chaplain of their Paris embassy, to spy on Catholic discoveries in America. His reports speeded the planting of English colonies there & earned him a sinecure in Bristol Cathedral.*

I HAVE thought it very requisite for thy further instruction and direction in this historie (Good Reader) to acquaint thee brieflie with the Methode and order which I have used in the whole course thereof: and by the way also to let thee understand by whose friendly aide in this my travell I have bene furthered: acknowledging that ancient speach to be no lesse true then ingenious, that the offence is great, *Non agnoscere per quos profeceris*, not to speake of them by whom a man in his indevours is assisted.

Concerning my proceeding therefore in this present worke, it hath bene this. Whatsoever testimonie I have found in any authour of authoritie appertaining to my argument, either stranger or naturall, I have recorded the same word for word, with his particular name and page of booke where it is extant. If the same were not reduced into our common language, I have first expressed it in the same termes wherein it is originally written, whether it were a Latine, Italian, Spanish or Portingall discourse, or whatsoever els, and thereunto in the next roome have annexed the signification and translation of the wordes in English. And to the ende that those men which were the paynefull and personall travellers might reape that good opinion and just commendation which they have deserved, and further, that every man might answere for himselfe, justifie his reports, and stand accountable for his owne doings, I have referred every voyage to his Author, which both in person hath performed, and in writing hath left the same: for I am not ignorant of Ptolomies assertion, that *Peregrinationis historia*, and not those wearie volumes bearing the titles of universall Cosmographie which some men that I could name have published as their owne, beyng in deed most untruly and unprofitablie ramassed and hurled together, is that which must bring us to the certayne and full discoverie of the world.

Moreover, I meddle in this worke with the Navigations onely of our owne nation: And albeit I alleage in a few places (as the matter and occasion required) some strangers as witnesses of the things done, yet are they none but such as either faythfully remember, or sufficiently confirme the travels of our owne people: of whom (to speake trueth) I have received more light in some respects, then all our owne Historians could affoord me in this case, Bale, Foxe, and Eden onely excepted.

And it is a thing withall principally to be considered, that I stand not upon any action perfourmed neere home, not in any part of Europe commonly frequented by our shipping, as for example: Not upon that victorious exploit not long since atchieved in our narrow Seas agaynst that monstrous Spanish army under the valiant and provident conduct of the right honourable the lord Charles Howard high Admirall of England: Not upon the good services of our two woorthie Generals in their late Portugall expedition: Not upon the two most fortunate attempts of our famous Chieftaine Sir Frauncis Drake, the one in the Baie of Cales upon a great part of the enimies chiefest shippes, the other neere the Islands upon the great Carrack of the East India, the first (though peradventure not the last) of that imployment, that ever discharged Molucca spices in English portes: these (albeit singular and happy voyages of our renowmed countrymen) I omit, as things distinct and without the compass of my prescribed limites, beyng neither of remote length and spaciousnesse, neither of search and discoverie of strange coasts, the chiefe subject of this my labour.

Thus much in brevitie shall serve thee for the generall order. I have disposed and digested the whole worke into 3. partes. In the first I have martialled all our voyages of any moment that have bene performed to the South and Southeast parts of the world, by which I chiefly meane that part of Asia which is neerest, and of the rest hithermost towards us: For I find that the oldest travels as well of the ancient Britains, as of the English, were ordinarie to Judea which is in Asia, termed by them the Holy land, principally for devotions sake according to the time, although I read in Joseph Bengorion a very authenticall Hebrew author, a testimonie of the passing of 20000. Britains valiant souldiours, to the siege and fearefull sacking of Jerusalem under the conduct of Vespasian and Titus the Romane

Emperour, a thing in deed of all the rest most ancient. But of latter dayes I see our men have pierced further into the East, have passed downe the mightie river Euphrates, have sayled from Balsara through the Persian gulfe to the Citie of Ormuz, and from thence to Chaul and Goa in the East India, which passages written by the parties themselves are herein to be read. To these I have added the Navigations of the English made for the parts of Africa, and either within or without the streights of Gibraltar: within, to Constantinople in Romania, to Alexandria, and Cayro in Egypt, to Tunez, to Goletta, to Malta, to Algier, and to Tripolis in Barbary: without, to Santa Cruz, to Asafi, to the Citie of Marocco, to the River of Senega, to the Isles of Cape Verde, to Guinea, to Benyn, and round about the dreadfull Cape of Bona Speranza, as far as Goa.

The north, and Northeasterne voyages of our nation I have produced in the second place, because our accesse to those quarters of the world is later and not so aunciant as the former: and yet some of our travailes that way be of more antiquitie by many hundred yeeres, then those that have bene made to the westerne coastes of America. Under this title thou shalt first finde the old northerne Navigations of our Brittish Kings, as of Arthur, of Malgo, of Edgar Pacificus the Saxon Monarch, with that also of Nicholaus de Linna under the north pole: next to them in consequence, the discoveries of the bay of Saint Nicholas, of Colgoieve, of Pechora, of the Isles of Vaigats, of Nova Zembla, and of the Sea eastwards towardes the river of Ob: after this, the opening by sea of the great Dukedome, and Empire of Russia, with the notable and strange journey of Master Jenkinson to Boghar in Bactria. Whereunto thou maist adde sixe of our voyages eleven hundred verstes up against the streame of Dwina to the towne of Vologhda: thence one hundred, and fourscore verstes by land to Yeraslave standing upon the mighty river of Volga: there hence above two thousand and five hundred versts downe the streame to the ancient marte Towne of Astracan, and so to the manifolde mouthes of Volga, and from thence also by ship over the Caspian sea into Media, and further then that also with Camels unto Georgia, Armenia, Hyrcania, Gillan, and the cheefest Cities of the Empire of Persia: wherein the Companie of Moscovie Marchants to the perpetuall honor of their Citie, and societie, have performed more then any one, yea then all the nations of Europe besides: which thing is also acknowledged by the most learned Cosmographers, and

Historiographers of Christendome, with whose testimonies I have concluded this second part.

Touching the westerne Navigations, and travailes of ours, they succeede naturallie in the third and last roome, forasmuch as those coastes, and quarters came last of all to our knowledge and experience. Herein thou shalt reade the attempt by Sea of the sonne of one of the Princes of Northwales, in sayling and searching towards the west more than 400. yeeres since: the offer made by Christopher Columbus that renowned Genouoys to the most sage Prince of noble memorie King Henrie the 7. with his prompt and cheerefull acceptation thereof, and the occasion whereupon it became fruitlesse, and at that time of no great effect to this kingdome: then followe the letters Patentes of the foresaid noble Prince given to John Cabot a Venetian and his 3. sonnes, to discover & conquer in his name, and under his Banners unknowen Regions: who with that royall incouragement & contribution of the king, and some assistance in charges of English Marchants departed with 5. sailes from the Port of Bristoll accompained with 300. Englishmen, and first of any Christians found out that mightie and large tract of lande and Sea, from the circle Arcticke as farre as Florida, as appeareth in the discourse thereof. The triumphant raigne of King Henry the 8. yelded some prosecution of this discoverie: for the 3. voyages performed, and the 4. intended for all Asia by his Majesties selfe, do confirme the same. Then ariseth the first English trade to Brasill, the first passing of some of our nation in the Spanish fleetes to the west Indies, and the huge Citie of Mexico in Nova Hispania. Then immediatlye ensue 3. voyages made by M. John Hawkins now Knight, then Esquire, to Hispaniola, and the gulfe of Mexico: upon which depende sixe verie excellent discourses of our men, whereof some for 15. or 16. whole yeeres inhabited in New Spaine, and ranged the whole Countrie, wherein are disclosed the cheefest secretes of the west India, which may in time turne to our no smal advantage. The next leaves thou turnest, do yeelde thee the first valiant enterprise of Sir Francis Drake upon Nombre de Dios, the mules laden with treasure which he surprised, and the house called the Cruzes, which his fire consumed: and therewith is joyned an action more venterous then happie of John Oxnam of Plimmouth written, and confessed by a Spanyard, which with his companie passed over the streight Istme of Darien, and building certaine pinnesses on the west shoare, was the first Englishman that entered the South sea. To passe over Master Frobisher and his actions, which I have also newly though briefely printed, and as it were revived, whatsoever Master John Davis hath performed in continuing that discovery, which Master Frobisher began for the northwest passage, I have faithfully at large communicated it with thee, that so the great good hope, & singular probabilities & almost certaintie therof, may be knowen of all men, that some may yet still prosecute so noble an action. Sir Humfrey Gilbert, that couragious Knight, and very expert in the mysteries of Navigation amongst the rest is not forgotten: his learned arguments for the passage before named, together with his last more commendable resolution then fortunate successe, are here both to be read. The continuance of the historie, produceth the beginnings, and proceedings of the two English Colonies planted in Virginia at the charges of sir Walter Raleigh, whose entrance upon those newe inhabitations had bene happie, if it had ben as seruiouslie followed, as it was cheerefully undertaken. I could not omit in this parte the two voyages made not long since to the Southwest, whereof I thinke the Spanyard hath had some knowledge, and felt some blowes: the one of Master Edward Fenton, and his consort Master Luke Warde: the other of Master Robert Withrington, and his hardie consort Master Christopher Lister as farre as 44. degrees of southerly latitude, set out at the direction and charge of the right honourable the Earle of Cumberland, both which in divers respectes may yelde both profite and pleasure to the reader, being carefully perused.

For the conclusion of all, the memorable voyage of Master Thomas Candish into the South sea, and from thence about the globe of the earth doth satisfie mee, and I doubt not but will fully content thee: which as in time it is later then that of Sir Frauncis Drake, so in relation of the Philippinaes, Japan, China, and the Isle of S. Helena it is more particular, and exact: and therfore the want of the first made by Sir Frauncis Drake will be the lesse: wherein I must confesse to have taken more then ordinarie paines, meaning to have inserted it in this worke: but being of late (contrary to my expectation) seriously delt withall, not to anticipate or prevent another mans paines and charge in drawing all the services of that worthie Knight into one volume, I have yeelded unto those my freindes which pressed me in the matter, referring the further knowledge of his proceedinges, to those intended discourses.

Now for the other part of my promise, I must crave thy further patience frendly reader, in acquainting thee with those vertuous gentlemen, and others which partly for their private affection to my selfe, but chiefely for their devotion to the furtherance of this my travaile, have yelded me their severall good assistances: for I accompt him unworthy of future favours, that is not thankefull for former benefites. In respect of a generall incouragement it were grosse ingratitude in mee to forget that man, whose onely name doth carrie with it sufficient estimation and love, Master Edward Dier, of whom my selfe and my intentions by his frendly meanes have bene made knowne to those, who in sundrie particulars have much steeded me. More specially in my first part, Master Richard Staper Marchant of London, hath furnished me with divers thinges touching the trade of Turkie, and other places in the East. Master William Burrowgh, Clarke of her Majesties navie, and Master Anthonie Jenkinson, both gentlemen of great experience, and observations in the north Regions, have much pleasured me in the second part. In the third and last besides myne owne extreme travaile in the histories of the Spanyards, my cheefest light hath bene received from Sir John Hawkins, Sir Walter Raleigh, and my kinseman Master Richard Hakluyt of the middle Temple.

And whereas in the course of this history often mention is made of many beastes, birds, fishes, serpents, plants, fruits, hearbes, rootes, apparell, armour, boates, and such other rare and strange curiosities, which wise men take great pleasure to reade of, but much more contentment to see: herein I my selfe to my singuler delight have bene as it were ravished in beholding all the premisses gathered together with no small cost, and preserved with no litle diligence, in the excellent Cabinets of my very worshipfull and learned friends M. Richard Garthe, one of the Clearkes of the pettie Bags, and M. William Cope Gentleman Ussier to the right Honourable and most prudent Counseller (the Seneca of our common wealth,) the Lord Burleigh, high Treasourer of England.

Nowe, because peradventure it would bee expected as necessarie, that the descriptions of so many parts of the world would farre more easily be conceived of the Readers, by adding Geographicall, and Hydrographicall tables thereunto, thou art by the way to be admonished, that I have contented my selfe with inserting into the worke one of the best generall mappes of the world onely, untill the comming out of a very large and most exact terrestriall Globe, collected and reformed according to the newest, secretest, and latest discoveries, both Spanish,

Portugall, and English, composed by M. Emmerie Mollineux of Lambeth, a rare Gentleman in his profession, being therein for divers yeeres, greatly supported by the purse and liberalitie of the worshipfull marchant M. William Sanderson.

This being the summe of those things which I thought good to admonish thee of (good Reader) it remaineth that thou take the profite and pleasure of the worke: which I wish to bee as great to thee, as my paines and labour have bene in bringing these rawe fruits unto this ripenesse, and in reducing these loose papers into this order.

Farewell.

1590c

THE JEW OF MALTA: A TRAGEDY
CHRISTOPHER MARLOWE
LONDON

Marlowe puts his age's most daring ideas into mouths of men made magnificent by laws they break, laws that finally damn them.
*DARING IDEAS In Christian ages Machiavelli was 1st to write of politics as if God had no hand in them & as if they were the work of selfish folk often too cowardly & stupid to work well. Heads of church & state who claimed to be God's deputies were appalled. Catholics & Protestants called him an atheist: noted his name had **mach**, German root of **make**, & **evil** in it. His Italian soul (says Marlowe here) entered the Duke of Guise who in 1572 led a massacre of French Protestants. The Duke's murder (a recent event) has let Machevil appear on a*

[Enter *Machevil* (as Prologue)]

*A*LBEIT *the world thinke* Machevill *is dead,*
Yet was his soule but flowne beyond the Alpes,
And now the Guize *is dead, is come from* France
To view this Land, and frolicke with his friends.
To some perhaps my name is odious,
But such as love me, gard me from their tongues,
And let them know that I am Machevill,
And weigh not men
         and therefore not mens words:
Admir'd I am of those that hate me most.
Though some speake openly against my bookes,
Yet will they reade me, and thereby attaine
To Peters *Chayre: And when they cast me off,*
Are poyson'd by my climing followers.
I count Religion but a childish Toy,
And hold there is no sinne but Ignorance.
Birds of the Aire will tell of murders past;
I am asham'd to heare such fooleries:
Many will talke of Title to a Crowne.
What right had Caesar to the Empery?
Might first made Kings,
         and Lawes were then most sure

When like the Dracos *they were writ in blood.*
Hence comes it, that a strong built Citadell
Commands much more then letters can import:
Which maxime had Phaleris *observ'd,*
H'had never bellowed in a brasen Bull
Of great ones envy; o'th poore petty wites,
Let me be envy'd and not pittied!
But whither am I bound, I come not, I,
To reade a lecture here in Britanie
But to present the Tragedy of a Jew,
Who smiles to see how full his bags are cramb'd,
Which mony was not got without my meanes.
I crave but this, Grace him as he deserves,
And let him not be entertain'd the worse
Because he favours me.
(Enter *Barabas* in his counting-house,
heapes of gold before him.)

London stage & thrill Christian audiences by saying all rulers are Machiavellian atheists in disguise. Marlowe also believed that. When a student he spied for the English government, through pretending to be Catholic among folk who plotted, with Spanish cash & Jesuit aid, to make England Catholic again. As a spy he was also spied upon. A state paper called him a homosexual who said Moses, Jesus & Mahomet were 3 impostors.

TWO TRAGICALL DISCOURSES OF MIGHTY TAMBURLAINE, THE SCYTHIAN SHEPHERD CHRISTOPHER MARLOWE: LONDON

c1590

In 1539 King Harry privatized church estates & 100 years after came civil war ending in a king beheaded. At the centre of this era more great dramatic poetry was written in London than in all Britain before or since. From this we deduce (dear Watson) there were more ideas, more folk discussing them, bigger audiences for ideas in London than before or since. Athens had flowered thus about 460 B.C. for the same reasons. In both cities the rich & those they depended on

[Part One: The Prologue]

*F*ROM *jygging vaines of riming mother wits,*
And such conceits as clownage keepes in pay,
Weele leade you to the stately tent of War:
Where you shall heare the Scythian Tamburlaine
Threatning the world with high astounding tearms
And scourging kingdoms with his conquering sword.
View but his picture in this tragicke glasse,
And then applaud his fortunes as you please.

[Part Two: The Prologue]

*T*HE *generall welcomes Tamburlain receiv'd,*
When he arrived last upon our stage,
Hath made our Poet pen his second part,
Wher death cuts off the progres of his pomp,
And murdrous Fates throwes al his triumphs down.

shared   profitable adventures, money & speech more intimately than before or since.

But what became of faire Zenocrate,
And with how manie cities sacrifice
He celebrated her sad funerall,
Himselfe in presence shal unfold at large.

1590c

THE TRAGICALL HISTORY OF THE LIFE AND DEATH OF DOCTOR FAUSTUS
CHRISTOPHER MARLOWE: LONDON

Money. Knowledge. Power. Privatizing church land made many richer & a lot poorer at first, but before safe banking the rich could only enlarge wealth by investing in trade, so for the first time since Chaucer tradesmen could pay to send sons to Oxford or Cambridge. Most such students became clergy, as universities mainly existed to make these. Some served royalty & nobility as tutors, agents & entertainers. No company could then act a play unless royalty or big nobles licensed them. Puritan laws now banned street theatre & guild miracle plays, but the English were so stage-struck that lords paid for private performances & lowered the cost by letting actors build & play in their own public theatres. The theatres made Marlowe (shoemaker's son, spy & England's 1st great poet-playwright) too famous for a secret agent. He was murdered at the age of 29.

[Enter Chorus.]

NOT marching in the fields of Thrasimen,
Where Mars did mate the warlicke Carthagens,
Nor sporting in the dalliance of love
In Courts of Kings, where state is over-turn'd,
Nor in the pompe of proud audacious deeds,
Intends our Muse to vaunt his heavenly verse;
Onely this, Gentles: we must now performe
The forme of Faustus fortunes, good or bad,
And now to patient judgements we appeale,
And speake for Faustus in his infancie.
Now is he borne, of parents base of stocke,
In Germany, within a Towne cal'd Rhodes:
At riper yeares to Wittenberg he went,
Whereas his kinsmen chiefly brought him up;
So much he profits in Divinitie,
The fruitfull plot of Scholerisme grac'd,
That shortly he was grac'd with Doctors name,
Excelling all, and sweetly can dispute
In th' heavenly matters of Theologie,
Till swolne with cunning, of a selfe conceit,
His waxen wings did mount above his reach,
And melting, heavens conspir'd his over-throw:
For falling to a divellish exercise,
And glutted now with learnings golden gifts,
He surfets upon cursed Necromancie:
Nothing so sweet as Magicke is to him,
Which he preferres before his chiefest blisse;
And this the man that in his study sits.

THE FAERIE QUEENE
EDMUND SPENSER
LONDON
1590

A LETTER OF THE AUTHORS EXPOUNDING HIS WHOLE INTENTION IN THE COURSE OF THIS WORKE: WHICH FOR THAT IT GIVETH GREAT LIGHT TO THE READER, FOR THE BETTER UNDERSTANDING IS HEREUNTO ANNEXED.

To the Right noble, and Valorous, Sir Walter Raleigh knight, Lo. Wardein of the Stanneryes, and her Majesties liefetenaunt of the County of Cornewayll.

S IR knowing how doubtfully all Allegories may be construed, and this booke of mine, which I have entituled the Faery Queene, being a continued Allegory, or darke conceit, I have thought good aswell for avoyding of gealous opinions and misconstructions, as also for your better light in reading therof, (being so by you commanded,) to discover unto you the general intention & meaning, which in the whole course thereof I have fashioned, without expressing of any particular purposes or by accidents therein occasioned. The generall end therefore of all the booke is to fashion a gentleman or noble person in vertuous and gentle discipline: Which for that I conceived should be most plausible and pleasing, being coloured with an historicall fiction, the which the most part of men delight to read, rather for variety of matter, then for profite of the ensample: I chose the historye of king Arthure, as most fitte for the excellency of his person, being made famous by many mens former workes, and also furthest from the daunger of envy, and suspition of present time. In which I have followed all the antique Poets historicall, first Homere, who in the Persons of Agamemnon and Ulysses hath ensampled a good governour and a vertuous man, the one in his Ilias, the other in his Odysseis: then Virgil, whose like intention was to doe in the person of Aeneas: after him Ariosto comprised them both in his Orlando: and lately Tasso dissevered them againe, and formed both

*The Merchant Taylors of London made a school where their sons were educated like gentry. Here Spenser, son of a Lancashire clothworker, construed Virgil, Ovid, & wrote his 1st verses. Later he called London **my most kindly nurse**. Charity & an allowance for poor students let him into Cambridge. Where Marlowe was recruited as a spy, Spenser met aristocrats who employed him as secretary, soldier & colonial administrator in their often bloody business of keeping control of Ireland. He was rewarded with part of Munster & lived there after 1586, working on this poem dedicated to the most high, mighty & magnificent Empress Elizabeth. Books I to III got printed in 1590, books IV to VI in 1596, & 2 more cantos after he died. An Irish war to expel colonists burnt his home & drove him back to London. In 1599 illness & (some say) hunger ended him. Lords & gentry were at his burial service in Westminster Abbey.*

parts in two persons, namely that part which they in Philosophy call Ethice, or vertues of a private man, coloured in his Rinaldo: The other named Politice in his Godfredo. By ensample of which excellente Poets, I labour to pourtraict in Arthure, before he was king, the image of a brave knight, perfected in the twelve private morall vertues, as Aristotle hath devised, the which is the purpose of these first twelve bookes: which if I finde to be well accepted, I may be perhaps encoraged, to frame the other part of polliticke vertues in his person, after that hee came to be king. To some I know this Methode will seme displeasaunt, which had rather have good discipline delivered plainly in ways of precepts, or sermoned at large, as they use, then thus clowdily enwrapped in Allegoricall devises. But such, me seeme, should be satisfide with the use of these dayesseeing all things accounted by their showes, and nothing esteemed of, that is not delightfull and pleasing to commune sence. For this cause is Xenophon preferred before Plato, for that the one in the exquisite depth of his judgement, formed a Commune welth such as it should be, but the other in the person of Cyrus and the Persians fashioned a government such as might best be: So much more profitable and gratious is doctrine by ensample, then by rule. So have I laboured to doe in the person of Arthure: whome I conceive after his long education by Timon, to whom he was by Merlin delivered to be brought up, so soone as he was borne of the Lady Igrayne, to have seene in a dream or vision the Faery Queen, with whose excellent beauty ravished, he awaking resolved to seeke her out, and so being by Merlin armed, and by Timon thoroughly instructed, he went to seeke her forth in Faerye land. In that Faery Queene I meane glory in my generall intention, but in particular I conceive the most excellent and glorious person of our soveraine the Queene, and her kingdome in Faery land. And yet in some places els, I doe otherwise shadow her. For considering she beareth two persons, the one of a most royall Queene or Empresse, the other of a most vertuous and beautifull Lady, this latter part in some places I doe expresse in Belphoebe, fashioning her name according to your own excellent conceipt of Cynthia, (Phoebe and Cynthia being both names of Diana.) So in the person of Prince Arthure I sette forth magnificence in particular, which vertue for that (according to Aristotle and the rest) itis the perfection of all the rest, and conteineth in it them all, therefore in the whole course I mention the deedes of Arthure applyable to that vertue, which I write of in that booke. But of the xii. other vertues, I make xii. other knights the patrones, for the more variety of the history: Of which these three bookes contayn three. The first of the knight of the Redcrosse, in whome I expresse Holynes: the second of Sir Guyon, in whome I sette forth Temperaunce: The third of Britomartis a Lady knight, in whom I picture Chastity. But because the beginning of the whole worke seemeth abrupte and as depending upon other antecedents, it needs that ye know the occasion of these three knights severall adventures. For the Methode of a Poet historical is not such, as of an Historiographer. For an Historiographer discourseth of affayres orderly as they were donne, accounting as well the times as the actions, but a Poet thrusteth into the middest, even where it most concerneth him, and there recoursing to the thinges forepaste, and divining of thinges to come, maketh a pleasing Analysis of all. The beginning therefore of my history, if it were to be told by an Historiographer should be the twelfth booke, which is the last, where I devise that the Faery Queene kept her Annual feaste xii. dayes, uppon which xii. severall dayes, the occasions of the xii. several adventures hapned, which being undertaken by xii. severall knights, are in these xii. books severally handled and discoursed. The first was this. In the beginning of the feast, there presented him selfe a tall clownishe younge man, who falling before the Queen of Faries desired a boone (as the manner then was) which during that feast she might not refuse: which was that hee might have the atchievement of any adventure, which during that feast should happen, that being graunted, he rested him on the floore, unfitte through his rusticity for a better place. Soone after entred a faire Ladye in mourning weedes, riding on a white Asse, with a dwarfe behind her leading a warlike steed, that bore the Armes of a knight, and his speare in the dwarfes hand. Shee falling before the Queene of Faeries, complayned that her father and mother an ancient King and Queene, had bene by an huge dragon many years shut up in a brasen Castle, who thence sufferd them not to yssew: and therefore besought the Faery Queene to assygne her some one of her knights to take on him that exployt. Presently that clownish person upstarting, desired that adventure: whereat the Queene much wondering, and the Lady much gainesaying, yet he earnestly importuned his desire. In the end the Lady told him that unlesse that armour which she brought, would serve him (that is the armour of a Christian man specified by Saint Paul v. Ephes.) that he could not succeed in that enterprise, which being forthwith put upon him with dewe furnitures thereunto, he seemed the goodliest man in al that company, and was well liked of the Lady. And eftesoones taking on him knighthood, and mounting on that straunge Courser, he went forth with her on that adventure: where beginneth the first booke, vz.

A gentle knight was pricking on the playne. &c.

The second day ther came in a Palmer bearing an Infant with bloody hands, whose Parents he complained to have bene slayn by an Enchaunteresse called Acrasia: and therfore craved of the Faery Queene, to appoint him some knight, to performe that adventure, which being assigned to Sir Guyon, he presently went forth with that same Palmer: which is the beginning of the second booke and the whole subject thereof. The third day there came in, a Groome who complained before the Faery Queene, that a vile Enchaunter called Busirane had in hand a most faire Lady called Amoretta, whom he kept in most grievous torment, because she would not yield him the pleasure of her body. Whereupon Sir Scudamour the lover of that Lady presently tooke on him that adventure. But being unable to performe it be reason of the hard Enchauntments, after long sorrow, in the end met with Britomartis, who succoured him, and reskewed his love.

But by occasion hereof, many other adventures are intermedled, but rather as Accidents, then intendments. As the love of Britomart, the overthrow of Marinell, the misery of Florimell, the vertuousnes of Belphoebe, the lasciviousnes of Hellenora, and many the like. Thus much Sir, I have briefly overronne to direct your understanding to the wel-head of the History, that from thence gathering the whole intention of the conceit, ye may as in a handfull gripe al the discourse, which otherwise may happily seeme tedious and confused. So humbly craving the continuaunce of your honorable favour towards me, and th'eternall establishment of your happines, I humbly take leave.

Yours most humbly affectionate, Ed. Spenser. 23. January. 1589.

THE FIRST BOOKE OF THE FAERIE QUEENE

L O I the man, whose Muse whilome did maske,
As time her taught,
   in lowly Shepheards weeds,
Am now enforst a far unfitter taske,
For trumpets sterne to chaunge mine Oaten reeds,
And sing of Knights and Ladies gentle deeds;
Whose prayses having slept in silence long,
Me, all too meane, the sacred Muse areeds

*In his first poems Virgil pictured himself as Tityrus, a shepherd playing an oatstalk mouth-organ. Spenser's first poems, **The Shepherd's Calendar**, followed Virgil by picturing England as a sheep-run (wool was still her main source of*

To blazon broad emongst her learned throng:
Fierce warres and faithfull loves
　　　　shall moralize my song.

Helpe then, O holy Virgin chiefe of nine,
Thy weaker Novice to performe thy will,
Lay forth out of thine everlasting scryne
The antique rolles, which there lye hidden still,
Of Faerie knights and fairest Tanaquill,
Whom that most noble Briton Prince so long
Sought through the world,
　　　　and suffered so much ill,
That I must rue his undeserved wrong:
O helpe thou my weake wit,
　　　　and sharpen my dull tong.

And thou most dreaded impe of highest Jove,
Faire Venus *sonne, that with thy cruell dart*
At that good knight so cunningly didst rove,
That glorious fire it kindled in his hart,
Lay now they deadly Heben bow apart,
And with thy mother milde come to mine ayde:
Come both, and with you bring triumphant Mart,
In loves and gentle jollities arrayd,
After his murdrous spoiles
　　　　and bloudy rage allayd.

And with them eke, O Goddesse heavenly bright,
Mirrour of grace and Majestie divine,
Great Lady of the greatest Isle, whose light
Like Phoebus *lampe*
　　　　throughout the world doth shine,
Shed thy faire beames into mine feeble eyne,
And raise my thoughts too humble and too vile,
To thinke of that true glorious type of thine,
The argument of mine afflicted stile:
The which to heare,
　　　　vouchsafe, O dearest dred a-while.

wealth) with Spenser (clothworker's son) as Colin Clout, poetic shepherd. **The Faerie Queene** *is his epic to the glory of Elizabeth's Protestant empire. The 1st lines are based on Virgil's short preface to the* **Aeneid**, *first translated into English by Douglas. (See foot of page 168.) A prayer to Roman gods then leads to a tale of sword & sorcery like that the Italians Boiardo & Ariosto had versified for fun. But Spenser is earnest. His knights & ladies are England's rulers as they* **should** *be: embodiments of Faith, Chastity, Justice. His monsters, savages & witches are images of the pope, the Irish, the Queen of Scots & also Spite, Rebellion, Deceit. Earlier poets showed saints & devils, in common words that made even God seem earthy & real. Spenser used strange words to make England Faerieland. Alliterations like* **his haughty helmet horrid all with gold** *was then as out-of-date as his spelling of* **faerie**. *So was chivalry. Elizabeth's knights were pirates, monopolists, & spymasters. To show purer realities Spenser devised a 9-line verse that mixed old & new speech so melodiously that Ben Jonson said it was* **no** *(real)* **language**.

1592

GREENES GROATS-WORTH OF WITTE,
Bought with a Million of Repentance.
ROBERT GREENE: LONDON

DESCRIBING THE FOLLIE OF YOUTH, THE FALSHOOD OF MAKESHIFTE FLATTERERS, THE MISERIE OF THE NEGLIGENT, AND MISCHIEFS OF DECEIVING COURTEZANS.

WRITTEN BEFORE HIS DEATH

[TO THE GENTLEMEN READERS]

*To get good jobs the university-taught sons of tradesmen & lesser gentry needed noble friends, but by 1580 some smart lads were avoiding becoming underpaid curates by writing for the London stage & book trade, which flourished as wildly as cinema & journalism now. Such writers were called **university wits** to mark them off from witty courtiers (like Raleigh) who used the same pubs, & from self-educated theatre folk like Shakespeare. Royalties, copyrights & banks did not exist so wits were paid in occasional hard-to-save lump sums. Rivalry was fierce; poverty & disease killed many of them young. Greene, a Norwich saddler's son, was the most reckless. He left wife and child to live with the sister of a notorious thief; wrote fine lyrics; rewrote aristocratic romances & Marlowe's **Dr. Faustus** in a more*

Gentlemen. The Swan sings melodiously before death, that in all his life time useth but a jarring sound. *Greene* though able inough to write, yet deeplyer serched with sicknes than ever heeretofore, sendes you his Swanne like songe, for that he feares he shall never againe carroll to you woonted love layes, never againe discover to you youths pleasures. How ever yet sickness, riot, Incontinence, have at once shown their extremitie yet if I recover, you shall all see, more fresh sprigs, then ever sprang from me, directing you how to live, yet not diswading ye from love. This is the last I have writ, and I feare me the last I shall writ. And how ever I have beene censured for some of my former bookes, yet Gentlemen I protest, they were as I had speciall information. But passing them, I commend this to your favourable censures, that like an Embrion without shape, I feare me will be thrust into the world. If I live to end it, it shall be otherwise: if not, yet will I commend it to your courtesies, that you may as well be acquainted with my repentant death, as you have lamented my careles course of life. But as *Nemo ante obitum felix*, so *Acta Exitus probat*: Beseeching therefore so to be deemed heereof as I deserve, I leave the worke to your likinges, and leave you to your delights.*OOOOOOOOOOOOOOOOOOOO*

GREENE TELLS HOW AVARICE, LUST, BAD COMPANY RUINED HIM AND WARNS THREE PLAYWRIGHTS (MARLOWE IS ONE) AGAINST ALL ACTORS, ESPECIALLY *SHAKESCENE!*

OOOOOOOOOOOOOOOOOOOOOOOOOOOOOOOOOOOOOOOOOOOOOOOO

Base minded men all three of you, if by my miserie you

be not warnd: for unto none of you (like mee) sought those burres to cleave: those Puppets (I meane) that spake from our mouths, those Anticks garnisht in our colours. Is it not strange, that I, to whom they all have beene beholding: is it not like that you, to whome they all have beene beholding, shall (were yee in that case as I am now) bee both at once of them forsaken? Yes trust then not: for there is an upstart Crow, beautified with our feathers, that with his *Tygers hart wrapt in a Players hyde*, supposes he is as well able to bombast out a blanke verse as the best of you: and beeing an absolute *Johannes fac totum*, is in his owne conceit the onely Shake-scene in a countrey. O that I might intreat your rare wits to be imploied in more profitable courses: & let those Apes imitate your past excellence, and never more acquaint them with your admired inventions.

crowd-pleasing style; tried to earn cash on his death bed with this tract against his own greed for gold, whoring, theatre going. He warns fellow wits against actors – **puppets who spake but with our breath** *– especially the actor Shakescene, now 28 years old, son of a Stratford burgher yet able to make successful plays from other men's work. Shakespeare turned a romance by Greene into* **A Winter's Tale** *20 years later.*

OF THE LAWES OF ECCLESIASTICALL POLITIE
RICHARD HOOKER: LONDON
1593

A PREFACE TO THEM THAT SEEKE (AS THEY TEARME IT) THE REFORMATION OF LAWES, AND ORDERS ECCLESIASTICALL, IN THE CHURCH OF ENGLAND.

CHAPTER 1: *THE CAUSE AND OCCASION OF HANDLING THESE THINGS AND WHAT MIGHT BE WISHED IN THEM FOR WHOSE SAKES SO MUCH PAINE IS TAKEN.*

THOUGH for no other cause, yet for this; that posteritie may know we have not loosely through silence permitted things to passe away as in a dreame, there shall be for mens information extant thus much concerning the present state of the Church of God established amongst us, and their carefull endevour which woulde have upheld the same. At your hands beloved in our Lord and Saviour Jesus Christ (for in him the love which we beare unto all that would but seeme to be borne of him, it is not the sea of your gall and bitternes that shall ever drown) I have no great cause

Elizabeth upset many of her clergy by upholding no doctrine but her own supremacy. When young she avoided conflict with Spain by acting as Catholic as a queen who rejects the pope can. She also distrusted Calvinists: they hated her ruling the church through bishops, but much of her revenue came from Calvinist merchants so she made no law to exclude them. In some pulpits Calvinist & Episcopal preachers

to looke for other then the selfesame portion and lot, which your maner hath bene hitherto to lay on them that concurre not in opinion and sentence with you. But our hope is that the God of peace shall (notwithstanding mans nature too impatient of contumelious malediction) inable us quietlie and even gladly to suffer all things, for that worke sake which we covet to performe. The wonderfull zeale and fervour wherewith ye have withstood the received orders of this Church was the first thing which caused me to enter into consideration, whether (as all your published bookes and writings peremptorilie mainteine) everie christian man fearing God stand bound to joyne with you for the furtherance of that which yee tearme *the Lords Discipline*. Wherein I must plainely confesse unto you, that before I examined your sundrie declarations in that behalfe, it could not settle in my head to thinke but that undoubtedly such numbers of otherwise right well affected and most religiouslie enclined mindes, had some marvelous reasonable inducements which led them with so great earnestnes that way. But when once, as neere as my slender abilitie woulde serve, I had with travaile and care performed that part of the Apostles advise and counsell in such cases whereby he willeth to *try all things*, and was come at the length so farre, that there remained only the other clause to be satisfied, wherein he concludeth that *what good is must be held*: there was in my poore understanding no remedie, but to set downe this as my finall resolute persuasion, *Surely the present forme of Church government which the lawes of this land have established, is such, as no lawe of God, nor reason of man hath hitherto bene alleaged of force sufficient to prove they do ill, who to the uttermost of their power withstand the alteration thereof.* Contrariwise, *The other which in stead of it we are required to accept, is only by error and misconceipt named the ordinance of Jesus Christ, no one proofe as yet brought forth whereby it may cleerely appeare to be so in very deede.* The explication of which two things I have heere thought good to offer into your owne hands, hartely beseeching you even by the meekenesse of Jesus Christ, whome I trust ye love; that, as ye tender the peace and quietnes of this Church, if there be in you that gracious humilitie which hath ever bene the crowne and glorie of a christianlie disposed mind, if your owne soules, heartes, and consciences, (the sound integritie whereof can but hardlie stand with the refusall of truth in personall respects) be, as I doubt not but they are, things most deere and pretious unto you, *Let not the faith which ye have in our Lord Jesus Christ,* be blemished *with partialities*, regard not who it is which speaketh, but waigh only what is spoken. Thinke not that ye reade the words of one, who bendeth him selfe as an adversarie against the truth which ye have alreadie embraced; but the words of one, who desireth even to embrace together with you the selfe same truth, if it be the truth, and for that cause (for no other God he knoweth) hath undertaken the burthensome labour of this painefull kinde of conference. For the plainer accesse whereunto, let it be lawfull for me to rip up to the verie bottome, how and by whome your Discipline was planted, at such time as this age we live in began to make first triall thereof.

CHAPTER 2: *THE FIRST ESTABLISHMENT OF NEW DISCIPLINE BY M. CALVINS INDUSTRY IN THE CHURCH OF GENEVA, AND THE BEGINNING OF STRIFE ABOUT IT AMONGST OUR SELVES.*

A FOUNDER IT HAD, whome, for mine owne part, I thinke incomparably the wisest man that ever the french Church did enjoy, since the houre it enjoyed him. His bringing up was in the studie of the Civill Lawe. Divine knowledge he gathered, not by hearing or reading so much, as by teaching others. For, though thousands were debters to him, as touching knowledge in that kinde; yet he to none but onely to God, the author of that most blessed fountaine, the booke of life, and of the admirable dexteritie of wit, together with the helpes of other learning which were his guides: til being occasioned to leave Fraunce, he fell at the length upon Geneva; which Citie, the Bishop and Cleargie thereof had a little before, (as some doe affirme) forsaken, being of likelyhood frighted with the peoples suddaine attempt for abolishment of popish religion: the event of which enterprise they thought it not safe for themselves to wait for in that place. At the comming of Calvin thither, the forme of their civill regiment was popular, as it continueth at this day: neither King, nor Duke, nor noble man of any authoritie or power over them, but officers chosen by the people yerely out of themselves, to order all things with publique consent. For spirituall government, they had no lawes at all agreed upon, but did what the Pastors of their soules by persuasion could win them unto. Calvin, being admitted one of their Preachers, and a divinitie reader amongst them, considered how dangerous it was that the whole estate of that Church should hang still on so slender a thred, as the liking of an ignorant multitude is, if it have power to change whatsoever it selfe listeth. Wherefore taking unto him two of the other ministers for more countenance of the action (albeit the rest were all against it) they moved, and in the end perswaded with much adoe the people to binde themselves by solemne oath, first never to admit the Papacie amongst them againe; and secondlie, to live in obedience unto such orders concerning the exercise of their religion, and the forme of their ecclesiasticall government, as those their true and faithfull Ministers of Gods word had agreeablie to Scripture set downe for that ende and purpose. When these things began to be put in ure, the people also (what causes moving them thereunto, themselves best knowe) began to repent them of that they had done, and irefully to champ upon the bit they had taken into their mouthes; the rather for that they grew by meanes of this innovation into dislike with some Churches neere about them, the benefite of whose good friendship their state could not well lacke. It was the manner of those times (whether through mens desire to enjoy alone the glorie of their owne enterprises, or else because the quicknes of their occasions required present dispatch,) so it was, that everie particular Church did that within it selfe, which some fewe of their owne thought good, by whome the rest were all directed. Such number of Churches then being, though free within themselves, yet smal, common conference before hand might have eased them of much aftertrouble. But a greater inconvenience it bred, that everie later endevoured to bee certaine degrees more removed from conformitie with the Church of Rome, then the rest before had bene: whereupon grewe marvelous great dissimilitudes, and by reason thereof, jealousies, hartburnings, jarres and discords amongst them.

OOOOOOOOOOOOOOOOOOOOOOOOOOOOOOOOOOOOOOOOOOOOOOOOOOOOOOOOOOOOOOOOO

HERE FOLLOWS AN ACCOUNT OF THE POLITICAL CONFUSIONS WHEREBY CALVIN WAS ENABLED TO BECOME RELIGIOUS AND CIVIL DICTATOR OF THE GENEVA CITY-STATE, AND GAVE IT THE CONSTITUTION HIS FOLLOWERS WISH TO IMPOSE EVERYWHERE.

OOOOOOOOOOOOOOOOOOOOOOOOOOOOOOOOOOOOOOOOOOOOOOOOOOOOOOOOOOOOOOOOO

The MOST EXCELLENT and LAMENTABLE TRAGEDIE of ROMEO and JULIET. WILLIAM SHAKESPEARE: LONDON

1596

[THE PROLOGUE: CORUS]

*T*WO housholds both alike in dignitie,
  (In faire Verona where we lay our Scene)
From auncient grudge, breake to new mutinie,
Where civill bloud makes civill hands uncleane:
From forth the fatall loynes of these two foes,
A paire of starre-crost lovers, take their life:
Whose misadventur'd pittious overthrowes,
Doth with their death burie their Parents strife.
The fearfull passage of their death-markt love,
And the continuance of their Parents rage:
Which but their childrens end
      nought could remove:
Is now the two houres trafficque of our Stage.
The which if you with patient eares attend,
What heare shall misse,
      our toyle shall strive to mend.

His dad, a glover, deals in grain, wool, timber, also lends money; is alderman & secret Catholic whose excuse for not going to Anglican church is danger of arrest for debt. Will leaves school, serves Catholic nobles with a private theatre in Lancashire. At 18 he weds a pregnant, propertied lass of 26. Greene damns him as a play-cobbling actor 10 years later. A plague shuts theatres so he versifies erotic tales by Plutarch & Ovid. Theatres open. Between 1594 & 1613 he writes 36 still-acted plays.

The SECOND PART of HENRY the FOURTH, LONDON, 1598

[Enter RUMOUR painted full of Tongues]

*O*PEN your eares; for which of you will stop
  The vent of hearing,
      when lowd Rumor speaks?
I from the Orient to the drooping West,
(Making the wind my poste-horse) still unfold
The acts commenced on this ball of earth,
Upon my tongues continuall slanders ride,
The which in every language I pronounce,
Stuffing the eares of men with false reports,
I speake of peace while covert enmity,
Under the smile of safety, woundes the world:
And who but Rumor, who but onely I,
Make fearefull musters, and prepar'd defence,
Whiles the bigge yeare,
      swolne with some other griefe,

Better audiences than attend later theatres inspire him. Courtiers, workmen, merchants, tradesmen & wives of these mix in a theatre he manages & partly owns, all keen to hear splendidly convincing words from splendidly daring, evil or absurd figures. Their standard is high. Some are more richly clad than those on stage. All talk the language of a Bible whose grand diction is excitingly modern, not staled by centuries of being chanted in the increasingly separate dialect of England's rulers. To please this public Will takes plots, characters, ideas from half the earlier books in this book & blends them with words from Italian novella, English fairy tale, travelogue, history, essay, play translated or written by contemporaries. His plays are so original that no rival authors attack him after the death of Greene, though attacking each other in play & pamphlet. They learned at college how Greeks & Romans made plays plausible: his are shaped by an actor's grasp of what holds audiences. He makes fantastic plots lifelike with surprisingly apt words, yet his history plays show nations at war – king lords clergy commoners scoundrels – with truth only Homer & Tolstoy equal. His comedies & tragedies mingle prose & verse yet are whole poems. None writing English after him can make such poetic plays. They lack the audiences.

Is thought with child by the sterne tyrant Warre?
And no such matter. Rumour is a pipe,
Blowne by surmizes, Jealousies conjectures,
And of so easie, and so plaine a stop,
That the blunt monster, with uncounted heads,
The still discordant wav'ring multitude,
Can play upon it. But what need I thus
(My wel knowne body) to anothomize
Among my houshold? why is Rumor here?
I runne before King Harries victorie,
Who in a bloudy field by Shrewsbury,
Hath beaten downe
               yong Hot-spurre and his troopes,
Quenching the flame of bold rebellion,
Even with the rebels bloud. But what meane I
To speake so true at first: my office is
To noyse abroad, that Harry Monmouth fell
Under the wrath of noble Hot-spurs sword,
And that the King before the Douglas rage,
Stoopt his annointed head as low as death.
This have I rumour'd
               through the peasant townes,
Betweene that royall field of Shrewsbury,
And this worme-eaten hold of ragged stone,
Where Hot-spurs father old Northumberland
Lies crafty sicke, the postes come tyring on,
And not a man of them brings other newes,
Than they have learnt of me,
               from Rumors tongues,
They bring smooth comforts false,
               worse then true wrongs.

THE LIFE OF HENRY THE FIFT, LONDON, c1599
                    [ENTER PROLOGUE]
O FOR a Muse of Fire, that would ascend
*   The brightest Heaven of Inventioun:*
A Kingdome for a Stage, Princes to Act,
And Monarchs to behold the swelling Scene.
Then should the Warlike Harry, like himselfe,

Assume the Port of Mars, and at his heeles
(Leasht in, like Hounds)
            should Famine, Sword, and Fire
Crouch for employment. But pardon,
            Gentles all:
The flat unraysed Spirits, that hath dar'd,
On this unworthy Scaffold, to bring forth
So great an Object. Can this Cock-Pit hold
The vastie fields of France?
            Or may we cramme
Within this Woodden O, the very Caskes
That did affright the Ayre at Agincourt?
O pardon: since a crooked Figure may
Attest in little place a Million,
And let us, Cyphers to this great Accompt,
On your imaginarie Forces worke.
Suppose within the Girdle of these Walls
Are now confin'd two mightie Monarchies,
Whose high, up-reared, and abutting Fronts,
The perillous narrow Ocean parts asunder.
Peece out our imperfections
            with your thoughts:
Into a thousand parts divide one Man,
And make imaginarie Puissance.
Thinke when we talk of Horses,
            that you see them
Printing their prowd Hoofes
            i' th' receiving Earth:
For 'tis your thoughts
            that now must deck our Kings,
Carry them here and there:
            Jumping o're Times;
Turning th' accomplishment of many yeeres
Into an Howre-glasse: for the which supplie,
Admit me Chorus to this Historie;
Who Prologue-like,
            your humble patience pray,
Gently to heare, kindly to judge our Play.

*Most writers put their own character into their work. Marlowe's heroes are all daring law-breakers, most of Jonson's are forceful humorists. Falstaff, King Lear, Cleopatra, Hamlet have nothing in common but imaginative words saying funny, deep or desperate things. They are Shakespeare's words, but had we been Falstaff, Cleopatra etc. in those situations we know WE would say them, so the plays are no clue to him. His love sonnets are earlier: 126 to a fair youth, 28 to a dark lady. By not naming them he excites gossip but is no mystery to friends & actors. His strong imagination writes plays; good business sense & a discretion (like his dad's) produces them profitably. A mild yet attentive manner, not bold & not servile, offends as few people as his plays & suits the court. It was Chaucer's manner. Like Chaucer his sympathy is with all he creates: even his monsters are human. Amid credible cruelties that make a nightmare of life he gives believable, kind, common words proving the world is still sane. His impersonal sympathy with so many people leads Ben Jonson, his friend & rival, to call him **soul of the age**.*

1601

Donne liked portraits of himself, but the 1 he wanted before this preface was never engraved, & the poem after it not completed. The soul of the fruit Eve plucked was to be shown entering many bodies, acquiring bad qualities from plants, birds, fishes & beasts before being born into bad people – Mahomet, Luther, Calvin, Queen Bess. (In 1601 she was old & unpopular.) **On a huge hill, Cragged & steep, truth stands & he that will Reach her, about must, & about must go.** *The biblical idea that the true path, though hard, is straight, was not true for Donne. The Renaissance had split his education, the Reformation his family. At university he was taught ancient science that harmonized every truth, yet heard of discoveries disproving it. The discoverers got damned as heretics by popes and Protestants who also damned each other. Donne's Catholic family had descended from Thomas More's. His brother died in jail for sheltering a Jesuit, his uncle WAS 1, yet Donne's ambition, wit & handsome looks fitted him for high offices in*

THE PROGRESSE OF THE SOULE
JOHN DONNE
LONDON

OTHERS at the Porches and entries of their Buildings set their Armes; I, my picture; if any colours can deliver a minde so plaine, and flat, and through light as mine. Naturally at a new Author, I doubt, and sticke, and doe not say quickly, good. I censure much and taxe; And this liberty costs mee more then others, by how much my owne things are worse then others. Yet I would not be so rebellious against my selfe, as not to doe it, since I love it; nor so unjust to others, to do it *sine talione*. As long as I give them as good hold upon mee, they must pardon mee my bitings. I forbid no reprehender, but him that like the Trent Councell forbids not bookes, but Authors, damning what ever such a name hath or shall write. None writes so ill, that he gives not some thing exemplary, to follow, or flie. Now when I beginne this booke, I have no purpose to come into any mans debt; how my stocke will hold out I know not; perchance waste, perchance increase in use; if I doe borrow any thing of Antiquitie, besides that I make account that I pay it to posterity, with as much and as good: You shall still finde mee to acknowledge it, and to thanke not him onely that hath digg'd out treasure for mee, but that hath lighted mee a candle to the place. All which I will bid you remember, (for I will have no such Readers as I can teach) is, that the Pithagorian doctrine doth not onely carry one soule from man to man, nor man to beast, but indifferently to plants also: and therefore you must not grudge to finde the same soule in an Emperour, in a Post-horse, and in a Mucheron, since no unreadinesse in the soule, but an indisposition in the organs workes this. And therefore though this soule could not move when it was a Melon, yet it may remember, and now tell mee, at what lascivious banquet it was serv'd. And though it could not speake, when it was a spider, yet it can remember, and now tell me, who used it for poyson to attaine dignitie. How ever the bodies have dull'd her other faculties, her memory hath ever been her owne, which makes me so seriously deliver you by her relation all her passages from her first making when she was that apple which Eve eate, to this time when she is hee, whose life you shall finde in the end of this booke.

[THE SECOND ANNIVERSARIE , 1612]

Nothing could make me sooner to confesse
That this world had an everlastingnesse,
Then to consider, that a yeare is runne,
Since both this lower world's,
*   and the Sunnes Sunne,*
The Lustre, and the vigor of this All,
Did set; 'twere blasphemie to say, did fall.
But as a ship which hath strooke saile,
*   doth runne*
By force of that force which before, it wonne:
Or as sometimes in a beheaded man,
Though at those two Red seas,
*   which freely ranne,*
One from the Trunke, another from the Head,
His soule be sail'd, to her eternall bed,
His eyes will twinckle,
*   and his tongue will roll,*
As though he beckned,
*   and cal'd backe his soule,*
He graspes his hands, and he pulls up his feet,
And seemes to reach, and to step forth to meet
His soule; when all these motions which we saw,
Are but as Ice, which crackles at a thaw:
Or as a Lute, which in moist weather, rings
Her knell alone, by cracking of her strings:
So struggles this dead world, now shee is gone;
For there is motion in corruption.

Protestant England. He became cynical toward all who thought truth simple & when 20 quit his old religion; studied law; joined raids on Spain led by Essex & Raleigh; at 26 was secretary to a noble statesman. His verses – satiric & erotic in a shockingly passionate, erudite yet conversational voice – were greatly admired. But he secretly wed a niece of his boss, was sacked for it, had to feed a growing family. He did so by jobs & presents got through flattering folk in the madly corrupt court of King James, who at last made him dean of St. Paul's Cathedral.

Donne wrote this poem to console the father of a girl who died a year earlier. He had never met her, & worked as sculptors then worked on tombs: commemorating the dead with images that morbidly amaze the living. Her death, he says, has robbed the world of motive power & at once tells why it still moves, using ship, beheaded man, ice, lute & any old corpse to prove that lifelessness can be active. This suggests everyone still alive is a kind of maggot: an idea too grotesquely scientific or religious for mere flattery.

1602

POETASTER, OR HIS ARRAIGNEMENT
BEN JONSON
LONDON

TO MY VERTUOUS, AND WORTHY FRIEND, MR. RICHARD MARTIN. Sir, a thankefull man owes a courtesie ever: the unthankefull, but when he needes it. To make mine owne marke appeare, and show by which of these seales I am known, I send you this peece of what may live of mine; for whose innocence, as for the Authors, you were once a noble and timely undertaker, to the greatest Justice of this kingdome. Enjoy now the delight of your goodnesse; which is to see that prosper, you preserv'd: and posteritie to owe the reading of that, without offence, to your name; which so much ignorance, and malice of the times, then conspir'd to have supprest.   Your true lover, Ben. Jonson.

THE PERSONS OF THE PLAY

Imagine this theatre open to the sky like an inn courtyard. It has a high balcony for some actions; underneath it a room hidden or exposed by drawing a curtain; before that a narrower stage like a flat cart with the audience on 3 sides. This stage lets actors move into what cinema speech calls close-up. It has a small trap door over a lift moved by weights on pulleys, to shoot those acting demons through. The start of the play is usually heralded by 3 trumpet calls. Today, after only 2 fanfares, a hideous figure rises in close-up, taller than life size & covered in writhing snakes. This play counterblasts poets who satirized Jonson in their plays, so without proper warning

Augustus Caesar	Lupus	Julia
Mecoenas	Tucca	Cytheris
Marc. Ovid	Crispinus	Plautia
Cor. Gallus	Hermogenes	Chloe
Propertius	De. Fannius	Maydes
Fus. Aristus	Albius	
Pub. Ovid	Minos	
Virgil	Histrio	
Horace	Pyrgus	
Trebatius	Lictors	

POETASTER
[AFTER THE SECOND SOUNDING]
ENVIE [ARISING IN THE MIDST OF THE STAGE]

L   *ight, I salute thee; but with wounded nerves:*
Wishing thy golden splendor, pitchy darknesse.
What's here? Th' Arraignment? I: This, this is it,
That our sunke eyes have wak't for, all this while:
Here will be subject for my snakes, and me.
Cling to my necke, and wrists, my loving wormes,
And cast you round, in soft, and amorous foulds
Till I doe bid, uncurle: Then, breake your knots,
Shoot out your selves at length, as your forc't stings
Would hide themselves within his malic't sides,

To whom I shall apply you. Stay! the shine
Of this assembly here offends my sight,
I'le darken that first, and out-face their grace.
Wonder not if I stare: These fifteene weekes
(So long as since the plot was but an embrion*)*
Have I, with burning lights mixt vigilant thoughts,
In expectation of this hated play:
To which (at last) I am arriv'd as Prologue*.*
Nor would I, you should looke for other lookes,
Gesture, or complement from me, then what
Th'infected bulke of Envie can afford:
For I am risse here with a covetous hope,
To blast your pleasures, and destroy your sports,
With wrestings, comments, applications,
Spie-like suggestions, privie whisperings,
And thousand such promooting sleights as these.
Marke, how I will begin: The Scene *is, ha!*
Rome? Rome? and Rome?
                    Cracke ey-strings, and your balles
Drop into earth; let me be ever blind.
I am prevented; all my hopes are crost,
Checkt, and abated; fie, a freezing sweate
Flowes forth at all my pores, my entrailes burne:
What should I doe? Rome? Rome?
              O my vext soule,
How might I force this to the present state?
Are there no players here? no poet-apes,
That come with basiliskes eyes,
              whose forked tongues
Are steept in venome, as their hearts in gall?
Eyther of these would helpe me;
              they could wrest,
Pervert, and poyson all they heare, or see,
With senselesse glosses, and allusions.
Now if you be good devils, flye me not.
You know what deare, and ample faculties
I have indow'd you with: Ile lend you more.
Here, take my snakes among you, come, and eate,

Envy springs up to anticipate the hisses of enemies in the audience.

This theatre has another freedom lost to later ages before cinema restored it. In a few seconds actors can move from Venice at midnight to Cyprus at noon, scenes being set by their words & action. The public need nothing else except (printed programmes not yet invented) a name on a placard by the stage. The placard today says ROME & infuriates Envy. Ben's comedies are usually peopled with critical satires on types of Londoner: confidence-trickster, shopkeeper, merchant, soldier, lord, lady, wife & prostitute: satires that get him jailed, once for joking about Scots parasites who came south with King James. Envy is enraged since a Roman setting for satire on bad poets gives less scope for charges of libel or sedition.

Ben was son of a clergyman, stepson of bricklayer. He went to Westminster School, founded by monks for the general public, now Protestant but still teaching commoners' sons. He laid bricks for his stepdad; went soldiering in Flanders; became an actor, poet & dramatist 2nd only to

*Shakespeare. They acted in each other's plays. That Ben was no university wit may explain his combative temper & prejudices against him, yet he was England's best Greek & Latin scholar. His style was modelled on Roman authors who believed plain words in a usual order worked best, if extraordinary subjects did not need more. Ben's adventurous age led many authors to make every phrase amusing or surprising. They used words & figures of speech that doctor, lawyer & preacher used to hold audience & tradesmen used to get buyers: pun, simile, metaphor, rhetorical query etc. Ben also uses these tricks but not to make a busy texture of words. As Envy sinks hellward down the demon trap she is halted with her shoulders above stage by an armed man who represents both Ben Jonson & **Truth**. He puts a foot on her head & thrusts her under. Jonson's words always tell what he sees as truth: unlike Shakespeare & Donne who often leave us to our own opinions. In the 18th century critics wanted truth to be as communal as possible so they ignored Donne.*

And while the squeez'd juice
         flowes in your blacke jawes,
Helpe me to damne the Authour. Spit it foorth
Upon his lines, and shew your rustie teeth
At everie word, or accent: or else choose
Out of my longest vipers, to stick downe
In your deep throats; and let the heads come forth
At your ranke mouthes;
         that he may see you arm'd
With triple malice, to hisse, sting, and teare
His worke, and him; to forge, and then declame,
Traduce, corrupt, apply, enforme, suggest:
O, these are gifts wherein your soules are blest.
What? doe you hide your selves?
         will none appeare?
None answere? what,
         doth this calme troupe affright you?
Nay, then I doe despaire: downe, sinke againe.
This travaile is all lost with my dead hopes.
If in such bosomes, spight have left to dwell,
Envie is not on earth, nor scarse in hell.

[THE THIRD SOUNDING]
PROLOGUE

Stay, Monster, ere thou sinke, thus on thy head
Set we our bolder foot; with which we tread
Thy malice into earth: So spight should die,
Despis'd and scorn'd by noble industrie.
If any muse why I salute the stage,
An armed Prologue; *know, 'tis a dangerous age:*
Wherein, who writes, had need present his Scenes
Fortie-fold proofe against the conjuring meanes
Of base detractors, and illiterate apes,
That fill up roomes in faire and formall shapes.
'Gainst these, have we put on this forc't defence:
Whereof the allegorie *and hid sence*
Is, that a well erected confidence
Can fright their pride,
         and laugh their folly hence.

Here now, put case our
      Authour should, once more,
Sweare that his play were good; he doth implore,
You would not argue him of arrogance:
How ere that common spawne of ignorance,
Our frie of writers, may beslime his fame,
And give his action that adulterate name.
Such ful-blowne vanitie he more doth lothe,
Then base dejection: There's a meane 'twixt both.
Which with a constant firmenesse he pursues,
As one, that knowes
      the strength of his owne muse.
And this he hopes all free soules will allow,
Others, that take it with a rugged brow,
Their moods he rather pitties, then envies:
His mind it is above their injuries.

Shakespeare's plays also held more truth than they could grasp but were too popular to ignore, so he was admired as a semi-illiterate genius. Poets (Dryden, Pope & Burns among them) loved Will but learned from Ben. He showed how Latin lyrics, satires, odes & private-letters-for-public-eyes could be modernized through English rhyme schemes. His London crowds of eccentric humorists were rediscovered for an industrial Britain by Dickens. Ben's songs are still sung.

ESSAYES of MICHAEL, LORD of MONTAIGNE **TRANSLATED BY JOHN FLORIO LONDON**

1603

[TO THE COURTEOUS READER]

READER, loe – here a well-meaning Booke. It doeth at the first entrance fore-warne thee, that in contriving the same, I have proposed unto my selfe no other then a familiar and private end: I have had no respect or consideration at all, either to thy service, or to my glory: my forces are not capable of any such desseigne. I have vowed the same to the particular commoditie of my kinsfolkes and friends: to the end, that loosing me (which they are likely to do ere long) they may therein finde some lineaments of my conditions and humours, and by that meanes reserve more whole, and more lively foster the knowledge and acquaintance they have had of me. Had my intention beene to forestall and purchase the worlds opinion and favour, I would surely have adorned my selfe more quaintly, or kept a more grave and solemne march. I desire therein to

This French lord read literature & law with famous tutors, knew court life, travelled in Germany & Italy, was for 13 years a city councillor in Bordeaux, later a satisfactory mayor, being a Catholic trusted by Calvinists when religious strife (which he hated) was deadly. At the age of 40 in 1571 he inherited a country estate & at leisure there wrote his essays. They revived tolerant doubts that Athenians had enjoyed, in a style so playful that censors ignored them. He found it odd that American cannibals used their prisoners more kindly than many Christians used each other; thought it best if all kept the faiths of their parents & did not war about them; noticed laws tend to outlaw the poorest & weakest.

Florio was son of a refugee Italian Protestant. Montaigne, said a critic of this translation, speaks now good English. In the essay on cannibalism & cruelty Shakespeare found material for **The Tempest, Hamlet, Lear.**

be delineated in mine owne genuine, simple and ordinary fashion, without contention, arte or studie; for it is my selfe I pourtray. My imperfections shall therein be read to the life, and my naturall forme discerned, so farreforth as publike reverence hath permitted me. For, if my fortune had beene to have lived among those nations, which yet are said to live under the sweete libertie of Natures first and uncorrupted lawes, I assure thee, I would most willingly have pourtrayed my selfe fully and naked. Thus gentle Reader my selfe am the groundworke of my booke: It is then no reason thou shouldest employ thy time about so frivolous and vaine a subject.

Therefore farewell.

From *Montaigne*, the first of March. 1580.

1605

First Booke of THE PROFISCIENCE & ADVANCE-MENT OF LEARNING, Divine & Humane.
FRANCIS BACON, Lord Verulam: LONDON
[TO THE KING]

Bacon's dad was in the small political clique Elizabeth depended on; James made Francis the English state prosecutor. Polonius in **Hamlet** *may portray him: full of smart wee sayings but too busy toadying to a corrupt king to do good. Bacon had suspects tortured, old friends beheaded, took bribes from both sides in cases he judged. By his hobby, the philosophy of science, he became who Pope called* **the wisest, brightest, meanest of mankind.**

Earlier philosophy (like religion) mainly

THERE WERE under the Lawe (excellent King) both dayly Sacrifices, and free will Offerings; The one proceeding upon ordinarie observance; The other uppon a devout cheerefulnesse: In like manner there belongeth to Kings from their Servants, both Tribute of dutie, and presents of affection: In the former of these, I hope I shal not live to be wanting, according to my most humble dutie, and the good pleasure of your Majesties employments: for the later, I thought it more respective to make choyce of some oblation, which might rather referre to the proprietie and excellencie of your individuall person, than to the businesse of your Crowne and State.

Wherefore representing your Majestie many times unto my mind, and beholding you not with the inquisitive eye presumtion, to discover that which the Scripture telleth me is inscrutable; but with the observant eye of dutie and admiration, leaving aside the other parts of your vertue and fortune, I have been touched, yea and possessed with an extreame woonder at those your vertues and faculties, which the Philosophers call intellectuall: The largenesse of your capacitie, the faithfulnesse of your memorie, the swiftnesse of your apprehension, the penetration of your Judgement, and the facilitie and order of your elocution; and I have often thought, that of all the persons living, that I have knowne, your Majestie were the best instance to make a man of *Platoes* opinion, that all knowledge is but remembrance, and that the minde of man by nature knoweth all things, and hath but her owne native and originall motions againe revived and restored: such a light of Nature I have observed in your Majestie, and such a readinesse to take flame, and blaze from the least occasion presented, or the least sparke of anothers knowledge delivered.

OOOOOOOOOOOOOOOOOOOOOOOOOOOOOOOOOOOOOOOOOOOOO

Therefore I did conclude with my selfe, that I could not make unto your Majesty a better oblation, then of some treatise tending to that end, whereof the summe will consist of these two partes: The former concerning the excellencie of learning and knowledge, and the excellencie of the merit and true glory, in the Augmentation and Propagation thereof: The latter, what the particuler actes and workes are, which have been imbraced and undertaken for the advancement of learning: And againe what defects and undervalewes I finde in such particuler actes: to the end, that though I cannot positively or affirmativelie advise your Majestie, or propound unto you framed particulers; yet I may excite your princely Cogitations to visit the excellent treasure of your owne mind, and thence to extract particulers for this purpose, agreeable to your magnanimitie and wisedome.

*dealt with ideal truth & virtue. Labourers & slaves had to know about physical things, but many wise people believed Aristotle had written all they need know of them in 330 BC. He wrote (for example) that heaviest solids fell fastest. It sounded logical so no one tested it before 1590 when Galileo proved all solids fall equally fast. Bacon was 1 of the 1st to see how experimental science would change the world & urge a government to assist it for the public good. This book suggests King James found a permanent society of scholars to test & publish new discoveries in every kind of science, thus improving British trade, farming & manufacture. Bacon also describes the mental barriers or conventions (he called them idols) that make folk prefer outworn ideas to evidence for new ones. But the king was a scholar who loved old ideas & feared witches. Quoting Angli-can liturgy he said this book was **like unto the peace of God that passeth all under-standing**. A generation elapsed before Bacon's ideas took root in heads containing fewer idols.*

1611

THE ILIADS OF HOMER, PRINCE OF POETS
Translated by **GEORGE CHAPMAN**
LONDON

TO THE HIGH BORNE PRINCE OF MEN HENRIE THRICE ROYAL
INHERITOR TO THE UNITED KINGDOMS OF GREAT BRITTAINE, &c.

OOOOOOOOOOOOOOOOOOOOOOOOOOOOOOOOOOOOOOOOOOOOOOOOOOOOOOOOOOOOOO

Chapman was a fine playwright who by 1614, helped by a Latin version of the original Greek, had put all Homer into English verse. Sometimes mistaken in sense & jogtrot in metre, it is also lively, sensible, sensuous. It moved Keats in 1815 to write his first great poem, which praised Chapman's loud, bold speech. In 1937 Ezra Pound said Chapman's verse should have cured other English poets of the pretentious rumble they had learned from Milton.

The first extract begs the crown prince to encourage poetry, describing man as a tree grown from the poetic seed in the fruit of his brain; for as living bodies are made by sexual love so poetry shapes speech, thought & truth. (In 16th-century Europe most history, science & philosophy were read as poetry, which had the prestige we allow to mathematical formula.)

The 2nd extract follows an attack on critics who damn

*A*nd lastly, great Prince, marke and pardon me
– As in a flourishing and ripe fruite Tree
Nature hath made the barke to save the Bole,
The Bole the sappe, the sappe to decke the whole
With leaves and branches, they to beare and shield
The usefull fruite, the fruite it selfe to yeeld
Guard to the kernell, and for that all those
(Since out of that againe the whole Tree growes):
So in our Tree of man, whose nervie Roote
Springs in his top, from thence even to his foote
There runnes a mutuall aide through all his parts,
All joyn'd in one to serve his Queene of Arts,
In which doth Poesie like the kernell lie
Obscur'd, though her Promethean facultie
Can create men and make even death to live –
For which she should live honor'd,
                    Kings should give
Comfort and helpe to her that she might still
Hold up their spirits in vertue, make the will
That governes in them to the power conform'd,
The power to justice – that the scandals storm'd
Against the poore Dame,
                    clear'd by your faire Grace,
Your Grace may shine the clearer. Her low place
Not shewing her, the highest leaves obscure.
Who raise her, raise themselves; and he sits sure
Whom her wing'd hand advanceth, since on it
Eternitie doth (crowning Vertue) sit.

OOOOOOOOOOOOOOOOOOOOOOOOOOOOOOOOOOOOOOOOOOOOOOOOOO

Forth then, ye Mowles,
                    sonnes of the earth, abhorre her;
Keepe still on in the durty vulgar way,

Till durt receive your soules, to which ye vow;
And with your poison'd spirits bewitch our thrifts.
Ye cannot so despise us as we you.
Not one of you above his Mowlehill lifts
His earthy Minde, but, as a sort of beasts,
Kept by their Guardians, never care to heare
Their manly voices, but, when in their fists
They breathe wild whistles and the beasts' rude eare
Heares their Curres barking, then by heapes they flie
Headlong together – so men beastly given
The manly soule's voice (sacred Poesie
Whose Hymnes the Angels ever sing in heaven)
Contemne and heare not; but when brutish noises
(For Gaine, Lust, Honour, in litigious Prose)
Are bellow'd-out and cracke the barbarous voices
Of Turkish Stentors, O! ye leane to those
Like itching Horse to blockes or high May-poles,
And breake nought but the wind of wealth, wealth, All
In all your Documents; your Asinine soules
(Proud of their burthens) feele not how they gall.
But as an Asse that in a field of weeds
Affects a thistle and falles fiercely to it,
That pricks and gals him, yet he feeds and bleeds –
Forbeares a while and licks, but cannont woo it
To leave the sharpnes, when (to wreake his smart)
He beates it with his foote, then backward kickes
Because the Thistle gald his forward part,
Nor leaves till all be eate, for all the prickes,
Then falles to others with as hote a strife,
And in that honourable warre doth waste
The tall heate of his stomacke and his life:
So, in this world of weeds you worldlings taste
Your most-lov'd dainties, with such warre buy peace,
Hunger for torment, vertue kicke for vice;
Cares for your states do with your states increase,
And, though ye dreame ye feast in Paradise,
Yet Reason's Day-light shewes ye at your meate –
Asses at Thistles, bleeding as ye eate.

English as unpoetic because, unlike Italian & French, it uses many short words. Chapman says these words flow most easily into poetry because – "Our Mono-syllables so kindly, fall, And meet, opposed in rhyme, as they did kiss", while foreign Latinate words jostle & collide in short verse lines like men with huge swords fighting in a narrow space. Chapman then damns all who do not like poetry as moles or beasts of burden, blind or deaf to human speech. The latter, driven by whistles & barks of their dads & tutors & by their own greed for wealth, study only commerce & law, harsh stuff for which they have no real taste. An ass madly chewing on what hurts him is Chapman's satire on the puritan merchant who, hating playhouses where English poetry thrives, reads nothing modern but sermons making him hate other kinds of Christian.

1611

THE HOLY BIBLE
A COMMITTEE OF HIGH ANGLICAN
CHURCHMEN: LONDON

TO THE MOST HIGH AND MIGHTIE PRINCE, JAMES BY THE GRACE OF GOD KING OF GREAT BRITAINE, FRANCE AND IRELAND, DEFENDER OF THE FAITH, &c. THE TRANSLATORS OF THE BIBLE WISH GRACE, MERCIE, AND PEACE, THROUGH JESUS CHRIST OUR LORD.

Mary Tudor had all Anglican church Bibles burnt. Elizabeth's clergy replaced them with a revision by Calvinists (John Knox 1 of them) trained in Geneva. The marginal notes implied that priests outrank kings. In 1603 Anglican Puritans asked King James to ban Catholic rituals still used in their church services. He refused, pleasing most of his bishops by instead ordering this new Bible based on a conservative version licensed by Henry VIII. More recent scholarship shaped it; there were no notes on church & state politics. Though a committee wrote it, & its speech was more solemn than Tyndal's, & scholars said the Geneva Bible was a truer translation, this became the most widespread & lasting best seller in history.

GREAT and manifold were the blessings (most dread Soveraigne) which Almighty God, the Father of all Mercies, bestowed upon us the people of England, when first he sent Your Majesties Royall Person to rule and raigne over us. For whereas it was the expectation of many, who wished not well unto our Sion, that upon the setting of that bright *Occidentall Starre*, Queen Elizabeth of most happy memory, some thicke and palpable cloudes of darknesse would so have overshadowed this land, that men should have bene in doubt which way they were to walke and that it should hardly be knowen, who was to direct the unsetled State: the appearance of Your Majestie, as of the *Sunne* in his strength, instantly dispelled those supposed and surmised mists, and gave unto all that were well affected, exceeding cause of comfort; especially when we beheld the government established in your Highnesse, and your hopefull Seed, by an undoubted Title, and accompanied with Peace and tranquillitie, at home and abroad.

oooooooooooooooooooooooooooooooooooooooooooooooooooooooooooooooo

AFTER MANY MORE FAWNING SENTENCES THIS TEAM OF
BISHOPS ASK FOR ROYAL PROTECTION –

oooooooooooooooooooooooooooooooooooooooooooooooooooooooooooooooo

So that, if on the one side we shall be traduced by Popish persons at home or abroad, who therefore will maligne us, because we are poore Instruments to make Gods holy Trueth to be yet more and more knowen unto the people, whom they desire still to keepe in ignorance and darknesse: or if on the other side, we shall be maligned by selfe-conceited brethren, who runne their owne wayes, and give liking unto nothing but what is framed by themselves, and hammered on their Anvile; we may rest secure, supported within by the trueth and innocencie of a good conscience, having walked the wayes of simplicitie and integritie, as before the Lord; And sustained without, by the powerful Protection of your Majesties grace and favour, which will ever give countenance to honest and Christian endevours, against bitter censures, and uncharitable imputations.

The Lord of heaven and earth blesse your Majestie with many and happy dayes, that as his Heavenly hand hath enriched your Highnesse with many singular, and extraordinary Graces; so you may be the wonder of the world in this later age, for happinesse and true felicitie, to the honour of that Great God, and the good of his Church, through Jesus Christ our Lord and onely Saviour.

[THE FIRST BOOKE OF MOSES, called GENESIS]

IN THE BEGINNING God created the Heaven, and the Earth. And the earth was without forme, and voyd, and darkenesse was upon the face of the deepe: and the Spirit of God mooved upon the face of the waters. And God said, Let there be light: and there was light. And God saw the light, that it was good: and God divided the light from the darkenesse. And God called the light, Day, and the darknesse he called Night: and the evening and the morning were the first day.

And God said, Let there be a firmament in the midst of the waters: and let it divide the waters from the waters. And God made the firmament; and divided the waters, which were under the firmament, from the waters, which were above the firmament: and it was so. And God called the firmament, Heaven: and the evening and the morning were the second day.

And God said, Let the waters under the heaven be gathered together unto one place, and let the dry land appeare: and it was so. And God called the drie land, Earth, and the gathering together of the waters called hee, Seas: and God saw that it was good. And God said, Let the Earth bring foorth grasse, the herbe yeelding seed, and the fruit tree, yeelding fruit after his kinde, whose seed is in it selfe, upon the earth: and it was so. And the earth brought foorth grasse, and herbe yeelding seed after his kinde, and the tree yeelding fruit, whose seed was in it selfe, after his kinde: and God saw that it was good. And the evening and the morning were the third day.

And God said, Let there bee lights in the firmament of the heaven, to divide the day from the night: and let them be for signes and for seasons, and for dayes and yeeres. And let them be for lights in the firmament of the heaven, to give light upon the earth: and it was so. And God made two great lights: the greater light to rule the day, and the lesser light to rule the night: he made the starres also. And God set them in the firmament of the heaven, to give light upon the earth: and to rule over the day, and over the night, and to divide the light from the darkenesse: and God saw that it was good. And the evening and the morning were the fourth day. And God said, Let the waters bring foorth aboundantly the moving creature that hath life, and foule that may flie above the earth in the open firmament of heaven. And God created great whales, and every living creature that moveth, which the waters brought forth aboundantly after their kinde, and every winged foule after his kinde: and God saw that it was good. And God blessed them, saying, Be fruitfull, and multiply, and fill the waters in the Seas, and let foule multiply in the earth. And the evening and the morning were the fift day.

And God said, Let the earth bring forth the living creature after his kinde, cattell, and creeping thing, and beast of the earth after his kinde: and it was so. And God made the beast of the earth after his kinde, and cattell after their kinde, and every thing that creepeth upon the earth, after his kinde: and God saw that it was good.

And God said, Let us make man in our Image, after our likenesse: and let them have dominion over the fish of the sea, and over the foule of the aire, and over the cattell, and over all the earth, and over every creeping thing that creepeth upon the earth. So God created man in his owne Image, in the Image of God created hee him; male and female created hee them. And God blessed them, and God said unto them, Be
fruitfull, and multiply, and replenish the earth, and subdue it, and
have dominion over the fish of the sea, and over the
foule of the aire, and over every living
thing that mooveth
upon the
earth.

THE KNIGHT OF THE BURNING PESTLE
FRANCIS BEAUMONT
LONDON

1613

When grocers & cooks ground their herbs by hand, pestles were as common as spoons but more comic: their shape & use as beater resembled a busy penis. In plays derived from knightly legends **the burning sword** *was a cliche. This title announces a play that, like the spoof Wild West film* **Blazing Saddles**, *mocks a popular heroic genre. Cervantes'* **Don Quixote** *had appeared in 1603. Its mockery of chivalry in the real world spread through Europe & influenced this satire on what folk want from their theatres.*

The comedy of getting a real or pretend part of an audience to perform is a trick as old as open-air markets, yet this play was 1st acted in a new sort of public theatre: roofed, with seats for everyone, & audiences who gladly paid more for them & the luxury of sitting with richer folk. These theatres for over 100 years performed more comedies & tragedies by Beaumont & his collaborators than all Marlowe, Shakespeare & Jonson's plays added together. Being

INDUCTION

Enter PROLOGUE

PROLOGUE. From all that's neere the Court,
           from all that's great,
   Within the compass of the Citty-wals
   We now have brought our Sceane.

Enter CITIZEN

CITIZEN. Hold your peace good-man boy.

PROLOGUE. What do you meane, sir?

CITIZEN. That you have no good meaning: This seven yeares there hath beene playes at this house, I have observed it, you have still girds at Citizens; and now you call your play, *The London Merchant*. Downe with your Title boy, down with your Title.

PROLOGUE. Are you a member of the noble Citty?

CITIZEN. I am.

PROLOGUE. And a Free-man?

CITIZEN. Yea, and a Grocer.

PROLOGUE. So Grocer, then by your sweet favour, we intend no abuse to the Citty.

CITIZEN. No sir, yes sir, if you were not resolv'd to play the Jacks, what need you study for new subjects, purposely to abuse your betters? why could you not be contented, as well as others, with the legend of *Whittington*, or the life and death of sir *Thomas Gresham*? with the building of the Royal Exchange? or the story of Queene *Elenor*, with the rearing of London Bridge upon wool-sackes?

PROLOGUE. You seeme to bee an understanding man: what would you have us do, sir?

CITIZEN. Why present something notably in honour of the Commons of the Citty.

PROLOGUE. Why what do you say to the life and

*licensed by the Stuarts the new theatres reflected their taste. James said Raleigh's history was **too saucy** **in its censure of kings:** few of Shakespeare's kings are **good** men; Marlowe's heroes are villains. High class acting troops & audiences began to think such plays impolite, though folk who hired standing room in cheap roofless theatres enjoyed them until 1642 when the Puritan parliament & civil war shut every theatre.*

*Plays by Beaumont & his partners had few astounding ambiguities, but were not shoddy or written only for snobs. A grocer & wife who push in among gentry on stage, then make the play include what **they** like, prove the play was written at a theatrical turning point. A fashion for plays mocking folk of his class has angered this citizen: he wants plays that glorify it with Shakespearean rant – Rafe's specimen speech is from Henry IV. He, his wife & Rafe are a mutual aid team too strong for a theatre to resist.*

death of fat *Drake*, or the repairing of Fleet-privies?

CITIZEN. I do not like that, but I will have a Citizen, and hee shall be of my own trade.

PROLOGUE. Oh you should have told us your minde a moneth since, our play is ready to begin now.

CITIZEN. 'Tis all one for that, I will have a Grocer, and he shall do admirable things.

PROLOGUE. What will you have him do?

CITIZEN. Marry I will have him -

WIFE.   (*below*)   Husband,   husband.

RAFE.   (*below*)   Peace   mistresse.

WIFE. Hold thy peace *Rafe*, I know what I do I warrant tee. Husband, husband.

CITIZEN. What sayst thou cunny?

WIFE. Let him kill a Lyon with a pestle husband, let him kill a Lyon with a pestle.

CITIZEN. So he shall, Il'e have him kill a Lyon with a pestle.

WIFE. Husband, shall I come up husband?

CITIZEN. I cunny. *Rafe* helpe your mistresse this way: pray gentlemen make her a little roome, I pray you sir lend me your hand to helpe up my wife: I thanke you sir. So.   (WIFE and RAFE *ascend.*)

WIFE. By your leave Gentlemen all, Im'e somthing troublesome, Im'e a stranger here, I was nere at one of these playes as they say, before; but I should have seen *Jane Shore* once, and my husband hath promised me any time this Twelve-moneth to carry me to the *Bold Beauchams*, but in truth he did not, I pray you beare with me.

CITIZEN. Boy, let my wife and I have a cupple stooles, and then begin, and let the Grocer do rare things.

PROLOGUE. But sir, we have never a boy to play him, every one hath a part already.

WIFE. Husband, husband, for Gods sake let *Rafe* play him, beshrew mee if I do not thinke hee will go beyond them all.

CITIZEN. Well remembred wife, come up *Rafe*: Il'e tell you Gentlemen, let them but lend him a suit of reparrell, and necessaries, and by Gad, if any of them all blowe winde in the taile on him, Il'e be hang'd.

WIFE. I pray you youth let him have a suit of reparrell, Il'e be sworne. Gentlemen, my husband tels you true, hee will act you sometimes at our house, that all the neighbours cry out on him: hee will fetch you up a couraging part so in the garret, that, that we are all as feard I warrant you, that wee quake againe: wee'l feare our children with himif they bee never so un-ruly, do but cry, *Rafe comes, Rafe comes* to them, and they'l be as quyet as Lambes. Hold up they head *Rafe*, shew the Gentlemen what thou canst doe, speake a huffing part, I warrant you the Gentlemen will accept of it.

CITIZEN. Do *Rafe*, do.

RAFE.   By heaven me thinkes it were an easie leap
>   To plucke bright honour from the pale-fac'd Moone,
>   Or dive into the bottome of the sea,
>   Where never fathame line touch't any ground,
>   And plucke up drowned honor from the lake of hell.

CITIZEN. How say you Gentlemen, is it not as I told you?

WIFE. Nay Gentlemen, hee hath played before, my husband sayes, *Musidorus* before the Warden of our Company.

CITIZEN. I, and hee should have played *Jeronimo* with a Shooemaker for a wager.

PROLOGUE. He shall have a suite of apparrell if he will go in.

CITIZEN. In *Rafe*, in *Rafe*, and set out the Grocery in their kinde, if thou lov'st me.   (*Exit RAFE*)

WIFE. I warrant our *Rafe* will looke finely when hee's drest.

PROLOGUE. But what will you have it called?

CITIZEN. *The Grocers honour*.

PROLOGUE. Me thinks *The Knight of the burning Pestle* were better.

WIFE. Il'e be sworne husband, thats as good a name as can be.

CITIZEN. Let it be so, begin, begin, my wife and I wil sit downe.

PROLOGUE. I pray you do.

CITIZEN. What stately musicke have you? you have shawmes.

PROLOGUE. Shawmes? no.

CITIZEN. No? Im'e a thiefe if my minde did not give me so. *Rafe* playes a stately part, and he must needs have shawmes: Il'e be at the charge of them my selfe, rather than wee'l be without them.

PROLOGUE. So you are like to be.

CITIZEN. Why and so I will be: ther's two shillings., let's have the waits of South-warke, they are as rare fellows as any are in England; and that will fetch them all or'e the water with a vengeance, as if they were mad.

PROLOGUE. You shall have them: will you sit downe then?

CITIZEN. I, come wife.

WIFE. Sit you merry all Gentlemen, Im'e bold to sit amongst you for my ease.

PROLOGUE. From all that's neere the Court, from all that's great,
> Within the compasse of the Citty-walles
> We now have brought our Sceane: fly farre from hence
> All private taxes, immodest phrases,
> What ere may but shew like vicious:
> For wicked mirth never true pleasure brings,
> But honest minds are pleas'd with honest things.

Thus much for that we do: but for *Rafes* part you must answer for your selfe.

CITIZEN. Take you no care for *Rafe*, hee'l discharge himselfe I warrant you.

WIFE. I faith Gentlemen Il'e give my word for *Rafe*.

1614 THE HISTORY OF THE WORLD
SIR WALTER RALEIGH
LONDON

OOOOOOOOOOOOOOOOOOOOOOOOOOOOOOOOOOOOOOOOOOOOOOOOOOOOOOOOOOOOOOOOOO

NOW FOR KING *HENRY* THE EIGHT: if all the pictures and Patternes of a mercilesse Prince were lost in the World, they might all againe be painted to the life, out of the story of this King. For how many servants did hee advance in hast (but for what vertue no man could suspect) and with the change of his fancy ruined againe; no man knowing for what offence? To how many others of more desert gave hee aboundant flowres from whence to gather hony, and in the end of Harvest burnt them in the Hive? How many wives did hee cut off, and cast off, as his fancy and affection changed? How many Princes of the bloud (whereof some of them for age could hardly crawle towards the block) with a world of others of all degrees (of whome our common Chronicles have kept the accompt) did he execute? Yea, in his very death-bed, and when he was at the point to have given his accompt to GOD for the aboundance of bloud already spilt: He imprisoned the Duke of *Norfolke* the Father; and executed the Earle of *Surrey* the sonne; the one, whose deservings he knew not how to value, having never omitted any thing that concerned his owne honour, and the Kings service; the other, never having committed anything worthy of his least displeasure: the one exceeding valiant and advised; the other, no lesse valiant than learned, and of excellent hope. But besides the sorrowes which hee heaped upon the Fatherlesse, and widdowes at home: and besides the vaine enterprises abroad, wherein it is thought that hee consumed more Treasure, than all our victorious Kings did in their severall Conquests: what causelesse and cruel warres did he make upon his owne Nephew King *James* the fift? What Lawes and Wills did he devise, to establish this Kingdome in his owne issues? using his sharpest weapons to cut off, and cut downe those branches, which sprang from the same roote that him-selfe did. And in the end (notwithstanding these his so many irreligious provisions) it pleased GOD to take away all his owne, withoute increase; though, for themselves in their severall kindes, all Princes of eminent vertue. For these wordes of *Samuel* to Agag King of the *Amalekites,* have beene verified upon many others: *As thy sword hath made other women childlesse: so shall thy mother be childlesse among other women.* And that bloud, which the same King *Henry* affirmed, that the cold aire of *Scotland* had frozen up in the North, GOD hath diffused by the sunshine of his grace: from whence *His Majesty* now living, and long to live, is descended. Of whome I may say it truely, That if all the malice of the world were infused into one eie: yet could it not discerne in His life, even to this daie, any one of those foule spots, by which the Consciences of

*Raleigh's preface (too long to print entire) begins by saying that he has only written a history to ease **inmost & soul-piercing wounds**, as history shows that greed & injustice lead to destruction, & that rulers refuse to learn from it. To prove this he harshly portrays the English kings since **the violence of the Norman conquest**. The words opposite follow his abuse of Henry VII. He had reason for a low opinion of royalty.*

Elizabeth had rewarded his courage & skill as a soldier & sailor with knighthood, jobs, estates & licence to export woven wool. He saw North America could become part of an English empire as great as Spain's & lost a fortune trying to colonise it. He raided Spanish ships & cities, explored the Orinoco, brought Europe its 1st tobacco & potatoes, was MP for Devon. A fine writer & poet, he helped clever poorer men such as Marlowe, Spenser, Dr Harvey who found how blood circulates. Drake & Essex feared him as a rival, cabinet ministers because he was not their tool. They were glad when he enraged the queen by wooing a lady in her court without asking royal *permission. (She would have denied it.) Disliking Raleigh became a fashion. His pride, eccentric pals & chemical experiments suggested black arts. Shakespeare's only hit at a living celebrity is a dark hint about a **school of night**, the secret society where Raleigh & co. were said to promote atheism & magic. In 1603 James Stuart became king of England & Raleigh was tried for treason. He was accused of having been in Spanish pay.*

The truth was that James wanted an alliance with Spain & the Spanish wanted Raleigh dead: he was the enemy they most feared. James had also been told that as Elizabeth lay dying, Raleigh had said that if England became a republic like Venice it would need no Scots king. All this was widely known but could not be admitted. Edward Coke, crown attorney, had no proofs or witnesses so got Raleigh condemned to death by misquoting law & bullying the court. Raleigh answered him with quiet wit that renewed his lost popularity. James feared public opinion in this foreign land where he had no great army. On the axeman's scaffold Raleigh heard

all the forenamed Princes (in effect) have beene defiled; nor any droppe of that innocent bloud on the sword of his justice, with which the most that fore-went him, have stayned both their hands and fame. And for this Crowne of *England*; it may truely be avowed, That he hath received it even from the hand of GOD, and hath stayed the time of putting it on, howsoever he were provoked to hasten it: That Hee never tooke revenge of any man, that foughte to put him beside it: That Hee refused the assistance of Her enemies, that wore it long, with as great glory as ever Princesse did, That *His Maiesty* entred not by a breach, nor by bloud; but by the Ordinary gate, which his owne right set open; and into which, by a generall love and Obedience, Hee was received. And howsoever *His Majesties* praeceding title to this Kingdome, was preferred by many Princes (witnesse the Treaty at *Cambray* in the yeare, 1559) yet hee never pleased to dispute it, during the life of that renowned *Lady*, his Praedecessor; no, notwithstanding the injury of not being declared Heire, in all the time of Her long reigne.

Neither ought wee to forget, or neglect our thankefulnesse to GOD for the uniting of the Northerne parts of Brittany to the South, to wit of Scotland to England, which though they were severed but by small brookes and bancks, yet by reason of the long continewed warre, and the cruelties exercised upon each other, in the affection of the Nations, they were infinitly severed. This I say is not the least of Gods blessings which *His Majesty* hath brought with him unto this Land: No, put all our petty greevances together, and heap them up to their hight, they wil appeare but as a Mole-hil, compared with the Mountaine of this concord. And if all the Historiens since then have acknowledged the uniting of the Red-Rose, and the White, for the greatest happinesse, (Christian Religion excepted) that ever this Kingdome received from GOD, certainely the peace betweene the two Lions of gold and gules, and the making them one, doth by many degrees exceed the former; for by it, besides the sparing of our british bloud, heretofore and during the difference so often & aboundantly shed, the state of England is more assured, the Kingdom more inabled to recover her auntient honor and rights, and by it made more invincible, than by all our former alliances, practices, policies an'd conquests.

ooooooooooooooooooooooooooooooooooooooooooooo
How-so-ever, I know that it will bee said by many, That I might have beene more pleasing to the Reader, if I had written the Story of mine owne times; having been permitted to draw water as neare the Well-head as another. To this I answer, that who-so-ever in writing a moderne Historie, shall follow truth too neare the heeles, it may happily strike out his teeth. There is no Mistress or Guide, that hath led her followers and servants into greater miseries. He that goes after her too farre off, looseth her sight, and looseth him-selfe: and hee that walkes after her at a middle distance; I know not whether I should call that kinde of course Temper or Basenesse. It is true, that I never travailed after mens opinions, when I might have made the best use of them: and I have now too few daies remayning, to imitate those, that either out of extreame ambition, or extreame cowardise, or both, doe yet, (when death hath them on his shoulders) flatter the world, betweene the bed and the grave. It is enough for me (being in that state I am) to write of the eldest times: wherein also why may it not be said, that in speaking of the past, I point at the present, and taxe the vices of those that are yet lyving, in their persons that are long since dead; and have it laid to my charge? But this I cannot helpe, though innocent. And certainely if there be any, that finding themselves spotted like the Tigers of old time, shal finde fault with me for painting them over a new; they shall therein accuse themselves justly, and me falsly.

he would not be killed but jailed for life.

*The Tower of London had apartments for noble prisoners. Elizabeth had been 1. Between 1603 & 1614 Raleigh wrote four books there, mainly for Prince Henry, James' eldest son, who often visited him. Before 1900 all British crown princes made friends their parents disliked. James, though no fool, was a messy cowardly pedant compared with the last of the old queen's heroic captains. The contrast is as great between their books. In **Basilikon Doron** James wrote that kings are appointed by God so bad kings, like bad weather or plague, are punishments all subjects must accept. This history describes folk uniting in nations & republics that single rulers ruin. He wanted Henry to avoid ruin by working with & through parliament. Henry died young. Only the history's 1st part (ending with a Greek empire falling to the Roman republic) got printed. It was popular despite royal dislike. In 1616 Francis Bacon told James that Raleigh, having been convicted of treason in 1603, needed no new trial to be legally beheaded. So he WAS.*

For I protest before the Majesty of GOD, That I malice no man under the Sunne. Impossible I know it is to please all: seeing few or none are so pleased with themselves, or so assured of themselves, by reason of their subjection to their passions; but that they seeme diverse persons in one and the same day. Seneca hath said it, and so do I: *Unus mihi pro populo erat*: and to the same effect *Epicurus, Hoc ego non multis sed tibi*; or (as it hath since lamentably fallen out) I may borrow the resolution of an ancient Philosopher, *Satis est unus, Satis est nullus*. For it was for the service of that inestimable *Prince Henry*, the successive hope, and one of the greatest of the Christian World, that I undertooke this Worke. It pleased him to peruse some part thereof, and to pardon what was amisse. It is now left to the world without a Maister: from which all that is presented, hath received both blows and thanks. *Eadem probamus, eadem reprehendimus: hic exitus est omnis iudicii, in quo lis secundum plures datur*. But these discourses are idle. I know that as the charitable will judge charitably: so against those, *qui gloriantur in malitia*, my present adversitie hath disarmed mee. I am on the ground already; and therefore have not farre to fall: and for rysing againe, as in the Naturall privation there is no recession to habit; so it is seldome seene in the privation politique. I doe therefore for-beare to stile my Readers *Gentle, Courteous*, and *Friendly*, thereby to beg their good opinions, or to promise a second and third volume (which I also intend) if the first receive grace and good acceptance. For that which is already done, may be thought enough; and too much: and it is certaine, let us claw the Reader with never so many courteous phrases; yet shall we ever-more be thought fooles, that write foolishly. For conclusion; all the hope I have lies in this, That I have already found more ungentle and uncourteous Readers of my Love towards them, and well-deserving of them, than ever I shall doe againe. For had it beene otherwise, I should hardly have had this leisure, to have made my selfe a foole in print.

THE ANATOMY OF MELANCHOLY
ROBERT BURTON
OXFORD
1621

THE AUTHOR'S ABSTRACT OF MELANCHOLY,

*W*HEN I goe musing all alone,
   Thinking of divers things fore-known,
When I build castles in the aire,
Void of sorrow and void of feare,
Pleasing my selfe with phantasmes sweet,
Me thinkes the time runnes very fleet.
     All my joyes to this are folly,
     Naught so sweet as melancholy.

Me thinkes I heare, me thinkes I see
Ghosts, goblins, feinds, my phantasie
Presents a thousand ougly shapes,
Headlesse beares, blacke men, and apes,
Dolefull outcries, and fearefull fightes,
My sad and dismall soule affrightes.
     All my griefes to this are jolly
     None so damn'd as Melancholy.

Ile' not change life with any King,
I ravisht'am: can the world bring
More joy, then still to laugh and smile,
In pleasant toyes time to beguile?
Doe not, O doe not trouble mee,
So sweet content I feele and see.
     All my joyes to this are folly,
     None so devine as melancholy.

Ile' change my state with any wretch,
Thou canst from gaole or dunghill fetch:
My paine, past cure, another Hell,
I may not in this torment dwell,
Now desperate I hate my life,
Lend me a halter or a knife.
     All my griefes to this are jolly,
     Naught so damn'd as melancholy.

Elizabeth, a virgin, did not like married clergy but could only force celibacy on clergy in Oxford & Cambridge. Her law made tutors there eccentric until 1890 when parliament abolished it. Burton, an Oxford don, loved maths & astrology. A cheerful, boyish man, he wrote this huge book on madness, mainly the sort called **melancholy***. This, from the Greek words for* **black humour***, was a sullen, nervous state of mind, thought to afflict strong thinkers. It fascinated this mentally adventurous age. Hamlet is the best of many characters showing it on stage. Burton's book is an encyclopaedia of what, over centuries, poets, doctors, philosophers wrote about madness. He applied their words to his own experience so Milton, Sterne, Dr. Johnson, Byron, Melville (all melancholy humorists) learned from his long, solemn, often ironic sentences. These verses from a rhymed preface describe what is now called manic-depressive cycles. They prove speech was then so healthy that even an Oxford tutor could make good plain poetry.*

1629

*Coke knew & could quote customs & acts of parliament framing English law far better than anyone alive. He soon became Crown attorney when juries were punished for verdicts kings disliked. He bullied courts, suppressed evidence & became 1 of England's biggest land owners. Bacon, who was even more servile to the Crown, got Coke made Chief Justice, a higher post but allowing less money from bribes. As kings no longer supported Coke above the law he decided they should be brought under it. He had pleased Elizabeth by hiding an edict confirming **Magna Carta**, the 1218 code promising fair jury trials to all. He had helped James break this code. He now risked his life by declaring (at times the sole judge to do so) the supremacy of common law over royal privilege, & wrote his 4 Institutes to rescue that law from dead languages. As an MP he used it to stop Charles II arresting or taxing without his property-owning senate agreeing. This greedy, spiteful, well-*

The INSTITUTES of THE LAWS of ENGLAND or, a Commentary upon LITTLETON
EDWARDO COKE: LONDON

DEO, PATRIAE, TIBI.

[PROEMIUM]

OUR AUTHOR, a Gentleman of an ancient and fairedescended family *de Littleton*, took his name of a towne so called, as that famous chiefe justice *Sir John de Markham*, and divers of our profession and others have done.

OOOOOOOOOOOOOOOOOOOOOOOOOOOOOOOOOOOOOOOOOOOOOO

He that is desirous to see his picture, may in the Churches of Frankley and Hales Owen see the grave and reverend countenance of our Author, the outward man, but he hath left this Book, as a figure of that higher and nobler part (that is) of the excellent and rare endowments of his minde, especially in the profound knowledge of the fundamentall Lawes of this Realme. He that diligently reades this his excellent Worke, shall behold the childe and figure of his mind, which the more often he beholds in the visiall line, & well observes him, the more shall he justly admire the judgment of our Author, and increase his owne. This onely is desired, that he had written of other parts of the Law, and specially of the rules of good pleading (the heart-string of the Common Law) wherein he excelled, for of him might the saying of our English Poet be verified:

There to he could indite and maken a thing,
There was no Wight could pinch at his writing.

So farre from exception, as none could pinch at it. This skill of good pleading he highly in this Worke commended to his sonne, and under his name to all other Students sons of his Law. He was learned also in that Art, which is so necessary to a compleat Lawyer (I meane) Logicke, as you shall perceive by reading of these Institutes, wherein are observed his Syllogismes, Inductions, and other arguments; and his Definitions, Descriptions, Divisions, Etymologies, Derivations,

Significations, and the like. Certaine it is that when a great learned man (who is long in making) dyeth, much learning dyeth with him. That this Booke is the ornament of the Common Law, and the most perfect and absolute Work that ever was written in any humane Science: and that it is a Work of as absolute perfection in his kinde, and as free from errour, as any Book that I have knowne to be written of any humane learning, shall to the diligent and observing Reader of these Institutes, be made manifest, and we by them (which is but a Commentary upon him) be deemed to have fully satisfied that, which we in former times have so confidently affirmed and assumed. His greatest commendation, because it is of greatest profit to us, is, that by this excellent Worke, which he had studiously learned of others, he faithfully taught all the professors of the Law in succeeding ages. The victory is not great to overthrow his opposites, for there was never any learned man in the Law, that understood our Author, but concurred with me in his commendation. For whatsoever excelleth hath just honour due to it. Such, as in words have endeavored to offer him disgrace, never understood him, and therfore we leave them in their ignorance, and with that by these our Labours, they may know the truth, and bee converted. But herein we will proceed no further, for it is meere folly to confute absurd opinions with too much curiosity.

And albeit, our Author in his three Books cites not many authorities, yet he holdeth no opinion in any of them, but is proved and approved by these two faithfull witnesses in matter of Law, Authority, and Reason. Certaine it is, when he raiseth any question, and sheweth the reason on both sides, the latter opinion is his owne, and is consonant to Law. We have knowne many of his cases drawne in question, but never could finde any judgement given

*read bully became leader of the most popular party in the House of Commons. After the civil war his **Institutes** were famed as foundations of English liberty & justice.*

*Europe's laws grew from old Roman codes, except in England. The rulers & lawyers here used a tangle of edicts from Saxon, Norman, Catholic & later days that even judges with Royal support found confusing. So Coke's **Institutes** pruned the tangle down to a line of precedents rooted like a tree in King Alfred's time & aided to stronger growth by William the Waster & all who followed him – a progressive view. Coke hid how greatly he had reshaped the laws he explained by calling his book a **commentary**; and it made legal business easier for lawyers, so soon replaced the account of property rights Littleton had written (around 1480, in obsolete French) as best English guide to legal practices. By still basing them on precedent instead of principle it made sure most prosperous men could keep what they got by work or cunning or inheritance.*

against any of them, which we cannot affirme of any other Booke or Edition of our law. In the raigne of our late Soveraigne Lord King *James* of famous and ever blessed memory; It came in question upon a demurrer in Law, whether the release to one trespasser should be availeable or no, to his companion. Sir *Henry Hobart* that honourable Judge, and great Sage of the Law, and those reverend and learned Judges *Warburton, Winch,* and *Nichols* his companions, gave judgement according to the opinion of our Author, and openly said, That they owed so great reverence to *Littleton,* as they would not have his Case disputed or questioned, and the like you shall finde in this part of the Institutes. Thus much (though not so much as his due) have we spoken of him, both to set out his life, because he is our Author, and for the imitation of him by others of our profession.

OOOOOOOOOOOOOOOOOOOOOOOOOOOOOOOOOOOOOOOOOOOOOOOOOOOOOOOOOOOOOO

Our hope is, that the yong Student, who heretofore meeting and wrastling with difficult terms and matter, was at the first discouraged (as many have bin) may by reading these Institutes, have the difficulty and darknesse both of the Matter, and of the Termes and Words of Art facilitated, and explained unto him, to the end he may proceed in his Study cheerfully, and with delight.

This part we have (and not without president) published in English; a worke necessarie, and yet heretofore not undertaken by any, albeit in all other professions there are the like. We have left our Author to speake his owne language, and have translated him into English, to the end that any of the Nobilitie, or Gentrie of this Realme, or of any other estate, or profession whatsoever, that will bee pleased to read him and these Institutes, may understand the language wherin they are written.

I cannot conjecture that the generall communicating of these Lawes in the English tongue can worke any inconvenience, but introduce great profit, seeing that *Ignorantia iuris non excusat,* Ignorance of the Law excuseth not. And herein I am justified by the Wisdome of a Parliament; the words whereof be, *That the Lawes and Customes of this Realme the rather should bee reasonably perceived and knowne, and better understood by the tongue used in this Realme, and by so much every man might the better governe himselfe without offending of the Law, and the better keepe, save, and defend his heritage and possessions. And in divers Regions and Countries where the King, the Nobles, and other of the sayd Realme have beene, good governance and full right is done to every man, because that the Lawes and Customes bee learned and used in the Tongue of the Countrey:* as more at large by the said Act, and the purview thereof may appeare, *Et neminem oportet esse sapientiorem Legibus*, No man ought to be wiser than the Law.

And true it is that our Books of Reports and statutes in ancient times were written in such French as in those times was commonly spoken and written by the French themselves. But this kind of French that our Author hath used is most commonly written and read, and very rarely spoken, and therefore cannot be either pure, or well pronounced. Yet the change thereof (having been so long accustomed) should be without any profit, but not without great danger and difficulty: For so many ancient Termes and words drawne from that legall French, are grown to be *Vocabula artis*, Vocables of Art, so apt & significant to expresse the true sense of the Laws, & are so woven into the laws themselves, as it is in a manner impossible to change them, neither ought legall termes to be changed.

OOOOOOOOOOOOOOOOOOOOOOOOOOOOOOOOOOOOOOOOOOOOOOOOOOOOOOOOOOOOOOOOO

Before I entred into any of these parts of our Institutes, I acknowledging mine own weaknesse and want of judgement to undertake so great Workes, directed my humble Suit and Prayer to the Author of all Goodnesse and Wisedome, out of the Booke of *Wisedome*; Oh Father and God of mercie, give me wisedome, the Assistant of thy seats; Oh, send her out of thy holy Heavens, and from the seat of thy Greatnesse, that she may be present with me, and labour with mee, that I may know what is pleasing unto thee, *Amen*.

Our Author hath divided his whole Worke into three Bookes: in his first he hath divided Estates in Lands and Tenements, in this manner; For, *Res per divisionem melius aperiuntur*.

A Figure of the Division of Possessions

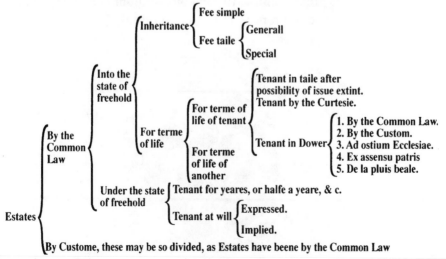

Our Authour dealt onely with the Estates and termes abovesayd; Somewhat Wee shall speake of Estates by force of certaine Statutes, as of Statute Merchant, Statute Staple, and *Elegit*, (whereof our Authour intended to have written) and likewise to Executors to whom lands are devised for payment of debts, and the like.

I shall desire, That the learned Reader will not conceive any opinion against any part of this painfull and large Volume, untill hee shall have advisedly read over the whole, and diligently searched out and well considered of the severall Authorities, Proofes, and Reasons which we have cited and set downe for warrant and confirmation of our opinions throughout this whole worke.

Mine advice to the Student is, That before he reade any part of our Commentaries upon any Section, that first he reade againe and againe our Author himselfe in that Section, and doe his best endeavours, first of himselfe, and then by conference with others, (which is the life of Study) to understand it, and then to reade our Commentary thereupon, and no more at any one time, than he is able with delight to beare away, and after to meditate thereon, which is the life of reading. But of this Argument we have for the better direction of our Student in his Study, spoken in our Epistle to our first Booke of *Reports*.

And albeit the Reader shall not at any one day (do what he can) reach to the meaning of our Author, or of our Commentaries, yet let him no way discourage himselfe, but proceed; for on some other day, in some other place, that doubt will be cleared. Our Labors herein are drawn out to this great Volume, for that our Authour is twice repeated, once in French, and againe in English.

3 NATIONAL BODIES REJECT THEIR HEAD

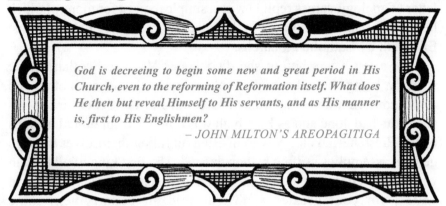

> *God is decreeing to begin some new and great period in His Church, even to the reforming of Reformation itself. What does He then but reveal Himself to His servants, and as His manner is, first to His Englishmen?*
> — *JOHN MILTON'S AREOPAGITIGA*

SCOTS KINGS HAD CHIEFLY RULED WITH HELP from their Catholic clergy. They had no archbishop but the pope who accepted the king's advice on church appointments, even to making abbots of their bastard infants. But between 1542 and 61 Scotland had an absent infant queen married to the king of France, English garrisons on her soil, nobles in the pay of France or England, often of both. With Protestant faith as excuse or with no excuse these nobles seized Church property leaving most clergy as poor as parish priests. Along with their congregations many turned Calvinist - they could only afford a church without rich hierarchies, buildings and vestments, one in which priests were appointed by their congregations, not by bishops in the pay of a lord or king. This had been the earliest form of Christianity, for it let the believer feel superior to riches and those who enjoyed them. It was the only kind of church that could flourish in a nation whose governors were divided by foreign interference. The short reign of Mary, Queen of Scots did not end this anarchy.

She was the only living grandchild of Henry VIII, as wilful as he but without his great fortune. In 1563 she married another heir to the English throne in a catholic ceremony; in 1564 she bore a son; in 1565 was deposed for marrying a protestant suspected of murdering her child's father. Next year she fled to England, leaving Scotland ruled again by cliques of nobles squabbling for possession of an infant king. This king, however, would inherit the throne of his great-aunt Elizabeth if he agreed with her Protestant parliament. Young James Stuart took care to be agreeable. He was twenty one when English lords persuaded Elizabeth to sign his mother's death warrant. Elizabeth wrote him a letter of apology. James replied with a simple request for money (which he received) and did not join in the international outcry raised against Elizabeth by Catholic monarchs.

For a few years before she died James VI gave Scotland some stability, being shrewd enough to play cliques against each other and avoid confrontations. He wanted to command the Scots kirk as his ancestors had done and as Elizabeth was doing. He appointed bishops over a Presbyterian clergy who insisted on ruling themselves through general assemblies as if no bishop existed. The first king of all Britain was a droll fellow. On leaving Scotland to mount the English throne in 1603 ("for your greater good", he told his countrymen) some complained that the English called the Scots a beggarly people. "I'll make them as beggarly as yourselves," said the king, and attempted it. Elizabeth had spent as little as possible on all but clothes. James kept such a riotous court, such reckless favourites, gave such wasteful balls and banquets that he had to sell peerages and Crown lands and keep petitioning parliament for money. But since helping Henry VIII privatise church property parliament had grown stronger, especially the House of Commons whose MPs handled money more carefully than the House of Peers. They raised objections, made conditions and James, though deriding them for questioning his God-appointed self, followed Elizabeth's example of not breaking with them.

But from the security of south Britain he worked to unite his new empire by passing laws that caused a British civil war in his own century and Irish ones ever since. He banned General Assemblies of the Scottish Church and gave Scottish bishops powers of coercion. Presbyterian clergy who came to London to complain he arrested as trouble-makers. And while oppressing the Presbyterian Church where it was most popular he tried to subdue Ireland by giving Scots Presbyterians lands in Ulster from which Irish Catholics were evicted. He boasted he was doing deeds with his pen that his ancestors could not do with their swords and licensed a company which established the first permanent English colony in America: Virginia.

His son Charles was sober and hard-working, a scholar who took kingship seriously. By marrying a French king's sister he made alliances that kept peace with France and Spain, Britain's only dangerous rivals. He still wanted a regular army to enforce his decrees in Britain. If war grew popular he could call on the House of Commons for money to hire regular troops, otherwise The Commons felt England's navy was sufficient defence and that the king's decrees, if agreeable to them, needed no regular army. They knew the French king (Charles' brother in law) had overruled parliaments since a Catholic church, aristocracy and regular army let him tax France as he liked: only national bankruptcy 150 years later made a French king call another national assembly. But Charles believed (like his father and the royal Louis) that kings were appointed by God to be bosses, not partners of middle class assemblies. By thrift and forced loans he ruled England without parliament for eleven years, making magistrates pay more money in poor relief than kings before and kings after him, while stopping the enclosure of common ground. He appointed an archbishop who declared God liked old-fashioned games on Sunday and semi-pagan, semi-Catholic holidays like May Day, Christmas and Easter. He also forbade Calvinist forms of worship in England and sacked clergy who insisted on them. Some tough English Calvinists emigrated to Holland where all could worship as they liked, but hated this lax attitude to religion so crossed the Atlantic to Massachusetts and built the independent, intolerant rural state they desired. Other parties of adventurous, independent-minded folk, mostly more liberal, followed their example. King Charles was too shy and austere to be popular but though he annoyed employers with his poor relief tax and his church that gave their men frequent holidays, he would never have provoked English civil war had he not tried to rule Ireland and Scotland.

He sent Ireland an Anglican viceroy who managed Catholics and Calvinists by playing them against each other. It inflamed them into mutual massacre AND defying the king's government. The width of the Irish sea at first stopped this disrupting England. Scotland did that. Ministers of religion there prayed as The Holy Ghost moved them, sometimes praying publicly that God open kings' eyes to the truth. That seemed treason to Charles. Anglican prayer books prevented such a service so he decided to impose them on Scotland. Scots law gave him powers extinct in England and no Scots parliament had ever limited an adult Stuart monarch. He also knew poverty was the main Scottish trouble and meant to reduce it as John Knox had proposed, by taxing owners of estates that had belonged to the monasteries, thus creating a fund that would finance schools and relieve the poor. Had he first come north and worked with the clergy to increase their pay and power he might have pushed his new prayer book onto them. He began by employing a deputy to impose the Anglican service. It provoked a mob riot encouraged by solid citizens who had no wish to pay taxes and ministers who preferred their own way of praying. They wrote a Covenant, a legal contract binding Scotland to God and the Presbyterian faith. Hundreds of clergy, burghers and lairds signed it.

Charles sent armies against the Covenanters which were defeated. He agreed to pay the Scots a huge indemnity, had to summon England's parliament to ask for money, in return gave promises he broke. Parliament refused to be disbanded so he moved to Oxford and raised an army to conquer London. It failed, but his cavaliers won skirmishes until parliament got an army officered by small landowners and tradesmen promoted for merit in battle. It contained every sort of dissenter from the Anglican church except Catholics, and Britain has never had an army more efficient. Cromwell, a middle-aged MP, emerged as commander. With Scots aid he defeated the king's troops decisively. Not parliament but this new army imprisoned and beheaded Charles after judging him guilty of tyranny, treason and murder – he had ordered war against his subjects, at one point scheming to fight the parliament army with aid from Catholic Ireland. Cromwell's army subdued south Ireland with vile massacres and land clearances on a scale making earlier colonists seem mild.

Charles' son fled to Scotland where native Calvinists and Cavaliers crowned him Charles II of Britain and invaded England, one party hoping to make a Calvinist Kirk supreme there, the other hoping to make their Anglican king head of every church. Cromwell's forces conquered the Scots and Scotland. By then he had abolished parliament and ruled Britain by martial law. Parliamentary and Cromwellian rule tolerated many popular political and religious viewpoints that were not obviously Catholic, so outside the theatres (which were banned) good vernacular English literature went on flourishing in south Britain, though it stopped being courtly, and was never truly courtly again. But for two or three centuries the most popular institutions in Scotland and Ireland were churches persecuted by an absent government, so their literature was nearly all depressed into propaganda and complaint.

Between Two Revolutions

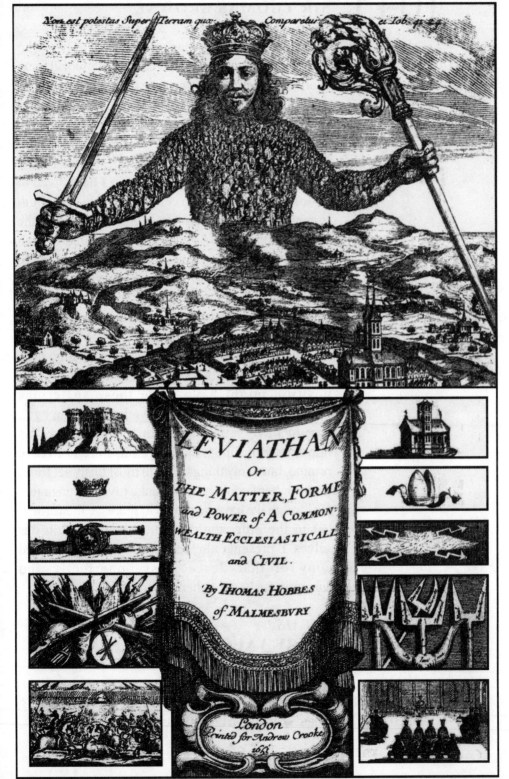

Non est potestas Super Terram quæ Comparetur ei. Iob. 41. 24

LEVIATHAN
Or
THE MATTER, FORME
and POWER of A COMMON-
WEALTH ECCLESIASTICALL
and CIVIL.

By THOMAS HOBBES
of MALMESBVRY

London
Printed for Andrew Crooke.
1651.

1643

*Between 1641 & 1660 the print trade boomed as government was in too big a flux to censor it. Among books loudly urging & scorning old & new ways to run church & state this gentle essay on a doctor's faith was reviled but popular. Doctors were suspected then of atheism: Browne admits he is more liable to superstition, is an Anglican who sees more good than evil in all Christianities, & thinks it unchristian to hate Turks, Infidels & Jews. His tolerance is not (like Montaigne's) got by doubting all authority but good sense; he feels that in a way known only to God **most** authorities may be right so should not be quarreled over. His long ornate sentences show more love of ancient lore than of new discovery. Printed 1st from a bad M.S. copy without the author's knowledge, he had it correctly printed next year with this preface.*

RELIGIO MEDICI
SIR THOMAS BROWNE
LONDON

CERTAINLY that man were greedy of life, who should desire to live when all the world were at an end, and be must needs be very impatient, who would repine at death in the societie of all things that suffer under it. Had not almost every man suffered by the presse; or were not the tyranny thereof become universall; I had not wanted reason for complaint: but in times wherein I have lived to behold the highest perversion of that excellent invention; the name of his Majesty defamed, the honour of Parliament depraved, the writings of both depravedly, anticipatively, counterfeitly imprinted; complaints may seeme ridiculous in private persons, and men of my condition may be as incapable of affronts, as hopelesse of their reparations. And had not the duty I owe unto the importunitie of friends, and the allegeance I must ever acknowledge unto truth prevayled with me; the inactivitie of my disposition might have made these sufferings continuall, and time that brings other things to light, should have satisfied me in the remedy of its oblivion. But things evidently false are not onely printed, but many things of truth most falsly set forth. In this latter I could not but thinke my selfe engaged: for though we have no power to redresse the former, yet in the other the reparation being within our selves, I present unto the world a full and intended copy of that Peece most imperfectly and surreptitiously published before.

1646

POEMS
HENRY VAUGHAN
LONDON

[To All Ingenious Lovers of Poesy]

GENTLEMEN, to you alone, whose more refined *Spirits* out-wing these dull Times, and soar above the drudgerie of durty Intelligence, have I made sacred these *Fancies*: I know the yeares, and what course entertainment they affoord Poetry. If any shall question that *Courage* that durst send me abroad so late, and revell it thus in the *Dregs* of an *Age*, they have my silence: only,

Languescente seculo, liceat aegrotari;

My more calme *Ambition*, amidst the common noise, hath thus exposed me to the World: You have here a *Flame*, bright only in its owne *Innocence*, that kindles nothing but a generous thought; which though it may warm the Bloud, the fire at highest is but *Platonick* and the *Commotion*, within these limits, excludes *Danger*; For the *Satyre*, it was of purpose borrowed, to feather some slower Houres; And what you see here, is but the *Interest*; It is one of his, whose *Roman* Pen had as much true *Passion*, for the infirmities of that state, as we should have *Pity*, to the distractions of our owne: Honest (I am sure) it is, and offensive cannot be, except it meet with such *Spirits* that will quarrell with *Antiquitie*, or purposely *Arraigne* themselves; These indeed may thinke, that they have slept out so many *Centuries* in this *Satyre*, and are now awaked; which, had it been still *Latine*, perhaps their Nap had been Everlasting; But enough of these, – It is for you only that I have adventured thus far, and invaded the Presse with *Verse*; to whose more noble *Indulgence*, I shall now leave it; and so am gone. N.H.V.

Vaughan was in many ways not a man of his time: Anglican Royalist in faith & politics, in philosophy a Hermetic. Like his twin brother Thomas he believed in natural magic. His 1st language was perhaps Welsh, his life in Wales quiet & contemplative. He studied law before practising medicine. A kind of conversion, a mental awakening led to **Silex Scintillans**, *Latin for* **flashing flint**, *a book illustrated with God's arm wielding a hammer striking sparks from a stone heart. His pain was maybe caused by a brother William's death in the civil war, but (& this is another way he is outside his time) the sublime yet matter-of-fact poems touch the eternal –* **I saw eternity the other night/like a great ring of pure & endless light***.*

HESPERIDES,
or The Works both Humane and Divine of
ROBERT HERRICK ESQ.: LONDON

1648

TO THE MOST ILLUSTRIOUS, AND MOST HOPEFULL
PRINCE, CHARLES, PRINCE of *WALES*.

*W*ELL may my Book come forth
like Publique Day,
When such a Light as You are leads the way:
Who are my Works Creator, and alone
The Flame of it, and the Expansion

Priest, Poet, Royalist, Herrick was born a London goldsmith's son in 1591. Despite his dad's reputed suicide the estate was not

forfeited to the Crown as was then usual. Raised by his uncle Sir William, also a gold-smith, Herrick earned a BA & MA from Cam-bridge & was ordained to Dean Priory, a small community in Devon. He became known as a Cavalier poet around 1620-30, publishing this with its defiant dedication to the future Charles II, then a fugitive, with the king his father a prisoner soon to be executed. Like other Cavalier poets Herrick liked hyperbole so likens Charles to God, his Work's Creator *& the sun giving light to the universe:* So all my Morne & Evening Stars from You/ have their Existence & their Influence too*. He lost his living under the Protectorate until the restored monarchy returned it in 1660. He died in 1674, aged 84.*

And look how all those heavenly Lamps acquire
Light from the Sun, that inexhausted Fire:
So all my Morne, *and* Evening Stars *from You*
Have their Existence, *and their* Influence *too.*
Full is my Book of Glories; but all These
By You become Immortall Substances.
For these Transgressions which thou here dost see,
Condemne the Printer, Reader, and not me;
Who gave him forth good Grain, though he mistook
The Seed; so sow'd these Tares throughout my Book.

[The Argument of his Book]

I SING of Brooks, *of* Blossomes, Birds, *and* Bowers:
Of April, May, *of* June *and* July-*Flowers.*
I sing of May-poles, Hock-carts, Wassails, Wakes,
Of Bride-grooms, Brides, *and of their* Bridall-cakes.
I write of Youth, *of* Love, *and have Accesse*
By these, to sing of cleanly-Wantonnesse.
I sing of Dewes, *of* Raines, *and piece by piece*
Of Balme, *of* Oyle, *of* Spice, *and* Amber-Greece.
I sing of Times trans-shifting; *and I write*
How Roses *first came* Red, *and* Lillies White.
I write of Groves, *of* Twilight, *and I sing*
The Court of Mab, *and of the* Fairie-King.
I write of Hell; *I sing (and ever shall)*
Of Heaven, *and hope to have it after all.*

1651

THE RULE AND EXERCISES
OF HOLY DYING
JEREMY TAYLOR: LONDON

Between 1641 & 1660 London was not an aristocratic capital. First the king, then a middleclass parlia-ment, then Cromwell ruled with as few peers as possible while asking the rest to manage their country estates & stay out of politics. Most did.

TO THE RIGHT HONOURABLE AND NOBLEST
LORD, RICHARD, EARL OF CARBERY, ETC.

MY LORD, I am treating your Lordship as a Roman Gentleman did Saint *Augustine* and his Mother; I shall entertain you in a charnel-house, and carry your Meditations awhile into the chambers of Death, where you shall find the rooms dressed up with melancholy arts, and fit to converse with your most retired thoughts, which begin with a sigh, and proceed in deep consideration, and end in a holy resolution. The sight that *S. Augustin* most noted in that house of sorrow, was the body of *Caesar* clothed with all the dishonours of corruption that you can suppose in a six months burial. But I know that, without pointing, your first thoughts will remember the change of a greater beauty, which is now dressing for the brightest immortality, and from her bed of darkness calls to you to dress your Soul for that change which shall mingle your bones with that beloved dust, and carry your Soul to the same Quire, where you may both sit and sing for ever. My Lord, it is your dear Ladies *Anniversary*, and she deserved the *biggest honour*, and the *longest memory*, and the *fairest monument*, and the most solemn mourning: and in order to it, give me leave (My Lord) to cover her Hearse with these following sheets. This Book was intended first to minister to her Piety; and she desired all good people should partake of the advantages which are here recorded: she knew how to live rarely well, and she desired to know how to die; and God taught her by an experiment. But since her work is done, and God supplied her with provisions of his own, before I could minister to her, and perfect what she desired, it is necessary to present to your Lordship those bundles of Cypress which were intended to dress her closet, but come now to dress her Hearse. My Lord, both your Lordship and my self have lately seen and felt such sorrows of Death, and such sad departure of dearest friends, that it is more then high time we should think our selves nearly concerned in the accidents. Death hath come so near to you as to fetch a portion from your very heart; and now you cannot chuse but dig your own grave, and place your cofin in your eye, when the Angel hath dressed your scene of sorrow and meditation with so particular and so near an object: and therefore, as it

*Others were fined, exiled, wounded or killed in battle or on scaffolds. Those who stayed quiet could worship as Anglicans in private chapels, though bishops were banned & Archbishop Laud beheaded. Taylor, son of a Cambridge barber, studied divinity there & at Oxford. He was chaplain to Laud, to Charles I, to the royal army, then to Earl of Carbery after the royal defeat. Taylor wrote what some call **the most enduring monuments of sacred eloquence in English**. Half the religious writing still read in English appeared in this hopeful, troubled age, for great writing (an extraordinary union of strong feeling & thought) is not evoked easily by untroubled faith. To live so that we die sure of having done God's will is (Taylor thinks) hard & yet nothing else is worth doing. It strengthens his dark sentences. He wrote **The Liberty of Prophecy** in 1646 defending religious tolerance. Charles II (crowned king again in 1660) made Taylor privy councillor & bishop of Ireland. Taylor went there & ejected 36 Presbyterian ministers.*

is my duty, I am come to minister to your pious thoughts, and to direct your sorrows, that they may turn into vertues and advantages.

OOOOOOOOOOOOOOOOOOOOOOOOOOOOOOOOOOOOOOOOOOOOOOOOOOOOOOOOOOOOOOOOOOOOOOOOO

THE EARL OF CARBERY IS SO JUST, CHARITABLE AND PIOUS THAT, TO MAKE HIM WHOLLY PLEASING TO GOD, HIS PRIEST MUST TEACH HIM THE EXERCISE OF CONSIDERING DEATH.

OOOOOOOOOOOOOOOOOOOOOOOOOOOOOOOOOOOOOOOOOOOOOOOOOOOOOOOOOOOOOOOOOOOOOOOOO

My Lord, it is a great art to die well, and to be learnt by men in health, by them that can discourse and consider, by those whose understanding and acts of reason are not abated with fear or pains: and as the greatest part of Death is passed by the preceding years of our life, so also in those years are the greatest preparations to it; and he that prepares not for Death before his last sickness, is like him that begins to study Philosophy when he is going to dispute publicly in the facultie. All that a sick and dying man can doe is but to exercise those vertues which he before acquired, and to perfect that repentance which was begun more early. And of this (My Lord) my book I think is a good testimony; not only because it represents the vanity of a late and sick-bed repentance, but because it contains in it so many precepts and meditations, so many propositions and various duties, such forms of exercise, and the degrees and difficulties of so many graces which are necessary preparatives to a holy Death, that the very learning the duties requires study and skill, time and understanding in the ways of godliness: and it were very vain to say so much is necessary, and not to suppose more time to learn them, more skill to practise them, more opportunities to desire them, more abilities both of body and minde then can be supposed in a sick, amazed, timorous, and weak person; whose natural acts are disabled, whose senses are weak, whose discerning faculties are lessened, whose principles are made intricate and intangled, upon whose eye sits a cloud, and the heart is broken with sickness, and the liver pierced through with sorrows, and the strokes of Death. And therefore (My Lord) it is intended by the necessitie of affairs, that the precepts of *dying well* be part of the studies of them that live in health, and the daies of discourse and understanding, which in this case hath another degree of necessity superadded; because in other notices, an imperfect study may be supplied by a frequent exercise and a renewed experience; here if we practise imperfectly once, we shall never recover the errour: for we die but once; and therefore it will be necessary that our skill be more exact, since it is not to be mended by trial, but the actions must be for ever left imperfect, unless the habit be contracted with study and contemplation before-hand.

oooooooooooooooooooooooooooooooooooooooooooooooooooooooooooooooooo

INFIRMITIES OF AGE DO NOT MAKE THE UNGODLY MORE ACCEPTABLE TO GOD; NOR SHOULD A PRIEST TELL MIDDLING PEOPLE THAT THEY ARE CERTAIN OF SALVATION; A BAD MAN ON THE BRINK OF DEATH WILL ALMOST CERTAINLY GO TO HELL BECAUSE A TRUE REPENTANCE IS THEN ALMOST IMPOSSIBLE. EXTREME UNCTION AND PRAYERS FOR THE DEAD ARE ALSO USELESS.

oooooooooooooooooooooooooooooooooooooooooooooooooooooooooooooooooo

My work here is not to please the speculative part of men, but to minister to practice, to preach to the weary, to comfort the sick, to assist the penitent, to reprove the confident, to strengthen weak hands and feeble knees, having scarce any other possibilities left me of doing alms, or exercising that charity by which we shall be judged at dooms-day. It is enough for me to be an under-builder in the house of God, and I glory in the imploiment, I labour in the foundations; and therefore the work needs no Apology for being plain, so it be strong and well laid. But (my Lord) as mean as it is, I must give God thanks for the desires and the strength, and next to him, to you for that opportunity and little portion of leisure which I had to do it in: for I must acknowledge it publicly (and besides my praiers, it is all the recompence I can make you) my being quiet I owe to your Interest, much of my support to your bounty, and many other collateral comforts I derive from your favour and nobleness. My Lord, because I much honour you, and because I would doe honour to my self, I have written your name in the entrance of my Book: I am sure you will entertain it, because the design related to your dear Lady, and because it may minister to your spirit in the day of visitation, when God shall call for you to receive your reward for your charity and your noble piety, by which you have not only endeared very many persons, but in great degrees have obliged me to be,

My noblest Lord,

Your Lordships most thankfull and most humble Servant,

JER. TAYLOR

1651

THE LAW OF FREEDOM ON A PLATFORM
Or, True Magistracy Restored.
GERRARD WINSTANLEY: LONDON

HUMBLY PRESENTED TO OLIVER CROMWELL, GENERAL OF THE COMMON-WEALTH'S ARMY. AND TO ALL ENGLISH-MEN MY BRETHERN WHETHER IN CHURCH-FELLOWSHIP, OR NOT IN CHURCH-FELLOWSHIP, BOTH SORTS WALKING AS THEY CONCEIVE ACCORDING TO THE ORDER OF THE GOSPEL: AND FROM THEM TO ALL THE NATIONS IN THE WORLD. WHEREIN IS DECLARED, WHAT IS KINGLY GOVERNMENT, AND WHAT IS COMMONWEALTH'S GOVERNMENT.

In thee, O England, is the Law arising up to shine,
If thou receive and practise it, the crown it will be thine.
If thou reject, and still remain a froward Son to be,
Another Land will it receive, and take the crown from thee.
           Revel.11.15, Dan. 7.27.

To get allies in their war with King Charles the parliament gentry promised poorer folk a share in government, promises soon broken by army commanders (nicknamed **grandees***) who took estates from royalist losers. That a fair society was still remote grew plain in the 1640s when bad harvests & high prices forced starvation on the poor. Unemployed folk started planting corn, oats & beans on common land. Local gentry (who were able to enclose commons by act of parliament) invoked common law & combined to drive them off. One of these* **diggers** *(as they were called)*

SIR, GOD hath honoured you with the highest honour of any man since Moses's time, to be the head of a people who have cast out an oppressing Pharaoh. For when the Norman power had conquered our forefathers, he took the free use of our English ground from them, and made them his servants. And God hath made you a successful instrument to cast out that conqueror, and to recover our land and liberties again, by your victories, out of that Norman hand.

That which is yet wanting on your part to be done is this, to see the oppressor's power to be cast out with his person; and to see that the free possession of the land and liberties be put into the hands of the oppressed commoners of England.

For the crown of honour cannot be yours, neither can those victories be called victories on your part, till the land and freedoms won be possessed by them who adventured person and purse for them.

Now you know, Sir, that the kingly conqueror was not beaten by you only as you are a single man, nor by the officers of the Army joined to you; but by the hand and assistance of the commoners, whereof some came in person and adventured their lives with you; others stayed at home and planted the earth and paid taxes and free-quarter to maintain you that went to war.

So that whatsoever is recovered from the conqueror is recovered by a joint consent of the commoners: therefore it is all equity, that all the commoners who assisted you should be set free from the conqueror's power with you: as David's law was, *The spoil shall be divided between them who went to war, and them who stayed at home.*

And now you have the power of the land in your hand, you must do one of these two things: first, either set the land free to the oppressed commoners who assisted you and paid the Army their wages; and then you will fulfil the Scriptures and your own engagements, and so take possession of your deserved honour:

Or secondly, you must only remove the conqueror's power out of the King's hand into other men's, maintaining the old laws still; and then your wisdom and honour is blasted for ever, and you will either lose yourself, or lay the foundation of greater slavery to posterity than you ever knew.

OOOOOOOOOOOOOOOOOOOOOOOOOOOOOOOOOOOOOOOOO

"But shall not one man be richer than another?" There is no need of that; for riches make men vainglorious, proud, and to oppress their brethern; and are the occasion of wars.

No man can be rich, but he must be rich either by his own labours, or by the labours of other men helping him. If a man have no help from his neighbour, he shall never gather an estate of hundreds and thousands a year. If other men help him to work, then are those riches his neighbours' as well as his; for they may be the fruit of other men's labours as well as his own.

But all rich men live at ease, feeding and clothing themselves by the labours of other men, not by their

was a ruined cloth merchant & cowherd who saw that if the poor cultivated common lands, waste land, Crown forests & parks of the gentry their poverty would end, but laws made by rich folk stopped this. Poverty was therefore not a punishment for disobeying a kind of eternal landlord, as the landlord's clergy said, it was the crime of greedy men robbing their brothers. Winstanley here asks Cromwell, now head of Britain, to divide all untilled land & former Catholic church lands among the poor while abolishing rents that let rich folk live without working. He wanted a nation of co-operative communes with no law or army to maintain social inequity, but since a revolutionary army would have to found it he addresses Cromwell. But that general (like Napoleon & Lenin) held power because a new rich class & some old survivors knew he would save their goods & means of enlarging them from levellers like Winstanley. Many like him then tramped about preaching & writing that a new heaven & earth must still be built. Where & how he & they later lived & died is not known.

own; which is their shame, and not their nobility; for it is a more blessed thing to give than to receive. But the rich men receive all they have from the labourer's hand, and what they give, they give away other men's labours, not their own. Therefore they are not righteous actors in the earth.

"But shall not one man have more titles of honour than another?"

Yes. As a man goes through offices, he rises to titles of honour till he comes to the highest nobility, to be a faithful commonwealth's man in Parliament House. Likewise he who finds out any secret in nature shall have a title of honour given him, though he be a young man. But no man shall have any title of honour till he win it by industry, or come to it by age or office-bearing. Every man that is above sixty years of age shall have respect as a man of honour by all others that are younger, as is shewed hereafter.

"Shall every man count his neighbour's house as his own, and live together as one family?"

No. Though the earth and storehouses be common to every family, yet every family shall live apart as they do; and every man's house, wife, children and furniture for ornament of his house, or anything which he hath fetched in from the store-houses, or provided for the necessary use of his family, is all a property to that family, for the peace thereof. And if any man offer to take away a man's wife, children or furniture of his house, without his consent, or disturb the peace of his dwelling, he shall suffer punishment as an enemy to the commonwealth's government, as is mentioned in the platform following.

"Shall we have no lawyers?"

There is no need of them, for there is to be no buying and selling; neither any need to expound laws, for the bare letter of the law shall be both judge and lawyer, trying every man's actions. And seeing we shall have successive Parliaments every year, there will be rules made for every action a man can do.

But there is to be officers chosen yearly in every parish, to see the laws executed according to the letter of the laws; so that there will be no long work in trying of offences, as it is under kingly government, to get the lawyers money and to enslave the commoners to the conqueror's prerogative law or will. The sons of contention, Simeon and Levi, must not bear rule in a free commonwealth.

At the first view you may say, "This is a strange government." But I pray judge nothing before trial. Lay this platform of commonwealth's government in one scale, and lay monarchy or kingly government in the other scale, and see which give true weight to righteous freedom and peace. There is no middle path between these two, for a man must either be a free and true commonwealth's man, or a monarchical tyrannical royalist.

If any say, "This will bring poverty"; surely they mistake. For there will be plenty of all earthly commodities, with less labour and trouble than now it is under monarchy. There will be no want, for every man may keep as plentiful a house as he will, and never run into debt, for common stock pays for all.

If you say, "Some will live idle": I answer, No. It will make idle persons to become workers, as is declared in the platform: there shall be neither beggar nor idle person.

If you say, "This will make men quarrel and fight": I answer, No. It will turn swords into ploughshares, and settle such a peace in the earth, as nations shall learn wars no more. Indeed the government of kings is a breeder of wars, because men being put into the straits of poverty are moved to fight for liberty, and to take one another's estates from them, and to obtain mastery. Look into all armies, and see what they do more, but make some poor, some rich; put some into freedom, and others into bondage. And is not this a plague among mankind?

Well, I question not but what objections can be raised against this commonwealth's government, they shall find an answer in this platform following. I have been something large, because I could not contract my self into a lesser volume, having so many things to speak of.

I do not say, nor desire, that every one shall be compelled to practise this commonwealth's government; for the spirits of some will be enemies at first, though afterwards will prove the most cordial and true friends thereunto.

Yet I desire that the commonwealth's land, which is the ancient commons and waste land, and the lands newly got in by the Army's victories out of the oppressors' hands, as parks, forests, chases and the like, may be set free to all that have lent assistance, either of person or purse, to obtain it; and to all that are willing to come in to the practice of this government and be obedient to the laws thereof. And for others who are not willing, let them stay in the way of buying and selling, which is the law of the conqueror, till they be willing.

And so I leave this in your hand, humbly prostrating my self and it before you; and remain

A true lover of commonwealth's government, peace and freedom
Gerrard Winstanley Novemb. 5, 1651

1651

Hobbes was son of an absconding vicar and his uncle, a prosperous glover, paid for an education. He became tutor, friend and factotum to the aristocracy, was secretary to Francis Bacon, knew Ben Jonson and also Harvey, discoverer of the circulation of the blood. Harvey, Galileo & Descartes decided him to become a philosopher who would describe all mankind as a union of parts in physical motion, anatomically, psychologically and politically. He avoided the British civil war by living in France, returning at the age of 63, when his best book, Leviathan, was about to be published. In those days it could have been published nowhere else, for censorship of the press had been put in the hands of Milton who did not censor revolutionary ideas. During Hobbes' absence a deadly efficient English puritan army, originally formed to protect the rights of the smaller landlords and rich burgesses, had tried and decapitated the second king to rule all Britain, allowed and dismissed a couple of republican parliaments, and in the year this book was printed defeated an invading army of Scots and Irish led by the

LEVIATHAN, or the Matter, Forms and Power of a Commonwealth, Ecclesiasticall and Civil
THOMAS HOBBES: LONDON

NATURE (the Art whereby God hath made and governes the World) is by the *Art* of man, as in many other things, so in this also imitated, that it can make an Artificial Animal. For seeing life is but a motion of Limbs, the begining whereof is in some principall part within; why may we not say, that all *Automata* (Engines that move themselves by springs and wheeles as doth a watch) have an artificiall life? For what is the *Heart*, but a *Spring*; and the *Nerves*, but so many *Strings*; and the *Joynts*, but so many *Wheeles*, giving motion to the whole Body, such as was intended by the Artificer? *Art* goes yet further, imitating that Rationall and most excellent worke of Nature, *Man*. For by art is created that great *Leviathan* called a *Common-wealth*, or *State*, (in latine *Civitas*) which is but an Artificiall Man; though of greater stature and strength than the Naturall, for whose protection and defence it was intended; and in which, the *Soveraignty* is an Artificiall *Soul*, as giving life and motion to the whole body; The *Magistrates*, and other *Officers* of Judicature and Execution, artificiall *Joynts*; *Reward* and *Punishment* (by which fastned to the seate of the Soveraignty, every joynt and member is moved to performe his duty) are the *Nerves*, that do the same in the Body Naturall; The *Wealth* and *Riches* of all the particular members, are the *Strength*; *Salus Populi* (the *peoples safety*) its *Businesse*; *Counsellors*, by whom all things needfull for it to know, are suggested unto it, are the *Memory*; *Equity* and *Lawes*, an artificiall *Reason* and *Will*; *Concord*, *Health*; *Sedition*, *Sicknesse*; and *Civill war*, *Death*. Lastly, the *Pacts* and *Covenants*, by which the parts of this Body Politique were at first made, set together, and united, rememble that *Fiat*, or the *Let us make man*, pronounced by God in the Creation.

To describe the Nature of this Artificiall man, I will consider

First, the *Matter* thereof, and the *Artificer*; both which is *Man*.

Secondly, *How*, and by what *Covenants* it is made; what are the *Rights* and just *Power* or *Authority* of a *Soveraigne*; and what it is that *preserveth* and *dissolveth* it.

Thirdly, what is a *Christian Common-wealth*.

Lastly, what is the *Kingdome of Darkness*.

Concerning the first, there is a saying much unsurped of late, That *Wisedome* is acquired, not by reading of *Books*, but of *Men*. Consequently whereunto, those persons, that for the most part can give no other proof of being wise, take great delight to shew what they think they have read in men, by uncharitable censures of one another behind their backs. But there is another saying not of late understood, by which they might learn truly to read one another, if they would take the pains; and that is, *Nosce teipsum, Read thy self*: which was not meant, as it is now used, to countenance, either the barbarous state of men in power, towards their inferiors; or to encourage men of low degree, to a sawcie behaviour towards their betters; But to teach us, that for the similitude of the thoughts, and Passions of one man, to the thoughts, and Passions of another, whosoever looketh into himself, and considereth what he doth, when do does *think, opine, reason, hope, feare*, &c, and upon what grounds; he shall thereby read and know, what are the thoughts, and Passions of all other men, upon the like occasions. I say the similitude of *Passions*, which are the same in all men, *desire, feare, hope*, &c; not the similitude of *the objects* of the Passions, which are the things *desired, feared, hoped*, &c: for these the constitution individuall, and particular education do so vary, and they are so easie to be kept from our knowledge, that the characters of mans heart,

third king to rule all Britain, who barely escaped to the continent.

In the Introduction a consciously late Renaissance, late Protestant Englishman who feels capable of grasping EVERYTHING is challenging like minds to join him in a universe which is harder and drier, but also simpler and more excitingly intelligible than they had hitherto noticed. Like Milton, Hobbes fears neither God nor government because he thinks he can justify both. His conscious influences are not (as in Milton's case) the Bible, Virgil and Ariosto, but Euclid, Bacon, Galileo and Descartes. He is also so enraptured by recent improvements of the printing press, the musket and the clock that he does not believe he is using a poetic metaphor when he describes men and their nations as different sizes of mechanical doll; he thinks he is being modern and scientific. In this he resembles our own theorists who are so awed by their comprehension of developments in the computer industry that they tell us people are essentially computers.

He said all human action came from selfish appetite, & laughter was a sense of glory got from suddenly seeing others worse than we. He said uncivilised folk lived in a *chaos of unending war with each other, but some had contracted into nations when they saw their lives & property would be safer if they helped 1 tyrant crush all others who threatened them. This was how firm government was made. Churches were good parts of government when they taught folk to obey the main ruler. Hobbes claimed this agreed perfectly with those who thought churches & states invented by God to reward virtue & punish sins – Leviathan showed the natural way God worked, as the Bible showed the spiritual. But to most British Christians the words **atheist** & **Hobbist** meant the same. Charles II was a Hobbist. He enjoyed Hobbes' humour.*

blotted and confounded as they are, with dissembling, lying, counterfeiting, and erroneous doctrines, are legible onely to him that searcheth hearts. And though by mens actions wee do discover their designe sometimes; yet to do it without comparing them with our own, and distinguishing all circumstances, by which the case may come to be altered, it to decypher without a key, and be for the most part deceived, by too much trust, or by too much diffidence; as he that reads, is himself a good or evil man.

But let one man read another by his actions never so perfectly, it serves him onely with his acquaintance, which are but few. He that is to govern a whole Nation, must read in himself, not this, or that particular man; but Man-kind: which though it be hard to do, harder than to learn any Language, or Science; yet, when I shall have set down my own reading orderly, and perspicuously, the pains left another, will be onely to consider, if he also find not the same in himself. For this kind of Doctrine, admitteth no other Demonstration.

1653 THE COMPLEAT ANGLER
or the Contemplative Man's Recreation
IZAAK WALTON: LONDON

[To the Reader of this Discourse: but especially To the honest Angler]

I THINK fit to tell thee these following truths; that I did not undertake to write, or to publish this discourse of *fish* and *fishing*, to please my self, and that I wish it may not displease others; for, I have confest there are many defects in it. And yet, I cannot doubt, but that by it, some readers may receive so much *profit* or *pleasure*, as if they be not very busie men, may make it not unworthy the time of their perusall; and this is all the confidence that I can put on concerning the merit of this Book.

And I wish the Reader also to take notice, that in writing of it, I have made a recreation, of a recreation; and that it might prove so to thee in the reading, and not to read *dull*, and *tediously*, I have in severall places mixt some innocent Mirth; of which, if thou be a severe, sowr complexioned man, then I here disallow thee to be a competent Judg. For Divines say, *there are offences given*; and *offences taken, but not given*. And I am the willinger to justifie this *innocent Mirth*, because the whole discourse is a kind of picture of my owne disposition, at least of my disposition in such daies and times as I allow my self, when honest Nat. and R.R. and I go a fishing together; and let me adde this, that he that likes not the discourse, should like the pictures of the *Trout* and other fish, which I may commend, because they concern not myself.

And I am also to tel the Reader, that in that which is the more usefull part of this discourse; that is to say, the observations of the *nature* and *breeding*, and *seasons*, and *catching of fish*, I am not so simple as not to think but that he may find exceptions in some of these; and therefore I must intreat him to know, or rather note, that severall Countreys, and severall Rivers alter the *time* and *manner* of fishes Breeding; and therefore if he bring not candor to the reading of this Discourse, he shall both injure me, and possibly himself too by too many Criticisms.

Now for the Art of catching fish; that is to say, how to make a man that was none, an Angler by a book: he that undertakes it, shall undertake a harder task then *Hales*, that in his printed Book, called the private School of defence, undertook by it to teach the Art of Fencing, and was laught at for his labour. Not but that something usefull might be observed out of that Book; but that Art was not to be taught by words; nor is the Art of Angling. And yet, I think, that most that love that Game, may here learn something that may be worth their money, if they be not needy: and if they be, then my advice is, that they forbear; for, I write not to get money, but for pleasure; and this discourse boasts of no more: for I hate to promise much, and fail.

George Orwell says English culture differs from other nations by appearing in private hobbies rather than public societies. If we admit that many public societies in Britain behave as if private it is still true that good writing & other work has been done for fun by folk living on private fortunes. Walton was a London ironmonger or draper related by 2 marriages to high Anglican clergy. When 51 he retired & mainly lived with them, usually in their country homes. A great Russian said farmers & hunters are the only folk to truly enjoy a countryside: meaning that others treat it as a picnic park. Isaac Walton would have added anglers to that short list. His preface truly says this is no great angling guide. What it gives, often in dialogue, is enjoyment of fields & streams in an ideal England of cottagers & milkmaids who reward a gentleman's gift of trouts by singing the songs of Kit Marlow & Walter Raleigh. This is an England that many have wanted to invent again, & have done so in a few places for short times. This slight book therefore lasted, as Walton anticipated.

But pleasure I have found both in the *search* and *conference* about what is here offered to thy view and censure; I wish thee as much in the perusal of it, and so might here take my leave; but I will stay thee a little longer by telling thee, that whereas it is said by many, that in *Fly-fishing* for a *Trout*, the Angler must observe his twelve Flyes for every Month; I say, if he observe that, he shall be as certain to catch fish, as they that make Hay by the fair dayes in Almanacks, and be no surer: for doubtless, three or four *Flyes* rightly made, do serve for a *Trout* all *Summer*; and for *Winter-flies*, all *Anglers* know, they are as useful as an *Almanack* out of date.

Of these (because no man is born an *Artist* nor an *Angler*) I thought fit to give thee this notice. I might say more, but it is not fit for this place; but if this Discourse which follows shall come to a second impression, which is possible, for slight books have been in this Age observed to have that fortune; I shall then for thy sake be glad to correct what is faulty, or by a conference with any to explain or enlarge what is defective: but for this time I have neither a willingness nor leasure to say more, then wish thee a *rainy evening* to read this book in, and *that the east wind may never blow when thou goest a fishing*. Farewel.

1653

GARGANTUA AND PANTAGRUEL BY DOCTOR FRANCIS RABELAIS, translated by SIR THOMAS URQUHART: LONDON
[THE AUTHORS PROLOGUE]

M ost Noble and Illustrious Drinkers, and you thrice precious Pockified blades, (for to you, and none else do I dedicate my writings) *Alcibiades*, in that Dialogue of *Plato's*, which is entituled *The Banquet*, whil'st he was setting forth the praises of his Schoolmaster *Socrates* (without all question the Prince of Philosophers) amongst other discourses to that purpose said, that he resembled the *Silenes*. *Silenes* of old were little boxes, like those we now may see in the shops of Apothecaries, painted on the outside with wanton toyish figures, as *Harpyes, Satyrs, bridled Geese, horned Hares, saddled Ducks, flying Goats, Thiller Harts*, and other suchlike counterfeted pictures at discretion, to excite people unto laughter, as *Silenus* himself, who was the foster-father of good *Bacchus*, was wont to do: but within those capricious caskets were carefully preserved and kept many rich jewels, and fine drugs, such as *Balme, Ambergreece, Amamon, Musk, Civet*, with several kindes of precious stones, and other things of great price. Just such another thing was *Socrates*, for to have eyed his outside, and esteemed of him by his exterior appearance, you would not have given the peel of a Oinion for him, so deformed he was in body, and riduculous in his gesture: he had a sharp pointed nose, with the look of a Bull, and countenance of a foole: he was in his carriage simple, boorish in his apparel, in fortune poore, unhappy in his wives, unfit for all offices in the Common-wealth, always laughing, tipling, and merrily carousing to every one, with continual gybes and jeeres, the better by those meanes to conceale his divine knowledge: now opening this boxe you would have found within it a heavenly and inestimable drug, a more then humane understanding, an admirable vertue, matchlesse learning, invincible courage, unimitable sobriety, certaine contentment of minde, perfect assurance, and an incredible misregard of all that, for which men commonly do so much watch, run, saile, fight, travel, toyle and turmoile themselves.

Whereunto (in your opinion) doth this little flourish of a preamble tend? For so much as you, my good disciples, and some other jolly fooles of ease and leasure, reading the pleasant titles of some books of our invention, as *Gargantua, Pantagruel, Whippot*, the dignity of Cod-peeces, of Peas and Bacon with a Commentary, etc., are too ready to judge, that there is nothing in them but jests, mockeries, lascivious discourse, and recreative lies; but because the outside (which is the title) is usually (without and farther enquiry) entertained with scoffing and derision: but truly it is very unbeseeming to make so light account of the works of men, seeing your selves avouch that it is not the habit makes the Monk, many being Monasterially accoutred, who inwardly are nothing

*Urquhart of Cromarty, an Anglican cavalier from north-east Scotland, saw himself as 1 of the few bright mental sparks remaining in a nation ruined by stupid greedy Presbyterians & levellers to whom he owed cash. His epigrams & geometry book are not very good. A few sceptics suggest his universal language (in which, he claimed, a 7-syllable word said what needed at least 95 words in other tongues) only existed in his tale of how the only MS explaining it was used (after the battle of Worcester) to wipe bums & wrap sweets. Yet of Scottish writing in those days Urquhart's **Rabelais** & 3 booklets he got printed when jailed in London are all that still give pleasure. His prose is a voice enjoying words for jokes they play & ornaments they invent. Rabelais & Shakespeare had this verbal gusto, using it more soberly. The infant Gargantua's penis is given 13 pet names by his doting nurses: Urquhart gives 38. For 9 animal sounds in French he gives 72. His learning was more from dictionaries than shaped art, yet this book is the best translation in English after the King James Bible.*

less then monachal, and that there are of those that weare *Spanish* caps, who have but little of the valour of *Spaniards* in them. Therefore is it, that you must open the book, and seriously consider of the matter treated in it, then shall you finde that it containeth things of farre higher value then the boxe did promise; that is to say, that the subject thereof is not so foolish, as by the Title at the first sight it would appear to be.

And put the case that in the literal sense, you meet with purposes merry and solacious enough, and consequently very correspondent to their inscriptions, yet must not you stop there as at the melody of the charming Syrens, but endeavour to interpret that in a sublimer sense, which possibly you intended to have spoken in the jollitie of your heart; did you ever pick the lock of a cupboard to steal a bottle of wine out of it? Tell me truly, and if you did call to minde the countenance which then you had? or, did you ever see a Dog with a marrow-bone in his mouth, (the beast of all other, saies *Plato, lib.2, de Republica*, the most Philosophical). If you have seene him, you might have remarked with what devotion and circumspectnesse he wards and watcheth it; with what care he keeps it: how fervently he holds it: how prudently he gobbets it: with what affection he breaks it: and with what diligence he sucks it: To what end all this? what moveth him to take all these paines? what are the hopes of his labour? what doth he expect to reap thereby? nothing but a little marrow: True it is, that this little is more savoury and delicious than the great quantities of other sorts of meat, because the marrow (as *Galen* testifieth, *3. facult. nat.* and *II de usu partium*) is a nourishment most perfectly elaboured by nature.

In imitation of this Dog, it becomes you to be wise, to smell, feele and have in estimation these faire goodly books, stuffed with high conceptions, which though seemingly easie in the pursuit, are in the cope and encounter somewhat difficult; and then like him you must by a sedulous Lecture, and frequent meditation break the bone, and suck out the marrow; that is, my allegorical sense, or the things I to my self propose to be signified by these *Pythagorical* Symbols, with assured hope, that in so doing, you will at last attaine to be both well-advised and valiant by the reading of them: for in the perusal of this Treatise, you shall finde another kinde of taste, and a doctrine of a more profound and abstruse consideration, which will disclose unto you the most glorious Sacraments, and dreadful mysteries, as well in what concerneth your Religion, as matters of the publike State, and Life oeconomical.

Do you beleeve upon your conscience, that *Homer* whil'st he was a couching his *Iliads* and *Odysses*, had any thought upon those Allegories, which *Plutarch*, *Heraclides*, *Ponticus*, *Fristatius*, *Cornutus* squeesed out of him, and which *Politian* filched againe from them: if you trust it, with neither hand nor foot do you come neare to my opinion, which judgeth them to have beene as little dreamed of by *Homer*, as the Gospel-sacraments were by *Ovid* in his *Metamorphosis*, though a certaine gulligut Fryer and true bacon-picker would have undertaken to prove it, if perhaps he had met with as very fools as himself, (and as the Proverb saies) a lid worthy of such a kettle: if you give no credit thereto, why do not you the same in these jovial new chronicles of mine; albeit when I did dictate them, I thought upon no more then you, who possibly were drinking (the whil'st) as I was; for in the composing of this lordly book, I never lost nor bestowed any more, nor any other time then what was appointed to serve me for taking of my bodily refection, that is, whil'st I was eating and drinking. And indeed that is the fittest, and most proper hour, wherein to write these high matters and deep Sciences: as *Homer* knew very well, the Paragon of all Philologues, and *Ennius*, the father of the Latine Poets (as *Horace* calls him) although a certain sneaking jobernol alledged that his Verses smelled more of the wine then oile.

So saith a *Turlupin* or a new start-up grub of my books, but a turd for him. The fragrant odour of the wine; O how much more dainty, pleasant, laughing, celestial and delicious it is, then that smell of oile! And I will glory as much when it is said of me, that I have spent more on wine then oile, as did *Demosthenes*, when it was told him, that his expense on oile was greater than on wine; I truly hold it for an honour and praise to be called and reputed a frolick *Gualter*, and a Robin goodfellow; for under this name am I welcome in all choise companies of *Pantagruelists*: it was upbraided to *Demosthenes* by an envious surly knave, that his Orations did smell like the sarpler or wrapper of a foul and filthy oile-vessel; for this cause interpret you all my deeds and sayings in the perfectest sense; reverence the cheese-like brain that feeds you with these faire billevezees, and trifling jollities, and do what lies in you to keep me alwayes merry. Be frolick now my lads, cheer up your hearts, and joyfully read the rest, with all the ease of your body and profit of your reines; but hearken joltheads, you viedazes, or dickens take ye, remember to drink a health to me for the like favour again, and I will pledge you instantly,

Tout ares metys.

1660

*When Charles 1st's head got struck off all the parliament supporters there applauded as if at a play. So did Pepys, a tailor's son and schoolboy. In 1660, 1st year of his diary, he hoped nobody remembered that. He was soon Admiralty secretary in Charles II's cabinet. This amorous husband, busy citizen, hard-working civil servant wrote out all he saw, heard, felt & imagined during the great plague, the fire of London, the invasion of the Thames by a Dutch fleet. Using a cypher & shorthand that made the diary meaningless to all but his own eyes he filled 6 volumes. When sight failed him in 1669 he hid these behind other books in a specially made case. This was given to a Cambridge college where he had been a charity student. The diary was found & finally decoded in 1822 when Pepys' good work for the Royal Navy was forgotten. At once the vitality & truth of his writing was recognised; but critics from Macauley to R.L. Stevenson were so unused to complete honesty about human male animals that they said Pepys wrote well because he was stupid: too stupid to omit the trivia & indecencies they enjoyed reading but only a fool would record. Later research shows Pepys was a kind patron of good music, trusted secretary of the Royal Society, & efficient MP for Harwich & Sandwich. In 1938 a biography by Bryant called Pepys **Saviour of the Navy.** Charles II avoided blame for political action by leaving it to others, & early in his reign royal dockyards, ships, supplies & payments were so badly run by men who used them for private gain that in war with Holland the Dutch sailed up the Thames & landed on any coast of England*

DIARY
SAMUEL PEPYS
LONDON

BLESSED BE GOD, at the end of the last year I was in very good health, without any sense of my old pain, but upon taking of cold. I lived in Axe Yard, having my wife, and servant Jane, and no other in family than us three.

The condition of the State was thus: viz. the Rump, after being disturbed by my Lord Lambert, was lately returned to sit again. The officers of the Army all forced to yield. Lawson lies still in the river, and Monk is with his army in Scotland. Only my Lord Lambert is not yet come into the Parliament, nor is it expected that he will, without being forced to it. The new Common Council of the City do speak very high: and had sent to Monk their sword-bearer to acquaint him with their desires for a free and full Parliament, which is at present the desires and the hopes and the expectations of all: twenty-two of the old secluded members having been at the House-door the last week to demand entrance, but it was denied them; and it is believed that neither they nor the people will be satisfied till the House be filled. My own private condition very handsome, and esteemed rich, but indeed very poor; besides my goods of my house, and my office, which at present is somewhat uncertain. Mr. Downing master of my office.

Jan. 1st. 1660 (Lord's day). This morning (we living lately in the garret) I rose, put on my suit with great skirts, having not lately worn any other clothes but them. Went to Mr. Gunning's chapel at Exeter House, where he made a very good sermon upon these words:

"That in the fulness of time God sent his Son, made of a woman," etc.; showing that by "made under the law" is meant the circumcision, which is solemnized this day. Dined at home in the garret, where my wife dressed the remains of a turkey; and in the doing of it she burned her hand. I stayed at home the whole afternoon, looking over my accounts; then went with my wife to my father's, and in going observed the great posts which the City workmen set up at the Conduit in Fleet Street.

they liked. Elizabeth's courtiers had also managed her navy for personal gain, but were practical merchants & seamen who dealt directly & steadily with their workers. Charles II's courtiers thought such skill & dealings beneath them, so a tailor's busy son reformed the navy. Charles II was no fool & supported him. Lord Macaulay, also a reforming civil servant but in early Victorian days, did not see Pepys was a major politician as Pepys described meetings of the king's privy council after saying how Mrs Pepys burnt her hand while basting a turkey.

HUDIBRAS
SAMUEL BUTLER
LONDON

1663

[CANTO 1: THE ARGUMENT]

Sir Hudibras *his passing worth,*
The manner how he sally'd forth:
His Arms and Equipage are shown;
His Horse's Vertues, and his own.
Th' Adventure of the Bear *and* Fiddle
Is sung, but breaks off in the middle.

*W*HEN civil *Fury first grew high,*
And men fell out they knew not why;
When hard words, Jealousies *and* Fears,
Set Folks together by the ears,
And made them fight, like mad or drunk,
For Dame Religion *as for Punk,*
Whose honesty they all durst swear for,
Though not a man of them knew wherefore:
When Gospel-trumpeter, *surrounded*
With long-ear'd rout, to Battel sounded,
And Pulpit, Drum Ecclesiastick,
Was beat with fist, instead of a stick:
Then did Sir Knight *abandon dwelling,*
And out he rode a Colonelling.

Charles II & those who got him crowned king again loved this long poem mocking the lower middle classes who had defeated them in war. Like Don Quixote a Puritan magistrate has misadventures in a nation that rejects or exploits him. The brisk couplets hit out smartly at mob politics, religious fanatics, law & medicine. The hero is a dull clown made to be sneered at: a poor caricature of a class whose faith & energy had changed Britain. But having reduced kingly power with Puritan aid nobility & gentry after restoration were happy to laugh at Puritans as unfashionable folk.

Butler was a farmer's son who lived by working as an upper servant of the aristocracy. There was no copyright law then. Despite having written this bestselling poem that was reprinted for years, & despite a gift of £300 from the king, which kept him out of debtor's jail, he would have been buried in a pauper's grave if a London lawyer had not befriended him.

1667

THE HISTORY OF THE ROYAL SOCIETY OF
LONDON, *for the Improving of Natural Knowledge*
THOMAS SPRAT: LONDON

[TO THE KING]

SIR, Of all the Kings of *Europe*, Your Majesty was the first, who confirm'd this Noble Design of *Experiments*, by Your own Example, and by a Public Establishment. An *Enterprize* equal to the most renoun'd Actions of the best *Princes*. For, to increase the Powers of all Mankind, and to free them from the bondage of Errors, is greater Glory than to enlarge *Empire*, or to put Chains on the necks of Conquer'd *Nations*.

What Reverence all *Antiquity* had for the *Authors* of *Natural Discovery*, is evident by the Diviner sort of Honor they conferr'd on them. Their Founders of *Philosophical Opinions* were only admir'd by their own Sects, Their *Valiant Men* and *Generals* did seldome rise higher than to *Demy-Gods* and *Heros*. But the *Gods* they Worshipp'd with *Temples* and *Altars*, were those who instructed the World to *Plow*, to *Sow*, to *Plant*, to *Spin*, to *build Houses*, and to find out *New Countries*. This Zeal indeed, by which they express'd their Gratitude to such Benefactors, degenerated into Superstition: yet it has taught us, That a higher degree of Reputation is due to *Discoverers*, than to the *Teachers of Speculative Doctrines*, nay even to *Conquerors* themselves.

Nor has the *True God* himself omitted to shew his value of *Vulgar Arts*. In the whole *History* of the first *Monarchs* of the World, from *Adam* to *Noah*, there is no mention of their *Wars*, or their *Victories*: All that is Recorded is this, They liv'd so many years, and taught their *Posterity* to keep *Sheep*, to till the *Ground*, to plant *Vineyards*, to dwell in *Tents*, to build *Cities*, to play on the *Harp* and *Organs*, and to work in *Brass* and *Iron*. And if they deserv'd a *Sacred Remembrance*, for one *Natural* or *Mechanical Invention*, Your Majesty will certainly obtain *Immortal Fame*, for having establish'd a perpetual Succession of *Inventors*.

I am,

(May it please Your Majesty)

Your Majesties most humble, and most obedient Subject, and Servant,

THO. SPRAT.

[To the Royal Society]

I.

PHILOSOPHY the great and only Heir
Of all that Human Knowledge which has bin
Unforfeited by Mans rebellious Sin,
Though full of years He do appear,
(Philosophy, I say, and call it, He,
For whatsoe're the Painters Fancy be,
It a Male Virtu seems to me)
Has still bin kept in Nonage till of late,
Nor manag'd or enjoy'd his vast Estate:
Three or four thousand years
                              one would have thought,
To ripeness and perfection might have brought
A Science so well bred and nurst,
And of such hopeful parts too at the first.
But, oh, the Guardians and the Tutors then,
(Some negligent, and some ambitious men)
Would ne're consent to set him Free,
Or his own Natural Powers to let him see,
Lest that should put an end to their Autoritie.

II.

That his own busines he might quite forgit,
They' amus'd him with the sports of wanton Wit,
With the Desserts of Poetry they fed him,
Instead of solid meats t'encreas his force;
Instead of vigorous exercise, they led him
Into the pleasant Labyrinths of ever-fresh Discours:
Instead of carrying him to see
The Riches which doe hoorded for him lye
In Natures endless Treasurie,
They chose his Eye to entertain
(His curious but not covetous Eye)
With painted Scenes, and Pageants of the Brain.
Some few exalted Spirits this latter Age has shown,
That labour'd to assert the Liberty
(From Guardians, who were now Usurpers grown)
Of this Old Minor *still,* Captiv'd *Philosophy;*

*A new Britain & new age are evoked in this dedication & preface by men sure they are helping to make them. A remark by a poet of a later revolutionary age explains this. Shelley said modern poetry & science began when reform broke open the mental jail of Catholicism. He was wrong about Italy (a Catholic stronghold) in centuries when she imported wealth from 3 continents. Like old Greece her cities had societies where clever & powerful men, some of them princes of the Church, met to promote knowledge, art & trade. Italians 1st reached & named America & proved moon & planets were also worlds. Popes only said the universe **must** be earth-centred when thoroughly alarmed by Protestant competitors, religious wars & trade shifting westward. But Shelley's idea was true of England. Marlowe & Bacon could have left nothing memorable in that pastoral land when ecclesiastical courts arrested folk for writing profoundly in their own tongue.*

But England now traded in slaves, fish, tobacco, sugar, fabric, spice & raw material around Atlantic, Baltic, Mediterranean &

Indian coasts. London housed a quarter million souls, more than Amsterdam & Paris joined. A king's effort to rule this & 2 other lands through ecclesiastical courts instead of parliament produced a parliament that put king, bishops & ecclesiastical courts down & out for 18 years. In those years the English worshipped & met to discuss faith & politics as freely as citizens of republican Holland. An assembly of Presbyterian divines in 1643 agreed on a **Confession of Faith** *but failed to force it on everyone. It said everyone is so evil that we deserve eternal torture & will get it, except a few who God (**out of his meer good Pleasure**) chooses to save. It did not mention charity, hugely enlarged The 10 Commandments, & was a bracing religion for hard workers in harsh climates who expected little from others. In America until the 19th century, & Scotland & Ulster until the 20th, schoolchildren were made to recite a form of the Confession but in most of England folk wanted a kinder God. Milton, recalling an earlier effort by Archbishop Laud to force conformity on Britain, declared New Presbyter is but old Priest writ*

But 'twas Rebellion call'd to fight
For such a long oppressed Right.
Bacon *at last, a mighty Man, arose,*
Whom a wise King and Nature chose
Lord Chancellour of both their Laws,
And boldly undertook the injur'd Pupils caus.
III.
Autority, which did a Body boast,
Though 'twas but Air condens'd,
         and stalk'd about,
Like some old Giants more Gigantic Ghost,
To terrifie the Learned Rout
With the plain Magique of tru Reasons Light,
He chac'd out of our sight,
Nor suffer'd Living Men to be misled
By the vain shadows of the Dead:
To Graves, from whence it rose,
         the conquer'd Phantome fled;
He broke that Monstrous God which stood
In midst of th'Orchard, and the whole did claim,
Which with a useless Sith of Wood,
And something else not worth a name,
(Both vast for shew, yet neither fit
Or to Defend, or to Beget;
Ridiculous and senceless Terrors!) made
Children and superstitious Men afraid.
The Orchards open now, and free;
Bacon has broke that Scar-crow Deitie;
Come, enter, all that will,
Behold the rip'ned Fruit,
         come gather now your Fill.
Yet still, methinks, we fain would be
Catching at the Forbidden Tree,
We would be like the Deitie,
When Truth and Falshood, Good and Evil, we
Without the Sences aid within our selves would see;
For 'tis God only who can find
All Nature in his Mind.

IV.

From Words, which are but Pictures of the Thought,
(Though we our Thoughts
                   from them perversly drew)
To Things, the Minds right Object, he it brought,
Like foolish Birds to painted Grapes we flew;
He fought and gather'd for our use the Tru;
And when on heaps the chosen Bunches lay,
He prest them wisely the Mechanic way,
Till all their juyce did in one Vessel joyn,
Ferment into a Nourishment Divine,
The thirsty Souls refreshing Wine.
Who to the life an exact Piece would make,
Must not from others Work a Copy take;
No, not from Rubens *or* Vandike;
Much less content himself to make it like
Th'Idaeas and the Images which ly
In his own Fancy, or his Memory.
No, he before his sight must place
The Natural and Living Face;
The real Object must command
Each Judgment of his Eye,
                   and Motion of his Hand.

V.

From these and all long Errors of the way,
In which our wandring Praedecessors went,
And like th'old Hebrews *many years did stray*
In Desarts but of small extent,
Bacon, *like* Moses, *led us forth at last,*
The barren Wilderness he past,
Did on the very Border stand
Of the blest promis'd Land,
And from the Mountains Top of his Exalted Wit,
Saw it himself, and shew'd us it.
But Life did never to one Man allow
Time to Discover Worlds, and Conquer too;
Nor can so short a Line sufficient be
To fadome the vast depths of Natures Sea:

large. He saw the Commonwealth as a free market for ideas as well as goods, where most folk would choose the best if choice was not limited by government. The army of parliament shared that opinion. No other army has so combined discipline & democracy.

It excluded men of title, promoting for merit only, so officers (as in the armies of revolutionary France) were from trades that nobles thought servile. When not fighting or marching the regiments recombined in various religious & political groups to worship God or debate. These groups chose their own cleric or chairman who, if of low army rank, was now able to rebuke or to silence any officer at their meeting. Yet in war the strict obedience & courage of this army was always victorious. It was paid by gifts & sale of estates taken from beaten royalists & Irish Catholics, so the army helped busy men with new ideas become landed gents. By rackrenting tenants in Ireland (where no law restrained them) & by farming in new, more productive ways they got cash to buy shares in new business. Rent, land-yield, manufacture, trade, colonial

growth fed each other
until Britain had the
biggest industrial em-
pire in the world, so
Cromwell's army at last
strengthened an upper
class it began by
deposing. But it also
renewed that great
dissenting faith of the
English Lollards: that
God's will **can** be done
on earth as it is in
heaven: a tradition often
pushed down afterward
but never extinguished.
Evangelist sects that
still flourish started
then, including the
Quakers who founded
Pennsylvania.

   The excitement of
new ideas, markets &
inventions   brought
together these: –
Robert Boyle, Earl of
Cork's son who, by work
on expanding gases & a
molecular   theory,
began modern che-
mistry. Founder of East
India Company. He
hoped trade with the
Orient would plant the
Christian faith there;
had visited Accademia
dei Lincei in Italy to
which Galileo belonged.
Robert Hooke, chemist,
geometrist, botanist;
discoverer of law gov-
erning elastic bodies;
improver of telescope,
microscope, quadrant,
spring watch & clock;
city surveyor, planner,
architect. **Christopher
Wren,** Architect. **John
Wilkins,** Cromwell's
brother-in-law, Bishop

The work he did we ought t'admire,
And were unjust if we should more require
From his few years, divided 'twixt th'Excess
Of low Affliction, and high Happiness:
For who on things remote can fix his sight,
That's always in a Triumph, or a Fight?
VI.
From you, great Champions, we expect to get
These spacious Countries but discover'd yet;
Countries where yet instead of Nature, we
Her Images and Idols worship'd see:
These large and wealthy Regions to subdu,
Though Learning has whole Armies at command,
Quarter'd about in every Land,
A better Troop she ne're together drew.
Methinks, like Gideon's *little Band,*
God with Design has pickt out you,
To do these noble Wonders by a Few:
When the whole Host he saw, They are (said he)
Too many to O'recome for Me;
And now he chuses out his Men,
Much in the way that he did then:
Not those many whom he found
Idely extended on the ground,
To drink with their dejected head
The Stream just so as by their Mouths it fled:
No, but those Few who took the Waters up,
And made of their laborious Hands the Cup.
VII.
Thus you prepar'd; and in the glorious Fight
Their wondrous pattern too you take:
Their old and empty Pitchers first they brake,
And with their Hands then lifted up the Light.
Io! Sound too the Trumpets here!
Already your victorious Lights appear;
New Scenes of Heven already we espy,
And Crowds of golden Worlds on high;
Which from the spacious Plains of Earth and Sea,

Could never yet discover'd be
By Sailers or Chaldaeans *watchful Eye.*
Natures great Works no distance can obscure,
No smalness her near Objects can secure,
Y' have taught the curious Sight to press
Into the privatest recess
Of her imperceptible Littleness.
She with much stranger Art than his who put
*All th'*Iliads *in a Nut,*
The numerous work of Life does into Atomes shut.
Y' have learn'd to Read her smallest Hand,
And well begun her deepest Sense to Understand.
VIII.
Mischief and tru Dishonour fall on those
Who would to laughter or to scorn expose
So Virtuous and so Noble a Design,
So Human for its Use, for Knowledge so Divine.
The things which these proud men despise, and call
Impertinent, and vain, and small,
Those smallest things of Nature let me know,
Rather than all their greatest Actions Doe.
Whoever would Deposed Truth advance
Into the Throne usurp'd from it,
Must feel at first the Blows of Ignorance,
And the sharp Points of Envious Wit.
So when by various turns of the Celestial Dance,
In many thousand years
A Star, so long unknown, appears,
Though Heven itself more beauteous by it grow,
It troubles and alarms the World below,
Does to the Wise a Star, to Fools a Meteor show.
IX
With Courage and Success you the bold work begin;
Your Cradle has not Idle bin:
None e're but Hercules *and you could be*
At five years Age worthy a History.
And ne're did Fortune better yet
Th'Historian to the Story fit:

of Chester who wrote of life on the moon & how to fly there. With some other like minds they called themselves (since they had no fixed meeting place) **The Invisible College**. They thought experimental science a highway to truth; that it had been blocked by superstition since old Greece decayed, & they were reopening it as Bacon had foretold. Cowley's poem speaks of this, & their wish to use words that refer directly to things, & avoid rhetorical tricks & ornaments.

In 1660 Charles II was British king again but an ambassador of France told Louis XIV that the land was still republican. Louis was richest man in Europe as he directly taxed French industry, trade & colonies. Charles II got so little of the great wealth flowing into London that he took a secret pension from Louis in return for a promise (which he broke) to become Catholic. But chemistry was 1 of his hobbies & he was glad when the Invisible College went public, made him chief member & called itself **The Royal Society**. With the constitution of a private club, it is still aiding research & sharing scientific news.

*But for great truths to be found in a flea's guts & the moon's craters struck many as a huge joke. So Cowley, then thought **the best of poets**, was elected to dignify this history with this introduction. The shift from a more royal to a more commercial & scientific style of writing is shown by contrasting Shakespeare & Donne's rich, intricate lines & Cowley's more prosaic ones.*

As you from all Old Errors free
And purge the Body of Philosophy;
So from all Modern Folies He
Has vindicated Eloquence and Wit.
His candid Stile like a clean Stream does slide,
And his bright Fancy all the way
Does like the Sun-shine in it play;
It does like Thames, *the best of Rivers, glide,*
Where the God does not rudely overturn,
But gently pour the Crystal Urn,
And with judicious hand
                    does the whole Current guide.
T' has all the Beauties Nature can impart,
And all the comely Dress without the paint of Art.

1668

PARADISE LOST
JOHN MILTON
LONDON

Entitled THE VERSE & added to the 2nd edition, this preface was probably written because a critic of the 1st complained it did not rhyme. A political manifesto underlies this answer. Milton believes kings, like rhyme, are also a troublesome modern bondage invented by a barbarous age.

Milton's dad had been rejected by his own Catholic dad for turning Protestant, & prospered by writing legal documents & moneylending. He paid a Scots Presbyterian to teach his son but was no puritan, being a fine musician. Maybe his wife's early death led

THE MEASURE is *English* Heroic Verse without Rime, as that of *Homer* in *Greek*, and *Virgil* in *Latin*; Rime being no necessary Adjunct or true Ornament of Poem or good Verse, in longer Works especially, but the Invention of a barbarous Age, to set off wretched matter and lame Meeter; grac't indeed since by the use of some famous modern Poets, carried away by Custom, but much to thir own vexation, hindrance, and constraint to express many things otherwise, and for the most part worse then else they would have exprest them. Not without cause therefore some both *Italian* and *Spanish* Poets of prime note have rejected Rime both in longer and shorter Works, as have also long since our best *English* Tragedies, as a thing of it self, to all judicious eares, triveal and of no true musical delight; which consists only in apt Numbers, fit quantity of Syllables, and the sense variously drawn out from one Verse into another, not in the jingling sound of like endings, a fault avoyded by the learned Ancients both in Poetry and all good Oratory. This neglect then of Rime so little is to be taken for a defect, though it may seem so perhaps to vulgar Readers, that it rather is to be esteem'd an example set, the first in *English*, of ancient liberty recover'd to Heroic Poem from the troublesome and modern bondage of Rimeing.

[THE ARGUMENT of the First Book]
The first Book proposes first in brief the whole Subject, Mans disobedience, and the loss thereupon of Paradise wherein he was plac't: *Then touches* the prime cause of his fall, the Serpent, or rather Satan in the Serpent; who revolting from God, and drawing to his side many Legions of Angels, was by the command of God driven out of Heaven with all his Crew into the great Deep. *Which action past over, the Poem hasts into the midst of things, presenting* Satan with his Angels fallen into Hell, describ'd here, not in the Center (*for Heaven and Earth may be suppos'd as yet not made, certainly not yet accurst*) but in a place of utter darknesse, fitliest call'd *Chaos.* Here *Satan* with his Angels lying on the burning Lake, thunderstruck and astonisht, after a certain space recovers, as from confusion, calls up him who next in Order and Dignity lay by him; they confer of thir miserable fall. *Satan* awakens all his Legions, who lay till then in the same manner confounded; they rise, thir Numbers, array of Battel, thir chief Leaders nam'd, according to the Idols known afterwards in *Canaan* and the Countries adjoyning. To these *Satan* directs his Speech, comforts them with hope yet of regaining Heaven, but tells them lastly of a new World and new kind of Creature to be created, according to an ancient Prophesie or report in Heaven; *for that Angels were long before this visible Creation, was the opinion of many ancient Fathers.* To find out the truth of this Prophesie, and what to determin thereon he refers to a full Councell. What his Associates

him to educate the boy with unusual deference toward his talent. Milton became consciously scholarly, poetic & virtuous - for he who would write well hereafter of laudable things ought himself to be a true poem. He wished to write as well as Homer about war, but with nobler reasons; to write as well as Virgil about creating nations, but republics, not empires; to write like Moses (then thought author of Genesis) about the earliest things, but as a Christian who knew world history; to show heaven, earth & hell with Dante's scope, but as a Protestant who read Galileo. He studied & wrote their 4 tongues so well that parliament made him its foreign secretary & defender against denunciations for killing Charles 1st. He went blind writing tracts for parliament & others urging social reform, especially easy divorce for men. His royalist wife had left him, only returning with the king's defeat. This gave his epic a climax. A terrifically creative, foreseeing God goads his chief angel to revolt & invade Eden, thus making a husband & wife defy God, quarrel, learn they need each

*other, beg forgiveness &
enter a world inclined
to disasters, but where
errors can teach us to
do better. The **Aeneid**
hero is shown a vision
of his efforts at last
making a better world
through imperial Rome.
Milton could not, as he
had hoped, console the
parents of mankind with
visions of descendants
entering a pure British
Protestant Republic. He
shows them a future of
free people, out of
luxury, folly & sloth,
submitting to tyrants
again & again. This, of
course, was Walter
Raleigh's historical
vision.*

*Milton believed
rhetoric essential to
great poetry because
easy, trivial talk was
common to courtiers &
irresponsible idiots. He
used the grammar of 4
other tongues to enrich
Shakespearian blank
verse, building sen-
tences with so many
clauses that at a 1st
reading their solemn
music must be heard
aloud to make sense.*

thence attempt. *Pandemonium* the Palace of *Satan*
rises, suddenly built out of the Deep: The infernal
Peers there sit in Counsel.

[BOOK I]

*O F Mans First Disobedience, and the Fruit
Of that Forbidden Tree, whose mortal tast
Brought Death into the World, and all our woe,
With loss of Eden, till one greater Man
Restore us, and regain the blissful Seat,
Sing Heav'nly Muse, that on the secret top
Of Oreb, or of Sinai, didst inspire
That Shepherd, who first taught the chosen Seed,
In the Beginning how the Heav'ns and Earth
Rose out of Chaos: Or, if Sion Hill
Delight thee more, and Siloa's Brook that flow'd
Fast by the Oracle of God; I thence
Invoke thy aid to my adventrous Song,
That with no middle flight intends to soar
Above th' Aonian Mount, while it pursues
Things unattempted yet in Prose or Rhime.
And chiefly Thou O Spirit, that dost prefer
Before all Temples th' upright heart and pure,
Instruct me, for Thou know'st; Thou from the first
Wast present, and with mighty wings outspread
Dove-like satst brooding on the vast Abyss,
And mad'st it pregnant: What in me is dark
Illumine, what is low raise and support;
That to the highth of this great Argument
I may assert th' Eternal Providence,
And justifie the wayes of God to men.*

1670

POEMS OF FELICITY
THOMAS TRAHERNE
LONDON

[The Author to the Critical Peruser]

*T HE NAKED TRUTH in many faces shewn,
Whose inward Beauties very few hav known,*

A simple Light, transparent Words, a Strain
That lowly creeps, yet maketh Mountains plain,
Brings down the highest Mysteries to sense
And keeps them there; that is Our Excellence:
At that we aim; to th' end thy Soul might see
With open Eys they Great Felicity,
Its Objects view, and trace the glorious Way
Wherby thou may'st thy Highest Bliss enjoy.

No curling Metaphors that gild the Sence,
Nor Pictures here, nor painted Eloquence;
No florid Streams of Superficial Gems,
But real Crowns & Thrones & Diadems!
That Gold on Gold should hiding shining ly
May well be reckon'd baser Heraldry.

An easy Stile drawn from a native vein,
A clearer Stream than that which Poets feign,
Whose bottom may, how deep so'ere, be seen,
Is that which I think fit to win Esteem:
Els we could speak Zamzummin *words, & tell*
A Tale in tongues that sound like Babel-Hell;
In Meteors speak, in blazing Prodigies,
Things that amaze, but will not make us wise.

On shining Banks we could nigh Tagus *walk;*
In flow'ry Meads of rich Pactolus *talk;*
Bring in the Druids, *& the* Sybills *view;*
See what the Rites are which the Indians *do;*
Derive along the channel of our Quill
The Streams that flow from high Parnassus *hill;*
Ransack all Nature's Rooms, & add the things
Which Persian *Courts enrich; to make Us Kings:*
To make us Kings indeed! Not verbal Ones,
But reall Kings, exalted unto Thrones;
And more than Golden Thrones! 'Tis this I do,
Letting Poëtick Strains & Shadows go.

Traherne, like Vaughan, was a true mystic & a contemplative clergyman. Son of a shoemaker in Hereford & orphaned early, he was brought up by a wealthy uncle, studied at Oxford & in 1660 was ordained as a village rector in the restored Church of England, later becoming chaplain in a noble's household. His poems & inspired prose were in manuscript until 1896 when some were bought for a few pence by a collector from a bookstall in London. They were anonymous, but a literary detective discovered the author through the 1 book he had printed when alive: **Roman Forgeries**, *an anti-Catholic polemic. More manuscript was rescued in 1967 from a burning rubbish tip. "Someone up there" clearly wanted these works read, but not exactly as Traherne wrote them. Research shows some poems were revised by his brother Philip, to make the rhythms & theology more conventional.*

Traherne is in the British tradition of Pelagius, Juliana of Norwich, Vaughan, Milton & the artists Blake, Gill, Spencer: folk so sure God is good & made our body for *pleasure that the idea of original sin hardly interests them. St. Augustine, Luther & Calvin believed all children so naturally evil that babies who died without baptism would be tortured in hell & deserve to be. Traherne thinks sin an adult disease infants can teach us how to cure if, like them, we accept the universe as a wonderfully made gift. The millions of grotesque creatures, the endless suns & other worlds now seen through microscopes & telescopes were not, to him, alarming evidence of human insignificance, but new proof of God's unlimited creative generosity. He writes to show **ALL THINGS...** to be **Objects of Happiness**. His best poems convey what he called **Felicity**: the spiritual state of **enjoying the world aright**. Consciousness expanding, awareness-heightening, mantric are newer words for them.*

I cannot imitat their vulgar Sence
Who Cloaths admire, but not the Man they fence
Against the Cold; and while they wonder at
His Rings, his precious Stones, his Gold & Plate;
The middle piece, his Body & his Mind,
They over-look; no Beauty in them find:
God's Works they slight, their own *they magnify,*
His they contemn, or careless pass them by;
Their woven Silks & wel-made Suits they prize,
Valu their Gems, but not their useful Eys:
Their precious Hands, their Tongues & Lips divine,
Their polisht Flesh where whitest Lillies join
With blushing Roses & with saphire Veins,
The Bones, the Joints, & that which els remains
Within that curious Fabrick, Life & Strength,
I' th' wel-compacted bredth & depth & length
Of various Limbs, that living Engins be
Of glorious worth; God's Work they will not see:
Nor yet the Soul, *in whose concealed Face,*
Which comprehendeth all unbounded Space,
GOD may be seen; tho she can understand
The Length of Ages & the Tracts of Land
That from the Zodiac *do extended ly*
Unto the Poles, *and view* Eternity.
Ev'n thus do idle Fancies, Toys, & Words,
(Like gilded Scabbards sheathing rusty Swords)
Take vulgar Souls; who gaze on rich Attire
But God's diviner Works do ne'r admire.

1675

THE COUNTRY-WIFE, A COMEDY
WILLIAM WYCHERLEY
LONDON

[THE PERSONS]

MR. *HORNER*	MR. *HARCOURT*	MR. *DORILANT*
MR. *PINCHWIFE*	MR. *SPARKISH*	SIR *JASPAR FIDGET*
MRS. *MARGERY PINCHWIFE*	MRS. *ALITHEA*	MY LADY *FIDGET*
MRS. *DAINTY FIDGET*	MRS. *SQUEAMISH*	OLD LADY *SQUEAMISH*
A *BOY*	A *QUACK*	LUCY, ALITHEA'S *MAID*

[PROLOGUE, spoken by Mr. *Hart* at the Theatre Royal]

*P*OETS *like Cudgel'd Bullys, never do*
At first, or second blow, submit to you;
But will provoke you still, and ne're have done,
Till you are weary first, with laying on:
The late so bafled Scribler of this day,
Though he stands trembling, bids me boldly say,
What we, before most Playes are us'd to do,
For Poets out of fear, first draw on you;
In a fierce Prologue, the still Pit defie,
And e're you speak, like Castril, *give the lye;*
But though our Bayses Batles *oft I've fought,*
And with bruis'd knuckles, their dear Conquests bought;
Nay, never yet fear'd Odds upon the Stage,
In Prologue dare not Hector with the Age,
But wou'd take Quarter from your saving hands,
Though Bayse *within all yielding Countermands,*
Says you Confed'rate Wits no Quarter give,
Ther'fore his Play shan't ask your leave to live:
Well, let the vain rash Fop, by huffing so,
Think to obtain the better terms of you;
But we the Actors humbly will submit,
Now, and at any time, to a full Pit;
Nay, often we anticipate your rage,
And murder Poets for you, on our Stage:
We set no Guards upon our Tyring-Room,
But when with flying Colours, there you come,
We patiently you see, give up to you,
Our Poets, Virgins, nay our Matrons too.

Charles II had no faith in religion or virtue but some in tolerant politeness. He shared 1 of his mistresses with Wycherley, a courtier when the court licensed only 2 public theatres. Their best comedies, like all new fashions then, were based on French ones coarsened to please the British. They show fashionable men & women politely & elaborately duping one another to get sex & riches. Only contemptible folk **earn** *a living in these plays that usually end with a gallant rake wedding a rich virgin. Milton saw such folk as damned souls but Wycherley makes their hells of deceit, lust & greed amuse by energy, repartee & satire. He began an English middle class comic tradition ending in Noël Coward.*

The **Bayse** *here mentioned is Dryden, poet laureate who sought favour with critics in dearer seats by mocking some in the cheaper - the Pit.*

THE PILGRIM'S PROGRESS *from this world to that which is to come delivered under the similitude of a dream:* JOHN BUNYAN: LONDON

[The Author's Apology For His Book]

*W*HEN *at the first I took my Pen in hand,*
Thus for to write; I did not understand
That I at all should make a little Book
In such a mode; Nay, I had undertook

1678

The first 36 lines of this describe how a middle-aged Baptist preacher became a creative artist. While writing a *tract to persuade ordinary Christians that Christ should be a real presence for them, he remembers Christ called himself THE WAY, & suddenly THE WAY stops being symbolic. (Flannery O' Connor said to a lady who praised the symbolism of the Mass, **If it's just a symbol the hell with it!**) THE WAY becomes a world he is creating – creating, partly, from memory. It is his own journey through life leaving wife & children for religion's sake, meeting companions who help or distract him, giant despair, kind women, the valley of the shadow, cruel judges, wrongful imprisonment & final liberation. The power entering Bunyan here is the Holy Ghost that Milton prayed to at the start of **Paradise Lost**, declaring it God's creative power in all minds, for it originally shaped world, life & mind together. Thomas Macaulay is Bunyan's best commentator, Extracts from his essay in the 1830 **Edinburgh Review** are printed boldly below.*

Bunyan's father owned a small cottage near Elsted, a Bedfordshire village where he lived by mending kettles & pans. His son

*To make another; which when almost done,
Before I was aware, I this begun.
    And thus it was: I writing of the Way
And Race of Saints in this our Gospel-Day,
Fell suddenly into an Allegory
About their Journey, and the way to Glory,
In more than twenty things, which I set down;
This done, I twenty more had in my Crown,
And they again began to multiply,
Like sparks that from the coals of Fire do flie.
Nay then, thought I, if that you breed so fast,
I'll put you by your selves, lest you at last
Should prove ad infinitum, and eat out
The Book that I already am about.
Well, so I did; but yet I did not think
To shew to all the World my Pen and Ink
In such a mode; I only thought to make
I knew not what: nor did I undertake
Thereby to please my Neighbour; no not I,
I did it mine own self so gratifie.
    Neither did I but vacant seasons spend
In this my Scribble; Nor did I intend
But to divert my self in doing this,
From worser thoughts, which make me do amiss.
    Thus I set Pen to Paper with delight,
And quickly had my thoughts in black & white.
For having now my Method by the end;
Still as I pull'd, it came; and so I penn'd
It down, until it came at last to be
For length & breadth the bigness which you see.
    Well, when I had thus put mine ends together,
I shew'd them others, that I might see whether
They would condemn them, or them justifie:
And some said, let them live; some, let them die:
Some said, John, print it; others said, Not so:
Some said, It might do good; others said, No.
    Now was I in a straight, and did not see
Which was the best thing to be done by me:*

At last I thought, Since you are thus divided,
I print it will, and so the case decided.
For, thought I; Some I see would have it done,
Though others in that Channel do not run;
To prove then who advised for the best,
Thus I thought fit to put it to the test.
I further thought, if now I did deny
Those that would have it thus, to gratifie,
I did not know, but hinder them I might,
Of that which would to them be great delight.

    For those that were not for its coming forth;
I said to them, Offend you I am loth;
Yet since your Brethren pleased with it be,
Forbear to judge, till you do further see.

    If that thou wilt not read, let it alone;
Some love the meat, some love to pick the bone:
Yea, that I might them better palliate,
I did too with them thus Expostulate.

    May I not write in such a stile as this?
In such a method too, and yet not miss
Mine end, thy good? why may it not be done?
Dark Clouds bring Waters,
              when the bright bring none;
Yea, dark, or bright, if they their silver drops
Cause to descend, the Earth, by yielding Crops,
Gives praise to both, and carpeth not at either,
But treasures up the Fruit they yield together:
Yea, so commixes both, that in her Fruit
None can distinguish this from that, they suit
Her well, when hungry: but if she be full,
She spues out both, &
            makes their blessings null.
    You see the ways the Fisher-man doth take
To catch the Fish; what Engins doth he make?
Behold! how he ingageth all his Wits,
Also his Snares, Lines, Angles, Hooks & Nets:
Yet Fish there be, that neither Hook, nor Line,
Nor Snare, nor Net, nor Engin can make thine;

John, born 1628, became the same kind of self-employed man, a class rich in independent thinkers, where stimulus to thought exists; & this was

– the time of a great stirring of the public mind. To the regularity of one intolerant church had succeeded the license of innumerable sects, drunk with the sweet & heady must of their new liberty. The history of Bunyan is the history of an excitable mind in an age of excitement.

Young Bunyan enjoyed the sports & arts of other small towns: hockey, dancing, bell-ringing & tales of the English folk-heroes. At 16 he enlisted as a private in the army of the parliamentary. Two years later he left it & married a woman who brought religious books to his house, probably the **Bible** *&* **Foxe's Book of Martyrs**, *for shortly after he read these constantly. He gave up the sports & arts he enjoyed, & thought himself a reformed character until one day he overheard some poor women gossiping about Jesus in a way which showed they found him a real &*

comforting presence.
Bunyan did not. To him Christ was a reminder, not experience of salvation. He passed into a state which the Age of Faith called **the dark night of the soul**, & the Age of Reason **religious melancolia**. Our own age lumps it together with several other mental conditions under that holdall label, **schizophrenia**. Bunyan lived among folk who thought fear of damnation was rational so he was allowed to toil, weep, debate & suffer until he found God in his own heart. He grew sane, cheerful, prayed publicly in fields or by invitation in private houses. He wrote hot gospel tracts while still mending pans & kettles, as he refused money for praying & preaching. When King Charles was restored to his throne Bunyan was told to stop preaching by the magistrates, as people in power thought public speeches not licensed by a bishop would lead to revolt. Bunyan spent the next 12 years in Bedford County Jail, with some weeks out on parole when the jailor was lenient. He could have left at any time had he promised to crush his will to preach

They must be grop'd for, and be tickled too,
Or they will not be catcht, what e're you do.
How doth the Fowler seek to catch his Game,
By divers means, all which one cannot name?
His Gun, his Nets, his Lime-twigs, light & bell:
He creeps, he goes, he stands; yea, who can tell
Of all his postures? Yet there's none of these
Will make him master of what Fowls he please.
Yea, he must Pipe, and Whistle to catch this;
Yet if he does so, that Bird he will miss.

    If that a Pearl may in a Toads-head dwell,
And may be found too in an Oister-shell;
If things that promise nothing, do contain
What better is then Gold; who will disdain,
(That have an inkling of it,) there to look,
That they may find it? Now my little Book,
(Tho void of all those paintings that may make
It with this or the other man to take,)
Is not without those things that do excel
What do in brave, but empty notions dwell.

    Well, yet I am not fully satisfied,
That this your Book will stand, when soundly try'd.

    Why, what's the matter? It is dark, what tho?
But it is feigned, what of that I tro?
Some men by feigning words as dark as mine,
Make truth to spangle, and its rayes to shine.
But they want solidness: Speak man thy mind:
They drown'd the weak; Metaphors make us blind.

    Solidity, indeed becomes the Pen
Of him that writeth things Divine to men:
But must I needs want solidness, because
By Metaphors I speak; was not Gods Laws,
His Gospel-laws, in older time held forth
By Types, Shadows and Metaphors? Yet loth
Will any sober man be to find fault
With them, lest he be found for to assault
The highest Wisdom. No, he rather stoops,
And seeks to find out what by pins and loops,

By Calves, and Sheep; by Heifers, and by Rams;
By Birds and Herbs, and by the blood of Lambs;
God speaketh to him: And happy is he
That finds the light, & grace that in them be.
    Be not too forward therefore to conclude,
That I want solidness; that I am rude:
All things solid in shew, not solid be;
All things in parables despise not we,
Lest things most hurtful lightly we receive;
And things that good are, of our souls bereave.
    My dark and cloudy words they do but hold
The Truth, as Cabinets inclose the Gold.
    The Prophets used much by Metaphors
To set forth Truth; Yea, who so considers
Christ, his Apostles too, shall plainly see,
That Truths to this day in such Mantles be.
    Am I afraid to say that Holy Writ,
Which for its Stile, and Phrase, puts down all Wit,
Is every where to full of all these things,
(Dark Figures, Allegories,) yet there springs
From that same Book, that lustre, & those rayes
Of light, that turns our darkest nights to days.
    Come, let my Carper, to his Life now look,
And find There darker Lines, then in my Book
He findeth any. Yea, and let him know,
That in his best things there are worse lines too.
    May we but stand before impartial men,
To his poor One, I durst adventure Ten,
That they will take my meaning in these lines
Far better than his lies in Silver Shrines.
Come, Truth, although in Swadling-clouts, I find
Informs the Judgement, rectifies the Mind,
Pleases the Understanding, makes the Will
Submit; the Memory too it doth fill
With what doth our Imagination please;
Likewise, it tends our troubles to appease.
    Sound words I know Timothy is to use;
And old Wives Fables he is to refuse,

– the one talent in him which (Milton says) it is death to hide.

The jail was a very communal place, as only the rich in those days could afford solitary confinement. He converted several fellow prisoners & a jailor, earned money for wife & children by making laces for shoes & stomachers. He also wrote religious tracts. When working on 1 the Holy Ghost entered & produced this book.

In 1672 Charles II passed the Declaration of Indulgence in order to earn the secret pension he got from French King Louis for restoring British Catholicism. A 1st step was allowing folk to worship how they liked, as when Cromwell ruled. Bunyan was released, licensed to preach, & 2 years later published his Pilgrim's Progress.

The Pilgrim's Progress stole silently into the world. Not a single copy of the first edition is known to be in existence. The fame of Bunyan during his life, & during the century which followed his death was great, but was almost wholly confined to religious families of the lower or middle classes. Very seldom was he during that time

mentioned with respect
by any writer of great
literary eminence.

It is a significant
circumstance that, till
a recent period, all the
numerous editions of
the Pilgrim's Progress
were evidently meant
for the cottage & the
servants' hall. The
paper, the printing, the
plates were all of the
meanest description.
In general, when the
educated minority &
the common people
differ about the merit
of a book, the opinion
of the educated mino-
rity prevails. Pilgrim's
Progress is perhaps
the only book which,
after the lapse of a
hundred years, the
educated minority has
come over to the
opinion of the com-
mon people.

The vocabulary is
the vocabulary of the
common people.
There is not an expres-
sion, if we except a few
technical terms of
theology, which would
puzzle the rudest
peasant. Many pages
do not contain a single
word of more than two
syllables. Yet no writer
has said more exactly
what he meant to say.
For magnificence, for
pathos, for vehement
exhortation, for every
purpose of the poet,
the orator & the
divine, this homely
dialect – the dialect of

But yet grave Paul him no where doth forbid
The use of Parables; in which lay hid
That Gold, those Pearls, & precious stones that were
Worth digging for; & that with greatest care.

Let me add one word more, O Man of God!
Art thou offended? dost thou wish I had
Put forth my matter in another dress,
Or that I had in things been more express?
Three things let me propound, then I submit
To those that are my betters, (as is fit.)

1. I find not that I am denied the use
Of this my method, so I no abuse
Put on the Words, Things, Readers, or be rude
In handling Figure, or Similitude,
In application; but, all that I may,
Seek the advance of Truth, this or that way:
Denied, did I say? Nay, I have leave,
(Example too, and that from them that have
God better please'd by their words or ways,
Than any Man that breatheth now adays,)
Thus to express my mind, thus to declare
Things unto thee that excellentest are.

2. I find that men (as high as Trees) will write
Dialogue-wise; yet no Man doth them slight
For writing so: Indeed if they abuse
Truth, cursed be they, and the craft they use
To that intent; but yet let Truth be free
To make her Salleys upon Thee, and Me,
Which way it pleases God. For who knows how,
Better then he that taught us first to Plow,
To guide our Mind and Pens for his Design?
And he makes base things usher in Divine.

3. I find that holy Writ in many places,
Hath semblance with this method, where the cases
Doth call for one thing to set forth another:
Use it I may then, and yet nothing smother
Truths golden Beams; Nay, by this method may
Make it cast forth its rayes as light as day.

And now, before I do put up my Pen,
I'le shew the profit of my Book, and then
Commit both thee, and it unto that hand
That pulls the strong down, & makes weak ones stand.

This Book it chaulketh out before thine eyes,
The man that seeks the everlasting Prize:
It shews you whence he comes, whither he goes,
What he leaves undone; also what he does:
It also shews you how he runs, and runs,
Till he unto the Gate of Glory comes.

It shews too, who sets out for life amain,
As if the lasting Crown they would attain:
Here also you may see the reason why
They loose their labour, and like fools do die.

This Book will make a Traveller of thee,
If by its Counsel thou wilt ruled be;
It will direct thee to the HolyLand,
If thou wilt its Directions understand:
Yea, it will make the sloathful, active be;
The Blind also, delightful things to see.
Art thou for something rare, and profitable?
Wouldest thou see a Truth within a Fable?
Art thou forgetful? wouldest thou remember
From New-years-day to the last of December?
Then read my fancies, they will stick like Burs,
And may be to the Helpless, Comforters.

This Book is writ in such a Dialect,
As may the minds of listless men affect:
It seems a Novelty, and yet contains
Nothing but sound and honest Gospel-strains.

Would'st thou divert thy self from Melancholly?
Would'st thou be pleasant, yet be far from folly?
Would'st thou read Riddles, and their Explanation?
Or else be drownded in thy Contemplation?
Dost thou love picking-meat? or would'st thou see
A man i' th Clouds, & hear him speak to thee?
Would'st thou be in a Dream, and yet not sleep?
Or would'st thou in a moment Laugh and Weep?

plain working men – *was sufficient. There is* *no book in our liter-* *ature which shows* *how rich the old* *unpolluted English* *language is in its own* *proper wealth, & how* *little it has been* *improved by all it has* *borrowed.*

The verses opposite *show the truth of the* *last statement. They are* *an argument for the* *religious imagination* *cast in verse. Bunyan,* *like Milton, felt argu-* *ment needed artisic* *forms.* **The Pilgrim's** **Progress**, *a Protestant* **Piers Plowman**, *des-* *cribes England as the* *dream of a Christian* *trying to save his soul.* *He meets vices &* *virtues of neighbours,* *friends & local gentry* *drawn with the strong* *plain realism of Defoe.* *His own weaknesses* *attack him shaped like* *earthy monsters in old* *English fairy tales.* *Dialogues, if long, are* *printed as in plays.* *When happy a hero or* *heroine will sing as in* *musical comedy. One* *song is now a popular* *hymn. The only other* *by a great English* *writer is Blake's* **Jerusalem**. *In this* *preface is fine poetry:* **Dark clouds bring** **waters when the bright** **bring none**: *could be a* *common proverb* *nobody today re-*

*members. It could
have been written by
Shakespeare or by
Blake.*

*Wouldest thou loose thy self, and catch no harm?
And find thy self again without a charm?
Would'st read thy self, and read thou know'st not what
And yet know whether thou art blest or not,
By reading the same lines? O then come hither,
And lay my Book, thy Head & Heart together.*

1681

THE ROVER: PART TWO
MRS. APHRA BEHN
LONDON

[PROLOGUE spoken by Mr. SMITH]

*A middle class woman
with all the plebeian
virtues: humour, vitality,
courage, wrote Woolf.
Aphra, a child, goes to
Surinam with her dad,
barber made ruler of
this American colony
through Cromwell. The
workers are African
slaves, & Aphra is told
of Oroonoko. Surinam
is given to Holland in
exchange for Nieuw
Amsterdam, now called
New York. At 18 she is
in London, wife of a
Dutch merchant. Her
wit, beauty & husband's
connections soon make
her welcome at court.
With France, the Dutch
republic is England's
main trade rival: ahead
of her in agriculture,
philosophy, science,
law, art; tolerating all
faiths; home of Descartes
& Spinoza & Rembrandt. In 1666 Mr Behn
dies. Sent to spy on
Holland, Aphra's report
on Dutch plan to burn
Thames dockyards is
true, ignored & unpaid.*

*I*N VAIN we labour to reform the Stage,
*Poets have caught too the Disease o' th' Age,
That Pest, of not being quiet when they're well,
That restless Fever, in the Brethren, Zeal;
In publick Spirits call'd,*
        *Good o' th' Commonweal.
Some for this Faction cry, others for that,
The pious Mobile for they know not what:
So tho by different ways the Fever seize,
In all 'tis one and the same mad Disease.
Our Author too, as all new Zealots do,
Full of Conceit and Contradiction too,
'Cause the first Project took, is now so vain,
T'attempt to play the old Game o'er again:
The Scene is only chang'd; for who wou'd lay
A Plot, so hopeful, just the same dull way?
Poets, like Statesmen, with a little change,
Pass off old Politicks for new and strange;
Tho the few Men of Sense decry't aloud,
The Cheat will pass with the unthinking Croud:
The Rabble 'tis we court, those powerful things,
Whose Voices can impose even Laws on Kings.
A Pox of Sense and Reason, or dull Rules,
Give us an Audience that declares for Fools;
Our Play will stand fair: we've Monsters too,
Which far exceed your City Pope for Show.
Almighty Rabble, 'tis to you this Day*

Our humble Author dedicates the Play,
From those who in our lofty Tire sit,
Down to the dull Stage Cullies of the Pit,
Who have much Money, and but little Wit:
Whose useful Purses, and whole empty Skulls
To private Int'rest make ye Publick Tools;
To work on Projects which the wiser frame,
And of fine Men of Business get the Name.
You who have left caballing here of late,
Imploy'd in matters of a mightier weight;
To you we make our humble Application,
You'd spare some time from your dear new
    Vocation,
Of drinking deep, then settling the Nation,
To countenance us, whom Commonwealths of old
Did the most politick Diversion hold.
Plays were so useful thought to Government,
That Laws were made for their Establishment;
Howe'er in Schools differing Opinions jar,
Yet all agree i' th' crouded Theatre,
Which none forsook in any Change or War,
That, like their Gods, unviolated stood,
Equally needful to the publick Good.
Throw then, Great Sirs, some vacant hours away,
And your Petitioners shall humbly pray, &c.

Poverty strikes, & jail for debt. To earn a living wage she starts to write & succeeds: a deed of more historic worth (says Mrs Woolf) **than any Crusade or Wars of Roses.** *Until then saints & queens were the only women who spoke their minds publicly. Aphra proves to a very competitive male society that by WRITING her mind a middle class widow can also prosper. Her books are popular for over a century, especially with French democrats. The start of* **Oroonoko** *tells why. Though a royalist she sees folk as naturally good, & evil caused by institutions like that of slavery. Her plays are brisk & manly. Her prologue refers to an anti-Catholic mob that had made king & politicians pass oppressive laws they later tried to undo.*

OROONOKO: The History of The Royal Slave 1688

I DO NOT PRETEND, in giving you the History of this *ROYAL SLAVE*, to entertain my Reader with the Adventures of a feign'd *Hero*, whose Life and Fortunes Fancy may manage at the Poet's Pleasure; nor in relating the Truth, design to adorn it with any Accidents, but such as arrived in earnest to him: And it shall come simply into the World, recommended by its own proper Merits, and natural Intrigues; there being enough of Reality to support it, and to render it diverting, without the Addition of Invention.

I was myself an Eye-witness to a great Part of what you will find here set down; and what I could not be Witness of, I receiv'd from the Mouth of the chief Actor in this History, the *Hero* himself, who gave us the whole Transactions of his Youth: And I shall omit, for Brevity's Sake, a thousand little Accidents of his Life, which, however pleasant to us, where History was scarce, and Adventures very rare, yet might prove tedious and heavy to my Reader, in a World where he finds Diversions for every Minute, new and strange. But we who were perfectly charm'd with the Character of this great Man, were curious to gather every Circumstance of his Life.

The Scene of the last Part of his Adventures lies in a Colony in *America*, called *Surinam*, in the *West-Indies*.

But before I give you the story of this *Gallant Slave*, 'tis fit I tell you the Manner of bringing them to these new *Colonies*; those they make Use of there, not being *Natives* of the Place: for those we live with in perfect Amity, without daring to command 'em; but, on the contrary, caress 'em with all the brotherly and friendly Affection in the World; trading with them for their Fish, Venison, Buffaloes Skins, and little Rarities; as *Marmosets*, a sort of Monkey, as big as a Rat or Weasel, but of a marvellous and delicate Shape, having Face and Hands like a Human Creature; and *Cousheries*, a little Beast in the Form and Fashion of a Lion, as big as a Kitten, but so exactly made in all Parts like that Noble Beast, that it is it in *Miniature*: Then for little *Paraketoes*, great *Parrots*, *Muckaws*, and a thousand other Birds and Beasts of wonderful and surprizing Forms, Shapes and Colours: For Skins of prodigious Snakes, of which there are some three-score Yards in Length; as is the Skin of one that may be seen at his Majesty's *Antiquary's*; where are also some rare Flies, of amazing Forms and Colours, presented to 'em by myself: some as big as my Fist, some less; and all of various Excellencies, such as Art cannot imitate. Then we trade for Feathers, which they order into all Shapes, make themselves little short Habits of 'em, and glorious Wreaths for their Heads, Necks, Arms and Legs, whose Tinctures are unconceivable. I had a Set of these presented to me, and I gave 'em to the *King's Theatre*; it was the Dress of the *Indian Queen*, infinitely admir'd by Persons of Quality; and it was inimitable. Besides these, a thousand little Knacks, and Rarities in Nature; and some of Art, as their Baskets, Weapons, Aprons, &c. We dealt with 'em with Beads of all Colours, Knives, Axes, Pins and Needles, which they us'd only as Tools to drill Holes with in their Ears, Noses and Lips, where they hang a great many little Things; as long Beads, Bits of Tin, Brass or Silver beat thin, and any shining Trinket. The Beads they weave into Aprons about a Quarter of an Ell long, and of the same Breadth; working them very prettily in Flowers of several Colours; which Apron they wear just before 'em, as *Adam* and *Eve* did the Fig-leaves; the Men wearing a long Stripe of Linen, which they deal with us for. They thread these Beads also on long Cotton-threads, and make Girdles to tie their Aprons to, which come twenty times, or more, about the Waste, and then cross, like a Shoulder-belt, both Ways, and round their Necks, Arms and Legs. This Adornment, with their long black Hair, and the Face painted in little Specks or Flowers here and there, makes 'em a wonderful Figure to behold. Some of the Beauties, which indeed are finely shap'd, as almost all are, and who have pretty Features, are charming and novel; for they have all that is called Beauty, except the Colour, which is a reddish Yellow; or after a new Oiling, which they often use to themselves, they are of the Colour of a new Brick, but smooth, soft and sleek. They are extreme modest and bashful, very shy, and nice of being touch'd. And tho' they are all thus naked, if one lives forever among 'em, there is not to be seen an indecent Action, or Glance: and being continually us'd to see one another so unadorned, so like our first Parents before the Fall, it seems as if they had no Wishes, there being nothing to heighten Curiosity: but all you can see, you see at once, and every Moment see; and where there is no Novelty, there can be no Curiosity. Not but I have seen a handsome young *Indian*, dying for love of a very beautiful young *Indian* Maid; but all his Courtship was, to fold his Arms, pursue her with his Eyes, and Sighs were all his Language: Whilst she, as if no such Lover were present, or rather as if she desired none such, carefully guarded her Eyes from beholding him; and never approach's him, but she look'd down with all the blushing Modesty I have seen in the most Severe and Cautious of our World. And these People represented to me a absolute *Idea* of the first State of Innocence, before Man knew how to sin: And 'tis most evident and plain, that simple Nature is the most harmless, inoffensive and virtuous Mistress. 'Tis she alone, if she were permitted, that better instructs the World, than all the Inventions of Man: Religion would here but destroy that Tranquillity they possess by Ignorance; and Laws would but teach 'em to know Offences, of which now they have no Notion. They once made Mourning and Fasting for the Death of the *English* Governor, who had given his Hand to come on such a Day to 'em, and neither came nor sent; believing, when a Man's Word was past, nothing but Death could or should prevent his keeping it: And when they saw he was not dead, they ask'd him what Name they had for a Man who promis'd a Thing he did not do? The Governor told them, Such a Man was a Lyar, which was a Word of Infamy to a Gentleman. Then one of 'em reply'd, *Governor, you are a Lyar, and guilty of that Infamy.* They have a native Justice, which knows no Fraud; and they understand no Vice, or Cunning, but when they are taught by the *White* Men. They have Plurality of Wives; which, when they grow old, serve those that succeed 'em, who are young, but with a Servitude easy and respected; and unless they take Slaves in War, they have no other Attendants.

Those on that *Continent* where I was, had no King; but the oldest War-Captain was obey'd with great Resignation.

A War-Captain is a Man who has led them on to Battle with Conduct and Success; of whom I shall have Occasion to speak more hereafter, and of some other of their Customs and Manners, as they fall in my Way.

With these People, as I said, we live in perfect Tranquillity, and good Understanding, as it behoves us to do; they knowing all the Places where to seek the best Food of the Country, and the Means of getting it; and for very small and invaluable Trifles, supplying us with what 'tis almost impossible for us to get: for they do not only in the Woods, and over the *Sevana's*, in Hunting, supply the Parts of Hounds, by swiftly scouring thro' those almost impassible Places, and by the mere Activity of their Feet, run down the nimblest Deer, and other eatable Beasts; but in the Water, one would think they were Gods of the Rivers, or Fellow-Citizens of the Deep; so rare an Art they have in swimming, diving and almost living in Water; by which they command the less swift Inhabitants of the Floods. And then for shooting, what they cannot take, or reach with their Hands, they do with Arrows; and have so admirable an Aim, that they will split almost an Hair, and at any Distance that an Arrow can reach: they will shoot down Oranges, and other Fruit, and only touch the Stalk with the Dart's Point, that they may not hurt the Fruit. So that they being on all Occasions very useful to us, we find it absolutely necessary to caress 'em as Friends, and not to treat 'em as Slaves; nor dare we do otherwise, their Numbers so far surpassing ours in that Continent.

Those then whom we make use of to work in our Plantations of

Sugar, are *Negroes*, Black-Slaves altogether, who are transported thither in this Manner.

Those who want Slaves, make a Bargain with a Master, or a Captain of a Ship, and contract to pay him so much apiece, a Matter of twenty Pound a Head, for as many as he agrees for, and to pay for 'em when they shall be deliver'd on such a Plantation: So that when there arrives a Ship laden with Slaves, they who have so contracted, go aboard, and receive their Number by Lot; and perhaps in one Lot that may be for ten, there may happen to be three or four Men, the rest Women and Children. Or there be more or less of either Sex, you are obliged to be contented with your Lot.

Coramantien, a country of Blacks so called, was one of those Places in which they found the most advantageous Trading for these Slaves, and thither most of our great Traders in that Merchandize traffick; for that Nation is very warlike and brave: and having a continual Campaign, being always in Hostility with one neighbouring Prince or other, they had the Fortune to take a great many Captives: for all they took in Battle were sold as Slaves; at least those common Men who could not ransom themselves. Of these Slaves so taken, the General only has all the Profit; and of these Generals our Captains and Masters of Ships buy all their Freights.

THE INSTITUTIONS OF THE LAW OF SCOTLAND
JAMES DALRYMPLE,
VISCOUNT OF STAIR: EDINBURGH
[TO THE KING]

1681

MAY IT Please Your Majesty,
I do humbly present to Your MAJESTY a Summary of the Laws and Customes of Your ancient Kingdom of SCOTLAND, *which can be no where so fitly Placed, as under the Rayes of Your Royal Protection*: I am confident it will tend to the Honour and Renoun of Your MAJESTY, and Your Princely Progenitors, that You have Governed this Nation so long and so happily, by such just and convenient Laws, which are here offered to the view of the World, in a Plain, Rational, and Natural Method; In which, Material Justice (the common

Dalrymple, born 1619, was first of all :–
1 Covenanting soldier. 2 Philosophy professor at Glasgow University. 3 Judge appointed by General Monk, ruler of Scotland for Cromwell. After Cromwell's death he advised Monk to call a free parliament & helped to restore Charles II, so though Presbyterian became Viscount Stair & chief Scots law lord. In 1679 James, Charles' brother,

*came north & tried, as his dad & grandad had tried, to make Scotland Anglican. James, being Catholic, saw Anglicans as heretics but more governable heretics than the Presbyterians. Stair left his legal practice & worked on this book. It did for Scots law what Coke's work did for English. Scottish law till then was diffuse, chaotic & corrupt. Stair had sat in meetings called by parliament to report on it & done nothing. He now rewrote that law making it practical & respected, with Scots cases illustrating his Dutch adaption of a Roman code. **Material Justice (the common Law of the World)** was deduced from self-evident principles. The common law of England was differently based, on precedents. Both decided the ownership of property, but their separate logics meant that after the union of parliaments in 1707 English lawyers could not handle Scottish business, even though the richest Scottish proprietors lived in London. Edinburgh's legal aristocracy thus stayed in Scotland when she had no other.*

When James became king Stair went to Holland, returning with William of Orange in the 1689 revolution.

Law of the World) is in the first place orderly deduced from self evident Principles, thorow all the several private Rights thence arising: And in the next place, the Expedients of the most Polite Nation, for Ascertaining and Expeding the Rights and Interests of Mankind, are Applyed in their proper places; especially these which have been invented or followed by *this Nation*; so that a great part of what is here offered, is common to most *Civil Nations*, and is not like to be displeasing to the Judicious and Sober any where, who dote not so much upon their own Customes, as to think that none else are worthy of their notice. There is not much here asserted upon meer Authority, or imposed for no other reason but *quia majoribus placuerunt*; but the rational Motives inductive of the several Laws and Customes, are therewith held forth: And though the Application of those common Rules, to the varietie of Cases determined by our Statutes, our ancient Customes, and the more recent Decisions of our Supream Courts, be peculiar to us; Yet even the *Quadrancy* of these to the common Dictates of Reason and Justice, may make them the less displeasing; and that no Nation hath so few words of Art, but that almost all our Terms are near the Common and Vulgar Acceptation; Yea, the Historical Part relating the Helps and Expedients for Clearing and Securing the Rights of Men out of the Word of God; the Moral and Judicial Law contained therein; the Civil, Canon and Feudal Laws, and many Customes of the Neighbouring Nations Digested, as they fall in with the Common Rules of Justice, may probably be acceptable to these who may, and will allow time for their perusal, *a quint and gliding Stile*, much less the Flourishes of Eloquence, the ordinarie *Condiment and Vernish which qualifie the pains of Reading*, could not justlie be expected in a Treatise of Law, which of all

Subjects doth require the most *Plain and Accurate Expressions*; to ballance which, the Nausiating burden of Citations, are as much as can be left out.*0000000000000000000000000000000000000000000000000*

KING CHARLES II IS CONGRATULATED ON A SCOTS ANCESTRY MORE ANCIENT THAN OTHER NOBLE LINES.

0000000000000000000000000000000000000000000000000000000000000

It is yet a greater glory to Your Royal Family, that You have been Christian Kings before any other Family in *Christendom* were Kings: and that You and Your Subjects of *Scotland* have been least under the Yoke of *Rome*, in Your Sacred or Civil Interest; their Arms could never subdue You, but they turned on the Defensive; and to exclude Your Valour, two of their most famous Emperors, *Severus* and *Hadrian*, were at an incredible Coast to build two Walls from Sea to Sea, the foundations of which are yet known, and a great part of *Hadrian's* Wall, from *Carleisle* to *Newcastle* is still standing. And albeit the Roman Art did prevail more than their Arms, in procuring a Subordination and dependence of this Church to the Bishops of Rome, and acceptance of the Services and Ceremonies which they imbraced not for many Centuries after they were Christians; yet in their greatest devotion to the See of *Rome*, they keeped always a considerable Reserve; so that it was Barratrie (that is, Proscription, Banishment, and loss of Lands and Goods) to purchase Benefices from the Court of *Rome*; Yea, it was not lawful to go to *Rome* without the Kings Licence: And the *Roman* Yoke hath by the good Providence of God, been fully rejected by three successive Kings, during the space of an hundred twenty three years; and we have returned to the true, ancient and Apostolick Faith of Christ, warranted by the holy Canon of the Scripture: And Your Majesty is the King in the World of the purest Religion, and it is Your greatest glory and interest, to be Zealous and valient for it, both at home and abroad, the steady pursuance whereof, made a Distaff not only peaceable and secure at home, but terrible to the Popish Kingdoms abroad.

I have as distinctly and clearly as I could by this Essay, given a view of Law and of our Customes, and the Decisions of the Session since the Institution of the Colledge of Justice, as they have been remarked and reported by the most eminent Judges and Pleaders from time to time, which I hope shall be more Inlarged and Improven by others. It hath been my aim and endeavour more then twenty years, in which I have served Your Majesty as a Senator of Your Colledge of Justice; Of which by Your Majesties Favour, I have been President near eleven years. It is but little short of fourty years since I have followed the Study and Practice of Law, constantly and diligently, so that these who will not deny me Reason and Capacity, can hardly deny my Knowledge and Experience in the Subject I write of; my modesty did not permit me to publish it, least it should be Judicially Cited where I sat: But now becoming old, I have been prevailed with to Print it, while I might oversee the Press; It was not vanity and ambition that set me on Work, but being so long a Servant to God and Your Majestie, in the matter of Justice, I thought it my Duty, not to smother my Thoughts of the Immaculate Righteousness of God Almighty, in His Moral Law, and of the justness and fitness of Your Majesties Laws, that I might promote Your Honour and Service, and the good of Your Subjects, which shall ever be the sincere endeavour of

Your MAJESTIES most humble, most affectionate and obedient Servant and Subject,

JA. DALRYMPLE.

1687

THE HIND AND THE PANTHER
JOHN DRYDEN
LONDON

Dryden's many works in verse, drama & criticism, his clear strong language, his leading part in public controversy brought him fame but his character is strangely elusive. He was child of a country vicarage when Puritans ruled the church & his early verses praise Cromwell's victories. Like most of England's middle class he became a hearty royalist when Charles II was crowned, crisply flattering aristocrats & feeding the fashionable taste of his age in poem

[TO THE READER]

THE NATION is in too high a Ferment, for me to expect either fair War, or even so much as fair Quarter from a *Reader* of the opposite Party. All men are engag'd either on this side or that: and tho' Conscience is the common *Word*, which is given by both, yet if a Writer fall among Enemies, and cannot give the Marks of *Their* Conscience, he is knock'd down before the Reasons of his own are heard. A *Preface*, therefore, which is but a bespeaking of Favour, is altogether useless. What I desire the *Reader* should know concerning me, he will find in the Body of the Poem; if he have but the patience to peruse it. Only this Advertisement let him take before hand, which relates to the Merits of the Cause. No general Characters of Parties, (call 'em either Sects or Churches) can be so fully and exactly drawn, as to

Comprehend all the several Members of 'em; at least all such are as receiv'd under that Denomination. For example; there are some of the Church by Law Establish'd, who envy not Liberty of Conscience to Dissenters; as being well satisfied that, according to ther own Principles, they ought not to persecute them. Yet these, by reason of their fewness, I could not distinguish from the Numbers of the rest with whom they are Embodied in one common Name: On the other side there are many of our Sects, and more indeed then I could reasonably have hop'd, who have withdrawn themselves from the Communion of the *Panther*; and embrac'd this Gracious Indulgency of His Majesty in point of Toleration. But neither to the one nor the other of these is this Satyr any way intended: 'tis aim'd only at the refractory and disobedient on either side. For those who are come over to the Royal Party are consequently suppos'd to be out of Gunshot. Our Physicians have observ'd, that in Process of Time, some Diseases have abated of their Virulence, and have in a manner worn out their Malignity, so as to be no longer Mortal: and why may not I suppose the same concerning some of those who have formerly been Enemies to Kingly Government, As well as Catholick Religion? I hope they have now another Notion of both, as having found, by Comfortable Experience, that the Doctrine of Persecution is far from being an Article of our Faith.

'Tis not for any Private Man to Censure the Proceedings of a Foreign Prince: but, without suspicion of Flattery, I may praise our own, who has taken contrary Measures, and those more suitable to the Spirit of Christianity. Some of the Dissenters in their Addresses to His Majesty have said that *He has restor'd God to his Empire over Conscience*: I Confess I dare not stretch the Figure to so great a boldness: but I may safely say, that Conscience is the

& play. The Stuarts appointed him poet laureate & Historiographer Royal, yet he was 1 of the earliest to praise **Paradise Lost** by republican Milton. Dryden too wished to write a great epic, but had to earn money by shorter work, for he had married into the nobility. He later wrote to a friend **I am still drudging on, always a poet but never a good one**. That was too severe. His limits as epic & lyric poet were compensated by a command of poetic reasoning, wit & satire that went through enemies (his position & talent made many) like a dose of salts. He wrote 2 long poems about the knotty, intertwined roots of politics & religion. **Religio Laici** (1682) defended Anglicanism: this defends Catholicism. James II, an open Catholic had become king & Dryden a convert. James now annoyed his Protestant subjects by giving Catholics high places in the army, universities & law courts till even Anglican bishops (who did not mind a Catholic king if he kept **their** church the most powerful) grew alarmed. **The Hind & The Panther** is a political beast-fable

Royalty and Prerogative of every Private man. He is absolute in his own Breast, and accountable to no Earthly Power, for that which passes only betwixt God and Him. Those who are driven into the Fold are, generally speaking, rather made Hypocrites then Converts.

This Indulgence being granted to all the Sects, it ought in reason to be expected, that they should both receive it, and receive it thankfully. For at this time of day to refuse the Benefit, and adhere to those whom they have esteem'd their Persecutors, what is it else, but publickly to own that they suffer'd not before for Conscience sake; but only out of Pride and Obstinacy to separate from a Church for those Impositions, which they now judge may be lawfully obey'd? After they have so long contended for their Classical Ordination, (not to speak of Rites and Ceremonies) will they at length submit to an Episcopal? if they can go so far out of Complaisance to their old Enemies, methinks a little reason should perswade 'em to take another step, and see whether that wou'd lead 'em.

Of the receiving this Toleration thankfully, I shall say no more, than that they ought, and I doubt not they will consider from what hands they receiv'd it. 'Tis not from a *Cyrus*, a Heathen Prince, and a Foreigner, but from a Christian King, their Native Sovereign: who expects a Return in *Specie* from them; that the Kindness which He has Graciously shown them, may be retaliated on those of his own perswasion.

As for the Poem in general, I will only thus far satisfie the *Reader*: That it was neither impos'd on me, nor so much as the Subject given me by any man. It was written during the last Winter and the beginning of this Spring; though with long interruptions of ill health, and other hindrances. About a Fortnight before I had finish'd it, His Majesties Declaration for Liberty of Conscience came abroad: which, if I had so soon expected, I might have spar'd my self the labour of writing many things which are contain'd in the third part of it. But I was alwayes in some hope, that the Church of *England* might have been perswaded to have taken off the *Penal Lawes* and the *Test*, which was one Design of the Poem when I propos'd to my self the writing of it.*000000000000000*
DRYDEN SAYS NO-ONE SUGGESTED THE POEM TO HIM, NOR WOULD IT GIVE SO MANY ARGUMENTS FOR RELIGIOUS TOLERATION HAD HE KNOWN THE KING OF BRITAIN WAS ABOUT TO PROCLAIM IT.
000000000000000000000000000000000000000000000000000000000000000

I have but one word more to say concerning the Poem as such, and abstracting from the Matters either Religious or Civil which are handled in it. The *first part*, consisting most in general Characters and Narration, I have endeavour'd to raise, and give it the Majestick Turn of Heroick Poesie. The *second*, being Matter of Dispute, and chiefly concerning Church Authority, I was oblig'd to make as plain and perspicuous as possibly I cou'd: yet not wholly neglecting the Numbers, though I had not frequent occasions for the Magnificence of Verse. The *third*, which has more of the Nature of Domestick Conversation, is, or ought to be more free and familiar than the two former.

There are in it two *Episodes*, or *Fables*, which are interwoven with the main Design; so that they are properly parts of it, though they are also distinct Stories of themselves. In both of these I have made use of the Common Places of *Satyr*, whether true or false, which are urg'd by the Members of the one Church against the other: At which I hope no *Reader* of either Party will be scandaliz'd; because they are not of my Invention: but as old to my knowledge, as the Times of *Boccace* and *Chawcer* on the one side, and as those of the Reformation on the other.

THE HIND AND THE PANTHER

A MILK white Hind, *immortal and unchang'd,*
Fed on the lawns and in the forest rang'd;
Without unspotted, innocent within,
She fear'd no danger, for she knew no sin.
Yet had she oft been chas'd with horns and hounds
And Scythian shafts; and many winged wounds
Aim'd at her Heart; was often forc'd to fly,
And doom'd to death, though fated not to dy.

 Not so her young; for their unequal line
Was Heroe's make, half humane, half divine.
Their earthly mold obnoxious was to fate,
Th' immortal part assum'd immortal state.
Of these a slaughtered army lay in bloud,
Extended o'er the Caledonian *wood,*
Their native walk; whose vocal bloud arose
And cry'd for pardon on their perjur'd foes;
Their fate was fruitful, and the sanguin seed,
Endu'd with souls, encreas'd the sacred breed.

derived from Aesop through medieval allegory. The Panther is Anglicanism, the Hind Catholicism, the lion is King. They can live well together (Dryden suggests) if defended from Baptist boars, Presbyterian wolves, Congregationalist bears, Quaker hares & Atheist monkeys. He warns Catholics against superstition, Anglicans against pompous ignorance. But a fable needs a good plot & most of this is a long religious debate in which the hind scores most points. There are fine passages: A down-

hill Reformation rolls
apace; *Calvin's vice is*
innate antipathy to
kings; *but the poem is*
not one of Dryden's
best. It was published
in Britain's 3 capital
cities just after James'
Declaration of In-
dulgence *allowed*
everyone to worship as
they pleased. A royal
subsidy must have paid
for the printing, so
Dryden's claim to have
written it without royal
favour does not
convince.
  High-minded
Protestants called
Dryden a time-server
because he reflected so
many changes in
English religion &
politics. But he stayed
Catholic under the
penal laws of Calvinist
King William, lost his
place at court, had to
pay higher taxes, live
outside London & could
not own a horse – the
equivalent of a private
car in a land without
public transport.

So Captive Israel *multiply'd in chains,*
A numerous Exile; and enjoy'd her pains.
With grief and gladness mixt, their mother view'd
Her martyr'd offspring, and their race renew'd;
Their corps to perish, but their kind to last,
So much the deathless plant
                    the dying fruit surpass'd.
        Panting and pensive now she ranged alone,
And wander'd in the kingdoms once Her own.
The common Hunt
                    though from their rage restrain'd
By sov'reign power, her company disdain'd:
Grin'd as They pass'd, and with a glaring eye
Gave gloomy signs of secret enmity.
'Tis true, she bounded by, and trip'd so light,
They had not time to take a steady sight,
For truth has such a face and such a meen
As to be lov'd needs only to be seen.
        The bloudy Bear, *an* Independent *beast,*
Unlick'd to form, in groans her hate express'd.
Among the timorous kind the Quaking Hare
Profess'd neutrality, but would not swear.
Next her, the Buffoon Ape, *as Atheists use,*
Mimick'd all Sects and had his own to chuse:
Still when the Lyon look'd, his knees he bent,
And pay'd at Church a Courtier's Complement.

ALTERATIONS

All, all, of a piece throughout:
Thy Chase had a Beast in view;
Thy Wars brought nothing about;
Thy Lovers were all untrue.
'Tis well an Old Age is out,
And time to begin a New.
– DRYDEN'S SECULAR MASQUE, CHRISTMAS 1700

DRYDEN'S SONG SUMMARIZES A NEAR CENTURY of British government. *Thy Chase had a Beast in view* was the reign of that keen huntsman, James the 1st of Britain, who viewed but never seized the fattest deer of all: absolute power. His son Charles lost his head struggling for that. *Thy Wars brought nothing about* refers to civil war that seemed a detour from one Stuart king to another. *Thy Lovers were all untrue* points at Charles II and his brother James, faithless to the British church and state because both were in the pay of Catholic France. James was deposed without bloodshed in 1688 and allowed to skedaddle abroad. His enemies did not want another royal martyr.

The almost dreamlike unanimity by which lords and clergy, squires and merchants replaced him came from sharing a new kind of prosperity. Elizabeth's richest courtiers had jewels, pearls and gold sewn to their clothing. Like the rich speech of their plays and poetry this was practical as well as splendid. In a land with no police force portable wealth was safer on their bodies than in houses, and they wore swords to defend it. But England now had a dependable banking system. Dress and language became plainer for gentry who wore swords as badges of rank more than weapons for defence.

In 1694 a Scots businessman called Paterson persuaded the government to finance war with France by creating its own bank, the Bank of England, which has financed British wars ever since. The largest English fortunes no longer hung on a wheel that might fling the wealthy down to deaths as horrid as those of peasants in a famine. Foreign war could now protect and increase their property and investments, civil war in England would damage them, so has never happened again. Alexander Pope (a Catholic) said: *A King may be a tool, a thing of straw; but if he serves to frighten our enemies it is well enough; a scarecrow is a thing of straw, but it protects the corn.* The enemies he referred to were a populace in revolt, the corn was private property. The Houses of Lords and Commons agreed. By putting hereditary millionaires of Dutch or German birth at the head of Church and State and keeping the appointment of MPs and clergy to themselves the richest landlords and merchants gave their money market the utmost power. This system has lasted with periodic adjustments for over 300 years. Edmund Burke published a defence of it in 1790 which Roger Scruton on page 426 calls *the first major statement of modern Conservatism.*

In 1707 Scotland was pulled into this system by English statesmen who bribed Scottish ones to abolish their Edinburgh parliament and become a fraction of London's. They succeeded because England at last accepted Presbyterianism as the Scottish state church. Having no hierarchy the ministers were still parish priests, but earned extra by running parish schools; thus Scots manual workers were often as literate as some of England's middle class, with results we shall see. Dublin still had a parliament but one wholly subordinate to Westminster. It represented a small Anglican plutocracy who harshly exploited a big Catholic labour force too poor to escape, and oppressed Calvinists settlers who, being richer, began emigrating in droves to North America.

Here twelve east coast colonies had more democratic versions of the London parliament. In each a governor sent from Britain represented the king, the Lords were the few big land owners, the Commons an assembly elected by householders of many religions. That was why the last Catholic Stuart king had tried to outlaw the American states assemblies & why Calvinist William's government legalised them again.

These colonies were growing fast through immigration
and because (among those who were not slaves)
fewer folk died of hunger and dirty
housing than in Britain.
This also had results.

ESTABLISHMENT

THE HOUSE OF COMMONS
IN SIR ROBERT WALPOLE'S ADMINISTRATION
1. Sir Robert Walpole. **2.** The Right Hon. Arthur Onslow.
3. Sidney Godolphin, Father of the House. **4.** Sir Joseph Jekyll. **5.** Colonel Onslow.
6. Edward Stables, Esq., Clerk of the House of Commons. **7.** Sir James Thornhill.
8. Mr Aske, Clerk Assistant, House of Commons.

1690

DON SEBASTIAN, KING OF PORTUGAL
JOHN DRYDEN
LONDON

A prolific, successful playwright, Dryden got most of his income by the theatre, especially after the revolution of 1689 when he lost a lot by remaining a Catholic. This, his 1st stage play for 7 years, has an interestingly prickly prose preface, at times boastful, at times defensive, often mentioning my enemies. It explains how plays are cut for theatrical performance so must differ from a text lovingly restored for print, & claims that readers alone will be able to appreciate the play's clearness of conception, its lustre & masculine vigour. This rhyming prologue (Spoken by a Woman) was delivered straight from the stage to a fashionable audience & is a direct appeal to its good humour. The indication that an audience & playwright can agree to disagree on faith & politics is a sign of a new age. Don Sebastian is a heroic tragedy, 1 of the best examples in English of a genre Corneille & Racine had given France. Dryden thought their imperial unities produced plays with better plots than Shakespeare's, though the latter had livelier

[PROLOGUE, Spoken by a Woman]

*T*HE *Judge remov'd, tho he's no more My Lord,*
May plead at Bar, or at the Council-Board:
So may cast Poets write; there's no Pretension,
To argue loss of Wit from loss of Pension.
Your looks are cheerful; and in all this place
I see not one, that wears a damning face.
The British *Nation, is too brave to show,*
Ignoble vengeance, on a vanquish'd foe.
At least be civil to the Wretch imploring;
And lay your Paws upon him, without roaring:
Suppose our Poet was your foe before;
Yet now, the bus'ness of the Field is o'er;
'Tis time to let your Civil Wars alone,
When Troops are into Winter-quarters gone.
Jove *was alike to* Latian *and to* Phyrgian;
And you well know, a Play's of no Religion.
Take good advice, and please your selves this day;
No matter from what hands you have the Play.
Among good Fellows ev'ry health will pass,
That serves to carry round another glass:
When, with full bowls of Burgundy *you dine,*
Tho at the Mighty Monarch you repine,
You grant him still most Christian, in his Wine.
Thus far the Poet, but his brains grow Addle;
And all the rest is purely from this Noddle.
You've seen young Ladies at the Senate door,
Prefer Petitions, and your grace implore;
How ever grave the Legislators were,
Their Cause went ne'er the worse for being fair.
Reasons as weak as theirs, perhaps I bring;
But I cou'd bribe you, with as good a thing.
I heard him make advances of good Nature;
That he for once, wou'd sheath his cutting Satyr:
Sign but his Peace, he vows he'll ne'er again
The sacred Names of Fops and Beaus profane.

Strike up the Bargain quickly; for I swear,
As Times go now, he offers very fair.
Be not too hard on him, with Statutes neither,
Be kind; and do not set your Teeth together,
To stretch the Laws, as Coblers do their Leather.
Horses, by Papists are not to be ridden;
But sure the Muses Horse was ne'er forbidden.
For in no Rate-Book, it was ever found
That Pegasus *was valued at Five-pound:*
Fine him to daily Drudging and Inditing;
And let him pay his Taxes out, in Writing.

characters. This play about incest & moral & political intrigue has an engagingly exotic North African setting. The blank verse lacks Elizabethan colloquial energy but unfolds a well-made, convincing tragedy. It is a dark, bold play.

THE WORKS OF VIRGIL IN ENGLISH: THE AENEIS 1697
[EXTRACTS FROM DEDICATION TO EARL OF MUSGRAVE]

A HEROICK Poem, truly such, is undoubedly the greatest Work which the Soul of Man is capable to perform. The Design of it, is to form the Mind to Heroick Virtue by Example; 'tis convey'd in Verse, that it may delight, while it instructs: The Action of it is always one, entire, and great. The least and most trivial Episodes, or under-Actions, are parts either necessary, or convenient to carry on the main Design: all things must be Grave, Majestical, and Sublime: Nothing of a Foreign Nature, like the trifling Novels, which *Ariosto* and others have inserted in their Poems: By which the Reader is miss-led into another sort of Pleasure. One raises the Soul and hardens it to Virtue, the other softens it again and unbends it into Vice. If this Oeconomy must be observ'd in the minutest Parts of an Epick Poem, which, to a common Reader, seem to be detach'd from the Body, and almost independent of it; what Soul, tho' sent into the World with great advantages of Nature, cultivated with the liberal Arts and Sciences; conversant with Histories of the Dead, and enrich'd with Observations on the Living, can be sufficient to inform the whole Body of so great a Work?*OOOOOOOOOOOOOOOOOOOOOOOOOOOOOOOOOOOOOO* SOME USE HOMER'S EPIC TO DECRY VIRGIL'S.

*At the end of his life Dryden mainly lived by translation. His version of Virgil was a huge undertaking & perhaps amounted to the epic he had vainly longed to write. He described 3 sorts of translation: **word by word**, which can give meaning but lacks music & rhythm: **imitation**, where idea & words of an earlier poem inspire a new 1 as Donne translated Juvenal; **paraphrase**, by which Dryden hopes **to make Virgil speak such English as he himself would have spoken, if he had been born in England & in this present age**. Dryden's robustly confident translation has the direct speech Puritan founders of the Royal Society AND modern royalists liked.*

They begin with the Moral of his Poem, which I own not to be so Noble as that of *Homer*. But without contradicting my Opinion, I can shew that *Virgil*'s was as useful to the *Romans* of his Age, as *Homer*'s was to the *Grecians* of his; in what time soever he may have liv'd and flourish'd. *Homer*'s Moral was to urge the necessity of Union, and good understanding betwixt Confederate States and Princes engag'd in a War with a Mighy Monarch: as also of Discipline in an Army, and obedience in the several Chiefs, to the Supream Commander of the joynt Forces. To inculcate this, he sets forth the ruinous Effects of Discord in the Camp of those Allies, by the quarrel betwixt the General, and the next in Office under him. *Homer* liv'd when the *Median* Monarchy was grown formidable to the *Grecians*: and the joint Endeavours of his Country-men, were little enough to preserve their common Freedom, from an encroaching Enemy. Such was his Moral, which all Cricks have allow'd to be more Noble than that of *Virgil*: though not adapted to the times in which the *Roman* Poet liv'd. Had *Virgil* flourish'd in the Age of *Ennius*, and address'd to *Scipio*, he had probably taken the same Moral, or some other not unlike it. For then the Romans were in as much danger from the *Carthaginian* Commonwealth, as the *Grecians* were from the *Assyrian*, or *Median* Monarchy. But we are to consider him as writing his Poem in a time when the Old Form of Government was subverted, and a new one just Established by *Octavius Caesar*: In effect by force of Arms, but seemingly by the Consent of the *Roman* People. He saw, beside, that the Commonwealth was lost without ressource: The Heads of it destroy'd; the Senate new moulded, grown degenerate; and either bought off, or thrusting their own Necks into the Yoke, out of fear of being forc'd. Yet I may safely affirm for our great Author (as Men of good Sense are generally Honest) that he was still of Republican principles in his Heart.*0000000000000000*

[VIRGIL'S *AENEIS*: BOOK 1]

By calling the poet of Augustus an inward republican Dryden is excusing himself for praising Cromwell then exalting later kings, & an English majority who, though not poets, did so too. William of Orange now ruled England AND the Dutch republic. Both nations had overseas empires.

Arms, and the Man I sing, who, forc'd by Fate,
And haughty Juno*'s unrelenting Hate;*
Expell'd and exil'd, left the Trojan *Shoar:*
Long Labours, both by Sea and Land he bore,
And in the doubtful War, before he won
The Latian *Realm, and built the destin'd Town:*
His banish'd Gods restor'd to Rites Divine,
And setl'd sure Succession in his Line:
From whence the Race of Alban *Fathers come,*
And the long Glories of Majestick Rome.

AN ESSAY CONCERNING HUMANE UNDERSTANDING
JOHN LOCKE: LONDON

1690

[THE EPISTLE TO THE READER]

READER, I Here put into thy Hands, what has been the diversion of some of my idle and heavy Hours: If it has the good luck to prove so of any of thine, and thou hast but half so much Pleasure in reading, as I had in writing it, thou wilt as little think thy Money, as I do my Pains, ill bestowed. Mistake not this, for a Commendation of my Work; nor conclude, because I was pleased with the doing of it, that therefore I am fondly taken with it now it is done. He that hawks at Larks and Sparrows, has no less Sport, though a much less considerable Quarry, than he that flies at nobler Game: And he is little acquainted with the Subject of this Treatise, the UNDERSTANDING who does not know, that as it is the most elevated Faculty of the Soul, so it is employed with a greater, and more constant Delight than any of the other.

Locke's father was a country-town lawyer & Puritan who fought for parliament: a kind man. His son was keen to investigate the 3 great questions which were still considered religious matters, but his Oxford college was run by Calvinists who banned free enquiry, & after 1660 England was ruled by equally intolerant Anglicans. It was also hard to discuss big questions calmly with leaders of the dissenting sects, their ideas & words were often inspired by the Holy Ghost, so not always open to human reason.

OOOOOOOOOOOOOOOOOOOOOOOOOOOOOOOOOOOOOOOOOOOOOOOOOOOOOOOOOOOOOOOO

ALL WHO INCREASE THEIR UNDERSTANDING BY CAREFUL THOUGHT, EVEN A LITTLE, ENJOY A PLEASURE DENIED TO THOSE WHO LIVE ON SCRAPS OF BORROWED OPINIONS. LOCKE HAS LET LOOSE HIS THOUGHTS AND FOLLOWED THEM IN WRITING, HOPING THAT THE READER WILL ENJOY FOLLOWING TOO, THOUGH HE MAY DISAGREE WITH LOCKE'S CONCLUSIONS. THE BOOK IS NOT FOR THOSE CONTENT WITH THEIR POWERS OF UNDERSTANDING. IT WAS WRITTEN TO SOLVE DIFFICULTIES WHICH STOPPED LOCKE'S DISCUSSIONS WITH FRIENDS REACHING CONCLUSIONS, SINCE NEITHER HE NOR THEY HAD FIRST AGREED ON WHAT THEIR WORDS MEANT. HIS FRIENDS FOUND THIS ESSAY USEFUL: HE HOPES SOME READERS WILL DO SO TOO.

OOOOOOOOOOOOOOOOOOOOOOOOOOOOOOOOOOOOOOOOOOOOOOOOOOOOOOOOOOOOOOOO

The Commonwealth of Learning, is not at this time without Master-

Locke taught Greek, studied medicine, joined Royal Society so met Boyle, Hooke & Newton. They debated big questions calmly & found answers no one could doubt, answers confirmed by the logic of mathematics, by the measure of weight & extent in repeatable experiments & by true report of experiments. Locke then became the secretary of a great Whig politician who was also inclined to civil & religious liberties. That was dangerous & Locke evaded dangers by flitting to France & Holland, returning from there with William of Orange in 1689. By then he had become famed as a philosopher.

Like Hobbes he based his politics on the way humanity 1st contracted into states. Hobbes thought we did it out of exhaustion, letting a strong boss unite us since without him our wildly selfish natures made warfare perpetual. But Locke thought we had always been social animals so early kingdoms, like families & tribes, were voluntary structures. This meant kings using armed force to rule their subjects were

Builders, whose mighty Designs, in advancing the Sciences, will leave lasting Monuments to the Admiration of Posterity; But every one must not hope to be a *Boyle*, or a *Sydenham*; and in an Age that produces such Masters, as the Great – *Huygenius*, and the incomparable Mr. *Newton*, with some other of that Strain; 'tis Ambition enough to be employed as an Under-Labourer in clearing Ground a little, and removing some of the Rubbish, that lies in the way to Knowledge; which certainly had been very much more advanced in the World, if the Endeavours of ingenious and industrious Men had not been much cumbred with the learned but frivolous use of uncouth, affected, or unintelligible Terms, introduced into the Sciences, and there made an Art of, to that Degree, that Philosophy, which is nothing but the true Knowledge of Things, was thought unfit, or uncapable to be brought into well-bred Company, and polite Conversation. Vague and insignificant Forms of Speech, and Abuse of Language, have so long passed for Mysteries of Science; And hard or misapply'd Words, with little or no meaning, have, by Prescription, such a Right to be mistaken for deep Learning, and heighth of Speculation, that it will not be easie to persuade, either those who speak, or those who hear them, that they are but the Covers of Ignorance, and hindrance of true Knowledge. To break in upon the Sanctuary of Vanity and Ignorance, will be, I suppose, some Service to Humane Understanding: Though so few are apt to think, they deceive, or are deceived in the Use of Words; or that the Language of the Sect they are of, has any Faults in it, which ought to be examined or corrected, that I hope I shall be pardon'd, if I have in the Third Book dwelt long on this Subject; and endeavoured to make it so plain, that neither the inveterateness of the Mischief, nor the prevalency of the Fashion, shall be any Excuse

for those, who will not take Care about the meaning of their own Words, and will not suffer the Significancy of their Expressions to be enquired into.*OOOOOOOOOOOOOOOOOOOOOOOOOOOOOOOOOOOOOOO*
AN ESSAY IS AN ATTEMPT TO WEIGH SOMETHING EXACTLY OR DO SOMETHING DIFFICULT. LOCKE WANTS HIS BOOK CRITICIZED AS THE SECOND OF THESE. *OOOOOOOOOOOOOOOOOOOOOOOOOOOOOOOOOOOOOOOO*

The Booksellers preparing for the fourth Edition of my *Essay*, gave me notice of it, that I might, if I had leisure, make any additions or alterations I should think fit. Whereupon I thought it convenient to advertise the Reader, that besides several corrections I have made here and there, there was one alteration which it was necessary to mention, because it ran through the whole Book, and is of consequence to be rightly understood. What I thereupon said, was this:

Clear and distinct Ideas are terms, which though familiar and frequent in Men's Mouths, I have reason to think every one, who uses, does not perfectly understand. And possibly 'tis but here and there one, who gives himself the trouble to consider them so far as to know what he himself, or others precisely mean by them; I have therefore in most places chose to put *determinate* or *determined*, instead of clear and distinct, as more likely to direct Men's thoughts to my meaning in this matter. By those denominations, I mean some object in the Mind, and consequently *determined*, i.e. such as it is there seen and perceived to be. This I think may fitly be called a *determinate* or *determin'd* Idea, when such as it is at any time objectively in the Mind, and so *determined* there, it is annex'd, and without variation *determined* to a name or articulate sound, which is to be steadily the sign of that very same object of the Mind, or *determinate* Idea.

breaking a natural law & subjects were right to replace them. The founders of republics in America & France were inspired by this & also (alas!) by his idea that right to own a thing originated in a fixed use of it. This gave the 1st settlers invading a land the right to evict nomads already living there.

Locke knew that science needs exactly measured mass, time & distance. Most of what we see, hear & feel is not measurable. This led him to think mass, time, space had reality lacking in colour, sound, scent & feelings, which occur as things outside us strike eyes, ears & bodily organs. This meant all that we directly notice is more real, maybe, than thoughts & dreams but is ideas too, so liable to mislead if logic (preferably numerical logic) does not confirm it. This set British philosophers seeking a numerical base for justice which they at last named political economy, & led Blake to call Locke a devil who had made people see the universe as a colourless, feelingless machine. Locke did not intend that; he meant only to end conflicts about

To explain this a little more particularly. By *determinate*, when applied to a *simple Idea*, I mean that simple appearance, which the Mind has in its view, or perceives in it self, when that Idea is said to be in it: By *determined*, when applied to a *complex Idea*, I mean such an one as consists of a determinate number of certain simple or less complex Ideas, joyn'd in such a proportion and situation, as the Mind has before its view, and sees in it self when that Idea is present in it, or should be present in it, when a Man gives a name to it. I say *should* be: because it is not every one, nor perhaps any one, who is so careful of his Language, as to use no Word, till he views in his Mind the precise *determined* Idea, which he resolves to make it the sign of. The want of this is the cause of no small obscurity and confusion in Men's thoughts and discourses.

I know there are not Words enough in any Language to answer all the variety of Ideas, that enter into Men's discourses and reasonings. But this hinders not, but that when any one uses any term, he may have in his Mind a *determined* Idea, which he makes it the sign of, and to which he should keep it steadily annex'd during that present discourse. Where he does not, or cannot do this, he in vain pretends to *clear or distinct Ideas*: 'Tis plain his are not so: and therefore there can be expected nothing but obscurity and confusion, where such terms are made use of, which have not such a precise determination.

Upon this Ground I have thought *determined* Ideas a way of speaking less liable to mistake, than *clear* and *distinct*: and where Men have got such determined Ideas of all, that they reason, enquire, or argue about, they will find a great part of their Doubts and Disputes at an end. The greatest part of the Questions and Controversies that perplex Mankind depending on the doubtful and uncertain use of Words, or (which is the same) *indetermined Ideas*, which they are made to stand for. I have made choice of these terms to signifie, 1. Some immediate object of the Mind, which it perceives and has before it distinct from the sound it uses as a sign of it. 2. That this Idea thus *determined*, i.e. which the Mind has in it self, and knows, and sees there be *determined* without any change to that name, and that name *determined* to that precise Idea. If Men had such *determined* Ideas in their enquiries and discourses, they would both discern how far their own enquiries and discourses went, and avoid the greatest part of the Disputes and Wranglings they have with others.

Besides this the Bookseller will think it necessary I should advertise the Reader, that there is an addition of two Chapters wholly new; the one *of the Association of Ideas*, the other *of Enthusiasm*. These with some other larger additions never before printed, he has engaged to print by themselves after the same manner, and for the same purpose as was done when this Essay had the Second Impression.

I will tell you in 3 words what the book is. – It is a history. – A history! of who? what? where? when? Don't hurry yourself - It is a history-book, Sir, of what passes in a man's own mind; & if you will say so much of the book, & no more, believe me, you will cut no contemptible figure in a metaphysic circle.

A TALE OF A TUB WRITTEN FOR THE UNIVERSAL IMPROVEMENT OF MANKIND JONATHAN SWIFT: LONDON [THE PREFACE]

1704

THE Wits of the present Age being so very numerous and penetrating, it seems, the Grandees of *Church* and *State* begin to fall under horrible Apprehensions, lest these Gentlemen during the Intervals of a long Peace, should find leisure to pick Holes in the weak sides of Religion and Government. To prevent which, there has been much Thought employ'd of late upon certain Projects for taking off the Force and Edge of those formidable Enquirers, from canvasing and reasoning upon such delicate Points. They have at length fixed upon one,

Like all Swift's work published in his lifetime this appeared anonymously. It blends parodies of all literary forms. The subtitle mocks Royal Society forecasts for science, Locke's essay to clarify thinking & company prospectuses aimed at the investors' greed. It precedes a satire against nearly everything in England, & was written to defend the distracted Anglican Church.

Its archbishop & bishops had begun a revolution by breaking their oath of loyalty to a Catholic king who issued an edict for universal tolerance. The honest among them then refused to swear loyalty to a Calvinist king about to tolerate Dissenters. Supported by parliament he then replaced them with a more docile archbishop & bishops: a difficult foundation to defend religiously. Swift did it by a parable.

Christianity is shown as 3 brothers. Their dad (God) gives the eldest (Catholicism) a coat (the Church) & the eldest embroiders it so gaudily that the cloth cannot be seen. The 2nd son (Calvinism) tears the embroidery off so violently that he rips the coat to rags & says this was the original state. The 3rd son (Anglicanism) mends it with some of the 1st son's thread & makes the coat decent & protective, neither beggarly nor gaudy.

*This defence of the English middle way annoyed Anglicans like Queen Anne who felt their Church was not protective patchwork but **true**, & wanted it accepted, not deeply examined. Swift agreed*

which will require some Time as well as Cost, to perfect. Mean while, the Danger hourly increasing, by new Levies of Wits all appointed (as there is Reason to fear) with Pen, Ink, and Paper, which may at an hour's Warning be drawn out into Pamphlets, and other Offensive Weapons, ready for immediate Execution: It was judged of absolute necessity, that some present Expedient be thought on, till the main Design can be brought to Maturity. To this End, at a Grand Committee, some Days ago, this important Discovery was made by a certain curious and refined Observer; That Sea-men have a Custom when they meet a *Whale*, to fling him out an empty *Tub*, by way of Amusement, to divert him from laying violent Hands upon the Ship. This Parable was immediately mythologiz'd; The *Whale* was interpreted to be *Hobs's Leviathan*, which tosses and plays with all other Schems of Religion and Government, whereof a great many are hollow, and dry, and empty, and noisy, and wooden, and given to Rotation. This is the *Leviathan* from whence the terrible Wits of our Age are said to borrow their Weapons. The *Ship* in danger, is easily understood to be its old Antitype the *Commonwealth*. But, how to analyze the *Tub*, was a Matter of Difficulty; when after long Enquiry and Debate, the literal Meaning was preserved: And it was decreed, that in order to prevent these *Leviathans* from tossing and sporting with the *Commonwealth*, (which of it self is too apt to *fluctuate*) they should be diverted from their Game by a *Tale of a Tub*. And my Genius being conceived to lye not unhappily that way, I had the Honor done me to be engaged in the Performance.

This is the sole Design in publishing the following Treatise, which I hope will serve for an *Interim* of some Months to employ those unquiet Spirits, till the perfecting of that great Work; into the Secret of which, it is reasonable the courteous

Reader should have some little Light. It is intended that a large Academy be erected, capable of containing nine thousand seven hundred forty and three Persons; which by modest Computation is reckoned to be pretty near the current Number of *Wits* in this Island. These are to be disposed into the several Schools of this Academy, and there pursue those Studies to which their Genius most inclines them. The Undertaker himself will publish his Proposals with all convenient speed, to which I shall refer the curious Reader for a more particular Account, mentioning at present only a few of the principal Schools. There is, first, a large *Pedarastick* School, with *French* and *Italian* Masters. There is also, the *Spelling* School, *a very spacious Building*: The School of *Looking-Glasses*: The School of *Swearing*: The School of *Criticks*: The School of *Salivation*: The School of *Hobby-Horses*: The School of *Poetry*: The School of *Tops*: The School of *Spleen*: The School of *Gaming*; with many others too tedious to recount. No Person to be admitted Member into any of these Schools, without an Attestation under two sufficient Persons Hands, certifying him to be a *Wit*.

But, to return. I am sufficiently instructed in the principal Duty of a Preface, if my Genius were capable of arriving at it. Thrice have I forced my Imagination to take the *Tour* of my Invention, and thrice it has returned empty; the latter having been wholly drained by the following Treatise. Not so, my more successful Brethren the *Moderns*, who will by no means let slip a Preface or Dedication, without some notable distinguishing Stroke, to surprize the Reader at the Entry, and kindle a wonderful Expectation of what is to ensue. Such was that of a most ingenious Poet, who solliciting his Brain for something new, compared himself to the *Hangman*, and his Patron to the *Patient*: This was *Insigne*,

upon the last point, but with disturbing gusto: Yesterday I saw a woman flayed; you can have no conception of how much it changed her, for the worse. But the queen's Tory prime minister, Robert Harley, knew this pungent writer could help him. Tale of a Tub disparaged wars & armies, calling them colleges in which violent madmen could graduate to honours. A new parliamentary system of 2 opposed parties had begun & the parties were now divided over a war.

An English-Dutch-Austrian army led by Churchill won battle after battle against France (now England's biggest trade rival) in a seemingly endless war. Taxes to finance it fell heavily on the country squires, who were Anglican, Tory, & had a majority of MPs in the Commons. The war was favoured by a majority of lords who led the Whigs, a mainly city-based party, but they feared a country land-owners revolt as Tory leaders feared to upset share prices. The Whigs thought the war too popular for the Tory prime minister to end it. This 2-party system often put men in office who went on doing as their enemies had done, if that kept them in office. But by hiring folk to defend their policies & attack opponents in regular newspapers & special pamphlets they also tried to win votes & alter public opinion. All factions did that, so Anne's reign grew as rich in journalism as Elizabeth's was in poetic drama. Defoe, England's 1st realistic novelist, was editor & reporter for Harley's journals, but the best journalist was Swift.

*Born in Dublin of English folk he became Anglican vicar in an Irish parish & often a guest of rich & clever Londoners who enjoyed his wit. He hoped, with their aid, to become a bishop. He liked wielding power secretly, wrote for Harley, & refused pay to avoid seeming a hireling. He helped to end the war quickly by proving the many victories had enriched city bankers, brokers & generals who could now live well without more. For this Swift got to be Dean of a Dublin cathedral: not the job he had craved. He hated Ireland but it Irished him. **Gulliver's Travels** describes England like a witty reporter seeing more in a game than the players can. It is he who began the IRISH ENGLISH tradition.*

recens, indictum ore alio. When I went thro' that necessary and noble Course of Study, I had the happiness to observe many such egregious Touches, which I shall not injure the Authors by transplanting: Because I have remarked, that nothing is so very tender as a Modern Piece of *Wit*, and which is apt to suffer so much in the Carriage. Some things are extreamly witty *to day*, or *fasting*, or *in this Place,* or *at eight a Clock*, or *over a Bottle*, or *spoken by* Mr. Whatdicall'um, or *in a Summer's Morning*: Any of which, by the smallest Transposal or Misapplication, is utterly annihilate. Thus, *Wit* has its Walks and Purlieus, out of which it may not stray the breadth of a Hair, upon peril of being lost. The *Moderns* have artfully fixed this *Mercury*, and reduced it to the Circumstances of Time, Place and Person. Such a Jest there is, that will not pass out of *Convent-Garden*; and such a one, that is no where intelligible but at *Hide-Park Corner*. Now, tho' it sometimes tenderly affects me to consider, that all the towardly Passages I shall deliver in the following Treatise, will grow quite out of date and relish with the first shifting of the present Scene; yet I must need subscribe to the Justice of this Proceeding: because, I cannot imagine why we should be at Expence to furnish Wit for succeeding Ages, when the former have made no sort of Provision for ours; wherein I speak the Sentiment of the very newest, and consequently the most Orthodox Refiners, as well as my own. However, being extreamly sollicitous that every accomplish'd Person who has got into the Taste of Wit calculated for this present Month of *August* 1697, should descend to the very *bottom* of all the *Sublime* throughout this Treatise; I hold it fit to lay down this general Maxim. Whatever Reader desires to have a thorow Comprehension of an Author's Thoughts, cannot take a better Method, than by putting himself into the Circumstances and

Posture of Life, that the Writer was in, upon every important Passage as it flowed from his Pen; For this will introduce a Parity and strict Correspondence of Idea's between the Reader and the Author. Now, to assist the diligent Reader in so delicate an Affair, as far as brevity will permit, I have recollected, that the shrewdest Pieces of this Treatise, were conceived in Bed, in a Garrat: At other times (for a Reason best known to my self) I thought fit to sharpen my Invention with Hunger; and in general, the whole Work was begun, continued, and ended, under a long course of Physick, and a great want of Money. Now, I do affirm, it will be absolutely impossible for the candid Peruser to go along with me in a great many bright Passages, unless upon the several Difficulties emergent, he will please to capacitate and prepare himself by these Directions. And this I lay down as my principal *Postulatum*.

Because I have profess'd to be a most devoted Servant of all *Modern* Forms; I apprehend some curious *Wit* may object at me, for proceeding thus far in a Preface, without declaiming according to the Custom, against the Multitude of Writers, whereof the whole Multitude of Writers most reasonably complains. I am just come from perusing some hundreds of Prefaces, wherein the Authors do at the very beginning address the gentle Reader concerning this enormous Grievance. Of these I have preserved a few Examples, and shall set them down as near as my Memory has been able to retain them.

One begins thus;

For a Man to set up for a Writer, when the Press swarms with, &c.

Another;

The Tax upon Paper does not lessen the Number of Scriblers, who daily pester, &c.

Another;

When every little Would-be-wit takes Pen in hand, 'tis vain to enter the Lists, &c.

Another;

To observe what Trash the Press swarms with, &c.

Another;

SIR. It is meerly in Obedience to your Commands that I venture into the Publick; for who upon a less Consideration would be of a Party with such a Rabble of Scribblers, &c.

Now, I have two Words in my own Defence, against this Objection. First: I am far from granting the Number of Writers, a Nuisance to our

Nation, having strenuously maintained the contrary in several Parts of the following Discourse. Secondly: I do not well understand the Justice of this Proceeding, because I observe many of these polite Prefaces, to be not only from the same Hand, but from those who are most voluminous in their several Productions: Upon which I shall tell the Reader a short Tale.

A Mountebank in Lecester-Fields *had drawn a huge Assembly about him. Among the rest, a fat unweildy Fellow, half stifled in the Press, would be every fit crying out, Lord! what a filthy Crowd is here; Pray, good People, give way a little; Bless me! what a Devil has rak'd this Rabble together: Z—ds, what squeezing is this! Honest Friend, remove your Elbow. At last a Weaver that stood next him could hold no longer: A Plague confound you (said he) for an over-grown Sloven; and who (in the Devil's Name) I wonder, helps to make up the Crowd half so much as your self? Don't you consider (with a Pox) that you take up more room with that Carcass than any five here? Is not the Place as free for us as for you? Bring your own Guts to a reasonable Compass (and be d—n'd) and then I'll engage we shall have room enough for us all.*

There are certain common Privileges of a Writer, the Benefit whereof, I hope there will be no Reason to doubt; particularly, that where I am not understood, it shall be concluded, that something very useful and profound is coutcht underneath: And again, that whatever Word or Sentence is printed in a different Character, shall be judged to contain something extraordinary either of *Wit* or *Sublime*.

As for the Liberty I have thought fit to take of praising my self, upon some Occasions or none; I am sure it will need no Excuse, if a Multitude of great Examples be allowed sufficient Authority: For, it is here to be noted, that Praise was originally a Pension paid by the World; but the *Moderns* finding the Trouble and Charge too great in collecting it, have lately bought out the *Fee-Simple*; since which time, the Right of Presentation is wholly in our selves.

For this Reason it is, that when an Author makes his own Elogy, he uses a certain Form to declare and insist upon his Title, which is commonly in these or the like Words, *I speak without Vanity*; which I think plainly shews it to be a Matter of Right and Justice. Now, I do here once for all declare, that in every Encounter of this Nature, thro' the following Treatise, the Form aforesaid is imply'd; which I mention, to save the Trouble of repeating it on so many Occasions.

'Tis a great Ease to my Conscience that I have writ so elaborate and useful a Discourse without one grain of Satyr intermixt; which is the sole Point wherein I have taken Leave to dissent from the famous Originals of our Age and Country. I have observ'd some Satyrists to use the Publick much at the rate that Pedants do a naughty Boy ready hors'd for Discipline; First expostulate the Case, then plead the Necessity of the Rod, from great Provocations, and conclude every Period with a Lash. Now, if I know anything of Mankind, these Gentlemen might very well spare their Reproof and Correction: For, there is not through all Nature another so callous and insensible a Member as the *World's Posteriors*, whether you apply to it the *Toe* or the *Birch*. Besides, most of our late Satyrists seem to lye under a sort of Mistake, that because *Nettles* have the Prerogative to Sting, therefore all *other Weeds* must do so too. I make not this Comparison out of the least Design to detract from these worthy Writers: For it is well known among *Mythologists*, that *Weeds* have the Preeminence over all other Vegetables; and therefore the first *Monarch* of this Island, whose Taste and Judgment were so acute and refined, did very wisely root out the *Roses* from the Collar of the *Order*, and plant the *Thistles* in their stead, as the nobler Flower of the two. For which Reason it is conjectured by profounder Antiquaries, that the Satyrical Itch, so prevalent in this Part of our Island, was first brought among us from beyond the *Tweed*. Here may it long flourish and abound: May it survive and neglect the Scorn of the World, with as much Ease and Contempt, as the World is insensible to the Lashes of it. May their own Dullness, or that of their Party, be no Discouragement for the Authors to proceed; but let them remember, it is with *Wits* as with *Razors*, which are never so apt to cut those they are employ'd on, as when they have *lost their Edge*: Besides, those whose Teeth are too rotten to bite, are best of all others qualified to revenge that Defect with their Breath.

I am not like other Men, to envy or undervalue the Talents I cannot reach; for which Reason I must needs bear a true Honor to this large eminent Sect of our *British* Writers. And I hope, this little Panegyrick will not be offensive to their Ears, since it has the Advantage of being only designed for themselves. Indeed, Nature her self has taken Order, that Fame and Honor should be purchased at a better Penyworth by Satyr, than by any other Productions of the Brain; the World being soonest provoked to *Praise* by *Lashes*, as Men are to *Love*. There is a Problem in an ancient Author, why Dedications, and other Bundles of Flattery run all upon stale musty Topicks, without the smallest Tincture of any thing New; not only to the torment and nauseating of the *Christian* Reader, but (if not suddenly prevented) to the universal spreading of that pestilent Disease, the Lethargy in this Island: Whereas, there is very little Satyr which has not something in it untouch'd before. The Defects of the former are usually imputed to the want of Invention among those who are Dealers in that kind: But, I think, with a great deal of Injustice; the Solution being easy and natural. For, the Materials of Panegyrick being very few in Number, have been long since exhausted: For, as Health is but one Thing, and has been always the same, whereas Diseases are by thousands, besides new and daily Additions: So, all the Virtues that have been ever in Mankind, are to be counted upon a few Fingers; but his Follies and Vices are innumerable, and Time adds hourly to the Heap. Now, the utmost a poor Poet can do, is to get by heart a List of the Cardinal Virtues, and deal them with his utmost Liberality to his Hero or his Patron: He may ring the Changes as far as it will go, and vary his Phrase till he has talk'd round; but the Reader quickly finds, it is all Pork, with a little variety of Sawce: For there is no inventing Terms of Art beyond our Idea's; and when Idea's are exhausted, Terms of Art must be so too

But, tho' the Matter for Panegyrick were as fruitful as the Topicks of Satyr, yet would it not be hard to find out a sufficient Reason, why the latter will be always better received than the first. For, this being bestowed only upon one or a few Persons at a time, is sure to raise Envy, and consequently ill Words from the rest, who have no share in the Blessing: But Satyr being levelled at all, is never resented for an Offence by any, since every individual Person makes bold to understand it of others, and very wisely removes his particular Part of the Burthen upon the Shoulders of the World, which are broad enough, and able to bear it. To this purpose, I have sometimes reflected upon the Difference between *Athens* and *England* with respect to the Point before us. In the *Attick* Commonwealth, it was the Priviledge and Birth-right of every Citizen and Poet, to rail aloud and in publick, or to expose upon the Stage by Name, any Person they pleased, tho' of the greatest Figure, whether a *Creon*, an *Hyperbolus*, an *Alcibiades*, or a *Demosthenes*: But, on the other side, the least reflecting Word let fall against the

People in general, was immediately caught up, and revenged upon the Authors, however considerable for their Quality or their Merits. Whereas, in *England* it is just the Reverse of all this.

Here, you may securely display your utmost *Rhetorick* against Mankind, in the Face of the World; tell them, *"That all are gone astray; That there is none that doth good, no not one; That we live in the very Dregs of Time; That Knavery and Atheism are Epidemick as the Pox; That Honesty is fled with Astraea;"* with any other Common Places *equally* new and eloquent, which are furnished by the *Splendida bilis*. And when you have done, the whole Audience, far from being offended, shall return you Thanks, as a Deliverer of precious and useful Truths. Nay further; It is but to venture your Lungs, and you may Preach in *Covent-Garden* against Foppery and Fornication, and *something else*: Against Pride, and Dissimulation, and Bribery, at *White-Hall*: You may expose Rapine and Injustice in the *Inns* of *Court Chapel*: And in a *City* Pulpit be as fierce as you please, against Avarice, Hypocrisy and Extortion. 'Tis but a *Ball* bandied to and fro, and every Man carries a *Racket* about Him to strike it from himself among the rest of the Company. But on the other side, whoever should mistake the Nature of things so far, as to drop but a single Hint in publick, How *such a one* starved half the Fleet, and half poyson'd the rest: How *such a one* from a true Principle of *Love* and *Honor*, pays no Debts but for *Wenches* and *Play*: How *such a one* has got a Clap, and runs out of his Estate: How *Paris* bribed by *Juno* and *Venus*, loath to offend either Party, slept out the whole Cause on the Bench: Or, how *such an Orator* makes long Speeches in the Senate, with much Thought, little Sense, and to no Purpose. Whoever, I say, should venture to be thus particular, must expect to be imprisoned for *Scandalum Magnatum*; to have *Challenges* sent him; to be sued for *Defamation*; and to be *brought before the Bar of the House*.

But, I forget that I am expatiating on a Subject, wherein I have no Concern, having neither a Talent nor an Inclination for Satyr; On the other side, I am so entirely satisfied with the whole present Procedure of human Things, that I have been for some Years preparing Materials towards *A Panegyrick upon the World*; to which I intended to add a Second Part, entitled, *A Modest Defence of the Proceedings of the Rabble in all Ages*. Both these I had Thoughts to publish by way of Appendix to the following Treatise; but finding my Common-Place-Book fill much slower than I had reason to expect, I have chosen to defer them to another Occasion. Besides, I have been unhappily prevented in that Design, by a certain Domestick Misfortune, in the Particulars whereof, tho' it would be very seasonable, and much in the *Modern* way, to inform the *gentle Reader*, and would also be of great Assistance towards extending this Preface into the Size now in Vogue, which by Rule ought to be *large* in Proportion as the subsequent Volume is *small*; Yet I shall now dismiss our impatient Reader from any further Attendance at the *Porch*; and having duly prepared his Mind by a preliminary Discourse, shall gladly introduce Him to the sublime Mysteries that ensue.

1704

Concentration on maths when 14 made Isaac useless to a twice-widowed mother running her farm in Lincolnshire: he was helped to Cambridge by a clergyman uncle. Like Leonardo da Vinci he lacked parental love when small & sought certainties in lonely intense thought & experiment; thus when academic educations gave misleading ideas about material science both men found right ways into it, hid them, & even so were helped by folk who recognised their genius. When 24 Newton found a fast way to measure change in mass & energy now called infinitesimal calculus. He kept it secret. Yet this lonely, depressed & at times paranoid man was put in university posts, controlled the Royal

OPTICKS *or, A Treatise of the Reflections, Refractions, Inflections and Colours of Light*
SIR ISAAC NEWTON: LONDON
[ADVERTISEMENT]

PART of the ensuing Discourse about Light was written at the Desire of some Gentlemen of the *Royal-Society*, in the Year 1675, and then sent to their Secretary, and read at their Meetings, and the rest was added about twelve Years after to complete the Theory; except the third Book, and the last Proposition of the Second, which were since put together out of scatter'd Papers. To avoid being engaged in Disputes about these Matters, I have hitherto delayed the printing, and should still have delayed it, had not the Importunity of Friends prevailed upon me. If any other Papers writ on this Subject are got out of my Hands they are imperfect, and were perhaps written before I had tried all the Experiments here set down, and fully satisfied my self about the Laws of Refractions and Composition of Colours. I have here publish'd what I think proper to come abroad, wishing that it may not be translated into another Language without my Consent.

The Crowns of Colours, which sometimes appear about the Sun and Moon, I have endeavoured to give an Account of; but for want of sufficient Observations leave that Matter to be farther examined. The Subject of the Third Book I have also left imperfect, not having tried all the Experiments which I intended when I was about these Matters, nor repeated some of those which I did try, until I had satisfied my self about all their Circumstances. To communicate what I have tried, and leave the rest to others for farther Enquiry, is all my Design in publishing these Papers.

In a Letter written to Mr. *Leibnitz* in the year 1679, and published by Dr. *Wallis*, I mention'd a Method by which I had found some general Theorems about squaring Curvilinear Figures, or comparing them with the Conic Sections, or other the simplest Figures with which they may be compared. And some Years ago I lent out a Manuscript containing such Theorems, and having since met with some Things copied out of it, I have on this Occasion made it publick, prefixing to it an *Introduction*, and subjoining a *Scholium* concerning that Method. And I have joined with it another small Tract concerning the Curvilinear Figures of the Second Kind, which was also written many Years ago, and made known to some Friends, who have solicited the making it publick.

I.N. *April 1, 1704.*

HYMNS AND SPIRITUAL SONGS
ISAAC WATTS
LONDON

[THE PREFACE]

WHILE we sing the Praises of our God in his Church, we are employ'd in that part of Worship which of all others is the nearest a-kin to Heaven; and 'tis pity that this of all others should be perform'd the worst upon Earth. The Gospel brings us nearer to the heavenly State than all the former Dispensations of God amongst Men: And in these last Days of the Gospel we are brought

Mint, received wealth, fame & leisure for research. By defying James II's interference in Cambridge Newton was made MP for it & gave Swift an idea in Gulliver's 3rd voyage. It shows a land ruled by a flying university full of Isaac Newtons.

With a formula explaining movement of planets, falling apples & erratic tides on the Chinese coast Newton proved every body in the universe attracts every other body. With a prism he split white sunlight into all other colours. For 200 years before radio scanning every new astronomic discovery was found through a reflecting telescope he devised. This preface hints that Leibniz, who discovered calculus separately & published it, stole the idea.

1709

Protestants use Bibles, Catholics, prayer books, Anglicans, both. All but the wee Scottish Free Kirk use hymn books. The Wee Frees' 17th-century service has not been amended by Isaac Watts.

The 1st Christians were also Jews, so had services like those in

*synagogues & sang psalms, supposedly by King David, containing terrible curses of the Jews' enemies. In Latin these entered Catholic church services with chants to Jesus & to God's merciful mother. Luther, Calvin & Knox rid their services of female stuff, using psalms modernised with a vengeance. Watts says that circa 1710 psalms are sung without true feeling, & the biblical patchwork of prayer recited in Protestant churches is in parts unchristian. A popular Dissenting preacher, he was a small man who liked children. Anglican Dr Johnson called him 1 who **every Christian church would rejoice to have adopted**. He quietly reformed the services of nearly all British churches, not by rejecting anything in their creeds, but by adding songs praising God's goodness & mercy. Thomas Hardy & D. H. Lawrence, greatest of English poet-novelists, as children attended separate Anglican & Methodist services, later losing faith in the Gods worshipped there. They never lost faith in the Holy Communion of the hymns, as their poetry tells us.*

almost within sight of the Kingdom of our Lord; yet we are very much unacquainted with the Songs of the *New Jerusalem*, and unpractis'd in the Work of Praise. To see the dull Indifference, the negligent and the thoughtless Air that sits upon the Faces of a whole Assembly, while the Psalm is on their Lips, might tempt even a charitable Observer to suspect the Fervency of inward Religion; and 'tis much to be fear'd that the Minds of most of the Worshippers are absent or unconcern'd. Perhaps the Modes of Preaching in the best Churches still want some Degrees of Reformation, nor are the Methods of Prayer so perfect as to stand in need of no Correction or Improvement: But of all our Religious Solemnities *Psalmodie* is the most unhappily manag'd. That very Action which should elevate us to the most delightful and divine Sensations, doth not only flat our Devotion, but too often awakens our Regret, and touches all the Springs of Uneasiness within us.

I have been long convinc'd, that one great Occasion of this Evil arises from the Matter and Words to which we confine all our Songs. Some of 'em are almost opposite to the Spirit of the Gospel: Many of them foreign to the State of the New-Testament, and widely different from the present Circumstances of Christians. Hence it comes to pass, that when spiritual Affections are excited within us, and our Souls are raised a little above this Earth in the beginning of a Psalm, we are check'd on a sudden in our Ascent toward Heaven by some Expressions that are more suited to the Days of *Carnal Ordinances*, and fit only to be sung in the *Worldly Sanctuary*. When we are just entring into an Evangelic Frame by some of the Glories of the Gospel presented in the brightest Figures of *Judaism*, yet the very next Line perhaps which the Clerk parcels out unto us, hath something in it so extreamly *Jewish* and cloudy, that darkens our Sight of God the Saviour: Thus by keeping too close to David in the House of God, the Vail of *Moses* is thrown over our Hearts. While we are kindling into Divine Love by the Meditations of the *loving Kindness of God, and the Multitude of his tender Mercies*, within a few Verses some dreadful Curse against Men is propos'd to our Lips; That *God would add Iniquity unto their Iniquity, not let 'em come into his Righteousness, but blot 'em out of the Book of the Living*, Psal. 69. 16, 27, 28. which is so contrary to the New Commandment, *of loving our Enemies*; and even under the Old Testament is best accounted for, by referring it to the Spirit of Prophetic Vengeance. Some Sentences of the *Psalmist* that are expressive of the Temper of our own Hearts and the Circumstances of our Lives may compose our Spirits to Seriousness, and allure us to a sweet Retirement within our selves; but we meet with a following Line which so peculiarly belongs but to one Action or Hour of the Life of *David* or *Asaph*, that breaks off our Song in the midst; our Consciences are affrighted lest we should speak a Falsehood unto God: Thus the Powers of our Souls are shock'd on a sudden, and our Spirits ruffled before we have time to reflect that this may be sung only as a History of antient Saints: And perhaps in some Instances that *Salvo* is hardly sufficient neither. Besides, it almost always spoils the Devotion by breaking the Uniform Thread of it. For while our Lips and our Hearts run on sweetly together, applying the Words to our own Case, there is something of Divine Delight in it: But at once we are forced to turn off the Application abruptly, and our Lips speak nothing but the Heart of *David*: Thus our own Hearts are as it were forbid the Pursuit of the Song, and then the Harmony and the Worship grow dull of meer necessity.

Many Ministers and many private Christians have long groan'd under this Inconvenience, and have wish'd rather than attempted a Reformation: At their importunate and repeated Requests I have for some Years past devoted many Hours of leisure to this Service. Far be it from my Thoughts to lay aside the Book of Psalms in public Worship few can pretend so great a Value for 'em as my self: It is the most artful, most Devotional and Divine Collection of Poesy; and nothing can be suppos'd more proper to raise a pious Soul to Heaven than some parts of that Book; never was a piece of Experimental Divinity so nobly written, and so justly reverenced and admired: But it must be acknowledged still, that there are a thousand Lines in it which were not made for a Church in our Days, to assume as its own: There are also many Deficiencies of Light and Glory, which our Lord *Jesus* and his Apostles have supply'd in the Writings of the New Testament; and with this Advantage I have compos'd these spiritual Songs which are now presented to the World. Nor is the Attempt vain-glorious or presuming; for in respect of clear Evangelic Knowledge, *The least in the Kingdom of Heav'n is greater than all the Jewish Prophets*, Mat. 11.11.

oooooooooooooooooooooooooooooooooooooooooooooooooooooooooooo

WATTS SAYS HIS HYMNS FITTED TO WELL KNOWN TUNES, EXPRESS PIETY ACCORDING TO PASSIONS OF LOVE, FEAR, HOPE, DESIRE, SORROW, WONDER OR JOY. HE HOPES NO CHRISTIAN SECT FINDS OFFENCE IN HIS WORDS, INVITES THOSE WHO DO TO CHANGE THEM.

1710

THE WAY OF THE WORLD
WILLIAM CONGREVE
LONDON

*Born in Yorkshire but educated in Ireland where his army-officer dad was sent, Congreve studied law in London & published **Incognita** (1692) a novel that Dr Johnson said he could endorse but not endure. Next year his 1st play **The Old Bachelor** was a Drury Lane success when only that theatre was licensed by King William. Wycherley & Etherege, best of the restoration dramatists, had retired or died & Congreve's comedies of idle young men's plots to wed rich heiresses were for wider & less brutal audiences than courtiers of Charles II. He joined a company that opened London's*

[PROLOGUE]

*O*F those few Fools, who with ill Stars are curst,
   Sure scribling Fools,
         call'd Poets, fare the worst:
For they're a sort of Fools which Fortune makes,
And after she has made 'em Fools, forsakes.
With Nature's Oafs 'tis quite a diff'rent Case,
For Fortune favours all her Idiot-Race:
In her own Nest the Cuckow-Eggs we find,
O'er which she broods to hatch the Changling-Kind.
No Portion for her own she has to spare,
So much she doats on her adopted Care.
    Poets are Bubbles, by the Town drawn in,
Suffer'd at first some trifling Stakes to win:
But what unequal Hazards do they run!
Each time they write they venture all they've won:
The Squire that's butter'd still, is sure to be undone.
This Author, heretofore, has found your Favour,
But pleads no Merit from his past Behaviour;
To build on that might prove a vain Presumption,

Shou'd Grants to Poets made, admit Resumption:
And in Parnassus *he must lose his Seat,*
If that be found a forfeited Estate.
　　　He owns, with Toil,
　　　　　　　he wrought the following Scenes,
But if they're naught ne'er spare him for his Pains:
Damn him the more; have no Commiseration
For Dulness on mature Deliberation.
He swears he'll not resent one hiss'd-of Scene
Nor, like those peevish Wits, his Play maintain,
Who, to assert their Sense, your Taste arraign.
Some Plot we think he has, and some new Thought;
Some Humour too, no Farce; but that's a Fault.
Satire, he thinks, you ought not to expect;
For so Reform'd a Town, who dares Correct?
To Please, this Time, has been his sole Pretence,
He'll not instruct, lest it shou'd give Offence.
Shou'd he by chance a Knave or Fool expose,
That hurts none here, sure here are none of those.
In short, our Play shall (with your leave to shew it)
Give you one Instance of a Passive Poet.
Who to your Judgments yields all Resignation;
So Save or Damn, after your own Discretion.

*2nd playhouse in the Haymarket. Characters in his plays are wits who can make jokes since they see humour in others, & those who **are** jokes since they cannot. Hero & heroine are always witty & fashionable, so while mocking the monetary greed, lust & folly of a fashionable crowd they make us feel superior parts of it. Such comedies were attacked by critics in a Society for the Reformation of Morals who said dramas caused the indecencies they displayed: still a popular argument. Congreve's plays were all written before he was 30. He became Secretary to the Island of Jamaica & amazed Voltaire by saying he did not wish to be thought a writer, but a gentleman.*

A TREATISE CONCERNING THE PRINCIPLES OF HUMAN KNOWLEDGE GEORGE BERKELEY: DUBLIN

1710

WHAT I here make Publick has, after a long and scrupulous Inquiry, seem'd to me evidently true, and not unuseful to be known, particularly to those who are tainted with Scepticism, or want a Demonstration of GOD, or the Natural Immortality of the Soul. Whether it be so or no, I am content the Reader shou'd impartially Examine. Since I do not think my self any farther concern'd for the Success of what I have Written, than as it is agreeable to *Truth*. But to the end *This* may not suffer, I make it my Request that the Reader suspend

*Born & educated like Swift in a land whose native speech he did not know, the Anglican Bishop of Cloyne was scathing of Locke's philosophy: **In Ireland we think otherwise**. Locke said that extent, weight, duration, & movement of bodies are primary: have a reality not found in scent, sound, colour -*

secondary things, for a rose has only scent when smelled, wind only sounds when heard etc. Such events are ideas in the mind, like thoughts & dreams, so insubstantial. No! said Berkeley, for extent & weight are not more real to us than noise & colours. "Primary qualities" are equally dependent on active perception. All things exist by perceiving and being perceived. We experience brute data maintained for us by an outer perceiver, & Berkeley called it God. Philosophy in England, Christian or not, still found more reward in Locke's primary ideas of measurable quality. The English search for a morality based on numbers was not diverted by Berkeley. He entered European thought by changing the minds of Hume & Kant.

his Judgment, till he was once, *at least*, read the whole through with that degree of Attention and Thought which the subject Matter shall seem to deserve. For as there are some Passages that, taken by themselves, are very liable (nor cou'd it be remedied) to gross Misinterpretation, and to be charged with most absurd Consequences, which, nevertheless, upon an intire perusal will appear not to follow from them: So likewise, tho' the whole shou'd be read over, yet, if this be done Transiently, 'tis very probable my Sense may be mistaken; but to a Thinking Reader, I flatter my self, it will be throughout Clear and Obvious. As for the Characters of Novelty and Singularity, which some of the following Notions may seem to bear, 'tis, I hope, needless to make any Apology on that account. He must surely be either very weak, or very little acquainted with the Sciences, who shall reject a Truth, that is capable of Demonstration, for no other Reason but because it's newly known and contrary to the Prejudices of Mankind. Thus much I thought fit to premise, in order to prevent, if possible, the hasty Censures of a sort of Men, who are too apt to condemn an Opinion before they rightly comprehend it.

1711

Ireland was then the most likely place for Englishmen with small fortunes to enlarge them. Their initiative bred a 2nd generation of Anglo-Irish wits who sought fame in England. Steele was one. As trooper in a regiment of guards he came to a London

THE TATLER, VOLUME 4
RICHARD STEELE
LONDON

[THE PREFACE]

IN THE last *Tatler* I promised some Explanation of Passages and Persons mention'd in this Work, as well as some Account of the Assistances I have had in the Performance. I shall do this in very few Words; for when a Man has no Design but to speak plain Truth, he may say a great deal in a very narrow Compass. I have in the Dedication of the First Volume made my Acknowledgments to Dr. *Swift*, whose pleasant Writings, in the Name of *Bickerstaff*, created an Inclination in the Town towards any Thing that could appear in the same Disguise. I must acknowledge also, that at my first entring upon this Work, a certain uncommon Way of Thinking, and a Turn in Conversation peculiar to that agreeable Gentleman, rendered his Company very advantageous to one whose Imagination was to be continually employed upon obvious and common Subjects, though at the same Time obliged to treat them in a new and unbeaten Method. His Verses on the *Shower in Town*, and the *Description of the Morning*, are Instances of the Happiness of that Genius, which could raise such Pleasing Idea's upon Occasions so barren to an ordinary Invention.

where intellectual life was centred in coffee houses. Here men of leisure met to discuss fashion, literature & politics as reported in gossip & news sheets. Voltaire noticed that English writers were given jobs & sinecures that in other nations only went to courtiers: patronage in London had moved from court to parliament. Steele, a devout Protestant, wrote for the Whigs, got jobs & pay by it, was too reckless to save money.

OOOOOOOOOOOOOOOOOOOOOOOOOOOOOOOOOOOOOOOOOOOOOOOOOOOOOOOOOOOOOOOO

STEELE THANKS OTHER CONTRIBUTORS; SAYS HIS SATIRICAL PORTRAITS, ESPECIALLY OF CLERGY, ARE BASED ON PEOPLE OF BOTH PARTIES IN POLITICS AND RELIGION, SO CANNOT BE THOUGHT BIASED.

OOOOOOOOOOOOOOOOOOOOOOOOOOOOOOOOOOOOOOOOOOOOOOOOOOOOOOOOOOOOOOOO

I really have acted in these Cases with Honesty, and am concerned it should be thought otherwise: For Wit, if a Man had it, unless it be directed to some useful End, is but a wanton frivolous Quality; all that one should value himself upon in this Kind is, that he had some honourable Intention in it.

As for this Point, never Hero in Romance was carried away with a more furious Ambition to conquer Giants and Tyrants, than I have been in extirpating Gamesters and Duellists. And indeed, like one of those Knights too, though I was calm before, I am apt to fly out again, when the Thing that first disturbed me is presented to my Imagination. I shall therefore leave off when I am well, and fight with Windmills no more: Only shall be so Arrogant as to say of my self, that in Spite of all the Force of Fashion and Prejudice, in the Face

In those days rich hooligans in the House of Lords & Commons introduced to London the manners of blood sports; thought rape of working class women a manly game & duelling another. No law or police existed to stop them. Steele had nearly killed a man in a duel; loathed having done it; began this paper to spread good manners through witty articles making vice look unfashionable. He used a pseudonym invented by Dean Swift (Isaac Bickerstaff) & moral reformers approved.

of all the World, I alone bewailed the Condition of an *English* Gentleman, whose Fortune and Life are at this Day precarious; while His Estate is liable to the Demands of Gamesters, through a false Sense of Justice; and to the Demands of Duellists, through a false Sense of Honour. As to the First of these Orders of Men, I have not one Word more to say of them: As to the latter, I shall conclude all I have more to offer against them (with Respect to their being prompted by the Fear of Shame) by applying to the Duellists what I think Dr. *South* says somewhere of the Lyar, *He is a Coward to Man, and a Brave to God.*

1711

Steele's **Tatler** *had articles suggesting a moderate Whiggism. He soon dropped them for essays on literature & society that pleased all parties & let him use contributions from Tories like Swift. Then Addison contributed in a style so gracefully flowing that shortly he was filling nearly all the issues. After no. 271 Steele ended* **The Tatler***: Addison & he then launched* **The Spectator***. It was even more popular & became the 1st journal to be republished in book form. Steele imagined a club of middle-class gents, at once typical yet amusingly eccentric. Addison described them charmingly & readers bought issues hoping again to encounter a favourite character. This formula was such a success that in 1836 publishers commis-*

THE SPECTATOR, FIRST NUMBER
JOSEPH ADDISON
LONDON

[No.1 THURSDAY, MARCH 1,1711]
Non fumam ex fulgore, sed ex fumo dare lucem
Cogitat, ut speciosa dehinc miracula promat. Hor.

I HAVE observed, that a Reader seldom peruses a Book with Pleasure 'till he knows whether the Writer of it be a black or a fair Man, of a mild or cholerick Disposition, Married or a Batchelor, with other Particulars of the like nature, that conduce very much to the right Understanding of an Author. To gratify this Curiosity, which is so natural to a Reader, I design this Paper, and my next, as Prefatory Discourses to my following Writings, and shall give some Account in them of the several Persons that are engaged in this Work. As the chief Trouble of Compiling, Digesting and Correcting will fall to my Share, I must do my self the Justice to open the Work with my own History.

I was born to a small Hereditary Estate, which, according to the Tradition of the Village where it lies, was bounded by the same Hedges and Ditches in *William* the Conqueror's Time that it is at present, and has been delivered down from Father to Son whole and entire, without the Loss or Acquisition of a single Field or Meadow, during the space of six hundred Years. There runs a Story in the Family, that when my Mother was gone with Child of me about three Months, she dreamt that she was brought to Bed of a Judge: Whether this might proceed from a Law-Suit which was then depending in the Family, or my Father's being a Justice of the Peace, I cannot determine; for I am not so vain as to think it presaged any Dignity that I should arrive at in my future Life, though that was the Interpretation which the Neighbourhood put upon it. The Gravity of my Behaviour at my very first Appearance in the World, and all the Time that I sucked, seemed to favour my Mother's Dream: For, as she has often told me, I threw away my Rattle before I was two Months old, and would not make use of my Coral 'till they had taken away the Bells from it.

As for the rest of my Infancy, there being nothing in it remarkable, I shall pass it over in Silence. I find, that, during my Nonage, I had the Reputation of a very sullen Youth, but was always a Favourite of my School-Master, who used to say, *that my Parts were solid and would wear well*. I had not been long at the University, before I distinguished my self by a most profound Silence: For, during the Space of eight Years, excepting in the publick Exercises of the College, I scarce uttered the Quantity of an hundred Words; and indeed do not remember that I ever spoke three Sentences together in my whole Life. Whilst I was in this Learned Body I applied my self with so much Diligence to my Studies, that there are very few celebrated Books, either in the Learned or the Modern Tongues, which I am not acquainted with.

Upon the Death of my Father I was resolved to travel into Foreign Countries, and therefore left the University, with the Character of an odd unaccountable Fellow, that had a great deal of Learning, if I would but show it. An insatiable Thirst after Knowledge carried me into all the Countries

sioned from Dickens, a young reporter, a series of comic articles about the Pickwick Club & it made him a popular novelist. Dickens also wished for a better society, but his pages contained too many of the lower classes to be much read for polite instruction. Meanwhile The Spectator *(wrote Dr Johnson in 1776)* **is too well known to be praised: It comprises precepts of criticism, sallies of invention, descriptions of life & lectures of virtue. It employs wit in the cause of truth, makes elegance subservient to piety, & has for over half a century supplied the English nation ... with principles of speculation, & rules of practice.** *Johnson's prose is more heavily Latinate & magisterial than Addison's but modelled on it. Swift & Defoe wrote more plainly but their prose, as the century advanced, sounded too close to brute facts for polite ears. The prose of Addison fits detached spectators expressing amusement at both the ways of poorer people & those who think themselves superior. With personal variation this is the voice used by English prose until native Scots, American & Irish voices are heard.*

of *Europe*, in which there was any thing new or strange to be seen; nay, to such a Degree was my Curiosity raised, that having read the Controversies of some great Men concerning the Antiquities of *Egypt*, I made a Voyage to *Grand Cairo*, on purpose to take the Measure of a Pyramid; and as soon as I had set my self right in that Particular, returned to my Native Country with great Satisfaction.

I have passed my latter Years in this City, where I am frequently seen in most publick Places, tho' there are not above half a dozen of my select Friends that know me; of whom my next Paper shall give a more particular Account. There is no Place of general Resort, wherein I do not often make my Appearance; sometimes I am seen thrusting my Head into a Round of Politicians at *Will*'s, and listening with great Attention to the Narratives that are made in those little Circular Audiences. Sometimes I smoak a Pipe at *Child*'s; and whilst I seem attentive to nothing but the *Post-Man*, overhear the Conversation of every Table in the Room. I appear on *Sunday* Nights at St. *James*'s Coffee-House, and sometimes join the little Committee of Politicks in the Inner-Room, as one who comes there to hear and improve. My Face is likewise very well known at the *Grecian*, the *Cocoa-Tree*, and in the Theaters both of *Drury-Lane*, and the *Hay-Market*. I have been taken for a Merchant upon the *Exchange* for above these ten Years, and sometimes pass for a *Jew* in the Assembly of Stock-Jobbers at *Jonathan*'s. In short, where-ever I see a Cluster of People I always mix with them, tho' I never open my Lips but in my own Club.

Thus I live in the World, rather as a Spectator of Mankind, than as one of the Species; by which means I have made my self a Speculative Statesman, Soldier, Merchant and Artizan, without ever medling with any Practical Part in Life. I am very well versed in the Theory of an Husband, or a Father, and can discern the Errors in the Oeconomy, Business, and Diversion of others, better than those who are engaged in them; as Standers-by discover Blots, which are apt to escape those who are in the Game. I never espoused any Party with Violence, and am resolved to observe an exact Neutrality between the Whigs and Tories, unless I shall be forc'd to declare my self by the Hostilities of either side. In short, I have acted in all the parts of my Life as a Looker-on, which is the Character I intend to preserve in this Paper.

I have given the Reader just so much of my History and Character, as to let him see I am not altogether unqualified for the Business I have undertaken. As for other Particulars in my Life and Adventures, I shall insert them in following Papers, as I shall see occasion. In the mean time, when I consider how much I have seen, read and heard, I begin to blame my own Taciturnity; and since I have neither Time nor Inclination to communicate the Fulness of my Heart in Speech, I am resolved to do it in Writing; and to Print my self out, if possible, before I Die. I have been often told by my Friends, that it is Pity so many useful Discoveries which I have made, should be in the Possession of a Silent Man. For this Reason therefore, I shall publish a Sheet-full of Thoughts every Morning, for the Benefit of my Contemporaries; and if I can any way contribute to the Diversion or Improvement of the Country in which I live, I shall leave it, when I am summoned out of it, with the secret Satisfaction of thinking that I have not Lived in vain.

There are three very material Points which I have not spoken to in this Paper, and which, for several important Reasons, I must keep to my self, at least for some Time: I mean, an Account of my Name, my Age, and my Lodgings. I must confess I would gratify my Reader in any thing that is reasonable; but as for these three Particulars, though I am sensible they might tend very much to the Embellishment of my Paper, I cannot yet come to a Resolution of communicating them to the Publick. They would indeed draw me out of that Obscurity which I have enjoy'd for many Years, and expose me in publick Places to several Salutes and Civilities, which have been always very disagreeable to me; for the greatest Pain I can suffer, is the being talked to, and being stared at. It is for this Reason likewise, that I keep my Complexion and Dress, as very great Secrets; tho' it is not impossible, but I may make Discoveries of both in the Progress of the Work I have undertaken.

After having been thus particular upon my self, I shall in to-Morrow's Paper give an Account of those Gentlemen who are concerned with me in this Work. For, as I have before intimated, a Plan of it is laid and concerted (as all other Matters of Importance are) in a Club. However, as my Friends have engaged me to stand in the Front, those who have a mind to correspond with me, may direct their Letters *To The Spectator*, at Mr. *Buckley*'s in *Little Britain*. For I must further acquaint the Reader, that tho' our Club meets only on *Tuesdays* and *Thursdays*, we have appointed a Committee to sit every Night, for the Inspection of all such Papers as may contribute to the Advancement of the Publick Weal.

1714

London's rapid growth kept her the biggest city on earth for 3 centuries. She grew by her immigrants. Until flush lavatories were common around 1900 more died than were born there, a majority killed young by dirt, overcrowding & hunger. Increasing nastiness around the richest of all trade & money markets could not be ignored, nor could the crime it fostered.

Moralists said laziness & vice caused poverty & blamed the poor. They could not blame infants left to beg or starve in the streets. Charities to care for them had the support of Addison & others, for until then many Catholic nations had better charitable hospices than England. Mandeville, a Dutch doctor practising in London, believed the moralists & charitable folk equally wrong.

His fable is in verse, with glosses in prose. They describe the social contract as a benign conspiracy turning our private vices (of which vanity is chief) into public benefits. The chastity of women, courage of soldiers, honesty of all classes is enforced by fear of

THE FABLE OF THE BEES
or PRIVATE VICES, PUBLICK BENEFITS
BERNARD MANDEVILLE: LONDON

[THE PREFACE]

LAWS and Government are to the Political Bodies of Civil Societies, what the Vital Spirits and Life it self are to the Natural Bodies of Animated Creatures; and as those that study the Anatomy of Dead Carkasses may see, that the chief Organs and nicest Springs more immediately required to continue the Motion of our Machine, are not hard Bones, strong Muscles and Nerves, nor the smooth white Skin that so beautifully covers them, but small trifling Films and little Pipes that are either overlook'd, or else seem inconsiderable to Vulgar Eyes; so they that examine into the Nature of Man, abstract from Art and Education, may observe, that what renders him a Sociable Animal, consists not in his desire of Company, good Nature, Pity, Affability, and other Graces of a fair Outside; but that his vilest and most hateful Qualities are the most necessary Accomplishments to fit him for the largest, and according to the World, the happiest and most flourishing Societies.

The following Fable, in which what I have said is set forth at large was printed above eight Years ago in a Sixpenny Pamphlet call'd, *The Grumbling Hive*; or *Knaves turn'd Honest*; and being soon after Pyrated, cry'd about the Streets in a Half-penny Sheet. Since the first publishing of it I have met with several that either wilfully or ignorantly mistaking the Design, would have it, that the Scope of it was a Satyr upon Virtue and Morality, and the whole wrote for the Encouragement of Vice. This made me resolve, whenever it should be reprinted, some way or other to inform the Reader of the real Intent this little Poem was wrote with. I do not dignify these few loose Lines with the Name of

Poem, that I would have the Reader expect any Poetry in them, but barely because they are Rhime, and I am in reallity puzled what name to give them; for they are neither Heroick nor Pastoral, Satyr, Burlesque nor Heroi-comick; to be a Tale they want Probability, and the whole is rather too long for a Fable. All I can say of them is, that they are a Story told in Dogrel, which without the least design of being witty, I have endeavour'd to do in as easy and familiar a Manner as I was able: The Reader shall be welcome to call them what he pleases. 'Twas said of Montagne, that he was pretty well vers'd in the Defects of Mankind, but unacquainted with the Excellencies of Humane Nature: If I fare no worse, I shall think my self well used.

What Country soever in the Universe is to be understood by the Bee-Hive represented here, it is evident from what is said of the Laws and Constitution of it, the Glory, Wealth, Power and Industry of its Inhabitants, that it must be a large, rich and warlike Nation that is happily governed by a limited Monarchy. The Satyr therefore to be met with in the following Lines upon the several Professions and Callings, and almost every Degree and Station of People was not made to injure and point to particular Persons, but only to shew the Vileness of the Ingredients that all together compose the wholesome Mixture of a well order'd Society; in order to extol the wonderful Power of Political Wisdom, by the help of which so beautiful a Machine is rais'd from the most contemptible Branches. For the main design of the Fable, (as it is breefly explain'd in the Moral) is to shew the Impossibility of enjoying all the most elegant Comforts of Life that are to be met with in an industrious, wealthy and powerful Nation, and at the same time be bless'd with all the Virtue and Innocence that can be wish'd for in a Golden Age;

contempt. Love of luxury has so stimulated industry & trade that many poor now enjoy goods that the rich once lacked, but industry & trade only thrive with badly paid, ignorant workers, so charity that feeds & teaches the poor is bound to destroy our prosperity – labourers are to England what slaves were to Greece & Rome. Yes, poverty also causes crime but without crime judges, lawyers, jailors would be unemployed. The church also profits by vice & crime which persuade the prosperous to pay clergy to preach against theft & fraud. But robbery & fraud, like extravagance, can also benefit the public by restoring to its use funds hoarded by the thrifty. Mandeville says unselfish virtues exist, but cannot make strong, rich & highly cultured nations.

This defence of the English economy was denounced as evil & impious by press & pulpit & became a best seller. Adam Smith's **Moral Sentiments** *(1759) said it alarmed friends of virtue (Berkeley & Watts among them) by bordering upon the truth. It gave social science a necessary key by showing all actions, selfish or benign, had unintended results.*

from thence to expose the Unreasonableness and Folly of those, that desirous of being an opulent and flourishing People, and wonderfully greedy after all the Benefits they can receive as such, are yet always murmuring at and exclaiming against those Vices and Inconveniencies, that from the beginning of the World to this present Day, have been inseparable from all Kingdoms and States that ever were fam'd for Strength, Riches and Politeness at the same time.

To do this, I first slightly touch upon some of the Faults and Corruptions the several Professions and Callings are generally charg'd with. After that I shew that those very Vices of every Particular Person by skilful Management were made subservient to the Grandeur and worldy Happiness of the whole. Lastly, by setting forth what of necessity must be the consequence of general Honesty and Virtue and National Temperance, Innocence and Content, I demonstrate that if Mankind could be cured of the Failings they are Naturally guilty of they would cease to be capable of being rais'd into such vast, potent and polite Societies, as they have been under the several great Common-wealths and Monarchies that have flourish'd since the Creation.

If you ask me why I have done all this, *cui bono*? And what Good these Notions will produce; truly besides the Reader's Diversion, I believe none at all; but if I was ask'd what Naturally ought to be expected from 'em, I wou'd answer, That in the first Place the People, who continually find Fault with others, by reading them, would be taught to look at home, and examining their own Consciences, be made asham'd of always railing at what they are more or less guilty of themselves; and that in the next, those who are so fond of the Ease and Comforts, and reap all the Benefits that are the Consequence of a great and flourishing Nation, would learn more patiently to submit to those Inconveniencies, which no Government upon Earth can remedy, when they should see the Impossibility of enjoying any great share of the first, without partaking likewise of the latter.

This I say ought naturally to be expected from the publishing of these Notions, if People were to be made better by any thing that could be said to them; but Mankind having for so many Ages remain'd still the same, notwithstanding the many instructive and elaborate Writings, by which their Amendment has been endeavour'd, I am not so vain as to hope for better success from so inconsiderable a Trifle.

Having allow'd the small Advantage this little Whim is likely to produce, I think my self oblig'd to shew, that it cannot be prejudicial to any; for what is published, if it does no good, ought at least to do no harm: In order to this I have made some Explanatory Notes, to which the Reader will find himself refer'd in those Passages that seem to be most liable to Exceptions.

The Censorious that never saw the *Grumbling Hive*, will tell me, that whatever I may talk of the Fable, it not taking up a Tenth part of the Book, was only contriv'd to introduce the *Remarks*; that instead of clearing up the doubtful or obscure Places, I have only pitch'd upon such as I had a Mind to expatiate upon; and that far from striving to extenuate the Errors committed before I have made Bad worse, and shewn my self a more bare-fac'd Champion for Vice, in the rambling Digressions, than I had done in the Fable itself.

I shall spend no time in answering these Accusations; where Men are prejudic'd, the best Apologies are lost; and I know that those who think it Criminal to suppose a necessity of Vice in any Case whatever, will never be reconcil'd to any part of the Performance; but if this be thoroughly examin'd all the Offence it can give, must result from the wrong Inferences that may perhaps be drawn from it, and which I desire no body to make. When I assert, that Vices are inseparable from great and potent Societies, and that it is impossible their Wealth and Grandeur should subsist without, I do not say that the particular Members of them who are guilty of any, should not be continually reprov'd, or not be punish'd for them when they grow into Crimes.

There are, I believe, few People in *London*, of those that are at any time forc'd to go a foot, but what could wish the Streets of it much cleaner than generally they are; whilst they regard nothing but their own Cloaths and private Conveniency; but when once they come to consider, that what offends them is the result of the Plenty, great Traffick and Opulency of that mighty City, if they have any Concern in its Welfare, they will hardly ever wish to see the Streets of it less dirty. For if we mind the Materials of all sorts that must supply such an infinite number of Trades and Handicrafts, as are always going forward; the vast quantity of Victuals, Drink and Fewel that are daily consum'd in it, and the Waste and Superfluities that must be produc'd from them; the multitudes of Horses and other Cattle that are always dawbing the Streets, the Carts, Coaches and more heavy Carriages that are perpetually wearing and breaking the Pavement of them, and above all the numberless swarms of People that are continually harrassing and trampling through every part of them. If, I say, we mind all these, we shall find that every Moment must produce new Filth, and considering how far distant the great Streets are from the River side, what Cost and Care soever be bestow'd to remove the Nastiness almost as fast as 'tis made, it is impossible *London* should be more cleanly before it is less flourishing. Now would I ask if a good Citizen, in consideration of what has been said, might not assert, that dirty Streets are a necessary Evil inseparable from the Felicity of *London* without being the least hindrance to the cleaning of Shoes, or sweeping of Streets, and consequently without any Prejudice either to the *Blackguard* or the *Scavingers*.

But if, without any regard to the Interest or Happiness of the City, the Question was put, What Place I thought most pleasant to walk in? No body can doubt but before the stinking Streets of *London*, I would esteem a fragrant Garden, or a shady Grove in the Country. In the same manner, if laying aside all worldy Greatness and Vain Glory, I should be ask'd where I thought it was most probable that Men might enjoy true Happiness, I would prefer a small peaceable Society, in which Men neither envy'd nor esteem'd by Neighbours, should be contented to live upon the Natural Product of the Spot they inhabit, to a vast multitude abounding in Wealth and Power, that should always be conquering others by their Arms Abroad, and debauching themselves by Foreign Luxury at Home.

Thus much I had said to the Reader in the First Edition; and have added nothing by way of Preface in the Second. But since that, a violent Out-cry has been made against the Book, exactly answering the Expection I always had of the Justice, the Wisdom, the Charity, and Fair-dealing of those whose Goodwill I despair'd of. It has been presented by the Grand-Jury, and condemn'd by thousands who never saw a word of it. It has been preach'd against before my Lord Mayor; and an utter Refutation of it is daily expected from a Reverend Divine, who has call'd me Names in the Advertisements, and threatened to answer me in two Months time for above five Months together. What I have to say for my self, the Reader will see in my Vindication at the end of the Book, where he will likewise find the Grand-Jury's Presentment, and a Letter to the Right Honourable Lord *C*. which is very Rhetorical beyond Argument or Connexion. The Author shews a fine Talent for Invectives, and great Sagacity in discovering Atheism, where others can find none. He is zealous against wicked Books, points at the Fable of the Bees, and is very angry with the Author: he bestows four strong Epithets on the Enormity of his Guilt, and by several elegant Innuendo's to the Multitude, as the Danger there is in suffering such Authors to live, and the Vengeance of Heaven upon a whole Nation, very charitably recommends him to their Care.

Considering the length of this Epistle, and that it is not wholly levell'd at me only, I thought at first to have made some Extracts from it of what related to my self; but finding, on a nearer Enquiry, that what concern'd me was so blended and interwoven with what did not, I was oblig'd to trouble the Reader with it entire; not without Hopes that, prolix as it is, the Extravagancy of it will be entertaining to those who have perused the Treatise it condemns with so much Horror.

THE ILIAD OF HOMER
ALEXANDER POPE
LONDON

1715

[PREFACE]

HOMER is universally allow'd to have had the greatest Invention of any Writer whatever. The Praise of Judgment *Virgil* has justly contested with him, and others may have their Pretensions as to particular Excellences; but his Invention remains yet unrival'd. Nor is it a Wonder if he has ever been acknowledg'd the greatest of Poets, who most excell'd in That which is the very Foundation of Poetry. It is the Invention that in different degrees distinguishes all great Genius's: The utmost Stretch of human Study, Learning, and Industry, which master everything besides, can never attain to this. It furnishes Art with all her Materials, and without it Judgment itself can at best but *steal wisely*: For Art is only like a prudent Steward that lives on managing the Riches of Nature. Whatever Praises may be given to Works of Judgment, there is not even a single Beauty in them but is owing to the Invention. As in the most regular Gardens, however

Pope was born in 1688, his dad a linen draper, both parents elderly Catholics. They retired to a house by Windsor Forest when Catholics were legally forbidden to live in London. Their care kept Pope alive as spinal tuberculosis deformed & stunted him: he could not stand without an iron corset. Friendship & security helped Pope live to be 56 but tubercular ill health at first drove him as fast as young Keats. Home tuition & close imitation of fine poets from Chaucer to Dryden matured his talent. At 14, to learn French &

Italian, he insisted on visits to London; at 17 knew Wycherley & Congreve; at 24 his verse was printed & praised by Steele & Addison. A bishop visiting the royal palace heard Swift telling Queen Anne's courtiers that the best poet in England was Mr Pope (a papist), who had begun a translation of Homer into English for which he would have them all subscribe: "For," says he, "he shall not begin to print till I have a thousand guineas for him." An equivalent sum in 2000AD would be £20,000. At that time Swift (as Dr Johnson wrote later) dictated the political opinions of the English nation.

From Chaucer Dryden had learned to satirically portray & firmly translate. Pope learned from both, yet never drudged for a king or aristocracy, being the 1st poet to live an independent life by bookwriting. The Iliad enabled him to buy a villa on the Thames at Twickenham & create a miniature landscape garden, an interest relevant to images in this preface. They suggest that cultivation produces less vigorous poetry than grows wild in heroic ages, but that better social order has its own poetry.

Art may carry the greatest Appearance, there is not a Plant or Flower but is the Gift of Nature. The first can only reduce the Beauties of the latter into a more obvious Figure, which the common Eye may better take in, and is therefore more entertain'd with. And perhaps the reason why most Criticks are inclin'd to prefer a judicious and methodical Genius to a great and fruitful one, is, because they find it easier for themselves to pursue their Observations through an uniform and bounded Walk of Art, than to comprehend the vast and various Extent of Nature.

Our Author's Work is a wild Paradise, where if we cannot see all the Beauties so distinctly as in an order'd Garden, it is only because the Number of them is infinitely greater. 'Tis like a copious Nursery which contains the Seeds and first Productions of every kind, out of which those who follow'd him have but selected some particular Plants, each according to his Fancy, to cultivate and beautify. If some things are too luxuriant, it is owing to the Richness of the Soil; and if others are not arriv'd to Perfection or Maturity, it is only because they are over-run and opprest by those of a stronger Nature.

It is to the Strength of this amazing Invention we are to attribute that unequal'd Fire and Rapture, which is so forcible in *Homer*, that no Man of a true Poetical Spirit is Master of himself while he reads him. What he writes is of the most animated Nature imaginable; every thing moves, every thing lives, and is put in Action. If a council be call'd, or a Battle fought, you are not coldly inform'd of what was said or done as from a third Person; the Reader is hurry'd out of himself by the Force of the Poet's Imagination, and turns in one place to a Hearer, in another to a Spectator. The Course of his Verses resembles that of the Army he describes,

Οι δΠ αρ ισαν, ως ει τε πυρι Χθων πασα νεμοιτο.

– *They pour along like a Fire that sweeps the whole*

Earth before it. 'Tis however remarkable that his Fancy, which is every where vigorous, is not discover'd immediately at the beginning of his Poem in its fullest Splendor: It grows in the Progress both upon himself and others, and becomes on Fire like a Chariot-Wheel, by its own Rapidity. Exact Disposition, just Thought, correct Elocution, polish'd Numbers, may have been found in a thousand; but this Poetical *Fire*, this *Vivida vis animi*, in a very few. Even in Works where all those are imperfect or neglected, this can over-power Criticism, and make us admire even while we disapprove. Nay, where this appears, tho' attended with Absurdities, it brightens all the Rubbish about it, 'till we see nothing but its own Splendor. This *Fire* is discern'd in *Virgil*, but discern'd as through a Glass, reflected, and more shining than warm, but every where equal and constant; In *Lucan* and *Statius*, it bursts out in sudden, short, and interrupted Flashes: In *Milton*, it glows like a Furnace kept up to an uncommon Fierceness by the Force of Art: In *Shakespear*, it strikes before we are aware, like an accidental Fire from Heaven: But in *Homer*, and in him only, it burns every where clearly, and every where irresistibly.

0000000000000000000000000000000000000000000000000000000000

[The First Book of the Iliad]

The Wrath of Peleus *' Son,*

           to Greece the direful Spring

Of all the Grecian *Woes, O Goddess, sing!*

That Wrath which hurl'd to Pluto *'s gloomy Reign*

The Souls of mighty Chiefs untimely slain;

Whose Limbs unbury'd on the naked Shore

Devouring Dogs and hungry Vultures tore.

Since Great Achilles *and* Atrides *strove,*

Such was the Sov'reign Doom,

           and such the Will of Jove.

   Declare, O Muse! in what ill-fated Hour

Sprung the fierce Strife,

           from what offended Pow'r?

Latona 's Son a dire Contagion spread,

And heap'd the Camp

           with Mountains of the Dead;

The King of Men his Rev'rend Priest defy'd,

And, for the King's Offence, the People dy'd.

*Sir Thomas More & friends put teachers of Greek in charge of English schools so that high-born people would learn the exact words of Jesus. This led to civil war. Wars about religion made it unfashionable, with the unintended result of the poshest schools teaching the words of Homer. Most of those aspiring to the height of genteel literature found Pope's **Iliad** easier. Though true to plot & deeds he gives Homer's heroic crooks, bullies & quarrelsome Gods a civilising polish of balanced, magisterial rhymed couplet.*

1722

*Defoe: London butcher's son. Efficient hosiery merchant, accountant, factory boss, he loses cash in business risks. A smart journalist, he prints pamphlet urging that dissent from the Anglican church be bloodily punished. This delights Tory extremists until news that Defoe (a dissenter) wrote it gets them ridiculed. He is jailed then bailed out by Tory lords who pay him to spy, run a press agency, write a seemingly independent newspaper for them. He knows London citizens love history, biography, travels full of weird facts that show God's providence, since they think God bans fiction. Facts excite Defoe's commercial imagination. He invents them; prints **Robinson Crusoe** as a true tale warning all youths in the **middle station of life** to do as dad orders & never go to sea; quietly lets that moral disappear. Crusoe ends ruling a busy island of faithful blacks. Moll Flanders, whore and thief, repents & ends prosperous too. Defoe's convincing lies led to realistic social novels that Dr Leavis in 1948 called **The Great Tradition**.*

THE FORTUNES AND MISFORTUNES OF THE FAMOUS MOLL FLANDERS, &c.
DANIEL DEFOE: LONDON
[THE PREFACE]

THE WORLD is so taken up of late with Novels and Romances, that it will be hard for a private History to be taken for Genuine, where the Names and other Circumstances of the Person are concealed, and on this Account we must be content to leave the Reader to pass his own Opinion upon the ensuing Sheets, and take it just as he pleases.

The Author is here supposed to be writing her own History, and in the very beginning of her Account she gives the Reasons why she thinks fit to conceal her true Name, after which there is no Occasion to say any more about that.

It is true, that the original of this Story is put into new Words, and the Stile of the famous Lady we here speak of, is a little alter'd, particularly she is made to tell her own Tale in modester Words than she told it at first; the Copy which came first to Hand, having been written in Language more like one still in *Newgate* than one grown Penitent and Humble, as she afterwards pretends to be.

The Pen employ'd in finishing her Story, and making it what you see it to be, has had no little Difficulty to put it into a Dress fit to be seen, and to make it speak Language fit to be read: When a Woman debauch'd from her Youth, nay, even being the Off-spring of Debauchery and Vice, comes to give an Account of all her vicious Practices, and even to descend to the particular Occasions and Circumstances, by which she first became wicked, and of all the progressions of Crime, which she ran through in Threescore Years, an Author must be hard put to it to wrap it up so clean, as not to give room, especially for vicious Readers, to turn it to his Disadvantage.

All possible Care however has been taken to give no lew'd Ideas, no immodest Turns in the new dressing up this Story, No, not to the worst part of her Expressions; to this Purpose some of the vicious part of her Life, which could not be modestly told, is quite left out, and several other Parts are very much shorten'd; what is left 'tis hop'd will not offend the chastest Reader, or the modestest Hearer; and as the best use is to be made even of the worst Story, the Moral 'tis hop'd will keep the Reader serious, even where the Story might incline him to be otherwise: To give the History of a wicked Life repented of, necessarily requires that the wicked part should be make as wicked as the real History of it will bear; to illustrate and give a Beauty to the Penitent part, which is certainly the best and brightest if related with equal Spirit and Life.

It is suggested there cannot be the same Life, the same Brightness and Beauty in relating the penitent Part, as in the criminal Part: If there is any Truth in that Suggestion, I must be allow'd to say, 'tis because there is not the same taste and relish in the Reading; and indeed it is too true that the difference lies not in the real worth of the Subject so much as in the Gust and Palate of the Reader.

But as this Work is chiefly recommended to those who know how to read it, and how to make the good Uses of it, which the Story all along recommends to them; so it is to be hop'd that such Readers will be much more pleas'd with the Moral than the Fable, with the Application than with the Relation, and with the end of the Writer than with the Life of the Person written of.

There is in this Story abundance of delightful Incidents, and all of them usefully apply'd. There is an agreeable turn Artfully given them in the relating, that naturally Instructs the Reader, either one way, or another. The first part of her lew'd Life with the young Gentleman at Colchester, has so many happy turns given it to expose the Crime, and warn all whose Circumstances are adapted to it, of the ruinous End of such things, and the foolish thoughtless and abhor'd Conduct of both the Parties, that it abundantly attones for all the lively Description she gives of her Folly and Wickedness.

The Repentance of her Lover at Bath, and how brought by the just alarm of his Fit of Sickness to abandon her; the just Caution given there against even the lawful Intimacies of the dearest Friends, and how unable they are to preserve the most solemn Resolutions of

Virtue without divine Assistance; these are parts, which to a just Discernment will appear to have more real Beauty in them, than all the amorous Chain of Story, which introduces it.

In a word, as the whole Relation is carefully garbled of all the Levity and Looseness that was in it: So it is applied, and with the utmost care to vertuous and religious Uses. None can without being guilty of manifest Injustice, cast any Reproach upon it, or upon our Design in publishing it.

The Advocates for the Stage, have in all Ages, made this the great Argument to perswade People that their Plays are useful, and that they ought to be allow'd in the most civiliz'd, and in the most religious Government; namely, that they are apply'd to vertuous Purposes, and that by the most lively Representations, they fail not to recommend Virtue, and generous Principles, and to discourage and expose all sorts of Vice and Corruption of Manners; and were it true that they did so, and that they constantly adhered to that Rule, as the Test of their acting on the Theatre, much might be said in their Favour.

Throughout the infinite variety of this Book, this Fundamental is most strictly adhered to; there is not a wicked Action in any Part of it, but is first or last rendered Unhappy and Unfortunate: There is not a superlative Villain brought upon the Stage, but either he is brought to an unhappy End, or brought to be a Penitent: There is not an ill thing mention'd but it is condemn'd, even in the Relation, nor a vertuous just thing, but it carries its Praise along with it: What can more exactly answer the Rule laid down, to recommend, even those Representations of things which have so many other just Objections lying against them? Namely, of Example, of bad Company, obscene Language, and the Like.

OOOOOOOOOOOOOOOOOOOOOOOOOOOOOOOOOOOOOOOOOOOOOOOOOOOOOOOOOOOOOOOOOOOO

We cannot say indeed, that this History is carried on quite to the End of the Life of this famous *Moll Flanders*, for no Body can write their own Life to the full End of it, unless they can write it after they are dead; but her Husband's Life being written by a third Hand, gives a full Account of them both, how long they liv'd together in that Country, and how they came both to *England* again, after about eight Years, in which time they were grown very Rich, and where she liv'd it seems, to be very old; but was not so extraordinary a Penitent, as she was at first; it seems only that indeed she always spoke with abbhorence of her former Life, and of every Part of it.

In her last Scene at *Maryland*, and *Virginia*, many pleasant things happen'd, which makes that part of her Life very agreeable, but they are not told with the same Elegancy as those accounted for by herself; so it is still to the more Advantage that we break off here.

THE EVER GREEN, ALLAN RAMSAY EDINBURGH

1724

I HAVE observed that *Readers* of the best and most exquisite Discernment frequently complain of our *modern Writings*, as filled with affected Delicacies and studied Refinements, which they would gladly exchange for that natural Strength of Thought and Simplicity of Stile our Forefathers practised: To such, I hope, the following *Collection of Poems* will not be displeasing.

When these good old *Bards* wrote, we had not yet made Use of imported Trimming upon our Cloaths, nor of Foreign Embroidery in our Writings. Their *Poetry* is the Product of their own Country, not pilfered and spoiled in the Transportation from abroad: Their Images are native, and their *Landskips* domestick; copied from those Fields and Meadows we every Day behold.

The Morning rises (in the Poets Description) as she does in the Scottish Horizon. We are not carried to *Greece* or *Italy* for a Shade, a Stream or a Breeze. The *Groves* rise in our Valleys; the *Rivers* flow from our own Fountains, and the *Winds* blow upon our own Hills. I find not Fault with those Things, as they are in *Greece* or *Italy*: But with a *Northern Poet* for fetching his Materials from these Places, in a Poem, of which his own Country is the Scene; as our *Hymners* to the *Spring* and *Makers* of *Pastorals* frequently do.

This *Miscellany* will likewise recommend

The thing most like a government in Scotland after her kings left was a poor, bellicose kirk that had tried to outlaw poetry, art & music not found in the Bible & Calvinist theology. But in 1707 leading Scots joined a parliament that seemed to represent everyone. It negotiated like an equal with England till, succumbing to bribes & threats, the leaders went south to become a fraction of England's parliament. Ramsay, an Edinburgh wig-maker, felt betrayed as did most Scots: feared his whole culture might 1 day vanish south. To defend it he printed songs kept evergreen by working folk who kirk & State had not uprooted. Ramsay was only 1 who reacted to Union by gathering & reprinting vernacular Scots poetry, ancient & contemporary. This gave later writers a confidence to create new things with it.

itself, by the Diversity of Subjects and Humour it contains. The grave Description and the wanton Story, the moral Saying and the mirthful Jest, will illustrate and alternately relieve each other.

The *Reader* whose Temper is spleen'd with the *Vices* and *Follies* now in Fashion, may gratifie his Humour with the *Satyres* he will here find upon the *Follies* and *Vices* that were uppermost two or three Hundred Years ago. The Man, whose Inclinations are turned to *Mirth*, will be pleased to know how the good Fellow of a former Age told his jovial Tale; and the *Lover* may divert himself with the old fashioned *Sonnet* of an amorous Poet in Q. Margaret and Q. Mary's Days. In a Word, the following *Collection* will be such another Prospect to the Eye of the Mind, as to the outward Eye is the various Meadow, where Flowers of different Hue and Smell are mingled together in a beautiful Irregularity.

I hope also the *Reader*, when he dips into these *Poems*, will not be displeased with this Reflection, That he is stepping back into the Times that are past, and that exist no more. Thus the *Manners* and *Customs* then in Vogue, as he will find them here described, will have all the Air and Charm of *Novelty*; and that seldom fails of exciting Attention and pleasing the Mind. Besides, the *Numbers*, in which these *Images* are conveyed, as they are not now commonly practised, will appear new and amusing.

OOOOOOOOOOOOOOOOOOOOOOOOOOOOOOOOOOOOOOOOOOOOOOOOOOOOOOOOOOOOOOOOOOOO

There is nothing can be heard more silly than one's expressing his *Ignorance* of his *native Language*; yet such there are, who can vaunt of acquiring a tolerable Perfection in the *French* or *Italian* Tongues, if they have been a Forthnight in *Paris* or a Month in *Rome*: But shew then the most elegant Thoughts in a *Scots* Dress, they as disdainfully as stupidly condemn it as barbarous. But the true Reason is obvious: Every one that is born never so little superior to the *Vulgar*, would fain distinguish themselves from them by some Manner or other, and such, it would appear, cannot arrive at a better *Method*. But this affected Class of Fops give no Uneasiness, not being numerous; for the most part of our Gentlemen, who are generally Masters of the most useful and politest *Languages*, can take Pleasure (for an Change) to speak and read their own.

THE BEGGAR'S OPERA
JOHN GAY
LONDON

1728

[INTRODUCTION – BEGGAR, PLAYER]

BEGGAR. If Poverty be a Title to Poetry, I am sure No-body can dispute mine. I own myself of the Company of Beggars; and I make one at their Weekly Festivals at St. *Giles*'s. I have a small Yearly Salary for my Catches, and am welcome to a Dinner there whenever I please, which is more than most Poets can say.

PLAYER. As we live by the Muses, 'tis but Gratitude in us to encourage Poetical Merit where-ever we find it. The Muses, contrary to all other Ladies, pay no Distinction to Dress, and never partially mistake the Pertness of Embroidery for Wit, nor the Modesty of Want for Dulness. Be the Author who he will, we push his Play as far as it will go. So (though you are in Want) I wish you Success heartily.

BEGGAR. This Piece I own was originally writ for the celebrating the Marriage of *James Chanter* and *Moll Lay*, two most excellent Ballad-Singers. I have introduc'd the Similes that are in your celebrated *Operas*: the *Swallow*, the *Moth*, the *Bee*, the *Ship*, the *Flower*, &c. Besides, I have a Prison Scene, which the Ladies always reckon charmingly pathetick. As to the Parts, I have observ'd such a nice Impartiality to our two Ladies, that it is impossible for either of them to take Offence. I hope I may be forgiven, that I have not made my Opera throughout unnatural, like those in vogue; for I have no Recitative: Excepting this, as I have consented to have neither Prologue nor Epilogue, it must be allow'd an Opera in all its forms. The Piece indeed hath been heretofore frequently represented by ourselves in our great Room at St. *Giles*'s, so that I cannot too often acknowledge your Charity in bringing it now on the Stage.

The Scriblerus Club contained Swift, Pope & Gay, Tories wanting a Stuart, not German king. They met to plan attacks on the Whigs now in power & their talks led to ideas in **Gulliver's Travels***, in Pope's satires, & this opera. The Hanoverian court had made operas about romantic lovers fashionable. Romantic stories of love among simple rural folk still sold. Swift suggested a romance among whores, thieves & turnkeys in Newgate jail. Crime now made the rich feel so insecure that folk arrested for a theft were liable to hang unless, like the most successful thieves, they could hire lawyers & false witnesses to get them acquitted. In Gay's opera London is ruled by 2 gangs in league with each other: fraudulent beggars & receivers of stolen goods, also Macheath, highway robber who cheats them all. This hit at Whigs, Tories & prime minister Walpole, with British tunes, was the last good English opera before 1875. Brecht & Weill modernised it for the 20th century.*

PLAYER. But I see 'tis time for us to withdraw; the Actors are preparing to begin. Play away the Ouverture.   *Exeunt.*

1729 *THE DUNCIAD, VARIORUM* ALEXANDER POPE LONDON

[MARTINUS SCRIBLERUS OF THE POEM]

THIS Poem, as it celebrateth the most grave and antient of things, Chaos, Night and Dulness, so is it of the most grave and antient kind. *Homer*, (saith *Aristotle*) was the first who gave the *Form*, and (saith *Horace*) who adapted the *Measure*, to heroic poesy. But even before this, may be rationally presumed from what the antients have left written, was a piece by *Homer* composed, of like nature and matter with this of our Poet. For of Epic sort it appeareth to have been, yet of matter surely not unpleasant, witness what is reported of it by the learned Arcbishop *Eustathius*, in Odyss. κ. And accordingly *Aristotle* in his poetic, chap. 4. doth further set forth, that as the Iliad and Odyssey gave example to Tragedy, so did this poem to Comedy its first Idaea.

From these authors also it shou'd seem, that the Hero or chief personage of it was no less obscure, and his *understanding* and *sentiments* no less quaint and strange (if indeed not more so) than any of the actors in our poem. *Margites* was the name of this personage, whom Antiquity recordeth to have been *Dunce the First*; and surely from what we hear of him, not unworthy to be the root of so spreading a tree, and so numerous a posterity. The poem therefore celebrating him, was properly and absolutely a *Dunciad*; which tho' now unhappily lost, yet is its nature sufficiently known by the infallible tokens aforesaid. And thus it doth appear, that the first Dunciad was the first Epic poem, written by *Homer* himself, and anterior even to the Iliad or Odyssey.

Now forasmuch as our Poet had translated those two famous works of *Homer* which are yet left; he did conceive it in some sort his duty to imitate that also which was lost: And was therefore induced to bestow on it the same Form which *Homer*'s is reported to have had, namely that of Epic poem, with a title also framed after the antient *Greek* manner, to wit, that of *Dunciad*.

Wonderful it is, that so few of the moderns have been stimulated to attempt some Dunciad! Since in the opinion of the multitude, it might cost less pain and oil, than an imitation of the greater Epic. But possible it is also that on due reflection, the maker might find it easier to paint a *Charlemagne*, a *Brute* or a *Godfry*, with just pomp and dignity heroic, than a *Margites*, a *Codrus*, a *Flecknoe*, or a *Tibbald*.

We shall next declare the occasion and the cause which moved our Poet to this particular work. He lived in those days, when (after providence had permitted the Invention of Printing as a scourge for the Sins of the learned) Paper also became so cheap, and printers so numerous, that a deluge of authors cover'd the land: Whereby not only the peace of the honest unwriting subject was daily molested, but unmerciful demands were made of his applause, yea of his money, by such as would neither earn the one, or deserve the other: At the same time, the Liberty of the Press was so unlimited, that it grew dangerous to refuse them either: For they would forthwith publish slanders unpunish'd, the authors being anonymous; nay the immediate publishers thereof lay sculking under the wings of an Act of Parliament, assuredly intended for better purposes.

Now our author living in those times, did conceive it an endeavour well worthy an honest satyrist, to dissuade the dull and punish the malicious, *the only way that was left*. In that public-spirited view he laid the plan of this Poem, as the greatest service he was capable (without much hurt or being slain) to render his dear country. First, taking things from their original, he considereth the Causes creative of such authors, namely *Dulness* and *Poverty*; the one born with them, the other contracted, by neglect of their proper talent thro' self conceit of greater abilities. This truth he wrapped in an *Allegory* (as the constitution of Epic poesy requires).

0000000000000000000000000000000000000000000000000000000000000

VIRGIL'S *AENEID* TOLD HOW THE GODDESS OF WISDOM MOVED THE TROJAN CAPITAL TO ITALY: THE *DUNCIAD* WILL TELL HOW THE GODDESS OF DULNESS MOVED HER GOVERNMENT. SHE LIVED WITH POVERTY AT SMITHFIELD, CENTRE OF THE BUTCHERMEAT AND PRINTING TRADE, UNTIL NOBLE STATESMEN (MOSTLY WHIGS) BROUGHT HER TO THE FASHIONABLE PART OF LONDON BY PAYING JOURNALISTS, BOOKSELLERS AND CRITICS TO WRITE, PUBLISH AND PRAISE DULL BOOKS.

0000000000000000000000000000000000000000000000000000000000000

Though banned in the theatre, literary wars continued in the press. Pope's enemies called him a faulty scholar & bitter papist dwarf. In this poem he replied by calling them dull. Milton showed history as a process in which greed & luxury kept undoing democracy. In The Dunciad Pope has civilisation created by God's word & classical poetry, then uncreated by commercial publicity swamping intelligence with trivial ideas & details, so sciences & arts fall apart & all end in obscure chaos: a modern idea. He provides footnotes to tell future ages of the poor writers & booksellers he mocks. He invokes Swift, now a dean in Dublin, who had recently defeated a government plan to cheapen Irish money by writing a series of pamphlets against it, signing them Drapier.

BOOK THE FIRST

Books and the Man I sing, the first who brings
The Smithfield Muses to the Ear of Kings.
Say great Patricians! (since your selves inspire
These wond'rous works; so Jove and Fate require)
Say from what cause, in vain decry'd and curst,
Still Dunce the second reigns like Dunce the first?

In eldest time, e'er mortals writ or read,
E'er Pallas issued from the Thund'rer's head,
Dulnes o'er all possess'd her antient right,
Daughter of Chaos and eternal Night¹:
Fate in their dotage this fair idiot gave,
Gross as her sire, and as her mother grave,
Laborious, heavy, busy, bold, and blind,
She rul'd, in native Anarchy, the mind.

Still her old empire to confirm, she tries,
For born a Goddess, Dulness never dies.

O thou! whatever Title please thine ear,
Dean, Drapier, Bickerstaff, or Gulliver!
Whether thou chuse Cervantes' serious air,
Or laugh and shake in Rab'lais' easy Chair,
Or praise the Court, or magnify Mankind²,
Or they griev'd Country's copper chains unbind;
From thy Bæotia tho' Her Pow'r retires³,
Grieve not at ought our sister realm acquires⁴:
Here pleas'd behold her mighty wings out-spread,
To hatch a new Saturnian age of Lead⁵.

---

1 Daughter of Chaos, &c. The beauty of this whole Allegory being purely of the Poetical kind, we think it not our proper business as a Scholiast, to meddle with it; but leave it (as we shall in general all such) to the Reader: remarking only, that Chaos (according to Hesiod, Qeogonia) was the Progenitor of all the Gods. Scribl.

2 Or praise the Court, &c. Ironicé, alluding to Gulliver's Representations of both – The next line relates to the Papers of the Drapier against Wood's Copper Coin in Ireland, which upon the great discontent of the people, his Majesty has graciously recalled.

3 From thy Bæotia Bæotia of old lay under the Raillery of the neighbouring Wits, as Ireland does now; tho' each of those nations produced one of the greatest Wits, and Greatest Generals, of their age.

4 Grieve not, &c. Ironicé iterum. The Politicks of England and Ireland were at this time by some thought to be opposite, or interfering with each other: Dr. Swift of course was in the interest of the latter, our Author of the former.

5 A new Saturnian Age of Lead The ancient Golden Age is by Poets stiled Saturnian; but in the Chymical language, Saturn is Lead.

AN ESSAY ON MAN
ALEXANDER POPE
LONDON
1734

[THE DESIGN]

HAVING proposed to write some Pieces on Human Life and Manners, such as (to use my Lord *Bacon's* expression) *come home to Men's Business and Bosoms*, I thought it more satisfactory to begin with considering Man in the Abstract, his Nature and his State: since to prove any moral Duty, to inforce any moral Precept, or to examine the Perfection or Imperfection of any Creature whatsoever, it is necessary first to know what *Condition and Relation* it is placed in, and what is the proper *End* and *Purpose* of its *Being*.

The Science of Human Nature is, like all other Sciences, reduced to a *few, clear Points*: There are not many certain Truths in this World. It is therefore in the Anatomy of the Mind as in that of the Body; more Good will accrue to mankind by attending to the large, open, and perceptible parts, than by studying too much such finer nerves and vessels as will for ever escape our observation. The *Disputes* are all upon these last, and I will venture to say, they have less sharpen'd the *Wits* than the *Hearts* of Men against each other, and have diminished the Practise, more than advanced the Theory, of Morality. If I could flatter my self that this Essay has any Merit, it is in steering betwixt Doctrines seemingly opposite, in passing over Terms utterly unintelligible, and in forming out of all a *temperate* yet not *inconsistent*, and a *short* yet not *imperfect* System of Ethics.

This I might have done in Prose; but I chose Verse, and even Rhyme, for two reasons. The one will appear obvious; that Principles, Maxims, or Precepts so written, both strike the reader more strongly at first, and are more easily retained by him afterwards. The other may seem odd but is true; I found I could express them more *shortly* this way than in Prose itself, and nothing is more certain than that much of the *Force* as well as *Grace* of Arguments or Instructions depends on their Conciseness. I was unable to treat this part of my subject more in *detail*, without becoming dry and tedious; or more poetically, without sacrificing Perspicuity to Ornament, without wandring from the Precision, or breaking the Chain of Reasoning. If any man can unite all these, without diminution of any of them, I freely confess he will compass a thing above my capacity.

Epistle 1. Of the Nature and State of MAN with respect to the UNIVERSE

After attacking the dominant stupidity he saw as England's main defect (Georges I & II were famous dunces) Pope wished to show humanity in a larger way & do for his age what Milton's **Paradise Lost** *sought to do –* **justify the ways of God to man.** *He was therefore attempting what philosophy since Descartes & Hobbes had been attempting: to derive a moral code from natural existence instead of the bible & poetic imagery. It had to be a universal vision without original sin, hell, Christ's birth, crucifixion & salvation - all that Christians thought the truths of their faith, & fought about, & that English gentry agreed to keep private as Dissent was encouraged by it. Dr Johnson disliked the essay for leaving so much out:* **Never were penury of knowledge & vulgarity of sentiment so happily disguised,** *he said. Pope wrote it as 4 letters to St John Irvine, a Tory statesman out of work for trying to restore the Stuarts, & who had suggested the plan of the work. Pope chose a letter form because his subject was* **mixt with Argument, which of its Nature** *approacheth to Prose.*

Awake, my ST. JOHN! leave all meaner things
To low ambition, and the pride of Kings,
Let us (since Life can little more supply
Than just to look about us and to die)
Expatiate free o'er all this scene of Man;   5
A mighty maze! but not without a plan;
A Wild, where weeds and flow'rs promiscuous shoot,
Or Garden, tempting with forbidden fruit.
Together let us beat this ample field,
Try what the open, what the covert yield;   10
The latent tracts, the giddy heights explore
Of all who blindly creep, or sightless soar;
Eye Nature's walks, shoot Folly as it flies,
And catch the Manners living as they rise;
Laugh where we must, be candid where we can;   15
But vindicate the ways of God to Man.

   I. Say first, of God above, or Man below,
What can we reason, but from what we know?
Of Man what see we, but his station here,
From which to reason, or to which refer?   20
Thro' worlds unnumber'd tho' the God be known,
'Tis ours to trace him only in our own.
He, who thro' vast immensity can pierce,
See worlds on worlds compose one universe,
Observe how system into system runs,   25
What other planets circle other suns,
What vary'd being peoples ev'ry star,
May tell why Heav'n has made us as we are.
But of this frame the bearings, and the ties,
The strong connections, nice dependencies,   30
Gradations just, has thy pervading soul
Look'd thro'? or can a part contain the whole?
   Is the great chain, that draws all to agree,
And drawn supports, upheld by God, or thee?   34
OOOOOOOOOOOOOOOOOOOOOOOOOOOOOOOOOOOOOOOOOOOO

   III. Heav'n from all creatures
               hides the book of Fate,

All but the page prescrib'd, their present state;
From brutes what men, from men what spirits know:
Or who could suffer Being here below?   80
The lamb thy riot dooms to bleed to-day,
Had he thy Reason, would he skip and play?
Pleas'd to the last, he crops the flow'ry food,
And licks the hand just rais'd to shed his blood.
Oh blindness to the future! kindly giv'n,   85
That each may fill the circle mark'd by Heav'n;
Who sees with equal eye, as God of all,
A hero perish, or a sparrow fall,
Atoms or systems into ruin hurl'd,
And now a bubble burst, and now a world.   90
   Hope humbly then; with trembling pinions soar;
Wait the great teacher Death, and God adore!
What future bliss, he gives not thee to know,
But gives that Hope to be thy blessing now.
Hope springs eternal in the human breast: 95
Man never Is, but always To be blest:
The soul, uneasy and confin'd from home,
Rests and expatiates in a life to come.
   Lo! the poor Indian, whose untutor'd mind
Sees God in clouds, or hears him in the wind;   100
His soul proud Science never taught to stray
Far as the solar walk, or milky way;
Yet simple Nature to his hope has giv'n,
Behind the cloud-topt hill, an humbler heav'n;
Some safer world in depth of woods embrac'd,   105
Some happier island in the watry waste,
Where slaves once more their native land behold,
No fiends torment, no Christians thirst for gold!
To Be, contents his natural desire,
He asks no Angel's wing, no Seraph's fire;   110
But thinks, admitted to that equal sky,
His faithful dog shall bear him company,
   IV. Go, wiser thou! and in thy scale of sense
Weigh thy Opinion against Providence;
Call Imperfection what thou fancy'st such,   115

That led to Matthew Arnold's quip that Pope is a classic of prose not poetry. The 1st letter argues that our discontent is the 1 flaw in a world where some irregularities noticed by scientists are part of a harmony beyond their scope. The 2nd letter describes our social harmony rising from selfish passion controlled by reason, so that lust leads to care of wife & child, other passions to activity a nation needs: **The merchant's toil, the sage's indolence, the monk's humility, the hero's pride, All, all alike find reason on their side.** *Letter 3 blends Milton & Locke ideas in a historical view. Peaceful early tribes founded cities, united under kings to get rich by warfare, & justified the crime by adopting false gods. Predatory states were unstable so even their rulers needed to reform them:* **Forc'd into virtue thus by self-defence, Ev'n Kings learned justice & benevolence.** *Nobody now should fight over politics & religion for* **In Faith & Hope the world will disagree, but all Mankind's concern is charity.** *The last book defends British social order:* **Order is Heav'ns first law, &**

this confest; Some are, & must be greater than the rest, More rich, more wise. Yet all can be happy by thinking right & meaning well. If some good people seem to suffer, only God knows who is truly good. This resembles the philosophy of Dr Pangloss who thought all is for the best in this best of possible worlds, & the earthquakes destroying Lisbon & Lima served mankind by proving both cities on a volcanic fault. Yet Voltaire, creator of Pangloss, called Pope's essay **The Most beautiful, the most useful, & the most sublime didactic poem ever written ·in any language**. It implied that monarchy limited by legislature is best, & he wished France to adopt that. But this poem went into most European tongues for it also suggested most nations are now as good as possible. That was not Pope's fixed opinion. In a poem on the Use of Riches he talks of how much is owned by the vicious, how much wasted on useless display, & how a day will come when vast private parks of the nobility will be planted with corn. He was no aristocrat, but a member of the hard-working middle-classes.

Say, here he gives too little, there too much;
Destroy all creatures for thy sport or gust,
Yet cry, If Man's unhappy, God's unjust;
If Man alone ingross not Heav'n's high care,
Alone made perfect here, immortal there: 120
Snatch from his hand the balance and the rod,
Re-judge his justice, be the GOD of GOD!
    In Pride, in reas'ning Pride, our error lies;
All quit their sphere, and rush into the skies.
OOOOOOOOOOOOOOOOOOOOOOOOOOOOOOOOOOOOOOOOOOOOO
    All are but parts of one stupendous whole,
Whose body, Nature is, and God the soul;
That, chang'd thro' all, and yet in all the same,
Great in the earth, as in th' aethereal frame,   270
Warms in the sun, refreshes in the breeze,
Glows in the stars, and blossoms in the trees,
Lives thro' all life, extends thro' all extent,
Spreads undivided, operates unspent,
Breathes in our soul, informs our mortal part,   275
As full, as perfect, in a hair as heart;
As full, as perfect, in vile Man that mourns,
As the rapt Seraph that adores and burns;
To him no high, no low, no great, no small;
He fills, he bounds, connects, and equals all.   280
    X. Cease then, nor ORDER Imperfection name:
Our proper bliss depends on what we blame.
Know thy own point: This kind, this due degree
Of blindness, weakness, Heav'n bestows on thee.
Submit — In this, or any other sphere,   285
Secure to be as blest as thou canst bear:
Safe in the hand of one disposing Pow'r,
Or in the natal, or the mortal hour.
All Nature is but Art, unknown to thee;
All Chance, Direction, which thou canst not see;   290
All Discord, Harmony, not understood;
All partial Evil, universal Good:
And, spite of Pride, in erring Reason's spite,
One truth is clear, "Whatever IS, is RIGHT."

A TREATISE OF HUMAN NATURE an Attempt to Introduce the Experimental Method of Reasoning Into Moral Subjects **DAVID HUME: LONDON**

1739

[ADVERTISEMENT]

MY design in the present work is sufficiently explain'd in the *introduction*. The reader must only observe, that all the subjects I have there plann'd out to my self, are not treated of in these two volumes. The subjects of the *understanding* and *passions* make a compleat chain of reasoning by themselves; and I was willing to take advantage of this natural division, in order to try the taste of the public. If I have the good fortune to meet with success, I shall proceed to the examination of *morals*, *politics*, and *criticism*; which will compleat this *Treatise of human nature*. The approbation of the public I consider as the greatest reward of my labours; but am determin'd to regard its judgment, whatever it be, as my best instruction.

[INTRODUCTION]

NOTHING is more usual and more natural for those, who pretend to discover any thing new to the world in philosophy and the sciences, than to insinuate the praises of their own systems, by decrying all those, which have been advanced before them. And indeed were they content with lamenting that ignorance, which we still lie under in the most important questions, that can come before the tribunal of human reason, there are few, who have an acquaintance with the sciences, that would not readily agree with them. 'Tis easy for one of judgment and learning, to perceive the weak foundation even of those systems, which have obtained the greatest credit, and have carried their pretensions highest to accurate and profound reasoning. Principles taken upon trust, consequences lamely deduced from them, want of coherence in the parts, and of evidence in the whole, these are

*In search of certainty Descartes, a Catholic, looked into his mind & deduced we have 2 certainties: a thinking self or immortal soul, & **God** who made that. Much more exists, but it keeps altering so is never certain. Hume, son of a Presbyterian Scots laird, was nearly maddened as a child by fear of burning in hell for ever. He looked into his mind & saw it alter with each cluster of thoughts, memories & sense of surroundings composing it. Hume's discovery that he was not eternally fixed in a self, so death need not be feared, pleased him to the end of his days. It also led him to think God too was not a fixture. He imagined his masterpiece, this book, when a 15-year-old student of law at Edinburgh University. When 20 & clerking for a Bristol merchant he planned it thoroughly, & wrote it between 23 & 25 when living cheap in France. It embraced Locke & Berkeley but went far beyond them in clearing away religious, philosophic & political dogma. He showed how rhetoric makes these, fostering a passionate **ought** on a* *factual is until temporary souls & social contracts get called eternal. He also undermined scientific dogma by saying that no matter how many experiments confirm a formula & how often a formula succeeds, a strong probability, not an eternal natural law, is proved. When homing to Scotland he had this published. It **fell dead born from the press** & entered the philosophy of Europe when later writings on faith, trade & history made him famous. He was then in a movement of thinkers who met in Paris, Glasgow & Edinburgh & had no official title, though its members developed physical sciences that London's Royal Society hardly bothered with since the geniuses who founded it had died. **Enlightenment** was the movement's nickname & Kant said it applied to those who thought for themselves instead of accepting established ideas through fear, laziness or stupidity. Hume had now argued that Bible miracles did not prove Christianity true, that the vitality of the universe was the only necessary God, & death did not alarm him. He proved the last point in 1776, dying cheerfully from cancer of the bowels.*

every where to be met with in the systems of the most eminent philosophers, and seem to have drawn disgrace upon philosophy itself.

Nor is there requir'd such profound knowledge to discover the present imperfect condition of the sciences, but even the rabble without doors may judge from the noise and clamour, which they hear, that all goes not well within. There is nothing which is not the subject of debate, and in which men of learning are not of contrary opinions. The most trivial question escapes not our controversy, and in the most momentous we are not able to give any certain decision. Disputes are multiplied, as if every thing was uncertain; and these disputes are managed with the greatest warmth, as if every thing was certain. Amidst all this bustle 'tis not reason, which carries the prize, but eloquence; and no man needs ever despair of gaining proselytes to the most extravagant hypothesis, who has art enough to represent it in any favourable colours. The victory is not gained by the men at arms, who manage the pike and the sword; but by the trumpeters, drummers, and musicians of the army.

From hence in my opinion arises that common prejudice against methaphysical reasonings of all kinds, even amongst those, who profess themselves scholars, and have a just value for every other part of literature. By metaphysical reasonings, they do not understand those on any particular branch of science, but every kind of argument, which is any way abstruse, and requires some attention to be comprehended. We have so often lost our labour in such researches, that we commonly reject them without hesitation, and resolve, if we must for ever be a prey to errors and delusions, that they shall at least be natural and entertaining. And indeed nothing but the most determined scepticism, along with a great degree of indolence, can justify this aversion to metaphysics. For if truth be at all within the reach of human capacity, 'tis certain it must lie very deep and abstruse; and to hope we shall arrive at it without pains, while the greatest geniuses have failed with the utmost pains, must certainly be esteemed sufficiently vain and presumptuous. I pretend to no such advantage in the philosophy I am going to unfold, and would esteem it a strong presumption against it, were it so very easy and obvious.

'Tis evident, that all the sciences have a relation, greater or less, to human nature; and that however wide any of them may seem to run from it, they still return back by one passage or another. Even *Mathematics*, *Natural Philosophy*, and *Natural Religion*, are in some measure dependent on the science of Man; since they lie under the cognizance of men, and are judged of by their powers and faculties. 'Tis impossible to tell what changes and improvements we might make in these sciences were we thoroughly acquainted with the extent and force of human understanding, and cou'd explain the nature of the ideas we employ, and of the operations we perform in our reasonings. And these improvements are the more to be hoped for in natural religion, as it is not content with instructing us in the nature of superior powers, but carries its views farther, to their disposition towards us, and our duties towards them; and consequently we ourselves are not only the beings, that reason, but also one of the objects, concerning which we reason.

If therefore the sciences of Mathematics, Natural Philosophy, and Natural Religion, have such a dependence on the knowledge of man, what may be expected in the other sciences, whose connexion with human nature is more close and intimate? The sole end of logic is to explain the principles and operations of our reasoning faculty, and the nature of our ideas: morals and criticism regard our tastes and sentiments: and politics consider men as united in society, and dependent on each other. In these four sciences of *Logic*, *Morals*, *Criticism*, and *Politics*, is comprehended almost every thing, which it can any way import us to be acquainted with, or which can tend either to the improvement or ornament of the human mind.

Here then is the only expedient, from which we can hope for success in our philosophical researches, to leave the tedious lingring method, which we have hitherto followed, and instead of taking now and then a castle or village on the frontier, to march up directly to the capital or center of these sciences, to human nature itself; which being once masters of, we may every where else hope for an easy victory. From this station we may extend our conquests over all those sciences, which more intimately concern human life, and may afterwards proceed at leisure to discover more fully those, which are the objects of pure curiosity. There is no question of importance, whose decision is not compriz'd in the science of man; and there is none, which can be decided with any certainty, before we become acquainted with that science. In pretending therefore to explain the principles of human nature, we in effect propose a compleat system of the sciences, built on a foundation almost entirely new, and the only one upon which they can stand with any security.

And as the science of man is the only solid foundation for the other sciences, so the only solid foundation we can give to this science itself must be laid on experience and observation. 'Tis no astonishing reflection to consider, that the application of experimental philosophy to moral subjects should come after that to natural at the distance of above a whole century; since we find in fact, that there was about the same interval betwixt the origins of these sciences; and that reckoning from Thales to Socrates, the space of time is nearly equal to that betwixt my Lord Bacon and some late philosophers in *England*, who have begun to put the science of man on a new footing, and have engaged the attention, and excited the curiosity of the public. So true it is, that however other nations may rival us in poetry, and excel us in some other agreeable arts, the improvements in reason and philosophy can only be owing to a land of toleration and of liberty.

Nor ought we to think, that this latter improvement in the science of man will do less honour to our native country than the former in natural philosophy, but ought rather to esteem it a greater glory, upon account of the greater importance of that science, as well as the necessity it lay under of such a reformation. For to me it seems evident, that the essence of the mind being equally unknown to us with that of external bodies, it must be equally impossible to form any notion of its powers and qualities otherwise than from careful and exact experiments, and the observation of those particular effects, which result from its different circumstances and situations. And tho' we must endeavour to render all our principles as universal as possible, by tracing up our experiments to the utmost, and explaining all effects from the simplest and fewest causes, 'tis still certain we cannot go beyond experience; and any hypothesis, that pretends to discover the ultimate original qualities of human nature, ought at first to be rejected as presumptuous and chimerical.

I do not think a philosopher, who would apply himself so earnestly to the explaining the ultimate principles of the soul, would show himself a great master in that very science of human nature, which he pretends to explain, or very knowing in what is naturally satisfactory to the mind of man. For nothing is more certain, than that despair has almost the same effect upon us with enjoyment, and that we are no sooner acquainted with the impossibility of satisfying any desire, than the desire itself vanishes. When we see, that we have arrived at the utmost extent of human reason, we sit down contented; tho' we be perfectly satisfied in the main of our ignorance, and perceive that we can give no reason for our most general and most refined principles, beside our experience of their reality; which is the reason of the mere vulgar, and what it required no study at first to have discovered for the most particular and most extraordinary phaenomenon. And as this impossibility of making any farther progress is enough to satisfy the reader, so the writer may derive a more delicate satisfaction from the free confession of his ignorance, and from his prudence in avoiding that error, into which so many have fallen, of imposing their conjectures and hypotheses on the world for the most certain principles. When this mutual contentment and satisfaction can be obtained betwixt the master and scholar, I know not what more we can require of our philosophy.

But if this impossibility of explaining ultimate principles should be esteemed a defect in the science of man, I will venture to affirm, that 'tis a defect common to it with all the sciences, and all the arts, in which we can employ ourselves, whether they be such as are cultivated in the schools of the philosophers, or practised in the shops of the meanest artizans. None of them can go beyond experience, or establish any principles which are not founded on that authority. Moral philosophy has, indeed, this peculiar disadvantage, which is not found in natural, that in collecting its experiments, it cannot make them purposely, with premeditation, and after such a manner as to satisfy itself concerning every particular difficulty which may arise. When I am at a loss to know the effects of one body upon another in any situation, I need only put them in that situation, and observe what results from it. But should I endeavour to clear up after the same manner any doubt in moral philosophy, by placing myself in the same case with that which I consider, 'tis evident this reflection and premeditation would so disturb the operation of my natural principles, as must render it impossible to form any just conclusion from the phaenomenon. We must therefore glean up our experiments in this science from a cautious observation of human life, and take them as they appear in the common course of the world, by men's behaviour in company, in affairs, and in their pleasures. Where experiments of this kind are judiciously collected and compared, we may hope to establish on them a science, which will not be inferior in certainty, and will be much superior in utility to any other of human comprehension.

1742

The History of the Adventures of JOSEPH ANDREWS, and of His Friend Mr. Abraham Adams. **HENRY FIELDING: LONDON** WRITTEN IN IMITATION OF THE MANNER OF CERVANTES, AUTHOR OF DON QUIXOTE.

18th-century Cambridge & Oxford were not big centres of learning. They taught sons of gentry & nobility to know each other & (if they chose) to become Anglican clergy. Those wishing to learn more went to universities in Scotland or oversea. Henry Fielding, son of a general, left Eton & studied literature at Leyden. He wanted to live by it & succeeded at first with versions of Molière's comedies & burlesques of other stage plays, but **The Beggar's Opera** *led him to burlesque the government.* **Pasquin & The Historical Register 1737** *were so popular, annoyed such mighty politicians that they made England's Lord Chancellor censor*

[PREFACE]

AS it is possible the mere *English* reader may have a different Idea of Romance with the Author of these little Volumes; and may consequently expect a kind of Entertainment, not to be found, nor which was even intended, in the following Pages; it may not be improper to premise a few Words concerning this kind of Writing, which I do not remember to have seen hitherto attempted in our Language.

The Epic as well as the Drama is divided into Tragedy and Comedy. *Homer*, who was the Father of this Species of Poetry, gave us a Pattern of both these, tho' that of the latter kind is entirely lost; which *Aristotle* tells us, bore the same relation to Comedy which his *Iliad* bears to Tragedy. And perhaps, that we have no more Instances of it among the Writers of Antiquity, is owing to the Loss of this great Pattern, which, had it survived, would have found its Imitators equally with the other Poems of this great Original.

And farther, as this Poetry may be Tragic or Comic, I will not scruple to say it may be likewise either in Verse or Prose: for tho' it wants one particular, which the Critic enumerates in the constituent Parts of an Epic Poem, namely Metre; yet, when any kind of Writing contains all its other parts, such as Fable, Action, Characters, Sentiments, and Diction, and is deficient in Metre only; it seems, I think, reasonable to refer it to the Epic; at least, as no Critic hath thought proper to range it under any other Head, nor to assign it a particular Name to itself.

Thus the *Telemachus* of the Arch-Bishop of *Cambray* appears to me of the Epic Kind, as well as the *Odyssey* of *Homer*; indeed, it is much fairer and more reasonable to give it a Name common with that Species from which it differs only in a single Instance, than to confound it with those which it resembles in no other. Such are those voluminous Works commonly called *Romances*, namely, *Clelia*, *Cleopatra*, *Astraea*, *Cassandra*, the *Grand Cyrus*, and innumerable others which contain, as I apprehend, very little Instruction or Entertainment.

Now a comic Romance is a comic Epic-Poem in prose; differing from Comedy, as the serious Epic from Tragedy: its Action being more extended and comprehensive; containing a much larger Circle of Incidents, and introducing a greater Variety of Characters. It differs from the serious Romance in its Fable and Action, in this; that as in the one these are grave and solemn, so in the other they are light and ridiculous: it differs in its Characters, by introducing Persons of inferiour Rank, and consequently of inferiour Manners, whereas the grave Romance, sets the highest before us; lastly in its Sentiments and Diction, by preserving the Ludicrous instead of the Sublime. In the Diction I think, Burlesque itself may be sometimes admitted; of which many Instances will occur in this Work, as in the Descriptions of the Battles, and some other Places, not necessary to be pointed out to the

of stage plays. He banned political satire, forbad further performances of work by Fielding & Gay, & stunted British drama until 1967. Gay lived on by becoming a house guest of rich aristocrats. Fielding became a lawyer & part-time journalist.

In 1741 appeared Richardson's **Pamela, or Virtue Rewarded,** *a best-selling romance in the form of letters* **published** *(they say)* **to cultivate Principles of Virtue & Religion.** *It tells how a lovely maidservant resists a nobleman's efforts to enjoy her body, until he buys it in lawful marriage. This blend of sex, moral sentiment & financial self-interest provoked Fielding to burlesque it in a tale about Pamela's brother Joseph, a footman who resists assault by the lustful noblewoman* **he** *works for. Booksellers were then publishers too & reduced risks of expense on a new book by issuing it in short serial volumes, pressing the author to write more or less according to sales. The 1st volume of* **Joseph Andrews** *sold out. As Fielding wrote the 2nd he knew burlesque, his starting place, had grown into something else: a vision of folk in every social class presented with* *ironic relish. The Canterbury Tales gave this & Shakespeare & Jonson's plays, but the authors had been poets. Critics thought prose should give moral instruction, so Defoe & Richardson disguised their novels as sermons & warnings. Fielding's tolerance of human failings, love of absurdity even in good folk, his pictures of many who did not aspire to the manners of gentry struck most reviewers as bad for readers who enjoyed them. Dickens, Twain, Hardy, D. H. Lawrence later underwent that criticism. This preface says novels can have the epic scope of the Odyssey or Iliad, but these epics had kingly heroes & gods. Only ancient comedy showed many commoners, so Fielding, like Pope in his Dunciad preface, uses a lost comic epic by Homer to justify his own, & says ridicule of vice & folly is as likely to end them as sermons. He was no friend to crime & on becoming magistrate of Middlesex created the 1st mobile police force in Britain. He wanted laws to make the rural poor starve or beg at home, & stop bringing hunger & crime to London where they rot among themselves: rob among their betters.*

Classical Reader; for whose Entertainment those Parodies or Burlesque Imitations are chiefly calculated.

But tho' we have sometimes admitted this in our Diction, we have carefully excluded it from our Sentiments and Characters: for there it is never properly introduced, unless in Writings of the Burlesque kind, which this is not intended to be. Indeed, no two Species of Writing can differ more widely than the Comic and the Burlesque: for as the latter is ever the Exhibition of what is monstrous and unnatural, and where our Delight, if we examine it, arises from the surprizing Absurdity, as in appropriating the Manners of the highest to the lowest, or *è converso*; so in the former, we should ever confine ourselves strictly to Nature from the just Imitation of which, will flow all the Pleasure we can this way convey to a sensible Reader. And perhaps, there is one Reason, why a Comic Writer should of all others be the least excused for deviating from Nature, since it may not be always so easy for a serious Poet to meet with the Great and the Admirable; but Life every where furnishes an accurate Observer with the Ridiculous.

I have hinted this little, concerning Burlesque; because, I have often heard that Name given to Performances, which have been truly of the Comic kind, from the Author's having sometimes admitted it in his Diction only; which as it is the Dress of Poetry, doth like the Dress of Men establish Characters, (the one of the whole Poem, and the other of the whole Man,) in vulgar Opinion, beyond any of their greater Excellencies: But surely, a certain Drollery in Style, where the Characters and Sentiments are perfectly natural, no more constitutes the Burlesque, than an empty Pomp and Dignity of Words, where every thing else is mean and low, can entitle any Performance to the Appellation of the true Sublime.

00

BURLESQUE IS ABSURD EXAGGERATION, LIKE CARICATURE IN ART, WHICH CAN SHOW A NOSE BIGGER THAN ITS FACE. A COMIC NOVEL MAY USE SOME OF IT, BUT THE BEST COMEDY DEPENDS ON TRUTH TO LIFE AS SEEN IN HOGARTH'S PAINTINGS. ONLY THE VICIOUS ARE AMUSED BY HORRID CRUELTY BUT VANITY AND HYPOCRISY DESERVE RIDICULE.

0000000000000000000000000000000000000000000000000000000000000000

I might observe that our *Ben Johnson*, who of all Men understood the *Ridiculous* the best, hath chiefly used the hypocritical Affectation.

Now from Affectation only, the Misfortunes and Calamities of Life, or the Imperfections of Nature, may become the Objects of Ridicule. Surely he hath a very ill-framed Mind, who can look on Ugliness, Infirmity, or Poverty, as ridiculous in themselves: nor do I believe any Man living who meets a dirty Fellow riding through the Streets in a Cart, is struck with an Idea of the Ridiculous from it; but if he should see the same Figure descend from his Coach and Six, or bolt from his Chair with his Hat under his Arm, he would then begin to laugh, and with justice. In the same manner, were we to enter a poor House, and behold a wretched Family shivering with Cold and languishing with Hunger, it would not incline us to Laughter, (at least we must have very diabolical Natures, if it would:) but should we discover there a Grate, instead of Coals, adorned with Flowers, empty Plate or China Dishes on the Sideboard, or any other Affectation of Riches and Finery either on their Persons or in their Furniture; we might then indeed be excused, for ridiculing so fantastical an Appearance. Much less are natural Imperfections the objects of Derision: but when Ugliness aims at the Applause of Beauty, or Lameness endeavours to display Agility; it is then that these unfortunate Circumstances, which at first moved our Compassion, tend only to raise our Mirth.

The Poet carries this very far:

> *None are for being what they are in Fault,*
> *But for not being what they would be thought.*

Where if the Metre would suffer the Word *Ridiculous* to close the first Line, the Thought would be rather more proper. Great Vices are the proper Objects of our Detestation, smaller Faults of our Pity: but Affectation appears to me the only true Source of the Ridiculous.

But perhaps it may be objected to me, that I have against my own Rules introduced Vices, and of a very black Kind into this Work. To which I shall answer: First, that it is very difficult to pursue a Series of human Actions, and keep clear from them. Secondly, That the Vices to be found here, are rather the accidental Consequences of some human Frailty, or Foible, than Causes habitually existing in the Mind. Thirdly, That they are never set forth as the Objects of Ridicule but Destestation. Fourthly, That they are never the principal Figure at that time on the Scene; and lastly, they never produce the intended Evil.

Having thus distinguished *Joseph Andrews* from the Productions of Romance Writers on the one hand, and Burlesque Writers on the other, and given some few very short Hints (for I intended no more) of this Species of Writing, which I have affirmed to be hitherto unattempted in our Language; I shall leave to my good-natur'd Reader to apply my Piece to my Observations, and will detain him no longer than with a Word concerning the Characters in this Work.

And here I solemnly protest, I have no Intention to vilify or asperse any one: for tho' every thing is copied from the Book of Nature, and scarce a Character or Action produced which I have not taken from my own Observations and Experience, yet I have used the utmost Care to obscure the Persons by such different Circumstances, Degrees, and Colours, that it will be impossible to guess at them with any degree of Certainty; and if it ever happens otherwise, it is only where the Failure characterized is so minute, that it is a Foible only which the Party himself may laugh at as well as any other.

As to the Character of *Adams*, as it is the most glaring in the whole, so I conceive it is not to be found in any Book now extant. It is designed a Character of perfect Simplicity; and as the Goodness of his Heart will recommend him to the Good-natur'd; so I hope it will excuse me to the Gentlemen of his Cloth; for whom, while they are worthy of their sacred Order, no Man can possibly have a greater Respect. They will therefore excuse me, notwithstanding the low Adventures in which he is engaged, that I have made him a Clergyman; since no other Office could have given him so many Opportunities of displaying his worthy Inclinations.

CLARISSA
SAMUEL RICHARDSON
LONDON 1747

THE HISTORY OF A YOUNG LADY: COMPREHENDING THE MOST
IMPORTANT CONCERNS OF PRIVATE LIFE, AND PARTICULARLY
SHOWING THE DISTRESS THAT MAY ATTEND THE MISCONDUCT
BOTH OF PARENTS AND CHILDREN, IN RELATION TO MARRIAGE.

[PREFACE]

THE following History is given in a Series of Letters, written principally in a double, yet separate, Correspondence;

Between Two young Ladies of Virtue and Honour, bearing an inviolable Friendship for each other, and writing upon the most interesting Subjects: And

Between Two Gentlemen of free Lives; one of them glorying in his Talents for Stratagem and Invention, and communicating to the other, in Confidence, all the secret Purposes of an intriguing Head, and resolute Heart.

But it is not amiss to premise, for the sake of such as may apprehend Hurt to the Morals of Youth from the more freely-written Letters, That the Gentlemen, tho' professed Libertines as to the Fair Sex, and making it one of their wicked Maxims, to keep no Faith with any of the Individuals of it who throw themselves into their Power, are not, however, either Infidels or Scoffers: Nor yet such as think themselves freed from the Observance of those other moral Obligations, which bind Man to Man.

On the contrary, it will be found, in the Progress of the Collection, that they very often make such Reflections upon each other, and each upon himself, and upon his Actions, as reasonable Beings, who disbelieve not a future State of Rewards and Punishments (and who one day propose to reform) must sometimes make:– One of them actually reforming, and antidoting the Poison which some might otherwise apprehend would be spread by the

His dad, a Derbyshire joiner, sent his son to the Merchant Taylors School in London attended by Spenser. From there he was apprenticed to a printer. Like Hogarth's industrious apprentice he worked hard & wed his master's daughter, began his own firm & prospered greatly. He was small, plump, prim & he liked female company. When a schoolboy he wrote love-letters for a group of maid-servants. As a London printer he composed a specimen letter book showing how to write business & marriage proposals, & accept or reject them, & invoke legal action. Romans were the 1st to make public art of private letters in poetry & moral teaching. Paul's gospels used the form & Jonson, Donne, Pope, Burns in later British poetry. Richardson was 1st to see that a fictional sequence of letters could tell a story by linking different, very intimate views of the same plot. The plot he found most exciting (&

*so did many readers) was pursuit, capture & ravishing of a virgin by a gentleman rake. His 1st version of the plot was damaged by Pamela's unconvincing happiness in wedlock with a man she never respected or liked, & the readiness of the aristocracy to accept a former serving maid as one of themselves. A parody called **Shamela**, maybe by Fielding & coarser than **Joseph Andrews**, joked about that.*

Richardson again used his plot & turned it into a convincing tragedy. For monetary reasons then thought normal, Clarissa's middle-class family are forcing her to a hateful marriage. Her need to escape is used by Lovelace as a way to abduct her. Both are intelligent & capable of loving each other. His sexual haste kills love, her, then him.

gayer Pen, and lighter Heart, of the other.

And yet that other, [altho' in unbosoming himself to a *Select Friend*, he discover Wickedness enough to intitle him to general Hatred] preserves a Decency, as well in his Images, as in his Language, which is not always to be found in the Works of some of the most celebrated modern Writers, whose Subjects and Characters have less warranted the Liberties they have taken.

Length will be naturally expected, not only from what has been said, but from the following Considerations:

That the Letters on both Sides are written while the Hearts of the Writers must be supposed to be wholly engaged in their Subjects: The Events at the Time generally Dubious:– So that they abound, not only with critical Situations; but with what may be called *instantaneous* Descriptions and Reflections; which may be brought home to the Breast of the youthful Reader:– As also, with affecting Conversations; many of them written in the Dialogue or Dramatic Way.

To which may be added, that the Collection contains not only the History of the excellent Person whose Name it bears, but includes The Lives, Characters, and Catastrophes, of several others, either principally or incidentally concerned in the Story.

OOOOOOOOOOOOOOOOOOOOOOOOOOOOOOOOOOOOOOOOOOOOOOOOOOOOOOOOOOOOOOOOO

SOME ADVISED LIMITING THE BOOK TO THE HEROINE'S TRAGEDY BY SHORTENING: OTHERS SAID IT WAS MORE INSTRUCTIVE AND AMUSING AS IT STOOD.

OOOOOOOOOOOOOOOOOOOOOOOOOOOOOOOOOOOOOOOOOOOOOOOOOOOOOOOOOOOOOOOOO

*When **Clarissa** appeared Richardson received a letter from Fielding full of the heartiest praise, **though we are Rivals for that Coy Mrs Fame**. Dr Johnson said there was as big a difference*

Others, likewise gave *their* Opinions. But no Two being of the same Mind, as to the Parts which could be omitted, it was resolved to present to the World, the Two First Volumes, by way of Specimen; and to be determined with regard to the rest by the Reception those should meet with.

If that be favourable, Two others may soon follow;

the whole Collection being ready for the Press: That is to say, If it be not found necessary to abstract or omit some of the Letters, in order to reduce the Bulk of the Whole.

Thus much in general. But it may not be amiss to add, in particular, that in the great Variety of Subjects which this Collection contains, it is one of the principal Views of the Publication,

To caution Parents against the *undue* Exertion of their natural Authority over their Children, in the great Article of Marriage:

And Children against preferring a Man of Pleasure to a Man of Probity, upon that dangerous, but too commonly received Notion, That a *Reformed Rake makes the best Husband.*

between Richardson & Fielding as between a man who knew how a watch was made & one who could tell the hour by looking on the dial & that there is more knowledge of the heart in one letter of Richardson's, than in all Tom Jones.

Clarissa excelled by ending with a heroine NOT happily married, with plenty of money, loveable friends & the hope of many children: an end that flattened British plays & novels for centuries.

A DICTIONARY OF THE ENGLISH LANGUAGE 1755
SAMUEL JOHNSON: LONDON

IN WHICH THE WORDS ARE DEDUCED FROM THEIR ORIGINALS, AND ILLUSTRATED IN THEIR DIFFERENT SIGNIFICATIONS BY EXAMPLES FROM THE BEST WRITERS

[PREFACE]

IT IS THE FATE of those who toil at the lower employments of life, to be rather driven by the fear of evil, than attracted by the prospect of good; to be exposed to censure, without hope of praise; to be disgraced by miscarriage, or punished for neglect, where success would have been without applause, and diligence without reward.

Among these unhappy mortals is the writer of dictionaries; whom mankind have considered, not as the pupil, but the slave of science, the pionier of literature, doomed only to remove rubbish and clear obstructions from the paths of Learning and Genius, who press forward to conquest and glory, without bestowing a smile on the humble drudge that facilitates their progress. Every other authour may aspire to praise; the lexicographer can only hope to escape reproach, and even this negative recompense has been yet granted to very few.

I have, notwithstanding this discouragement, attempted a dictionary of the *English* language, which, while it was employed in the cultivation

Of great strength in body & mind, though both were diseased, he became wise & good. His dad was an erudite bookseller impoverished by reading more than selling his stock: was also a devout Anglican & Tory Jacobite who thought disputes about religion & politics were pointless. From him son Sam (born 1709 in the Staffordshire market town of Lichfield) got his great learning, & beliefs, & maybe some eccentric habits. Sam grew big but with eyes damaged, face bloated by a tubercular skin disease, mind liable to depressions in which he could hardly move because he felt God could not love him. Poverty was another affliction. At Oxford his mental gifts were recognised while his dirty raggedness got him small charities he violently rejected. He had to leave when his father died in his 2nd year; failed as a teacher because his twitching face & surly manner repelled folk; married a widow whose income could not keep both of them, & went to London with a play theatres rejected. In those days statesmen no longer looked out for good authors. As Pope had declared in The

of every species of literature, has itself been hitherto neglected, suffered to spread, under the direction of chance, into wild exuberance, resigned to the tyranny of time and fashion, and exposed to the corruptions of ignorance, and caprices of innovation.

When I took the first survey of my undertaking, I found our speech copious without order, and energetick without rules: wherever I turned my view, there was perplexity to be disentangled, and confusion to be regulated; choice was to be made out of boundless variety, without any established principle of selection; adulterations were to be detected, without a settled test of purity; and modes of expression to be rejected or received, without the suffrages of any writers of classical reputation or acknowledged authority.

Having therefore no assistance but from general grammar, I applied myself to the perusal of our writers; and noting whatever might be of use to ascertain or illustrate any word or phrase, accumulated in time the materials of a dictionary, which, by degrees, I reduced to method, establishing to myself, in the progress of the work, such rules as experience and analogy suggested to me; experience, which practice and observation were continually increasing; and analogy, which, though in some words obscure, was evident in others.

OOOOOOOOOOOOOOOOOOOOOOOOOOOOOOOOOOOOOOOOOOOOOOO

In examining the orthography of any doubtful word, the mode of spelling by which it is inserted in the series of the dictionary, is to be considered as that to which I give, perhaps not often rashly, the preference. I have left, in the examples, to every authour his own practice unmolested, that the reader may balance suffrages, and judge between us: but this question is not always to be determined by reputed or by real learning; some men, intent upon greater things, have thought little on sounds and derivations; some, knowing in the ancient tongues, have neglected those in which our words are commonly to be sought. Thus *Hammond* writes *fecibleness* for *feasibleness*, because I suppose he imagined it derived immediately from the *Latin*; and some words, such as *dependant*, *dependent*; *dependance*, *dependence*, vary their final syllable, as one or other language is present to the writer.

In this part of the work, where caprice has long wantoned without controul, and vanity sought praise by petty reformation, I have endeavoured to proceed with a scholar's reverence for antiquity, and a grammarian's regard to the genius of our tongue. I have attempted few alterations, and among those few, perhaps the greater part is from the modern to the ancient practice; and I hope I may be allowed to recommend to those, whose thoughts have been, perhaps, employed too anxiously on verbal singularities, not to disturb, upon narrow views, or for minute propriety, the orthography of their fathers. It has been asserted, that for the law to be *known*, is of more importance than to be *right*. Change, says *Hooker*, is not made without inconvenience, even from worse to better. There is in constancy and stability a general and lasting advantage, which will always overbalance the slow improvements of gradual correction. Much less ought our written language to comply with the corruptions of oral utterance, or copy that which every variation of time or place makes different from itself, and imitate those changes, which will again be changed, while imitation is employed in observing them.

This recommendation of steadiness and uniformity does not proceed from an opinion, that particular combinations of letters have much influence on human happiness; or that truth may not be successfully taught by modes of spelling fanciful and erroneous: I am not yet so lost in lexicography, as to forget that *words are the*

Dunciad, nobody in power now needed strong wits. Bribes, not pamphlets, won votes & booksellers had hordes of competing writers to choose from. Even popular Henry Fielding sometimes pawned his coat to buy a dish of tripe. By translation & hack work Sam lived for 10 years, at times homeless & sleeping in church porches, as did thousands then, while increasingly known as 1 of England's greatest scholars. Bad eyesight blinded him to details, just reasoning let him grasp general truths, making him excel as a critic & moralist. His prose was often wordy with Latinisms which many readers thought virtues then. In 1747 a team of booksellers advanced him £1575 to make a dictionary that would fix the words & spelling of English.

*Establishing a language through a book is as old as the forgotten scribes who 1st wrote **Genesis**, the **Iliad** & **Mahabharata**. Confucius & Mahomet did it, & Dante when he wrote his epic in the Tuscan dialect while adding a selection of words & usages from other parts of Italy. But Italian dialects were so many & well-written that academies in Venice, Rome, Milan etc* *could not agree on a standard speech. In 1635 Richelieu got Louis XIII to found the Académie Française, a group of 40 salaried authors. He did so to bring literature under state control, ordering from them a dictionary & grammatic rules so that, from now onward, schools could teach French as a uniform tongue. The Académie did this so well, made French so fine a tool of exact polite logic that German & Russian courtiers preferred it to their own tongues, & Lingua Franca was used by international diplomacy until 1918. Defoe, Swift & others wanted a similar body to preserve their own language. They feared that without even a good dictionary to define it, German kings, courtiers who thought French more polite, & 2 universities which taught only dead languages would soon make Shakespeare, Milton & Pope sound as antique as Chaucer. But parliament felt it paid enough to beat France in battle without an expensive academy like that of their despotic enemy: so the dictionary at last depended on London booksellers & Johnson.*

The 40 French academicians had

daughters of earth, and that things are the sons of heaven. Language is only the instrument of science, and words are but the signs of ideas: I wish, however, that the instrument might be less apt to decay, and that signs might be permanent, like the things which they denote.

OOOOOOOOOOOOOOOOOOOOOOOOOOOOOOOOOOOOOOOOOOOOOOOOOOO

That part of my work on which I expect malignity most frequently to fasten, is the *Explanation*; in which I cannot hope to satisfy those, who are perhaps not inclined to be pleased, since I have not always been able to satisfy myself. To interpret a language by itself is very difficult; many words cannot be explained by synonimes, because the idea signified by them has not more than one appellation; nor by paraphrase, because simple ideas cannot be described. When the nature of things is unknown, or the notion unsettled and indefinite, and various in various minds, the words by which such notions are conveyed, or such things denoted, will be ambiguous and perplexed. And such is the fate of hapless lexicography, that not only darkness, but light, impedes and distresses it; things may be not only too little, but too much known, to be happily illustrated. To explain, requires the use of terms less abstruse than that which is to be explained, and such terms cannot always be found; for as nothing can be proved but by supposing something intuitively known, and evident without proof, so nothing can be defined but by the use of words too plain to admit a definition.

OOOOOOOOOOOOOOOOOOOOOOOOOOOOOOOOOOOOOOOOOOOOOOOOOO

But many seeming faults are to be imputed rather to the nature of the undertaking, than the negligence of the performer. Thus some explanations are unavoidably reciprocal or circular, as *hind, the female of the stag*; *stag, the male of the hind*: sometimes easier words are changed into harder, as *burial* into *sepulture* or *interment*, *drier* into *desiccative*, *dryness* into *siccity* or *aridity*, *fit* into *paroxysm*; for the easiest word, whatever it be, can never be translated into one more easy. But easiness and difficulty are merely relative, and if the present prevalence of our language should invite foreigners to this dictionary, many will be assisted by those words which now seem only to increase or produce obscurity. For this reason I have endeavoured frequently to join a *Teutonick* and *Roman* interpretation, as to cheer to *gladden*, or *exhilarate*, that every learner of *English* may be assisted by his own tongue.

The solution of all difficulties, and the supply of all defects, must be sought in the examples, subjoined to the various senses of each word, and ranged according to the time of their authours.

When first I collected these authorities, I was desirous that every quotation should be useful to some other end than the illustration of a word; I therefore extracted from philosophers principles of science; from historians remarkable facts; from chymists complete processes; from divines striking exhortations; and from poets beautiful descriptions. Such is design, while it is yet at a distance from execution. When the time called upon me to range this accumulation of elegance and wisdom into an alphabetical series, I soon discovered that the bulk of my volumes would fright away the student, and was forced to depart from my scheme of including all that was pleasing or useful in *English* literature, and reduce my transcripts very often to clusters of words, in which scarcely any meaning is retained; thus to the weariness of copying, I was condemned to add the vexation of expunging. Some passages I have yet spared, which may relieve the labour of verbal searches, and interperse with verdure and flowers the dusty desarts of barren philology.

*taken 40 years over theirs. By hiring 6 assistants (5 of them Scottish) Johnson hoped to do the job in 3 years. He took 8, with no help from a great nobleman & politician who at 1st seemed to offer that. From then on Johnson thought patronage a curse on literature. He raised cash by writing **The Rambler**, a twice-weekly magazine like **The Tatler**, & made a home for his wife in London. The preface regrets that she did not live to see his great work finished. It is still 1 of the few dictionaries that are a pleasure to read. He shows by quotation how words & meanings alter from the time of Shakespeare to his own & enjoys declaring his Toryism. When Whigs held power by patronage he defined a pension as:* **pay given to a state hireling to betray his country**. *Though now England's most famous author he was arrested for debt, bailed out by printer-novelist Richardson, would have died poor if George III, a Tory king, had not granted him a state pension. He could thus give a home to old friends who would have been destitute without his generosity.*

The examples, thus mutilated, are no longer to be considered as conveying the sentiments or doctrine of their authours; the word for the sake of which they are inserted, with all its appendant clauses, has been carefully preserved: but it may sometimes happen, by hasty detruncation, that the general tendency of the sentence may be changed: the divine may desert his tenets, or the philosopher his system.

Some of the examples have been taken from writers who were never mentioned as masters of elegance or models of stile; but words must be sought where they are used; and in what pages, eminent for purity, can terms of manufacture or agriculture be found? Many quotations serve no other purpose, than that of proving the bare existence of words, and are therefore selected with less scrupulousness than those which are to teach their structures and relations.

My purpose was to admit no testimony of living authours, that I might not be misled by partiality, and that none of my cotemporaries might have reason to complain; nor have I departed from this resolution, but when some performance of uncommon excellence excited my veneration, when my memory supplied me, from late books, with an example that was wanting, or when my heart, in the tenderness of friendship, solicited admission for a favourite name.

So far have I been from any care to grace my pages with modern decorations, that I have studiously endeavoured to collect examples and authorities from the writers before the restoration, whose works I regard as *the wells of English undefiled*, as the pure sources of genuine diction. Our language, for almost a century, has, by the concurrence of many causes, been gradually departing from its original *Teutonick* character, and deviating towards a *Gallick* structure and phraseology, from which it ought to be our endeavour to recal it, by making our ancient volumes the ground-work of stile, admitting among the additions of later times, only such as may supply real deficiencies, such as are readily adopted by the genius of our tongue, and incorporate easily with our native idioms.

But as every language has a time of rudeness antecedent to perfection, as well as of false refinement and declension, I have been cautious lest my zeal for antiquity might drive me into times too remote, and croud my book with words now no longer understood. I have fixed *Sidney*'s work for the boundary, beyond which I make few excursions. From the authours which rose in the time of *Elizabeth*, a speech might be formed adequate to all the purposes of use and elegance. If the language of theology were extracted from *Hooker* and the translation of the Bible; the terms of natural knowledge from *Bacon*; the phrases of policy, war, and navigation from *Raleigh*; the dialect of poetry and fiction from *Spenser* and *Sidney*; and the diction of common life from *Shakespeare*, few ideas would be lost to mankind, for want of *English* words, in which they might be expressed.

ooooooooooooooooooooooooooooooooooooooooooooooooooooooooo

I have sometimes, though rarely, yielded to the temptation of exhibiting a genealogy of sentiments, by shewing how one authour copied the thoughts and diction of another: such quotations are indeed little more than repetitions, which might justly be censured, did they not gratify the mind, by affording a kind of intellectual history.

ooooooooooooooooooooooooooooooooooooooooooooooooooooooooo

When first I engaged in this work, I resolved to leave neither words nor things unexamined, and pleased myself with a prospect of the hours which I should revel away in feasts of literature, the obscure recesses of northern learning, which I should enter and ransack, the treasures with which I expected every search into those neglected mines to reward my labour, and the triumph with which I should display my acquisitions to mankind. When I had thus enquired into the original of words, I resolved to show likewise my attention to things; to pierce deep into every science, to enquire the nature of every substance of which I inserted the name, to limit every idea by a definition strictly logical, and exhibit every production of art or nature in an accurate description, that my book might be in place of all other dictionaries whether appellative or technical. But these were the dreams of a poet doomed at last to wake a lexicographer. I soon found that it is too late to look for instruments, when the work calls for execution, and that whatever abilities I had brought to my task, with those I must finally perform it. To deliberate whenever I doubted, to enquire whenever I was ignorant, would have protracted the undertaking without end, and, perhaps, without much improvement; for I did not find by my first experiments, that what I had not of my own was easily to be obtained: I saw that one enquiry only gave occasion to another, that book referred to book, that to search was not always to find, and to find was not always to be informed; and that thus to persue perfection, was, like the first inhabitants of Arcadia, to chace the sun, which, when they had reached the hill where he seemed to rest, was still beheld at the same distance from them.

I then contracted my design, determining to confide in myself, and no longer to solicit auxiliaries, which produced more incumbrance than assistance: by this I obtained a least one advantage, that I set limits to my work, which would in time be finished, though not completed.

0000000000000000000000000000000000000000000000000000000000000000

That many terms of art and manufacture are omitted, must be frankly acknowledged; but for this defect I may boldly allege that is was unavoidable: I could not visit caverns to learn the miner's language, nor take a voyage to perfect my skill in the dialect of navigation, nor visit the warehouses of merchants, and shops of artificers, to gain the names of wares, tools and operations, of which no mention is found in books; what favourable accident, or easy enquiry brought within my reach, has not been neglected; but it had been a hopeless labour to glean up words, by courting living information, and contesting with the sullenness of one, and the roughness of another.

To furnish the academicians *della Crusca* with words of this kind, a series of comedies called *la Fiera*, or *the Fair*, was professedly written by *Buonaroti*; but I had no such assistant, and therefore was content to want what they must have wanted likewise, had they not luckily been so supplied.

Nor are all words which are not found in the vocabulary, to be lamented as omissions. Of the laborious and mercantile part of the people, the diction is in a great measure casual and mutable; many of their terms are formed for some temporary or local convenience, and though current at certain times and places, are in others utterly unknown. This fugitive cant, which is always in a state of increase or decay, cannot be regarded as any part of the durable materials of a language, and therefore must be suffered to perish with other things unworthy of preservation.

0000000000000000000000000000000000000000000000000000000000000000

Of the event of this work, for which, having laboured it with so much application, I cannot but have some degree of parental fondness, it is natural to form conjectures. Those who have been persuaded to think well of my design, require that it should fix our language, and put a stop to those alterations which time and chance have hitherto been suffered to make in it without opposition. With this consequence

I will confess that I flattered myself for a while; but now begin to fear that I have indulged expectation which neither reason nor experience can justify. When we see men grow old and die at a certain time one after another, from century to century, we laugh at the elixir that promises to prolong life to a thousand years; and with equal justice may the lexicographer be derided, who being able to produce no example of a nation that has preserved their words and phrases from mutability, shall imagine that his dictionary can embalm his language, and secure it from corruption and decay, that it is in his power to change sublunary nature, or clear the world at once from folly, vanity, and affectation.

With this hope, however, academies have been instituted, to guard the avenues of their languages, to retain fugitives, and repulse intruders; but their vigilance and activity have hitherto been vain; sounds are too volatile and subtile for legal restraints; to enchain syllables, and to lash the wind, are equally the undertakings of pride, unwilling to measure its desires by its strength. The *French* language has visibly changed under the inspection of the academy; the stile of *Amelot*'s translation of father *Paul* is observed by *Le Courayer* to be *un peu passé*; and no *Italian* will maintain, that the diction of any modern writer is not perceptibly different from that of *Boccace*, *Machiavel*, or *Caro*.

Total and sudden transformations of a language seldom happen; conquests and migrations are now very rare: but there are other causes of change, which, though slow in their operation, and invisible in their progress, are perhaps as much superiour to human resistance, as the revolutions of the sky, or intumescence of the tide. Commerce, however necessary, however lucrative, as it depraves the manners, corrupts the language; they that have frequent intercourse with strangers, to whom they endeavour to accommodate themselves, must in time learn a mingled dialect, like the jargon which serves the traffickers on the *Mediterranean* and *Indian* coasts. This will not always be confined to the exchange, the warehouse, or the port, but will be communicated by degrees to other ranks of the people, and be at last incorporated with the current speech.

There are likewise internal causes equally forcible. The language most likely to continue long without alteration, would be that of a nation raised a little, and but a little, above barbarity, secluded from strangers, and totally employed in procuring the conveniencies of life; either without books, or, like some of the *Mahometan* countries, with very few: men thus busied and unlearned, having only such words as common use requires, would perhaps long continue to express the same notions by the same signs. But no such constancy can be expected in a people polished by arts, and classed by subordination, where one part of the community is sustained and accommodated by the labour of the other. Those who have much leisure to think, will always be enlarging the stock of ideas, and every increase of knowledge, whether real or fancied, will produce new words, or combinations of words. When the mind is unchained from necessity, it will range after convenience; when it is left at large in the fields of speculation, it will shift opinions; as any custom is disused, the words that expressed it must perish with it; as any opinion grows popular, it will innovate speech in the same proportion as it alters practice.

As by the cultivation of various sciences, a language is amplified, it will be more furnished with words deflected from their original sense; the geometrician will talk of a courtier's zenith, or the excentrick virtue of a wild hero, and the physician of sanguine expectations and phlegmatick delays. Copiousness of speech will give opportunities to capricious choice, by which some words will be preferred, and others degraded; vicissitudes of fashion will enforce the use of new, or extend the signification of known terms. The tropes of poetry will make hourly encroachments, and the metaphorical will become the current sense: pronunciation will be varied by levity or ignorance, and the pen must at length comply with the tongue; illiterate writers will at one time or other, by publick infatuation, rise into renown, who, not knowing the original import of words, will use them with colloquial licentiousness, confound distinction, and forget propriety. As politeness increases, some expressions will be considered as too gross and vulgar for the delicate, others as too formal and ceremonious for the gay and airy; new phrases are therefore adopted, which must, for the same reasons, be in time dismissed. *Swift*, in his petty treatise on the *English* language, allows that new words must sometimes be introduced, but proposes that none should be suffered to become obsolete. But what makes a word obsolete, more than general agreement to forbear it? and how shall it be continued, when it conveys an offensive idea, or recalled again into the mouths of mankind, when it has once by disuse become unfamiliar, and by unfamiliarity unpleasing.

There is another cause of alteration more prevalent than any other, which yet in the present state of the world cannot be obviated. A mixture of two languages will produce a third distinct from both, and they will always be mixed, where the chief part of education, and the most conspicuous accomplishment, is skill in ancient or in foreign tongues. He that has long cultivated another language, will find its words and combinations croud upon his memory; and haste and negligence, refinement and affectation, will obtrude borrowed terms and exotick expressions.

The great pest of speech is frequency of translation. No book was ever turned from one language into another, without imparting something of its native idiom; this is the most mischievous and comprehensive innovation; single words may enter by thousands, and the fabrick of the tongue continue the same, but new phraseology changes much at once; it alters not the single stones of the building, but the order of the columns. If an academy should be established for the cultivation of our stile, which I, who can never wish to see dependance multiplied, hope the spirit of *English* liberty will hinder or destroy, let them, instead of compiling grammars and dictionaries, endeavour, with all their influence, to stop the licence of translatours, whose idleness and ignorance, if it be suffered to proceed, will reduce us to babble a dialect of *France*.

If the changes that we fear be thus irresistible, what remains but to acquiesce with silence, as in the other insurmountable distresses of humanity? it remains that we retard what we cannot repel, that we palliate what we cannot cure. Life may be lengthened by care, though death cannot be ultimately defeated: tongues, like governments, have a natural tendency to degeneration; we have long preserved our constitution, let us make some struggles for our language.

In hope of giving longevity to that which its own nature forbids to be immortal, I have devoted this book, the labour of years, to the honour of my country, that we may no longer yield the palm of philology to the nations of the continent. The chief glory of every people arises from its authours: whether I shall add any thing by my own writings to the reputation of *English* literature, must be left to time: much of my life has been lost under the pressures of disease; much has been trifled away; and much has always been spent in provision for the day that was passing over me; but I shall not think my employment useless or ignoble, if by my assistance foreign nations, and distant ages, gain access to the propagators of knowledge, and understand the teachers of truth; if my labours afford light to the repositories of science, and add celebrity to *Bacon*, to *Hooker*, to *Milton*, and to *Boyle*.

When I am animated by this wish, I look with pleasure on my book, however defective, and deliver it to the world with the spirit of a man that has endeavoured well. That it will immediately become popular I have not promised to myself: a few wild blunders, and risible absurdities, from which no work of such multiplicity was ever free, may for a time furnish folly with laughter, and harden ignorance in contempt; but useful diligence will at last prevail, and there never can be wanting some who distinguish desert; who will consider that no dictionary of a living tongue ever can be perfect, since while it is hastening to publication, some words are budding, and some falling away; that a whole life cannot be spent upon syntax and etymology, and that even a whole life would not be sufficient; that he, whose design includes whatever language can express, must often speak of what he does not understand; that a writer will sometimes be hurried by eagerness to the end, and sometimes faint with weariness under a task, which *Scaliger* compares to the labours of the anvil and the mine; that what is obvious is not always known, and what is known is not always present; that sudden fits of inadvertency will surprize vigilance, slight avocations will seduce attention, and casual eclipses of the mind will darken learning; and that the writer shall often in vain trace his memory at the moment of need, for that which yesterday he knew with intuitive readiness, and which will come uncalled into his thoughts tomorrow.

In this work, when it shall be found that much is omitted, let it not be forgotten that much likewise is performed; and though no book was ever spared out of tenderness to the authour, and the world is little solicitous to know whence proceeded the faults of that which it condemns; yet it may gratify curiosity to inform it, that the *English Dictionary* was written with little assistance of the learned, and without any patronage of the great; not in the soft obscurities of retirement, or under the shelter of academick bowers, but amidst inconvenience and distraction, in sickness and in sorrow: and it may repress the triumph of malignant criticism to observe, that if our language is not here fully displayed, I have only failed in an attempt which no human powers have hitherto completed. If the lexicons of ancient tongues, now immutably fixed, and comprised in a few volumes, be yet, after the toil of successive ages, inadequate and delusive; if the aggregated knowledge, and co-operating diligence of the *Italian* academicians, did not secure them from the censure of *Beni*, if the embodied criticks of *France*, when fifty years had been spent upon their work, were obliged to change its oeconomy, and give their second edition another form, I may surely be contented without the praise of perfection, which, if I could obtain, in this gloom of solitude, what would it avail me? I have protracted my work till most of those whom I wished to please, have sunk into the grave, and success and miscarriage are empty sounds: I therefore dismiss it with frigid tranquillity, having little to fear or hope from censure or from praise.

FRAGMENTS of ANCIENT POETRY collected in the Scotish Highlands & translated from the Galic or Erse by JAMES MACPHERSON: EDINBURGH

1760

The destruction of monastic libraries in Scotland left her (unlike Wales & Ireland) with hardly any early Gaelic writing. In 1759 Edinburgh littérateurs who regretted this met a young Inverness school-teacher: he showed them fragments of Gaelic epic by (he said) an ancient bard, Ossian, which could still be found in the Highlands. His hearers had no Gaelic but his trans- lations convinced them, so they paid him to tour the north collecting & translating more. This work became a best- selling book. Dr. Johnson called it fake, but the fake simplicity of these lines: **The blue waves of Erin roll in light. The mountains are covered with day. Grey torrents pour their noisy streams. Two green hills, with aged oaks, surround a narrow plain** refreshed readers used to nature poems starting: **From brightening fields of ether fair disclosed, / Child of** **the sun, refulgent summer** comes. *The voice of fashion- able poetry was now so genteel that it made Mac- pherson's fake simplicity sound Homeric. Despite Dr Johnson, fashionable taste & Jefferson & Napoleon & Goethe put Ossian with Homer. Macpherson (Borges says) sacrificed honesty* to *the greater glory of Scotland, besides writing the first romantic poem in European Literature.*

THE LIFE AND OPINIONS OF TRISTRAM SHANDY, GENTLEMAN. LAURENCE STERNE: YORK

1760

[TO THE RIGHT HONOURABLE MR. PITT]

SIR, Never poor Wight of a Dedicator had less hopes from his Dedication, than I have from this of mine; for it is written in a bye corner of the kingdom, and in a retired thatch'd house, where I live in a constant endeavour to fence against the infirmities of ill health, and

*Born in Ireland in 1713, an army officer's son, graduate of Cambridge, ordained clergyman & inveterate philanderer, Sterne led a suitably Shandean patchy life, much of it separated from his wife, though he was paid to preach in York Cathedral. He must always have been a storyteller, but the 1st 2 volumes of what would be a 9-volume book appeared to much fashionable acclaim in his 47th year, the last in 1767, a year before he died. The book is wilful, exuberant, bawdy, gleefully plagiarising, eccentric & humane. It delights in its fiction, freely acknowledging the conversation that joins author & reader, & using every device that late 20th-century critics label **post-modernist**. He is also a slyly self-conscious cultivator of kindly feelings. Note how his dedication flatters a prime minister while pretending not to, & says he is poor & ill while seeming to avoid self-pity. He was also master of the erotic insinuation. This short 1st chapter laments an interrupted coupling which the writer says gave him life & many weaknesses of mind & body. He was unusually tall & thin, & is said to have appeared post mortem in a Cambridge dissecting theatre.*

other evils of life, by mirth; being firmly persuaded that every time a man smiles, – but much more so, when he laughs, that it adds something to this Fragment of Life.

I humbly beg, Sir, that you will honour this book by taking it – (not under your Protection, – it must protect itself, but) – into the country with you; where, if I am ever told, it has made you smile, or can conceive it has beguiled you of one moment's pain – I shall think myself as happy as a minister of state; – perhaps much happier than any one (one only excepted) that I have ever read or heard of.

I am, great Sir,

(and what is more to your Honour)

I am, good Sir,

Your Well-wisher,

and most humble

Fellow-Subject,

The Author.

[CHAPTER ONE]

I wish either my father or my mother, or indeed both of them, as they were in duty both equally bound to it, had minded what they were about when they begot me; had they duly consider'd how much depended upon what they were then doing; – that not only the production of a rational Being was concern'd in it, but that possibly the happy formation and temperature of his body, perhaps his genius and the very cast of his mind; – and, for aught they knew to the contrary, even the fortunes of his whole house might take their turn from the humours and dispositions which were then uppermost: – Had they duly weighed and considered all this, and proceeded accordingly, – I am verily persuaded I should have made a quite different figure in the world, from that, in which the reader is likely to see me. – Believe me, good folks, this is not so inconsiderable a thing as many of you may think it; – you have all, I dare say, heard of the animal spirits, as how they are transfused from father to son, *&c. &c.* – and a great deal to that purpose: – Well, you may take my word, that nine parts in ten of a man's sense or his nonsense, his successes and miscarriages in this world depend upon their motions and activity, and the different tracks and trains you put them into; so that when they are once set a-going, whether right or wrong, 'tis not a half-penny matter, – away they go cluttering like hey-go mad; and by treading the same steps over and over again, they presently make a road of it, as plain and as smooth as a garden walk, which, when they are once used to, the Devil himself sometimes shall not be able to drive then off it.

Pray, my dear, quoth my mother, *have you not forgot to wind up the clock? – Good G– !* cried my father, making an exclamation, but taking care to moderate his voice at the same time, – *Did ever woman, since the creation of the world, interrupt a man with such a silly question?* Pray, what was your father saying? – Nothing.

COMMENTARIES ON THE LAWS OF ENGLAND
SIR WILLIAM BLACKSTONE: OXFORD
1765
[INTRODUCTION TO THE STUDY OF ENGLISH LAWS : SUMMARISED IN ITALICS WITH EXTRACTS]

In Scotland and mainland Europe most wealthy, educated folk have studied their country's laws. These are based on codes of Roman and Byzantine emperors, unlike English common law which grew out of unwritten British, Anglo-Saxon and Danish customs. Our laws, saith Lord Bacon, are mixed as our language: and as our language is so much the richer, our laws are more complete. *King Alfred put them in writing; Norman conquest violated them; King John's barons retrieved them by getting Habeus Corpus law and trial by jury; Edward the First strengthened them by making a permanent high court at Westminster. English monarchs defended common law against Roman law used by the Catholic church, so common law finally triumphed with English Protestantism, making –*

In the 18th century's 2nd half a fear of innovations developed in south Britain. King George III was trying to rule. He disliked all politicians wiser than he. Most were, so new acts by House of Commons were thrown out by the House of Lords which the king packed with servile numskulls. Johnson was trying to stop change in English speech with his dictionary. In this book Blackstone tried to stop change in law by teaching gentry to use what existed. Coke had simplified law for lawyers. Blackstone, a less pushy man, made it available to anyone who could read. In his profession he was a slow starter but gave such excellent private legal tuition to a Mr. Viner that Viner gave Oxford University a big sum of money to endow a Chair of Law with Blackstone the 1st occupant. His lectures became this 1st plain statement of English law at a surprisingly late date. It pleased a Tory government, which made him an MP & judge. On logical & political grounds his views were disputed but reformers needed his clear showing of existing law as much as Tories who wanted no change. Sometimes little change was needed. Poaching increased as private parliamentary bills let more gentry enclose common land. New laws to exile or hang peasants living as they had lived for centuries were justified by the game laws of William the Conqueror. Blackstone was valued as highly in America whose States were managed by gentlemen with large properties by using all the law they could master. Owners of estates, slaves & businesses found the

A land, perhaps the only one in the universe, in which political and civil liberty is the very end and scope of the constitution. This liberty, rightly understood, consists in the power of doing whatever the law permits; which is only to be effected by a general conformity of all orders and degrees to those equitable rules of action, by which the meanest individual is protected from the insults and oppression of the greatest . . . It is the glory of English law that an Englishman cannot be affected either in his property, his liberty, or his person, but by the unanimous decision of twelve of his neighbours and equals. *Parts of the common law may startle the student because at first sight they do not make sense and seem unduly tortuous, but closer study will show the law is like –* an old Gothic castle, erected in the days of chivalry, but fitted up for a modern inhabitant. The moated ramparts, the embattled towers, and the trophied halls are magnificent and venerable, but useless. The interior apartments, now converted into rooms of convenience, are cheerful and commodious, though their approaches are winding and difficult.

But English law is in danger: only practising lawyers know it, not those who rule the nation. Gentlemen of rank and distinction with the leisure to enter parliament have, from ignorance, made new laws when they should have revoked or amended old. Sir Edward Coke had said such additions were hard to reconcile with common law. And if this inconvenience was so heavily felt in the reign of Queen Elizabeth, you may judge how evil is increased in later times when the statute book is swelled to ten times a larger bulk. *Ignorant magistrates may also abuse the law.* But how much more serious and affecting is the case of a superior judge, if without any skill in the laws he will boldly venture to decide a question upon which the welfare and subsistence of whole families may depend! *Since the House of*

Lords is the nation's final court of appeal even an English nobleman should be master of those points upon which it is his birthright to decide . . . Yet, vast as this trust is, it can no where be so properly reposed, as in the noble hands where our excellent constitution has placed it, because, from the independence of their fortune and dignity of their station, they are presumed to employ that leisure which is the consequence of both, in attaining a more extensive knowledge of the laws than those of inferior rank.

Commentaries so very useful that much of it was written into the legal constitution of the USA they created. Blackstone was not a democrat and would have been amazed that his book helped a modern democracy into being; pleased this made law the USA's dominant profession. . On page 406 is another view of him.

ENCYCLOPAEDIA BRITANNICA
EDITOR: WILLIAM SMELLIE
EDINBURGH

1768

OR, A DICTIONARY OF ARTS & SCIENCES DIGESTED INTO DISTINCT TREATISES OR SYSTEMS BY A SOCIETY OF GENTLEMEN IN SCOTLAND

The Greeks & Romans thought of putting all knowledge in 1 book & Pliny (23-79AD) did it with all he discovered about natural history, geography, medicine & art. Chinese emperors got encyclopaedias by having scholars unite instructive parts of every book available. In Europe discoveries kept making the best efforts obsolete, but an English dictionary of scientific & technical terms (of a sort that Johnson's dictionary mainly omitted since gentlemen had no use for them) was issued by Ephraim Chambers in 1728 & translated into other tongues. In France it suggested to Diderot the plan of an encyclopaedia to which all the best writers he knew could contribute. It

UTILITY ought to be the principal intention of every publication. Wherever this intention does not plainly appear, neither the books nor their authors have the smallest claim to the approbation of mankind.

To diffuse the knowledge of Science, is the professed design of the following work. What methods, it may be asked, have the compilers employed to accomplish this design? Not to mention original articles, they have had recourse to the best books upon almost every subject, extracted the useful parts, and rejected whatever appeared trifling or less interesting. Instead of dismembering the Sciences, by attempting to treat them intelligibly under a multitude of technical terms, they have digested the principles of every science in the form of systems or distinct treatises, and explained the terms as they occur in the order of the alphabet, with *would tell how to make every product from brass & gunpowder to rouge & velvet, give the exact design of all useful tools & machines, & explain old & new science & philosophy. He printed 24 volumes from 1751 to 1772 & as they contained writing by Voltaire, Rousseau & other free thinkers was often in danger of arrest. In south Britain his example was not much noticed at 1st, but the north was now making money by using new ideas in farming, trade & industries. Scottish universities lectured on them. A traffic of publications flowed between Edinburgh & Paris.*

*Smellie was printer for Edinburgh University. He typeset Latin classics, work by Hume & Adam Smith & the 1st book of Burns' poems. His university contact let him attend lectures on subjects from Hebrew to zoology. Learning led to book making. He co-authored a popular work of home medicine, translated into English the **Histoire Naturelle** of Buffon, & with Bell (an engraver) & Mac-Farquarson (who had money) became the society that made the 1st **Britannica**. Smellie was the main compiler. When later asked his*

references to the sciences to which they belong.

As this plan differs from that of all the Dictionaries of Arts and Sciences hitherto publshed, the compilers think it necessary to mention what they imagine gives it a superiority over the common method. A few words will answer this purpose. Whoever has had occasion to consult Chambers, Owen, &c. or even the volumious French Encyclopedie, will have discovered the folly of attempting to communicate science under the various technical terms suggested in alphabetical order. Such an attempt is repugnant to the very idea of science, which is a connected series of conclusions deduced from self-evident or previously discovered principles and relations of different parts of science, laid in one uninterrupted chain. But where is the man who can learn the principles of any science from a Dictionary compiled upon the alphabetic plan? We will, however, venture to affirm, that any man of ordinary parts, may, if he chuses, learn the principles of Agriculture, of Astronomy, of Botany, of Chemistry, &c. &c. from the ENCYCLOPAEDIA BRITANNICA.

WE must acknowledge, that, in some instances, we have deviated from the plan. Under the words BOTANY and NATURAL HISTORY it would have been an endless, and perhaps an useless task, to have given the generic distinctions of every plant, and of every animal. These are to be found under the names of the plants and animals themselves. The same observation may be made with respect to **Mineralogy, Materia Medica, Pathology, Physiology**, and **Therapeutics**. These are so interwoven with **Anatomy, Botany, Chemistry**, and **Medicine**, that, in a work of this kind, it was almost impossible, without many unnecessary repetitions, to treat them as distinct sciences. Indeed, properly speaking, they are not sciences, but parts or accessories of sciences, which, by the dexterity of teachers and authors, have been exhibited under as separate.

WITH regard to errors in general, whether under the denomination of mental, typographical, or accidental, we are able to point out a greater number than any critic. Men acquainted with the innumarable difficulties attending their work of an extensive nature will make proper allowances. To these we appeal, and shall rest satisfied with their judgment.

method of work he said **scissors & paste**. *The ground floor he laid was broad enough for others to build & improve upon. Later editors could pay 1st-class specialists for entries. The* **Britannica** *was Edinburgh-based till the London* **Times** *bought it in 1903, New York got it in the 1920s.*

THE EXPEDITION OF HUMPHRY CLINKER
TOBIAS SMOLLETT
LONDON

1771

TO MR. HENRY DAVIS, BOOKSELLER IN LONDON

Abergavenny, Aug. 4.

RESPECTED SIR, I have received your esteemed favour of the 13th ultimo, whereby it appeareth, that you have perused those same Letters, the which were delivered unto you by my friend the reverend Mr. Hugo Behn; and I am pleased to find you think they may be printed with a good prospect of success; in as much as the objections you mention, I humbly conceive, are such as may be redargued, if not entirely removed – And, first, in the first place, as touching what prosecutions may arise from printing the private correspondence of persons still living, give me leave, with all due submission, to observe, that the Letters in question were not written and sent under the seal of secrecy; that they have no tendency to the *mala fama*, or prejudice of any person whatsoever; but rather to the information and edification of mankind: so that it becometh a sort of duty to promulgate them *in usum publicum*. Besides, I have consulted Mr. Davy Higgins, an eminent attorney of this place, who, after due inspection and consideration, declareth, That he doth not think the said Letters contain any matter which will be held actionable in the eye of the law.

Orwell said Smollett was **Scotland's best** *novelist because he is outside an English tradition where vice is punished & virtues neatly rewarded; hero & heroine may be at fault but are mostly good folk so come to do as well on earth as they will in heaven. Smollett has rogues & snobs for heroes. They fight on the slightest provocation & amuse themselves by planned seductions & hideous practical jokes. Most novelists then tried to promote cleaner ways by showing them as if normal, but in Smollett's rambling & messy novels appears the world painted by Hogarth where filth & corruption are the* *norm. By ruling out "good" motives & showing no respect whatever for human dignity, Smollett attains a truthfulness (says Orwell) that more serious novelists have missed. In Roderick Random the hero is smitten by V.D. Out of work in France he joins the army there (it is nearer than the British) fights his own countrymen on a German battlefield & after, on a Frenchman insulting Britain, duels with him. It shows how little the wars British & French governments were fighting for the trade of Europe, India & America interested most of the citizens.*

*Sterne nicknamed Smollett **Dr Smellfungus** to imply he revelled in filth he showed. While **Humphrey Clinker** is not his best novel it shows Bath & London as heavens for nice young ladies, hells for any with modern ideas of hygiene. Smollett was a trained doctor.*

Finally, if you and I should come to a right understanding, I do declare *in verbo sacerdotis*, that, in case of any such prosecution, I will take the whole upon my own shoulders, even *quoad* fine and imprisonment, though, I must confess, I should not care to undergo flagellation: *Tam ad turpitudinem, quam ad amaritudinem poenae spectans* – Secondly, concerning the personal resentment of Mr. Justice Lismahago, I may say, *non flocci facio* – I would not willingly vilipend any Christian, if, peradventure, he deserveth that epithet: albeit, I am much surprised that more care is not taken to exclude from the commission all such vagrant foreigners as may be justly suspected of disaffection to our happy constitution, in church and state – God forbid that I should be so uncharitable, as to affirm positively, that the said Lismahago is no better than a Jesuit in disguise; but this I will assert and maintain, *totis viribus*, that, from the day he qualified, he has never been once seen *intra templi parietes*, that is to say, within the parish church.

Thirdly, with respect to what passed at Mr. Kendal's table, when the said Lismahago was so brutal in his reprehensions, I must inform you, my good sir, that I was obliged to retire, not by fear arising from his minatory reproaches, which, as I said above, I value not of a rush; but from the sudden effect produced by a barbel's roe, which I had eaten at dinner, not knowing, that the said roe is at certain seasons violently cathartic, as Galen observeth in his chapter περι ιχθυς.

Fourthly, and lastly, with reference to the manner in which I got possession of these Letters, it is a circumstance that concerns my own conscience only; suffice it to say, I have fully satisfied the parties in whose custody they were; and, by this time, I hope I have also satisfied you in such ways, that the last hand may be put to our agreement, and the work proceed with all convenient expedition; in

which hope I rest,
> respected sir,
>> your very humble servant,
>>> Jonathan Dustwich

P.S. I propose, *Deo volente*, to have the pleasure of seeing you in the great city, towards All-hallowtide, when I shall be glad to treat with you concerning a parcel of MS. sermons, of a certain clergyman deceased; a cake of the right leaven, for the present taste of the public. *Verbum sapienti*, &c.

TO THE REVD. MR. JONATHAN DUSTWICH

SIR, I received yours in course of post, and shall be glad to treat with you for the MS. which I have delivered to your friend Mr. Behn; but can by no means comply with the terms proposed. Those things are so uncertain – Writing is all a lottery – I have been a loser by the works of the greatest men of the age – I could mention particulars, and name names; but don't chuse it – The taste of the town is so changeable. Then there have been so many letters upon travels lately published – What between Smollett's, Sharp's, Derrick's, Thickness's, Baltimore's, and Baretti's, together with Shandy's Sentimental Travels, the public seems to be cloyed with that kind of entertainment – Nevertheless, I will, if you please, run the risque of printing and publishing, and you shall have half the profits of the impression – You need not take the trouble to bring up your sermons on my account – No body reads sermons but Methodists and Dissenters – Besides, for my own part, I am quite a stranger to that sort of reading; and the two persons, whose judgment I depended upon in those matters, are out of the way; one is gone abroad, carpenter of a man of war; and the other has been silly enough to abscond, in order to avoid a prosecution for blasphemy – I'm a great loser by his going off – He has left a manual of devotion half finished on my hands, after having received money for the whole copy – He was the soundest divine, and had the most orthodox pen of all my people; and I never knew his judgment fail, but in flying from his bread and butter on this occasion.

By owning you was not put in bodily fear by Lismahago, your preclude yourself from the benefit of a good plea, over and above the advantage of binding him over. In the late war, I inserted in my evening paper, a paragraph that came by the post, reflecting upon the behaviour of a certain regiment in battle. An officer of said regiment came to my shop, and, in the presence of my wife and journeyman, threatened to cut off my ears – As I exhibited marks of bodily fear, more ways than one, to the conviction of the byestanders, I bound him over; my action lay, and I recovered. As for flagellation, you have nothing to fear, and nothing to hope, on that head – There has been but one printer flogged at the cart's tail these thirty years; that was Charles Watson; and he assured me it was no more than a flea-bite. C – S – has been threatened several times by the House of L –; but it came to nothing. If an information should be moved for, and granted against you, as the editor of those Letters, I hope you will have honesty and wit enough to appear and take your trial – If you should be sentenced to the pillory, your fortune is made – As times go, that's a sure step to honour and preferment. I shall think myself happy if I can lend you a lift; and am, very sincerely,

yours,
Henry Davis.

London, Aug. 10th.

Please my kind service to your neighbour, my cousin Madoc – I have sent an Almanack and Court-kalendar, directed for him at Mr. Sutton's, bookseller, in Gloucester, carriage paid, which he will please to accept as a small token of my regard. My wife, who is very fond of toasted cheese, presents her compliments to him, and begs to know if there's any of that kind, which he was so good as to send us last Christmas, to be sold in London.   H.D.

1771

AUTOBIOGRAPHY
BENJAMIN FRANKLIN
LONDON

*Franklin was born in Philadelphia in 1706, 15th of 17 children. An early career as a printer led him to publish pamphlets, papers & the popular annual **Poor Richard's Almanac**. He called it a **proper vehicle for conveying instruction among the common people, who bought scarcely any other books**. He was*

TWYFORD, AT THE BISHOP OF ST. ASAPH'S 1771

DEAR SON, I have ever have a Pleasure in obtaining any little Ancedotes of my Ancestors. You may remember the Enquiries I made among the Remains of my Relations when you were with me in England; and the Journey I took for that purpose. Now imagining it may be equally agreeable to you to know the Circumstances of *my* Life, many of which you are yet unacquainted with; and expecting a Weeks uninterrupted Leisure in my present Country Retirement, I sit down to write them for you. To which I have besides some other Inducements. Having emerg'd from the Poverty and Obscurity in which I was born and bred, to a State of Affluence and some Degree of Reputation in the World, and having gone so far thro' Life with a considerable Share of Felicity, the conducing Means I made use of, which, with the Blessing of God, so well succeeded, my Posterity may like to know, as they may find some of them suitable to their own Situations, and therefore fit to be imitated. That Felicity, when I reflected on it, has induc'd me sometimes to say, that were it offer'd to my Choice, I should have no Objection to a Repetition of the same Life from its Beginning, only asking the Advantage Authors have in a second Edition to correct some Faults of the first. So would I if I might, besides correcting the Faults, change some sinister Accidents and Events of it for others more favourable, but tho' this were deny'd, I should still accept the Offer. However, since such a Repetition is not to be expected, the next Thing most like living one's Life over again, seems to be a *Recollection* of that Life; and to make that Recollection as durable as possible, the putting it down in Writing. Hereby, too, I shall indulge the Inclination so natural in old Men, to be talking of themselves and their own past Actions, and I shall indulge it, without being troublesome to others who thro' respect to Age might think themselves oblig'd to give me a Hearing, since this may be read or not as any one pleases. And lastly, (I may as well confess it, since my Denial of it will be believ'd by no body) perhaps I shall a good deal gratify my own *Vanity*. Indeed I scarce ever heard or saw the introductory Words, *Without Vanity I may say*, &c. but some vain thing immediately follow'd. Most People dislike Vanity in others whatever Share they have of it themselves, but I give it fair Quarter wherever I meet with it,

elected his State's representative, & after 1757, America's leading diplomat in England, negotiating about taxation. As a scientist he discovered the Gulf Stream & nature of electricity; invented the lightning rod & bifocal spectacles; received honorary degrees from Oxford & Edinburgh universities. In 1776 he revised Thomas Jefferson's **USA Declaration of Independence**, *short-ening the wordy opening to read* **We hold these truths to be self-evident, that all men are created equal**, *& is said to have remarked at the signing,* **We must all hang together or, most assuredly, we shall all hang separately.***

As Ambassador to Versailles he got the French Monarchy to help the new USA democracy fight free of Britain: which D.H. Lawrence later saw as a sign of deep-seated hypocrisy, but before everything else he was intensely practical. He came home in 1783, was later elected President of the State of Pennsylvania. A joyfully bawdy man, among his aperçus are:– **Time is money, Man is a tool-making animal**, *&* **In this world nothing can be certain except death and taxes**.*

being persuaded that it is often productive of Good to the Possessor and to others that are within his Sphere of Action: And therefore in many Cases it would not be quite absurd if a Man were to thank God for his Vanity among the other Comforts of Life.

1776

When the 18th century began most notable thinkers & scientists believed in life after death, used a bible & form of worship as a guide to it, yet did not publicly discuss their faiths because the natural world now seemed the only work of God on which they could agree through mathematical logic & experiment. This book made Bentham (1748-1832) leader of those social reformers, later called **Utilitarians***, who rejected imaginary & unmeasurable worlds outside nature. He was a London lawyer's son, a qualified barrister who studied theories of law because he did not need to practise. He rejected the social contract theory that Blackstone had taken from Hobbes & that obliged folk to obey ancestral laws more or less blindly. He held that real rights exist only in working laws that are justified by promoting greatest happiness among most people, they are the only force*

A FRAGMENT ON GOVERNMENT ; or, a Comment on the Commentaries
JEREMY BENTHAM : LONDON

THE AGE we live in is a busy age; in which knowledge is rapidly advancing towards perfection. In the natural world, in particular, every thing teems with discovery and with improvement. The most distant and recondite regions of the earth traversed and explored – the all-vivifying and subtle element of the air so recently analyzed and made known to us – are striking evidences, were all others wanting, of this pleasing truth.

Correspondent to *discovery* and *improvement* in the natural world, is *reformation* in the moral; if that which seems a common notion be, indeed, a true one, that in the moral world there no longer remains any matter for *discovery*. Perhaps, however, this may not be the case: perhaps among such observations as would be best calculated to serve as grounds for reformation, are some which, being observations of matters of fact hitherto either incompletely noticed, or not at all would, when produced, appear capable of bearing the name of discoveries: with so little method and precision have the consequences of this fundamental axiom, *it is the greatest happiness of the greatest number that is measure of right and wrong*, been as yet developed.

Be this as it may, if there be room for making, and if there be use in publishing, *discoveries* in the *natural* world, surely there is not much less room for making, nor much less use in proposing, *reformation* in the *moral*. If it be a matter of importance and of use to us to be made acquainted with *distant* countries, surely it is not a matter of much less importance, nor of much less use to us, to be made better and better acquainted with the chief means of living happily in our *own*: If it be of importance and of use to us to know the principles of the element we breathe, surely it is not of much less importance nor of much less use to comprehend the principles, and endeavour at the improvement of those *laws*, by which alone we breathe it in security. If to this endeavour we should fancy any Author, especially any Author of great name, to *be*, and as far as could in such case be expected, to *avow himself* a determined and persevering enemy, what should we say of him? We should say that the interests of reformation, and through them the welfare of mankind, were inseparably connected with the downfall of his works: of a great part, at least, of the esteem and, influence, which these works might under whatever title have acquired.

Such an enemy it has been my misfortune (and not mine only) to see, or fancy at least I saw, in the Author of the celebrated *Commentaries on the Laws of England*; an Author whose works have had beyond comparison a more extensive circulation, have obtained a greater share of esteem, of applause, and consequently of influence (and that by a title on many grounds so indisputable) than any other writer who on that subject has ever yet appeared.

It is on this account that I conceived, some time since, the design of pointing out some of what appeared to me the capital blemishes of that work, particularly this grand and fundamental one, the antipathy to reformation; or rather, indeed, of laying open and exposing the universal inaccuracy and confusion which seemed to my apprehension to pervade the whole.

binding a people to governments. Earthly joy & pain, he thought, explained the actions of humanity as completely as Newton's formula explained the movement of lifeless bodies. John Mill (Scots journalist, economist & radical) convinced him that democracy was a worthwhile goal. Makers of the French Republic admired him, made him honorary citizen: he said their Declaration of the Rights of Man was **nonsense on stilts.** *He tested all things by their practical use. His ideas for a wagon train running between London & Edinburgh, a Panama canal & frozen peas were premature. He & his associates at last ended hanging for theft & transportation for poaching. They had British jails made to feed & treat prisoners alike, no matter what their social rank, & the 1st English university open to students of any or no religion. Like most Utilitarians Bentham kept his atheism from public view under the general agreement not to discuss religion or attack an established church, but he avoided a Christian burial & now sits, as he willed, embalmed, in his usual clothes, in a cupboard of London University.*

OOOOOOOOOOOOOOOOOOOOOOOOOOOOOOOOOOOOOOOOOOOOOOOOOOOOOOOOOOOOO

A COMMENTARY ON LAWS SHOULD TELL HOW THEY ARE USED UNFAIRLY BESIDES SAYING WHAT THEY ARE. PURELY TECHNICAL INFORMATION CAN BE USED TO BLOCK JUSTICE, BUT REFORM NEEDS MORE INFORM- ATION. BLACKSTONE'S COMMENTARY ARRANGES LAWS UNDER PURELY TECHNICAL HEADINGS SO CAN CONCLUDE THAT IN ENGLISH LAW *EVERYTHING IS AS IT SHOULD BE*, THOUGH IT MAKES CATHOLICISM A CRIME AND DENIES LEGAL PROTECTION TO STREET TRADERS. THE NATURAL WAY TO ARRANGE LAWS IS UNDER THEIR USEFULNESS (BENTHAM CALLS IT UTILITY) IN REDUCING MISERY OR PROMOTING HAPPINESS.

0000000000000000000000000000000000000000000000000000000000

The mischievousness of a bad Law would be detected, at least the utility of it would be rendered suspicious, by the difficulty of finding a place for it in such an arrangement: while, on the other hand, a *technical* arrangement is a sink that with equal facility will swallow any garbage that is thrown into it.

That this advantage may be possessed by a natural arrangement, is not difficult to conceive. Institutions would be characterized by it in the only universal way in which they can be characterized; by the nature of the several *modes* of *conduct* which, by prohibiting, they constitute *offences*.

These offences would be collected into classes denominated by the various modes of their *divergency* from the common *end*; that is, as we have said, by their various forms and degrees of *mischievousness*: in a word, by those properties which are *reasons* for their being made *offences*: and whether any such mode of conduct possesses any such property is a question of experience. Now, a bad Law is that which prohibits a mode of conduct that is *not* mischievous. Thus would it be found impracticable to place the mode of conduct prohibited by a bad law under any denomination of offence, without asserting such a matter of fact as is contradicted by experience. Thus cultivated, in short, the soil of Jurisprudence would be found to repel in a manner every evil institution; like that country which refuses, we are told, to harbour any thing venomous in its bosom.

The *synopsis* of such an arrangement would at once be a compendium of *expository* and of *censorial* Jurisprudence: nor would it serve more effectually to instruct the *subject*, than it would to justify or reprove the *Legislator*.

Such a synopsis, in short, would be at once a map, and that an universal one, of Jurisprudence as it *is*, and a slight but comprehensive sketch of what it *ought to be*.

OOOOOOOOOOOOOOOOOOOOOOOOOOOOOOOOOOOOOOOOOOOOOOOOOOOOOOOOOOOOOOOO

To return to our Author. Embarrassed, as a man must needs be, by this blind and intractable nomenclature, he will be found, I conceive, to have done as much as could reasonably be expected of a writer so circumstanced; and more and better than was done before by any one.

In one part, particularly, of his Synopsis, several fragments of a sort of method which is, or at least comes near to, what may be termed a natural one, are actually to be found. We there read of "*corporal injuries*"; of "offences against *peace*"; against "*health*"; against "*personal security*"; "*liberty*": – "*property*": – light is let in, though irregularly, at various places.

In an unequal imitation of this Synopsis that has lately been performed upon what is called the *Civil Law*, *all* is technical. All, in short, is darkness. Scarce a syllable by which a man would be led to suspect, that the affair in hand were an affair that happiness or unhappiness was at all concerned in.

To return, once more, to our Author's Commentaries. Not even in a *censorial* view would I be understood to deem them altogether without merit. For the institutions commented on, where they are capable of good reasons, good reasons are every now and then given: in which way, so far as it goes, one-half of the Censor's task is well accomplished. Nor is the dark side of the picture left absolutely untouched. Under the head of "Trial by Jury," are some very just and interesting remarks on the yet-remaining imperfections of that mode of trial: and under that of "Assurances by matter of Record," on the lying and extortious jargon of *Recoveries*. So little, however, are these particular remarks of a piece with the general disposition, that shews itself so strongly throughout the work, indeed so plainly adverse to the general maxims that we have seen, that I can scarce bring myself to attribute them to our Author. Not only disorder is announced by them, but remedies, well-imagined remedies, are pointed out. One would think some Angel had been
sowing wheat among our Author's
thistles.

OOO

The chief employment of this Essay, as we have said, has necessarily been *to overthrow*. In the little, therefore, which has been done by it in the way of *setting up*, my view has been not so much to think for the Reader, as to put him upon thinking for himself. This I flatter myself with having done on several interesting topics; and this is all that at present I propose.

Among the few positions of my own which I have found occasion to advance, some I observe which promise to be far from popular. These it is likely may give rise to very warm objections: objections which in themselves I do not wonder at, and which in their motive I cannot but approve. The people are a set of masters whom it is not in a man's power in every instance fully to please, and at the same time faithfully to serve. He that is resolved to persevere without deviation in the line of truth and utility, must have learnt to prefer the still whisper of enduring approbation, to the short-lived bustle of tumultuous applause.

Other passages too there may be, of which some farther explanation may perhaps not unreasonably be demanded. But to give these explanations, and to obviate those objections, is a task which, if executed at all, must be referred to some other opportunity. Consistency forbad our expatiating so far as to lose sight of our Author: since it was the line of his course that marked the boundaries of ours.

1776

THE HISTORY OF THE DECLINE AND FALL OF THE ROMAN EMPIRE
EDWARD GIBBON: LONDON
[FIRST PARAGRAPH OF CHAPTER I
FIRST VOLUME]

Rome at its mightiest is deliberately praised here in words Britons used to praise their own empire, & is then shown collapsing into heaps of ruin through 1300 years of tyranny, civil war, Christianity, barbarian invasion & Mahomedan conquest. Gibbon thought history little more than the register of the crimes,

IN THE SECOND CENTURY of the Christian era, the Empire of Rome comprehended the fairest part of the earth, and the most civilized portion of mankind. The frontiers of that extensive monarchy were guarded by ancient renown and disciplined valour. The gentle, but powerful, influence of laws and manners had gradualy cemented the union of the provinces. Their peaceful inhabitants enjoyed and abused the advantages of wealth and luxury.

The image of a free constitution was preserved with decent reverence; the Roman senate appeared to possess the sovereign authority, and devolved on the emperors all the executive powers of government. During a happy period of more than fourscore years, the public administration was conducted by the virtue and abilities of Nerva, Trajan, Hadrian and the two Antonines. It is the design of this, and of the two succeeding chapters, to describe the prosperous condition of their empire; and afterwards, from the death of Marcus Antoninus, to deduce the most important circumstances of its decline and fall; a revolution which will ever be remembered, and is still felt, by the nations of the earth.

follies & misfortunes of mankind & shows it with witty relish as a warning against the destructive force of religious enthusiasm. He later calls his own civilisation safer than Rome's because it has no central government. All European nations are in it; their wars no longer menace lives & property of the polite; no barbarous invaders can defeat the explosive weapons of their armed forces.

PREFACE TO THE LAST VOLUME

OOOOOOOOOOOOOOOOOOOOOOOOOOOOOOOOOOOOOOOOOOOOOOOOOOOOOOOOOOOOO

GIBBON CONGRATULATES HIMSELF ON LIVING TO FINISH THIS GREAT AND POPULAR WORK, THEN SAYS:

OOOOOOOOOOOOOOOOOOOOOOOOOOOOOOOOOOOOOOOOOOOOOOOOOOOOOOOOOOOOO

I shall soon revisit the banks of the lake of Lausanne, a country which I have known and loved from my early youth. Under a mild government, amidst a beauteous landskip, in a life of leisure and independence, and among a people of easy and elegant manners, I have enjoyed, and may again hope to enjoy, the varied pleasures of retirement and society. But I shall ever glory in the name and character of an Englishman: I am proud of my birth in a free and enlightened country; and the approbation of that country is the best and most honourable reward of my labours. Were I ambitious of any other Patron than the public, I would inscribe this work to a Statesman, who, in a long, a stormy, and at length an unfortunate administration, had many political opponents, almost without a personal enemy: who has retained, in his fall from power, many faithful and

Rent from family land let Gibbon become a historian by studying at Lausanne on Lake Geneva. As a youth he was sent to lodge with a Calvinist cleric there: he had converted to Catholicism & his dad wanted him cured. He became a sceptic & later still an MP & a commissioner of trade under North, a prime minister who provoked the American revolution by obeying George III. Gibbon, then the only English writer with a European outlook, was much more appalled to see civilised France grow enthusiastic & have a revolution too.

disinterested friends; and who, under the pressure of severe infirmity, enjoys the lively vigour of his mind, and the felicity of his incomparable temper. Lord North will permit me to express the feelings of friendship in the language of truth: but even truth and friendship should be silent, if he still dispensed the favours of the crown.

In a remote solitude, vanity may still whisper in my ear, that my readers, perhaps, may enquire, whether, in the conclusion of the present work, I am now taking an everlasting farewell. They shall hear all that I know myself, all that I could reveal to the most intimate friend. The motives of action or silence are now equally balanced, nor can I pronounce in my most secret thoughts, on which side the scale will preponderate. I cannot dissemble that six ample quartos must have tried, and may have exhausted, the indulgence of the Public; that, in the repetition of similar attempts, a successful Author has much more to lose than he can hope to gain; that I am now descending into the vale of years; and that the most respectable of my countrymen, the men whom I aspire to imitate, have resigned the pen of history about the same period of their lives. Yet I consider that the annals of ancient and modern times may afford many rich and interesting subjects; that I am still possessed of health and leisure; that by the practice of writing, some skill and facility must be acquired; and that in the ardent pursuit of truth and knowledge, I am not conscious of decay. To an active mind, indolence is more painful than labour; and the first months of my liberty will be occupied and amused in the excursions of curiosity and taste. By such temptations, I have been sometimes seduced from the rigid duty even of a pleasing and voluntary task: but my time will now be my own; and in the use or abuse of independence, I shall no longer fear my own reproaches or those of my friends. I am fairly entitled to a year of jubilee: next summer and the following winter will rapidly pass away; and experience only can determine whether I shall still prefer the freedom and variety of study to the design and composition of a regular work, which animates, while it confines, the daily application of the Author. Caprice and accident may influence my choice; but the dexterity of self-love will contrive to applaud either active industry, or philosophic repose.

Downing Street, May 1, 1788.

AN INQUIRY INTO THE NATURE AND CAUSES OF THE WEALTH OF NATIONS ADAM SMITH: LONDON

1776

[INTRODUCTION AND PLAN OF THE WORK]

THE annual labour of every nation is the fund which originally supplies it with all the necessaries and conveniences of life which it annually consumes, and which consist always, either in the immediate produce of that labour, or in what is purchased with that produce from other nations.

According therefore, as this produce, or what is purchased with it, bears a greater or smaller proportion to the number of those who are to consume it, the nation will be better or worse supplied with all the necessaries and conveniences for which it has occasion.

But this proportion must in every nation be regulated by two different circumstances; first, by the skill, dexterity, and judgment with which labour is generally applied in it; and, secondly, by the proportion between the number of those who are employed in useful labour, and that of those who are not so employed. Whatever be the soil, climate, or extent of territory of any particular nation, the abundance or scantiness of its annual supply must, in that particular situation, depend upon those two circumstances.

Their abundance or scantiness of this supply too seems to depend more upon the former of those two circumstances than upon the latter. Among the savage nations of hunters and fishers, every individual who is able to work, is more or less employed in useful labour, and endeavours to provide, as well as he can, the necessaries and conveniences of life, for himself, and such of his family or tribe as are either too old, or too young, or too infirm to go a hunting and fishing. Such nations, however, are so miserably poor, that, from mere want, they are frequently reduced, or, at least, think themselves reduced, to the necessity sometimes

His dad, controller of customs at Kirkcaldy, died before his birth in 1723. Smith became head of Scots customs in 1778. In between he taught literature at Edinburgh University, logic & philosophy at Glasgow, conversed on finance & the material grounds of mind with French encyclopaed-ists, but was often with his mother in Kirkcaldy as there he had peace to study & write. Being childless & comfortable with little, he secretly donated money he did not need to charities. His 1st book analysed virtue & based it on sympathy: doing unto others what would help us, if we were thus. His 2nd book was so successful that before a London dinner Pitt, then prime minister, insisted Smith enter the room 1st as everyone else was now his pupil. The Wealth of Nations was based on his per-ception that the 50-mile-wide plain between Clyde & Forth was an international market. Local industry gave it cloth, pottery & hard-ware. Farmers brought wool, drovers highland cattle, fishers their catch. Glasgow ship owners gave it sugar, cotton, tobacco from their estates in Jamaica & America. All raw material Scotland did not buy was sold to England or Europe, surplus cloth & goods to the Americas. Inventive manual workers, coal & iron mining & a money market helped. Land rents funded new business & expanded its capital. This capitalism now held the wealth of England & France too, where monarchs & 1 central government (things capitalism did not need & Scotland mainly lacked) blinded folk to much of it till they read Smith's book. From then on wealthy economists invoked it when persuading their government to serve a money market before all else. They ignored that it said productive labour, not money, is the only true measure of wealth; that kings, lawyers, armed forces & some of the most respectable orders of society are as unproductive as domestic servants; that businessmen's advice should be regarded with suspicion as they generally have an interest to deceive & even oppress the public, that no society can surely flourish & be happy of which the greater part are miserable & poor. Smith's 1st book had said kind feeling is prior to selfishness in making nations. It was his physiological substitute for the Lockean social contract.

of directly destroying, and sometimes of abandoning their infants, their old people, and those afflicted with lingering diseases, to perish with hunger, or to be devoured by wild beasts. Among civilized and thriving nations, on the contrary, though a great number of people do not labour at all, many of whom consume the produce of ten times, frequently of a hundred times more labour than the greater part of those who work; yet the produce of the whole labour of the society is so great, that all are often abundantly supplied, and a workman, even of the lowest and poorest order, if he is frugal and industrious, may enjoy a greater share of the necessaries and conveniences of life than it is possible for any savage to acquire.

The causes of this improvement, in the productive powers of labour, and the order, according to which its produce is naturally distributed among the different ranks and conditions of men in the society, make the subject of the First Book of this Inquiry.

Whatever be the actual state of the skill, dexterity, and judgment with which labour is applied in any nation, the abundance or scantiness of its annual supply, must depend, during the continuance of that state, upon the proportion between the number of those who are annually employed in useful labour, and that of those who are not so employed. The number of useful and productive labourers, it will hereafter appear, is every where in proportion to the quantity of capital stock which is employed in setting them to work, and to the particular way in which it is so employed. The Second Book, therefore, treats of the nature of capital stock, of the manner in which it is gradually accumulated, and of the different quantities of labour which it puts into motion, according to the different ways in which it is employed.

Nations tolerably well advanced as to skill, dexterity, and judgment, in the application of labour, have followed very different plans in the general conduct or direction of it; and those plans have not all been equally favourable to the greatness of its produce. The policy of some nations has given extraordinary encouragement to the industry of the country; that of others to the industry of towns. Scarce any nation has dealt equally and impartially with every sort of industry. Since the downfall of the Roman empire, the policy of Europe has been more favourable to arts, manufactures, and commerce, the industry of towns; than to agriculture, the industry of the country. The circumstances which seem to have introduced and established this policy are explained in the Third Book.

Though those different plans were, perhaps, first introduced by the private interests and prejudices of particular orders of men, without any regard to, or foresight of, their consequences upon the general welfare of the society; yet they have given occasion to very different theories of political œconomy; of which some magnify the importance of that industry which is carried on in towns, others of that which is carried on in the country. Those theories have had a considerable influence, not only upon the opinions of men of learning, but upon the public conduct of princes and sovereign states. I have endeavoured, in the Fourth Book, to explain, as fully and distinctly as I can, those different theories, and the principal effects which they have produced in different ages and nations.

In what has consisted the revenue of the great body of the people, or what is the nature of those funds which, in different ages and nations, have supplied their annual consumption, is treated of in these four first Books. The Fifth and last Book treats of the revenue of the sovereign, or commonwealth. In this Book I have endeavoured to show; first, what are the necessary expences of the sovereign, or commonwealth; which of those expences ought to be defrayed by the general contribution of the whole society; and which of them, by that of some particular part only, or of some particular members of the society; secondly, what are the different methods in which the whole society may be made to contribute towards defraying the expences incumbent on the whole society, and what are the principal advantages and inconveniences of each of those methods: and, thirdly and lastly, what are the reasons and causes which have induced almost all modern governments to mortgage some part of this revenue, or to contract debts, and what have been the effects of those debts upon the real wealth, the annual produce of the land and labour of the society.

1776

THE AMERICAN DECLARATION OF INDEPENDENCE
THOMAS JEFFERSON: PHILADELPHIA

THE UNANIMOUS DECLARATION OF
THE THIRTEEN UNITED STATES OF AMERICA

WHEN in the Course of human events, it becomes necessary for one people to dissolve the political bands which have connected them with another, and to assume among the powers of the earth, the separate and equal station to which the Laws of Nature and of Nature's God entitle them, a decent respect to the opinions of mankind requires that they should declare the causes which impel them to the separation. We hold these truths to be self-evident, that all men are created equal, that they are endowed by their Creator with certain unalienable Rights, that among these are Life, Liberty and the pursuit of Happiness. That to secure these rights, Governments are instituted among Men, deriving their just powers from the consent of the governed, That whenever any Form of Government becomes destructive of these ends, it is the Right of the People to alter or to abolish it, and to institute new Government, laying its foundation on such principles and organizing its powers in such form, as to them shall seem most likely to effect their Safety and Happiness. Prudence, indeed, will dictate that Governments long established should not be changed for light and transient causes; and accordingly all experience hath shewn, that mankind are more disposed to suffer, while evils are sufferable, than to right themselves by abolishing the forms to which they are accustomed. But when a long train of abuses and usurpations, pursuing invariably the same Object evinces a design to reduce them under absolute Despotism, it is their right, it is their duty, to throw off such Government, and to provide new Guards for their future security. Such has been the patient sufferance of these Colonies; and such is now the necessity which constrains them to alter their former Systems of Government. The history of the present King of Great Britain is a history of repeated injuries and usurpations, all having in direct object the establishment of an absolute Tyranny over these States.

To prove this, let Facts be submitted to a candid world.

Throughout this century Britain & France fought for empire in Europe, India, Africa, the Caribbean. To stop Britain's Atlantic colonies spreading to the Pacific the French built a line of forts from Quebec down to Louisiana. Virginian militia led by George Washington attacked a fort & started warfare in America. French colonists, though fewer than British, had more redskin allies & were beaten by the Royal Navy keeping French troops out & landing British troops who took Quebec. Britain wanted compensation for defending its colonies so tried to tax them, but colonial assemblies were as money-minded as Britain's parliament & could now rule their states without it. As popular resistance to taxes grew violent the assemblies sent represent-atives to a continental con-gress. From Virginia came Jefferson, landlord, slave-owner, lawyer. He wrote this declaration. The rest amended & signed.

The only earlier document declaring the independence of a nation was written by an abbot of Arbroath in 1320 & signed by landlords & clan chiefs. They too had come to lead what began as popular resistance to the Westminster government & their declar-ation promised freedom from foreign rule to everyone in Scotland. But Jefferson's Declaration was a social contract 1st imagined by Hobbes & Locke. By signing, the delegates of the states swore that the American people gave them the right to make a new government if, & only if, it guarded all people's equal right to Life, Liberty & the pursuit of Happiness. The word **Happiness** replaced **Property** in the 1st draft as slaves WERE property so unable to pursue it. Many who signed this contract meant it to exclude slaves, redskins, women & others too poor to be allowed a vote, for these were not people with a capital P.

To others this declaration was & is a true statement of the democratic idea – a goal to keep working for. But politicians must barter & compromise. Founders of the republic who disliked slavery kept quiet about it as they needed the slave-owners' help. Jefferson, as 3rd USA president, did many good things. Shame at the com-promises they required led him, when writing his epitaph, to say only that he had founded Virginia's University, made laws that stopped religions deciding state appointments, & had written the Declaration of American Independence. It was 1st of those North American state documents whose clear strong speech was the USA's best early literature. The clarity was from the Bible & Calvinist sermons, logical style from Coke & Blackstone, a pithy raciness from journalism by Franklin & Tom Paine: men who encouraged Americans to win the war for democracy.

A VOYAGE TOWARDS THE SOUTH POLE, AND ROUND THE WORLD CAPTAIN JAMES COOK: LONDON 1777

The son of a Scottish farm labourer who emigrated to Yorkshire, Cook learned to sail ships on a North Sea coal carrier & in his spare time taught himself to be the greatest navigator & marine carto-grapher of his age. The British government put him in command of 3 Pacific expedi-tions in 1768–71, 1772–75, 1777–78, to advance trade,

science & find a southern continent as big as North America & as profitable. He killed the last idea by sailing further south than men had ever done, charting undiscovered islands, New Zealand & East Australia. (The government ships that next went there carried convicts the USA then refused, as black slaves could be driven harder.) His book has no fine

preface; is based on diaries describing natural phenomena & Pacific people accurately, vividly & without racial prejudice. He ate all he saw natives eat, & disgusted his men & saved them from scurvy (which had killed most folk on long sea voyages) by making them eat vegetables and fruit. Hawaiian islanders killed him in 1779.

1787

POEMS:
CHIEFLY IN THE SCOTTISH DIALECT
ROBERT BURNS: EDINBURGH
[TO THE NOBLEMEN AND GENTLEMEN OF THE
CALEDONIAN HUNT]

MY Lords, and Gentlemen, A Scottish Bard, proud of the name, whose ambition is to sing in his Country's service, where shall he so properly look for patronage as to the illustrious Names of his Native Land; those who bear the honours and inherit the virtues of their Ancestors? – The Poetic Genius of my Country found me as the prophetic bard Elijah did Elisha – at the *plough*; and threw her inspiring *mantle* over me. She bade me sing the loves, joys, rural scenes and rural pleasures of my natal Soil, in my native tongue: I tuned my wild, artless notes, as she inspired. – She whispered me to come to this ancient metropolis of Caledonia, and lay my Songs under your protection: I now obey her dictates. Though indebted to your goodness, I do not approach you, my Lords and Gentlemen, in the usual stile of dedication, to thank you for past favours; that path is so hackneyed by prostituted Learning, that honest Rusticity is ashamed of it. – Nor do I present this Address with the soul of a servile Author, looking for a continuation of favours: I was bred to the Plough, and am independent. I come to claim the common Scottish name with you, my illustrious Countrymen; and to tell the world that I glory in the title. I congratulate my Country, that the blood of her ancient heroes still runs uncontaminated; and that from your courage, knowledge, and public spirit, she may expect protection, wealth, and liberty. In the last place, I proffer my warmest wishes to the Great Fountain of Honour, the Monarch of the Universe, for your welfare and happiness. When you go forth to waken the Echoes, in the ancient and favourite amusement of your Forefathers, may Pleasure ever be of your party; and may Social-joy await your return! When harassed in courts or camps with the justlings of bad men and bad measures, may the honest consciousness of injured Worth attend your return to your native Seats; and may Domestic Happiness, with a smiling welcome, meet you at your gates! May Corruption shrink at your kindling indignant glance; and may tyranny in the Ruler and licentiousness in the People equally find you an inexorable foe!

I have the honour to be, with sincerest gratitude and highest respect,
My Lords And Gentlemen, Your most devoted humble servant.
ROBERT BURNS, April 4, 1787.

[A Dedication to Gavin Hamilton Esq;]

*E*XPECT na, Sir, in this narration,
A fleechan, fleth'ran Dedication,
*To roose you up, an' ca' you guid,
An' sprung o' great an' noble bluid;
Because ye're sirnam'd like* His Grace,
*Perhaps related to the race:
Then when I'm tir'd – and sae are* ye,
*Wi' monie a fulsome, sinfu' lie,
Set up a face, how I stop short,
For fear your modesty be hurt.*

*This may do – maun do, Sir, wi' them wha
Maun please the Great-folk for a wamefou;
For me! sae laigh I need na bow,
For,* LORD *be thanket,* I can plough;
*And when I downa yoke a naig,
Then,* LORD *be thanket,* I can beg;
*Sae I shall say, an' that's nae flatt'rin,
It's just* sic Poet *an'* sic Patron.

*The Poet, some guid Angel help him,
Or else, I fear, some ill ane skelp him!
He may do weel for a' he's done yet,
But only – he's no just begun yet.
The Patron, (Sir, ye maun forgie me,
I winna lie, come what will o' me)
On ev'ry hand it will allow'd be,
He's just – nae better than he should be.*

*I readily and freely grant,
He downa see a poor man want;
What's no his ain, he winna tak it;
What ance he says, he winna break it;
Ought he can lend he'll no refus't,
Till aft his guidness is abus'd;
And rascals whyles that do him wrang,
Ev'n that, he does na mind it lang:*

The prose dedication has no Scots folk-speech for here Burns shows readers he can write the South British dialect also. Like Spenser & Milton in **The Shepherd's Calendar** & *Lycidas* he artfully calls himself an artless rustic, knowing he is a thoroughly educated poet & (unlike them) a real farmer also. By asking the Monarch of the Universe to help Scots gentry overcome bad men & bad measures in courts & camps & tyranny in the Ruler he is siding with the reformers who opposed war with the USA & wanted a British democracy to end control of parliament by a king & lords. The VERSE dedication shows the full range of his vocabulary & thought in lowland Scots vernacular. From Pope he has learned to turn a private letter into a public statement of faith: faith in the body, not soul, as the source of our virtues. To know how such a bilingual democrat occurred, look back to North America.

That all men are created equal was self-evident to many there, for by uniting in militias that expelled redskins they got limitless cheap land. Each farm & estate, whether the owner & his family or his slaves worked it, fed & clad its people with hardly any rent or taxes, so small farmers could claim social equality with great landlords. Not so in England, where they were losing ground to them. Rents were raised while the rich used new crops & methods to get more produce from fewer workers. But these methods let thin soil in the Scots lowlands be cultivated for the 1st time. Landlords let out parcels of it for low rent to folk who toiled to make it pay, after

which rent (of course) was raised,
but for a while farmers of that
class felt nobody but God & his
weather was over them. Burns'
dad had been gardener at a big
house & won that hard independence in a series of poor
upland Ayrshire farms. He had
no capital so a bad harvest would
ruin him. When 13 his eldest son
Robert strained his heart toiling
to save a harvest in foul weather.
It made him a prey to fits of
depression & killed him at 37, but
his mind was formed by the
independent republic of a small
farm with an unusually broad
outlook.

   From his mother & an old
farm worker, Betty Davidson, he
learned Scots stories, ballads &
songs. His dad & a neighbour
paid a university student to teach
their children in vacations.
Robert read Shakespeare, Milton,
some French, Ramsay's **Ever
Green**, Hary's **Wallace** (that
**poured a Scottish prejudice in
my veins**), Locke, Richardson,
Sterne, & Robert Fergusson, the
Scots vernacular poet who died
at 24 in an Edinburgh Bedlam:
**my elder brother in Misfortune/
By far my elder Brother in the
muse**. When 15 he **1st committed
the sin of RHYME** in a song
made for a girl he had partnered
when harvesting & was soon a
great sinner. He had a quizzical
interest in the Scots kirk, then
split between moderates who did
not think most folk were damned
& old Calvinists who KNEW they
were. His 1st satirical verse was
against old Calvinists. He joined
the freemasons, widespread at
this time for they asserted
brotherhood across social
barriers many now thought
absurd. The founders of the USA,

As Master, Landlord, Husband, Father,
He does na fail his part in either.

But then, nae thanks to him for a' that;
Nae godly symptom ye can ca' that;
It's naething but a milder feature,
Of our poor, sinfu', corrupt Nature:
Ye'll get the best o' moral works,
'Mang black Gentoos, and Pagan Turks,
Or Hunters wild on Ponotaxi,
Wha never heard of Orth–d–xy.
That he's the poor man's friend in need,
The GENTLEMAN in word and deed,
It's no through terror of D–mn–t–n;
It's just a carnal inclination.

Morality, thou deadly bane,
Thy tens o' thousands thou hast slain!
Vain is his hope, whase stay an' trust is,
In moral Mercy, Truth and Justice!

No – stretch a point to catch a plack;
Abuse a Brother to his back;
Steal thro' the winnock frae a wh–re,
But point the Rake that taks the door;
Be to the Poor like onie whunstane,
And haud their noses to the grunstane;
Ply ev'ry art o' legal thieving;
No matter – stick to sound believing.

Learn three-mile pray'rs, an' half-mile graces,
Wi' weel spread looves, an' lang, wry faces;
Grunt up a solemn, lengthen'd groan,
And damn a' Parties but your own;
I'll warrant then, ye're nae Deceiver,
A steady, sturdy, staunch Believer.

O ye wha leave the springs o' C–lv–n,

For gumlie dubs *of your ain delvin!*
Ye sons of Heresy and Error,
Ye'll some day *squeel in quaking terror!*
When Vengeance draws the sword in wrath,
And in the fire throws the sheath;
When Ruin, with his sweeping besom,
Just frets till Heav'n *commission gies him;*
While o'er the Harp *pale Misery moans,*
And strikes the ever-deep'ning tones,
Still louder shrieks, and heavier groans!

Your pardon, Sir, for this digression,
I maist forgat my Dedication;
But when Divinity comes cross me,
My readers still are sure to lose me.
So Sir, you see 'twas nae daft vapour,
But I maturely thought it proper,
When a' my works I did review,
To dedicate *them, Sir, to* YOU:
Because (ye need na tak it ill)
I thought them something like yoursel.

Then patronize them wi' your favor,
And your Petitioner shall ever –
I had amaist said, ever pray,
But that's a word I need na say:
For prayin I hae little skill o't;
I'm baith dead-sweer, an' wretched ill o't;
But I'se repeat each poor man's pray'r,
That kens or hears about you, Sir –

"May ne'er Misfortune's gowling bark,
"Howl thro' the dwelling o' the CLERK!
"May ne'er his gen'rous, honest heart,
"For that same gen'rous spirit smart!
"May K———'s far-honor'd name
"Lang beet his hymeneal flame,
"Till H———'s, at least a diz'n,

French encyclopaedists, German & English princes & Mozart were members. The companionship of lairds, lawyers & tradesmen after a week of open-air slogging fed Burns' faith in social union & scorn of claims to a higher authority. He started a club of bachelor youths who swore to pursue sexual joy & support illegitimate offspring. Burns added 4 to families he supported after his father died, but made 2 legitimate by wedding Jean Armour, their mother. But before that he printed by subscription this book of poems. He was 27.

Great writing is only quickly & lastingly popular when it uses common speech uncommonly well. Shakespeare did that. *Hamlet* uses words from the trades of manual workers, words Dr Johnson thought polite folk did not need. The polite practised a diction soon called **The King's (or Queen's) English** & as far from the speech of commoners & tradesmen as possible. Since Pope all big poetic efforts except **The Deserted Village** & Gray's **Elegy** had been warped by genteel diction. Posh Scots used it when writing & when on business in England, often relaxing into common Scots at home. These poems to a mouse, louse, haggis, whisky, lawyers & devil, with tender love songs, satirical prayer & reflective epistle made sense to all Scots ranks & many others. In 1787 it was printed in London, pirated in Dublin, Belfast, New York, Philadelphia. Burns earned enough to visit Edinburgh, tour Scotland & rent what looked a better farm. Famed as a national bard, he was still outside the class who obtained well-paid, leisurely

work. The farm failed. He
became exciseman, patrolling a
coast to police & measure
imports. In spare moments he
tackled the only writing his
divided time allowed.

He collected over 300 lyrics
in the speech of the Lowland
commoners which he wanted to
live long beyond him. Editing
different versions into 1,
completing fragments with his
own words yet keeping the
vernacular idiom, fitting each
lyric to a popular old tune, he
gave classic form to some of the
world's best songs. Though
commissioned by publishers he
refused to be paid, saying the
songs were not his but the Scots
people's. Until the end of his short
troubled life he also added brave
songs of his own that most Scots
now think THEIR property.

Like most British democrats
Burns thought the French
Revolution was starting a better
age for everyone, & still thought
so when King Louis & his wife
were beheaded for trying to join
the Austrians at war with France.
This got him shunned by middle-
class neighbours & threatened
with loss of work. It also inspired
him to write 2 of his most popular
songs, **Scots Wha Hae Wi'
Wallace Bled** in praise of
freedom, & **A Man's a Man for
A' That** praising social equality
& mocking monarchs & nobility.
In 1999 promoters of a new Scots
parliament chose the last as a
national anthem. It was sung in
public before the Queen, lords
and newly elected Commons in
Edinburgh. At a banquet given
to these dignitaries afterwards it
was sung again, but the verses
satirising inherited privilege and
wealth were omitted.

"Are frae their nuptial labors risen:
"Five bonie Lasses round their table,
"And sev'n braw fellows, stout an' able,
"To serve their King an' Country weel,
"By word, or pen, or pointed steel!
"May Health and Peace, with mutual rays,
"Shine on the ev'ning o' his days;
"Till his wee, curlie John's *ier-oe,*
"When ebbing life nae mair shall flow,
"The last, sad, mournful rites bestow!"

I will not wind a lang conclusion,
With complimentary effusion:
But whilst your wishes and endeavours,
Are blest with Fortune's smiles and favours,
I am, Dear Sir, with zeal most fervent,
Your much indebted, humble servant.

But if, which Pow'rs above prevent,
That iron-hearted Carl, Want,
Attended, in his grim advances,
By sad mistakes, *and* black mischances,
While hopes, and joys, and pleasures fly him,
Make you as poor a dog as I am,
Your humble servant then no more;
For who would humbly serve the Poor?
But by a poor man's hopes in Heav'n!
While recollection's pow'r is giv'n,
If, in the vale of humble life,
The victim sad of Fortune's strife,
I, through the tender-gushing tear,
Should recognise my Master *dear,*
If friendless, low, we meet together,
Then, Sir, your hand –
                    my FRIEND *and* BROTHER.

FRANCE REMADE

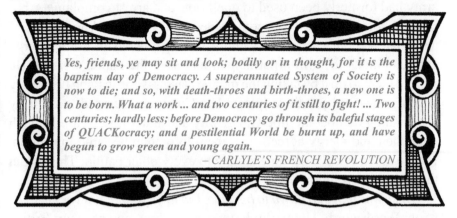

AT THE END OF THE EIGHTEENTH CENTURY
Robert Burns became the greatest living poet in English, mainly because he used strong forms of speech common among lowland Scots. In south Britain poetry was blighted by a genteel assumption that common speech-forms, like common people, were not truly civilised. A social shake-up was needed to help a new generation of poets write strongly of universal things, a shake-up as great as the Black Death, Protestant Reformation and parliamentary wars. France supplied it.

France was Europe's richest centralised monarchy, a land owned by families so ancient and exclusive that compared with them British royalty and nobility were all *parvenus*. As in Britain the king and great landlords chose the clergy (a Catholic clergy) leaving administration, law and finance to a middle class. But the British middle class was large, open to successful tradesmen, had wealthy members who spoke in parliament and joined the aristocracy. The French bourgeoisie were a small part of so large a nation, as exclusive as their nobility and with no say in government. Yet France led Europe in military organisation, palace architecture, polite manners and literature. French speech was so fashionable among European ruling classes that Sam Johnson feared English might become a French dialect.

Yet a vast French majority were peasants whose work fed, clothed and fuelled the rest, and were taxed to the verge of hunger and sometimes starvation by unproductive nobility who obstinately refused to pay taxes, supported a world-wide imperial war that Britain won, and by 1787 had reduced France to bankruptcy. The monarchy could not pay its servants' wages and interest on loans it had incurred. This caused outcries. The army had formerly been used to quell riots and arrest complainers, but now the soldiers themselves complained of pay arrears. After a century and a half without a national assembly the king ordered his Lords, Clergy and Commons to form a parliament and save the nation's credit. He wished them to do it by taxing the middle classes while leaving hereditary wealth, titles and privilege intact. The Commons decided to do it by establishing democratic liberty, equality and fraternity for all. Enough noblemen and clergy agreed with them to outnumber any opposition. France again felt she set an example to every other nation. This began the French Revolution.

Bliss was it in that dawn to be alive, But to be young was very heaven wrote Wordsworth. He was in France at the time, one of many British radicals who hoped their country would follow where France led. Britain too had a huge population with no say in a government whose king and House of Lords were superior to taxation, and mainly used the national revenue to pension their supporters and wage war. But the French democrats were forced to wage war too. Noblemen who feared to lose their great estates supported an invasion ordered by foreign kings determined to smash the new republic. French citizens quickly improvised armies whose amazing counter-attacks made Austria, Germany and Italy parts of a new French empire, but that came later.

In its seven-year existence the revolutionary government, by public execution or indiscriminate massacre, ordered or caused the killing of roughly four thousand people: aristocrats, bourgeoisie, royalty, peasants and leaders of the revolution itself. This number is (very roughly of course) a nearly two hundredth part of those killed in the seven-year war between Austria and Prussia thirty years before, a war that enlarged one nation at the expense of the other, did no harm to the monarchs who ordered it, gave hope of a better future to nobody. The Revolution killings sprang from a great effort at social betterment, so are still used as a terrible warning by writers who find deaths caused by well-established governments (even death through famine and poverty) natural and lawful.

So once again, as in the time of Langland and Tyndal, Shakespeare and Milton, minds were stirred by great events. They loosed the hold of gentility on the best English authors, except in sexual matters. In the 19th century prudishness banned honest writing about sexual love, even
by Irish, Scots and Americans on whom
gentility never had much hold.

THE DISTURBED ESTABLISHMENT

Eighteen hundred years: Man was a dream.
Shadows of men in fleeting bands upon the winds
Divide, the heavens of Europe
The cloud bears hard on Albions shore

1790

Burke's **Reflections** are perhaps the first major statement of modern Conservatism as a social & political philosophy. Written in response to the French Revolution & before the Reign of Terror, it was soon recognised as a true prophecy of what was to come, while giving a philosophical account of its inevitability. Burke defended old traditions, "prejudice" & inherited authority against what he saw as the invented "rights" & botched constitution of the new Republic of France. **The Rights of Man,** he argued, make no sense if the duties of man are not firmly specified & upheld by custom. He disputed the liberal philosophy of the social contract that Rousseau expounded & the Revolutionaries upheld, foreseeing that, unless moderated by custom & deference, it excused tyranny. He argued that society is indeed a contract – but not, as in democratic theory, between the living only. It is a long-term partnership between the living, the dead & the unborn. The members of the Revolutionary National Assembly, by enforcing their right to control all

REFLECTIONS ON THE REVOLUTION IN FRANCE

EDMUND BURKE: LONDON

AND ON THE PROCEEDINGS IN CERTAIN SOCIETIES IN LONDON RELATIVE TO THAT EVENT: IN A LETTER INTENDED TO HAVE BEEN SENT TO A GENTLEMAN IN PARIS.

DEAR SIR, You are pleased to call again, and with some earnestness, for my thoughts on the late proceedings in France. *OOOOOOOOOOOOOOOOOOOO* You see, Sir, by the long letter I have transmitted to you, that though I do most heartily wish that France may be animated by a spirit of rational liberty, and that I think you bound, in all honest policy, to provide a permanent body in which that spirit may reside, and an effectual organ by which it may act, it is my misfortune to entertain great doubts concerning several points in your late transactions.

You imagined, when you wrote last, that I might possibly be reckoned among the approvers of certain proceedings in France, from the solemn public seal of sanction they have received from two clubs of gentlemen in London, called the Constitutional Society, and the Revolution Society.

I certainly have the honour to belong to more clubs than one, in which the constitution of this kingdom, and the principles of the glorious Revolution, are held in high reverence; and I reckon myself among the most forward in my zeal for maintaining that constitution and those principles in their utmost purity and vigour. It is because I do so that I think it necessary for me that there should be no mistake. Those who cultivate the memory of our Revolution, and those who are attached to the constitution of this kingdom, will take good care how they are involved with persons, who under the pretext of zeal towards the Revolution and constitution too frequently wander from their true principles; and are ready on every occasion to depart from the firm but cautious and deliberate spirit which produced the one, and which presides in the other. Before I proceed to answer the more material particulars in your letter, I shall beg leave to give you such information as I have been able to obtain of the two clubs which have thought proper, as bodies, to interfere in the concerns of France; first assuring you, that I am not, and that I have never been, a member of either of those societies.

The first, calling itself the Constitutional Society, or Society for Constitutional Information, or by some such title, is, I believe, of seven or eight years standing. The institution of this society appears to be of a charitable, and so far of a laudable nature: it was intended for the circulation, at the expense of the members, of many books, which few other would be at the expense of buying; and which might lie on the hands of the booksellers, to the great loss of an useful body of men. Whether the books, so charitably circulated, were ever as charitably read, is more than I know. Possibly several of them have been exported to France; and, like goods not in request here, may with you have found a market. I have heard much talk of the lights to be drawn from books that are sent from hence. What improvements they have had in their passage (as it is said some liquors are meliorated by crossing the sea) I cannot tell: but I never heard a man of common judgment, or the least degree of information, speak a word in praise of the greater part of the publications circulated by that society; nor have their proceedings been accounted, except by some of themselves, as of any serious consequence.*OOOOOOOOOOOOOOOOOOOO*
BUT A GROUP OF RELIGIOUS DISSENTERS CALLED THE REVOLUTION SOCIETY HAVE CONGRATULATED THE FRENCH NATIONAL ASSEMBLY AND BEEN THANKED BY IT.
OOOOOOOOOOOOOOOOOOOOOOOOOOOOOOOOOOOOOOOOOO

the resources of France, had jeopardised their inheritance & had also instituted a habit of squandering it without regard for future generations, in response to a crisis they were themselves causing. Burke eloquently defended aristocracy as the guardian of basic liberties, monarchy as a way of understanding the ultimate arbitrariness of human fate, inherited religion as instilling that piety without which nobody is satisfied with life on earth. He castigated the shallow logic of the Revolutionaries, their hubristic confidence that they could devise from the small stock of reason in their own heads a substitute for the bank of reason stored over very many centuries, in custom, tradition & ancient laws. The style of the **Reflections** *is subtle & imaginative, a masterly union of abstract philosophy & concrete evocation. It also has some notoriously sentimental purple passages. Despite these flaws the* **Reflections** *are revered by Conservatives, as they contain the core conceptions of their world-view, made fully articulate for the first time.*

In the ancient principles and conduct of the club, so far at least as they were declared, I see nothing to which I could take exception. I think it probable, that for some purpose, new members have entered among them; and that some truly Christian politicians, who love to dispense benefits, but are careful to conceal the hand which distributes the dole, have made them the instruments of their pious designs. Whatever I have reason to suspect I shall speak of nothing as of a certainty but what is public.

For one, I should be sorry to be thought, directly or indirectly, concerned in their proceedings. I certainly take my full share, along with the rest of the world, in my individual and private capacity, in speculating on what has been done, or is doing, on the public stage, in any place ancient or modern; in the republic of Rome, or in the republic of Paris; but having no general apostolical mission, being a citizen of a particular state, and being bound up, in a considerable degree, by its public will, I should think it at least improper and irregular for me to open a formal public correspondence with the actual government of a foreign nation, without the express authority of the government under which I live.

1791 *RIGHTS OF MAN, Being an answer to Mr. Burke's attack on the French Revolution* **THOMAS PAINE: LONDON**

TO GEORGE WASHINGTON, PRESIDENT OF THE
UNITED STATES OF AMERICA

SIR, I PRESENT YOU a small Treatise in defence of those Principles of Freedom which your exemplary Virtue hath so eminently contributed to establish. – That the Rights of Man may become as universal as your Benevolence can wish, and that you may enjoy the Happiness of seeing the New World regenerate the Old, is the Prayer of

SIR, Your much obliged, and

Obedient humble Servant,

THOMAS PAINE.

[PREFACE TO THE ENGLISH EDITION]

FROM THE PART Mr. Burke took in the American Revolution, it was natural that I should consider him a friend to mankind; and as our acquaintance commenced on that ground, it would have been more agreeable to me to have had cause to continue in that opinion, than to change it.

At the time Mr. Burke made his violent speech last winter in the English

Parliament against the French Revolution and the National Assembly, I was in Paris, and had written him, but a short time before, to inform him how prosperously matters were going on. Soon after this, I saw his advertisement of the Pamphlet he intended to publish: As the attack was to be made in a language but little studied, and less understood, in France, and as every thing suffers by translation, I promised some of the friends of the Revolution in that country, that whenever Mr. Burke's Pamphlet came forth, I would answer it. This appeared to me the more necessary to be done, when I saw the flagrant misrepresentations which Mr. Burke's Pamphlet contains; and that while it is an outrageous abuse on the French Revolution, and the principles of Liberty, it is an imposition on the rest of the world.

I am the more astonished and disappointed at this conduct in Mr. Burke, as (from the circumstance I am going to mention), I had formed other expectations.

I had seen enough of the miseries of war, to wish it might never more have existence in the world, and that some other mode might be found out to settle the differences that should occasionally arise in the neighbourhood of nations. This certainly might be done if Courts were disposed to set honestly about it, or if countries were enlightened enough not to be made the dupes of Courts. The people of America had been bred up in the same prejudices against France, which at that time characterized the people of England; but experience and an acquaintance with the French Nation have most effectually shown to the Americans the falsehood of those prejudices; and I do not believe that a more cordial and confidential intercourse exists between any two countries than between America and France.

When I came to France in the Spring of 1787, the Archbishop of Toulouse was then Minister, and at that time highly esteemed. I became much acquainted with the private Secretary of that Minister, a man of an

*This was Britain's most influential pamphlet, its author a tradesman who went to America, served the US army & government, & was rewarded by Congress. Back in England he became friendly with Burke & other Whig MPs who opposed King George's Tories. With the French Revolution most Whigs became Tory too, & Burke wrote his defence of the hereditary elites. Paine addressed this rebuttal to the 95% of Britons denied the vote by their birthplace, poverty or religion. In language as plain as any Quaker meeting house & as streamlined as a piece of Shaker furniture, he said Burke offered them **perpetual serfdom under the authority of the dead over the living**, as he defended inherited privileges that let a few families use parliament to enrich themselves & their supporters & fight wars for profit. They would never let parliament be reformed by folk outside it so the people should elect their own representatives to a National Convention that would adopt a constitution like the French, declaring –*

1 Men are born to

free & equal rights; so titles should be founded only on public usefulness.

2 All political groups should aim to preserve everyone's right to liberty, property, safety & their right to resist oppression.

3 No single PER-SON or GROUP has right to rule a nation when not entitled by an assembly representing all the people.

In a chapter called **Ways & Means** *he showed how taxes now spent on pensions & grants to the rich could fund public schools, health-care & old age pensions for all.*

Pitt's cabinet offered Paine 1000 guineas (about a quarter million in today's money) for the copyright. He refused & beat censorship by swiftly having a big cheap edition printed, then avoided arrest for sedition by escaping to France. The book was a best-seller, especially in Scotland where the Society of Friends of the People held 4 National Conventions, each with more Plebeian members than the last, before the leaders were arrested. Burns A Man's a Man for A' That *gave Paine's ideas universal expression. (P.S. The rumour that Burke had been awarded a state pension was true.)*

enlarged benevolent heart; and found, that his sentiments and my own perfectly agreed with respect to the madness of war, and the wretched impolicy of two nations, like England and France, continually worrying each other, to no other end than that of a mutual increase of burdens and taxes. That I might be assured I had not misunderstood him, nor he me, I put the substance of our opinions into writing, and sent it to him; subjoining a request, that if I should see among the people of England, any disposition to cultivate a better understanding between the two nations than had hitherto prevailed, how far I might be authorized to say that the same disposition prevailed on the part of France? He answered me by letter in the most unreserved manner, and that not for himself only, but for the Minister, with whose knowledge the letter was declared to be written.

I put this letter into the hands of Mr. Burke almost three years ago, and left it with him, where it still remains; hoping, and at the same time naturally expecting, from the opinion I had conceived of him, that he would find some opportunity of making a good use of it, for the purpose of removing those errors and prejudices, which two neighbouring nations, from the want of knowing each other, had entertained, to the injury of both.

When the French Revolution broke out, it certainly afforded to Mr. Burke an opportunity of doing some good, had he been disposed to it; instead of which, no sooner did he see the old prejudices wearing away, than he immediately began sowing the seeds of a new inveteracy, as if he were afraid that England and France would cease to be enemies. That there are men in all countries who get their living by war, and by keeping up the quarrels of Nations, is as shocking as it is true; but when those who are concerned in the government of a country, make it their study to sow discord, and cultivate prejudices between Nations, it becomes the more unpardonable.

With respect to a paragraph in this Work alluding to

Mr. Burke's having a pension, the report has been some time in circulation, at least two months; and as a person is often the last to hear what concerns him the most to know, I have mentioned it, that Mr. Burke may have an opportunity of contradicting the rumour, if he thinks proper.

THE MARRIAGE OF HEAVEN AND HELL
WILLIAM BLAKE
LONDON

1791

[THE ARGUMENT]

*R*INTRAH *roars & shakes*
          his fires in the burdend air;
Hungry clouds swag on the deep.

Once meek, and in a perilous path,
The just man kept his course along
The vale of death.
Roses are planted where thorns grow,
And on the barren heath
Sing the honey bees.

Then the perilous path was planted:
And a river, and a spring
On every cliff and tomb;
And on the bleached bones
Red clay brought forth.

Till the villain left the paths of ease,
To walk in perilous paths, and drive
The just man into barren climes.

Now the sneaking serpent walks
In mild humility,
And the just man rages in the wilds
Where lions roam.

Rintrah roars & shakes
          his fires in the burdend air;
Hungry clouds swag on the deep.

These verses give images in plain speech, telling us that (as a later poet said) **Times They Are A-Changing**, *& turbulently. What else they say is obscure. It is in a tradition forcibly obscured by rulers who thought it dangerous & polite folk who thought it rude: the English Bible tradition. Begun by Lollards, renewed by Tyndal, for 3 centuries it informed all great writing, secular & religious, inspiring both Anglicans & those who beheaded an Anglican king. Most rulers disliked it. By 1700 English universities & public schools mainly taught Greek & Latin classics promoting the cool, oligarchic virtues of courage in battle, & generosity when sharing loot. That & the French tongue became* POLITE *education. The native tradition was left to Dissenting artisans & tradesmen who still thought God's word & love needed discussion, still described mental & social states in Bible words. Only by rebellion had such folk a say in how their land was ruled. Blake, an engraver living by book illustration, was 1 of many who thought the established church & government a whore serving a dragon, & welcomed the Revolution. When parliament banned republican books in 1793, Blake helped Paine escape to France. His own subversive prophetic books were too obscure to alarm a censor, unlike* **The Rights of Man**.

1792

*Her shifty & often drunk dad wasted inherited cash, left family care to a wife who left it to Mary, eldest of 3 daughters. Mary learned how to depend on her own judgment, also learned foreign tongues. With her sisters she started a small private school. It failed but she was kindly encouraged by Dr. Johnson, then got work from a Dissenting publisher, also called Johnson. He printed her novel, stories & French & German translations, some illustrated by Blake. She was now in a group Burke suspected of treason since it sent letters to congratulate the French National Assembly. Before Paine wrote a **Vindication of the Rights of Man** against Burke's **Reflections on the Revolution**, Mary wrote another. This book upon **The Rights of Women** was printed 2 years later, just before she visited Paris to report on the Revolution from its centre. She was held there for 2 years by the outbreak of war between France & Britain & by an American she loved. Liberty in politics & sex*

VINDICATION OF THE RIGHTS OF WOMEN: with strictures on political and moral subjects
MARY WOLLSTONECRAFT: LONDON

AFTER considering the historic page, and viewing the living world with anxious solicitude, the most melancholy emotions of sorrowful indignation have depressed my spirits, and I have sighed when obliged to confess that either Nature has made a great difference between man and man, or that the civilization which has hitherto taken place in the world has been very partial. I have turned over various books written on the subject of education, and patiently observed the conduct of parents and the management of schools; but what has been the result? – a profound conviction that the neglected education of my fellow-creatures is the grand source of the misery I deplore; and that women, in particular, are rendered weak and wretched by a variety of concurring causes, originating from one hasty conclusion. The conduct and manners of women, in fact, evidently prove that their minds are not in a healthy state; for, like the flowers which are planted in too rich a soil, strength and usefulness are sacrificed to beauty; and the flaunting leaves, after having pleased a fastidious eye, fade, disregarded on the stalk, long before the season when they ought to have arrived at maturity. – One cause of this barren blooming I attribute to a false system of education, gathered from the books written on this subject by men who, considering females rather as women than human creatures, have been more anxious to make them alluring mistresses than rational wives; and the understanding of the sex has been so bubbled by this specious homage, that the civilized women of the present century, with a few exceptions, are only anxious to inspire love, when they ought to cherish a nobler ambition, and by their abilities and virtues exact respect.

In a treatise, therefore, on female rights and manners, the works which have been particularly written for their improvement must not be overlooked, especially when it is asserted, in direct terms, that the minds of women are enfeebled by false refinement; that the books of instruction, written by men of genius, have had the same tendency as more frivolous productions; and that, in the true style of Mahometanism, they are only considered as females, and not as a part of the human species, when improvable reason is allowed to be the dignified distinction which raises men above the brute creation, and puts a natural sceptre in a feeble hand.

Yet, because I am a woman, I would not lead my readers to suppose that I mean violently to agitate the contested question respecting the equality or inferiority of the sex; but as the subject lies in my way, and I cannot pass it over without subjecting the main tendency of my reasoning to misconstruction, I shall stop a moment to deliver, in a few words, my opinion. – In the government of the physical world it is observable that the female, in general, is inferior to the male. The male pursues, the female yields – this is the law of nature; and it does not appear to be suspended or abrogated in favour of woman. This physical superiority cannot be denied – and it is a noble prerogative! But not content with this natural pre-eminence, men endeavour to sink us still lower, merely to render us alluring objects for a moment; and women, intoxicated by the adoration which men, under the influence of their senses, pay them, do not seek to obtain a durable interest in their hearts, or to become the friends of the fellow creatures who find amusement in their society.

I am aware of an obvious inference: – from every quarter have I heard exclamations against

often connect. (At this time Blake would have taken a concubine if his wife had not forbade him.) Mary's lover was untrue & left her with their child after she rejected his offer of financial support. She tried to drown herself – was rescued – regained her will to live – began doing so with William Godwin, an atheist, pacifist, & then Britain's most famed thinker. He believed that material know-ledge & virtue had advanced so far they could never be set back. He wrote that nature's law is good & gives us all a right to health & leisure; that human law is bad, being based on force, & marriage bad because, like slavery, it turns people into property. He taught that governments & churches, riches & poverty would end when folk saw they could be happier without. His ideas enchanted Coleridge, Wordsworth, also Shelley who became his lifelong disciple. Mary grew pregnant & married Godwin – secretly, for they had both decried mar-riage. At 38 she died giving birth to a girl who came to write **Frankenstein.**

masculine women; but where are they to be found? If by this appellation men mean to inveigh against their ardour in hunting, shooting, and gaming, I shall most cordially join in the cry; but if it be against the imitation of manly virtues, or, more properly speaking, the attainment of those talents and virtues, the exercise of which ennobles the human character, and which raise females in the scale of animal being, when they are comprehensively termed mankind; – all those who view them with a philosophic eye must, I should think, wish with me, that they may every day grow more and more masculine.

This discussion naturally divides the subject. I shall first consider women in the grand light of human creatures, who, in common with men, are placed on this earth to unfold their faculties; and afterwards I shall more particularly point out their peculiar designation.

I wish also to steer clear of an error which many respectable writers have fallen into; for the instruction which has hitherto been addressed to women, has rather been applicable to *ladies*, if the little indirect advice, that is scattered through Sandford and Merton, be excepted; but, addressing my sex in a firmer tone, I pay particular attention to those in the middle class, because they appear to be in the most natural state. Perhaps the seeds of false-refinement, immorality, and vanity, have ever been shed by the great. Weak, artificial beings, raised above the common wants and affections of their race, in a premature unnatural manner, undermine the very foundation of virtue, and spread corruption through the whole mass of society! As a class of mankind they have the strongest claim to pity; the education of the rich tends to render them vain and helpless, and the unfolding mind is not strengthened by the practice of those duties which dignify the human character. – They only live to amuse themselves, and by the same law which in nature invariably produces certain effects, they soon only afford barren amusement. But as I purpose taking a separate view of the different ranks of society, and of the moral character of women, in each, this hint is, for the present, sufficient; and I have only alluded to the subject, because it appears to me to be the very essence of an introduction to give a cursory account of the contents of the work it introduces.

My own sex, I hope, will excuse me, if I treat them like rational creatures, instead of flattering their *fascinating* graces, and viewing them as if they were in a state of perpetual childhood, unable to stand alone. I earnestly wish to point out in what true dignity and human happiness consists. – I wish to persuade women to endeavour to acquire strength, both of mind and body, and to convince them that the soft phrases, susceptibility of heart, delicacy of sentiment, and refinement of taste, are almost synonymous with epithets of weakness, and that those beings who are only the objects of pity and that kind of love, which has been termed its sister, will soon become objects of contempt. Dismissing then those pretty feminine phrases, which the men condescendingly use to soften our slavish dependence, and despising that weak elegancy of mind, exquisite sensibility, and sweet docility of manners, supposed to be the sexual characteristics of the weaker vessel, I wish to show that elegance is inferior to virtue, that the first object of laudable ambition is to obtain a character as a human being, regardless of the distinction of sex; and that secondary views should be brought to this simple touchstone.

This is a rough sketch of my plan; and should I express my conviction with the energetic emotions that I feel whenever I think of the subject, the dictates of experience and reflection will be felt by some of my readers. Animated by this important object, I shall disdain to cull my phrases or polish my style; – I aim at being useful, and sincerity will render me unaffected; for, wishing rather to persuade by the force of my arguments, than dazzle by the elegance of my language, I shall not waste my time in rounding periods, nor in fabricating the turgid bombast of artificial feelings, which, coming from the head, never reach the heart. – I shall be employed about things, not words! – and, anxious to render my sex more respectable members of society, I shall try to avoid that flowery diction which has slided from essays into novels, and from novels into familiar letters and conversations. These pretty nothings – these caricatures of the real beauty of sensibility, dropping glibly from the tongue, vitiate the taste, and create a kind of sickly delicacy that turns away from simple unadorned truth; and a deluge of false sentiments and overstretched feelings, stifling the natural emotions of the heart, render the domestic pleasures insipid, that ought to sweeten the exercise of those severe duties, which educate a rational and immortal being for a nobler field of action.

The education of women has, of late, been more attended to than formerly; yet they are still reckoned a frivolous sex, and ridiculed or pitied by the writers who endeavour by satire or instruction to improve them. It is acknowledged that they spend many of the first years of their lives in acquiring a smattering of accomplishments: meanwhile strength of body and mind are sacrificed to libertine notions of beauty, to the desire of establishing themselves, – the only way women can rise in the world, – by marriage. And this desire making mere animals of them, when they marry they act as such children may be expected to act: – they dress; they paint, and nickname God's creatures. – Surely these weak beings are only fit for a seraglio! – Can they be expected to govern a family, or take care of the poor babes whom they bring into the world?

If then it can be fairly deduced from the present conduct of the sex, from the prevalent fondness for pleasure which takes place of ambition and those nobler passions that open and enlarge the soul; that the instruction which women have received has only tended, with the constitution of civil society, to render them insignificant objects of desire – mere propagators of fools! – if it can be proved that in aiming to accomplish them, without cultivating their understandings, they are taken out of their sphere of duties, and made ridiculous and useless when the short-lived bloom of beauty is over, I presume that *rational* men will excuse me for endeavouring to persuade them to become more masculine and respectable.

Indeed the word masculine is only a bugbear: there is little reason to fear that women will acquire too much courage or fortitude; for their apparent inferiority with respect to bodily strength, must render them, in some degree, dependent on men in the various relations of life; but why should it be increased by prejudices that give a sex to virtue, and confound simple truths with sensual reveries?

Women are, in fact, so much degraded by mistaken notions of female excellence, that I do not mean to add a paradox when I assert, that this artificial weakness produces a propensity to tyrannize, and gives birth to cunning, the natural opponent of strength, which leads them to play off those contemptible infantine airs that undermine esteem even whilst they excite desire. Do not foster these prejudices, and they will naturally fall into their subordinate, yet respectable station, in life. It seems scarcely necessary to say that I now speak of the sex in general. Many individuals have more sense than their male relatives; and, as nothing preponderates where there is a constant struggle for an equilibrium, without it has naturally more gravity, some women govern their husbands without degrading themselves, because intellect will always govern.

LYRICAL BALLADS, with a few other poems
WILLIAM WORDSWORTH
LONDON

1798

[ADVERTISEMENT]

IT is the honourable characteristic of Poetry that its materials are to be found in every subject which can interest the human mind. The evidence of this fact is to be sought, not in the writings of Critics, but in those of Poets themselves.

The majority of the following poems are to be considered as experiments. They were written chiefly with a view to ascertain how far the language of conversation in the middle and lower classes of society is adapted to the purposes of poetic pleasure. Readers accustomed to the gaudiness and inane phraseology of many modern writers, if they persist in reading this book to its conclusion, will perhaps frequently have to struggle with feelings of strangeness and aukwardness: they will look round for poetry, and will be induced to enquire by what species of courtesy these attempts can be permitted to assume that title. It is desirable that such readers, for their own sakes, should not suffer the solitary word Poetry, a word of very disputed meaning, to stand in the way of their gratification; but that, while they are perusing this book, they should ask themselves if it contains a natural delineation of human passions, human characters, and human incidents; and if the answer be favourable to the author's wishes, that they should consent to be pleased in spite of that most dreadful enemy to our pleasures, our own pre-established codes of decision.

Readers of superior judgment may disapprove of the style in which many of these pieces are executed. It must be expected that many lines and phrases will not exactly suit their taste. It will perhaps appear to them, that wishing to avoid the prevalent fault of the day, the author has sometimes descended too low, and that many of his expressions are too familiar, and not of sufficient dignity. It is apprehended, that the more conversant the reader is with our elder writers, and with those in modern times who have been the most successful in painting manners and passions, the fewer complaints of this kind will he have to make.

An accurate taste in poetry, and in all the other arts, Sir Joshua Reynolds has observed, is an acquired talent, which can only be produced by severe thought, and a long continued intercourse with the best models of composition. This is mentioned not with so ridiculous a purpose as to prevent the most inexperienced reader from judging for himself; but merely to temper the rashness of decision, and to suggest that if poetry be a subject on which much time has not been bestowed, the judgment may be erroneous, and that in many cases it necessarily will be so.

   The tale of Goody Blake and Harry Gill is founded on a well-authenticated fact which happened in Warwickshire. Of the other poems in the collection, it may be proper to say that they are either absolute inventions of the author, or facts which took place within his personal observation or that of his friends. The poem of the Thorn, as the reader will soon discover, is not supposed to be spoken in the author's own person: the character of the loquacious narrator will sufficiently shew itself in the course of the story. The Rime of the Ancyent Marinere was professedly written in imitation of the style, as well as of the spirit of the elder poets; but with a few exceptions, the Author believes that the language adopted in it has been equally intelligible for these three last centuries. The lines entitled Expostulation and Reply, and those which follow, arose out of conversation with a friend who was somewhat unreasonably attached to modern books of moral philosophy.

POEM, LATER CALLED THE PRELUDE, ADDRESSED BY WORDSWORTH TO S.T. COLERIDGE MANUSCRIPT OF INTRODUCTION c1799

O H there is blessing in this gentle breeze
*   That blows from the green fields*
*   and from the clouds*
And from the sky: it beats against my cheek
And seems half conscious of the joy it gives.
O welcome Messenger! O welcome Friend!
A Captive greets thee, coming from a house
Of bondage, from yon City's walls set free,
A prison where he hath been long immured.
Now I am free, enfranchis'd and at large,
May fix my habitation where I will.
What dwelling shall receive me? In what Vale
Shall be my harbour? Underneath what grove
Shall I take up my home, and what sweet stream
Shall with its murmur lull me to my rest?

*The **Lyrical Ballads** preface above introduces poems whose metre is more popular & speech plainer than English readers expect & main theme is the hard lives of rural labourers. In a later version Wordsworth will say that since Milton's time poetry has been tied by stilted diction to a narrow (moneyed) class of passions & subjects, &*

The earth is all before me: with a heart
Joyous, nor scar'd at its own liberty
I look about, and should the guide I chuse
Be nothing better than a wandering cloud
I cannot miss my way. I breathe again;
Trances of thought and mountings of the mind
Come fast upon me: it is shaken off,
As by miraculous gift 'tis shaken off,
That burthen of my own unnatural self,
The heavy weight of many a weary day
Not mine, and such as were not made for me.
Long months of peace (if such bold word accord
With any promises of human life)
Long months of ease and undisturb'd delight
Are mine in prospect: whither shall I turn
By road or pathway or through open field,
Or shall a twig or any floating thing
Upon the river, point me out my course?
Enough that I am free; for months to come
May dedicate myself to chosen tasks;
May quit the tiresome sea and dwell on shore,
If not a settler on the soil, at least
To drink wild water, and to pluck green herbs,
And gather fruits fresh from their native bough.
Nay more, if I may trust myself, this hour
Hath brought a gift that consecrates my joy;
For I, methought, while the sweet breath of Heaven
Was blowing on my body, felt within
A corresponding mild creative breeze,
A vital breeze which travell'd gently on

O'er things which it had made, and is become
A tempest, a redundant energy
Vexing its own creation. 'Tis a power
That does not come unrecogniz'd, a storm,
Which, breaking up a long continued frost,
Brings with it vernal promises, the hope
Of active days, of dignity and thought,

should reflect the glory & pain of a larger nature & humanity. In 1799 he does not want to be thought a radical urging social reform: such folk are being arrested by a government that fears revolution. Wordsworth & Coleridge (whose **Rime of the Ancyent Marinere** is the 1st ballad) are or were recently democrats, so have a government spy sniffing after them. William builds many clauses into complex sentences to convey (like a man aiming to look genteel by constantly adjusting his dress) that he is not addressing the common folk he writes about, so his verses aim at poetic, not political change. His readers take this for granted. Some Whig & Tory critics deplore his low-class subjects, but the ballads are reprinted to more & more praise of his truth, tenderness & love of Nature. After that prose preface to **Lyrical Ballads**, the opening of **The Prelude** sounds as fresh as the breeze in its 1st line.

Of prowess in an honourable field,
Pure passions, virtue, knowledge, and delight,
The holy life of music and of verse.

Thus, far, O Friend! did I, not used to make
A present joy the matter of my song,
Pour out that day my soul in measured strains
Even in the very words which I have here
Recorded: to the open fields I told
A prophecy: poetic numbers came
Spontaneously, and clothed in priestly robe
My spirit, thus singled out, as it might seem,
For holy services: great hopes were mine;
My own voice cheered me, and, far more, the mind's
Internal echo of the imperfect sound;
To both I listened, drawing from them both
A cheerful confidence in things to come.

Whereat, being not unwilling now to give
A respite to this passion, I paced on
Gently, with careless steps; and came, ere long,
To a green shady place, where down I sate
Beneath a tree, slackening my thoughts by choice,
And settling into gentler happiness.
'Twas autumn, and a calm and placid day,
With warmth, as much as needed, from a sun
Two hours declined towards the west; a day
With silver clouds, and sunshine on the grass,
And in the sheltered grove where I was couched
A perfect stillness. On the ground I lay
Passing through many thoughts, yet mainly such
As to myself pertained. I made a choice
Of one sweet Vale, whither my steps should turn,
And saw, methought, the very house and fields
Present before my eyes: nor did I fail
To add, meanwhile, assurance of some work
Of glory there forthwith to be begun,
Perhaps too there performed. Thus long I lay

Wordsworth (to be called W after this) & his family called it Coleridge's poem. That great critic was 2 years younger than W & only 25 in 1795 when they became friends, but he was sure W could be as great as Milton if he wrote a poem on man, nature & society informed by modern thought, so the blank verse & sentences of **The Prelude** *are Miltonic. It can claim (so far) to be the last great very long poem in English, yet it begins a new kind of writing. Homer's, Virgil's & Milton's epics start by giving the theme* **(Achilles' wrath/Arms & the man/Man's first disobedience)** *& do not depict the author:* **The Prelude** *starts with a declaration of independence as W exults in a newfound freedom.* **Piers Plowman** *&* **Canterbury Tales** *also start with spring weather & a poet on holiday from a city, but Langland's & Chaucer's self-portraits are ironic & lead us into crowds jostled by social & religious aims. W joys at first in having no aim. Lines 15 to 19 reverse the end of*

Cheered by the genial pillow of the earth
Beneath my head, soothed by a sense of touch
From the warm ground, that balanced me, else lost
Entirely, seeing nought, nought hearing, save
When here and there, about the grove of oaks
Where was my bed, an acorn from the trees
Fell audibly, and with a startling sound.

Thus occupied in mind, I lingered here
Contented, nor rose up until the sun
Had almost touched the horizon; bidding then
A farewell to the city left behind,
Even with the chance equipment of that hour
I journeyed towards the Vale which I had chosen.
It was a splendid evening, and my soul
Did once again make trial of the strength
Restored to her afresh; nor did she want
Aeolian visitations; but the harp
Was soon defrauded, and the banded host
Of harmony dispersed in straggling sounds,
And lastly utter silence! "Be it so;
It is an injury," said I, "to this day
To think of any thing but present joy."
So, like a peasant I pursued my road
Beneath the evening sun, nor had one wish
Again to bend the Sabbath of that time
To a servile yoke. What need of many words?
A pleasant loitering journey, through two days
Continued, brought me to my hermitage.

I spare to speak, my friend, of what ensued,
The admiration and the love, the life
In common things – the endless store of things,
Rare, or at least so seeming, every day
Found all about me in one neighbourhood –
The self-congratulation, the complete
Composure, and the happiness entire.
But speedily a longing in me rose

Paradise Lost where Adam & Eve are evicted from their happy garden into a wilderness: **some natural tears they shed, but wiped them soon;/The world was all before them, where to choose/Their place of rest, and Providence their guide./They, hand in hand with wandering steps and slow,/Through Eden took their solitary way.** *An angel has told them their children will build cities in this wilderness & endure tyranny in there. W leaves in London* **the burthen of my most un-natural self** *& enters a land that seems all happy garden without peasants or landlords. But his free flow of energy renews a wish to make a poem that inspires others. Lines 177 to 234 recall known & unknown freedom-fighters he had thought to glorify in verse, also the poem he & Coleridge now prefer:* **some philosophic song/of Truth that cherishes our daily life.** *Unable to write this poem he feels an idle waster until the question in line 272 recalls his Lake-district infancy. From then on he discovers the great poem in his own life story – he will make it by recollecting the growth of his own* *mind. I had nothing to do but describe how I felt & thought, he said in a letter of 1805. How easy – how hard! He does it by presenting & linking spots of time – events that gave deep insights, the most vital being earliest. He was orphaned when young & describes a childhood of unrestricted play almost pagan in its wildness – swimming, boating, skating, riding, climbing. Fair seed-time had my soul, and I grew up/Fostered alike by beauty and by fear. (i.305). Why fear? One of the spots of time describes how at the age of 8 he used to steal out at night to snare woodcocks, and some-times snatched birds from somebody else's snare, his guilt trans-formed imaginatively into low breathings coming after him, & the sound of steps almost as silent as the turf they trod (i.305). It is quite natural to hear un-explained sounds in the countryside at night, but Wordsworth projects this into a wider sense of intrusion: he hurries on, scudding from snare to snare under the stars & moon, as if he was troubling the peace that was among them. More than guilt, it is a sudden sense of the whole world of nature in which man*

To brace myself to some determined aim,
Reading or thinking, either to lay up
New stores, or rescue from decay the old
By timely interference: I had hopes
Still higher, that with a frame of outward life
I might endure, might fix in a visible home
Some portion of those phantoms of conceit
That had been floating loose about so long,
And to such beings temperately deal forth
The many feelings that oppressed my heart.
But I have been discouraged; gleams of light
Flash often from the east, then disappear
And mock me with a sky that ripens not
Into a steady morning: if my mind,
Remembering the sweet promise of the past,
Would gladly grapple with some noble theme,
Vain is her wish; where'er she turns she finds
Impediments from day to day renewed.

And now it would content me to yield up
Those lofty hopes awhile, for present gifts
Of humbler industry. But, O dear Friend!
The Poet, gentle creature as he is,
Hath, like the Lover, his unruly times;
His fits when he is neither sick nor well,
Though no distress be near him but his own
Unmanageable thoughts: the mind itself,
The meditative mind, best pleased, perhaps,
While she as duteous as the mother dove
Sits brooding, lives not always to that end,
But hath less quiet instincts, goadings on
That drive her as in trouble through the groves;
With me is now such passion, which I blame
No otherwise than as it lasts too long.

When, as becomes a man who would prepare
For such a glorious work, I through myself
Make rigorous inquisition, the report

Is often cheering; for I neither seem
To lack that first great gift, the vital soul,
Nor general Truths, which are themselves a sort
Of Elements and Agents, Under-powers,
Subordinate helpers of the living mind:
Nor am I naked in external things,
Forms, images, nor numerous other aids
Of less regard, though won perhaps with toil
And needful to build up a Poet's praise.
Time, place, and manners, these I seek, and these
I find in plenteous store, but nowhere such
As may be singled out with steady choice;
No little band of yet remembered names
Whom I, in perfect confidence, might hope
To summon back from lonesome banishment,
And make them inmates in the hearts of men
Now living, or to live in times to come.
Sometimes, mistaking vainly, as I fear,
Proud spring-tide swellings for a regular sea,
I settle on some British theme, some old
Romantic tale by Milton left unsung;
More often resting at some gentle place
Within the groves of Chivalry, I pipe
Among the shepherds, with reposing knights
Sit by a fountain side, and hear their tales.
Sometimes, more sternly moved, I would relate
How vanquished Mithridates northward passed,
And, hidden in the cloud of years, became
That Odin, Father of a race by whom
Perished the Roman Empire: how the friends
And followers of Sertorius, out of Spain,
Flying, found shelter in the Fortunate Isles,
And left their usages, their arts and laws,
To disappear by a slow gradual death,
To dwindle and to perish one by one,
Starved in those narrow bounds: but not the soul
Of Liberty, which fifteen hundred years
Survived, and, when the European came

may be an intruder, but when he sees the figure of a shepherd standing on a hillside above a bank of mist he feels humanity too has natural grandeur. These are truths he carries into his schooling & university days, into his decision to be a poet & his life in London. No bible god or earthly authority enters his poem. They are not even rejected – they have no part. The only supernatural event is an Arab in a dream who saves science & art (contained in a stone & sea-shell) from a flood that drown humanity: the dream was Coleridge's! W has faith in no power but nature & his own imagination, no government better than affection, no evil worse than poverty & injustice. This was the faith of the French revolution. W tells of his delight in its early days & how he yielded up moral questions in despair at its terror & massacres. Meetings with Coleridge & Dorothy (a sister W had been divided from when a child) restore his faith in nature, imagination, affection & poetry. He thanks Calvert, another friend who made his poetry possible by leaving him money to work at it. All

With skill and power that could not be withstood,
Did, like a pestilence, maintain its hold
And wasted down by glorious death that race
Of natural heroes: or I would record
How, in tyrannic times, some unknown man,
Unheard of in the chronicles of kings,
Suffered in silence for the love of Truth;
How that one Frenchman, through continued force
Of meditation on the inhuman deeds
Of the first conquerors of the Indian Isles,
Went single in his ministry across
The Ocean; not to comfort the oppressed,
But, like a thirsty wind, to roam about
Withering the Oppressor: how Gustavus found
Help at his need in Dalecarlia's mines:
How Wallace fought for Scotland; left the name
Of Wallace to be found, like a wild flower,
All over his dear Country; left the deeds
Of Wallace, like a family of Ghosts,
To people the steep rocks and river banks,
Her natural sanctuaries, with a local soul

Of independence and stern liberty.
Sometimes it suits me better to shape out
Some tale from my own heart, more near akin
To my own passions and habitual thoughts;
Some variegated story, in the main
Lofty, with interchange of gentler things.
But deadening admonitions will succeed
And the whole beauteous fabric seems to lack
Foundation, and, withal, appears throughout
Shadowy and unsubstantial. Then, last wish,
My last and favourite aspiration, then
I yearn towards some philosophic song
Of Truth that cherishes our daily life;
With meditations passionate from deep
Recesses in man's heart, immortal verse
Thoughtfully fitted to the Orphean lyre;
But from this awful burden I full soon

Take refuge and beguile myself with trust
That mellower years will bring a riper mind
And clearer insight. Thus from day to day
I live, a mockery of the brotherhood
Of vice and virtue, with no skill to part
Vague longing that is bred by want of power
From paramount impulse not to be withstood,
A timorous capacity from prudence,
From circumspection, infinite delay.
Humility and modest awe themselves
Betray me, serving often for a cloak
To a more subtle selfishness; that now
Doth lock my functions up in blank reserve,
Now dupes me by an over-anxious eye
That with a false activity beats off
Simplicity and self-presented truth.
Ah! better far than this, to stray about
Voluptuously through fields and rural walks,
And ask no record of the hours, given up
To vacant musing, unreproved neglect
Of all things, and deliberate holiday.
Far better never to have heard the name
Of zeal and just ambition, than to live
Thus baffled by a mind that every hour
Turns recreant to her task; takes heart again,
Then feels immediately some hollow thought
Hang like an interdict upon her hopes.
This is my lot; for either still I find
Some imperfection in the chosen theme,
Or see of absolute accomplishment
Much wanting, so much wanting, in myself,
That I recoil and droop, and seek repose
In indolence from vain perplexity,
Unprofitably travelling towards the grave,
Like a false steward who hath much received
And renders nothing back. Was it for this
That one, the fairest of all rivers, loved
To blend its murmurs with my nurses song?

a republic with equal rights for all, rejects the notion that popular government, social equality or new philosophy caused the Terror. He blames it on the old French regime's injustice as Carlyle was later to do. Had any version been printed before 1840 it would have linked **W** with the radical poets Burns, Shelley & Byron, radical action like machine-breaking, Rebecca riots & Chartism. So **The Prelude**, named & edited by **W**'s wife, was printed in 1850 after his death. By then most of his readers thought the nature he loved was nothing but the landscapes enjoyed by city folk on holiday. J.S. Mill & George Eliot were among a few who saw he meant a very great deal more than that.

1798

ESSAY ON THE PRINCIPLE OF POPULATION
THOMAS MALTHUS: LONDON

This preface sets the tone of what follows. The manner is gentle but the Essay *embodies a hard doctrine on **the great question: can** the general state of humanity be improved? Malthus, an Anglican clergyman, accepts that most labourers have short, miserable lives. He does not, like many clergy, say this is a punishment for their sins, & agrees with Godwin & Paine that a more equal share of wealth would do them good – but not for long. He argues that better wages, food & homes for all would, in 1 generation, lead to them having as many healthy, long-lived children as richer folk, quadrupling the people in a nation before the food supply could be more than doubled. Malthus' idea that food supply limits the numbers of a species is true: it helped Darwin discover evolution by natural selection. The Green Party accept it, & those who know our hugely expanding numbers press on the limits of a finite planet, & want governments to fight disease & famine by urging conservation & birth control.*

THE FOLLOWING *Essay* owes its origin to a conversation with a friend, on the subject of Mr. Godwin's essay on "Avarice and Profusion" in his *Enquirer*. The discussion started the general question of the improvement of society; and the Author at first sat down with an intention of merely stating his thoughts to his friend, upon paper, in a clearer manner than he thought he could do in conversation. But as the subject opened upon him, some ideas occurred, which he did not recollect to have met with before; and as he conceived that every least light, on a topic so generally interesting, might be received with candour, he determined to put his thoughts in a form for publication.

The *Essay* might, undoubtedly, have been rendered much more complete by a collection of a greater number of facts in elucidation of the general argument. But a long and almost total interruption from very particular business, joined to a desire (perhaps imprudent) of not delaying the publication much beyond the time that he originally proposed, prevented the Author from giving to the subject an undivided attention. He presumes, however, that the facts which he has adduced will be found to form no inconsiderable evidence for the truth of his opinion respecting the future improvement of mankind. As the Author contemplates this opinion at present, little more appears to him to be necessary than a plain statement, in addition to the most cursory view of society, to establish it.

It is an obvious truth, which has been taken notice of by many writers, that population must always be kept down to the level of the means of subsistence; but no writer that the Author recollects has inquired particularly into the means by which this level is effected: and it is a view of these means which forms, to his mind, the strongest obstacle in the way to any very great future improvement of society. He hopes it will appear that, in the discussion of this interesting subject, he is actuated solely by a love of truth, and not by any prejudices against any particular set of men, or of opinions. He professes to have read some of the speculations on the future improvement of society in a temper very different from a wish to find them visionary, but he has not acquired that command over his understanding which would enable him to believe what he wishes, without evidence, or to refuse his assent to what might be unpleasing, when accompanied with evidence.

The view which he has given of human life has a melancholy hue, but he feels conscious that he has drawn these dark tints from a conviction that they are really in the picture, and not from a jaundiced eye or an inherent spleen of disposition. The theory of mind which he has sketched in the two last chapters accounts to his own understanding in a satisfactory manner for the existence of most of the evils of life, but whether it will have the same effect upon others must be left to the judgement of his readers.

If he should succeed in drawing the attention of more able men to what he conceives to be the principal difficulty in the way to the improvement of society and should, in consequence, see this difficulty removed, even in theory, he will gladly retract his present opinions and rejoice in a conviction of his error.

*Malthus had no faith in these. He said labouring people always grow too many for the food they produce, so social equality can only spread hunger to the wealthy. He said earthly misery was enforced by a natural law **so deeply seated that no human ingenuity could reach it**, & gave a mathematic formula for the law. It seemed to take **the great question** of social betterment away from moral philosophy & give it to science. Political economy was now being promoted as a science. The industry of Britain had made it the world's greatest international money market. The economists (Ricardo, McCulloch & Senior) said the government's main job was to preserve high interest on bank loans, which would suffer if taxes were used to reduce poverty. They made Malthus' formula a strong article of their faith. Senior said the more than three-quarter million Irish killed by the potato famine were too few for the nation's good. Malthus' formula was also taken by prosperous Christians to be a law of nature AND God: a law that, if heeded, fixed their place in the world as firmly as Newton's laws placed the planets.*

1800

Maria, born in England to Anglo-Irish gentry, received a broad, free-thinking education as her dad was a keen rationalist, inventor & promoter of her books. **Castle Rackrent** *was begun in 1793 on their Irish estate & based (as the title tells) on bad though quite usual landlords of her own class. But she did not write it in the voice of her own class. In 1834 she described how the voice came to her. The only character drawn from the life in 'Castle Rackrent' is Thady himself, the teller of the story. He was an old steward (not very old, though, at that time; I added to his age, to allow him time for generations of the family) – I heard him when first I came to Ireland, & his dialect struck me, & his character, & I became so acquainted with it, that I could think & speak in it without effort: so that when, for mere amusement, without any ideas of publishing, I began to write a family history as Thady would tell it, he seemed to stand beside me & dictate & I wrote as fast as my pen could go, the characters*

CASTLE RACKRENT, An Hibernian tale from the manners of the Irish squires, before 1782
MARIA EDGEWORTH: LONDON

THE prevailing taste of the public for anecdote has been censured and ridiculed by critics, who aspire to the character of superior wisdom: but if we consider it in a proper point of view, this taste is an incontestible proof of the good sense and profoundly philosophic temper of the present times. Of the numbers who study, or at least who read history, how few derive any advantage from their labors! The heroes of history are so decked out by the fine fancy of the professed historian; they talk in such measured prose, and act from such sublime or such diabolical motives, that few have sufficient taste, wickedness or heroism, to sympathize in their fate. Besides, there is much uncertainty even in the best authenticated ancient or modern histories; and that love of truth, which in some minds is innate and immutable, necessarily leads to a love of secret memoirs and private anecdotes. We cannot judge either of the feelings or of the characters of men with perfect accuracy from their actions or their appearance in public; it is from their careless conversations, their half finished sentences, that we may hope with the greatest probability of success to discover their real characters. The life of a great or of a little man written by himself, the familiar letters, the diary of any individual published by his friends, or by his enemies after his decease, are esteemed important literary curiosities. We are surely justified in this eager desire to collect the most minute facts relative to the domestic lives, not only of the great and good, but even of the worthless and insignificant, since it is only by a comparison of their actual happiness or misery in the privacy of domestic life, that we can form a just estimate of the real reward of virtue, or the real punishment of vice. That the great are not as happy as they seem, that the external circumstances of fortune and rank do not constitute felicity, is asserted by every moralist; the historian can seldom, consistently with his dignity, pause to illustrate this truth, it is therefore to the biographer we must have recourse. After we have beheld splendid characters playing their parts on the great theatre of the world, with all the advantages of stage effect and decoration, we anxiously beg to be admitted behind the scenes, that we may take a nearer view of the actors and actresses.

Some may perhaps imagine, that the value of biography depends upon the judgment and taste of the biographer; but on the contrary it may be maintained, that the merits of a biographer are inversely as the extent of his intellectual powers and of his literary talents. A plain unvarnished tale is preferable to the most highly ornamented narrative. Where we see that a man has the power, we may naturally suspect that he has the will to deceive us, and those who are used to literary manufacture know how much is often sacrificed to the rounding of a period or the pointing an antithesis. That the ignorant may have their prejudices as well as the learned cannot be disputed, but we see and despise vulgar errors; we never bow to the authority of him who has no great name to sanction his absurdities. The partiality which blinds a biographer to the defects of his hero, in proportion as it is gross ceases to be dangerous; but if it be concealed by the appearance of candor, which men of great abilities best know how to assume, it endangers our judgment sometimes and sometimes our morals. If her Grace the Duchess of Newcastle, instead of penning her lord's elaborate eulogium, had undertaken to write the life of Savage, we should not have been in any danger of mistaking an idle, ungrateful libertine, for

all imaginary.

Thady's Anglo-Irish speech, like the Scots of Burns, has variety of tone that teachers of polite English tried to iron out. By using the voice of an old & un-scrupulous servant, a parasite feeding on a parasitic dynasty, Maria moved herself from Anglo to Irish, female to male, upper to under class with no loss of intelligence & a gain in vitality. Efforts to found an Irish republic halted her writing. Protestant aristocrats, backed by France, led a rising of Catholic peasants & Ulster Orangemen. The unstable alliance was smashed by the British army, then bribery & threats (as in 1707 Edinburgh) welded the parliament in Dublin city onto London's. **Castle Rackrent** *was published in the year of Irish union with Britain, & in the same year Maria Edgeworth's father wrote:* **We hear from good authority that the king was much pleased with Castle Rackrent – he rubbed his hands & said, "What what – I know something now of my Irish subjects."** *(George III was given to snorting* **what what**, *& loved for it.)*

a man of genius and virtue. The talents of a biographer are often fatal to his reader. For these reasons the public often judiciously countenances those, who without sagacity to discriminate character, without elegance of style to relieve the tediousness of narrative, without enlargement of mind to draw any conclusions from the facts they relate, simply pour forth anecdotes and retail conversations, with all the minute prolixity of a gossip in a country town.

The author of the following memoirs has upon these grounds fair claims to the public favor and attention: he was an illiterate old steward, whose partiality to the *family* in which he was bred and born must be obvious to the reader. He tells the history of the Rackrent family in his vernacular idiom, and in the full confidence that Sir Patrick, Sir Murtagh, Sir Kit, and Sir Condy Rackrent's affairs, will be as interesting to all the world as they were to himself. Those who were acquainted with the manners of a certain class of the gentry of Ireland some years ago, will want no evidence of the truth of honest Thady's narrative: to those who are totally unacquainted with Ireland, the following Memoirs will perhaps be scarcely intelligible, or probably they may appear perfectly incredible. For the information of the *ignorant* English reader a few notes have been subjoined by the editor, and he had it once in contemplation to translate the language of Thady into plain English; but Thady's idiom is incapable of translation, and besides, the authenticity of his story would have been more exposed to doubt if it were not told in his own characteristic manner. Several years ago he related to the editor the history of the Rackrent family, and it was with some difficulty that he was persuaded to have it committed to writing; however, his feelings for "*the honor of the family,*" as he expressed himself, prevailed over his habitual laziness, and he at length completed the narrative which is now laid before the public. The Editor hopes his readers will observe, that these are "tales of other times;" that the manners depicted in the following pages are not those of the present age: the race of the Rackrents has long since been extinct in Ireland, and the drunken Sir Patrick, the litigious Sir Murtagh, the fighting Sir Kit, and the slovenly Sir Condy, are characters which could no more be met with at present in Ireland, than Squire Western or Parson Trulliber in England. There is a time when individuals can bear to be rallied for their past follies and absurdities, after they have acquired new habits and a new consciousness. Nations as well as individuals gradually lose attachment to their identity, and the present generation is amused rather than offended by the ridicule that is thrown upon their ancestors.

Probably we shall soon have it in our power, in a hundred instances, to verify the truth of these observations. When Ireland loses her identity by an union with Great Britain, she will look back with a smile of good-humoured complacency on the Sir Kits and Sir Condys of her former existence.

NATURAL THEOLOGY: Evidence of Existence & Attributes of the Deity, collected from appearances of Nature : **WILLIAM PALEY: LONDON**

1802

[STATE OF THE ARGUMENT]

IN crossing a heath, suppose I pitched my foot against a *stone*, and were asked how the stone came to be there, I might possibly answer, that, for any thing I knew to the contrary, it had lain there for ever: nor would it perhaps be very easy to shew the absurdity of this answer. But suppose I had found a *watch* upon the ground, and it should be enquired how the watch happened to be in that place, I should hardly think of the answer which I had before given, that, for any thing I knew, the watch might have always been there. Yet why should not this answer serve for the watch, as well as for the stone? Why is it not as admissible in the second case, as in the first? For this reason, and for no other, viz. that, when we come to inspect the watch, we perceive (what we could not discover in the stone) that its several parts are framed and put together for a purpose, e.g. that they are so formed and adjusted as to produce motion, and that motion so regulated as to point out the hour of the day; that, if the several parts had been differently shaped from what they are, of a different size from what they are, or placed after any other manner, or in any other order, than that in which they are placed, either no motion at all would have been carried on in the machine, or

For a century exact classifying had shown how cunningly animals & plants fit their unique places in the world, how intricately they are orchestrated to feed & fertilize each other. The theory that heat alone gives birth to life in dead matter was being disproved by the microscope, so the Jewish idea that an eternal mind had made the world & living things to fit each other again seemed more likely than a Greek view that it evolved by chance. Yet dead matter was never more lively! Carlyle called his century **a machine age***, Owen called his factory workers human machinery. Paley used a watch to prove God a divine mechanic.*

The study of human anatomy was in its early stages, but Paley was up to date in drawing his illustrations from

current medical textbooks. That technical expertise lent credibility to his argument, and ensured its influence until Darwin (who read Paley at Cambridge when studying for the church in 1831) offered a different account of the natural world in **The Origin of Species**.

Wordsworth and Coleridge (who also studied Paley as undergraduates) regarded him as second only to Locke as an unimaginative, narrow-gauge thinker; the sort of philosopher who (as Keats put it), **would clip an angel's wings**. *To Shelley & Byron he was also conservative, his conviction in a designing creator leading all too easily to the conclusion that whatever is, is right, as God had made birds for air, worms for soil & (as a hymn put it) the rich man in his castle, the poor man at his gate. The social order as it stood, said Paley, was a continuation of God's natural order.* **At the banquet of life there are no free seats**, *he said, when opposing a plan for the government to provide jobs in a peace-time trade slump, by paying folk to build & mend roads & harbours, as it paid them to fight in war time.*

none which would have answered the use, that is now served by it. To reckon up a few of the plainest of these parts, and of their offices, all tending to one result: – We see a cylindrical box containing a coiled elastic spring, which, by its endeavour to relax itself turns round the box. We next observe a flexible chain (artificially wrought for the sake of flexure) communicating the action of the spring from the box to the fusee. We then find a series of wheels, the teeth of which catch in, and apply to, each other, conducting the motion from the fusee to the balance, and from the balance to the pointer; and at the same time, by the size and shape of those wheels, so regulating that motion, as to terminate in causing an index, by an equable and measured progression, to pass over a given space in a given time. We take notice that the wheels are made of brass, in order to keep them from rust; the springs of steel, no other metal being so elastic; that over the face of the watch there is placed a glass, a material employed in no other part of the work, but, in the room of which, if there had been any other than a transparent substance, the hour could not be seen without opening the case. This mechanism being observed (it requires indeed an examination of the instrument, and perhaps some previous knowledge of the subject, to perceive and understand it; but being once, as we have said, observed and understood), the inference, we think, is inevitable; that the watch must have had a maker; that there must have existed, at some time and at some place or other, an artificer or artficers who formed it for the purpose which we find it actually to answer; who comprehended its construction, and designed its use.

I. Nor would it, I apprehend, weaken the conclusion, that we had never seen a watch made; that we had never known an artist capable of making one; that we were altogether incapable of executing such a piece of workmanship ourselves, or of understanding in what manner it was performed: all this being no more than what is true of some exquisite remains of ancient art, of some lost arts, and, to the generality or mankind, of the more curious productions of modern manufacture. Does one man in a million know how oval frames are turned? Ignorance of this kind exalts our opinion of the unseen and unknown artist's skill, if he be unseen and unknown, but raises no doubt in our minds of the existence and agency of such an artist, at some former time, and in some place or other. Nor can I perceive that it varies at all the inference, whether the question arise concerning a human agent, or concerning an agent of a different species, or an agent possessing, in some respects, a different nature.

II. Neither, secondly, would it invalidate our conclusion, that the watch sometimes went wrong, or that it seldom went exactly right. The purpose of the machinery, the design, and the designer, might be evident, and in the case supposed would be evident, in whatever way we accounted for the irregularity of the movement, or whether we could account for it or not. It is not necessary that a machine be perfect, in order to shew with what design it was made: still less necessary, where the only question is, whether it were made with any design at all.

III. Nor, thirdly, would it bring any uncertainty into the argument, if there were a few parts of the watch, concerning which we could not discover, or had not yet discovered, in what manner they conduced to the general effect; or even some parts, concerning which we could not ascertain, whether they conduced to that effect in any manner whatever. For, as to the first branch of the case; if, by the loss, or disorder, or decay of the parts in question, the movement of the watch were found in fact to be stopped, or disturbed, or retarded, no doubt would remain in our minds as to the utility or intention of these parts, although we should be unable to investigate the manner according to which, or the connection by which, the ultimate effect depended upon their action or assistance: and the more complex is the machine, the more likely is this obscurity to arise. Then, as to the second thing supposed, namely, that there were parts, which might be spared without prejudice to the movement of the watch, and that we had proved this by experiment,– these superfluous parts, even if we were completely assured that they were such, would not vacate the reasoning which we had instituted concerning other parts. The indication of contrivance remained, with respect to them, nearly as it was before.

IV. Nor, fourthly, would any man in his senses think the existence of the watch, with its various machinery, accounted for, by being told that it was one out of possible combinations of material forms; that whatever he had found in the place where he found the watch, must have contained some internal configuration or other; and that this configuration might be the structure now exhibited, viz. of the works of a watch, as well as a different structure.

V. Nor, fifthly, would it yield his enquiry more satisfaction to be answered, that there existed in things a principle of order, which had disposed the part of the watch into their present form and situation. He never knew a watch made by the principle of order; not can he even form to himself an idea of what is meant by a principle of order, distinct from the intelligence of the watch-maker.

VI. Sixthly, he would be surprised to hear, that the mechanism of the watch was no proof of contrivance, only a motive to induce the mind to think so:

VII. And not less surprised to be informed, that the watch in his hand was nothing more than the result of the laws of metallic nature. It is a perversion of language to assign any law, as the efficient, operative, cause of any thing. A law presupposes an agent; for it is only the mode, according to which an agent proceeds: it implies a power; for it is the order, according to which that power acts. Without this agent, without this power, which are both distinct from itself, the law does nothing; is nothing. The expression, "the law of metallic nature," may sound strange and harsh to a philosophic ear, but it seems quite as justifiable as some others which are more familiar to him, such as, "the law of vegetable nature" – "the law of animal nature," or indeed as "the law of nature" in general, when assigned as the cause of phaenomena, in exclusion of agency and power; or when it is substituted into the place of these.

VIII. Neither, lastly, would our observer be driven out of his conclusion, or from his confidence in its truth, by being told that he knew nothing at all about the matter. He knows enough for his argument. He knows the utility of the end: he knows the subserviency and adaptation of the means to the end. These points being known, his ignorance of other points, his doubts concerning other points, affect not the certainty of his reasoning. The consciousness of knowing little, need not beget a distrust of that which he does know.

JERUSALEM
WILLIAM BLAKE
LAMBETH: LONDON

1804

SHEEP　　　　TO THE PUBLIC　　　　GOATS

AFTER my three years slumber on the banks of the Ocean, I again display my Giant forms to the Public: My former Giants & Fairies having reciev'd the highest reward possible; the love and friendship of those with whom to be connected is to be blessed: I cannot doubt that this more consolidated & extended Work will be as kindly recieved – The Enthusiasm of the following Poem, the Author hopes no Reader will think presumptuousness or arrogance when he is reminded that the Ancients entrusted their love to their writing, to the full as enthusiastically as I have who Acknowledge mine for my Saviour and Lord, for they were wholly absorb'd in their Gods. I also hope the Reader will be with me wholly One in Jesus our Lord, Who is the God of Fire and Lord of Love to Whom the Ancients look'd, and saw His day afar off, with trembling & amazement.

　　The Spirit of Jesus is continual forgiveness of Sin: he who waits to be righteous before he enters into the Saviours Kingdom, the Divine Body; will never enter there. I am perhaps the most sinful of men! I pretend not to holiness! yet I pretend to love, to see, to converse with daily, as man with man, & the more to have an interest in the Friend of Sinners. Therefore Dear Reader forgive what you do not approve, & love me for this energetic exertion of my talent.

Reader! lover of books! lover of heaven,
And of that God from whom all books are given
Who in mysterious Sinais awful cave
To Man the wondrous art of writing gave,
Again he speaks in thunder and in fire!
Thunder of Thought, & flames of fierce desire;

Blake's **Giant forms** *illustrate the poems he wrote out, engraved & coloured by hand. He is here defending the enthusiasm that most 18th-century thinkers rejected as a cause of revolution, but Blake embraced as the inspiration of all true art, especially the Bible. He felt it most in the love & generosity of Jesus, while believing* **God only Acts & Is, in existing beings & men.** *Since imagined gods rule people's actions as much as hunger & thirst Blake thought them just as real, so he has been called a mystic: also a madman, for he could imagine as a presence any god or person he read of, a handy talent to an illustrator. He hated Homer's & Virgil's epics because they praised men who made war for revenge, loot & other people's land, & showed gods promoting these wars. But the god he hated most was the official god of Britain's state church whom he called* **Nobodaddy,** *for it was now mainly worshipped as a wholly bodiless abstraction who ruled a mechanical universe by Newton's mathematics, & in 1688 had founded*

*the British establish-
ment that ruled by the
maths of political
economists. Its clergy
backed wars to expand
imperial trading, while
preaching that riches &
poverty were decreed by
god's **natural** laws.
Blake thought this god
(often pictured as a
terrible old bearded
law-giver, cursing &
punishing folk) was not
a creator & certainly
not Christian, but a
devil rulers had raised
to help them hold down
their subjects. Blake
was 1 of these skilled
craftsmen who created
(said Smith) the wealth
of nations. A parliament
of landed proprietors
denied them any say in
their own government.
It feared creative energy
(which was Jesus, in
Blake's religion) so had
warped the teaching of
Jesus into a law of
obedience to THEM,
though Jesus had been
crucified by their pre-
decessors because his
love & forgiveness had
made all penal laws
completely obsolete.*

1804

*The gloss above is a
crude outline of
Blake's ideas: ideas
formed by wider
reading than that of
any poet then, except
Coleridge & Shelley.*

*Even from the depths of Hell his voice I hear
Within the unfathomd caverns of my Ear.
Therefore I print; nor vain my types shall be:
Heaven, Earth & Hell,
      henceforth shall live in harmony.*

OF THE MEASURE, IN WHICH THE FOLLOWING
POEM IS WRITTEN.

We who dwell on Earth can do nothing of ourselves, everything is conducted by Spirits, no less than Digestion or Sleep.

When this Verse was first dictated to me I consider'd a Monotonous Cadence like that used by Milton & Shakspeare & all writers of English Blank Verse, derived from the modern bondage of Rhyming; to be a necessary and indispensible part of Verse. But I soon found that in the mouth of a true Orator such monotony was not only awkward, but as much a bondage as rhyme itself. I therefore have produced a variety in every line, both of cadences & number of syllables. Every word and every letter is studied and put into its fit place; the terrific numbers are reserved for the terrific parts, the mild & gentle for the mild & gentle parts, and the prosaic, for inferior parts; all are necessary to each other, Poetry Fetter'd, Fetters the Human Race. Nations are Destroy'd, or Flourish, in proportion as Their Poetry, Painting, and Music, are Destroy'd or Flourish! The Primeval State of Man was Wisdom, Art, and Science.

MILTON
WILLIAM BLAKE
LAMBETH: LONDON

THE Stolen and Perverted Writings of Homer & Ovid: of Plato & Cicero, which all Men ought to contemn: are set up by artifice against the Sublime of the Bible, but when the New Age is at leisure to Pronounce; all will be set right; & those Grand Works of the more ancient & consciously & professedly Inspired Men will hold their proper rank, & the Daughters of Memory shall become the Daughters of Inspiration. Shakspeare & Milton were both curbd by the general malady & infection from the silly Greek & Latin slaves of the Sword.

Rouze up O Young Men of the New Age! set your foreheads against the ignorant Hirelings! For we have Hirelings in the Camp, the Court, & the University: who would if they could, for ever depress Mental & prolong Corporeal War. Painters! on you I call! Sculptors! Architects! Suffer not the fashionable Fools to depress your powers by the prices they pretend to give for contemptible works or the expensive advertizing boasts that they make of such works; believe Christ & his Apostles that there is a Class of Men whose whole delight is in Destroying. We do not want either Greek or Roman Models if we are but just & true to our own Imaginations, those Worlds of Eternity in which we shall live for ever; in Jesus our Lord.

And did those feet in ancient time
* Walk upon Englands mountains green:*
And was the holy Lamb of God
* On Englands pleasant pastures seen!*

And did the Countenance Divine
* Shine forth upon our clouded hills?*
And was Jerusalem builded here,
* Among these dark Satanic Mills?*

Bring me my Bow of burning gold:
* Bring me my Arrows of desire:*
Bring me my Spear: O clouds unfold:
* Bring me my Chariot of Fire!*

I will not cease from Mental Fight,
* Nor shall my Sword sleep in my hand:*
Till we have built Jerusalem,
* In Englands green & pleasant Land.*

"Would to God that all the Lord's people were Prophets." Numbers xi.29.

*Blake's best poetry is **Songs of Innocence & Experience** which tell of lovely & dreadful truths he found among people in & around London. Later he wrote epics like Hindu & Greek legends & Wagner's **Ring** in which mental & historic forces appear as gods & mighty people. Blake shows Los, Vala, Urizen, Newton & Milton struggle over **Jerusalem** - England as she **should** be. The scenery is extreme: huge waves through which the spine of an unformed god hurtles & **soft moony female spaces**. As Alice said of a later poem, "It seems to fill my head with ideas – only I don't quite know what they are." They show modern states where there is **A pretence of Art to destroy Art; a pretence of Liberty to destroy Liberty** & where **The Giants of Albion...** (Blake's name for corporate greed)... **accumulate A World in which man is by his nature the Enemy of Man, In pride of selfhood.** His illustrations, unlike Wagner's music, do not excite us to care for his terrific people. Yet this preface to **Milton** ends with his most popular poem, a hymn that should be England's national anthem.*

1813

A NEW VIEW OF SOCIETY, Essays on the Formation of Human Character
ROBERT OWEN: LONDON

TO THE SUPERINTENDENTS OF MANUFACTORIES, AND TO THOSE INDIVIDUALS GENERALLY, WHO, BY GIVING EMPLOYMENT TO AN AGGREGATED POPULATION, MAY EASILY ADOPT THE MEANS TO FORM THE SENTIMENTS AND MANNERS OF SUCH A POPULATION.

In the 1793-1821 wars with France British textile firms couldn't fully supply, at first, government orders for uniforms, sailcloth & rope. Their workforce was limited by the many men at war until they got new machines that women & children could work. These were paid less than men, & public charities supplied the firms with orphans who worked for only food & bedding. At once the factory towns & cities grew faster & filthier, with coal-fired engines driving machinery to the limit of workers' endurance. They swiftly made a new rich class of factory owner, new middle class of works manager, new class of slum-housed worker.

Owen was Welsh. At 10 he went to work in a draper's shop, at 19 managed a cotton mill. He knew children work better when well-fed & rested; not starved & forced to stay awake by an overseer caning them. He became son-in-law & partner of David Dale, cloth

LIKE you, I am a manufacturer for pecuniary profit. But having for many years acted on principles the reverse in many respects of those in which you have been instructed, and having found my procedure beneficial to others and to myself, even in a pecuniary point of view, I am anxious to explain such valuable principles, that you and those under your influence may equally partake of their advantages.

In two Essays, already published, I have developed some of these principles, and in the following pages you will find still more of them explained, with some detail of their application to practice under the peculiar local circumstances in which I took the direction of the New Lanark Mills and Establishment.

By those details you will find that from the commencement of my management I viewed the population, with the mechanism and every other part of the establishment, as a system composed of many parts, and which it was my duty and interest so to combine, as that every hand, as well as every spring, lever, and wheel, should effectually co-operate to produce the greatest pecuniary gain to the proprietors.

Many of you have long experienced in your manufacturing operations the advantages of substantial, well-contrived, and well-executed machinery.

Experience has also shown you the difference

of the results between mechanism which is neat, clean, well-arranged, and always in a high state of repair; and that which is allowed to be dirty, in disorder, without the means of preventing unnecessary friction, and which therefore becomes, and works, much out of repair.

In the first case the whole economy and management are good; every operation proceeds with ease, order, and success. In the last, the reverse must follow, and a scene be presented of counteraction, confusion, and dissatisfaction among all the agents and instruments interested or occupied in the general process, which cannot fail to create great loss.

If, then, due care as to the state of your inanimate machines can produce such beneficial results, what may not be expected if you devote equal attention to your vital machines, which are far more wonderfully constructed?

When you shall acquire a right knowledge of these, of their curious mechanism, of their self-adjusting powers; when the proper main-spring shall be applied to their varied movements, – you will become conscious of their real value, and you will readily be induced to turn your thoughts more frequently from your inanimate to your living machines; you will discover that the latter may be easily trained and directed to procure a large increase of pecuniary gain, while you may also derive from them high and substantial gratification.

Will you then continue to expend large sums of money to procure the best devised mechanism of wood, brass, or iron; to retain it in perfect repair; to provide the best substance for the prevention of unnecessary friction, and to save it from falling into premature decay? – Will you also devote years of intense application to understand the connection of the various parts of these lifeless machines, to

merchant & builder of New Lanark, a cotton-spinning town in upper Clydesdale. Here well-made houses had gardens & orphans were taught to dance. Here Owen practised ideas he put in this book – company profits of over 5% should be spent on the welfare of the workers & upon a fund to feed them when trade grew slack. With the defeat of France, it did.

Discharged soldiers returned to a land of factories shut by the ending of government orders. Hunger & riots ensued. A parliamentary committee considered remedies, Owen's among them, but parliament, investors & his fellow factory-owners had no wish to share the new industrial wealth with common workers. The unemployed were given strong new police forces, an army barracks near each industrial city, & poor-houses that split child from parent, wife from husband. That made a Socialist of Owen. He travelled widely, founding co-operative societies through combinations of workers & shopkeepers. Aided by Owen, Ruskin, J.S.Mill & Morris, the Co-ops throve & joined with trade unions to make a Labour Party that elected its 1st MPs in 1874.

improve their effective powers, and to calculate with mathematical precision all their minute and combined movements? – And when in these transactions you estimate time by minutes, and the money expended for the chance of increased gain by fractions, will you not afford some of your attention to consider whether a portion of your time and capital would not be more advantageously applied to improve your living machines? From experience which cannot deceive me, I venture to assure you, that your time and money so applied, if directed by a true knowledge of the subject, would return you, not five, ten or fifteen per cent. for your capital so expended, but often fifty, and in many cases a hundred per cent.

I have expended much time and capital upon improvements of the living machinery; and it will soon appear that the time and money so expended in the manufactory at New Lanark, even while such improvements are in progress only, and but half their beneficial effects attained, are now producing a return exceeding fifty per cent., and will shortly create profits equal to cent. per cent. on the original capital expended in them.

Indeed, after experience of the beneficial effects from due care and attention to the mechanical implements, it became easy to a reflecting mind to conclude at once, that at least equal advantages would arise from the application of similar care and attention to the living instruments. And when it was perceived that inanimate mechanism was greatly improved by being made firm and substantial; that it was the essence of economy to keep it neat, clean, regularly supplied with the best substance to prevent unnecessary friction, and by proper provision for the purpose to preserve it in good repair; it was natural to conclude that the more delicate, complex, living mechanism, would be equally improved by being trained to strength and activity; and that it would also prove true economy to keep it neat and clean; to treat it with kindness, that its mental movements might not experience too much irritating friction; to endeavour by every means to make it more perfect; to supply it regularly with a sufficient quantity of wholesome food and other necessaries of life, that the body might be preserved in good working condition, and prevented from being out of repair, or falling prematurely to decay.

These anticipations are proved by experience to be just. Since the general introduction of inanimate mechanism into British manufactories, man, with few exceptions, has been treated as a secondary and inferior machine; and far more attention has been given to perfect the raw materials of wood and metals than those of body and mind. Give but due reflection to the subject, and you will find that man, even as an instrument for the creation of wealth, may be still greatly improved.

But, my friends, a far more interesting and gratifying consideration remains. Adopt the means which ere long shall be rendered obvious to every understanding, and you may not only partially improve those living instruments, but learn how to impart to them such excellence as shall make them infinitely surpass those of the present and all former times.

Here, then, is an object which truly deserves your attention; and, instead of devoting all your faculties to invent improved inanimate mechanism, let your thoughts be, at least in part, directed to discover how to combine the more excellent materials of body and mind, which, by a well devised experiment, will be found capable of progressive improvement.

Thus seeing with the clearness of noonday light, thus convinced with the certainty of conviction itself, let us not perpetuate the really unnecessary evils which our present practices inflict on this large proportion of our fellow-subjects. Should your pecuniary interests somewhat suffer by adopting the line of conduct now urged, many of you are so wealthy that the expense of founding and continuing at your respective establishments the institutions necessary to improve your animate machines would not be felt. But when you may have ocular demonstration, that, instead of any pecuniary loss, a well-directed attention to form the character and increase the comforts of those who are so entirely at your mercy, will essentially add to your gains, prosperity, and happiness, no reasons, except those founded on ignorance of your self-interest, can in future prevent you from bestowing your chief care on the living machines which you employ. And by so doing you will prevent an accumulation of human misery, of which it is now difficult to form an adequate conception.

That you may be convinced of this most valuable truth, which due reflection will show you is founded on the evidence of unerring facts, is the sincere wish of

THE AUTHOR.

1814

At his grandad's farm on the Scottish Borders Walter, sick son of an Edinburgh lawyer, was nursed back to health among peasants whose talk was his deepest layer of education. To them history was their own ballads of Border cattle raids & tales of the Covenanters & the Jacobite war in living memory. Scott's later huge reading of history & romances from Froissart to Goethe gave that a European con-text, but folklore & Shakespeare & Burns taught him most. Love of wild deeds & life was tempered by study to join his dad's law office. The advocates' library founded by Stair had documents & reports of trials in which kings & judges damned Scottish folk heroes as rebels. The Enlightenment philosophy taught him to assess all opinions without prejudice. His Tory love of ancient social forms did not make him refuse payment to destroy them. He 1st saw the Highlands as a young advocate when evicting, with a troop of soldiers, folk whose landlord wanted their glen for sheep pasture. Such evictions would soon unpeople the Highlands more than Ireland was unpeopled by famine;

WAVERLEY
SIR WALTER SCOTT
EDINBURGH

Chapter LXXII
[A POSTSCRIPT WHICH SHOULD HAVE BEEN A PREFACE]

Our journey is now finished, gentle reader; and if your patience has accompanied me through these sheets, the contract is, on your part, strictly fulfilled. Yet, like the driver who has received his full hire, I still linger near you, and make, with becoming diffidence, a trifling additional claim upon your bounty and good nature. You are as free, however, to shut the volume of the one petitioner as to close your door in the face of the other. This should have been a prefatory chapter, but for two reason: First, that most novel readers, as my own conscience reminds me, are apt to be guilty of the sin of omission respecting that same matter of prefaces; Secondly, that it is a general custom with that class of students to begin with the last chapter of a work; so that, after all, these remarks, being introduced last in order, have still the best chance to be read in their proper place. There is no European nation which, within the course of half a century or little more, has undergone so complete a change as this kingdom of Scotland. The effects of the insurrection of 1745, – the destruction of the patriarchal power of the Highland chiefs, - the abolition of the heritable jurisdictions of the Lowland nobility and barons, - the total eradication of the Jacobite party, which, averse to intermingle with the English/ or adopt their customs, long continued to pride themselves upon maintaining ancient Scottish manners and customs, commenced this innovation. The gradual influx of wealth and extension of commerce have since united to render the present people of Scotland a class of beings as different from their grandfathers as the existing English are from those of Queen Elizabeth's time. The political and economical effects of these changes have been traced by Lord Selkirk with great precision and accuracy. But the change, though steadily and rapidly progressive, has nevertheless been gradual; and, like those who drift down the stream of a deep and smooth river, we are not aware of the progress we have made until we fix our eye on the now distant point from which we have been drifted. Such of the present generation as can recollect the last twenty or twenty-five years of the eighteenth century will be fully sensible of the truth of this statement; especially if their acquaintance and connexions lay among those who in my younger time were facetiously called "folks of the old leaven," who still cherished a lingering, though hopeless, attachment to the house of Stuart. This race has now almost entirely vanished from the land, and with it, doubtless, much absurd political prejudice, but also many living examples of singular and disinterested attachment to the principles of loyalty which they received from their fathers, and of old Scottish faith, hospitality, worth, and honour. It was my accidental lot, though not born a Highlander (which may be an apology for much bad Gaelic), to reside during my childhood and youth among persons of the above description; and now, for the purpose of preserving some idea of the ancient manners of which I have witnessed the almost total extinction, I have embodied in imaginary scenes, and ascribed to fictitious characters, a part of the incidents which I then received from those who were actors in them. Indeed, the most romantic parts of this narrative are precisely those which have a foundation in fact. The exchange of mutual protection between a Highland gentleman and an officer of rank in the king's service,

yet Highlanders & Lowlanders he equally admired, writing very popular verse about knightly deeds among both until Byron (rich, handsome, radical, & a lord) put his contempt for society into even more popular verse. Scott then completed **Waverley** *& the public reacted (it was said)* **with an electric shock of delight.** *In the next 14 years he wrote 26 more novels. Wilkie Collins called him the* **King, Emperor, President & God Almighty of** *novelists. Translated, pirated, imitated across Europe & America, his work inspired 100s of plays, operas, pictures, some of which were masterpieces, but the* **Postscript** *here gives no clue why. It starts as laboriously polite as Wordsworth before his* **Lyrical Ballads.** *Scott could describe action as well as Swift, Fielding & Smollett, but his narrative voice is not witty & personal. It is a posh, unlocal speech used in 19th-century Britain & USA by most gentry & folk aiming to join them. Scott used it to introduce characters whose voices were far more local & personal than his own when he spoke as a magistrate in court. His young heroes also talk posh, are good natured, well mannered, brave in battle & lack individuality, so during political revolts they* *waver from side to side. Waverley is an English Tory who finds himself among the Highlanders who smashed King George's army at Prestonpans. Scott's novels show that folk always **waver** under political stress, if not fixed to a social position by habit, work, greed or strong ideas. He also shows how habit, work, greed & strong ideas in all social classes cause upheavals which every class blames on others. Shakespeare in his Falstaff plays was the 1 writer before Scott to show so many strongly representative folk in a national movement. Scott was a firm Tory but his revolutionary insights widened the social vision of every good novelist & history writer after him. **He taught us all,** Carlyle said, **that the past is filled by living men, not by protocols, state papers, controversies & abstractions of men.***

In 1820 George IV came to Scotland in the 1st royal visit since 1745. Scott used his prestige to make a Scottish vision of lairds & peasants, clanfolk & chieftains in a tartan social union loyal to the king, who was then much disliked in England. Scott got officials, landowners, pipers & street crowds to act so well that the foreign visitors loved the show & Scots officials &

together with the spirited manner in which the latter asserted his right to return the favour he had received, is literally true. The accident by a musket shot, and the heroic reply imputed to Flora, relate to a lady of rank not long deceased. And scarce a gentleman who was "in hiding" after the battle of Culloden but could tell a tale of strange concealments and of wild and hair's-breadth escapes as extraordinary as any which I have ascribed to my heroes. Of this, the escape of Charles Edward himself, as the most prominent, is the most striking example. The accounts of the battle of Preston and skirmish at Clifton are taken from the narrative of intelligent eye-witnesses, and corrected from the *History of the Rebellion* by the late venerable author of *Douglas*. The Lowland Scottish gentlemen and the subordinate characters are not given as individual portraits, but are drawn from the general habits of the period, of which I have witnessed some remnants in my younger days, and partly gathered from tradition. It has been my object to describe these persons, not by a caricatured and exaggerated use of the national dialect, but by their habits, manners, and feelings, so as in some distant degree to emulate the admirable portraits drawn by Miss Edgeworth, so different from the "Teagues" and "dear joys" who so long, with the most perfect family resemblance to each other, occupied the drama and the novel. I feel no confidence' however, in the manner in which I have executed my purpose. Indeed, so little was I satisfied with my production, that I laid it aside in an unfinished state, and only found it again by mere accident among other waste papers in an old cabinet, the drawers of which I was rummaging in order to accommodate a friend with some fishing-tackle, after it had been mislaid for several years. Two works upon similar subjects, by female authors whose genius is highly creditable to their country, have appeared in the interval; I mean Mrs. Hamilton's *Glenburnie* and the late accounts of

Highland Superstitions. But the first is confined to the rural habits of Scotland, of which it has given a picture with striking and impressive fidelity; and the traditional records of the respectable and ingenious Mrs. Grant of Laggan are of a nature distinct from the fictitious narrative which I have here attempted.

* * * *

I would willingly persuade myself that the preceding work will not be found altogether uninteresting. To elder persons it will recall scenes and characters familiar to their youth; and to the rising generation the tale may present some idea of the manners of their forefathers. Yet I heartily wish that the task of tracing the evanescent manners of his own country had employed the pen of the only man in Scotland who could have done it justice – of him so eminently distinguished in elegant literature, and whose sketches of Colonel Caustic and Umphraville are perfectly blended with the finer traits of national character. I should in that case have had more pleasure as a reader than I shall ever feel in the pride of a successful author, should these sheets confer upon me that envied distinction. And, as I have inverted the usual arrangement, placing these remarks at the end of the work to which they refer, I will venture on a second violation of form, by closing the whole with a dedication:—

THESE VOLUMES

BEING RESPECTFULLY INSCRIBED

TO

OUR SCOTTISH ADDISON,

HENRY MACKENZIE,

BY

AN UNKNOWN ADMIRER

OF

HIS GENIUS.

the tourist trade still enact it. In 1820 it hid from view evicted crofters, unemployment, new machines forcing down wages, protesters tried for sedition or hanged when government spies had tricked them into revolt. Like Brecht in East Germany Scott hoped his idea of a better nation would reform it. He was not pompous & saw himself as an entertainer writing for cash. He wrote fast & wrote himself to death at 61. His best books, set in Scotland's recent past, are his earliest. All have dull parts but Pushkin, Gogol, Tolstoy, Balzac, Manzoni, etc acclaimed him, so critics valued his work more than he did before 1930, when the finely shaped novels of Proust, Woolf, Joyce etc made **Old Mortality** *&* **Heart of Midlothian** *look as messy as* **Don Quixote** *&* **Pickwick Papers;** *& though Marx admired him Scottish Marxists despised him for writing about ancient clan loyalties while staying friendly with clan chiefs who burned down their tenants' homes or, sometimes with the help of lowland soldiers, drove them onto ships that took them to Canada. The Mackenzie named here was famed for a sentimental novel & critical articles that promoted the fame of Burns AND Scott.*

1816

Coleridge (he will be named C here) was an Anglican vicar's son, & a precocious scholar, & a most imaginative & impractical man. At Cambridge he shocked his people by deciding Christ should be our leader, not our god, & turning Unitarian; also becoming a democrat who planned to start a commune in America with Southey, a friend. All would be social equals there, farming the land before noon with mental work later – childcare shared by women – house chores by men – laundry by machine. He & Southey prepared for this by marrying a couple of sisters, but no others joined the scheme. To pay his way C became a writer of pacifist & radical journalism & tramped the country lecturing to Unitarian friends of liberty, as they called themselves. A splendid speaker & walker, he leapt over a gate & cut across a field to meet for the 1st time Dorothy, Words-worth's sister. This was in 1797. C & Words-worth had both written poetry & now met for the 1st time to discuss it. Both felt hampered by the formal diction

KUBLA KHAN, a Vision
SAMUEL TAYLOR COLERIDGE
LONDON

THE following fragment is here published at the request of a poet of great and deserved celebrity, and, as far as the Author's own opinions are concerned, rather as a psychological curiosity, than on the ground of any supposed *poetic* merits.

In the summer of the year 1797, the Author, then in ill health, had retired to a lonely farm-house between Porlock and Linton, on the Exmoor confines of Somerset and Devonshire. In consequence of a slight indisposition, an anodyne had been prescribed, from the effects of which he fell asleep in his chair at the moment that he was reading the following sentence, or words of the same substance, in "Purchas's Pilgrimage": "Here the Khan Kubla commanded a palace to be built, and a stately garden thereunto. And thus ten miles of fertile ground were inclosed with a wall." The Author continued for about three hours in a profound sleep, at least of the external senses, during which time he has the most vivid confidence, that he could not have composed less than from two to three hundred lines; if that indeed can be called composition in which all the images rose up before him as *things*, with a parallel production of the correspondent expressions, without any sensation or consciousness of effort. On awaking he appeared to himself to have a distinct recollection of the whole, and taking his pen, ink, and paper, instantly and eagerly wrote down the lines that are here preserved. At this moment he was unfortunately called out by a person on business from Porlock, and detained by him above an hour, and on his return to his room, found, to his no small surprise and mortification, that though he still retained some vague and dim recollection of the general purport of the vision, yet, with the exception of some eight or ten scattered lines and images, all the rest had passed away like the images on the surface of a stream into which a stone has been cast, but, alas! without the after restoration of the latter!

Then all the charm
Is broken – all that phantom-world so fair
Vanishes, and a thousand circlets spread,
And each mis-shape the other. Stay awhile,
Poor youth! who scarcely dar'st lift up thine eyes –
The stream will soon renew its smoothness, soon
The visions will return! And lo, he stays,
And soon the fragments dim of lovely forms
Come trembling back, unite, and now once more
The pool becomes a mirror.

Yet from the still surviving recollections in his mind, the Author has frequently purposed to finish for himself what had been originally, as it were, given to him. Σαρμον αδιον ασω: but the to-morrow is yet to come.

As a contrast to this vision, I have annexed a fragment of a very different character, describing with equal fidelity the dream of pain and disease.

[A FRAGMENT]

In Xanadu did Kubla Khan
A stately pleasure-dome decree:
Where Alph, the sacred river, ran
Through caverns measureless to man
*   Down to a sunless sea.*
So twice five miles of fertile ground
With walls and towers were girdled round:
And there were gardens bright with sinuous rills
Where blossomed many an incense-bearing tree;
And here were forests ancient as the hills,
Enfolding sunny spots of greenery.

But oh! that deep romantic chasm which slanted
Down the green hill athwart a cedarn cover!
A savage place! as holy and enchanted

*that classical educations, Pope's genius & Johnson's scholarship had established. Both wanted a poetry that spoke directly to the senses. Shakespeare & folk ballads did so; how could expensively taught moderns do it? Wordsworth felt that the speech of common people was enough like his own to be useful. C loved the words of sailors & explorers; saw poetry flowing through their books down from Hakluyt to Captain Cook, without interruption. Like Ezra Pound C had critical insights that inspired others. The Wordsworths inspired him as much as he them. Their best work was produced in 1797–98: Wordsworth's **Ruined Cottage**, **The Pedlar**, many of the **Lyrical Ballads**, the earliest version of **The Prelude**. Dorothy wrote her 1st & most intriguing journal & C his 3 great poems: **Kubla Khan**, **Christabel** & **The Ancient Mariner**. The last appeared in **Lyrical Ballads** but C thought the others incomplete. **Christabel** certainly was. They circulated in hand-written copies, & are now so well known that we cannot imagine how much they amazed the earliest readers.*

*The Ancient Mariner had been called **wild, unintelligible, a cock & bull story** by the reviewers despite its regular rhyme scheme. Here rhyme & metres shift with the images, a device Scott used (though less daringly) to give his own long poems variety. Byron learned it from Scott, then found **C** was the true originator, & persuaded John Murray, his publisher, to print the poems as they were, for a payment to **C** of £80. He needed it. His opium addiction had reached a new peak. He had fallen out with Wordsworth &, though now reconciled, they remained at a distance. His ambitions as a poet & philosopher seemed to have failed: he was chiefly known as a journalist & talker. He had abandoned his wife & children, who were supported by Southey, his wife's brother-in-law. **C** had also abandoned his early faith in democracy, as had Southey & Wordsworth. The 1st was now poet laureate, the 2nd would be. **C** was now an apologist for his life, so calls this poem a **fragment,** though it could not be more complete. Like **The Prelude** it shows a poet & poem being made. When **C** says he*

As e'er beneath a waning moon was haunted
By woman wailing for her demon-lover!
And from this chasm,
          with ceaseless turmoil seething,
As if this earth in fast thick pants were breathing,
A mighty fountain momently was forced;
Amid whose swift half-intermitted burst
Huge fragments vaulted like rebounding hail,
Or chaffy grain beneath the thresher's flail;
And 'mid these dancing rocks at once and ever
It flung up momently the sacred river.
Five miles meandering with a mazy motion
Through wood and dale the sacred river ran,
Then reached the caverns measureless to man,
And sank in tumult to a lifeless ocean:
And 'mid this tumult Kubla heard from afar
Ancestral voices prophesying war!

    The shadow of the dome of pleasure
    Floated midway on the waves;
    Where was heard the mingled measure
    From the fountain and the caves.
It was a miracle of rare device,
A sunny pleasure-dome with caves of ice!

    A damsel with a dulcimer
    In a vision once I saw:
    It was an Abyssinian maid,
    And on her dulcimer she played,
    Singing of Mount Abora.
    Could I revive within me
    Her symphony and song,
    To such a deep delight 'twould win me
That with music loud and long,
I would build that dome in air,
That sunny dome! those caves of ice!
And all who heard should see them there,
And all should cry, Beware! Beware!

His flashing eyes, his floating hair!
Weave a circle round him thrice,
And close your eyes with holy dread,
For he on honey-dew hath fed,
And drunk the milk of Paradise.

could rebuild Kubla's palace in words if he recalled the damsel's song, & so become a dangerously great poet, he has already done so.

NORTHANGER ABBEY
JANE AUSTEN
LONDON

1818

The heroines of Jane Austen's novels are single women who end up married, never unhappily. Her genius is to make the journey to that end one of wicked social observation, dramatic moral shifts & reassessments. Using ordinary mistakes within a narrow social group she shows desire & conscience muddled by self-deception. In **Northanger Abbey** *Catherine Morland only grows up when the man she loves helps her to stop reading the world in a way distorted by her reading of spooky gothic melodrama novels – fiction mocked by all the negatives of Austen's first chapter. In* **Pride & Prejudice**, *love is only rewarded when Elizabeth Bennet & Darcy, chiefly through conversations, adjust their skewed judgments of each other. Emma Wood-house's misplaced match-making, her*

[ADVERTISEMENT BY THE AUTHORESS]

THIS little word was finished in the year 1803, and intended for immediate publication. It was disposed of to a bookseller, it was even advertised, and why the business proceeded no farther, the author has never been able to learn. That any bookseller should think it worth while to purchase what he did not think it worth while to publish, seems extraordinary. But with this, neither the author nor the public have any other concern than as some observation is necessary upon those parts of the work which thirteen years have made comparatively obsolete. The public are entreated to bear in mind that thirteen years have passed since it was finished, many more since it was begun, and that during that period, places, manners, books, and opinions have undergone considerable changes.

[CHAPTER I]

No one who had ever seen Catherine Morland in her infancy, would have supposed her born to be an heroine. Her situation in life, the character of her father and mother, her own person and disposition, were all equally against her. Her father was a clergyman, without being neglected, or poor, and a very respectable man, though his name was Richard – and he had never been handsome. He had a considerable independence, besides two good livings – and he was not in the least addicted to locking up his daughters. Her mother was a woman of useful plain sense, with a good temper, and, what is more remarkable, with a good constitution.

She had three sons before Catherine was born; and instead of dying in bringing the latter into the world, as any body might expect, she still lived on – lived to have six children more – to see them growing up around her, and to enjoy excellent health herself. A family of ten children will be always called a fine family, where there are heads and arms and legs enough for the number; but the Morlands had little other right to the word, for they were in general very plain, and Catherine, for many years of her life, as plain as any. She had a thin awkward figure, a sallow skin without colour, dark lank hair, and strong features; – so much for her person; – and not less unpropitious for heroism seemed her mind. She was fond of all boys' plays, and greatly preferred cricket not merely to dolls, but to the more heroic enjoyments of infancy, nursing a dormouse, feeding a canary-bird, or watering a rose-bush. Indeed she had no taste for a garden; and if she gathered flowers at all, it was chiefly for the pleasure of mischief – at least so it was conjectured from her always preferring those which she was forbidden to take. – Such were her propensities – her abilities were quite as extraordinary. She never could learn or understand any thing before she was taught; and sometimes not even then, for she was often inattentive, and occasionally stupid. Her mother was three months in teaching her only to repeat the "Beggar's Petition;" and after all, her next sister, Sally, could say it better than she did. Not that Catherine was always stupid, – by no means; she learnt the fable of "The Hare and many Friends," as quickly as any girl in England. Her mother wished her to learn music; and Catherine was sure she should like it, for she was very fond of tinkling the keys of the old forlorn spinnet; so, at eight years old she began. She learnt a year, and could not bear it; – and Mrs. Morland, who did not insist on her daughters being accomplished in spite of incapacity or distaste, allowed her to leave off. The day which dismissed the music-master was one of the happiest of Catherine's life. Her taste for drawing was not superior; though whenever she could obtain the outside of a letter from her mother, or seize upon any other odd piece of paper, she did what she could in that way, by drawing houses and trees, hens and chickens, all very much like one another. – Writing and accounts she was taught by her father; French by her mother: her proficiency in either was not remarkable, and she shirked her lessons in both whenever she could. What a strange, unaccountable character! – for with all these symptoms of profligacy at ten years old, she had neither a bad heart nor a bad temper; was seldom stubborn, scarcely ever quarrelsome, and very kind to the little ones, with few interruptions of tyranny; she was moreover noisy and wild, hated confinement and cleanliness, and loved nothing so well in the world as rolling down the green slope at the back of the house.

Such was Catherine Morland at ten. At fifteen, appearances were mending; she began to curl her hair and long for balls; her complexion improved, her features were softened by plumpness and colour, her eyes gained more animation, and her figure more consequence. Her love of dirt gave way to an inclination for finery, and she grew clean as she grew smart; she had now the pleasure of sometimes hearing her father and mother remark on her personal improvement. "Catherine grows quite a good-looking girl, – she is almost pretty to day," were words which caught her ears now and then; and how welcome were the sounds! To look *almost* pretty, is an acquisition of higher delight to a girl who has been looking plain the first fifteen years of her life, than a beauty from her cradle can ever receive.

Mrs. Morland was a very good woman, and wished to see her children every thing they ought to be; but her time was so much occupied in lying-in and teaching the little ones, that her elder daughters were inevitably left to shift for themselves; and it was not very wonderful that Catherine, who had by nature nothing heroic about, should prefer cricket, base ball, riding on horseback, and running about the country at the age of fourteen, to books – or at least books of information – for, provided that nothing like useful knowledge could be gained from them, provided they were all story and no reflection, she had never any objection to books at all. But from fifteen to seventeen she was in training for a heroine; she read all such works as heroines must read to supply their memories with those quotations which are so serviceable and so soothing in the vicissitudes of their eventful lives.

1818

K: born 1795, London. His dad ran a livery stable, equivalent now of a garage. K studied medicine, loved poetry met Shelley, Byron & Coleridge, was published by Hunt, a radical editor who thought governments & poetry had taken a wrong turning since Shakespeare's day. Hunt lent K Chapman's **Homer** *& printed his early verses though K, as he says here, knew he would write better if he lived longer. When this book came out K was nursing a brother dying of TB, K's own illness. This preface was rejected as too self-critical by the publisher & K replaced it with an even sharper one. It did not sweeten the Tory reviewer who mocked the poem as the work of a cockney chemist's assistant. K's greatest poems were all written in the months before he died aged 26. Their melancholy, sensual music hypnotised most British readers into thinking them unearthly, & that poetry should be like that. K's intellectual vigour would have shocked them awake if he had lived to write more.*

ENDYMION: A POETIC ROMANCE
Dedicated to Thomas Chatterton
JOHN KEATS: LONDON

[THE REJECTED PREFACE]

IN a great nation, the work of an individual is of so little importance; his pleadings and excuses are so uninteresting; his "way of life" such a nothing; that a preface seems a sort of impertinent bow to strangers who care nothing about it.

A preface however should be down in so many words; and such a one that, by a glance over the type, the Reader may catch an idea of an Author's modesty, and non opinion of himself – which I sincerely hope may be seen in the few lines I have to write, notwithstanding certain proverbs of many ages' old which men find a great pleasure in receiving for gospel.

About a twelve month since, I published a little book of verses; it was read by some dozen of my friends who lik'd it; and some dozen who I was unacquainted with, who did not. Now when a dozen human beings, are at words with another dozen, it becomes a matter of anxiety to side with one's friends; – more especially when excited thereto by a great love of Poetry.

I fought under disadvantages. Before I began I had no inward feel of being able to finish; and as I proceeded my steps were all uncertain. So this Poem must rather be considered as an endeavour than a thing accomplish'd: a poor prologue to what, if I live, I humbly hope to do. In duty to the Public I should have kept it back for a year or two, knowing it to be so faulty: but I really cannot do so:– by repetition my favourite Passages sound vapid in my ears, and I would rather redeem myself with a new Poem – should this one be found of any interest.

I have to apologise to the lovers of simplicity for touching the spell of loveliness that hung about

Endymion: if any of my lines plead for me with such people I shall be proud.

It has been too much the fashion of late to consider men biggotted and addicted to every word that may chance to escape their lips: now I here declare that I have not any particular affection for any particular phrase, word or letter in the whole affair. I have written to please myself and in hopes to please others, and for a love of fame; if I neither please myself, nor others nor get fame, of what consequence is Phraseology?

I would fain escape the bickerings that all works, not exactly in chime, bring upon their begetters:– but this is not fair to expect, there must be conversation of some sort and to object shows a Man's consequence. In case of a London drizzle or a Scotch Mist, the following quotation from Marston may perhaps stead me as an umbrella for an hour or so: "let it be the Curtesy of my peruser rather to pity my self-hindering labours than to malice me."

One word more:– for we cannot help seeing our own affairs in every point of view – Should anyone call my dedication to Chatterton affected I answer as followeth:

"Were I dead Sir I should like a Book dedicated to me" –
Teignmouth March 19th 1818.

DON JUAN
BYRON
LONDON
1819

I

I want a hero: an uncommon want,
When every year and month sends forth a new one,
Till, after cloying the gazettes with cant,
* The age discovers he is not the true one;*
Of such as these I should not care to vaunt,
* I'll therefore take our ancient friend, Don Juan –*
We all have seen him, in the pantomime,
Sent to the devil somewhat ere his time.

II

Vernon, the butcher Cumberland, Wolfe, Hawke,
* Prince Ferdinand, Granby,*
*   Burgoyne, Keppel, Howe,*
Evil and good, have had their tithe of talk,

The noble Byron family had many extravagant eccentrics. One married a rich Scots girl & swiftly wasted her fortune. She brought up their son, who was lame but strong, in Aberdeen lodging houses. He was 10 when an uncle's death let him inherit the title, wealth & prestige of an English lord. He later used these as was expected of a Byron: gambling, whoring, drinking & over-eating, but compensated by bouts of abstinence &

hard exercise, boxing & swimming. But being (as he said) **half Scotch**, he felt outside as well as superior to **the twice two thousand** folk in fashionable London society. In the House of Lords he defended the machine wreckers. An air of gloomy & mysterious scorn came easy to him. The hero of his long poem, **Childe Harold's Pilgrimage,** is full of that & hatred of injustice. It made him very fashionable till rumours of adultery with his half sister closed polite English society to him. He then lived in Venice where he aided Italian revolutionaries & wrote this, his greatest poem.

The hero of it is, like Waverley, an attractive young man to whom things happen. Half of them are love affairs which involve him with shipwreck, slavery, battle & send him finally to England as an emissary & ex-lover of Catherine the Great. These adventures are only romantic in their variety, for Byron disliked fine poetic sentiments, preferring the ironic & earthy humour of Pope & Burns. He shows a world **stripped of the tinsel of sentiment**, where only sex diverts people from grasping wealth & power, & where religion & politeness are hypocrisy. His jocular use of

And fill'd their sign-posts then, like Wellesley now;
Each in their turn like Banquo's monarchs stalk,
  Followers of fame, "nine farrow" of that sow:
France, too, had Buonaparté and Dumourier
Recorded in the Moniteur and Courier.

III

Barnave, Brissot, Condorcet, Mirabeau,
  Petion, Clootz, Danton, Marat, La Fayette,
Were French, and famous people, as we know;
  And there were others, scarce forgotten yet,
Joubert, Hoche, Marceau, Lannes, Desaix, Moreau,
  With many of the military set,
Exceedingly remarkable at times,
But not at all adapted to my rhymes.

IV

Nelson was once Britannia's god of war,
  And still should be so, but the tide is turn'd;
There's no more to be said of Trafalgar,
  'Tis with our hero quietly inurn'd;
Because the army's grown more popular,
  At which the naval people are concern'd;
Besides, the prince is all for the land-service,
Forgetting Duncan, Nelson, Howe, and Jervis.

V

Brave men were living before Agamemnon
  And since, exceeding valourous and sage,
A good deal like him too, though quite the same none;
  But then they shone not on the poet's page,
And so have been forgotten: – I condemn none,
  But can't find any in the present age
Fit for my poem (that is, for my new one);
So, as I said, I'll take my friend Don Juan.

VI

Most epic poets plunge "in medias res"
  (Horace makes this the heroic turnpike road),
And then your hero tells, whene'er you please,
  What went before – by way of episode,
While seated after dinner at his ease,

Beside his mistress in some soft abode,
Palace, or garden, paradise, or cavern,
Which serves the happy couple for a tavern.

VII

That is the usual method, but not mine –
My way is to begin with the beginning;
The regularity of my design
Forbids all wandering as the worst of sinning,
And therefore I shall open with a line
(Although it cost me half an hour in spinning)
Narrating somewhat of Don Juan's father,
And also of his mother, if you'd rather.

slang & ostentatiously bad rhymes to keep a strict verse form running let him leave the Byronic pedestal & address the reader as an equal. He meant to lead his hero into France where, like Tom Paine, Juan would join the Revolutionary National Assembly, but Byron went to fight for the liberty of Greece & died of marsh fever there. We will never know how Juan would have fared in the only political body Byron respected.

PROMETHEUS UNBOUND a Lyrical Drama in Four Acts with other poems by PERCY BYSSHE SHELLEY: LONDON
[PREFACE]

1820

THE Greek tragic writers, in selecting as their subject any portion of their national history or mythology, employed in their treatment of it a certain arbitrary discretion. They by no means conceived themselves bound to adhere to the common interpretation or to imitate in story as in title their rivals and predecessors. Such a system would have amounted to a resignation of those claims to preference over their competitors which incited the composition. The Agamemnonian story was exhibited on the Athenian theatre with as many variations as dramas.

I have presumed to employ a similar licence. The "Prometheus Unbound" of Aeschylus supposed the reconciliation of Jupiter with his victim as the price of the disclosure of the danger threatened to his empire by the consummation of his marriage with Thetis. Thetis, according to this view of the subject, was given in marriage to Peleus, and Prometheus, by the permission of Jupiter, delivered from his captivity

In Greek mythology **Prometheus** *is a god who creates men to be the gods' slaves & is crucified by Zeus for then trying to free them.* **Prometheus** *resonates through the Shelley circle. Byron wrote a poem about him. In* **Frankenstein** *Mary Shelley reworked it while her husband wrote this remarkable unactable drama. Here Prometheus echoes the poet-narrator of the* **Ode to the West Wind** *who also recalls Jesus:* **I fall upon the thorns of life! I bleed!** *He is freed when the god of earthly tyranny is at last dethroned by a monstrous son he has generated; Demagorgon, who (like Robespierre or*

Napoleon) falls in pulling down the old corruption that bred him. Shelley prophesies that this will lead to the diviner day of universal brotherhood. Mary Shelley was its best critic. She said it enacted the theory that evil is not inherent in the system of the creation, where human destiny is concerned, but an accident that might be expelled.

Most reviewers saw no sense in it & especially scorned the preface: as mystical & mysterious as the drama, complained the Literary Gazette. It puzzled them because it mostly answers a review of Shelley's previous book, The Revolt of Islam. An anonymous critic described him as an unsparing imitator of Wordworth, to whose religious mind it must be matter, we think, of perpetual sorrow to see the philosophy which comes so pure & holy from his pen, degraded & perverted, as it continually is, by this miserable crew of atheists or pantheists. There were more charges, but that of being an imitator hurt Shelley most & inspired his words on contemporary writings (he means Wordworth, Coleridge & Byron);

by Hercules. Had I framed my story on this model, I should have done no more than have attempted to restore the lost drama of Aeschylus; an ambition, which if my preference to this mode of treating the subject had incited me to cherish, the recollection of the high comparison such an attempt would challenge might well abate. But, in truth, I was averse from a catastrophe so feeble as that of reconciling the Champion with the Oppressor of mankind. The moral interest of the fable, which is so powerfully sustained by the sufferings and endurance of Prometheus, would be annihilated if we could conceive of him as unsaying his high language and quailing before his successful and perfidious adversary. The only imaginary being resembling in any degree Prometheus, is Satan; and Prometheus is, in my judgement, a more poetical character than Satan, because, in addition to courage, and majesty, and firm and patient opposition to omnipotent force, he is susceptible of being described as exempt from the taints of ambition, envy, revenge, and a desire for personal aggrandisement, which, in the Hero of Paradise Lost, interfere with the interest. The character of Satan engenders in the mind a pernicious casuistry which leads us to weigh his faults with his wrongs, and to excuse the former because the latter exceed all measure. In the minds of those who consider that magnificent fiction with a religious feeling it engenders something worse. But Prometheus is, as it were, the type of the highest perfection of moral and intellectual nature, impelled by the purest and the truest motives to the best and noblest ends.

This Poem was chiefly written upon the mountainous ruins of the Baths of Caracalla, among the flowery glades and thickets of odoriferous blossoming trees, which are extended in ever winding labyrinths upon its immense platforms and dizzy arches suspended in the air. The bright blue sky of Rome, and the effect of the vigorous awakening of spring in that divinest climate, and the new life with which it drenches the spirits even to intoxication, were the inspiration of this drama.

The imagery which I have employed will be found, in many instances, to have been drawn from the operations of the human mind, or from those external actions by which they are expressed. This is unusual in modern poetry, although Dante and Shakspeare are full of instances of the same kind: Dante indeed more than any other poet, and with greater success. But the Greek poets, as writers to whom no resource of awakening the sympathy of their contemporaries was unknown, were in the habitual use of this power; and it is the study of their works, (since a higher merit would probably be denied me,) to which I am willing that my readers should impute this singularity.

One word is due in candour to the degree in which the study of contemporary writings may have tinged my composition, for such has been a topic of censure with regard to poems far more popular, and indeed more deservedly popular, than mine. It is impossible that any one who inhabits the same age with such writers as those who stand in the foremost ranks of our own, can conscientiously assure himself that his language and tone of thought may not have been modified by the study of the productions of those extraordinary intellects. It is true, that, not the spirit of their genius, but the forms in which it has manifested itself, are due less to the peculiarities of their own minds than to the peculiarity of the moral and intellectual condition of the minds among which they have been produced. Thus a number of writers possess the form, whilst they want the spirit of those whom, it is alleged, they imitate; because the former is the endowment of the age in which they live, and

the golden age of our literature (the Eliza-bethan); Milton: & imitation in general. The review also mocked Shelley's politics, saying He is really too young, too ignorant, too inexperienced, too vicious to undertake the task of reforming any world, but the little world within his own breast. The 2nd last paragraph answers that. Shelley evokes as allies Plato & Bacon (who wrote to improve folk) against Malthus & Paley who said it could not be done, so the preface gives Shelley's ideas of philosophy, politics, his literary canon & what he thinks is the function of poetry. The anonymous critic who wrote the review was John T. Coleridge, nephew of the poet, devout Anglican, also a lawyer who became a high court judge & editor of The Commentaries of Blackstone. He could not possibly approve of a republican pacifist atheist & vegetarian who, separated from a 1st wife, had eloped with Godwin's daughter AND step-daughter.

the latter must be the uncommunicated lightning of their own mind.

The peculiar style of intense and comprehensive imagery which distinguishes the modern literature of England, has not been, as a general power, the product of the imitation of any particular writer. The mass of capabilities remains at every period materially the same; the circumstances which awaken it to action perpetually change. If England were divided into forty republics, each equal in population and extent to Athens, there is no reason to suppose but that, under institutions not more perfect than those of Athens, each would produce philosophers and poets equal to those who (if we except Shakspeare) have never been surpassed. We owe the great writers of the golden age of our literature to that fervid awakening of the public mind which shook to dust the oldest and most oppressive form of the Christian religion. We owe Milton to the progress and developement of the same spirit: the sacred Milton was, let it ever be remembered, a republican, and a bold inquirer into morals and religion. The great writers of our own age are, we have reason to suppose, the companions and forerunners of some unimagined change in our social condition or the opinions which cement it. The cloud of mind is discharging its collected lightning, and the equilibrium between institutions and opinions is now restoring, or is about to be restored.

As to imitation, poetry is a mimetic art. It creates, but it creates by combination and representation. Poetical abstractions are beautiful and new, not because the portions of which they are composed had no previous existence in the mind of man or in nature, but because the whole produced by their combination has some intelligible and beautiful analogy with those sources of emotion and thought, and with the contemporary condition of them: one great poet is a masterpiece of nature which another not only ought to study, but must study. He might as wisely and as easily determine that his mind should no longer be the mirror of all that is lovely in the visible universe, as exclude from his contemplation the beautiful which exists in the writings of a great contemporary. The pretence of doing it would be a presumption in any but the greatest; the effect, even in him, would be strained, unnatural, and ineffectual. A poet is the combined product of such internal powers as modify the nature of others; and of such external influences as excite and sustain these powers; he is not one, but both. Every man's mind is, in this respect, modified by all the objects of nature and art; by every word and every suggestion which he ever admitted to act upon his consciousness; it is the mirror upon which all forms are reflected, and in which they compose one form. Poets, not otherwise than philosophers, painters, sculptors and musicians, are, in one sense, the creators, and, in another, the creations, of their age. From this subjection the loftiest do not escape. There is a similarity between Homer and Hesiod, between Aeschylus and Euripides, between Virgil and Horace, between Dante and Petrarch, between Shakspeare and Fletcher, between Dryden and Pope; each has a generic resemblance under which their specific distinctions are arranged. If this similarity be the result of imitation, I am willing to confess that I have imitated.

Let this opportunity be conceded to me of acknowledging that I have, what a Scotch philosopher characteristically terms, "a passion for reforming the world:" what passion incited him to write and publish his book, he omits to explain. For my part I had rather be damned with Plato and Lord Bacon, than go to Heaven with Paley and Malthus. But it is a mistake to suppose that I dedicate my poetical compositions solely to the direct enforcement of reform, or that I consider them in any degree as containing a reasoned system on the theory of human life. Didactic poetry is my abhorrence; nothing can be equally well expressed in prose that is not tedious and supererogatory in verse. My purpose has hitherto been simply to familiarize the highty refined imagination of the more select classes of poetical readers with beautiful idealisms of moral excellence; aware that until the mind can love, and admire, and trust, and hope, and endure, reasoned principles of moral conduct are seeds cast upon the highway of life which the unconscious passenger tramples into the dust, although they would bear the harvest of his happiness. Should I live to accomplish what I purpose, that is, produce a systematical history of what appear to me to be the genuine elements of human society, let not the advocates of injustice and superstition flatter themselves that I should take Aeschylus rather than Plato as my model.

The having spoken of myself with unaffected freedom will need little apology with the candid; and let the uncandid consider that they injure me less than their own hearts and minds by misrepresentation. Whatever talents a person may possess to amuse and instruct others, be they ever so inconsiderable, he is yet bound to exert them: if his attempt be ineffectual, let the punishment of an unaccomplished purpose have been sufficient; let none trouble themselves to heap the dust of oblivion upon his efforts; the pile they raise will betray his grave which might otherwise have been unknown.

1827

In the 1790s a French government split the nobility's big estates among the peasants, & in 1801 the government of Britain did so in reverse. Until then each person wanting part of a common had to get it by private acts of parliament. Now a general act let local boards sell remaining common land fast. They did. Estates & farms expanded. Clare saw & felt the change as a child of poor cottagers.

THE PARISH OR THE PROGRESS OF CANT
JOHN CLARE
LONDON

THIS POEM was begun & finished under the pressure of heavy distress with embittered feelings under a state of anxiety & oppression almost amounting to slavery – when the prosperity of one class was founded on the adversity & distress of the other – The haughty demand by the master to his labourer was work for the little I chuse to alow you & go to the parish for the rest – or starve – to decline working under such advantages was next to offending a magistrate & no opportunity was lost in marking the insult by some unqualified oppression – but better times & better prospects have opened a peace establishment of more sociable feeling & kindness – & to no one upon earth do I owe ill will.

1828

Noah Webster's Grammatical Institute of the English Language, renamed the American Spelling Book & known as the Blue-backed Speller, was 1st published in 1783. It eliminated unnecessary letters & archaic spellings, such as the u in labour. He later produced an American Grammar & an American Reader, also for use in American schools, but by his death, the Blue-backed Speller had sold 24 million copies. Webster's royalty was half a cent per copy.

THE AMERICAN DICTIONARY OF THE ENGLISH LANGUAGE
NOAH WEBSTER: NEW YORK

IN the year 1783, just at the close of the Revolution, I published an elementary book for facilitating the acquisition of our vernacular tongue, and for correcting a vicious pronunciation which prevailed extensively among the common people of this country. Soon after the publication of that work, – I believe in the following year, – that learned and respectable scholar, the Rev. Dr. Goodrich, of Durham, one of the trustees of Yale College, suggested to me the propriety and expediency of my compiling a Dictionary which should complete a system for the instruction of the citizens of this country in the language. At that time, I could not indulge the thought, much less the hope, of undertaking such a work, as I was neither qualified by research, nor had I the means of support, during the execution of the work, had I been disposed to undertake it. For many years, therefore, though I considered such a work as very desirable, yet it appeared to me impracticable, as I was under the necessity of devoting my time to other occupations for obtaining subsistence.

About thirty-five years ago, I began to think of attempting the compilation of a Dictionary. I was induced to this undertaking, not more by the suggestion of friends, than by my own experience of the want of such a work while reading modern books of science. In this pursuit I found almost insuperable difficulties, from the want of a dictionary for explaining many new words which recent discoveries in the physical sciences had introduced into use. To remedy this defect in part, I published my *Compendious Dictionary* in 1806, and soon after made preparations for undertaking a larger work.

My original design did not extend to an investigation of the origin and progress of our language, much less of other languages. I limited my views to the correcting of certain errors in the best English dictionaries, and to the supplying of words in which they are deficient. But after writing through two letters of the alphabet, I determined to change my plan. I found myself embarrassed, at every step, for want of a knowledge of the origin of words, which Johnson, Bailey, Junius, Skinner, and some other authors, do not afford the means of obtaining. Then, laying aside my manuscripts, and all books treating of language, except lexicons and dictionaries, I endeavored, by a diligent comparison of words having the same or cognate radical letters, in about twenty languages, to obtain a more correct knowledge of the primary sense of original words, of the affinities between the English and many other languages, and thus to enable myself to trace words to their source.

I had not pursued this course more than three or

To safeguard the Speller rights, Webster instigated state copyright laws, followed by a federal law in 1790. After a brief spell as a newspaper publisher he devoted his life to compiling the dictionary which bears his name, completing his manuscript at Cambridge University in 1825. Unable to find an English publisher, he arranged for it to be printed in New Haven with a specially imported German typeface.

*As well as extending the Speller's reforms by reversing the **re** in words such as **theatre**, Webster included American nouns, many of native origin, which had never been categorised – **prairie, corn, caribou** & **porcupine** – along with immigrant phrases such as **strudel** & **cookie**. He incorporated colloquialisms but excluded slang; the English raised their hats, Americans raised children.*

four years before I discovered that I had to unlearn a great deal that I had spent years in learning, and that it was necessary for me to go back to the first rudiments of a branch of erudition which I had before cultivated, as I had supposed, with success.

I spent ten years in this comparison of radical words, and informing a *Synopsis of the principal Words in twenty Languages, arranged in Classes under the primary Elements or Letters*. The result has been to open what are to me new views of language, and to unfold what appear to be the genuine principles on which these languages are constructed.

After completing this *Synopsis*, I proceeded to correct what I had written of the Dictionary, and to complete the remaining part of work. But before I had finished it, I determined on a voyage to Europe, with the view of obtaining some books and some assistance which I wanted, of learning the real state of the pronunciation of our language in England, as well as the general state of philology in that country, and of attempting to bring about some agreement or coincidence of opinions in regard to unsettled points in pronunciation and grammatical construction. In some of these objects, I failed; in others, my designs were answered.

It is not only important, but in a degree necessary, that the people of this country should have an *American Dictionary of the English Language*; for, although the body of the language is the same as in England, and it is desirable to perpetuate that sameness, yet some differences must exist. Language is the expression of ideas; and if the people of one country can not preserve an identity of ideas, they can not retain an identity of language. Now, an identity of ideas depends materially upon a sameness of things or objects with which the people of the two countries are conversant. But in no two portions of the earth, remote from each other, can such identity be found. Even physical objects must be different. But the principal differences between the people of this country and of all others arise from different forms of government, different laws, institutions, and customs. Thus the practice of *hawking* and *hunting*, the institution of *heraldry* and the *feudal system* of England, originated terms which formed, and some of which now form, a necessary part of the language of that country; but, in the United States, many of these terms are no part of our present language, and they can not be, for the things which they express do not exist in this country. They can be known to us only as obsolete or as foreign words. On the other hand, the institutions in this country which are new and peculiar give rise to new terms, or to new applications of old terms, unknown to the people of England, which can not be explained by them, and which will not be inserted in their dictionaries, unless copied from ours. Thus the terms *land-office, land-warrant, location of land, consociation* of churches, *regent* of a university, *intendant* of a city, *plantation, selectmen, senate, congress, court, assembly, escheat,* etc., are either words not belonging to the language of England, or they are applied to things in this country which do not exist in that. No person in this country will be satisfied with the English definitions of the words *congress, senate,* and *assembly, court,* etc.; for although these are words used in England, yet they are applied in this country to express ideas which they do not express in that country. With out present constitutions of government, *escheat* can never have its feudal sense in the United States.

But this is not all. In many cases, the nature of our governments and of our civil institutions requires an appropriate language in the definition of words, even when the words express the same things as in England. Thus the English dictionaries inform us that a *justice* is one deputed by the *king* to do right by way of judgment; he is a *lord* by his office; justices of the peace are appointed by the *king's commission* – language which is inaccurate in respect to this officer in the United States. So *constitutionally* is defined, by Chalmers, *legally*; but in this country the distinction between *constitution* and *law* requires a different definition. In the United States, a *plantation* is a very different thing from what it is in England. The word *marshal*, in this country, has one important application unknown in England, or in Europe.

A great number of words in our language require to be defined in a phraseology accommodated to the condition and institutions of the people in these States, and the people of England must look to an *American Dictionary* for a correct understanding of such terms.

The necessity, therefore, of a dictionary suited to the people of the United States is obvious; and I should suppose that, this fact being admitted, there could be no difference of opinion as to the time when such a work ought to be substituted for English dictionaries.

There are many other considerations of a public nature which serve to justify this attempt to furnish an American work which shall be a guide to the youth of the United States. Most of these are too obvious to require illustration.

One consideration, however, which is dictated by my own feelings, but which, I trust, will meet with approbation in correspondent feelings in my fellow-citizens, ought not to be passed in silence. It is this: "The chief glory of a nation," says Dr. Johnson, "arises from its authors." With this opinion deeply impressed on my mind, I have the same ambition which actuated that great man when he expressed a wish to give celebrity to Bacon, to Hooker, to Milton, and to Boyle.

I do not, indeed, expect to add celebrity to the names of Franklin, Washington, Adams, Jay, Madison, Marshall, Ramsay, Kent, Hare, Silliman, Cleaveland, Walsh, Irving, and many other Americans distinguished by their writings or by their science; but it is with pride and satisfaction that I can place them, as authorities, on the same page with those of Boyle, Hooker, Milton, Dryden, Addison, Ray, Milner, Cowper, Davy, Thomson, and Jameson.

A life devoted to reading and to an investigation of the origin and principles of our vernacular language, and especially a particular examination of the best English writers, with a view to a comparison of their style and phraseology with those of the best American writers, and with our colloquial usage, enables me to affirm, with confidence, that the genuine English idiom is as well preserved by the unmixed English of this country as it is by the best *English* writers. . . .It is true that many of our writers have neglected to cultivate taste and the embellishments of style; but even these have written the language in its genuine *idiom*. In this respect, Franklin and Washington, whose language is their hereditary mother tongue, unsophisticated by modern grammar, present as pure models of genuine English as Addison or Swift. But I may go further, and affirm, with truth, that our country has produced some of the best models of composition. The style of President Smith; of the authors of the *Federalist*; of Mr. Ames; of Dr. Mason; of Mr. Harper; of Chancellor Kent; of Mr. Barlow; of Dr. Channing; of Washington Irving; of the legal decisions of the Supreme Court of the United States; of the reports of legal decisions in some of the particular States; and many other writings, – in purity; in elegance, and in technical precision, is equaled only by that of the best British authors, and surpassed by that of no English compositions of a similar kind.

The United States commenced their existence under circumstances wholly novel and unexampled in the history of nations. They commenced with civilization, with learning, with science, with constitutions of free government, and with that best of gift of God to man, the Christian religion. Their population is now equal to that of England; in arts and sciences, our citizens are very little behind the most enlightened people of earth, – in some respects they have no superiors; and our language, within two centuries, will be spoken by more people in this country than any other language on earth, except the Chinese, in Asia – and even that may not be an exception.

It has been my aim in this work, now offered to my fellow-citizens, to ascertain the true principles of the language, in its orthography and structure; to purify it from some palpable errors, and reduce the number of its anomalies, thus giving it more regularity and consistency in its forms, both of words and sentences; and in this manner to furnish a standard of our vernacular tongue, which we shall not be ashamed to bequeath to *five hundred millions of people*, who are destined to occupy, and I hope to adorn, the vast territory within our jurisdiction.

If the language can be improved in regularity, so as to be more easily acquired by our own citizens and by foreigners, and thus be rendered a more useful instrument for the propagation of science, arts, civilization, and Christianity; if it can be rescued from the mischievous influence of sciolists, and that dabbling spirit of innovation which is perpetually disturbing its settled usages and filling it with anomalies; if, in short, our vernacular language can be redeemed from corruptions, and our philology and literature from degradation, – it would be a source of great satisfaction to me to be one among the instruments of promoting these valuable objects. If this object can not be effected, and my wishes and hopes are to be frustrated, my labor will be lost, and this work must sink into oblivion.

This Dictionary, like all others of the kind, must be left, in some degree, imperfect; for what individual is competent to trace to their source, and define in all their various applications, popular, scientific, and technical, *seventy* or *eighty thousand* words! It satisfies my mind that I have done all that my health, my talents, and my pecuniary means would enable me to accomplish. I present it to my fellow-citizens, not with frigid indifference, but with my ardent wishes for their improvement and their happiness; and for the continued increase of the wealth, the learning, the moral and religious elevation of character, and the glory, of my country.

To that great and benevolent Being, who, during the preparation of this work, has sustained a feeble constitution, amidst obstacles and toils, disappointments, infirmities, and depressions, – who has borne me and my manuscripts in safety across the Atlantic, and given me strength and resolution to bring the work to a close, – I would present the tribute of my most grateful acknowledgements. And if the talent which he intrusted to my care has not been put to the most profitable use in his service, I hope it has not been "kept laid up in a napkin," and that any misapplication of it may be graciously forgiven.

Noah Webster. New Haven, 1828.

1831

Son of actor-parents & orphaned when 3, P was adopted by a childless couple, educated expensively, enrolled in Virginia University &, due to a gambling debt, was removed in a year by his stepdad. For 3 years he served as a soldier – printed 2 poem books – entered West Point for officer training – was expelled for neglect of duty. At 22 (when he wrote this) he had decided to live by writing. On both the Atlantic shores magazines bought reviews & prose upon comic, exotic, romantic, supernatural, criminal & scientific matters. Blackwood's magazine in Edinburgh printed horror tales disguised as true report. In all these modes, apart from the comic, P achieved lasting & popular art. In hypnotic, seductive, wonderfully distinct words he wrote verse &

POEMS
EDGAR ALLAN POE
NEW YORK

[INTRODUCTORY LETTER]

DEAR B—Believing only a portion of my former volume to be worthy a second edition – that small portion I thought it as well to include in the present book as to republish by itself. I have therefore herein combined "Al Aaraaf" and "Tamerlane" with other poems hitherto unprinted. Nor have I hesitated to insert from the "Minor Poems," now omitted, whole lines, and even passages, to the end that being placed in a fairer light, and the trash shaken from them in which they were imbedded, they may have some chance of being seen by posterity.

It has been said that a good critique on a poem may be written by one who is no poet himself. This, according to *your* idea and *mine* of poetry, I feel to be false – the less poetical the critic, the less just the critique, and the converse. On this account, and because there are but few B—s in the world, I would be as much ashamed of the world's good opinion as proud of your own. Another than yourself might here observe, "Shakespeare is in possession of the world's good opinion, and yet Shakespeare is the greatest of poets. It appears then that the world judge correctly, why should you be ashamed of their favourable judgment?"*OOOOOOOOOOOOOOOOOOOOOOOO*

AS MOST FOLK NEITHER READ NOR ENJOY SHAKESPEARE THEIR *HIGH OPINION* OF HIM ONLY ECHOES THE *JUDGMENT* OF A VERY FEW WHO DO.

OOOOOOOOOOOOOOOOOOOOOOOOOOOOOOOOOOOOOOOOOOOOOOOOOOOO

I mentioned just now a vulgar error as regards criticism. I think the notion that no poet can form a correct estimate of his own writings is another. I remarked before that in proportion to the poetical talent would be the justice of a critique upon poetry. Therefore a bad poet would, I grant, make a false critique, and his self-love would infallibly bias his little judgment in his favour; but a poet, who is indeed a poet, could not, I think, fail of making a just critique; whatever should be deducted on the score of self-love might be replaced on account of his intimate acquaintance with the subject; in short, we have more instances of false criticism than of just where one's own writings are the test, simply because we have more bad poets than good. There are, of course, many objections to what I say: Milton is a great example of the contrary; but his opinion with respect to the "Paradise Regained" is by no means fairly ascertained. By what trivial circumstances men are often led to assert what they do not really believe! Perhaps an inadvertent word has descended to posterity. But, in fact, the "Paradise Regained" is little, if at all, inferior to the "Paradise Lost," and is only supposed so to be because men do not like epics, whatever they may say to the contrary, and reading those of Milton in their natural order, are too much wearied with the first to derive any pleasure from the second.

I dare say Milton preferred "Comus" to either – if so – justly.

As I am speaking of poetry, it will not be amiss to touch slightly upon the most singular heresy in its modern history – the heresy of what is called, very

prose poems evoking yearning or menacing dream kingdoms, like those in Shakespeare plays he names on page 490. Some verge on melodrama, a very common fault then. He thinks nothing is too strange, difficult, horrid or vast to be imaginatively grasped & analysed, so half his tales show death approached, experienced or survived. The **Imp of the Perverse** *defines what Freud later named* **The Death Wish**. *His analysis of how odd urges grow into weird deeds led him to invent modern crime novels & science fiction (Jules Verne, Stevenson, Conan Doyle, H. G. Wells learned from him) so most Anglo-Saxons thought him just a pedlar of morbid thrills. Baudelaire saw his writings were what Chesterton calls* **dark blossoms on a tree of thought**, *&, by translating him, inspired a new school of French poetry.* **Eureka**, *P's last prose poem, said 60 years before Einstein that space & time are identical, & 85 years before Hubble that all matter had exploded from 1 vast globe, & (what is not yet proved, but suspected) mind & matter are eternal & identical too.*

foolishly, the Lake School. Some years ago I might have been induced, by an occasion like the present, to attempt a formal refutation of their doctrine; at present it would be a work of supererogation. The wise must bow to the wisdom of such men as Coleridge and Southey, but being wise, have laughed at poetical theories so prosaically exemplified.

Aristotle, with singular assurance, has declared poetry the most philosophical of all writings – but it required a Wordsworth to pronounce it the most metaphysical. He seems to think that the end of poetry is, or should be, instruction; yet it is a truism that the end of our existence is happiness; if so, the end of every separate part of our existence, everything connected with our existence, should be still happiness. Therefore the end of instruction should be happiness; and happiness is another name for pleasure; – therefore the end of instruction should be pleasure: yet we see the above-mentioned opinion implies precisely the reverse.

To proceed : *ceteris paribus*, he who pleases is of more importance to his fellow-men than he who instructs, since utility is happiness, and pleasure is the end already obtained which instruction is merely the means of obtaining.*OOOOOOOOOOOOOOOOOOOOOOOOOOOOOOOOOOOOOOOOOOOOOO*

Against the subtleties which would make poetry a study – not a passion – it becomes the metaphysician to reason – but the poet to protest. Yet Wordsworth and Coleridge are men in years; the one imbued in contemplation from his childhood; the other a giant in intellect and learning. The diffidence, then, with which I venture to dispute their authority would be overwhelming did I not feel, from the bottom of my heart, that learning has little to do with the imagination – intellect with the passions – or age with poetry.

> *"Trifles, like straws, upon the surface flow;*
> *He who would search for pearls must dive below,"*

are lines which have done much mischief. As regards the greater truths, men oftener err by seeking them at the bottom than at the top; Truth lies in the huge abysses where wisdom is sought – not in the palpable palaces where she is found. The ancients were not always right in hiding the goddess in a well; witness the light which Bacon has thrown upon philosophy; witness the principles of our divine faith – that moral mechanism by which the simplicity of a child may overbalance the wisdom of a man.

We see an instance of Coleridge's liability to err, in his *Biographia Literaria* – professedly his literary life and opinions, but, in fact, a treatise *de omni scibili et quibusdam aliis*. He goes wrong by reason of his very profundity, and of his error we have a natural type in the contemplation of a star. He who regards it directly and intensely sees, it is true, the star, but it is the star without a ray – while he who surveys it less inquisitively is conscious of all for which the star is useful to us below – its brilliancy and its beauty.

As to Wordsworth, I have no faith in him. That he had in youth the feelings of a poet I believe – for there are glimpses of extreme delicacy in his writings – (and delicacy is the poet's own kingdom – his *El Dorado*) – but they have the appearance of a better day recollected; and glimpses, at best, are little evidence of present poetic fire; we know that a few straggling flowers spring up daily in the crevices of the glacier.

He was to blame in wearing away his youth in contemplation with the end of poetizing in his manhood. With the increase of his judgment the light which should make it apparent has faded away. His judgment consequently is too correct. This may not be understood, – but the old Goths of Germany would have understood it, who used to debate matters of importance to their State twice, once when drunk, and once when sober – sober that they might not be deficient in formality – drunk lest they should be destitute of vigour.

0000000000000000000000000000000000000000000000000000000000
POE JEERS AT WORDSWORTH'S DULLEST LINES.
0000000000000000000000000000000000000000000000000000000000

Of Coleridge, I cannot speak but with reverence. His towering intellect! his gigantic power! To use an author quoted by himself, *"J'ai trouvé souvent que la plupart des sectes ont raison dans une bonne partie de ce qu'elles avancent, mais non pas en ce qu'elles nient;"* and to employ his own language, he has imprisoned his own conceptions by the barrier he has erected against those of others. It is lamentable to think that such a mind should be buried in metaphysics, and, like the Nyctanthes, waste its perfume upon the night alone. In reading that man's poetry, I tremble like one who stands upon a volcano, conscious from the very darkness bursting from the crater, of the fire and the light that are weltering below.

What is Poetry? – Poetry! that Proteus-like idea, with as many appellations as the nine-titled Corcyra! "Give me," I demanded of a scholar some time ago, "give me a definition of poetry." "*Très-volontiers*;" and he proceeded to his library, brought me a Dr. Johnson, and overwhelmed me with a definition. Shade of the immortal Shakespeare! I imagine to myself the scowl of your spiritual eye upon the profanity of that scurrilous Ursa Major. Think of poetry, dear B—, think of poetry, and then think of Dr. Samuel Johnson! Think of all that is airy and fairy-like, and then of all that is hideous and unwieldy; think of his huge bulk, the Elephant! and then – and then think of the "Tempest" – the "Midsummer Night's Dream" – Prospero – Oberon – and Titania!

A poem, in my opinion, is opposed to a work of science by having, for its *immediate* object, pleasure, not truth; to romance, by having, for its object, an indefinite instead of a definite pleasure, being a poem only so far as this object is attained; romance presenting perceptible images with definite, poetry with indefinite sensations, to which end music is an essential, since the comprehension of sweet sound is our most indefinite conception. Music, when combined with a pleasurable idea, is poetry; music, without the idea, is simply music; the idea, without the music, is prose, from its very definitiveness.

What was meant by the invective against him who had no music in his soul?

To sum up this long rigmarole, I have, dear B—, what you, no doubt, perceive, for the metaphysical poets as poets, the most sovereign contempt. That they have followers proves nothing –

> *"No Indian prince has to his palace*
> *More followers than a thief to the gallows."*

1831   *FRANKENSTEIN or The Modern Prometheus*
MARY SHELLEY
LONDON
[INTRODUCTION]

THE Publishers of the Standard Novels, in selecting "Frankenstein" for one of their series, expressed a wish that I should furnish them with some account of the origin of the story. I am the more willing to comply, because I shall thus give a general answer to the question, so very frequently asked me – "How I, then a young girl, came to think of, and to dilate upon, so very hideous an idea?" It is true that I am very averse to bringing myself forward in print; but as my account will only appear as an appendage to a former production, and as it will be confined to such topics as have connection with my authorship alone, I can scarcely accuse myself of a personal intrusion.

It is not singular that, as the daughter of two persons of distinguished literary celebrity, I should very early in life have thought of writing. As a child I scribbled; and my favourite pastime, during the hours given me for recreation, was to "write stories." Still I had a dearer pleasure than this, which was the formation of castles in the air – the indulging in waking dreams – the following up trains of thought, which had for their subject the formation of a succession of imaginary incidents. My dreams were at once more fantastic and agreeable than my writings. In the latter I was a close imitator – rather doing as others had done, than putting down the suggestions of my own mind. What I wrote was intended at least for one other eye – my childhood's companion and friend; but my dreams were all my own; I accounted for them to nobody; they were my refuge when annoyed – my dearest pleasure when free.

I lived principally in the country as a girl, and passed a considerable time in Scotland. I made occasional visits to the more picturesque parts; but my habitual residence was on the blank and dreary northern shores of the Tay, near Dundee. Blank and dreary on retrospection I call them; they were not so to me then. They were the eyry of freedom, and the pleasant region where unheeded I could commune with the creatures of my fancy. I wrote then – but in a most common-place style. It was beneath the trees of the grounds belonging to our house, or on the bleak sides of the woodless mountains near, that my true compositions, the airy flights of my imagination, were born and fostered. I did not make myself the heroine of my tales. Life appeared to me too common-place an affair as regarded myself. I could not figure to myself that romantic woes or wonderful events would ever be my lot; but I was not confined to my own identity, and I could people the hours with creations far more interesting to me at that age, than my own sensations.

*For Mary's parents see pp. 432-3. Born in 1797, she grew up with step-mother & a dad famed for his book arguing that slavery, poverty, kings, lords, churches, war & marriage would be ended by democracy & science: a book now outmoded among those who preferred Malthus' justification of selfish ownership. Shelley met Mary when she was 16, he 21 & writing **Queen Mab**, an epic bringing Godwin's ideas to many more folk. Godwin was poor. Shelley gave money, for though in debt he was heir to a wealthy estate & could always raise cash for others. Mary & her step-sister (also 16) eloped abroad with Shelley. He left behind his 2 children & a pregnant wife he had eloped with when **she** was 16. He invited her later to join them in France. She refused. The 3 elopers tried a sexual commune with Shelley's friend Hogg until Mary bore a premature baby, who died. Then Shelley was diagnosed consumptive. His speed in devising new plans & rejecting the past was feverish, maybe, but his lovers felt he flew. Mary & he flew to Geneva, met Byron. Like Coleridge & the Wordsworths 19 years before, the trio* *stimulated each other. The men's best poetry followed this meeting but Mary's novel came 1st.*

*She had heard how steam, gas, electricity gave men such godlike power that making life – intelligent life! – was the 1 power they still lacked. That Mary had a new baby, her adored Willmouse, was perhaps irrelevant to the men but not to this fable about a new method of making folk. Out of 5 dangerous pregnancies only 1 child of Mary survived infancy. But this myth of revulsion against new-born life & guilt, dread, flight from its consequences is as true for men as women. It describes the horror of a naturally good person perverted by rejection. **Dr Jekyll & Mr Hyde** is better written but shallower, for Mary's monster is wise & sympathetic. I expected this, he says when his maker curses him, All men hate the wretched; how, then, I must be hated who am miserable beyond all living things! As she wrote this novel Mary heard that her gentle neglected half sister & Shelley's wife were both dead by suicide. Frankenstein, wealthy scientific creator of poor life he wants to disown, still rules our civilisation.*

After this my life became busier, and reality stood in place of fiction. My husband, however, was, from the first, very anxious that I should prove myself worthy of my parentage, and enrol myself on the page of fame. He was for ever inciting me to obtain literary reputation, which even on my own part I cared for then, though since I have become infinitely indifferent to it. At this time he desired that I should write, not so much with the idea that I could produce any thing worthy of notice, but that he might himself judge how far I possessed the promise of better things hereafter. Still I did nothing. Travelling, and the cares of a family, occupied my time; and study, in the way of reading, or improving my ideas in communication with his far more cultivated mind, was all of literary employment that engaged my attention.

In the summer of 1816, we visited Switzerland, and became the neighbours of Lord Byron. At first we spent our pleasant hours on the lake, or wandering on its shores; and Lord Byron, who was writing the third canto of Childe Harold, was the only one among us who put his thoughts upon paper. These, as he brought them successively to us, clothed in all the light and harmony of poetry, seemed to stamp as divine the glories of heaven and earth, whose influences we partook with him.

But it proved a wet, ungenial summer, and incessant rain often confined us for days to the house. Some volumes of ghost stories, translated from the German into French, fell into our hands. There was the History of the Inconstant Lover, who, when he thought to clasp the bride to whom he had pledged his vows, found himself in the arms of the pale ghost of her whom he had deserted. There was the tale of the sinful founder of his race, whose miserable doom it was to bestow the kiss of death on all the younger sons of his fated house, just when they reached the age of promise. His gigantic, shadowy form, clothed like the ghost in Hamlet, in complete armour, but with the beaver up, was seen at midnight, by the moon's fitful beams, to advance slowly along the gloomy avenue. The shape was lost beneath the shadow of the castle walls; but soon a gate swung back, a step was heard, the door of the chamber opened, and he advanced to the couch of the blooming youths, cradled in healthy sleep. Eternal sorrow sat upon his face as he bent down and kissed the forehead of the boys, who from that hour withered like flowers snapt upon the stalk. I have not seen these stories since then; but their incidents are as fresh in my mind as if I had read them yesterday.

"We will each write a ghost story," said Lord Byron; and his proposition was acceded to. There were four of us. The noble author began a tale, a fragment of which he printed at the end of his poem of Mazeppa. Shelley, more apt to embody ideas and sentiments in the radiance of brilliant imagery, and in the music of the most melodious verse that adorns our language, than to invent the machinery of a story, commenced one founded on the experiences of his early life. Poor Polidori had some terrible idea about a skull-headed lady, who was so punished for peeping through a key-hole – what to see I forget – something very shocking and wrong of course; but when she was reduced to a worse condition than the renowned Tom of Coventry, he did not know what to do with her, and was obliged to despatch her to the tomb of the Capulets, the only place for which she was fitted. The illustrious poets also, annoyed by the platitude of prose, speedily relinquished their uncongenial task.

I busied myself *to think of a story*, – a story to rival those which had excited us to this task. One which would speak to the mysterious fears of our nature, and awaken thrilling horror – one to make the reader dread to look round, to curdle the blood, and quicken the beatings of the heart. If I did not accomplish these things, my ghost story would be unworthy of its name. I thought and pondered – vainly. I felt that blank incapability of invention which is the greatest misery of authorship, when dull Nothing replies to our anxious invocations. *Have you thought of a story?* I was asked each morning, and each morning I was forced to reply with a mortifying negative.

Every thing must have a beginning, to speak in Sanchean phrase; and that beginning must be linked to something that went before. The Hindoos give the world an elephant to support it, but they make the elephant stand upon a tortoise. Invention, it must be humbly admitted, does not consist in creating out of void, but out of chaos; the materials must, in the first place, be afforded: it can give form to dark, shapeless substances, but cannot bring into being the substance itself. In all matters of discovery and invention, even of those that appertain to the imagination, we are continually reminded of the story of Columbus and his egg. Invention consists in the capacity of seizing on the capabilities of a subject, and in the power of moulding and fashioning ideas suggested to it.

Many and long were the conversations between Lord Byron and Shelley, to which I was a devout but nearly silent listener. During one of these, various philosophical doctrines were discussed, and among others the nature of the principle of life, and whether there was any probability of its ever being discovered and communicated. They talked of the experiments of Dr. Darwin, (I speak not of what the Doctor really did, or said that he did, but, as more to my purpose, of what was then spoken of as having been done by him,) who preserved a piece of vermicelli in a glass case, till by some extraordinary means it began to move with voluntary motion. Not thus, after all, would life be given. Perhaps a corpse would be re-animated; galvanism had given token of such things: perhaps the component parts of a creature might be manufactured, brought together, and endued with vital warmth.

Night waned upon this talk, and even the witching hour had gone by, before we retired to rest. When I placed my head on my pillow, I did not sleep, nor could I be said to think. My imagination, unbidden, possessed and guided me, gifting the successive images that arose in my mind with a vividness far beyond the usual bounds of reverie. I saw – with shut eyes, but acute mental vision, – I saw the pale student of unhallowed arts kneeling beside the thing he had put together. I saw the hideous phantasm of a man stretched out, and then, on the working of some powerful engine, show signs of life, and stir with an uneasy, half vital motion. Frightful must it be; for supremely frightful would be the effect of any human endeavour to mock the stupendous mechanism of the Creator of the world. His success would terrify the artist; he would rush away from his odious handy-work, horror-stricken. He would hope that, left to itself, the slight spark of life which he had communicated would fade; that this thing, which had received such imperfect animation, would subside into dead matter; and he might sleep in the belief that the silence of the grave would quench for ever the transient existence of the hideous corpse which he had looked upon as the cradle of life. He sleeps; but he is awakened; he opens his eyes; behold the horrid thing stands at his bedside, opening his curtains, and looking on him with yellow, watery, but speculative eyes.

I opened mine in terror. The idea so possessed my mind, that a thrill of fear ran through me, and I wished to exchange the ghastly image of my fancy for the realities around. I see them still; the very room, the dark *parquet*, the closed shutters, with the moonlight struggling through, and the sense I had that the glassy lake and white high Alps were beyond. I could not so easily get rid of my hideous phantom; still it haunted me. I must try to think of something else. I recurred to my ghost story, – my tiresome unlucky ghost story! O! if I could only contrive one which would frighten my reader as I myself had been frightened that night!

Swift as light and as cheering was the idea that broke in upon me. "I have found it! What terrified me will terrify others; and I need only describe the spectre which had haunted my midnight pillow." On the morrow I announced that I had *thought of a story*. I began that day with the words, *It was on a dreary night of November*, making only a transcript of the grim terrors of my waking dream.

At first I thought but of a few pages – of a short tale; but Shelley urged me to develope the idea at greater length. I certainly did not owe the suggestion of one incident, nor scarcely of one train of feeling, to my husband, and yet but for his incitement, it would never have taken the form in which it was presented to the world. From this declaration I must except the preface. As far as I can recollect, it was entirely written by him.

And now, once again, I bid my hideous progeny go forth and prosper. I have an affection for it, for it was the offspring of happy days, when death and grief were but words, which found no true echo in my heart. Its several pages speak of many a walk, many a drive, and many a conversation, when I was not alone; and my companion was one who, in this world, I shall never see more. But this is for myself; my readers have nothing to do with these associations.

I will add but one word as to the alterations I have made. They are principally those of style. I have changed no portion of the story, nor introduced any new ideas or circumstances. I have mended the language where it was so bald as to interfere with the interest of the narrative; and these changes occur almost exclusively in the beginning of the first volume. Throughout they are entirely confined to such parts as are mere adjuncts to the story, leaving the core and substance of it untouched.

M.W.S. London, October 15, 1831

1832

*Born of England's last independent peasants, this great poet wrote, like Burns, in his own people's voice. Editors translated the local words & idioms into those of posh people, so Clare saw the link between enclosure of land & language. Both allowed efficient administracy of each, at the cost of people who lost their right to roam without toll. His perceptions & his poverty led to Clare's enclosure in asylums. He broke out & fed on common grass in his 3-day search for a girl lost in his memory of childhood. His poetry, evoking the jewels of the morning hanging on grass blades, draws on the commonly held speech of **Revelations**, yet clearly describes a low morning sun's light spectrum being diffused through drops of dew.*

THE MIDSUMMER CUSHION
JOHN CLARE
MANUSCRIPT

ALTHOUGH the fourth attempt may bring with it additional need of apology I am so confident of meeting success from the kindness of my readers if I deserve it as to render apology needless & so averse in apologizing for sympathy to aid successes that I may not be found to deserve that I shall so far deviate from the common place licence of prefaces as to make none & merely occupy the space that a preface universally occupies to explain the title to these trifles.

It is a very old custom among villagers in summer time to stick a piece of greensward full of field flowers & place it as an ornament in their cottages which ornaments are called Misdummer Cushions and as these trifles are field flowers of humble pretentions & of various hues I thought the above cottage custom gave me an opportunity to select a title that was not inapplicable to the contents of the Volume – not that I wish the reader to imagine that by so doing I consider these Poems in the light of flowers that can even ornament a cottage by their presence – yet if the eye of beauty can feel even an hours entertainment in their perusal I shall take it as the proudest of praise & if the lover of simple images

& rural scenery finds anything to commend
my end & aim is gratified.

1832

Dread of controversy stopped Scott making novels about politics after 1745. Galt is our author from then until 1832. A sea captain's son born in 1779, he was

THE MEMBER, An Autobiography
JOHN GALT
LONDON

[DEDICATION TO WILLIAM HOLMES, Esq. M.P.]
The Girlands, Jan. 1, 1832.

MY DEAR SIR,
I beg leave to inscribe to you this brief Memoir of my parliamentary services, and I do so on the same principle that our acquaintance, Colonel Napier, refers

to as his motive in dedicating that interesting work, the History of the Peninsular War, to the Duke of Wellington. It was chiefly under your kind superintendence that I had the satisfaction of exerting myself as an independent member, really and cordially devoted to the public good, during many anxious campaigns; and now, retired for ever from the busy scene, it is natural that I should feel a certain satisfaction in associating your respected name with this humble record.

If the Reform Bill passes, which an offended Providence seems, I fear, but too likely to permit, your own far more brilliant and distinguished career as a patriotic senator is, probably, also drawing to conclusion; and withdrawn, like me, to a rural retreat, in the calm repose of an evening hour, no longer liable to sudden interruption, it may serve to amuse your leisure to cast an eye over the unpretending narrative of scenes and events so intimately connected in my mind with the recollection of your talents, zeal, and genius, in what, though not generally so considered by the unthinking mass, I have long esteemed nearly the most important situation which any British subject can fill; but which, alas! is perhaps destined to pass away and be forgotten, amidst this general convulsion so fatal to the established institutions of a once happy and contented country. If, indeed, my dear and worthy friend, the present horrid measure be carried into full effect, it is but too plain that the axe will have been laid to the root of the British Oak. The upsetting, short-sighted conceit of new-fangled theorems will not long endure either the aristocratic or the monarchic branches; and your old office, so useful and necessary even, under a well-regulated social system, will fall with the rest; for the sharp, dogged persons likely to be returned under the schedules, will need no remembrancer to call them to their congenial daily and nightly task of retrenchment and demolition.

a shipping clerk & a journalist in Greenock; studied law in London; toured European ports as a merchant's agent seeking ways round Napoleon's embargo on British trade; became secretary of a company settling immigrants in Canada; opened new roads there; worked for the British government; founded Guelph, a new city. For over a year he lobbied parliament to get compensation for Canadians who, in war with the USA, had suffered by supporting Britain. They had been promised compen-sation. Galt found the British Constitution shrugs off promises MPs feel will reduce company gains. Sharper businessmen than Galt profited by his skill & energy. He would have died poor had he not written: once writing himself out of debtors' jail. His novels sold well, in spite of lacking a coy romanticism that was replacing sexual honesty & would spoil many Victorian novels & lives. His publisher weakened the comedy of his last novel by editing references to sex, but nobody tried to rewrite his dialect. The Scotch, he wrote were lucky to possess the whole range of the English language, as well as their own, by which they enjoy an unusually rich vocabulary. His best works (Annals of the Parish, The Entail, The Provost & this) he called treatises on the history of society. In rich speech with dry wit he describes ordinary habits, needs, greed & trade changing 18th-century life into one nearer ours. Galt's Provost still thrives in local politics by ensuring every civic improvement, disaster, festival & government subsidy enriches him. Galt's Member, equally corrupt & smug, seemed extinct in Britain but re-entered parliament long before 2000. Galt's MP, enriched by trade, finds parliament very profitable for clever traders; then meets folk starving because of promises it breaks, grows uneasy with the system & retires. Published just before the 1832 Reform Bill, this mock dedication to a real Tory House of Commons whip has the (fictional) retired author with an estate big enough to secure him from every social reform but revolution. This mock dedication was added by Lockhart, Galt's publisher, also a lawyer, landowner & Scott's son-in-law. It shows such folk could see reform as more a joke than a serious threat.

A melancholy vista discloses itself to all rational understandings; – a church in tatters; a peerage humbled and degraded – no doubt, soon to be entirely got rid of; that poor, deluded man, the well-meaning William IV, probably packed off to Hanover; the three per cents down to two, at the very best of it; a graduated property tax sapping the vitals of order in all quarters; and, no question, parliamentary grants and pensions of every description no longer held sacred!

May you be strengthened to endure with firmness the evil day; and if the neighbourhood of London should become so disturbed as to render Fulham no more that sweet snug retirement I always considered it, sure am I, that by making my little sequestered place here your temporary abode during the raging of the storm, you would confer much real pleasure and honour on myself and family. We have capital fishing, both trout and salmon, close at hand; and the moors are well enough all about us, – what with blackcock, grouse, ptarmigan, and occasionally roes, of which the duke's woods near harbour many. Here we might watch afar off the rolling of the popular billows, and the howlings of the wind of change and perturbation, and bide our time.

Once more, dear Mr. Holmes, accept the sincere tribute of esteem and regard from your old friend and pupil,

and humble servant at command,

ARCHIBALD JOBBRY

P.S. Herewith you will receive 4 brace moorfowl, 2 ditto B. cocks, item 3 hares, one side of a roe, and one gallon whisky (*véritable antique*); which liberty please pardon.

Jan. 2.—I am credibly informed that the weavers of Guttershiels, over their cups on hogmanae and yesterday, were openly discussing the division of landed properties in this district! What have not these demented ministers to answer for?

REFORMING AN EXPANDED MIDDLE

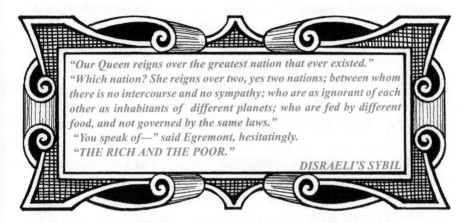

> "Our Queen reigns over the greatest nation that ever existed."
> "Which nation? She reigns over two, yes two nations; between whom there is no intercourse and no sympathy; who are as ignorant of each other as inhabitants of different planets; who are fed by different food, and not governed by the same laws."
> "You speak of—" said Egremont, hesitatingly.
> "THE RICH AND THE POOR."
>
> DISRAELI'S SYBIL

THAT NATURAL JUSTICE GAVE ALL MEN EQUAL right to vote for their own government was the faith of USA Republicans, French Revolutionaries and English reformers. It was shared by weavers, tenant farmers, dissenting clergy, industrialists and poets later called *romantic* by the Victorians. Defenders of royal and aristocratic privilege believed, of course, that what Burke called "the swinish multitude" should be excluded from political choice, and in this multitude they included all who were not Protestants with a landed estate. This pure Tory faith could not last. In 1829 the Anglo-Irish Duke of Wellington – conqueror of Napoleon, commander of Britain's armed forces and Tory prime minister – gave the vote to Catholic landlords, as the only way his government could keep control of Ireland.

By then Britain was the world's foremost industrial nation. It had a spreading railway network, imported material from every continent, exported machine-made goods and machines back, yet the manufacturing classes, though rich enough to have many friends in parliament, could hardly elect a single MP. In 1831 a majority of the Commons at last voted to reform the five-centuries-old electoral system and passed a bill they had rejected in 1797: a Liberal bill to take 143 seats from districts with no or hardly any voters and give them to counties and cities where nobody had voted. The House of Lords led by the Duke of Wellington rejected it. The king dithered. Public protest meetings erupted and rioters smashed windows in the palaces of the Duke and bishops who had also opposed the bill. A recently created civilian police could not restrain London mobs with middle-class sympathisers, so Britain seemed sliding into revolution. Events were maybe influenced by a fashionable London tailor with advertising facilities and radical ideas. He printed and widely distributed a poster headed GO FOR GOLD! advising Liberals with money in the Bank of England to withdraw it. Many did. This alarmed Britain's money market, so the king and a majority of lords swiftly made the bill law. Rotten boroughs vanished. Manchester, Birmingham, Leeds etc got parliamentary seats and there was widespread rejoicing, for a while.

The vote now belonged to adult males paying over £10 a year in house tax – the annual wage of sewing women and many labourers was less. Owners of big businesses and farms, bankers, shareholders, merchants, and lawyers could vote: not manual workers who had also been agitating for the vote since the 1790s. Apart from Socialist veterans like Robert Owen the middle class now overwhelmingly agreed with the aristocracy that votes for all was Utopian nonsense. A workers' party in the Commons might force them to raise their employees' wages and reduce their ability to compete – though at this time, as an industrial state, Britain had no competitors. Besides, the only nations where most adult males could vote were Switzerland (too small to consider), France (liable to revolutions), and the USA to which Liberal Britons felt morally superior – the most profitable American industries, unlike their own now, used slaves.

So after 1832 the British workers had less say in their own government and were far poorer than in 1790. An industrial and agricultural revolution had abolished the partially independent hand-loom weavers and cottagers by turning them into wage slaves: a new poor class whose labour created the wealth of the new rich. The British government had turned Australia into a huge jail for any poor who fought back by breaking game laws, toll gates, machines, or by forming trade unions. Before 1800 the British thought their nation divided among higher and lower *ranks*, the lowest having least money but not, because of that, an inevitable source of danger. From now on social ranks began to be called *classes*, named 1st 2nd and 3rd on railway carriage doors. The employing class took it for granted that the 2nd class was shallow, the 3rd class a deep reservoir of crime and disease. The Reform Bill did not cause this change, but confirmed it.

LIBERAL ENGLISH

1832
TO
1920

1843

PAST AND PRESENT
THOMAS CARLYLE
LONDON

[BOOK I. – PROEM : CHAPTER I. – MIDAS]

Born 1795 in Scottish border town, son of a builder. At 12 became student at Edinburgh University: no strange thing then, any could attend if tutors' fees were paid. He studied literature, especially German. Was school teacher; wrote entries for the Encyclopaedia Britannica (still an Edinburgh publication); married witty wife; farmed land she inherited; translated German philosophy & literature; corresponded with Goethe. Moved to London for access to library of the British Museum. His History of the French Revolution (like Marx's Das Kapital later) needed that. His radical theme & style shocked the History into fame; got it banned by monarchies restored, with British help, after Waterloo. It is written wholly in the present tense, & holds onto truths shared by great poets from Burns to Byron: politics are ruled by feelings, not statistics; states & churches without faith in equal justice for rich & poor are shams. Gibbon & Burke saw the French

THE condition of England, on which many pamphlets are now in the course of publication, and many thoughts unpublished are going on in every reflective head, is justly regarded as one of the most ominous, and withal one of the strangest, ever seen in this world. England is full of wealth, of multifarious produce, supply for human want in every kind; yet England is dying of inanition. With unabated bounty the land of England blooms and grows; waving with yellow harvests; thick-studded with workshops, industrial implements, with fifteen millions of workers, understood to be the strongest, the cunningest and the willingest our Earth ever had; these men are here; the work they have done, the fruit they have realised is here, abundant, exuberant on every hand of us: and behold, some baleful fiat as of Enchantment has gone forth, saying, "Touch it not, ye workers, ye master-workers, ye master-idlers; none of you can touch it, no man of you shall be the better for it; this is enchanted fruit!" On the poor workers such fiat falls first, in its rudest shape; but on the rich master-workers too it falls; neither can the rich master-idlers, nor any richest or highest man escape, but all are like to be brought low with it, and made "poor" enough, in the money sense or a far fataler one.

Of these successful skilful workers some two millions, it is now counted, sit in Workhouses, Poor-law Prisons; or have "out-door relief" flung over the wall to them, – the workhouse Bastille being filled to bursting, and the strong Poor-law broken asunder by a stronger. They sit there, these many months now; their hope of deliverance as yet small. In workhouses, pleasantly so-named, because work cannot be done in them. Twelve-hundred-thousand workers in England alone; their cunning right-hand lamed, lying idle in their sorrowful bosom; their hopes, outlooks, share of this fair world, shut-in by narrow walls. They sit there, pent up, as in a kind of horrid enchantment; glad to be imprisoned and enchanted, that they may not perish starved. The picturesque Tourist, in a sunny autumn day, through this bounteous realm of England, descries the Union Workhouse on his path. "Passing by the Workhouse of St.Ives in Huntingdonshire, on a bright day last autumn," says the picturesque Tourist, "I saw sitting on wooden benches, in front of their Bastille and within their ring-wall and its railings, some half-hundred or more of these men. Tall robust figures, young mostly or of middle age; of honest countenance, many of them thoughtful and even intelligent-looking men. They sat there, near by one another; but in a kind of torpor, especially in a silence, which was very striking. In silence: for, alas, what word was to be said? An Earth all lying round, crying, Come and till me, come and reap me; – yet we here sit enchanted! In the eyes and brows of these men hung the gloomiest expression, not of anger, but of grief and shame and manifold inarticulate distress and weariness; they returned my glance with a glance that seemed to say, 'Do not look at us. We sit enchanted here, we know not why. The Sun shines and the Earth calls; and, by the governing Powers and Impotences of this England, we are forbidden to obey. It is impossible, they tell us!' There was something that reminded me of Dante's Hell in the look of all this; and I rode swiftly away."

So many hundred thousands sit in workhouses: and other hundred thousands have not yet got even workhouses; and in thrifty Scotland itself, in Glasgow or Edinburgh City, in their dark lanes, hidden from all but the eye of God, and of rare Benevolence the minister of God, there are scenes

Revolution as damage done to lovely people by hasty idealists. Carlyle too admired & pitied Marie Antoinette, yet said history would be meaningless if a long-established, bankrupt, incompetent class of rulers had NOT driven people to revolt: said that a hungry French mob storming a palace did better than thousands of Irish starving to death in a peace blessed by landlords & British economists; that deaths of British orphans by brutal labour in factory & coal mine were as bad as the brutal killing of the French infant crown prince. This introduction tells his British readers that they too may provoke a revolt. He sees industry causes over-production, hence unemployment & **the shoemaker's child running barefoot, as her father has made too many shoes.** *He sounds like Isaiah & Micah – his parents were strict biblical Calvinists. German philosophy has taught him to see the world as the body (or garment) of a Spirit (or eternal idea) that all action reforms for better or worse, & he sees how machines* of woe and destitution and desolation, such as, one may hope, the Sun never saw before in the most barbarous regions where men dwelt. Competent witnesses, the brave and humane Dr. Alison, who speaks what he knows, whose noble Healing Art in his charitable hands becomes once more a truly sacred one, report these things for us: these things are not of this year, or of last year, have no reference to our present state of commercial stagnation, but only to the common state. Not in sharp fever-fits, but in chronic gangrene of this kind is Scotland suffering. A Poor-law, any and every Poor-law, it may be observed, is but a temporary measure; an anodyne, not a remedy: Rich and Poor, when once the naked facts of their condition have come into collision, cannot long subsist together on a mere Poor-law. True enough: – and yet, human beings cannot be left to die! Scotland too, till something better come, must have a Poor-law, if Scotland is not to be a byword among the nations. O, what a waste is there; of noble and thrice-noble national virtues; peasant Stoicisms, Heroisms; valiant manful habits, soul of a Nation's worth, – which all the metal of Potosi cannot purchase back; to which the metal of Potosi, and all you can buy with *it*, is dross and dust!

Why dwell on this aspect of the matter? It is too indisputable, not doubtful now to any one. Descend where you will into the lower class, in Town or Country, by what avenue you will, by Factory Inquiries, Agricultural Inquiries, by Revenue Returns, by Mining-Labourer Committees, by opening your own eyes and looking, the same sorrowful result discloses itself: you have to admit that the working body of his rich English Nation has sunk or is fast sinking into a state, to which, all sides of it considered, there was literally never any parallel. At Stockport Assizes, – and this too has no reference to the present state of trade, being of date prior to that, – a Mother and a Father are arraigned and found guilty of poisoning three of their children, to defraud a "burial-society" of some £3 8s. due on the death of each child: they are arraigned, found guilty; and the official authorities, it is whispered, hint that perhaps the case is not solitary, that perhaps you had better not probe farther into that department of things. This is in the autumn of 1841; the crime itself is of the previous year or season. "Brutal savages, degraded Irish," mutters the idle reader of Newspapers; hardly lingering on this incident. Yet it is an incident worth lingering on; the depravity, savagery and degraded Irishism being never so well admitted. In the British land, a human Mother and Father, of white skin and professing the Christian religion, had done this thing; they, with their Irishism and necessity and savagery, had been driven to do it. Such instances are like the highest mountain apex emerged into view; under which lies a whole mountain region and land, not yet emerged. A human Mother and Father had said to themselves, What shall we do to escape starvation? We are deep sunk here, in our dark cellar; and help is far. – Yes, in the Ugolino Hunger-tower stern things happen; best-loved little Gaddo fallen dead on his Father's knees!– The Stockport Mother and Father think and hint: Our poor little starveling Tom, who cries all day for victuals, who will see only evil and not good in this world: if he were out of misery at once; he well dead, and the rest of us perhaps kept alive? It is thought, and hinted; at last it is done. And now Tom being killed, and all spent and eaten, Is it poor little starveling Jack that must go, or poor little starveling Will? – What a committee of ways and means!

In starved seiged cities, in the uttermost doomed ruin of old Jerusalem fallen under the wrath of God, it was prophesied and said, "The hands of the pitiful women have sodden their own children." The stern Hebrew imagination could conceive no blacker gulf of wretchedness; that was the ultimatum of degraded god-punished man. And we here, in modern England, exuberant with supply of all kinds, besieged by nothing if it be not by invisible Enchantments, are we reaching that? – How come these things? Wherefore are they, wherefore should they be?

Nor are they of the St. Ives workhouses, of the Glasgow lanes, and Stockport cellars, the only unblessed among us. This successful industry of England, with its plethoric wealth, has as yet made nobody rich; it is an enchanted wealth, and belongs yet to nobody. We might ask, Which of us has it enriched? We can spend thousands where we once spent hundreds; but can purchase nothing good with them. In Poor and Rich, instead of noble thrift and plenty, there is idle luxury alternating with mean scarcity and inability. We have sumptuous garnitures for our Life, but have forgotten to *live* in the middle of them. It is an enchanted wealth; no man of us can yet touch it. The class of men who feel that they are truly better off by means of it, let them give us their name!

Many men eat finer cookery, drink dearer liquors, – with what advantage they can report, and their Doctors can: but in the heart of them, if we go out of the dyspeptic stomach, what increase of blessedness is there? Are they better, beautifuler, stronger, braver? Are they even what they call "happier"? Do they look with satisfaction on more things and human faces in this God's-Earth; do more things and human faces look with satisfaction on them? Not so. Human faces gloom discordantly, disloyally on one another. Things, if it be not mere cotton and iron things, are growing disobedient to man. The Master Worker is enchanted, for the present, like his Workhouse Workman; clamours, in vain hitherto, for a very simple sort of "Liberty:" the liberty "to buy where he finds it cheapest, to sell where he finds it dearest." With guineas jingling in every pocket, he was no whit richer; but now, the very guineas threatening to vanish, he feels that he is poor indeed. Poor Master Worker! And the Master Unworker, is not he in a still fataler situation? Pausing amid his game-preserves, with awful eye, – as he well may! Coercing fifty-pound tenants; coercing, bribing, cajoling; "doing what he likes with his own." His mouth full of loud futilities, and arguments to prove the excellence of his Corn-law; and in his heart the blackest misgiving, a desperate half-consciousness that his excellent Corn-law is *in*defensible, that his loud arguments for it are of a kind to strike men too literally *dumb*.

To whom, then, is this wealth of England wealth? Who is it that it blesses; makes happier, wiser, beautifuler, in any way better? Who has got hold of it, to make it fetch and carry for him, like a true servant, not like a false mock-servant; to do him any real service whatsoever? As yet no one. We have more riches than any Nation ever had before; we have less good of them than any Nation ever had before. Our successful industry is hitherto unsuccessful; a strange success, if we stop here! In the midst of plethoric plenty, the people perish; with gold walls, and full barns, no man feels himself safe or satisfied. Workers, Master Workers, Unworkers, all men, come to a pause; stand fixed, and cannot farther. Fatal paralysis spreading inwards, from the extremities, in St. Ives workhouses, in Stockport cellars, through all limbs, as if towards the heart itself. Have we actually got enchanted, then; accursed by some God? –

Midas longed for gold, and insulted the Olympians. He got gold, so that whatsoever he touched became gold, – and he, with his long ears, was little the better for it. Midas had misjudged the celestial music-tones; Midas has insulted Apollo and the gods: the gods gave him his wish, and a pair of long ears, which also were a good appendage to it. What a truth in these old Fables!

[CHAPTER II. – THE SPHINX]

How true, for example, is that other old Fable of the Sphinx, who sat by the wayside, propounding her riddle to the passengers, which if they could not answer she destroyed them! Such a Sphinx is this Life of ours, to all men and societies of men. Nature, like the Sphinx, is of womanly celestial loveliness and tenderness; the face and bosom of a goddess, but ending in claws and the body of a lioness. There is in her a celestial beauty which means celestial order, pliancy to wisdom; but there is also a darkness, a ferocity, fatality, which are infernal. She is a goddess, but one not yet disimprisoned; one still half-imprisoned, – the articulate, lovely still encased in the inarticulate, chaotic. How true! And does she not propound her riddles to us? Of each man she asks daily, in mild voice, yet with a terrible significance, "Knowest thou the meaning of this Day? What thou canst do Today; wisely attempt to do?" Nature, Universe, Destiny, Existence, howsoever we name this grand unnamable Fact in the midst of which we live and struggle, is as a heavenly bride and conquest to the wise and brave, to them who can discern her behests and do them; a destroying fiend to them who cannot. Answer her riddle, it is well with thee. Answer it not, pass on regarding it not, it will answer itself; the solution for thee is a thing of teeth and claws; Nature is a dumb lioness, deaf to thy pleadings, fiercely devouring. Thou art not now her victorious bridegroom; thou art her mangled victim, scattered on the precipices, as a slave found treacherous, recreant, ought to be and must.

With Nations it is as with individuals: Can they rede the riddle of Destiny? This English Nation, will it get to know the meaning of *its* strange new Today? Is there sense enough extant, discoverable anywhere or anyhow, in our united twenty-seven million heads to discern the same; valour enough in our twenty-seven million hearts to dare and do the bidding thereof? It will be seen! –

1847

THE PRINCESS; A MEDLEY
ALFRED, LORD TENNYSON
LONDON

*All that made wealthy Victorians contented is shown in harmony here: a private park to which (for a whole day!) the noble owner invites tenants from his lands outside, & half the folk of a nearby town. A ruined abbey on the estate must have once owned it. The present owner's house, in the Greek style, with busts, suggests a classical culture. Bright flowers show that his taste is not austere, fossils that science interests him. Curios link him to wild parts of the British Empire from Scotland to Oceania: horned heads indicate mighty hunters in the family. Weapons & a book tell of heroic ancestors in an age of chivalry and legend. Sir Walter & our poet (who seems just out of university), go past holiday makers revelling in **science & sport** to a picnic in the romantic ruin. A flirtatious chat follows with Walter's sister, a gay **half child half woman**, then a popular fictional type. (Middle-class dread of mature sex was then stronger. Doctors said*

[PROLOGUE]

*S*IR WALTER *Vivian all a summer's day*
Gave his broad lawns until the set of sun
Up to the people: thither flock'd at noon
His tenants, wife and child, and thither half
The neighbouring borough with their Institute
Of which he was the patron. I was there
From college, visiting the son, – the son
A Walter too,– with others of our set,
Five others: we were seven at Vivian-place.

And me that morning Walter show'd the house,
Greek, set with busts: from vases in the hall
Flowers of all heavens, and lovelier than their names,
Grew side by side; and on the pavement lay
Carved stones of the Abbey-ruin in the park,
Huge Ammonites, and the first bones of Time;
And on the tables every clime and age
Jumbled together; celts and calumets,
Claymore and snowshoe, toys in lava, fans
Of sandal, amber, ancient rosaries,
Laborious orient ivory sphere in sphere,
The cursed Malayan crease, and battle-clubs
From the isles of palm: and higher on the walls,
Betwixt the monstrous horns of elk and deer,
His own forefathers' arms and armour hung.

And "this" he said "was Hugh's at Agincourt;
And that was old Sir Ralph's at Ascalon:
A good knight he! we keep a chronicle
With all about him" – which he brought, and I
Dived in a hoard of tales that dealt with knights,
Half-legend, half-historic, counts and kings
Who laid about them at their wills and died;
And mixt with these, a lady, one that arm'd

Her own fair head, and sallying thro' the gate,
Had beat her foes with slaughter from her walls.

"O miracle of women," said the book,
"O noble heart who, being strait-besieged
By this wild king to force her to his wish,
Nor bent, nor broke, nor shunn'd a soldier's death,
But now when all was lost or seem'd as lost –
Her stature more than mortal in the burst
Of sunrise, her arm lifted, eyes on fire –
Brake with a blast of trumpets from the gate,
And, falling on them like a thunderbolt,
She trampled some beneath her horses' heels,
And some were whelm'd with missiles of the wall,
And some were push'd with lances from the rock,
And part were drown'd within the whirling brook:
O miracle of noble womanhood!"

So sang the gallant glorious chronicle;
And, I all rapt in this, "Come out," he said,
"To the Abbey: there is Aunt Elizabeth
And sister Lilia with the rest." We went
(I kept the book and had my finger in it)
Down thro' the park: strange was the sight to me;
For all the sloping pasture murmur'd, sown
With happy faces and with holiday.
There moved the multitude, a thousand heads:
The patient leaders of their Institute
Taught them with facts. One rear'd a font of stone
And drew, from butts of water on the slope,
The fountain of the moment, playing now
A twisted snake, and now a rain of pearls,
Or steep-up spout whereon the gilded ball
Danced like a wisp: and somewhat lower down
A man with knobs and wires and vials fired
A cannon: Echo answer'd in her sleep
From hollow fields: and here were telescopes
For azure views; and there a group of girls

men were weakened by it & only potential whores liked it. Meanwhile brothels & street sex markets spread VD as slumps in trade deprived low-class women of work in factories, thereby increasing the number & reducing the price of whores.)

The child-woman's prattle gets the poet telling this fable of a lovely princess who sets up a university for women. It excludes men under penalty of death. With 2 pals an ardent prince invades in drag, is exposed, & nearly slain in joust with the brother of the princess. So she nurses him to health & falls in love with him. They agree to wed as equals & work to make a world in which men will not tyrannise over women.

That romance was fuelled by Spenser's **Faerie Queen** *& by Scott's novel* **Ivanhoe**, *in which gallant men win lovely damsels by fighting for them. The prologue confronts historic fantasy with social fact. Mechanics Institutes were being sponsored by folk who saw a dangerous gulf between themselves & the poor (**think of the French Revolution!**) & wanted it bridged. The sponsors & members*

were often Owenites
& arranged outings to
the grounds of rich
patrons, with feasting,
sport & demonstration
of new discoveries in
science. Tennyson saw
such an event in 1842
at the country house
of a Kent landowner
whose sister he would
marry. The connection
between education for
workers & women is
only hinted here, but
to Victorian readers it
was obvious. When
The Princess appeared
in 1842 The Queen's
College for Women
was opened by F.D.
Maurice, Christian
Socialist & Anglican
priest, who had also
started a Working
Man's College. Out of
them came eventually
the opening of British
universities to women
& the working class.
The Princess, popular
for 6 decades because
of its romantic-young-
boy view of women,
was at last made to
look foolish by the
Suffragettes who did
not wait for men to
fight for them.
    Tennyson's dad
was forced by HIS
dad, a Lincolnshire
lawyer, to be a clergy-
man, & the cleric's
wife bore 12 offspring
inclined to poetry,
drug abuse & religious
mania. The 8th son
was given to declaring
in later years **I am the**

In circle waited, whom the electric shock
Dislink'd with shrieks and laughter: round the lake
A little clock-work steamer paddling plied
And shook the lilies: perch'd about the knolls
A dozen angry models jetted steam:
A petty railway ran: a fire-balloon
Rose gem-like up before the dusky groves
And dropt a fairy parachute and past:
And there thro' twenty posts of telegraph
They flash'd a saucy message to and fro
Between the mimic stations; so that sport
Went hand in hand with Science; otherwhere
Pure sport: a herd of boys with clamour bowl'd
And stump'd the wicket; babies roll'd about
Like tumbled fruit in grass; and men and maids
Arranged a country dance, and flew thro' light
And shadow, while the twangling violin
Struck up with Soldier-laddie, and overhead
The broad ambrosial aisles of lofty lime
Made noise with bees and breeze from end to end.

Strange was the sight and smacking of the time;
And long we gazed, but satiated at length
Came to the ruins. High-arch'd and ivy-claspt,
Of finest Gothic lighter than a fire,
Thro' one wide chasm of time and frost they gave
The park, the crowd, the house; but all within
The sward was trim as any garden lawn:
And here we lit on Aunt Elizabeth,
And Lilia with the rest, and lady friends
From neighbour seats: and there was Ralph himself,
A broken statue propt against the wall,
As gay as any. Lilia, wild with sport,
Half child half woman as she was, had wound
A scarf of orange round the stony helm,
And robed the shoulders in a rosy silk,
That made the old warrior from his ivied nook
Glow like a sunbeam: near his tomb a feast

Shone, silver-set; about it lay the guests,
And there we join'd them: then the maiden Aunt
Took this fair day for text, and from it preach'd
An universal culture for the crowd,
And all things great; but we, unworthier, told
Of college: he had climb'd across the spikes,
And he had squeezed himself betwixt the bars,
And he had breath'd the Proctor's dogs; and one
Discuss'd his tutor, rough to common men,
But honeying at the whisper of a lord;
And one the Master, as a rogue in grain
Veneer'd with sanctimonious theory.

But while they talk'd, above their heads I saw
The feudal warrior lady-clad; which brought
My book to mind: and opening this I read
Of old Sir Ralph a page or two that rang
With tilt and tourney; then the tale of her
That drove her foes with slaughter from her walls,
And much I praised her nobleness, and "Where,"
Ask'd Walter, patting Lilia's head(she lay
Beside him) "lives there such a woman now?"

Quick answer'd Lilia "There are thousands now
Such women, but convention beats them down:
It is but bringing up; no more than that:
You men have done it: how I hate you all!
Ah, were I something great! I wish I were
Some mighty poetess, I would shame you then,
That love to keep us children! O I wish
That I were some great princess, I would build
Far off from men a college like a man's,
And I would teach them all that men are taught;
We are twice as quick!" And here she shook aside
The hand that play'd the patron with her curls.

And one said smiling "Pretty were the sight
If our old halls could change their sex, and flaunt

last & most morbid of the Tennysons. Alfred was 4th son. Poets before him who doubted God believed in Nature & felt mankind a good part of it, & sure of being a better part with social equality. At Oxford Alfred shared this faith for a time. A passionately loved friend died. That made him a great poet, but only when he evoked loneliness, longing or death wish, or lost or remote glory. When not doing that his verses indicated how greatly Britain led mankind in our evolution from ape to angel, so an Irish poet called him Alfred **lawn** *Tennyson & a mere rhymester. British middle-class taste so appreciated his mix of 1st-class melancholy & 3rd-class confidence that this bisexual dipsomaniac chainsmoker (pipe), who in photographs & portraits resembles (as he said himself)* **a dirty monk**, *was made the Poet Laureate in 1850 when Wordsworth died, & a Peer of the Realm in 1882. This was mainly because, after viewing the fossils that proved man was the newest dominant creature on a planet that had millions of earlier, extinct ones, & after prophesying a future* of scientific marvels (aircraft etc), he called himself:– *An infant crying in the night; An infant crying for the light, And with no language but a cry.* Carlyle said *The Princess* was very gorgeous, fervid, luxuriant, but somnolent, indolent ... almost imbecile.

With prudes for proctors, dowagers for deans,
And sweet girl-graduates in their golden hair.
I think they should not wear our rusty gowns,
But move as rich as Emperor-moths, or Ralph
Who shines so in the corner; yet I fear,
If there were many Lilias in the brood,
However deep you might embower the nest,
Some boy would spy it."

                    At this upon the sward
She tapt her tiny silken-sandal'd foot:
"That's your light way; but I would make it death
For any male thing but to peep at us."

OOOOOOOOOOOOOOOOOOOOOOOOOOOOOOOOOOOOOOOOOOOOOOOOOOOOOOOOOOOOOOOOOOOOOO

1848

More political & social truths than all the professional politicians, publicists and moralists put together was Karl Marx's opinion of Thackeray. Born in India in 1811 and sent aged 5 to England where he was educated at Charterhouse & Cambridge, Thackeray originally wanted to become a painter. Through a mixture of dissipation & bad investment, he wasted an inheritance which might have let him do so & turned with great success to satirical journalism. The Book of Snobs, while vividly funny, is also of weighty intent. Of class distinction Thackeray wrote *It seems to me that all English society*

THE BOOK OF SNOBS By One of Themselves
WILLIAM MAKEPEACE THACKERAY
LONDON
PREFATORY REMARKS

[*The necessity of a work on Snobs, demonstrated from History, and proved by felicitous illustrations:– I am the individual destined to write that work – My vocation is announced in terms of great eloquence – I show that the world has been gradually preparing itself for the Work and the Man – Snobs are to be studied like other objects of Natural Science, and are a part of the Beautiful (with a large B). They pervade all classes – Affecting instance of Colonel Snobley.*]

WE have all read a statement, (the authenticity of which I take leave to doubt entirely, for upon what calculations I should like to know is it founded?) – we have all, I say, been favoured by perusing a remark, that when the times and necessities of the world call for a Man, that individual is found. Thus at the French Revolution (which the reader will be pleased to have introduced so early), when it was requisite to administer a corrective dose to the nation, Robespierre was found; a most foul and nauseous dose indeed, and swallowed eagerly by the patient, greatly to the latter's ultimate advantage: thus, when it became necessary to kick John Bull out of America, Mr. Washington stepped forward, and performed that job to satisfaction: thus, when the Earl of Aldborough was unwell, Professor Holloway appeared with his pills, and cured his lordship as per advertisement, &c. &c. Numberless instances might be adduced to show that when a nation is in great want, the relief is at hand; just as in the Pantomime (that microcosm) where when *Clown* wants anything – a warming-pan, a pump-handle, a goose, or a lady's tippet – a fellow comes sauntering out from behind the side-scenes with the very article in question.

Again, when men commence an undertaking, they always are prepared to show that the absolute necessities of the world demanded its completion.– Say it is a railroad: the directors begin by stating that "A more intimate communication between Bathershins and Derrynane Beg is necessary for the advancement of civilization, and demanded by the multitudinous acclamations of the great Irish people." Or suppose it is a newspaper: the prospectus states that "At a time when the Church is in danger, threatened from without by savage fanaticism and miscreant unbelief, and undermined from within by dangerous Jesuitism and suicidal Schism, a Want has been universally felt – a suffering people has looked abroad – for an Ecclesiastical Champion and Guardian. A body of Prelates and Gentlemen have therefore stepped forward in this our hour of danger and determined on establishing the *Beadle* newspaper," &c. &c. One or other of these points at least is incontrovertible: the public wants a thing, therefore it is supplied with it; or the public is supplied with a thing, therefore it wants it.

I have long gone about with a conviction on my mind that I had a work to do – a Work, if you like, with a great W; a Purpose to fulfil; a chasm to leap into,

is cursed by this mammonical superstition; and that we are sneaking and bowing and cringing on the one hand, or bullying and scorning on the other, from the lowest to the highest. The preface printed here, incidentally, shows him parodying Carlyle at his most oracular. After the publication of Vanity Fair, *a novel of Tolstoyan scope too bleakly true to be enjoyed by anyone under the age of 40, he changed. Whether through a particular desire to emulate the success of Dickens or through a general one for the good life, Thackeray drew back from what an audience seeking entertainment had seen as the cruelty of his earlier work. His writing became lighter, more superficial, and resigned to optimism.* **There's nothing new and there's nothing true, and it don't much sinnify,** *he used to say. Thackeray married in 1836 but less than 10 years later his wife was confined in a madhouse. Thereafter he led the life of a popular man of letters, part of that ostentatiously luxurious society he had ridiculed. He died of apoplexy at the age of 52.*

like Curtius, horse & foot; a Great Social Evil to Discover and to Remedy. That Conviction Has Pursued me for Years. It has Dogged me in the Busy Street; Seated Itself By Me in The Lonely Study; Jogged My Elbow as it Lifted The Wine-cup at The Festive Board; Pursued me through the Maze of Rotten Row; Followed me in Far Lands. On Brighton's Shingly Beach, or Margate's Sand, the Voice Outpiped the Roaring of the Sea; it Nestles in my Nightcap, and It Whispers, "Wake, Slumberer, thy Work Is Not Yet Done." Last Year, By Moonlight, in the Colosseum, the Little Sedulous Voice Came To Me and Said, "Smith, or Jones" (The Writer's Name is Neither Here nor There), "Smith or Jones, my fine fellow, this is all very well, but you ought to be at home writing your great work on SNOBS."

When a man has this sort of vocation it is all nonsense attempting to elude it. He must speak out to the nations; he must *unbusm* himself, as Jeames would say, or choke and die. "Mark to yourself," I have often mentally exclaimed to your humble servant, "the gradual way in which you have been prepared for, and are now led by an irresistible necessity to enter upon your great labour. First, the World was made: then, as a matter of course, Snobs; they existed for years and years, and were no more known than America. But presently, – *ingens patebat tellus,*– the people became darkly aware that there was such a race. Not above five-and-twenty years since, a name, an expressive monosyllable, arose to designate that race. That name has spread over England like railroads subsequently; Snobs are known and recognized throughout an Empire on which I am given to understand the Sun never sets. *Punch* appears at the ripe season, to chronicle their history: and the individual comes forth to write that history in *Punch*.

I have (and for this gift I congratulate myself with a Deep and Abiding Thankfulness) an eye for a Snob. If the Truthful is the Beautiful, it is Beautiful to study even the Snobbish; to track Snobs through history, as certain little dogs in Hampshire hunt out truffles; to sink shafts in society and come upon rich veins of Snob-ore. Snobbishness is like Death in a quotation from Horace, which I hope you never have heard, "beating with equal foot at poor men's doors, and kicking at the gates of Emperors." It is a great mistake to judge of Snobs lightly, and think they exist among the lower classes merely. An immense per-centage of Snobs, I believe, is to be found in every rank of this mortal life. You must not judge hastily or vulgarly of Snobs: to do so shows that you are yourself a Snob. I myself have been taken for one.

When I was taking the waters at Bagnigge Wells, and living at the

"Imperial Hotel" there, there used to sit opposite me at breakfast, for a short time, a Snob so insufferable that I felt I should never get any benefit of the waters so long as he remained. His name was Lieutenant-Colonel Snobley, of a certain dragoon regiment. He wore japanned boots and moustaches: he lisped, drawled, and left the "r's" of his words: he was always flourishing about, and smoothing his lacquered whiskers with a huge flaming bandanna, that filled the room with an odour of musk so stifling that I determined to do battle with that Snob, and that either he or I should quit the Inn. I first began harmless conversations with him; frightening him exceedingly, for he did not know what to do when so attacked, and had never the slightest notion that anybody would take such a liberty with him as to speak *first*: then I handed him the paper: then, as he would take no notice of these advances, I used to look him in the face steadily – and use my fork in the light of a toothpick. After two mornings of this practice, he could bear it no longer, and fairly quitted the place.

Should the Colonel see this, will he remember the Gent who asked him if he thought Publicoaler was a fine writer, and drove him from the Hotel with a four-pronged fork?

HISTORY OF ENGLAND
LORD MACAULAY
LONDON

1849

[CHAPTER I: INTRODUCTION]

I PURPOSE to write the history of England from the accession of King James the Second down to a time which is within the memory of men still living. I shall recount the errors which, in a few months, alienated a loyal gentry and priesthood from the House of Stuart. I shall trace the course of that revolution which terminated the long struggle between our sovereigns and their parliaments, and bound up together the rights of the people and the title of the reigning dynasty. I shall relate how the new settlement was, during many troubled years, successfully defended against foreign and domestic enemies; how, under that settlement, the authority of law and the security of property were found to be compatible with a liberty of discussion and of

"I wish," said Lord Melbourne, " that I was as cocksure of anything as Tom Macaulay is of everything."

The same Tom Macaulay could neither tie a bow nor shave without cutting his face. Raised in the strict accordances of the Clapham Sect of Evangelicals, who thought it profane to enjoy the Sabbath sunshine, Macaulay never married & lived a sheltered domestic life.

*An essay on Milton in the August 1825 issue of the **Edinburgh Review** brought him instant fame & for the*

next 20 years he provided the magazine with regular literary & historical pieces.

He entered parliament as a Whig in 1830 & in 1834 secured financial independence through a place on the Supreme Council of India. 4 years in India left him with the notion that lessons in English literature would elevate the natives & that their own literature contained nothing anyone need read. His knowledge of immediate social conditions was filtered through Commons debates. Macaulay insisted in 1842 that universal suffrage was "utterly incompatible with the very existence of civilisation".

*He acknowledged a debt to Sir Walter Scott & almost certainly created a historical market where none existed. Now remembered for his **Essays Critical and Historical** and the 2-volume **History of England**, rather than his **Lays of Ancient Rome**, his combination of description & certainty created a style others sought to copy, much against Macaulay's wishes. His conviction & brilliance can be disarming. Writing about anger, he exalts the shoemaker above the author: "It may be worse to be angry than to be wet. But shoes have kept millions from being wet; but we doubt whether Seneca ever kept anybody from being angry."*

individual action never before known; how, from the auspicious union of order and freedom, sprang a prosperity of which the annals of human affairs had furnished no example; how our country, from a state of ignominious vassalage, rapidly rose to the place of umpire among European powers; how her opulence and her martial glory grew together; how, by wise and resolute good faith, was gradually established a public credit fruitful of marvels which to the statesman of any former age would have seemed incredible; how a gigantic commerce gave birth to a maritime power, compared with which every other maritime power, ancient or modern, sinks into insignificance; how Scotland, after ages of enmity, was at length united to England, not merely by legal bonds, but by indissoluble ties of interest and affection; how, in America, the British colonies rapidly became far mightier and wealthier than the realms which Cortes and Pizarro had added to the dominions of Charles the Fifth; how, in Asia, British adventurers founded an empire not less splendid and more durable than that of Alexander.

Nor will it be less my duty faithfully to record disasters mingled with triumphs, and great national crimes and follies far more humiliating than any disaster. It will be seen that even what we justly account our chief blessings were not without alloy. It will be seen that the system which effectually secured our liberties against the encroachments of kingly power gave birth to a new class of abuses from which absolute monarchies are exempt. It will be seen that, in consequence partly of unwise interference, and partly of unwise neglect, the increase of wealth and the extension of trade produced, together with immense good, some evils from which poor and rude societies are free. It will be seen how, in two important dependencies of the crown, wrong was followed by just retribution; how imprudence and obstinacy broke the ties which bound the North American colonies to the parent state; how Ireland, cursed by the domination of race over race, and of religion over religion, remained indeed a member of the empire, but a withered and distorted member, adding no strength to the body politic, and reproachfully pointed at by all who feared or envied the greatness of England.

Yet, unless I greatly deceive myself, the general effect of this chequered narrative will be to excite thankfulness in all religious minds, and hope in the breasts of all patriots. For the history of our country during the last hundred and sixty years is eminently the history of physical, of moral, and of intellectual improvement. Those who compare the age on which their lot has fallen with a golden age which exists only in their imagination may talk of degeneracy and decay: but no man who is correctly informed as to the past will be disposed to take a morose or desponding view of the present.

I should very imperfectly execute the task which I have undertaken if I were merely to treat of battles and sieges, of the rise and fall of administrations, of intrigues in the palace, and of debates in the parliament. It will be my endeavour to relate the history of the people as well as the history of the government, to trace the progress of useful and ornamental arts, to describe the rise of religious sects and the changes of literary taste, to portray the manners of successive generations, and not to pass by with neglect even the revolutions which have taken place in dress, furniture, repasts, and public amusements. I shall cheerfully bear the reproach of having descended below the dignity of history, if I can succeed in placing before the English of the nineteenth century a true picture of the life of their ancestors.

UNPUBLISHED PREFACE TO SHIRLEY   1849
CHARLOTTE BRONTË
MANUSCRIPT: HAWORTH, YORKSHIRE

[A WORD TO THE "QUARTERLY", AUGUST 29th 1849]

THE PUBLIC is respectfully informed that with this Preface it has no manner of concern, the same being a private and confidential letter to a friend, and – what is more – a "lady-friend".

Currer Bell can have no hesitation as to the mode in which he ought to commence his epistle: he feels assured – his heart tells him that the individual who did him the honour of a small notice in the "Quarterly" –

*Charlotte Brontë was 3rd daughter of an Irish Anglican curate & a Cornish mother who died when she was five. A harsh boarding school helped to kill her 2 older sisters, & the 4 remaining Brontë children began inventing & sharing literary fantasy worlds. Later, with their father infirm & their brother Branwell a drug-addicted drunk, the sisters (all under pseudonyms surnamed Bell) hoped to support the family by writing. Charlotte's **Jane Eyre**, published 1st, brought fame & prurient speculation about the author. It showed a girl without good looks, money or connections being abused & bullied by others. It said that, given a comfortable home & a child to educate, she wanted more from life. An anonymous reviewer in the Quarterly (actually an Eleanor Rigby) denounced the book as revolutionary & guessed "Currer Bell" was female & a former governess. In the 19th century governessing was only a step more respectable than actressing & two steps above prostitution. Since the author showed scant knowledge of how fashionable (i.e. proper) women dressed, & since Thackeray had praised*

if not a woman, properly so called – is that yet more venerable character – an Old Woman. His ground then is clear and he falls to work upon it with much heart and comfort.

Dear Madam.

I daresay I should have written to you before but at the time your favour reached me I was engrossed with matters whereof I am dispensed from giving you the faintest outline of an account.

It is not my intention to go through your article from beginning to end: I merely wish to have a little quiet chat with you on one or two paragraphs.

In the first place, you appear alarmed with an idea that "the tone of mind and thought which has overthrown authority and violated every code, human and divine – abroad – and fostered Chartism and Rebellion – at home – is the same which has also written 'Jane Eyre'."

Let us not dwell on this subject: let us pass it lightly: if we trode with audacious emphasis, or if we confidingly sat down, both of us might fly abroad on the wings of sudden explosion. Any man's nose may here wind a Gunpowder Plot; the very savour and odour of the thing is traitorous. Permit me but to whisper – as you and I glide off, arm-in-arm and on tip-toe – Don't be too uneasy, dear Madam; take not on to any serious extent; be persuaded to keep as calm as may be. I am not at liberty to say more: we live in strange times – muffled in Mystery. Hush!

In the second place, you breathe a suspicion that Currer Bell, "for some sufficient reason" (Ah! Madam:

Skilled by a touch to deepen Scandal's tints
With all the kind mendacity of hints.)

"for some sufficient reason" has long forfeited the society of your sex. In this passage – Madam – we discover an undoubted Mare's nest: here is the cracked shell of the equine egg: there the colt making its escape à toutes jambes and alas! yonder – Truth scouring after it, catching it and finding the empty phantom vanish in her grasp. You should see – Ma'am, the figure Currer Bell can cut at a small party: you should watch him assisting at a tea-table; you should behold him holding skeins of silk or Berlin wool for the young ladies about whom he innocuously philanders, and who, in return, knit him comforters for winter-wear, or work him slippers for his invalid-member (he considers that rather an elegant expression – a nice substitute for – gouty foot; it was manufactured expressly for your refinement) you should see these things, for seeing is believing. Currer Bell forfeit the society of the better half of the human race? Heaven avert such a calamity – ! The idiot (inspired or otherwise) Sam. Richardson, could better have borne such a doom than he.

The idea by you propagated, if not by you conceived, that my book proceeded from the pen of Mr. Thackeray's governess caught my fancy singularly: I felt a little puzzled with it, at first, as – I make no doubt – did Mr. Thackeray – but, on the whole, it struck me as being in my line – in the line of any novel-wright – something boldly imaginative, – cunningly inventive, the reverse of trite. You say, you see no great interest in the question; I do: a very comical interest. What other "romantic rumours" have been current in Mayfair? You set my curiosity on edge. I have but a very vague notion of the occupations and manner of life of the inhabitants of Mayfair, but I rather suspect them of resembling the old Athenians who spent their time in nothing else but either to tell or to hear some new thing. Who invents the new things for their consumption? Who manufactures fictions to supply their cravings? I need not ask who vends them: you, Madam, are an active saleswoman; the pages of your "Quarterly" form a notable advertising medium.

*the book & (like Mr. Rochester) had a mad wife & a governess for his offspring, Rigby implied that Bell was Thackeray's mistress. Wounded & angry, Charlotte replied in this preface to her next novel, an **unromantic as Monday morning** book evoking the Luddite riots & calling Milton's Eve the first blue-stocking. It was written in the year when Branwell, Anne & Emily, Charlotte's entire literary circle, died of consumption. She was being cut by friends because her identity with Currer Bell was now public. At a London party Thackeray had introduced her as Jane Eyre. Even so the preface addresses the Quarterly's hack in gouty Bell persona, guessing her not only a woman but an old woman, for whom "he" would make allowance on the grounds of her frailty and ignorance. Her publishers, horrified, urged her to write about her dead sisters instead (better publicity). Charlotte refused & Shirley went preface-less. Being measured By some standard deemed becoming to my sex was an oft-felt hurt: **I wish all reviewers believed Currer Bell to be a man**, she wrote, **they would be more just to him**.*

Attentive to your stricture, I have made a point of ascertaining what that garment is which ladies, "roused in the night", assume in preference to "frock" or gown, as being at once "more convenient and more becoming". Candid – as I am sure you are, you will cheerfully allow that I have mastered it, and mastered it triumphantly; in proof whereof I point – not without exultation, to Mrs. Yorke in her Flannel Wrapper: chaste! simple! grand! severe! At this moment I recall another species of drapery whose dignity may be considered yet more recondite and impressive – the camisole or short night-jacket. On mature reflection however – it is my own unbiased opinion that the Wrapper – the Flannel Wrapper harmonises best with the genius of the British Nation to the folds of the Wrapper therefor I cling – and that from patriotic motives – the French – the Belgian women wear camisoles – and pretty figures they cut in them!

For the rest my accuracy is no novelty. Recollect, ma'am, it was only the shabby little governess whom I represented as putting on her "frock" and shawl – and as she possessed but three "frocks" (that class of persons often use the word "frock" where a "lady" would say "dress", if you observe, ma'am, as does also the domestic servant; – I like to put them on a level) in the world – a personage of your sagacity will have no difficulty in inferring that she was unlikely to boast any choce of garments more convenient and becoming; it may be questioned, indeed, whether it would not have been a piece of impertinent presumption in her to aspire to any such; at the same time two dowager ladies of quality, "roused in the night," are exhibited as "bearing down on Mr Rochester in vast white wrappers". Here, ma'am, is both a fitness of things and a concatenation accordingly. I discuss these points at length under the satisfactory conviction that I am writing to one who feels all their profound importance.

The other day I took the train down to Ingram Park to make personal inquiry of Miss Blanche Ingram's maid about the material of her lady's morning-dress. I am bound to confess that she shared your righteous indignation. "Crape!" she cried "her mistress never put on crape in a morning in her life, nor gauze neither!". "What was it then?" I petitioned to be informed – She told me "Barège" and proceeded to give a minute description of the pattern: you will have pleasure in hearing it repeated: A light blue ground, barred across with faint stripes of a deeper colour, figured with a pattern of small leaves mixed with zigzags, finished with a narrow silk stripe straight down. "Very neat" I pronounced it.

You will perhaps say, Ma'am, that "barège" is a fabric of more recent invention than the days of Miss Ingram's youth; in that case I can only answer, as the young ladies of a foreign establishment where I once taught English were wont briefly to answer when but too clearly convicted of fiction: "Tant pis!"

I had some thoughts of concluding my letter by a tender reproof of that rather coarse observation of yours relative to dessert-dishes and game – but I forbear – warning you only not to indulge too freely in the latter dish when very "high" – in that state it is not wholesome.

What a nice, pleasant gossip you and I have had together, Madam. How agreeable it is to twaddle at ones ease unmolested by a too fastidious public! Hoping to meet you one day again – and offering you such platonic homage as it becomes an old bachelor to pay

I am yours very devotedly

CURRER BELL

Allow me to add my address: Hay-lane Cottage Hay, Millcote. Should you ever come down to the North – pray do not forget this modest indication. N.B. I read all you said about governesses. My dear Madam – just turn out and be a governess yourself for a couple of years: the experiment would do you good: a little irksome toil – a little unpitied suffering – two years of uncheered solitude might perhaps teach you that to be callous, harsh and unsympathizing is not to be firm, superior and magnanimous.

It was a twinge of the gout which dictated that postscript.

KARL MARX: THE COMMUNIST PARTY MANIFESTO translated by Helen Macfarlane in The Red Republican Weekly: **LONDON**

1850

[PREFACE]

A frightful hobgoblin stalks throughout Europe. We are haunted by a ghost, the ghost of Communism. All the Powers of the Past have joined in a holy crusade to lay this ghost to rest, – the Pope and the Czar, Metternich and Guizot, French Radicals and German police agents. Where is the opposition which has not been accused of Communism by its enemies in Power? And where the opposition that has not hurled this blighting

At Berlin University Marx, Jewish lawyer's son, studied history, law, philosophy; became journalist & editor of democrat newspaper shut down for attack on government. In Paris he ran German émigré paper until the French expelled him; went to Brussels & here he

accusation at the heads of the more advanced oppositionists, as well as at those of its official enemies? Two things appear on considering these facts. I. The ruling Powers of Europe acknowledge Communism to be also a Power. II. It is time for the Communists to lay before the world an account of their aims and tendencies, and to oppose these silly fables about the bugbear of Communism, by a manifesto of the Communist Party.

CHAPTER I
BOURGEOIS AND PROLETARIANS.

Hitherto the history of Society has been the history of the battles between the classes composing it. Freemen and Slaves, Patricians and Plebeians, Nobles and Serfs, Members of Guilds and journeymen, – in a word, the oppressors and the oppressed, have always stood in direct opposition to each other. The battle between them has sometimes been open, sometimes concealed, but always continuous. A never-ceasing battle, which has invariably ended, either in a revolutionary alteration of the social system, or in the common destruction of the hostile classes.

In the earlier historical epochs we find almost everywhere a minute division of Society into classes or ranks, a variety of grades in social position. In ancient Rome we find Patricians, Knights, Plebeians, Slaves; in mediæval Europe, Feudal Lords, Vassals, Burghers, Journeymen, Serfs; and in each of these classes there were again grades and distinctions. Modern Bourgeois Society proceeded from the ruins of the feudal system, but the Bourgeois régime has not abolished the antagonism of classes.

New classes, new conditions of oppression, new forms and modes of carrying on the struggle, have been substituted for the old ones. The characteristic of our Epoch, the Era of the Middle-class, or

Bourgeoisie, is that the struggle between the various Social Classes, has been reduced to its simplest form. Society incessantly tends to be divided into two great camps, into two great hostile armies, the Bourgeoisie and the Proletariat.

The burgesses of the early Communes sprang from the Serfs of the Middle Ages and from this Municipal class were developed the primitive elements of the modern Bourgeoisie. The discovery of the New World, the circumnavigation of Africa, gave the Middle-class – then coming into being – new fields of action. The colonization of America, the opening up of the East Indian and Chinese Markets, the Colonial Trade, the increase of commodities generally and of the means of exchange, gave an impetus, hitherto unknown, to Commerce, Shipping, and Manufactures; and aided the rapid evolution of the revolutionary element in the old decaying, feudal form of Society. The old feudal way of managing the industrial interest by means of guilds and monopolies was not found sufficient for the increased demand caused by the opening up of these new markets. It was replaced by the manufacturing system. Guilds vanished before the industrial Middle-class, and the division of labour between the different corporations was succeeded by the division of labour between the workmen of one and the same great workshop.

But the demand always increased, new markets came into play. The manufacturing system, in its turn, was found to be inadequate. At this point industrial Production was revolutionised by machinery and steam. The modern industrial system was developed in all its gigantic proportions; instead of the industrial Middle-class we find industrial millionaires, chiefs of whole industrial armies, the modern Bourgeois, or Middle-class Capitalists. The discovery of America was the first step towards the

*Owenite Socialism only ways to help a corrupt system last slightly longer. His **Manifesto** ends by exhorting the workers of the world to unite – they have nothing to lose but their chains! That got Marx & his family expelled from Brussels. Britain & USA at that time allowed anyone in, (it lowered the cost of labour) so Engels helped them settle in London & gave them money when Marx's journalism did not pay for their food & rent. In the British Museum Reading Room Marx toiled on his reply to Tory economists, **Das Kapital**. Shaw said **it showed the 19th-century drifting like a cloud & changing shape as it did so**. Few Britons noticed. A German ambassador who wanted Marx's kind of Socialism banned in London (as it was in other European cities) was told by a member of the cabinet that the British method of aborting bad ideas is to let them be openly publicised. In London Marx endured nothing worse than poverty. Like earlier Jewish prophets he hated social injustice, saw why & how it throve, foresaw calamities it would bring. Micah said that descendants of those who believed* *him, after a dreadful time of trial, would see swords made into ploughshares, lions lie down with lambs in a peaceable kingdom. Marx said descendants of those who believed him, after worldwide revolutions, would at last lead a working-class dictatorship to abolish all social classes, making this a world without wars & governments & nations, where each would give their best & have all they needed. Marx foresaw great wars between capitalist states, & thought they would cause revolutions in the most modern industrial ones – not in Russia, China & Cambodia whose main industry was primitive agriculture. He could not have foreseen that Stalin, Mao & Pol Pot would use his words to justify massacre & forced labour. He foresaw the stock-market crash of 1929 & world trade depression after it, not how state investment in weapons races & warfare would get industries working again. He never foresaw his international Communism becoming a tool of Russian foreign policy.*

formation of a colossal market, embracing the whole world; whereby an immense developement was given to Commerce, and to the means of communication by sea and land. This again reacted upon the industrial system, and the developement of the Bourgeoisie, the increase of their Capital, the superseding of all classes handed down to modern times from the Middle Ages, kept pace with the developement of Production, Trade, and Steam communication.

We find, therefore, that the modern Bourgeoisie are themselves the result of a long process of developement, of a series of revolutions in the modes of Production and Exchange. Each of the degrees of industrial evolution, passed through by the modern Middle-class, was accompanied by a corresponding degree of political developement. This class was oppressed under the feudal régime, it then assumed the form of armed and self-regulating associations in the mediæval Municipalities; in one country we find it existing as a commercial republic, or free town; in another, as the third taxable Estate of the Monarchy; then during the prevalence of the manufacturing system (before the introduction of steam power) the Middle-class was a counterpoise to the Nobility in absolute Monarchies, and the groundwork of the powerful monarchical States generally. Finally, since the establishment of the modern industrial system, with its world-wide market, this class has gained the exclusive possession of political power in modern representative States. Modern Governments are merely Committees for managing the common affairs of the whole Bourgeoisie.

This Bourgeoisie has occupied an extremely revolutionary position in History. As soon as the Bourgeois got the upper hand, they destroyed all feudal, patriarchal, idyllic relationships between men. They relentlessly tore asunder the many-sided links of that feudal chain which bound men to their "natural superiors," and they left no bond of union between man and man, save that of bare self-interest, of cash payments. They changed personal dignity into market value, and substituted the single unprincipled freedom of trade for the numerous, hardly earned, chartered liberties of the Middle Ages. Chivalrous enthusiasm, the emotions of piety, vanished before the icy breath of their selfish calculations. In a word, the Bourgeoisie substituted shameless, direct, open spoliation, for the previous system of spoliation concealed under religious and political illusions. They stripped off that halo of sanctity which had surrounded the various modes of human activity, and had made them venerable, and venerated. They changed the physician, the jurisprudent, the priest, the poet, the philosopher, into their hired servants. They tore the touching veil of sentiment from domestic ties, and reduced family-relations to a mere question of hard cash. The Middle-classes have shown how the brutal physical force of the Middle Ages, so much admired by Reactionists, found its befitting complement in the laziest ruffianism. They have also shown what human activity is capable of accomplishing. They have done quite other kinds of marvellous work than Egyptian pyramids, Roman aqueducts, or Gothic Cathedrals; and their expeditions have far surpassed all former Crusades, and Migrations of nations.

The Bourgeoisie can exist only under the condition of continuously revolutionising machinery, or the instruments of Production. That is, perpetually changing the system of production, which again amounts to changing the whole system of social arrangements. Persistence in the old modes of Productions was, on the contrary, the first condition of existence for all the preceding industrial Classes. A continual change in the modes of Production, a never ceasing state of agitation and social insecurity, distinguish the Bourgeois-Epoch from all preceding ones. The ancient ties between men, their opinions and beliefs – hoar with antiquity – are fast disappearing, and the new ones become worn out ere they can become firmly rooted. Everything fixed and stable vanishes, everything holy and venerable is desecrated, and men are forced to look at their mutual relations, at the problem of Life, in the soberest, the most matter of fact way.

The need of an ever-increasing market for their produce, drives the Bourgeoisie over the whole globe – they are forced to make settlements, to form connections, to set up means of communication everywhere. Through their command of a universal market, they have given a cosmopolitan tendency to the production and consumption of all countries. To the great regret of the Reactionists, the Bourgeoisie have deprived the modern Industrial System of its national foundation. The old national manufactures have been, or are being, destroyed. They are superseded by new modes of industry, whose introduction is becoming a vital question for all civilized nations, whose raw materials are not indigenous, but are brought from the remotest countries, and whose products are not merely consumed in the home market, but throughout the whole world. Instead of the old national wants, supplied by indigenous products, we everywhere find new wants, which can be supplied only by the productions of the remotest lands and climes. Instead of the old local and national feeling of self-sufficingness and isolation, we find a universal intercourse, an inter-dependence, amongst nations. The same fact obtains in the intellectual world. The intellectual productions of individual nations tend to become common property. National one-sidedness and mental limitation are fast becoming impossible, and a universal literature is being formed from the numerous national and local literatures. Through the incessant improvements in machinery and the means of locomotion, the Bourgeoisie draw the most barbarous savages into the magic circle of civilization. Cheap goods are their artillery for battering down Chinese walls, and their means of overcoming the obstinate hatred entertained towards strangers by semi-civilized nations. The Bourgeoisie, by their competition, compel, under penalty of inevitable ruin, the universal adoption of their system of production; they force all nations to accept what is called civilization – to become Bourgeois – and thus the middle class fashions the world anew after its own image.

The Bourgeoisie has subjected the country to the ascendancy of the town; it has created enormous cities, and, by causing an immense increase of population in the manufacturing, as compared with the agricultural districts, has saved a great part of every people from the idiotism of country life. Not only have the Bourgeoisie made the country subordinate to the town, they have made barbarous and half-civilized tribes dependent on civilized nations, the agricultural on the manufacturing nations, the East on the West. The division of property, of the means of production, and of population, vanish under the

Bourgeois régime. It agglomerates population, it centralises the means of production, and concentrates property in the hands of a few individuals. Political centralization is the necessary consequence of this. Independent provinces, with different interests, each of them surrounded by a separate line of customs and under separate local governments, are brought together as one nation, under the same government, laws, line of customs, tariff, the same national class-interest. The Bourgeois régime has only prevailed for about a century, but during that time it has called into being more gigantic powers of production than all preceding generations put together. The subjection of the elements of nature, the developement of machinery, the application of chemistry to agriculture and manufacture, railways, electric telegraphs, steam ships, the clearing and cultivation of whole continents, canalizing of thousands of rivers; large populations,whole industrial armies, springing up, as if by magic! What preceding generation ever dreamed of these productive powers slumbering within society?*OOOOOOOOOOOOOOOOOOOOOOOOOOOOOOOOOOOOOOOOOOOOOOOOOOO* COMMERCIAL SOCIETIES CANNOT ESCAPE PERIODIC CRISES THEY ONLY OVERCOME BY CONQUERING NEW MARKETS OR EXPLOITING OLD ONES HARDER. THIS INCREASES THE NUMBER OF POOR UNTIL SOME OF THE RICH, SEEING IT IS THEIR ONLY CHANCE OF IMPROVEMENT, JOIN THE POOR IN A REVOLUTION MARX CALLS **INEVITABLE**.

OOOOOOOOOOOOOOOOOOOOOOOOOOOOOOOOOOOOOOOOOOOOOOOOOOOOOOOO

TWICE-TOLD TALES
NATHANIEL HAWTHORNE
BOSTON

1851

[PREFACE TO THE THIRD EDITION]

THE AUTHOR of *Twice-told Tales* has a claim to one distinction, which, as none of his literary brethren will care about disputing it with him, he need not be afraid to mention. He was, for a good many years, the obscurest man of letters in America. These stories were published in Magazines and Annuals, extending over a period of ten or twelve years, and comprising the whole of the writer's young manhood, without making (so far as he has

Here is Hawthorne at his craftiest & most ambivalent. He begins by characterizing himself as an obscure writer, whose style is remote & somehow bloodless, ignored by most contemporaries. Though he describes his tales as disembodied, sepia-tinted allegories, he wrote this Preface when his 1st novel, **The**

Scarlet Letter, enjoyed critical acclaim & commercial success. In the Genteel Tradition in American Literature (which was even more prudish than that of Victorian Britain), merely to publish a novel whose main theme was adultery was an achievement; to have it become such a best-seller as the The Scarlet Letter was extraordinary.

Hawthorne states enigmatically that, rather than being the written communic-ations of a solitary mind with itself, his style is that of a man of society. Indeed, far from being an unworldly bookish recluse (despite his years of seclusion in Salem), Hawthorne was a shrewd operator who used the Old Boy network of his Bowdoin College to obtain political appointments to the Salem Customs House & to the post of US consul in Liverpool. Yet the social dimen-sions of his work & its sweeping critique of American values in his own time (for example, his views on gender relations, his experi-ment in communitarian living at the Brook Farm collective, his economic radicalism) had to be cloaked in allegory or stashed safely in the Puritan past.

ever been aware) the slightest impression on the Public.

OOOOOOOOOOOOOOOOOOOOOOOOOOOOOOOOOOOOOOOOOOOOOOOO

THE FIRST TWO EDITIONS OF THIS BOOK WERE NOT PUBLISHED FOR THE AMERICAN PUBLIC BUT FOR HIS KNOWN AND UNKNOWN FRIENDS, SO HE IS SURPRISED AT THE VOGUE IT HAS GAINED. THIS IS BECAUSE HE IS ABLE TO CRITICISE HIS WRITINGS AS FAIRLY AS IF THEY HAD BEEN WRITTEN BY ANOTHER MAN.

OOOOOOOOOOOOOOOOOOOOOOOOOOOOOOOOOOOOOOOOOOOOOOOO

They have the pale tint of flowers that blossomed in too retired a shade – the coolness of a meditative habit, which diffuses itself through the feeling and observation of every sketch. Instead of passion, there is sentiment; and, even in what purport to be pictures of actual life, we have allegory, not always so warmly dressed in its habiliments of flesh and blood, as to be taken into the reader's mind without a shiver. Whether from lack of power, or an unconquerable reserve, the Author's touches have often an effect of tameness; the merriest man can hardly contrive to laugh at his broadest humor; the tenderest woman, one would suppose, will hardly shed warm tears at his deepest pathos. The book, if you would see anything in it, requires to be read in the clear, brown, twilight atmosphere in which it was written; if opened in the sunshine, it is apt to look exceedingly like a volume of blank pages.

With the foregoing characteristics, proper to the production of a person in retirement, (which happened to be the Author's category, at the time,) the book is devoid of others that we should quite as naturally look for. The sketches are not, it is hardly necessary to say, profound; but it is rather more remarkable that they so seldom, if ever, show any design on the writer's part to make them so. They have none of the abstruseness of idea, or obscurity of expression, which mark the written communications of a solitary mind with itself. They never need translation. It is, in fact, the style of a man of society. Every sentence, so far as it embodies thought or sensibility, may be understood and felt by anybody, who will give himself the trouble to read it, and will take up the book in a proper mood.

This statement of apparently opposite peculiarities leads us to a perception of what the sketches truly are. They are not the talk of a secluded man with his own mind and heart, (had it been so, they could hardly have failed to be more deeply and permanently valuable,) but his attempts, and very imperfectly successful ones, to open an intercourse with the world.

The Author would regret to be understood as speaking sourly or querulously of the slight mark, made by his earlier literary efforts, on the Public at large. It is so far the contrary, that he has been moved to write this preface chiefly, as affording him an opportunity to express how much enjoyment he has owed to these volumes, both before and since their publication. They are the memorials of very tranquil and not unhappy years. They failed, it is true – nor could it have been otherwise – in winning an extensive popularity. Occasionally, however, when he deemed them entirely forgotten, a paragraph or an article, from a native or foreign critic, would gratify his instincts of authorship with unexpected praise; – too generous praise, indeed, and too little alloyed with censure, which, therefore, he learned the better to inflict upon himself. And, by-the-by, it is a very suspicious symptom of a deficiency of the popular element in a book, when it calls forth no harsh criticism. This has been particularly the fortune of the Twice-told Tales. They made no enemies, and were so little known and talked about, that those who read, and chanced to like them, were apt to conceive the sort of kindness for the book, which a person naturally feels for a discovery of his own.

This kindly feeling, (in some cases, at least,) extended to the Author, who, on the internal evidence of his sketches, came to be regarded as a mild, shy, gentle, melancholic, exceedingly sensitive, and not very forcible man, hiding his blushes under an assumed name, the quaintness of which was supposed, somehow or other, to symbolize his personal and literary traits. He is by no means certain, that some of his subsequent productions have not been influenced and modified by a natural desire to fill up so amiable an outline, and to act in consonance with the character assigned to him; nor, even now, could he forfeit it without a few tears of tender sensibility. To conclude, however; – these volumes have opened the way to most agreeable associations, and to the formation of imperishable friendships; and there are many golden threads, interwoven with his present happiness, which he can follow up more or less directly, until he finds their commencement here; so that his pleasant pathway among realities seems to proceed out of the Dream-Land of his youth, and to be bordered with just enough of its shadowy foliage to shelter him from the heat of the day. He is therefore satisfied with what the TWICE-TOLD TALES have done for him, and feels it to be far better than fame.

Lenox, January 11, 1851.

1851

MOBY-DICK, OR, THE WHALE
HERMAN MELVILLE
LONDON

ETYMOLOGY
[SUPPLIED BY A LATE CONSUMPTIVE USHER TO A GRAMMAR SCHOOL]

*Hawthorne & Melville were friends & near neighbours when these books were published. The **pale usher** & **sub sub librarian** who introduce **Moby Dick** are parodies of the mild modest man Hawthorne pretended to be in **his** preface. M knew perfectly well that Hawthorne was tough & cunning, & in these 2 odd little prefaces is telling him: "Look! I can start a great book with twice as many dim pathetic characters than you do. Give it up!"*

M, like Chaucer, enjoyed making jokes most readers would miss. He also had a

THE PALE USHER – threadbare in coat, heart, body, and brain; I see him now. He was ever dusting his old lexicons and grammars, with a queer handkerchief, mockingly embellished with all the gay flags of all the known nations of the world. He loved to dust his old grammars; it somehow mildly reminded him of his mortality.

"While you take in hand to school others, and to teach them by what name a whale-fish is to be called in our tongue, leaving out, through ignorance, the letter H, which almost alone maketh up the signification of the word, you deliver that which is not true." *Hackluyt.*
"WHALE. * * * Sw. and Dan. *hval.* This animal is named from roundness or rolling; for in Dan. *hvalt* is arched or vaulted." *Webster's Dictionary.*
"WHALE. * * * It is more immediately from the Dut. and Ger. *Wallen*; A.S. Walw-ian, to roll, to wallow." *Richardson's Dictionary.*

TANIM,	Hebrew.
κητος,	Greek.
CETUS,	Latin.
WHAEL,	Anglo-Saxon.
HVAL,	Danish.
WAL,	Dutch.
HWAL,	Swedish.
HVALUR,	Icelandic.
WHALE,	English.
BALEINE,	French.
BALLENA,	Spanish.
PEKEE-NUEE-NEE,	Fegee.
PEHEE-NUEE-NEE,	Erromangoan.

[EXTRACTS SUPPLIED BY A SUB-SUB-LIBRARIAN.]

IT will be seen that this mere painstaking burrower and grub-worm of a poor devil of a Sub-Sub appears to have gone through the long Vaticans and street-stalls of the earth, picking up whatever random allusions to whales he could anyways find in any book whatsoever, sacred or profane. Therefore you must not, in every case at least, take the higgledy-piggledy whale statements, however authentic, in these extracts, for veritable gospel cetology. Far from it. As touching the ancient authors generally, as well as the poets here appearing, these extracts are solely valuable or entertaining, as affording a glancing bird's eye view of what has been promiscuously said, thought, fancied, and sung of Leviathan, by many nations and generations, including our own.

So fare thee well, poor devil of a Sub-Sub, whose commentator I am. Thou belongest to that hopeless, sallow tribe which no wine of this world will ever warm; and for whom even Pale Sherry would be too rosy-strong; but with whom one sometimes loves to sit, and feel poor-devilish, too; and grow convivial upon tears; and say to them bluntly, with full eyes

deep, ironic insight into the restless mobility of USA mankind, for he shared it.

Many Europeans who settled the east coast of North America did not settle down for long. Adventurous sons, sometimes with dads & uncles & more parties of immigrants, sought new wealth by pushing west, south & north with the blessing of expansionist senates. When the USA annexed much of Mexico, all Alaska & reached the Pacific coast, a readiness to get up & go where life seems better remained a USA tradition. Young Melville moved far & often. We will call him **M** *here.*

M *was born in 1819 New York to folk of Dutch-Scots origin who belonged to the earliest US aristocracy, being well-read cosmopolitan squires who felt more at home in Paris than London.* **M**'s *great uncle was a general & hero in the War of Independence. His charming dad tried & failed to support a family with inherited money, an import business & loans.* **M** *in his early teens was a store clerk; at 18 sailed to England as cabin boy; became a country* *school master (or usher); enrolled at 22 on a whaler bound for the Pacific & 18 months later deserted her on the island of Nukahiva. He hid in a woody glen for several weeks among kindly folk thought to be cannibals, then left by way of other ships & islands. This involved him in mutiny, jail & being a hand on the USA war ship that returned him to New York when 25. In the 5 following years he wrote 2 books of travel, 3 novels based on his adventures; got money & fame by them; married & took a farm which he worked while writing **Moby Dick**. An earlier novel, **Mardi**, had failed by starting realistically then describing an impossibly big South Sea atoll with as many islands as all our mental states & the world's nations combined. It had let him say what he felt about nearly everything. Many readers liked a plausible yarn, a poetic allegory or a political satire, few liked a novel mixing all 3. M foresaw **Moby Dick** would be better than **Mardi** & equally unpopular - it is my earnest desire to write those sort of books that are said to*

and empty glasses, and in not altogether unpleasant sadness – Give it up, Sub-Subs! For by how much the more pains ye take to please the world, by so much the more shall ye for ever go thankless! Would that I could clear out Hampton Court and the Tuileries for ye! But gulp down your tears and hie aloft to the royal-mast with your hearts; for your friends who have gone before are clearing out the seven-storied heavens, and making refugees of long-pampered Gabriel, Michael, and Raphael, against your coming. Here ye strike but splintered hearts together – there, ye shall strike unsplinterable glasses!

"And God created great whales." *Genesis*

"Leviathan maketh a path to shine after him; One would think the deep to be hoary." *Job*

"Now the Lord had prepared a great fish to swallow up Jonah." *Jonah*

"There go the ships; there is that Leviathan whom thou hast made to play therein." *Psalms*

"In that day, the Lord with his sore, and great, and strong sword, shall punish Leviathan the piercing serpent, even Leviathan that crooked serpent; and he shall slay the dragon that is in the sea." *Isaiah*

"He visited this country also with a view of catching horse- whales, which had bones of very great value for their teeth, of which he brought some to the King. ***The best whales were catched in his own country, of which some were forty-eight, some fifty yards long. He said that he was one of six who had killed sixty in two days." *Other or Octher's verbal narrative taken down from his mouth by King Alfred. A.D. 890.*

"And whereas all the other things, whether beast or vessel, that enter into the dreadful gulf of this monster's (whale's) mouth, are immediately lost and swallowed up, the sea-gudgeon retires into it in great

security, and there sleeps."   *Montaigne –*
Apology for Raimond Sebond
"Let us fly, let us fly! Old Nick take me if it is not Leviathan described by the noble prophet Moses in the life of patient Job."   *Rabelais*
"The great Leviathan that maketh the seas to seethe like a boiling pan."   *Lord Bacon's*
version of the Psalms
"Touching that monstrous bulk of the whale or ork we have received nothing certain. They grow exceeding fat, insomuch that an incredible quantity of oil will be extracted out of one whale."   *Ibid.*
"History of Life and Death"
"The sovereignest thing on earth is parmacetti for an inward bruise."   *King Henry*
"Very like a whale."   *Hamlet*
"Which to recure, no skill of leach's art
Mote him availle, but to returne againe
To his wound's worker, that with lovely dart,
Dinting his breast, had bred his restless paine,
Like as the wounded whale
to shore flies thro' the maine."
Spenser's "The Fairie Queen"
"What spermacetti is, men might justly doubt, since the learned Hosmannus in his work of thirty years, saith plainly, *Nescio quid sit.*"   *Sir T. Browne*
"Of Sperma Ceti and the Sperma Ceti Whale"
"By art is created that great Leviathan, called a Commonwealth or State – (in Latin, *Civitas*) which is but an artificial man."   *Hobbes's "Leviathan"*
opening sentence
"Silly Mansoul swallowed it without chewing, as if it had been a sprat in the mouth of a whale."
John Bunyan's "Holy war"
"That sea beast
Leviathan, which God of all his works
Created hugest that swim the ocean stream."
Milton's "Paradise Lost"

*'fail', he said to his father-in-law, so he needed a farm to keep his family, a farm not far from Hawthorne's cottage, for he wanted at least 1 under-standing reader. Hawthorne's fiction also was in chatty prose, gave seemingly sure facts from a democratic USA viewpoint, then tilted them into weirdness to suggest profoundly ambiguous truths. When **Moby Dick** was done M told Haw-thorne: **I have written a wicked book & feel as innocent as a lamb**. It has sexual (mainly homosexual) innuendoes too vast & blasphemous for any but brave & ex-perienced readers to see, or for any polite readers to admit they saw. He was safe from persecution by lawyers & reviewers on **that** account. It is a very tall sea story. A USA captain wants to kill a great white whale, because the 1st time he tried to do that it bit off his leg. Madly sure that the whale is an ultimate evil he goes after it with a crew officered by Yankees but drawn from every race & nation in the world. Whalers were international oil refineries, so common whales met on this*

quest to kill absolute evil are killed for business reasons, like industries that claim to defend us from evil government while selling weapons to **any** government. In D. H. Lawrence's study of US classical literature he says the ship is our civilisation, that the whale is natural life, that our businesses are killing, & if they finally succeed we will all be smashed as the ship is smashed by the dying whale. Like Webster, Whitman & others, **M** saw the US would eventually lead the world, but where? **To a better future!** believers in social progress replied, but if asked, **What must we do to achieve it?** The usual reply was **Mind your own business!** Liberal heads of state gave France, Britain & the USA the same advice. Said Guizot, Premier of France – **Enrich yourselves!** Lord Palmerston, Prime Minister of Britain, said – **Buy cheap & sell dear.** President Coolidge, shortly before the Wall Street crash of 1929, said – **The business of the USA is business.** Like Marx (who wrote in the **New York Daily Tribune**) M saw

"There Leviathan,
Hugest of living creatures, on the deep
Stretched like a promontory sleeps or swims,
And seems a moving land; and at his gills
Draws in, and at his trunk spouts out a sea."

Milton's "Paradise Lost"

"So close behind some promontory lie
The huge Leviathans to attend their prey,
And give no chace, but swallow in the fry,
Which through their gaping jaws mistake the way."

Dryden's "Annus Mirabilis"

"To fifty chosen sylphs of special note,
We trust the important charge, the petticoat.
Oft have we known that seven-fold fence to fail,
Tho' stiff with hoops and armed with ribs of whale."

Pope's "Rape of the Lock"

"A tenth branch of the king's ordinary revenue, said to be grounded on the consideration of his guarding and protecting the seas from pirates and robbers, is the right to *royal* fish, which are whale and sturgeon. And these, when either thrown ashore or caught near the coasts, are the property of the king."   *Blackstone*

"If we compare land animals in respect to magnitude, with those that take up their abode in the deep, we shall find they will appear contemptible in the comparison. The whale is doubtless the largest animal in creation."   *Goldsmith's "Natural History"*

"If you should write a fable for little fishes, you would make them speak like great whales."

Goldsmith to Johnson

"In the afternoon we saw what was supposed to be a rock, but it was found to be a dead whale, which some Asiatics had killed, and were then towing ashore. They seemed to endeavour to conceal themselves behind the whale, in order to avoid being seen by us."   *Cook's "Voyages"*

"Spain – a great whale stranded on the shores of Europe."   *Edmund Burke (somewhere)*

"The aorta of a whale is larger in the bore than the main pipe of the water-works at London Bridge, and the water roaring in its passage through that pipe is inferior in impetus and velocity to the blood gushing from the whale's heart."   *Paley's Theology*
"The whale is a mammiferous animal without hind feet."   *Baron Cuvier*
"In 40 degrees south, we saw Spermacetti Whales, but did not take any till the first of May, the sea being then covered with them."
Colnett's "Voyage for the Purpose of Extending the Spermacetti Whale Fishery"
"I built a cottage for Susan and myself and made a gateway in the form of a Gothic Arch, by setting up a whale's jaw bones." *Hawthorne's "Twice-told Tales"*
"She came to bespeak a monument for her first love, who had been killed by a whale in the Pacific ocean, no less than forty years ago."   *Ibid.*
"No, Sir, 'tis a Right Whale," answered Tom; "I saw his spout; he threw up a pair of as pretty rainbows as a Christian would wish to look at. He's a raal oil-butt, that fellow!"   *Cooper's "Pilot"*
"On one occasion I saw two of these monsters (whales) probably male and female, slowly swimming, one after the other, within less than a stone's throw of the shore (Terra Del Fuego) over which the beech tree extended its branches."
Darwin's "Voyage of a Naturalist"

*this blend of vague ideal & immediate greed **must** lead to smash. He could not imagine a workers' dictatorship making a Utopia after it, or a Carlyle-style dictator averting it – **M**'s ship of state has Cap'n Ahab dictating the course. So **M** shows the self-destructive quest with jocular gusto & ironic approval, seeing that the ship is **not** speeding to a destination ahead but fleeing from a world it cannot face. His lengthy epigraph, with quotes from King Alfred to Darwin & 16 other authors in THIS book, hints that **Moby Dick** is for the USA what the **Iliad** & **Aeneid** were for Greece & Rome: a summing up of the past in an epic to teach the future. The list of foreign words for **whale** claims a world-wide context for it.*

LONDON LABOUR AND THE LONDON POOR
HENRY MAYHEW
LONDON

1851

[PREFACE]

THE present volume is the first of an intended series, which it is hoped will form, when complete, a cyclopaedia of the industry, the want, and the vice of the great Metropolis.

It is believed that the book is curious for many reasons:

It surely may be considered curious as being the first attempt to

After running away from school to sail to Calcutta & from the Law to Journalism Mayhew succeeded as a comic dramatist & co-founder of Punch. A charming, jolly, friendly man, he settled in Germany for a time to write of the early life of Martin Luther, but his main achievement was to catch in print the voices of an extraordinary range of poor people: prostitutes, coster-mongers, men who scavenged the London sewers or collected dog shit. Effectively, he made people pay attention to the politically power-less who were resigned to silent poverty in a world growing ever more affluent. He wrote concisely, with an unfailing gift for the significant detail & the telling phrase, intro-ducing middle-class readers to uncom-fortable truths about poor people, emphas-izing the value of their contribution to the nation's wealth & the awful consequences of their being denied a fair share of the produce of their labour. Not overtly political, his faith lay mostly in the power of trade unionism: **Assuredly, he wrote, were it not for the trade societies, the country would have been destroyed by the greed of the capitalists long ago.**

publish the history of a people, from the lips of the people themselves – giving a literal description of their labour, their earnings, their trials, and their sufferings, in their own "unvarnished" language; and to pourtray the condition of their homes and their families by personal observation of the places, and direct communion with the individuals.

It may be considered curious also as being the first commission of inquiry into the state of the people, undertaken by a private individual, and the first "blue book" ever published in twopenny numbers.

It is curious, moreover, as supplying information concerning a large body of persons, of whom the public had less knowledge than of the most distant tribes of the earth – the government population returns not even numbering them among the inhabitants of the kingdom; and as adducing facts so extraordinary, that the traveller in the undiscovered country of the poor must, like Bruce, until his stories are corroborated by after investigators, be content to lie under the imputation of telling such tales, as travellers are generally supposed to delight in.

Be the faults of the present volume what they may, assuredly they are rather short-comings than exaggerations, for in every instance the author and his coadjutors have sought to understate, and most assuredly never to exceed the truth. For the ommissions, the author would merely remind the reader of the entire novelty of the task – there being no other similar work in the language by which to guide or check his inquiries. When the following leaves are turned over, and the two or three pages of information derived from books contrasted with the hundreds of pages of facts obtained by positive observation and investigation, surely some allowance will be made for the details which may still be left for others to supply. Within the last two years some thousands of the humbler classes of society must have been seen and visited with the especial view of noticing their condition and learning their histories; and it is but right that the truthfulness of the poor generally should be made known; for though checks have been usually adopted, the people have been mostly found to be astonishingly correct in their statements, – so much so indeed, that the attempts at deception are certainly the exceptions rather than the rule. Those persons who, from an ignorance of the simplicity of the honest poor, might be inclined to think otherwise, have, in order to be convinced of the justice of the above remarks, only to consult the details given in the present volume, and to perceive the extraordinary agreement in the statements of all the vast number of individuals who have been seen at different times, and who cannot possibly have been supposed to have been acting in concert.

The larger statistics, such as those of the quantities of fish and fruit, &c., sold in London, have been collected from tradesmen connected with the several markets, or from the wholesale merchants belonging to the trade specified – gentlemen to whose courtesy and co-operation I am indebted for much valuable information, and whose names, were I at liberty to publish them, would be an indisputable guarantee for the facts advanced. The other statistics have been obtained in the same manner – the best authorities having been invariably consulted on the subject treated of.

It is right that I should make special mention of the assistance I have received in the compilation of the present volume from MR. HENRY WOOD and MR. RICHARD KNIGHT (late of the City Mission), gentlemen who have been engaged with me from nearly the commencement of my inquiries, and to whose hearty co-operation both myself and the public are indebted for a large increase of knowledge. Mr. Wood, indeed, has contributed so large a proportion of the contents of the present volume that he may fairly be considered as one of its authors.

The subject of the Street-Folk will still require another volume, in order to complete it in that comprehensive manner in which I am desirous of executing the modern history of this and every other portion of the people. There still remain – the *Street-Buyers*, the *Street-Finders* the *Street-Performers*, the *Street-Artizans*, and the *Street-Labourers*, to be done, among the several classes of street-people; and the *Street Jews*, the *Street Italians* and *Foreigners*, and the *Street Mechanics*, to be treated of as varieties of the order. The present volume refers more particularly to the *Street-Sellers*, and includes special accounts of the *Costermongers* and the *Patterers* (the two broadly-marked varieties of street tradesmen), the *Street Irish*, the *Female Street-sellers* and the *Children Street-Sellers* of the metropolis.

My earnest hope is that the book may serve to give the rich a more intimate knowledge of the sufferings, and the frequent heroism under those sufferings, of the poor – that it may teach those who are beyond temptation to look with charity on the frailties of their less fortunate brethren – and cause those who are in "high places," and those of whom much is expected, to bestir themselves to improve the condition of a class of people whose misery, ignorance, and vice, amidst all the immense wealth and great knowledge of "the first city in the world," is, to say the very least, a national disgrace to us.

1852

Not long ago the term Uncle Tom was one of opprobrium. To young African-American militants Uncle Tom was a craven figure, enduring with resignation but without dignity the cruelty of slaveowning America. To traditional white academics **Uncle Tom's Cabin** *was an exercise in sentimental bathos which was not worthy of being called literature. Yet it, as the number one best-seller in 19th-century America, did more to overthrow slavery than any number of canonical works or pompous political speeches. In this preface Stowe stakes a radical claim for the political power of a literary text.*

UNCLE TOM'S CABIN; or Life Among the Lowly
HARRIET BEECHER STOWE
BOSTON

[PREFACE]

THE scenes of this story, as its title indicates, lie among a race hitherto ignored by the associations of polite and refined society; an exotic race, whose ancestors, born beneath a tropic sun, brought with them, and perpetuated to their descendants, a character so essentially unlike the hard and dominant Anglo-Saxon race, as for many years to have won from it only misunderstanding and contempt.

But, another and better day is dawning; every influence of literature, of poetry and of art, in our times, is becoming more and more in unison with the great master chord of Christianity, "good will to man."

The poet, the painter, and the artist, now seek out and embellish the common and gentler humanities of life, and, under the allurements of fiction, breathe a humanizing and subduing influence, favorable to the development of the great principles of Christian brotherhood.

The hand of benevolence is everywhere stretched out, searching into abuses, righting wrongs, alleviating distresses, and bringing to the knowledge and sympathies of the world the lowly, the oppressed, and the forgotten.

In this general movement, unhappy Africa at last is remembered; Africa, who began the race of civilization and human progress in the dim, gray dawn of early time, but who, for centuries, has lain bound and bleeding at the foot of civilized and Christianized humanity, imploring compassion in vain.

But the heart of the dominant race, who have been her conquerors, her hard masters, has at length been turned towards her in mercy; and it has been seen how far nobler it is in nations to protect the feeble than to oppress them. Thanks be to God, the world has at last outlived the slave-trade!

The object of these sketches is to awaken sympathy and feeling for the African race, as they exist among us; to show their wrongs and sorrows, under a system so necessarily cruel and unjust as to defeat and do away the good effects of all that can be attempted for them, by their best friends, under it.

In doing this, the author can sincerely disclaim any invidious feeling towards those individuals who, often without any fault of their own, are involved in the trials and embarrassments of the legal relations of slavery.

Experience has shown her that some of the noblest of minds and hearts are often thus involved; and no one knows better than they do, that what may be gathered of the evils of slavery from sketches like these, is not the half that could be told, of the unspeakable whole.

In the northern states, these representations may, perhaps, be thought caricatures; in the southern states are witnesses who know their fidelity. What personal knowledge the author has had, of the truth of incidents such as here are related, will appear in its time.

It is a comfort to hope, as so many of the world's sorrows and wrongs have, from age to age, been lived down, so a time shall come when sketches similar to these shall be valuable only as memorials of what has long ceased to be.

When an enlightened and Christianized community shall have, on the shores of Africa, laws, language and literature, drawn from among us, may then the scenes of the house of bondage be to them like the remembrance of Egypt to the Israelite, – a motive of thankfulness to Him who hath redeemed them!

For, while politicians contend, and men are swerved this way and that by conflicting tides of interest and passion, the great cause of human liberty is in the hands of one, of whom it is said:

> *"He shall not fail nor be discouraged*
> *Till He have set judgment in the earth."*
> *"He shall deliver the needy when he crieth,*
> *The poor, and him that hath no helper."*
> *"He shall redeem their soul from deceit and violence,*
> *And precious shall their blood be in His sight."*

1854

BLEAK HOUSE
CHARLES DICKENS
LONDON

*When **D** was 10 his dad, an unemployed clerk, was jailed for debt & the little boy filled bottles in a blacking factory. Later work as a newspaper reporter enlarged his view of society as a huge, unjust contraption ruled by grotesque adults & pressing hardest on children. **Bleak House** has (besides children abused by middle-class parents) 7 orphans, from Lord Chancellor's wards to Jo the street sweeper.*

*Dickens began it in 1851, some months after his father died & a year after finishing **David Copperfield**. It is the 1st of the 'dark', structurally complex*

[PREFACE]

A few months ago, on a public occasion, a Chancery Judge had the kindness to inform me, as one of a company of some hundred and fifty men and women not labouring under any suspicions of lunacy, that the Court of Chancery, though the shining subject of much popular prejudice (at which I thought the Judge's eye had a cast in my direction), was almost immaculate. There had been, he admitted, a trivial blemish or so in its rate of progress, but this was exaggerated, and had been entirely owing to the "parsimony of the public;" which guilty public, it appeared, had been until lately bent in the most determined manner on by no means enlarging the number of Chancery Judges appointed – I believe by Richard the Second, but any other king will do as well.

This seemed to me too profound a joke to be inserted in the body of this book, or I should have restored it to Conversation Kenge or to Mr. Vholes, with one or other of whom I think it must have originated. In such mouths I might have coupled it with an apt quotation from one of Shakespeare's Sonnets –

My nature is subdued
To what it works in, like the dyer's hand:
Pity me then, and wish I were renewed!

But as it is wholesome that the parsimonious public should know what has been doing, and still is doing, in this connection, I mention here that everything set forth in these pages concerning the Court of Chancery is substantially true, and within the truth. The case of Gridley is in no essential altered from one of actual occurrence, made public by a disinterested person who was professionally acquainted with the whole of the monstrous wrong from beginning to end. At the present moment there is a suit before the Court which was commenced nearly twenty years ago; in which from thirty to forty counsel have been known to appear at one time; in which costs have been incurred to the amount of seventy thousand pounds; which is a friendly suit; and which is (I am assured) no nearer to its termination now than when it was first begun. There is another well-known suit in Chancery, not yet decided, which was commenced before the close of the last century, and in which more than double the amount of seventy thousand pounds has been swallowed up in costs. If I wanted other authorities for JARNDYCE AND JARNDYCE, I could rain them on these pages, to the shame of – a parsimonious public. There is only one other point on which I offer a word of remark. The possibility of what is called Spontaneous Combustion has been denied since the death of Mr. Krook; and my good friend Mr. Lewes (quite mistaken, as he soon found, in supposing the thing to have been abandoned by all authorities) published some ingenious letters to me at the time when that event was chronicled, arguing that Spontaneous Combustion could not possibly be. I have no need to observe that I do not wilfully or

*works of his maturity, followed by **Hard Times**, **Little Dorrit**, **Great Expectations**. The story appeared in about 20 magazine instalments, revised for the book. It is told by 2 alternating 'voices', one belonging to a young woman, but **Bleak House** remains such a powerful work of art mainly through that glorious, worldly-wise 3rd-person voice opening the book. Dickens is such a bold artist! – heightening the drama by working in the present tense, a device learned from his friend Carlyle's history of the French Revolution. A fine amateur actor & director of stage plays, his sense of **performance** is crucial. In a superb interplay of oral & literary technique, he sets scenes & issues instructions like a cinema director, using his readers' imaginations as his technicians & actors to make the whole story. This present-tense narrative commands us: Imagine the scene!*

The 1st person voice is that of Esther Summerson, an illegitimate girl brought up by an unkind aunt. She attains her 'rightful' position in England's upper middle class through the offices of a wealthy benefactor, but 2 other wards in her position treat her with condescension. She does not resent this; is grateful. The text suggests Dickens approves of this. His main problem was not how to breathe life into such a shy little thing but how to do it each time her narrative resumed. He uses similar brush strokes over & over to keep her alive & consistent: in spite of some coyness he succeeds. Despite some inconsistency & persons who vanish for lengthy intervals (Young Smallweed for ever); despite some mealy-mouthed moralising, Bleak House is a mighty achievement. He presents a wide-screen view of a world where most folk representing law, government, philanthropy, religion & the arts are selfish shams. The exhumation of the Court of Chancery is fine & some of Dickens' best-kenned individuals traverse the pages.

negligently mislead my readers, and that before I wrote that description I took pains to investigate the subject. There are about thirty cases on record, of which the most famous, that of the Countess Cornelia de Bandi Cesenate, was minutely investigated and described by Giuseppe Bianchini, a prebendary of Verona, otherwise distinguished in letters, who published an account of it at Verona, in 1731, which he afterwards republished at Rome. The appearances beyond all rational doubt observed in that case, are the appearances observed in Mr. Krook's case. The next most famous instance happened at Rheims, six years earlier; and the historian in that case is LE CAT, one of the most renowned surgeons produced by France. The subject was a woman whose husband was ignorantly convicted of having murdered her; but, on solemn appeal to a higher court, he was acquitted, because it was shown upon the evidence that she had died the death to which this name of Spontaneous Combustion is given. I do not think it necessary to add to these notable facts, and that general reference to the authorities which will be found at page 329, the recorded opinions and experiences of distinguished medical professors, French, English, and Scotch, in more modern days; contenting myself with observing that I shall not abandon the facts until there shall have been a considerable Spontaneous Combustion of the testimony on which human occurrences are usually received.

In *Bleak House*, I have purposely dwelt upon the romantic side of familiar things. I believe I have never had so many readers as in this book. May we meet again.

[CHAPTER I : IN CHANCERY]

London. Michaelmas Term lately over, and the Lord Chancellor sitting in Lincoln's Inn Hall. Implacable November weather. As much mud in the streets, as if the waters had but newly retired from the face of the earth, and it would not be wonderful to meet a Megalosaurus, forty feet long or so, waddling like an elephantine lizard up Holborn Hill. Smoke lowering down from chimney-pots, making a soft black drizzle, with flakes of soot in it as big as full-grown snow-flakes – gone into mourning, one might imagine, for the death of the sun. Dogs, undistinguishable in mire. Horses, scarcely better; splashed to their very blinkers. Foot passengers, jostling one another's umbrellas, in a general infection of ill-temper, and losing their foot-hold at street-corners, where tens of thousands of other foot passengers have been slipping and sliding since the day broke (if the day ever broke), adding new deposits to the crust upon crust of mud, sticking at those points tenaciously to the pavement, and accumulating at compound interest.

Fog everywhere. Fog up the river, where it flows among green aits and meadows; fog down the river, where it rolls defiled among the tiers of shipping, and the waterside pollutions of a great (and dirty) city. Fog on the Essex marshes, fog on the Kentish heights. Fog creeping into the cabooses of collier-brigs; fog lying out on the yards, and hovering in the rigging of great ships; fog drooping on the gunwales of barges and small boats. Fog in the eyes and throats of ancient Greenwich pensioners, wheezing by the firesides of their wards; fog in the stem and bowl of the afternoon pipe of the wrathful skipper, down in his close cabin; fog cruelly pinching the toes and fingers of his shivering little 'prentice boy on deck. Chance people on the bridges peeping over the parapets into a nether sky of fog, with fog all round them, as if they were up in a balloon, and hanging in the misty clouds.

Gas looming through the fog in divers places in the streets, much as the sun may, from the spongey fields, be seen to loom by husbandman and ploughboy. Most of the shops lighted two hours before their time – as the gas seems to know, for it has a haggard and unwilling look.

The raw afternoon is rawest, and the dense fog is densest, and the muddy streets are muddiest, near that leaden-headed old obstruction, appropriate ornament for the threshold of a leaden-headed old corporation: Temple Bar. And hard by Temple Bar, in Lincoln's Inn Hall, at the very heart of the fog, sits the Lord High Chancellor in his High Court of Chancery.

Never can there come fog too thick, never can there come mud and mire too deep, to assort with the groping and floundering condition which this High Court of Chancery, most pestilent of hoary sinners, holds, this day, in the sight of heaven and earth.

1855

Whitman saw himself as belonging to a new age (an age of demo-cracy & science) & to a new place (the United States). He fully accepted the theme of the United States – **these states** *is one of his favourite phrases – & consciously sought to develop a new American poetry. His preface to the 1st (1855) edition of* **Leaves of Grass** *was among other things a manifesto for the new idea.* **The United States themselves are essentially the greatest poem. The genius of the United States is …most in the common people. In the beauty of poems are hence-forth the tuft & final applause of science.** *He associated the arts of the Old World with various artificialities, & his job in the New World was to break down such barriers* **(unscrew the locks from the doors!),** *to make the reader of his poetry think that he was being addressed, taken into confidence, in language that was not artless but was not arrogant or obscure. He made his living variously as compositor, teacher, government clerk, journalist &*

LEAVES OF GRASS
WALT WHITMAN
NEW YORK

AMERICA does not repel the past, or what the past has produced under its forms, or amid other politics, or the idea of castes, or the old religions – accepts the lesson with calmness – is not impatient because the slough still sticks to opinions and manners and literature, while the life which served its requirements has passed into the new life of the new forms – perceives that the corpse is slowly borne from the eating and sleeping rooms of the house – perceives that it waits a little while in the door – that it was fittest for its days – that its action has descended to the stalwart and well-shaped heir who approaches – and that he shall be fittest for his days.

The Americans of all nations at any time upon the earth, have probably the fullest poetical nature. The United States themselves are essentially the greatest poem. In this history of the earth hitherto, the largest and most stirring appear tame and orderly to their ampler largeness and stir. Here at last is something in the doings of man that corresponds with the broadcast doings of the day and night. Here is action untied from strings, necessarily blind to particulars and details, magnificently moving in masses. Here is the hospitality which for ever indicates heroes. Here the performance, disdaining the trivial, unapproach'd in the tremendous audacity of its crowds and groupings, and the push of its perspective, spreads with crampless and flowing breadth, and showers its prolific and splendid extravagance. One sees it must indeed own the riches of the summer and winter, and need never be bankrupt while corn grows from the ground, or the orchards drop apples, or the bays contain fish, or men beget children upon women.

Other states indicate themselves in their deputies

– but the genius of the United States is not best or most in its executives or legislatures, nor in its ambassadors or authors, or colleges or churches or parlors, nor even in its newspapers or inventors – but always most in the common people, south, north, west, east, in all its States, through all its mighty amplitude. The largeness of the nation, however, were monstrous without a corresponding largeness and generosity of the spirit of the citizen. Not swarming states, nor streets and steamships, nor prosperous business, nor farms, nor capital, nor learning, may suffice for the ideal of man – nor suffice the poet. No reminiscences may suffice either. A live nation can always cut a deep mark, and can have the best authority the cheapest – namely, from its own soul. This is the sum of the profitable uses of individuals or states, and of present action and grandeur, and of the subjects of poets. (As if it were necessary to trot back generation after generation to the eastern records! As if the beauty and sacredness of the demonstrable must fall behind that of the mythical! As if men do not make their mark out of any times! As if the opening of the western continent by discovery, and what has transpired in North and South America, were less than the small theatre of the antique, or the aimless sleep-walking of the middle ages!) The pride of the United States leaves the wealth and finesse of the cities, and all returns of commerce and agriculture, and all the magnitude of geography or shows of exterior victory, to enjoy the sight and realization of full-sized men, or one full-sized man unconquerable and simple.

The American poets are to enclose old and new, for America is the race of races. The expression of the American poet is to be transcendent and new. It is to be indirect, and not direct or descriptive or epic. Its quality goes through these to much more. Let the age and wars of other nations be chanted, and their

*editor, & insofar as these were routine activities they were violently broken into by the Civil War, when from 1863-1864 Whitman worked as a voluntary hospital orderly & assistant nurse. Out of this harrowing experience came the fine poems of **Drum-Taps** & the remarkable prose war-sketches of **Specimen Days**. Public events also impinged on his poetry, though less realistically, in his elegy on President Lincoln, **When lilacs last in the dooryard bloom'd**. But much of his verse is about **Walt Whitman, a Kosmos, of Manhattan the son**, most notably in the 60-page **Song of Myself**. This poem, despite its title, is not ingrown or solipsistic, but on the contrary shows the writer as outgoing, observant, sympathetic, a rememberer & a recorder, as a democratic poet should be. Its free verse does not preclude a good sense of structure: the poem proceeds in a huge arc of catharsis, moving through a series of at 1st pleasant & then cruel & terrible dramatic projections into other lives, pulling itself up (Section 38) with the line **Enough! Enough! Enough!**, & directing itself in the remainder* *towards a wonderfully affirmative reassertion of the tough persisting values of everyday life, summed up perhaps in a line like **the snag-toothed hostler with red hair redeeming sins past & to come**, where the ordinary, even the ugly, is raised to some enormous power. Whitman loved the materiality of things, & never shrinks from surface detail. But it is what he makes of this that matters, as is shown in a poem like **Crossing the Brooklyn Ferry**. He relished ferries, especially in a city like New York, where they were endlessly busy, & where he used to ride back & forth simply to mingle with & observe the variety of people. They became the symbol of a sort of eternal present, where he was avidly drinking in everything round about him, the people, the water, the gulls, the sky, the ships, the ware-houses, the barges, the foundry fires. All this is superficial, transient? Not so! Cities & the freight of waterfronts are **objects than which nothing else is more lasting...than which none else is perhaps more spiritual.** This accepting, liberating modernity is Whitman's great contribution to 19th-century poetry.*

eras and characters be illustrated, and that finish the verse. Not so the great psalm of the republic. Here the theme is creative, and has vista. Whatever stagnates in the flat of custom or obedience or legislation, the great poet never stagnates. Obedience does not master him, he masters it. High up out of reach he stands, turning a concentrated light – he turns the pivot with his finger – he baffles the swiftest runners as he stands, and easily overtakes and envelopes them. The time straying toward infidelity and confections and persiflage he withholds by steady faith. Faith is the antiseptic of the soul – it pervades the common people and preserves them – they never give up believing and expecting and trusting. There is that indescribable freshness and unconsciousness about an illiterate person, that humbles and mocks the power of the noblest expressive genius. The poet sees for a certainty how one not a great artist may be just as sacred and perfect as the greatest artist.

The power to destroy or remould is freely used by the greatest poet, but seldom the power of attack. What is past is past. If he does not expose superior models, and prove himself by every step he takes, he is not what is wanted. The presence of the great poet conquers – not parleying, or struggling, or any prepared attempts. Now he has passed that way, see after him! There is not left any vestige of despair, or misanthropy, or cunning, or exclusiveness, or the ignominy of a nativity or color, or delusion of hell or the necessity of hell – and no man thenceforward shall be degraded for ignorance or weakness or sin. The greatest poet hardly knows pettiness or triviality. If he breathes into anything that was before thought small, it dilates with the grandeur and life of the universe. He is a seer – he is individual – he is complete in himself – the others are as good as he, only he sees it, and they do not.

OOO

The land and sea, the animals, fishes and birds, the sky of heaven and the orbs, the forests, mountains and rivers, are not small themes – but folks expect of the poet to indicate more than the beauty and dignity which always attach to dumb real objects – they expect him to indicate the path between reality and their souls. Men and women perceive the beauty well enough – probably as well as he. The passionate tenacity of hunters, woodmen, early risers, cultivators of gardens and orchards and fields, the love of healthy women for the manly form, seafaring persons, drivers of horses, the passion for light and the open air, all is an old varied sign of the unfailing perception of beauty, and of a residence of the poetic in out-door people. They can never be assisted by poets to perceive – some may, but they never can. The poetic quality is not marshal'd in rhyme or uniformity, or abstract addresses to things, nor in melancholy complaints or good precepts, but is the life of these and much else, and is in the soul. The profit of rhyme is that it drops seeds of a sweeter and more luxuriant rhyme, and of uniformity that it conveys itself into its own roots in the ground out of sight. The rhyme and uniformity of perfect poems show the free growth of metrical laws, and bud from them as unerringly and loosely as lilacs and roses on a bush, and take shapes as compact as the shapes of chestnuts and oranges, and melons and pears, and shed the perfume impalpable to form. The fluency and ornaments of the finest poems or music or orations or recitations, are not independent but dependent. All beauty comes from beautiful blood and a beautiful brain. If the greatnesses are in conjunction in a man or woman, it is enough – the fact will prevail through the universe; but the gaggery and gilt of a million years will not prevail. Who troubles himself about his ornaments or fluency is lost. This is what you shall do: Love the earth and sun and the animals, despise riches, give alms to every one that asks, stand up for the stupid and crazy, devote your income and labor to others, hate tyrants, argue not concerning God, have patience and indulgence toward the people, take off your hat to nothing known or unknown, or to any man or number of men – go freely with powerful uneducated persons, and with the young, and with the mothers of families – re-examine all you have been told in school or church or in any book, and dismiss whatever insults your own soul; and your very flesh shall be a great poem, and have the richest fluency, not only in its words, but in the silent lines of its lips and face, and between the lashes of your eyes, and in every motion and joint of your body.

OOOOOOOOOOOOOOOOOOOOOOOOOOOOOOOOOOOOOOOOOOOOOOOOOOOOOOOOOOOOOOOOOO

Caution seldom goes far enough. It has been thought that the prudent citizen was the citizen who applied himself to solid gains, and did well for himself and for his family, and completed a lawful life without debt or crime. The greatest poet sees and admits these economies as he sees the economies of food and sleep, but has higher notions of prudence than to think he gives much when he gives a few slight attentions at the latch of the gate. The premises of the prudence of life are not the hospitality of it, or the ripeness and harvest of it. Beyond the independence of a little sum laid aside for burial-money, and of a few clap-boards around the shingles overhead on a lot of American soil own'd, and the easy dollars that supply the year's plain clothing and meals, the melancholy prudence of the abandonment of such a great being as a man is, to the toss and pallor of years of money-making, with all their scorching days and icy nights, and all their stifling deceits and underhand dodgings, or infinitesimals of parlors, or shameless stuffing while others starve, and all the loss of the bloom and odor of the earth, and of the flowers and atmosphere, and of the sea, and of the true taste of the women and men you pass or have to do with in youth or middle age, and the issuing sickness and desperate revolt at the close of a life without elevation or naiveté, (even if you have achiev'd a secure 10,000 a year, or election to Congress or the Governorship,) and the ghastly chatter of a death without serenity or majesty, is the great fraud upon modern civilization and forethought, blotching the surface and system which civilization undeniably drafts, and moistening with tears the immense features it spreads and spreads with such velocity before the reach'd kisses of the soul.

Ever the right explanation remains to be made about prudence. The prudence of the mere wealth and respectability of the most esteem'd life appears too faint for the eye to observe at all, when little and large alike drop quietly aside at the thought of the prudence suitable for immortality. What is the wisdom that fills the thinness of a year, or seventy or eighty years – to the wisdom spaced out by ages, and coming back at a certain time with strong reinforcements and rich presents, and the clear faces of wedding-guests as far as you can look, in every direction, running gaily toward you? Only the soul is of itself – all else has reference to what ensues. All that a person does or thinks is of consequence. Nor can the push of charity or personal force ever be anything else than the profoundest reason, whether it brings argument to hand or no. No specification is necessary – to add or subtract or divide is in vain. Little or big, learn'd or unlearn'd, white or black, legal or illegal, sick or well, from the first inspiration down the windpipe to the last expiration out of it, all that a male or female does that is vigorous and benevolent and clean is so much sure profit to him or her in the unshakable order of the universe, and through the whole scope of it forever. The prudence of the greatest poet answers at last the craving and glut of the soul, puts off nothing, permits no let-up for its own case or any case, has no particular sabbath or judgment day, divides not the living from the dead, or the righteous from the unrighteous, is satisfied with the present, matches every thought or act by its correlative, and knows no possible forgiveness or deputed atonement.

ooooooooooooooooooooooooooooooooooooooooooooooooooooooooooooooooo

There will soon be no more priests. Their work is done. A new order shall arise, and they shall be the priests of man, and every man shall be his own priest. They shall find their inspiration in real objects to-day, symptoms of the past and future. They shall not deign to defend immortality or God, or the perfection of things, or liberty, or the exquisite beauty and reality of the soul. They shall arise in America, and be responded to from the remainder of the earth.

The English language befriends the grand American expression – it is brawny enough, and limber and full enough. On the tough stock of a race who through all change of circumstances was never without the idea of political liberty, which is the animus of all liberty, it has attracted the terms of daintier and gayer and subtler and more elegant tongues. It is the powerful language of resistance – it is the dialect of common sense. It is the speech of the proud and melancholy races, and of all who aspire. It is the chosen tongue to express growth, faith, self-esteem, freedom, justice, equality, friendliness, amplitude, prudence, decision, and courage. It is the medium that shall wellnigh express the inexpressible.

No great literature, nor any like style of behavior or oratory, or social intercourse or household arrangements, or public institutions, or the treatment by bosses of employ'd people, nor executive detail, or detail of the army and navy, nor spirit of legislation or courts, or police or tuition or architecture, or songs or amusements, can long elude the jealous and passionate instinct of American standards. Whether or no the sign appears from the mouths of the people, it throbs a live interrogation in every freeman's and freewoman's heart, after that which passes by, or this built to remain. Is it uniform with my country? Are its disposals without ignominious distinctions? Is it for the ever-growing communes of brothers and lovers, large, well united, proud, beyond the old models, generous beyond all models? Is it something grown fresh out of the fields, or drawn from the sea for use to me to-day here? I know that what answers for me, an American, in Texas, Ohio, Canada, must answer for any individual or nation that serves for a part of my materials. Does this answer? Is it for the nursing of the young of the republic? Does it solve readily with the sweet milk of the nipples of the breasts of the Mother of Many Children?

America prepares with composure and good-will for the visitors that have sent word. It is not intellect that is to be their warrant and welcome. The talented, the artist, the ingenious, the editor, the statesman, the erudite, are not unappreciated – they fall in their place and do their work. The soul of the nation also does its work. It rejects none, it permits all. Only toward the like of itself will it advance half way. An individual is as superb as a nation when he has the qualities which make a superb nation. The soul of the largest and wealthiest and proudest nation may well go half-way to meet that of its poets.

1855 THE SONG OF HIAWATHA
HENRY WADSWORTH LONGFELLOW
BOSTON

Longfellow's Introduction reflects the fascination of his countrymen with Indians when many tribes were being eradicated. In 1855, stereotypes of Native Americans were shifting, from Indian as bloodthirsty barbarian to Indian as Noble Savage victim. Though Longfellow was perceptive and decent the insistent tom-tom beat of his verse represents the desire of the Anglo-American literary establishment to "play Indian", to annex images from another culture (just as his contemporaries were annexing Indian land) and thereby drown out twinges of conscience caused by the excesses of Manifest Destiny.

[INTRODUCTION]

SHOULD you ask me,
whence these stories?
Whence these legends and traditions,
With the odours of the forest,
With the dew and damp of meadows,
With the curling smoke of wigwams,
With the rushing of great rivers,
With their frequent repetitions,
And their wild reverberations,
As of thunder in the mountains?
I should answer, I should tell you,

"From the forests and the prairies,
From the great lakes
            of the Northland,
From the land of the Ojibways,
From the land of the Dacotahs,
From the mountains,
            moors, and fenlands,
Where the heron,
            the Shuh-shuh-gah,
Feeds among the reeds and rushes.
I repeat them as I heard them
From the lips of Nawadaha,
The musician, the sweet singer."

Should you ask where Nawadaha
Found these songs,
            so wild and wayward,
Found these legends and traditions,
I should answer, I should tell you,
"In the birds'-nests of the forest,
In the lodges of the beaver,
In the hoof-prints of the bison,
In the eyrie of the eagle!

"All the wild-fowl sang them to him,
In the moorlands and the fenlands,
In the melancholy marshes;
Chetowaik, the plover, sang them,
Mahng, the loon,
            the wild-goose, Wawa,
The blue heron, the Shuh-shuh-gah,
And the grouse, the Mushkodasa!"

If still further you should ask me,
Saying, "Who was Nawadaha?
Tell us of this Nawadaha,"
I should answer your inquiries
Straightway in such words as follow.

"In the Vale of Tawasentha,
In the green and silent valley,
By the pleasant water-courses,
Dwelt the singer Nawadaha.
Round about the Indian village
Spread the meadows
            and the corn-fields,
And beyond them stood the forest,
Stood the groves
            of singing pine-trees,
Green in Summer, white in Winter,
Ever sighing, ever singing.

"And the pleasant water-courses,
You could trace them
            through the valley,
By the rushing in the Spring-time,
By the alders in the Summer,
By the white fog in the Autumn,
By the black line in the Winter;
And beside them dwelt the singer,
In the Vale of Tawasentha,
In the green and silent valley.

"There he sang of Hiawatha,
Sang the Song of Hiawatha,
Sang his wondrous
            birth and being,
How he prayed
            and how he fasted,
How he lived, and toiled,
            and suffered,
That the tribes of men
            might prosper,
That he might advance his
people!"
OOOOOOOOOOOOOOOOOOOOOOOOOOOOOO
Read this Song of Hiawatha!

1859

THE ORIGIN OF SPECIES
CHARLES DARWIN
LONDON

Darwin belonged to a north-country family enriched by creative work in medicine & industry. Failing to find his vocation, 1st in medicine & then the Church, he sailed as a naturalist, when 22, aboard HMS Beagle, which from 1831 to 36 surveyed seas & lands south of the equator for the admiralty. His study of coral reefs, volcanoes, fossils & remote islands like the Galapagos group, each with its unique kind of animal, bird & plant, gave materials for work which, when he returned, soon made him known as a great scientist. He married &, his health poor, led the life of a country gent whose hobby was not hunting & shooting, but natural history.

Most astronomers & geologists had quietly abandoned the idea of a single creative act by God explaining the form of things, but no biologist had openly done so. Fossil proofs that millions of species had died before ours were evidence, said religious folk, that God had not ordered Noah to save them in his Ark. Many doubted that, but

[INTRODUCTION]

WHEN on board H.M.S. *Beagle*, as naturalist, I was much struck with certain facts in the distribution of the organic beings inhabiting South America, and in the geological relations of the present to the past inhabitants of that continent. These facts, as will be seen in the latter chapters of this volume, seemed to throw some light on the origin of species – that mystery of mysteries, as it has been called by one of our greatest philosophers. On my return home, it occurred to me, in 1837, that something might perhaps be made out on this question by patiently accumulating and reflecting on all sorts of facts which could possibly have any bearing on it. After five years' work I allowed myself to speculate on the subject, and drew up some short notes; these I enlarged in 1844 into a sketch of the conclusions which then seemed to me probable: from that period to the present day I have steadily pursued the same object. I hope that I may be excused for entering on these personal details, as I give them to show that I have not been hasty in coming to a decision.

My work is now (1859) nearly finished; but as it will take me many more years to complete it, and as my health is far from strong, I have been urged to publish this Abstract. I have more especially been induced to do this, as Mr. Wallace, who is now studying the natural history of the Malay Archipelago, has arrived at almost exactly the same general conclusions that I have on the origin of species. In 1858 he sent me a memoir on this subject, with a request that I would forward it to Sir Charles Lyell, who sent it to the Linnean Society, and it is published in the third volume of the Journal of that

Society. Sir C. Lyell and Dr. Hooker, who both knew of my work – the latter having read my sketch of 1844 – honoured me by thinking it advisable to publish, with Mr. Wallace's excellent memoir, some brief extracts from my manuscripts.

This Abstract, which I now publish, must necessarily be imperfect. I cannot here give references and authorities for my several statements; and I must trust to the reader reposing some confidence in my accuracy. No doubt errors will have crept in, though I hope I have always been cautious in trusting to good authorities alone. I can here give only the general conclusions at which I have arrived, with a few facts in illustration, but which, I hope, in most cases will suffice. No one can feel more sensible than I do of the necessity of hereafter publishing in detail all the facts, with references, on which my conclusions have been grounded; and I hope in a future work to do this. For I am well aware that scarcely a single point is discussed in this volume on which facts cannot be adduced, often apparently leading to conclusions directly opposite to those at which I have arrived. A fair result can be obtained only be fully stating and balancing the facts and arguments on both sides of each question; and this is here impossible.

I much regret that want of space prevents my having the satisfaction of acknowledging the generous assistance which I have received from very many naturalists, some of them personally unknown to me. I cannot, however, let this opportunity pass without expressing my deep obligations to Dr. Hooker, who, for the last fifteen years, has aided me in every possible way by his large stores of knowledge and his excellent judgment.

In considering the Origin of Species, it is quite conceivable that a naturalist, reflecting on the mutual affinities of organic beings, on their embryological

a convincing account of animal evolution was needed before it could be rationally argued. D's colleagues knew he was working on such an account, using the Malthus idea (of food supply limiting sizes of population) to say how species transform each other. He worked slowly, carefully. Not combative, aware that his book would cause uproars, he published (as he says here) only after learning that natural selection, the hub of his theory, had also been deduced by Wallace.

Origin of Species may be the last great revolutionary work of science in prose that any reader of English understands. Natural historians had not yet evolved to biologists, so specialist jargon did not hide what D meant. The world has not been particularly made for mankind. Our struggles to live are essential: not proofs of inferiority & not punishment for sins. Natural selection not only destroys life in competitive struggles for food, it links all life forms, "high" & "low", in an interdependent family whose members survive by alliances & adapting to each other. The accuracy of D's conclusions is amazing, for they were reached before the discovery of genetics & fossils of intermediate species. Only a few modifications of his theory are being discussed circa 2000. Fossils show life on earth divides roughly into 26 million-year periods, each 1 ending in vast extinctions (e.g. the dinosaurs). D said species died out or evolved into others at the same gradual rate of change. Later evidence suggests a periodic meteor blitz caused extinctions by sudden climate change, letting survivors evolve more swiftly while expanding into vacant territory. D thought natural selection not enough to explain the extravagance of (for example) the peacock's tail. Ultra-Darwinians now disagree with him.

*That the accident of a thicker fur or a sharper beak makes some creature fitter to survive & breed has no social moral. Liberal free traders faked one by arguing that folk with more money & guns were **naturally** fitter to exploit or kill those with less or none. This was the old Norman-French Right of Conquest in modern dress. Darwin was not responsible.*

relations, their geographical distribution, geological succession, and other such facts, might come to the conclusion that species had not been independently created, but had descended, like varieties, from other species. Nevertheless, such a conclusion, even if well founded, would be unsatisfactory, until it could be shown how the innumerable species inhabiting this world have been modified, so as to acquire that perfection of structure and coadaptation which justly excites our admiration. Naturalists continually refer to external conditions, such as climate, food, etc., as the only possible cause of variation. In one limited sense, as we shall hereafter see, this may be true; but it is preposterous to attribute to mere external conditions, the structure, for instance, of the woodpecker, with its feet, tail, beak, and tongue, so admirably adapted to catch insects under the bark of trees. In the case of the mistletoe, which draws its nourishment from certain trees, which has seeds that must be transported by certain birds, and which has flowers with separate sexes absolutely requiring the agency of certain insects to bring pollen from one flower to the other, it is equally preposterous to account for the structure of this parasite, with its relations to several distinct organic beings, by the effects of external conditions, or of habit, or of the volition of the plant itself.

It is, therefore, of the highest importance to gain a clear insight into the means of modification and coadaptation. At the commencement of my observations it seemed to me probable that a careful study of domesticated animals and of cultivated plants would offer the best chance of making out this obscure problem. Nor have I been disappointed; in this and in all other perplexing cases I have invariably found that our knowledge, imperfect though it be, of variation under domestication, afforded the best and safest clue. I may venture to express my conviction of the high value of such studies, although they have been very commonly neglected by naturalists.

From these considerations, I shall devote the first chapter of this Abstract to Variation under Domestication. We shall thus see that a large amount of hereditary modification is at least possible; and, what is equally or more important, we shall see how great is the power of man in accumulating by his Selection successive slight variations. I will then pass on to the variability of species in a state of nature; but I shall, unfortunately, be compelled to treat this subject far too briefly, as it can be treated properly only by giving long catalogues of facts. We shall, however, be enabled to discuss what circumstances are most favourable to variation. In the next chapter the Struggle for Existence amongst all organic beings throughout the world, which inevitably follows from the high geometrical ratio of their increase, will be considered. This is the doctrine of Malthus, applied to the whole animal and vegetable kingdoms. As many more individuals of each species are born than can possibly survive; and as, consequently, there is a frequently recurring struggle for existence, it follows that any being, if it vary however slightly in any manner profitable to itself, under the complex and sometimes varying conditions of life, will have a better chance of surviving, and thus be *naturally selected*. From the strong principle of inheritance, any selected variety will tend to propagate its new and modified form.

This fundamental subject of Natural Selection will be treated at some length in the fourth chapter; and we shall then see how Natural Selection almost inevitably causes much Extinction of the less improved forms of life, and leads to what I have called Divergence of Character. In the next chapter I shall discuss the complex and little-known laws of variation. In the five succeeding chapters, the most apparent and gravest difficulties in accepting the theory will be given: namely, first, the difficulties of transitions, or how a simple being or a simple organ can be changed and perfected into a highly developed being or into an elaborately constructed organ; secondly, the subject of Instinct, or the mental powers of animals; thirdly, Hybridism, or the infertility of species and the fertility of varieties when intercrossed; and fourthly, the imperfection of the Geological Record. In the next chapter I shall consider the geological succession of organic beings throughout time; in the twelfth and thirteenth, their geographical distribution throughout space; in the fourteenth, their classification or mutual affinities, both when mature and in an embryonic condition. In the last chapter I shall give a brief recapitulation of the whole work, and a few concluding remarks.

No one ought to feel surprise at much remaining as yet unexplained in regard to the origin of species and varieties, if he make due allowance for our profound ignorance in regard to the mutual relations of the many beings which live around us. Who can explain why one species ranges widely and is very numerous, and why another allied species has a narrow range and is rare? Yet these relations are of the highest importance, for they determine the present welfare, and, as I believe, the future success and modification of every inhabitant of this world. Still less do we know of the mutual relations of the innumerable inhabitants of the world during the many past geological epochs in its history. Although much remains obscure, and will long remain obscure, I can entertain no doubt, after the most deliberate study and dispassionate judgment of which I am capable, that the view which most naturalists until recently entertained, and which I formerly entertained – namely, that each species has been independently created – is erroneous. I am fully convinced that species are not immutable; but that those belonging to what are called the same genera are lineal descendants of some other and generally extinct species, in the same manner as the acknowledged varieties of any one species are the descendants of that species. Furthermore, I am convinced that Natural Selection has been the most important, but not the exclusive, means of modification.

1862

UNTO THIS LAST
JOHN RUSKIN
LONDON

*His 1st recorded utterance, at the age of 5, was a sermon, beginning, **People, be good**, a message Ruskin was to convey, 1 way or another, throughout his life. He was a natural moralist, a Christian born & bred who never lost the need to convert*

[PREFACE]

THE four following essays were published eighteen months ago in *The Cornhill Magazine*, and were reprobated in a violent manner, as far as I could hear, by most of the readers they met with.

Not a whit the less, I believe them to be the best, that is to say, the truest, rightest-worded, and most serviceable things I have ever written; and the last of them, having had especial pains spent on it, is probably the best I shall ever write.

"This," the reader may reply, "it might be, yet not therefore well written." Which in no mock humility, admitting, I yet rest satisfied with the work, though with nothing else that I have done; and purposing shortly to follow out the subjects opened in these papers, as I may find leisure, I wish the introductory statements to be within the reach of any one who may care to refer to them. So I republish the essays as they appeared. One word only is changed, correcting the estimate of a weight; and no word is added.

Although, however, I find nothing to modify in these papers, it is matter of regret to me that the most startling of all the statements in them – that respecting the necessity of the organisation of labour, with fixed wages – should have found its way into the first essay; it being quite one of the least important, though by no means the least certain, of the positions to be defended. The real gist of these papers, their central meaning and aim, is to give, as I believe for the first time in plain English – it has often been incidentally given in good Greek by Plato and Xenophon, and good Latin by Cicero and Horace – a logical definition of WEALTH: such definition being absolutely needed for a basis of economical science. The most reputed essay on that subject which has appeared in modern times, after opening with the statement that "writers on political economy profess to teach, or to investigate[1], the nature of wealth," thus follows up the declaration of its thesis: "Every one has a notion, sufficiently correct for common purposes, of what is meant by wealth." ... "It is no part of the design of this treatise to aim at metaphysical nicety of definition[2]."

others to his ways of thinking.

He was indifferent to nothing, enthusiastically embracing wonder & human achievement. In an age when it was fashionable to take the world & its changes more or less for granted, Ruskin was continuously bemused: I cannot express the amazed awe, the crushed humility, with which I sometimes watch a locomotive take its breath at a railway station, & think what work there is in its bars & wheels, & what manner of men they must be who dig brown ironstone out of the ground, & forge it into THAT!

Nor were his opinions always welcome. The Bradford businessmen who asked his advice on their proposed Exchange were indignant when he said taste is the only morality: Tell me what you like, & I'll tell you what you are, he told them.

For most of the 19th century his position was impregnable. On the death of Tennyson, Gladstone wanted to make him Poet Laureate; Tolstoy, Gandhi & Bernard Shaw considered him 1 of the greatest social reformers of his time. Ruskin societies were founded across the country & an Oxford College for working men was named after

---

1. Which? for where investigation is necessary, teaching is impossible.
2. "Principles of Poitical Economy." By J.S. Mill : Preliminary Remarks p.2.

Metaphysical nicety, we assuredly do not need; but physical nicety, and logical accuracy, with respect to a physical subject, we as assuredly do.

Suppose the subject of inquiry, instead of being House-law (*Oikonomia*), had been Star-law (*Astronomia*), and that, ignoring distinction between stars fixed and wandering, as here between wealth radiant and wealth reflective, the writer had begun thus: "Every one has a notion, sufficiently correct for common purposes, of what is meant by stars. Metaphysical nicety in the definition of a star is not the object of this treatise" – the essay so opened might yet have been far more true in its final statements, and a thousand-fold more serviceable to the navigator, than any treatise on wealth, which founds its conclusions on the popular conception of wealth, can ever become to the economist,

It was, therefore, the first object of these following papers to give an accurate and stable definition of wealth. Their second object was to show that the acquisition of wealth was finally possible only under certain moral conditions of society, of which quite the first was a belief in the existence and even, for practical purposes, in the attainability of honesty.

Without venturing to pronounce – since on such a matter human judgment is by no means conclusive – what is, or is not, the noblest of God's works, we may yet admit so much of Pope's assertion as that an honest man is among His best works presently visible, and, as things stand, a somewhat rare one; but not an incredible or miraculous work; still less an abnormal one. Honesty is not a disturbing force, which deranges the orbits of economy; but a consistent and commanding force, by obedience to which – and by no other obedience – those orbits can continue clear of chaos.

It is true, I have sometimes heard Pope

condemned for the lowness, instead of the height, of his standard: "Honesty is indeed a respectable virtue; but how much higher may men attain! Shall nothing more be asked of us than that we be honest?"

For the present, good friends, nothing. It seems that in our aspirations to be more than that, we have to some extent lost sight of the propriety of being so much as that. What else we may have lost faith in, there shall be here no question; but assuredly we have lost faith in common honesty, and in the working power of it. And this faith, with the facts on which it may rest, it is quite our first business to recover and keep: not only believing, but even by experience assuring ourselves, that there are yet in the world men who can be restrained from fraud otherwise than by the fear of losing employment[3]; nay, that it is even accurately in proportion to the number of such men in any State, that the said State does or can prolong its existance.

To these two points, then, the following essays are mainly directed. The subject of the organisation of labour is only casually touched upon; because, if we once can get a sufficient quantity of honesty in our captains, the organisation of labour is easy, and will develop itself without quarrel or difficulty; but if we cannot get honesty in our captains, the organisation of labour is for evermore impossible.

The several conditions of its possibility I purpose to examine at length in the sequel. Yet, lest the reader should be alarmed by the hints thrown out during the following investigation of first principles, as if they were leading him into unexpectedly dangerous ground, I will, for his better assurance, state at once the worst of the political creed at which I wish him to arrive.

1. First, that there should be training schools[4] for youth established, at Government cost, and under Government discipline, over the whole country; that every child born in the country should, at the parents' wish, be permitted (and, in certain cases, be under penalty required) to pass through them; and that, in these schools, the child should (with other minor pieces of knowledge hereafter to be considered)

---

3. The effectual discipline which is exercised over a workman is not that of his corporation, but of his customers. It is the fear of losing their employment which restrains his frauds, and corrects his negligence." ("Wealth of Nations," Book I. chap.10.)

4. It will probably be inquired by near-sighted persons, out of what funds such schools could be supported. The modes of direct provision for them I will examine hereafter; indirectly, they would be far more than self-supporting. The economy in crime alone (quite one of the most costly articles of luxury in the modern European market), which such schools would induce, would suffice to support them ten times over. Their economy of labour would be pure gain, and that too large to be presently calculable.

imperatively be taught, with the best skill of teaching that the country could produce, the following three things:–

(a) The laws of health, and the exercises enjoined by them;

(b) habits of gentleness and justice; and

(c) the calling by which he is to live.

2. Secondly, that, in connection with these training schools, there should be established also entirely under Government regulation, manufactories and workshops, for the production and sale of every necessary of life, and for the exercise of every useful art. And that, interfering no whit with private enterprise, nor setting any restraints or tax on private trade, but leaving both to do their best, and beat the Government if they could – there should, at these Government manufactories and shops, be authoritatively good and exemplary work done, and pure and true substance sold; so that a man could be sure if he chose to pay the Government price, that he got for his money bread that was bread, ale that was ale, and work that was work.

3. Thirdly, that any man, or woman, or boy, or girl, out of employment, should at once be received at the nearest Government school, and set to such work as it appeared, on trial, they were fit for, at a fixed rate of wages determinable every year: that, being found incapable of work through ignorance, they should be taught, or being found incapable of work through sickness, should be tended; but that being found objecting to work, they should be set, under compulsion of the strictest nature, to the more painful and degrading forms of necessary toil, especially to that in mines and other places of danger (such danger being, however, diminished to the utmost by careful regulation and discipline), and the due wages of such work be retained – cost of compulsion first abstracted – to be at the workman's command, so soon as he has come to sounder mind respecting the laws of employment.

4. Lastly, that for the old and destitute, comfort and home should be provided; which provision, when misfortune had been by the working of such a system sifted from guilt, would be honourable instead of disgraceful to the receiver. For (I repeat this passage out of my "Political Economy of Art," to which the reader is referred for farther detail) "a labourer serves his country with his spade, just as a man in the middle ranks of life serves it with sword, pen, or lancet. If the service be less, and, therefore, the wages during health less, then the reward when

health is broken may be less, but not less honourable; and it ought to be quite as natural and straightforward a matter for a labourer to take his pension from his parish, because he has deserved well of his parish, as for a man in higher rank to take his pension from his country, because he has deserved well of his country."

To which statement, I will only add, for conclusion, respecting the discipline and pay of life and death, that, for both high and low, Livy's last words touching Valerius Publicola, "*de publico est elatus*,"[5] ought not to be a dishonourable close of epitaph.

These things, then, I believe, and am about, as I find power, to explain and illustrate in their various bearings; following out also what belongs to them of collateral inquiry. Here I state them only in brief, to prevent the reader casting about in alarm for my ultimate meaning; yet requesting him, for the present, to remember, that in a science dealing with so subtle elements as those of human nature, it is only possible to answer for the final truth of principles, not for the direct success of plans: and that in the best of these last, what can be immediately accomplished is always questionable, and what can be finally accomplished, inconceivable.   DENMARK HILL 10th May 1862

---

5. P. Valerius, omnium consensu princeps belli pacisque artibus, anno post moritur; gloria ingenti, copiis familiaribus adeo exiguis, ut funeri sumtus deesset; de publico est elatus. Luxere matronae ut Brutum – Lib.II.c.xvi.

FELIX HOLT, THE RADICAL
 GEORGE ELIOT
 EDINBURGH 1866

[INTRODUCTION]

FIVE-AND-THIRTY years ago the glory had not yet departed from the old coach-roads: the great roadside inns were still brilliant with well-polished tankards, the smiling glances of pretty barmaids, and the repartees of jocose ostlers; the mail still announced itself by the merry notes of the horn; the hedge-cutter or the rick-thatcher might still know the exact hour by the unfailing yet otherwise meteoric apparition of the pea-green Tally-ho or the yellow Independent; and elderly gentlemen in pony-chaises, quartering nervously to make way for the rolling swinging swiftness, had not ceased to remark that times were finely changed since they used to see the pack-horses and hear the tinkling of their bells on this very highway.

In those days there were pocket boroughs, a Birmingham unrepresented in Parliament and compelled to make strong representations out of it, unrepealed corn-laws, three-and-sixpenny letters, a brawny and many-breeding pauperism, and other departed evils; but there were some pleasant things too, which have also departed. *Non omnia grandior aetas quae fugiamus habet*, says the wise goddess: you have not the best of it in all things, O youngsters! the elderly man has his enviable memories, and not the least of them is the memory of a long journey in mid-spring or autumn on the outside of a stage-coach. Posterity may be shot, like a bullet through a tube, by atmospheric pressure from Winchester to Newcastle: that is a fine result to have among our hopes; but the slow old-fashioned way of getting from one end of our country to the other is the better thing to have in the memory. The tube-journey can never lend much to picture and narrative; it is as barren as an exclamatory O! Whereas the happy outside passenger seated on the box from the dawn to the gloaming gathered enough stories of English life, enough of English labours in town and country, enough aspects of earth and sky, to make episodes for a modern Odyssey. Suppose only that his journey took him through that central plain, watered at one extremity by the Avon, at the other by the Trent. As the morning silvered the meadows with their long lines of bushy willows marking the watercourses, or burnished the golden corn-ricks clustered near the long roofs of some midland homestead, he saw the full-uddered cows driven from their pasture to the early milking. Perhaps it was the shepherd, head-servant of the farm, who drove them, his sheep-dog following with a heedless unofficial air as of a beadle in undress. The shepherd with a slow and slouching walk, timed by the walk of grazing beasts, moved aside, as if unwillingly, throwing out a monosyllabic hint to his cattle; his glance, accustomed to rest on things very near the earth, seemed to lift itself with difficulty to the coachman. Mail or stage coach for him belonged to that mysterious distant system of things called "Gover'ment," which, whatever it might be, was no business of his, any more than the most out-lying nebula or the coal-sacks of the southern hemisphere: his solar system was the parish; the master's temper and the casualties of lambing-time were his region of storms. He cut his bread and bacon with his pocket-knife, and felt no bitterness except in the matter of pauper labourers and the bad-luck that sent contrarious seasons and the sheep-rot. He and his cows were soon left behind, and the homestead too, with its pond overhung by elder-trees, its untidy kitchen-garden and cone-shaped yew-tree arbour. But everywhere the bushy hedgerows wasted the land with their straggling beauty, shrouded the grassy borders of the pastures with catkined hazels, and tossed their long blackberry branches on the corn-fields. Perhaps they were white with May, or starred with pale pink dogroses; perhaps the urchins were already nutting amongst them, or gathering the plenteous crabs. It was worth the journey only to see those hedgerows, the liberal homes of unmarketable beauty – of the purple-blossomed ruby-berried nightshade, of the wild convolvulus climbing and spreading in tendrilled strength till it made a great curtain of pale-green hearts and white trumpets, of the many-tubed honeysuckle which, in its most delicate fragrance, hid a charm more subtle and penetrating than beauty. Even if it were winter the hedgerows showed their coral, the scarlet haws, the deep-crimson hips, with lingering brown leaves to make a resting-place for the jewels of the hoar-frost. Such hedgerows were often as tall as the labourers' cottages dotted along the lanes, or clustered into a

from radicalism. In 1866 members of the Liberal Party (which had ruled since 1832) proposed a new reform bill giving the vote to men of a lower middle class. J.S. Mill tried & failed to have women included. The bill failed as many Liberals, Evans among them, thought it too radical. **Felix Holt** *was published in that year.*

It is set in the time of the 1st reform bill & describes 2 male radicals: Transome, a gentleman parliamentary candidate who provokes riot by demanding the vote for workmen; and Holt, a self-taught workman who fears riots will destroy social gains & tells local miners to seek self-improvement before the vote. As the opening shows, it is a richer novel than its simple moral that society should **change at a human pace** *– not too fast. Conservative reviewers approved.*

POLITICAL NOTE The Liberal defeat led to a government under Disraeli, a Tory radical. Few Conservatives liked him but only he knew how to entice electors. In 1867 he confounded the Liberals by giving more working men the vote than the Liberals had discussed – all who paid rates & many lodgers. (In 1918 women over 29 could vote. In 1929 the voting rights of both sexes were equalised.)

small hamlet, their little dingy windows telling, like thick-filmed eyes, of nothing but the darkness within. The passenger on the coach-box, bowled along above such a hamlet, saw chiefly the roofs of it: probably it turned its back on the road, and seemed to lie away from everything but its own patch of earth and sky, away from the parish church by long fields and green lanes, away from all intercourse except that of tramps. If its face could be seen, it was most likely dirty; but the dirt was Protestant dirt, and the big, bold, gin-breathing tramps were Protestant tramps. There was no sign of superstition near, no crucifix or image to indicate a misguided reverence: the inhabitants were probably so free from superstition that they were in much less awe of the parson than of the overseer. Yet they were saved from the excesses of Protestantism by not knowing how to read, and by the absence of handlooms and mines to be the pioneers of Dissent: they were kept safely in the *via media* of indifference, and could have registered themselves in the census by a big black mark as members of the Church of England.

But there were trim cheerful villages too, with a neat or handsome parsonage and grey church set in the midst; there was the pleasant tinkle of the blacksmith's anvil, the patient cart-horses waiting at his door; the basket-maker peeling his willow wands in the sunshine; the wheelwright putting the last touch to a blue cart with red wheels; here and there a cottage with bright transparent windows showing pots full of blooming balsams or geraniums, and little gardens in front all double daisies or dark wallflowers; at the well, clean and comely women carrying yoked buckets, and towards the free school small Britons dawdling on, and handling their marbles in the pockets of unpatched corduroys adorned with brass buttons. The land around was rich and marly, great corn-stacks stood in the rickyards – for the rick-burners had not found their way hither; the homesteads were those of rich farmers who paid no rent, or had the rare advantage of a lease, and could afford to keep their corn till prices had risen. The coach would be sure to overtake some of them on their way to their outlying fields or to the market-town, sitting heavily on their well-groomed horses, or weighing down one side of an olive-green gig. They probably thought of the coach with some contempt, as an accommodation for people who had not their own gigs, or who, wanting to travel to London and such distant places, belonged to the trading and less solid part of the nation. The passenger on the box could see that this was the district of protuberant optimists, sure that old England was the best of all possible countries, and that if there were any facts which had not fallen under their own observation, they were facts not worth observing: the district of clean little market-towns without manufacturers, of fat livings, aristocratic clergy, and low poor-rates. But as the day wore on the scene would change: the land would begin to be blackened with coal-pits, the rattle of handlooms to be heard in hamlets and villages. Here were powerful men walking queerly with knees bent outward from squatting in the mine, going home to throw themselves down in their blackened flannel and sleep through the daylight, then rise and spend much of their high wages at the ale-house with their fellows of the Benefit Club; here the pale eager faces of handloom-weavers, men and women, haggard from sitting up late at night to finish the week's work, hardly begun till the Wednesday. Everywhere the cottages and the small children were dirty, for the languid mothers gave their strength to the loom; pious Dissenting women, perhaps, who took life patiently, and thought that salvation depended chiefly on predestination, and not at all on cleanliness. The gables of Dissenting chapels now made a visible sign of religion, and of a meeting-place to counterbalance the ale-house, even in the hamlets; but if a couple of old termagants were seen tearing each other's caps, it was a safe conclusion that, if they had not received the sacraments of the Church, they had not at least given in to schismatic rites, and were free from the errors of Voluntaryism. The breath of the manufacturing town, which made a cloudy day and a red gloom by night on the horizon, diffused itself over all the surrounding country, filling the air with eager unrest. Here was a population not convinced that old England was as good as possible; here were multitudinous men and women aware that their religion was not exactly the religion of their rulers, who might therefore be better than they were, and who, if better, might alter many things which now made the world perhaps more painful than it need be, and certainly more sinful. Yet there were the grey steeples too, and the churchyards, with their grassy mounds and venerable headstones, sleeping in the sunlight; there were broad fields and homesteads, and fine old woods covering a rising ground, or stretching far by the roadside, allowing only peeps at the park and mansion which they shut in from the working-day world. In these midland districts the traveller passed rapidly from one phase of English life to another: after looking down on a village dingy with coal-dust, noisy with the shaking of looms, he might skirt a parish all of fields, high hedges, and deep-rutted lanes; after the coach had rattled over the pavement of a manufacturing town, the scene of riots and trades-union meetings, it would take him in another ten minutes into a rural region, where the neighbourhood of the town was only felt in the advantages of a near market for corn, cheese, and hay, and where men with a considerable banking account were accustomed to say that "they never meddled with politics themselves." The busy scenes of the shuttle and the wheel, of the roaring furnace, of the shaft and the pulley, seemed to make but crowded nests in the midst of the large-spaced, slow-moving life of homesteads and far-away cottages and oak-sheltered parks. Looking at the dwellings scattered amongst the woody flats and the ploughed uplands, under the low grey sky which overhung them with an unchanging stillness as if Time itself were pausing, it was easy for the traveller to conceive that town and country had no pulse in common, except where the handlooms made a far-reaching straggling fringe about the great centres of manufacture; that till the agitation about the Catholics in '29, rural Englishmen had hardly known more of Catholics than of the fossil mammals; and that their notion of Reform was a confused combination of rick-burners, trades-unions, Nottingham riots, and in general whatever required the calling-out of the yeomanry. It was still easier to see that, for the most part, they resisted the rotation of crops and stood by their fallows: and the coachman would perhaps tell how in one parish an innovating farmer, who talked of Sir Humphry Davy, had been fairly driven out by popular dislike, as if he had been a confounded Radical; and how, the parson having one Sunday preached from the words, "Break up your fallow-ground," the people thought he had made the text out of his own head, otherwise it would never have come "so pat" on a matter of business; but when they found it in the Bible at home, some said it was an argument for fallows (else why should the Bible mention fallows?), but a few of the weaker sort were shaken, and thought it was an argument that fallows should be done away with, else the Bible would have said, "Let your fallows lie;" and the next morning the parson had a stroke of apoplexy, which, as coincident with a dispute about fallows, so set the parish against the innovating farmer and the rotation of crops that he could stand his ground no longer, and transferred his lease.

The coachman was an excellent travelling companion and commentator on the landscape: he could tell the names of sites and persons, and explain the meaning of groups, as well as the shade of

Virgil in a more memorable journey; he had as many stories about parishes, and the men and women in them, as the Wanderer in the "Excursion," only his style was different. His view of life had originally been genial, and such as became a man who was well warmed within and without, and held a position of easy, undisputed authority; but the recent initiation of Railways had embittered him: he now, as in a perpetual vision, saw the ruined country strewn with shattered limbs, and regarded Mr. Huskisson's death as a proof of God's anger against Stephenson. "Why, every inn on the road would be shut up!" and at that word the coachman looked before him with the blank gaze of one who had driven his coach to the outermost edge of the universe, and saw his leaders plunging into the abyss. Still he would soon relapse from the high prophetic strain to the familiar one of narrative. He knew whose the land was wherever he drove; what noblemen had half-ruined themselves by gambling; who made handsome returns of rent; and who was at daggers-drawn with his eldest son. He perhaps remembered the fathers of actual baronets, and knew stories of their extravagant or stingy housekeeping; whom they had married, whom they had horsewhipped, whether they were particular about preserving their game, and whether they had had much to do with canal companies. About any actual landed proprietor he could also tell whether he was a Reformer or an Anti-Reformer. That was a distinction which had "turned up" in latter times, and along with it the paradox, very puzzling to the coachman's mind, that there were men of old family and large estate who voted for the Bill. He did not grapple with the paradox; he let it pass, with all the discreetness of an experienced theologian or learned scholiast, preferring to point his whip at some object which could raise no questions.

No such paradox troubled our coachman when, leaving the town of Treby Magna behind him, he drove between the hedges for a mile or so, crossed the queer long bridge over the river Lapp, and then put his horses to a swift gallop up the hill by the low-nestled village of Little Treby, till they were on the fine level road, skirted on one side by grand larches, oaks, and wych elms, which sometimes opened so far as to let the traveller see that there was a park behind them.

How many times in the year, as the coach rolled past the neglected-looking lodges which interrupted the screen of trees, and showed the river winding through a finely-timbered park, had the coachman answered the same questions, or told the same things without being questioned!

That? – oh, that was Transome Court, a place there had been a fine sight of lawsuits about. Generations back, the heir of the Transome name had somehow bargained away the estate, and it fell to the Durfeys, very distant connexions, who only called themselves Transomes because they had got the estate. But the Durfeys' claim had been disputed over and over again; and the coachman, if he had been asked, would have said, though he might have to fall down dead the next minute, that property didn't always get into the right hands. However, the lawyers had found their luck in it; and people who inherited estates that were lawed about often lived in them as poorly as a mouse in a hollow cheese; and, by what he could make out, that had been the way with these present Durfeys, or Transomes, as they called themselves. As for Mr. Transome, he was as poor, half-witted a fellow as you'd wish to see; but *she* was master, had come of a high family, and had a spirit – you might see it in her eye and the way she sat her horse. Forty years ago, when she came into this country, they said she was a pictur'; but her family was poor, and so she took up with a hatchet-faced fellow like this Transome. And the eldest son had been just such another as his father, only worse – a wild sort of half-natural, who got into bad company. They said his mother hated him and wished him dead; for she'd got another son, quite of a different cut, who had gone to foreign parts when he was a youngster, and she wanted her favourite to be heir. But heir or no heir, Lawyer Jermyn had had *his* picking out of the estate. Not a door in his big house but what was the finest polished oak, all got off the Transome estate.

If anybody liked to believe he paid for it, they were welcome. However, Lawyer Jermyn had sat on that box-seat many and many a time. He had made the wills of most people thereabout. The coachman would not say that Lawyer Jermyn was not the man he would choose to make his own will some day. It was not so well for a lawyer to be over-honest, else he might not be up to other people's tricks. And as for the Transome business, there had been ins and outs in time gone by, so that you couldn't look into it straight backward. At this Mr. Sampson (everybody in North Loamshire knew Sampson's coach) would screw his features into a grimace expressive of entire neutrality, and appear to aim his whip at a particular spot on the horse's flank. If the passenger was curious for further knowledge concerning the Transome affairs, Sampson would shake his head and say there had been fine stories in his time; but he never condescended to state what the stories were. Some attributed this reticence to a wise incredulity, others to a want of memory, others to simple ignorance. But at least Sampson was right in saying that there had been fine stories – meaning, ironically, stories not altogether creditable to the parties concerned.

And such stories often come to be fine in a sense that is not ironical. For there is seldom any wrong-doing which does not carry along with it some downfall of blindly-climbing hopes, some hard entail of suffering, some quickly-satiated desire that survives, with the life in death of old paralytic vice, to see itself cursed by its woeful progeny – some tragic mark of kinship in the one brief life to the far-stretching life that went before, and to the life that is to come after, such as has raised the pity and terror of men ever since they began to discern between will and destiny. But these things are often unknown to the world; for there is much pain that is quite noiseless; and vibrations that make human agonies are often a mere whisper in the roar of hurrying existence. There are glances of hatred that stab and raise no cry of murder; robberies that leave man or woman for ever beggared of peace and joy, yet kept secret by the sufferer – committed to no sound except that of low moans in the night, seen in no writing except that made on the face by the slow months of suppressed anguish and early morning tears. Many an inherited sorrow that has marred a life has been breathed into no human ear.

The poets have told us of a dolorous enchanted forest in the under world. The thorn-bushes there, and the thick-barked stems, have human histories hidden in them; the power of unuttered cries dwells in the passionless-seeming branches, and the red warm blood is darkly feeding the quivering nerves of a sleepless memory that watches through all dreams.

These things are a parable.

THE SUBJECTION OF WOMEN
JOHN STUART MILL
LONDON
1869

[INTRODUCTION]

THE OBJECT OF THIS ESSAY is to explain as clearly as I am able, the grounds of an opinion which I have held from the very earliest period when I had formed any opinions at all on social or political matters, and which, instead of being weakened or modified, has been constantly growing stronger by the progress of reflection and the experience of life: That the principle which regulates the existing social

Mill (1806-73) was born in London, son of the Scots philosopher James Mill, who tutored him to be the new leader of the British Benthamite Utilitarians. He was taught Greek at the age of 3, Latin & arithmetic at 8, logic at 12 & political economy at 13. An active social reformer & practical Malthusian, when 18 he was arrested for giving birth-control pamphlets to the poor. He had a successful 35-year pensioned career at the India Office & became an MP in 1865. He wrote prolifically, corresponded with Carlyle & Maurice, the theologian and champion of education for women & working men. His foremost book, A System of Logic, influenced Keynes & Bertrand Russell (who was Mill's godson). His book On Liberty said governments should not rule everyone by majority opinion, but protect those who disagreed with the majority, if they did so without injuring lives & property. Ideas of his importance vary. Russell says, He was not in the front rank of British thinkers; more recently he was called

relations between the two sexes – the legal subordination of one sex to the other – is wrong in itself, and now one of the chief hindrances to human improvement; and that it ought to be replaced by a principle of perfect equality, admitting no power or privilege on the one side, nor disability on the other.

The very words necessary to express the task I have undertaken, show how arduous it is. But it would be a mistake to suppose that the difficulty of the case must lie in the insufficiency or obscurity of the grounds of reason on which my conviction rests. The difficulty is that which exists in all cases in which there is a mass of feeling to be contended against. So long as an opinion is strongly rooted in the feelings, it gains rather than loses in stability by having a preponderating weight of argument against it. For if it were accepted as a result of argument, the refutation of the argument might shake the solidity of the conviction; but when it rests solely on feeling, the worse it fares in argumentative contest, the more persuaded its adherents are that their feeling must have some deeper ground, which the arguments do not reach.

OOOOOOOOOOOOOOOOOOOOOOOOOOOOOOOOOOOOOOOOOOOOO

MILL SAYS IT IS WIDELY ASSUMED THAT ANCIENT LAWS AND CUSTOMS NEED NO ARGUMENTS TO JUSTIFY THEM – THAT BY STILL EXISTING THEY PROVE THEY ARE NEEDED.

OOOOOOOOOOOOOOOOOOOOOOOOOOOOOOOOOOOOOOOOOOOOO

It is one of the characteristic prejudices of the reaction of the nineteenth century against the eighteenth, to accord to the unreasoning elements in human nature the infallibility which the eighteenth century is supposed to have ascribed to the reasoning elements. For the apotheosis of Reason, we have substituted that of Instinct; and we call everything instinct which we find in ourselves and for which we cannot trace any rational foundation. This idolatry, infinitely more degrading than the other, and the most pernicious of the false worships of the present day, of all of which it is now the main support, will probably hold its ground until it gives way before a sound psychology laying bare the real root of much that is bowed down to as the intention of Nature and the ordinance of God. As regards the present question, I am willing to accept the unfavourable conditions which the prejudice assigns to me. I consent that established custom, and the general feeling, should be deemed conclusive against me, unless that custom and feeling from age to age can be shown to have owed their existence to other causes than their soundness, and to have derived their power from the worse rather than the better parts of human nature. I am willing that judgment should go against me, unless I can show that my judge has been tampered with. The concession is not so great as it might appear; for to prove this, is by far the easiest portion of my task.

The generality of a practice is in some cases a strong presumption that it is, or at all events once was, conducive to laudable ends. This is the case, when the practice was first adopted, or afterwards kept up, as a means to such ends, and was grounded on experience of the mode in which they could be most effectually attained. If the authority of men over women, when first established, had been the result of a conscientious comparison between different modes of constituting the government of society; if, after trying various other modes of social organisation – the government of women over men, equality between the two, and such mixed and divided modes of government as might be invented – it had been decided, on the testimony of experience, that the mode in which women are wholly under the rule of men, having no share at all in public concerns, and each in private being under the legal obligation of obedience

the greatest British philosopher of the 19th century, bringing Britain's traditions of empiricism & liberalism to their Victorian apogee.

This book was inspired by the woman he loved & (after her husband died) married. It roused much antagonism, as Mary Wollstonecraft's call 77 years before for women's political & educational equality with men had been forgotten. Mill's strong writing & public campaign for wives' rights to their own property within their marriage (a right they had lost since the Wife of Bath's day) revived these demands. The Feminist movement owes much to him.

to the man with whom she has associated her destiny, was the arrangement most conducive to the happiness and well-being of both; its general adoption might then be fairly thought to be some evidence that, at the time when it was adopted, it was the best: though even then the considerations which recommended it may, like so many other primeval social facts of the greatest importance, have subsequently, in the course of ages, ceased to exist. But the state of the case is in every respect the reverse of this. In the first place, the opinion in favour of the present system, which entirely subordinates the weaker sex to the stronger, rests upon theory only; for there never has been trial made of any other; so that experience, in the sense in which it is vulgarly opposed to theory, cannot be pretended to have pronounced any verdict. And in the second place, the adoption of this system of inequality never was the result of deliberation, or forethought, or any social ideas, or any notion whatever of what conduced to the benefit of humanity or the good order of society. It arose simply from the fact that from the very earliest twilight of human society, every woman (owing to the value attached to her by men, combined with her inferiority in muscular strength) was found in a state of bondage to some man. Laws and systems of polity always begin by recognising the relations they find already existing between individuals. They convert what was a mere physical fact into a legal right, give it the sanction of society, and principally aim at the substitution of public and organised means of asserting and protecting these rights, instead of the irregular and lawless conflict of physical strength. Those who had already been compelled to obedience became in this manner legally bound to it. Slavery, from being a mere affair of force between the master and the slave, became regularised and a matter of compact among the masters, who, binding themselves to one another for common protection, guaranteed by their collective strength the private possessions of each, including his slaves. In early times, the great majority of the male sex were slaves, as well as the whole of the female. And many ages elapsed, some of them ages of high cultivation, before any thinker was bold enough to question the rightfulness, and the absolute social necessity, either of the one slavery or of the other. By degrees such thinkers did arise; and (the general progress of society assisting) the slavery of the male sex has, in all the countries of Christian Europe at least (though, in one of them, only within the last few years) been at length abolished.

MIDDLEMARCH
GEORGE ELIOT
EDINBURGH

1871

[PRELUDE]

WHO that cares much to know the history of man, and how the mysterious mixture behaves under the varying experiments of Time, has not dwelt, at least briefly, on the life of Saint Theresa, has not smiled with some gentleness at the thought of the little girl walking forth one morning hand-in-hand with her still smaller brother, to go and seek martyrdom in the country of the Moors? Out they toddled from rugged Avila, wide-eyed and helpless-looking as two fawns, but with human hearts, already beating to a national idea; until domestic reality met them in the shape of uncles, and turned them back from their great resolve. That child-pilgrimage was a fit beginning. Theresa's passionate, ideal nature demanded an epic life: what were many-volumed romances of chivalry and the social conquests of a brilliant girl to her? Her flame quickly burned up that light fuel; and, fed from within, soared after some illimitable satisfaction, some object which would never justify weariness, which would reconcile self-despair with the rapturous consciousness of life beyond self. She found her epos in the reform of a religious order.

That Spanish woman who lived three hundred years ago, was certainly not the last of her kind. Many Theresas have been born who found for themselves no epic life wherein there was a constant unfolding of far-resonant action; perhaps only a life of mistakes, the offspring of a certain spiritual grandeur ill-matched with the meanness of opportunity; perhaps a tragic failure which found no sacred poet and sank unwept into oblivion. With dim lights and tangled circumstance they tried to shape their thought and deed in noble agreement;

Virginia Woolf called this one of the few English novels written for grown-up people, for Austen's & Dickens' books end, like fairy tales, in marriage. The married folk in this middle-English market town want more from life, & those who want most are thwarted. A doctor, able & keen to run a modern public hospital, is reduced to serving the rich by a wife who wants to be idle & fashionable. A girl wanting to serve mankind by helping a genius weds a dry old scholar who only wants company. Eliot has the dry wit of Austen & Dickens' social range, yet her worst people are too like us to be just clowns or villains. Middlemarch has fewer drones than Bleak House, but is also ruled by money inherited, saved & lent; so the selfish & cautious dominate, brave idealists are mostly stunted by their prejudice. Yet this is not a depressing tale. Without faith in God but some in social better-ment Eliot shows the crushed hopes of obscure folk & lives warped by poverty & by riches make what is called HISTORY.

but after all, to common eyes their struggles seemed mere inconsistency and formlessness; for these later-born Theresas were helped by no coherent social faith and order which could perform the function of knowledge for the ardently willing soul. Their ardour alternated between a vague ideal and the common yearning of womanhood; so that the one was disapproved as extravagance, and the other condemned as a lapse.

Some have felt that these blundering lives are due to the inconvenient indefiniteness with which the Supreme Power has fashioned the natures of women: if there were one level of feminine incompetence as strict as the ability to count three and no more, the social lot of women might be treated with scientific certitude. Meanwhile the indefiniteness remains, and the limits of variation are really much wider than any one would imagine from the sameness of women's coiffure and the favourite love-stories in prose and verse. Here and there a cygnet is reared uneasily among the ducklings in the brown pond, and never finds the living stream in fellowship with its own oary-footed kind. Here and there is born a Saint Theresa, foundress of nothing, whose loving heart-beats and sobs after an unattained goodness tremble off and are dispersed among hindrances, instead of centering in some long-recognisable deed.

1872

THE MARTYRDOM OF MAN
WINWOOD READE
LONDON

[AUTHOR'S PREFACE]

*Holmes gave this book to Watson in **The Sign of Four**, calling it **1 of the most remarkable ever penned**. It surveys civilisation from its African & Asian roots to its spread through the world via Europe. Like Marx **R** saw the past as a prolonged tragedy, for social progress happened in lands where a large population exceeded the food supply, causing famine.*

IN 1862–3 I made a tour in Western Africa, and afterwards desired to revisit that strange country with the view of opening up new ground and of studying religion and morality among the natives. I was, however, unable to bear a second time the great expenses of African travel, and had almost given up the hope of becoming an explorer when I was introduced by Mr. Bates, the well-known Amazon traveller and Secretary of the Royal Geographical Society, to one of its Associates, Mr. Andrew Swanzy, who had long desired to do something in the cause of African discovery. He placed unlimited means at my disposal, and left me free to choose my own route. I travelled in Africa for two years (1868–70), and made a journey which is mentioned in the text. The narrative of my travels will be published in due course; I allude to them now in order to show that I have had some personal experience of savages. I wish also to take the first opportunity of thanking Mr. Swanzy for his assistance, which was given not only in the most generous but also in the most graceful manner.

With respect to the present work, I began it intending to prove that "Negroland" or Inner Africa is not cut off from the main-stream of events, as writers of philosophical history have always maintained, but connected by means of Islam with the lands of the East; and also that it has, by means of the slave-trade, powerfully influenced the moral history of Europe and the political history of the United States. But I was gradually led from writing the history of Africa into writing the history of the world. I could not describe the Negroland of ancient times without describing Egypt and Carthage. From Egypt I was drawn to Asia and to Greece; from Carthage I was drawn to Rome. That is the first chapter. Next, having to relate the progress of the Mohammedans in Central Africa, it was necessary for me to explain the nature and origin of Islam, but that religion cannot be understood without a previous study of Christianity and of Judaism, and those religions cannot be understood without a study of religion among savages. That is the second chapter. Thirdly, I sketched the history of the slave-trade, which took me back to the discoveries of the Portuguese, the glories of Venetian commerce, the revival of the arts, the Dark Ages, and the invasion of the Germans. Thus finding that my outline of universal history was almost complete, I determined in the last chapter to give a brief summary of the whole, filling up the parts omitted, and adding to it the materials of another work suggested several years ago by *The Origin of Species*.

One of my reasons for revisiting Africa was to

Calamity, said R, will then come & teach them by torture to invent. But nearly every invention has then served the users as a way to exploit others: never without eventual reactions. R said past exertions to escape calamities had been misled by Christianity spreading false ideas of human importance: Whether a man lives or dies is as much a matter of indifference to nature as whether a raindrop falls upon the field & feeds a blade of grass, or falls on a stone & is dried to death. If folk accepted this he hoped they would come to worship the divinity within them & work scientifically to help each other. He said sooner or later 3 inventions must end poverty in overcrowded Britain – a cleaner source of energy than steam power – air travel – flesh & flour made by chemical synthesis, so leaving land free to be made a garden all could enjoy. None will be rich & none poor ... immortality will be invented ...mankind will migrate into space & will cross the airless Saharas separating planet from planet & sun from sun, & be architects of worlds.

collect materials for this work, which I had intended to call *The Origin of Mind*. However, Mr. Darwin's *Descent of Man* has left little for me to say respecting the birth and infancy of the faculties and affections. I therefore merely follow in his footsteps, not from blind veneration for a great master, but because I find that his conclusions are confirmed by the phenomena of savage life. On certain minor points I venture to dissent from Mr. Darwin's views, as I shall show in my personal narrative, and there is probably much in this work of which Mr. Darwin will disapprove. He must therefore not be made responsible for all the opinions of his disciple.

0000000000000000000000000000000000000000000000000000000000000000

READE CITES WRITERS WHO INFORMED HIM ABOUT EGYPT, AFRICA, ASIA & EUROPE HISTORICALLY & SCIENTIFICALLY FROM HERODOTUS THROUGH HAKLUYT, SPINOZA, GIBBON, MACAULAY, IBN BATTUTA, DAVID LIVINGSTONE & MANY OTHER EXPLORERS, ADVENTURERS, SCHOLARS & SCIENTISTS.

0000000000000000000000000000000000000000000000000000000000000000

All the works of the above-named authors deserve to be carefully read by the student of universal history, and in them he will find references to the original authorities, and to all writers of importance on the various subjects treated of in this work.

As for my religious sentiments, they are expressed in opposition to the advice and wishes of several literary friends, and of the publisher, who have urged me to alter certain passages which they do not like, and which they believe will provoke against me the anger of the public. Now, as a literary workman I am thankful to be guided by the knowledge of experts, and I bow to the decisions of the great public, for whom alone I write, whom alone I care to please, and in whose broad unbiased judgment I place implicit trust. But in the matter of religion I listen to no remonstrance; I acknowledge no decision save that of the divine monitor within me. My conscience is my adviser, my audience, and my judge. It bade me write as I have written, without evasion, without disguise; it bids me to go on as I have begun, whatever the result may be. If therefore my religious opinions should be condemned, without a single exception, by every reader of the book, it will not make me regret having expressed them again. It is my earnest and sincere conviction that those opinions are not only true, but also that they tend to elevate and purify the mind. One thing at all events I know – that it has done me good to write this book, and therefore I do not think that it can injure those by whom it will be read.

THE CITY OF DREADFUL NIGHT
JAMES THOMSON
LONDON

1874

[PROEM]

*L*O, thus, as prostrate, "In the dust I write
   My heart's deep languor
             and my soul's sad tears."
Yet why evoke the spectres of black night
    To blot the sunshine of exultant years?
Why disinter dead faith from mouldering hidden?
Why break the seals of mute despair unbidden,
    And wail life's discords into careless ears?

Because a cold rage seizes one at whiles
        To show the bitter old and wrinkled truth
Stripped naked of all vesture that beguiles,
        False dreams, false hopes, false masks
                 and modes of youth;
Because it gives some sense of power and passion
In helpless impotence to try to fashion
        Our woe in living words howe'er uncouth.

Surely I write not for the hopeful young,
        Or those who deem their happiness of worth,
Or such as pasture and grow fat among
        The shows of life and feel
               nor doubt nor dearth,
Or pious spirits with a God above them
To sanctify and glorify and love them,
        Or sages who foresee a heaven on earth.

For none of these I write, and none of these
        Could read the writing if they deigned to try;
So may they flourish, in their due degrees,
        On our sweet earth and in their unplaced sky.
If any cares for the weak words here written,
It must be some one desolate, Fate-smitten,
        Whose faith and hope are dead, and who would die.

Thomson's mother was an evangelical Christian who brought him as a child to London; toiled as a dressmaker; died after placing him in a Church of Scotland orphanage. Calvinist teaching gave him a dark view of life that stayed when his faith in God ended. He served in Ireland as army schoolmaster & there met Sergeant Charles Bradlaugh, later editor of the **National Reformer** & Britain's 1st openly atheist MP. Both came to London where Thomson lived mainly by journalism, always in lodgings, often in rent arrears. He loved the poetry of Spenser & Shelley; learned Italian & German to enjoy Dante, Leopardi, Heine; trained as a poet by translating them. In this proem he claims only to write for those who feel life is a disease, yet his poem shows hopelessness in shapes so surprising & apt that in verse only Dante's hell is more horridly amusing. (Milton's hell is a very polite city.) Thomson's has no devils but is known to all who have tramped streets at night, homeless or afraid to go home. The **National**

*Reformer printed it.
Other editions were
praised by Herman
Melville & Karl Marx.
George Eliot said she
hoped **his distinct vision
& grand utterance
might now produce
heroic strains upon
human fellowship**. But
like millions then &
since Thomson had no
supporting community.
His income was from
journals that stopped
printing him or existing.
He became drunken,
homeless, destitute,
dying in a hospital
charity ward.*

Yes, here and there some weary wanderer
      In that same city of tremendous night,
Will understand the speech, and feel a stir
      Of fellowship in all-disastrous fight;
"I suffer mute and lonely, yet another
Uplifts his voice to let me know a brother
      Travels the same wild paths though out of sight."

O sad Fraternity, do I unfold
      Your dolorous mysteries shrouded from of yore?
Nay, be assured; no secret can be told
      To any who divined it not before:
None uninitiate by many a presage
Will comprehend the language of the message,
      Although proclaimed aloud for evermore.

1876

THE HUNTING OF THE SNARK
LEWIS CARROLL
LONDON

[PREFACE]

*Lewis Carroll, famously,
was also someone else:
the Oxford don, Charles
Lutwidge Dodgson
(1832–1898). The mixed
bag of Victorian don-
nish passions in his case
included mathematical
logic, nonsense, devout
Christianity, & photo-
graphing small girls,
often called Gertrude or
Constance, & frequently
without their clothes.
His most famous works,
**Alice's Adventures in
Wonderland** & **Through
the Looking-Glass** have
never yet gone out of
print.
    **The Hunting of the
Snark**, although a
longish, eight-part*

IF – and the thing is wildly possible – the charge of writing nonsense were ever brought against the author of this brief but instructive poem, it would be based, I feel convinced, on the line (in p.18) "*Then the bowsprit got mixed with the rudder sometimes.*"
In view of this painful possibility, I will not (as I might) appeal indignantly to my other writings as a proof that I am incapable of such a deed: I will not (as I might) point to the strong moral purpose of this poem itself, to the arithmetical principles so cautiously inculcated in it, or to its noble teachings in Natural History – I will take the more prosaic course of simply explaining how it happened.

    The Bellman, who was almost morbidly sensitive about appearances, used to have the bowsprit unshipped once or twice a week to be revarnished, and it more than once happened, when the time came for replacing it, that no one on board could remember which end of the ship it belonged to. They knew it was not of the slightest use to appeal to the Bellman about it – he would only refer to his Naval Code, and read out in pathetic tones Admiralty Instructions which none of them had ever been able to understand – so it generally ended in its being fastened on, anyhow, across the rudder. The helmsman[1] used to stand by with tears in his eyes: *he* knew it was all wrong, but alas! Rule 42 of the Code, *"No one shall speak to the Man at the Helm,"* had been completed by the Bellman himself with the words *"and the Man at the Helm shall speak to no one."* So remonstrance was impossible, and no steering could be done till the next varnishing day. During these bewildering intervals the ship usually sailed backwards.

As this poem is to some extent connected with the lay of the Jabberwock, let me take this opportunity of answering a question that has often been asked me, how to pronounce "slithy toves." The "i" in "slithy" is long, as in "writhe"; and "toves" is pronounced so as to rhyme with "groves." Again, the first "o" in "borogoves" is pronounced like the "o" in "borrow." I have heard people try to give it the sound of the "o" in "worry." Such is Human Perversity.

This also seems a fitting occasion to notice the other hard words in that poem. Humpty-Dumpty's theory, of two meanings packed into one word like a portmanteau, seems to me the right explanation for all.

For instance, take the two words "fuming" and "furious." Make up your mind that you will say both words, but leave it unsettled which you will say first. Now open your mouth and speak. If your thoughts incline ever so little towards "fuming," you will say "fuming-furious"; if they turn, by even a hair's breadth, towards "furious," you will say "furious-fuming"; but if you have that rarest of gifts, a perfectly balanced mind, you will say "frumious."

poem in anapaestic metre (Friends, Romans, and countrymen, lend me your ears! runs one line, somewhat misleadingly), is often seen as making up a sort of closely related non-trilogy with the Alice books. Carroll's preface, very modern-sounding in its nonchalant yet studied inconsequentiality, is addressed as much to the past prose romances as to the following verse one.

Its meaning is equally modern: one must bring one's own. Of course, nearly all hunts & searches are a kind of allegory. The snark itself one inevitably sees as a sort of shark: one character even dreams of it as a barrister, which perhaps aids this identification, even if the fact that you may serve it with greens, / And it's handy for striking a light helps maintain its elusiveness. But for that which has no determinate meaning, meaning may be eagerly sought for ever – hence the unending popularity of so many religious & philosophic systems. Behind all the variegated absurdities & astonishments of this shaggy dog story without the dog there is a nagging & inescapable

---

1. This office was usually undertaken by the Boots, who found in it a refuge from the Baker's constant complaints about insuffcient blacking of his three pairs of boots.

sense of pointlessness, suggesting that it may be a dazzlingly accurate if perhaps inadvertent allegory of terrestrial life. However, a mathematician should not (in line 340) call the third occurrence of a noise its **third repetition**.

Supposing that, when Pistol uttered the well known words –

"Under which king, Bezonian? Speak or die!"
Justice Shallow had felt certain that it was either William or Richard, but had not been able to settle which, so that he could not possibly say either name before the other, can it be doubted that, rather than die, he would have gasped out "Rilchiam!"

1876

The strange, winding route to literary fame of Gerard M. Hopkins, SJ, at first sight looks like a sure road to oblivion. After Oxford, aged 22, Gerard Manley Hopkins converted from Anglicanism to Roman Catholicism and embarked on the lengthy discipline of becoming a Jesuit priest. To help crush his strong sensual imagination (which he later said was far worse than R.L. Stevenson's Mr Hyde) he renounced his earlier frippery of writing verses – though not his maturing studies of Old English, Middle English, Latin, Greek and, most strikingly, Welsh. When he was 31, The Deutschland, a German ship bound for America, off course in appalling weather, ran aground on a notorious sandbank in the Thames Estuary, with great loss of life. Among the dead were 5 nuns. **The Times** *carried an inspiring paragraph about the tragedy, and Hopkins'*

THE WRECK OF THE DEUTSCHLAND
GERARD MANLEY HOPKINS
MANUSCRIPT: LONDON
TO THE HAPPY MEMORY OF FIVE FRANCISCAN NUNS, EXILES BY THE FALK LAWS, DROWNED BETWEEN MIDNIGHT AND MORNING OF DEC. 7TH, 1875

[PART THE FIRST]

1

Thou mastering me
God! giver of breath and bread;
World's strand, sway of the sea;
Lord of living and dead;
Thou hast bound bones and veins
        in me, fastened me flesh,
And after it almost unmade, what with dread,
Thy doing: and dost thou touch me afresh?
Over again I feel thy finger and find thee.

2

I did say yes
O at lightning and lashed rod;
Thou heardst me truer than tongue confess
Thy terror, O Christ, O God;
Thou knowest the walls, altar and hour and night:
The swoon of a heart that the sweep
        and the hurl of thee trod
Hard down with a horror of height:
And the midriff astrain with leaning of,
        laced with fire of stress.

3

The frown of his face
  Before me, the hurtle of hell
Behind, where, where was a, where was a place?
  I whirled out wings that spell
And fled with a fling of the heart
                    to the heart of the Host.
My heart, but you were dovewinged, I can tell,
  Carrier-witted, I am bold to boast,
To flash from the flame to the flame then,
                    tower from the grace to the grace.

4

  I am soft sift
  In an hourglass – at the wall
Fast, but mined with a motion, a drift,
  And it crowds and it combs to the fall;
I steady as a water in a well, to a poise, to a pane,
But roped with, always, all the way down from the tall
  Fells or flanks of the voel, a vein
Of the gospel proffer, a pressure,
                    a principle, Christ's gift.

5

  I kiss my hand
  To the stars, lovely-asunder
Starlight, wafting him out of it; and
  Glow, glory in thunder;
Kiss my hand to the dappled-with-damson west:
Since, tho' he is under the world's
                    splendour and wonder,
  His mystery must be instressed, stressed;
For I greet him the days I meet him, and bless
                    when I understand.

6

  Not out of his bliss
  Springs the stress felt
Nor first from heaven (and few know this)
  Swings the stroke dealt –
Stroke and a stress that stars and storms deliver,

superior hinted that a poem on the subject might not go unwelcomed by the Jesuit publication the **Month**. *This was enough to let the genie out of the cruelly lidded cruet where it had been trapped in strenuous silence for almost a decade.*

What emerged was a work of massively accomplished literary art; an Everest among local foothills. However, it took time for many, or indeed any, to volunteer the ascent. The century, never mind the **Month**, *was hardly prepared for handsome, hand-hewn rhymes like:* **leeward, drew her, endured** *(from Part 2 of the poem), nor for a great deal else. Even Robert Bridges, his poet friend, with whom Hopkins had a lively correspondence throughout his short adult life, thought his verses too odd to be great, though fortunately he kept copies. Hopkins died in 1889, after working as a parish priest in Wales, London & the slums of Liverpool & Glasgow. In 1918 Bridges arranged a first edition of the poems. Since then the summit has been crowded.*

I am soft sift / In an hourglass – at the wall / Fast, but mined with a motion, a drift, / And it crowds and it combs to a fall – who else could that possibly be? There is probably more poetry there than in the whole of decent old Robert Bridges' once vaunted **Collected Works.** *Hopkins rarely idles: he did not write for career reasons, nor to fill an elegant leisure hour. (His heavy religious duties left him few of those.) He sought the thisness of things; the dazzle and depth of the detail; the specificity of everything he observed; what he called its* **inscape.**

And yet – although the specific thing is supposedly gorgeous in its unique thisness, Hopkins rarely goes for long without asserting in a raised voice that this is only because it is always actually a glimpse of something else, some further quality presumed to be there but always in itself inobservable. God, in other words. More specifically, Jesus Christ – **the only just literary critic,** *among other accolades – the charismatic Rabbi who for traditionally obedient believers founded the Roman Catholic Church. Everything is Christ. Everything, the entire cosmos, all that exists, is unique, wonderful – and (Hopkins would say, because) full of the grandeur of something else. Ultimately, the* **thisness** *is always a* **thatness.** *Certainly those who think that Christ and the Church are very little of absolutely everything*

That guilt is hushed by,

                hearts are flushed by and melt –
But it rides time like riding a river
(And here the faithful waver,

                the faithless fable and miss).

7

  It dates from day
  Of his going in Galilee;
Warm-laid grave of a womb-life grey;
  Manger, maiden's knee;
The dense and the driven

                Passion, and frightful sweat;
Thence the discharge of it, there its swelling to be,
  Though felt before, though in high flood yet –
What none would have known of it,

             only the heart, being hard at bay,

8

  Is out with it! Oh,
  We lash with the best or worst
Word last! How a lush-kept plush-capped sloe
  Will, mouthed to flesh-burst,
Gush! – flush the man, the being with it,

                sour or sweet
Brim, in a flash, full! – Hither then, last or first,
To hero of Calvary, Christ's feet –
Never ask if meaning it, wanting it,

             warned of it – men go.

9

  Be adored among men,
  God, three-numberèd form;
Wring thy rebel, dogged in den,
  Man's malice, with wrecking and storm.
Beyond saying sweet, past telling of tongue,
Thou are lightning and love,

            I found it, a winter and warm;
Father and fondler of heart thou hast wrung:
Hast thy dark descending

           and most art merciful then.

10

With an anvil-ding
And with fire in him forge thy will
Or rather, rather then, stealing as Spring
Through him, melt him but master him still:
Whether at once, as once at a crash Paul,
Or as Austin, a lingering-out swéet skill,
Make mercy in all of us, out of us all
Mastery, but be adored, but be adored King.

are often left asking: What use to us is a fettered propagandist of spectacular literary skill? However, at the very least, possibly nowhere outside of Dante has an insistent and often aggressive credalism been so voluptuously well expressed.

MIXED ESSAYS
MATTHEW ARNOLD
LONDON

1879

[PREFACE]

THE FIRST ESSAY in this volume was published nearly twenty years ago, as preface to a work on Continental Schools, which has probably been read by specialists only. The other essays have appeared in well-known reviews.

The present volume touches a variety of subjects, and yet it has a unity of tendency; – a unity which has more interest for an author himself, no doubt, than for other people; but which my friendly readers, whose attention has long been my best encouragement and reward, will not unwillingly suffer me, perhaps, to point out to them.

Whoever seriously occupies himself with literature, will soon perceive its vital connexion with other agencies. Suppose a man to be ever so much convinced that literature is, as indisputably it is, a powerful agency for benefiting the world and for civilising it, such a man cannot but see that there are many obstacles preventing what is salutary in literature from gaining general admission, and from producing due effect. Undoubtedly, literature can of itself do something towards removing those obstacles, and towards making straight its own way. But it cannot do all.

English poets of the 19th century were hamstrung by the influence of Shelley & Keats, whose elevation to exemplary status had the effect of encouraging a poetry of mellifluous nostalgia – something of a paradox, as few poets had been more agitated by events in the real world than the Romantics. Unfortunately their posthumous reputations were stripped of the radicalism that had made them controversial figures during their lifetimes: Shelley was known less for **The Mask of Anarchy** *than for* **To a Skylark**, *while Keats was mythologised as the poet cut down in his prime by illness exacerbated by unkind reviews. Arnold failed to break free of this in* *his verse: The Scholar Gypsy, for all its lyricism, is unashamedly nostalgic for Oxford's dreaming spires, while Dover Beach hankers after a God whom Burns, Wordsworth, Shelley, Keats & Byron did not want, but later 19th-century English poets did. It is in Culture & Anarchy that Arnold's intellectual personality found its fullest expression. Having noted the breakdown of English society into barbarians (the landed gentry), philistines (the middle classes) & a brutalised working class, he envisaged the unification of people of all classes through a humane system of state education. As a schools inspector he was ideally placed to lobby for it. He went on to praise the achievements of the French Revolution (specifically for the reform of the French educational system), the Italians (for the aesthetic regard shown in the construction & organisation of their cities) & the Germans (for their high regard for the life of the mind), becoming 1 of the 1st Europeanists in British cultural history.*

In other words, literature is a part of civilisation; it is not the whole. What then is civilisation, which some people seem to conceive of as if it meant railroads and the penny post, and little more, but which is really so complex and vast a matter that a great spiritual power, like literature, is a part of it, and a part only? Civilisation is the humanisation of man in society. Man is civilised, when the whole body of society comes to live with a life worthy to be called *human*, and corresponding to man's true aspirations and powers.

The means by which man is brought towards this goal of his endeavour are various. It is of great importance to us to attain an adequate notion of them, and to keep it present before our minds. They may be conceived quite plainly, and enounced without any parade of hard and abstruse expression.

First and foremost of the necessary means towards man's civilisation we must name *expansion*. The need of expansion is as genuine an instinct in man as the need in plants for the light, or the need in man himself for going upright. All the conveniences of life by which man has enlarged and secured his existence – railroads and the penny post among the number – are due to the working in man of this force or instinct of expansion. But the manifestation of it which we English know best, and prize most, is the love of liberty.

The love of liberty is simply the instinct in man for expansion. Not only to find oneself tyrannised over and outraged is a defeat to this instinct; but in general, to feel oneself over-tutored, over-governed, *sate upon* (as the popular phrase is) by authority, is a defeat to it. Prince Bismarck says: "After all, a benevolent rational absolutism is the best form of government." Plenty of arguments may be adduced in support of such a thesis. The one fatal objection to it is that it is against nature, that is contradicts a vital instinct in man – the instinct of expansion. And man is not to be civilised or humanised, call it which you will, by thwarting his vital instincts. In fact, the benevolent rational absolutism always breaks down. It is found that the ruler cannot in the long run be trusted; it is found that the ruled deteriorate. Why? Because the proceeding is against nature.

The other great manifestation of the instinct of expansion is the love of equality. Of the love of equality we English have little; but, undoubetdly, it is no more a false tendency than the love of liberty. Undoubtedly, immense inequality of conditions and property is a defeat to the instinct of expansion; it depresses and degrades the inferior masses. The common people is and must be, as Tocqueville said, more uncivilised in aristocratic countries than in any others. A thousand arguments may be discovered in favour of inequality, just as a thousand arguments may be discovered in favour of absolutism. And the one insuperable objection to inequality is the same as the one insuperable objection to absolutism: namely, that inequality, like absolutism, thwarts a vital instinct, and being thus against nature, is against our humanisation. On the one side, in fact, inequality harms by pampering; on the other, by vulgarising and depressing. A system founded on it is against nature, and in the long run breaks down.

I put first among the elements in human civilisation the instinct of expansion, because it is the basis which man's whole effort to civilise himself presupposes. General civilisation presupposes this instinct, which is inseparable from human nature; presupposes its being satisfied, not defeated. The basis being given, we may rapidly enumerate the powers which, upon this basis, contribute to build up human civilisation. They are the power of conduct, the power of intellect and knowledge, the power of beauty, the power of social life and manners. Expansion, conduct, science, beauty, manners, – here are the conditions of civilisation, the claimants which man must satisfy before be can be humanised.

That the aim for all of us is to make civilisation pervasive and general; that the requisites for civilisation are substantially what have been here enumerated; that they all of them hang together, that they must all have their development, that the development of one does not compensate for the failure of others; that one nation suffers by failing in this requisite, and another by failing in that: such is the line of thought which the essays in the present volume follow and represent. They represent it in their variety of subject, their so frequent insistence on defects in the present actual life of our nation, their unity of final aim. Undoubtedly, that aim is not given by the life which we now see around us. Undoubtedly, it is given by "a sentiment of the ideal life." But then the ideal life is, in sober and practical truth, "none other than man's normal life, as we shall one day know it."

1884

Moby-Dick is the USA Iliad, this book its Odyssey. The hero goes by water through many isolated settlements in a vast rural republic with plenty of room for all but redskins. The only visible law is a public opinion inclined to tolerate anyone but a slave on the run. Folk from all social ranks talk together as equals, if not black & white, & even that colour bar is broken through by Huck. He is motherless, a nasty drunkard's son, the sort of child whom Dickens showed hungry or dying in workhouse or street. But the USA is still unenclosed & Huck can fish & trap food in wildernesses round a settlement & have pals & patrons among polite folk inside it. His liberty is envied by some of them & his freedom of speech shows why. Like the voices in the best of English literature before Bunyan died & in Burns' best poems, this

THE ADVENTURES OF HUCKLEBERRY FINN
MARK TWAIN: LONDON

[NOTICE]

PERSONS attempting to find a motive in this narrative will be prosecuted; persons attempting to find a moral in it will be banished; persons attempting to find a plot in it will be shot.

BY ORDER OF THE AUTHOR *per* G.G., CHIEF OF ORDNANCE

[EXPLANATORY]

IN this book a number of dialects are used, to wit: the Missouri negro dialect; the extremest form of the backwoods South-Western dialect; the ordinary "Pike-County" dialect; and four modified varieties of this last. The shadings have not been done in a haphazard fashion, or by guess-work; but pain - stakingly, and with the trustworthy guidance and support of personal familiarity with these several forms of speech.

I make this explanation for the reason that without it many readers would suppose that all these characters were trying to talk alike and not succeeding.

THE AUTHOR

[CHAPTER 1]

YOU don't know about me, without you have read a book by the name of *The Adventures of Tom Sawyer*, but that ain't no matter. That book was made by Mr. Mark Twain, and he told the truth, mainly. There was things which he stretched, but mainly he told the truth. That is nothing. I never seen anybody but lied, one time or another, without it was Aunt Polly, or the widow, or maybe Mary. Aunt Polly – Tom's Aunt Polly, she is – and Mary, and the Widow Douglas, is all told about in that book – which is mostly a true book; with some stretchers, as I said before.

Now the way that the book winds up, is this: Tom and me found the money that the robbers hid in the cave, and it made us rich. We got six thousand dollars apiece – all gold. It was an awful sight of money when it was piled up. Well, Judge Thatcher, he took it and put it out at interest, and it fetched us a dollar a day apiece, all the year round – more than a body could tell what to do with. The Widow Douglas, she took me for her son, and allowed she would civilize me; but it was rough living in the house all the time, considering how dismal regular and decent the widow was in all her ways; and so when I couldn't stand it no longer, I lit out. I got into my old rags and my sugar-hogshead again, and was free and satisfied. But Tom Sawyer he hunted me up and said he was going to start a band of robbers, and I might join if I would go back to the widow and be respectable. So I went back.

The widow she cried over me, and called me a poor lost lamb, and she called me a lot of other names, too, but she never meant no harm by it. She put me in them new clothes again, and I couldn't do nothing but sweat and sweat, and feel all cramped up. Well, then, the old thing commenced again. The widow rung a bell for supper, and you had to come to time. When you got to the table you couldn't go right to eating, but you had to wait for the widow to tuck down her head and grumble a little over the victuals, though there warn't really anything the matter with them. That is, nothing only everything was cooked by itself. In a barrel of odds and ends it is different; things get mixed up, and the juice kind of swaps around, and the things go better.

After supper she got out her book and learned me about Moses and the "Bulrushers"; and I was in a sweat

voice sounds like a nation's, not like a limited class in it.

Twain grew up in Hannibal, a town on the Mississipi, & played with boys like Huck. His dad, a cheery but careless storekeeper & lawyer, died leaving his family poor when T was 8. He wanted to be a pilot on the huge steam riverboats but 1st helped a brother on the Hannibal **Journal***; learned printing; as a printer went to work in New York & other towns, ending at Saint Louis. In 1851 when 26 he* **did** *become a Mississippi pilot. The Civil War ended that trade in 1861 so he went west to Nevada with a brother who was made lieutenant governor. He failed as a goldminer; began to do well in journalism; went to San Francisco; met writers (Artemus Ward & Bret Harte in particular) who mixed satires & reports on American life using phonetically rendered vernacular speech.* **T** *became greatest of them; an author, editor, lecturer famed & rich enough to wed a rich heiress. As America's increasing power & wealth attracted the attention of Europe* **T***'s books were read as enjoyable guides to the frontiers of an important new nation. They were* *denounced by prim critics for corrupting the purity of good English, but Oxford University gave him an honorary degree. He liked fame but had the wisdom to value it no more than Melville did, who had died in obscurity. His books have shallows, like the books of all authors compelled to write quickly. Scott & Balzac deteriorate to melodrama, Dickens to maudlin sentiment, D. H. Lawrence & Mac-Diarmid to diatribe & T into mere jocularity – even near the end of this, his best book. But the bible is not of equal value in every part & T's best jokes are profound. He saw us clearly,' by light of the most recent science: Man has been here 32,000 years. That it took a 100 million years to prepare the world for him is proof that that is what it was done for. I suppose it is. I dunno. If the Eiffel Tower represented the world's age, the skin of paint on the knob of the pinnacle at the summit would represent man's share of that age; & anyone would perceive that that skin was what the tower was built for. I reckon they would. I dunno. Poe, Melville, Whitman & Twain gave future US authors a tradition – a great wealth of examples.*

to find out all about him; but by and by she let it out that Moses had been dead a considerable long time; so then I didn't care no more about him; because I don't take no stock in dead people.

Pretty soon I wanted to smoke, and asked the widow to let me. But she wouldn't. She said it was a mean practice and wasn't clean, and I must try to not do it any more. That is just the way with some people. They get down on a thing when they don't know nothing about it. Here she was a-bothering about Moses, which was no kin to her, and no use to anybody, being gone, you see, yet finding a power of fault with me for doing a thing that had some good in it. And she took snuff too; of course that was all right, because she done it herself.

Her sister, Miss Watson, a tolerable slim old maid, with goggles on, had just come to live with her, and took a set at me now, with a spelling book. She worked me middling hard for about an hour, and then the widow made her ease up. I couldn't stood it much longer. Then for an hour it was deadly dull, and I was fidgety. Miss Watson would say, "Don't put your feet up there, Huckleberry"; and "Don't scrunch up like that, Huckleberry – set up straight"; and pretty soon she would say, "Don't gap and stretch like that, Huckleberry – why don't you try to behave?" Then she told me all about the bad place, and I said I wished I was there. She got mad, then, but I didn't mean no harm. All I wanted was to go somewheres; all I wanted was a change, I warn't particular. She said it was wicked to say what I said; said she wouldn't say it for the whole world; she was going to live so as to go to the good place. Well, I couldn't see no advantage in going where she was going, so I made up my mind I wouldn't try for it. But I never said so, because it would only make trouble, and wouldn't do no good.

Now she had got a start, and she went on and told me all about the good place. She said all a body would

have to do there was to go around all day long with a harp and sing for ever
and ever. So I didn't think much of it. But I never said so. I asked her if she
reckoned Tom Sawyer would go there, and she said, not by a considerable
sight. I was glad about that, because I wanted him and me to be together.

Miss Watson she kept pecking at me, and it got tiresome and lonesome.
By and by they fetched the niggers in and had prayers, and then everybody
was off to bed. I went up to my room with a piece of candle and put it on
the table. Then I set down in a chair by the window and tried to think of
something cheerful, but it warn't no use. I felt so lonesome I most wished
I was dead. The stars was shining, and the leaves rustled in the woods ever
so mournful; and I heard an owl, away off, who-whooing about somebody
that was dead, and a whippowill and a dog crying about somebody that
was going to die; and the wind was trying to whisper something to me and
I couldn't make out what it was, and so it made the cold shivers run over
me. Then away out in the woods I heard that kind of a sound that a ghost
makes when it wants to tell about something that's on its mind and can't
make itself understood, and so can't rest easy in its grave and has to go
about that way every night grieving. I got so downhearted and scared, I did
wish I had some company. Pretty soon a spider went crawling up my
shoulder, and I flipped it off and it lit in the candle; and before I could
budge it was all shrivelled up. That was an awful bad sign and would fetch
me bad luck, so I was scared and most shook the clothes off of me. I got up
and turned around in my tracks three times and crossed my breast every
time; then I tied up a little lock of my hair with a thread to keep witches
away. But I hadn't no confidence. You do that when you've lost a horse-
shoe you've found, instead of nailing it over the door, but I hadn't heard
anybody say it would keep off any bad luck when you'd killed a spider.

I set down again, a-shaking all over, and got out my pipe for a smoke;
for the house was all as still as death, now, and so the widow wouldn't
know. Well, after a long time I heard the clock away off in the town go
boom – boom – boom – twelve licks – and all still again – stiller than ever.
Pretty soon I heard a twig snap, down in the dark amongst the trees –
something was a-stirring. I set still and listened. Directly I could just barely
hear a *"me-yow! me-yow!"* down there. That was good! Says I, *"me-yow!
me-yow!"* as soft as I could, and then I put out the light and scrambled out
of the window on to the shed. Then I slipped down to the ground and
crawled in amongst the trees, and sure enough there
was Tom Sawyer waiting for me.

1884

**FERISHTAH'S FANCIES
ROBERT BROWNING
LONDON**

"His genius was jocular, but, when disposed, he could be very serious."
– Article on Shakespeare in Jeremy Collier's *Historical Dictionary*, 1701.
"You, Sir, I entertain you for one of my Hundred; only, I do not like the
fashion of your garments: you will say they are Persian: but let them
be changed." – *King Lear*, Act 3, Scene 6.

[PROLOGUE]

The rhetoric of mellifluous beauty inherited from Shelley & Keats was a trap in which many of the Victorians became inextricably enmeshed. Hopkins escaped it by abandoning his upper-class roots & working in the slums of Glasgow & Liverpool; Arnold through his work as a schools inspector. Browning escaped it by emigrating to Italy & becoming a foreigner. Hundreds of miles from home, it was easier for him to discover a new poetic voice far removed from that of his Romantic forebears – a difficult, knotty, alien voice which he knew the English public would not like, & probably not understand. The strangeness of his work extended to the psychological, philosophical & moral complexity of his poetic "characters"

*P*RAY, *Reader, have you eaten ortolans
    Ever in Italy?*
*Recall how cooks there cook them: for my plan's
    To – Lyre with Spit ally.*
*They pluck the birds, – some dozen luscious lumps,
    Or more or fewer, –*
*Then roast them, heads by heads and rumps by rumps,
    Stuck on a skewer.*
*But first,– and here's the point I fain would press, –
    Don't think I'm tattling! –*
*They interpose, to curb its lusciousness,
    – What 'twixt each fatling?*
*First comes plain bread, crisp, brown, a toasted square:
    Then, a strong sage-leaf:*
*(So we find books with flowers dried here and there
    Lest leaf engage leaf.)*
*First, food – then, piquancy – and last of all
    Follows the thirdling:*
*Through wholesome hard, sharp soft,
                                your tooth must bite
    Ere reach the birdling.*
*Now, were there only crust to crunch, you'd wince:
    Unpalatable!*
*Sage-leaf is bitter-pungent – so's a quince:
    Eat each who's able!*
*But through all three bite boldly – lo, the gust!
    Flavour – no fixture –*
Flies, permeating flesh and leaf and crust

In fine admixture.
So with your meal, my poem: masticate
Sense, sight and song there!
Digest these, and I praise your peptics' state,
Nothing found wrong there.
Whence springs my illustration who can tell?
– The more surprising
That here eggs, milk, cheese, fruit suffice so well
For gormandizing.
A fancy-freak by contrast born of thee,
Delightful Gressoney!
Who laughest "Take what is, trust what may be!"
That's Life true lesson, – eh?

MAISON DELAPIERRE, GRESSONEY ST. JEAN, VAL D'AOSTA, *September* 12, 83.

THE MASTER OF BALLANTRAE
ROBERT LOUIS STEVENSON
LONDON

1889

[PREFACE]

ALTHOUGH an old, consistent exile, the editor of the following pages revisits now and again the city of which he exults to be a native; and there are few things more strange, more painful, or more salutary, than such revisitations. Outside, in foreign spots, he comes by surprise and awakens more attention than he had expected; in his own city, the relation is reversed, and he stands amazed to be so little recollected. Elsewhere he is refreshed to see attractive faces, to remark possible friends; there he scouts the long streets, with a pang at heart, for the faces and friends that are no more. Elsewhere he is delighted with the presence of what is new, there tormented by the absence of what is old. Elsewhere he is content to be his present self; there he is smitten with an equal regret for what he once was and for what he once hoped to be.

He was feeling all this dimly, as he drove from the station, on his last visit; he was feeling it still as he

*& their unusual settings. This is particularly evident in the case of **Ferishtah's Fancies**, a late work in which the framework of an Indian fable by Bidpai provides the vehicle for an attack on some popular versions of Herbert Spencer's ideas on historical Christianity.*

Stevenson was a past master at importing the foreign into the homes of the "inhabitants of that United Kingdom, peopled from so many different stocks, babbling so many different dialects" – IMPERIA IN IMPERIO, foreign things at home. By making his readers travel the world, he made them aware of how foreign their own customs, languages & prejudices were. The Master of Ballantrae is a babble of various texts – mock memoirs, diaries, letters, legal accounts, gravestone epitaphs – that move the reader around the world, also back 100 years to that other foreign country – 18th-century Scotland. Travel unpicked the idea of empire, showed the dark double of imperial adventurism, incarnate in the evil genius of the Master. Writing from the other side of the world (Adirondack, the Marquesas, Tahiti, Honolulu), Stevenson plays with his world, constructs a post-Calvinist Scotland, parodies the Great Game of Empire, disinterring from the litter of past stories the body of evil History.

alighted at the door of his friend Mr. Johnstone Thomson, W.S., with whom he was to stay. A hearty welcome, a face not altogether changed, a few words that sounded of old days, a laugh provoked and shared, a glimpse in passing of the snowy cloth and bright decanters and the Piranesis on the dining-room wall, brought him to his bed-room with a somewhat lightened cheer, and when he and Mr. Thomson sat down a few minutes later, cheek by jowl, and pledged the past in a preliminary bumper, he was already almost consoled, he had already almost forgiven himself his two unpardonable errors, that he should ever have left his native city, or ever returned to it.

"I have something quite in your way," said Mr. Thomson. "I wished to do honour to your arrival; because, my dear follow, it is my own youth that comes back along with you; in a very tattered and withered state, to be sure, but – well! – all that's left of it."

"A great deal better than nothing," said the editor. "But what is this which is quite in my way?"

"I was coming to that," said Mr. Thomson: "Fate has put it in my power to honour your arrival with something really original by way of dessert. A mystery."

"A mystery?" I repeated.

"Yes," said his friend, "a mystery. It may prove to be nothing, and it may prove to be a great deal. But in the meanwhile it is truly mysterious, no eye having looked on it for near a hundred years; it is highly genteel, for it treats of a titled family; and it ought to be melodramatic, for (according to the superscription) it is concerned with death."

"I think I rarely heard a more obscure or a more promising annunciation," the other remarked. "But what is it?"

"You remember my predecessor's, old Peter M'Brair's business?"

"I remember him acutely; he could not look at me

without a pang of reprobation, and he could not feel the pang without betraying it. He was to me a man of a great historical interest, but the interest was not returned."

"Ah well, we go beyond him," said Mr. Thomson. "I daresay old Peter knew as little about this as I do. You see, I succeeded to a prodigious accumulation of the old law-papers and old tin boxes, some of them of Peter's hoarding, some of his father's, John, first of the dynasty, a great man in his day. Among other collections, were all the papers of the Durrisdeers."

"The Durrisdeers!" cried I. "My dear fellow, these may be of the greatest interest. One of them was out in the 'Forty-five; one had some strange passages with the devil – you will find a note of it in Law's 'Memorials,' I think; and there was an unexplained tragedy, I know not what, much later, about a hundred years ago – "

"More than a hundred years ago," said Mr. Thomson. "In 1783."

"How do you know that? I mean some death."

"Yes, the lamentable deaths of my Lord Durrisdeer and his brother, the Master of Ballantrae (attainted in the troubles)," said Mr. Thomson with something the tone of a man quoting. "Is that it?"

"To say truth," said I, "I have only seen some dim reference to the things in memoirs; and heard some traditions dimmer still, through my uncle (whom I think you knew). My uncle lived when he was a boy in the neighbourhood of St. Bride's; he has often told me of the avenue closed up and grown over with grass, the great gates never opened, the last lord and his old maid sister who lived in the back parts of the house, a quiet, plain, poor, humdrum couple it would seem – but pathetic too, as the last of that stirring and brave house – and, to the country folk, faintly terrible from some deformed traditions."

"Yes," said Mr. Thomson. "Henry Graeme Durie, the last lord, died in 1820; his sister, the Honourable Miss Katherine Durie, in 'Twenty-seven; so much I know; and by what I have been going over the last few days, they were what you say, decent, quiet people, and not rich. To say truth, it was a letter of my lord's that put me on the search for the packet we are going to open this evening. Some papers could not be found; and he wrote to Jack M'Brair suggesting they might be among those sealed up by a Mr. Mackellar. M'Brair answered, that the papers in question were all in Mackellar's own hand, all (as the writer understood) of a purely narrative character; and besides, said he, 'I am not bound to open them before the year 1889.' You may fancy if these words struck me: I instituted a hunt through all the M'Brair repositories; and at last hit upon that packet which (if you have had enough wine) I propose to show you at once."

In the smoking-room, to which my host now led me, was a packet, fastened with many seals and enclosed in a single sheet of strong paper thus endorsed:

Papers relating to the lives and lamentable deaths of the late Lord Durrisdeer, and his elder brother James, commonly called Master of Ballantrae, attainted in the troubles: entrusted into the hands of John M'Brair in the Lawnmarket of Edinburgh, W.S.; this 20th day of September Anno Domini 1789; by him to be kept secret until the revolution of one hundred years complete, or until the 20th day of September 1889: the same compiled and written by me,

EPHRAIM MACKELLAR,

For near forty years Land Steward on the estates of his Lordship.

As Mr. Thomson is a married man, I will not say what hour had struck when we laid down the last of the following pages; but I will give a few words of what ensued.

"Here," said Mr. Thomson, "is a novel ready to your hand: all you have to do is to work up the scenery, develop the characters, and improve the style."

"My dear fellow," said I, "they are just the three things that I would rather die than set my hand to. It shall be published as it stands."

"But it's so bald," objected Mr. Thomson.

"I believe there is nothing so noble as baldness," replied I, "and I am sure there is nothing so interesting. I would have all literature bald, and all authors (if you like) but one."

"Well, well," said Mr. Thomson, "we shall see."

1891 THE PICTURE OF DORIAN GRAY
OSCAR WILDE
LONDON

[THE PREFACE]

THE ARTIST is the creator of beautiful things. To reveal art and conceal the artist is art's aim. The critic is he who can translate into another manner or a new material his impression of beautiful things. The highest, as the lowest, form of criticism is a mode of autobiography.

Those who find ugly meanings in beautiful things are corrupt without being charming. This is a fault. Those who find beautiful meanings in beautiful things are the cultivated. For these there is hope. They are the elect to whom beautiful

things mean only Beauty.

There is no such thing as a moral or an immoral Book. Books are well written,

or badly written. That is all.

The nineteenth century dislike of Realism is the rage of Caliban seeing his own face in a glass. The nineteenth century dislike of Romanticism is the

rage of Caliban not seeing his own face in a glass.

The moral life of man forms part of the subject-matter of the artist, but the morality of art consists in the perfect use of an imperfect medium. No artist desires to prove anything. Even things that

are true can be proved.

No artist has ethical sympathies. An ethical sympathy in an artist is an unpardonable mannerism of style. No artist is ever morbid. The artist can express everything. Thought and language are to the artist

instruments of an art.

Vice and virtue are to the artist materials for an art. From the point of view of form, the type of all the arts is the art of the musician. From the point of

view of feeling, the actor's craft is the type.

All art is at once surface and symbol. Those who go beneath the surface do so at their peril. Those

who read the symbol do so at their peril.

It is the spectator, and not life, that art really mirrors. Diversity of opinion about a work of art shows that the work is new, complex, and vital. When critics disagree the artist is in accord with himself.

We can forgive a man for making a useful thing as long as he does not admire it. The only excuse for

making a useless thing is that one admires it

intensely.All art is quite useless.

With the publication of **Dorian Gray**, Oscar Wilde's reputation as a subversive became official. The eloquent Irishman became famous for his manifesto of Art for Art's Sake, dandyism which betrayed his homosexuality, & his witty disrespect for Victorian pieties. In **Soul of Man, Under Socialism**, this non-authoritarian socialist proposed that machinery could take the drudgery out of essential labour. In **The Critic as Artist** he wittily anticipated aspects of post-modernism, without its anti-individualist death-of-the-artist rhetoric. His social comedies brought him big acclaim, & his masterpiece is **The Importance of Being Earnest**, described by W. H. Auden as the only pure verbal opera in English. Success was brutally wiped out by a sodomy conviction & a sentence of hard labour. In Wilde's credo & meditation on his humiliation, **De Profundis**, he wrote: **Reformations in Morals are as meaningless and vulgar as Reformations in Theology.** But while to propose to be a better man is a piece of unscientific cant, to have become a deeper man is the privilege of those who have suffered. In prison he found comfort in a mysticism beyond churches: in the hotel bedroom where he died the wallpaper remained an affront (**One or the other of us will have to go**).

1892

Kipling was, as Keating observed, the 1st important Victorian writer not to be scared of the working class. It is the common soldier who made the British Empire – & the ballads, with their music-hall rhythms, cockney slang & exotic locations, show his voice booming throughout the imperial universe. Kipling is double-natured: apologist for racial imperialism & spokesman for the unruly subalterns of the world. He seems at first to be making demi-gods out of the Empire-building gentlemen entrepreneurs, like his recently deceased friend Balestier to whom the poem is dedicated. But in the context of the volume, the real makers are the lower ranks, the strong men & roaring boys of the working class. Kipling's God may be an imperialist, but God's agents are from the underworld, the luciferic "single men in barracks".

BARRACK-ROOM BALLADS
RUDYARD KIPLING
LONDON

[INTRODUCTORY POEM : TOMMY]

I went into a public-'ouse to get a pint o'beer,
The publican 'e up an' sez, "We serve no
   red-coats here."
The girls be'ind the bar they laughed
   an' giggled fit to die,
I outs into the street again an' to myself sez I:
 O it's Tommy this, an' Tommy that,
   an' "Tommy, go away";
 But it's "Thank you, Mister Atkins,"
   when the band begins to play,
 The band begins to play, my boys,
   the band begins to play,
 O it's "Thank you, Mister Atkins,"
   when the band begins to play.

I went into a theatre as sober as could be,
They gave a drunk civilian room,
   but 'adn't none for me;
They sent me to the gallery
   or round the music-'alls,
But when it comes to fightin',
   Lord! they'll shove me in the stalls!
 For it's Tommy this, an' Tommy that,
   an' "Tommy, wait outside";
 But it's "Special train for Atkins"
   when the trooper's on the tide,
 The troopship's on the tide, my boys,
   the troopship's on the tide,
 O it's "Special train for Atkins"
   when the trooper's on the tide.

Yes, makin' mock o' uniforms
   that guard you while you sleep
Is cheaper than them uniforms,
   an' they're starvation cheap;

An' hustlin' drunken soldiers when they're goin' large a bit
Is five times better business than paradin' in full kit.
   Then it's Tommy this, an' Tommy that, an' "Tommy, 'ow's yer soul?"
   But it's "Thin red line of 'eroes" when the drums begin to roll,
   The drums begin to roll, my boys, the drums begin to roll,
   O it's "Thin red line of 'eroes" when the drums begin to roll.

We aren't no thin red 'eroes, nor we aren't no blackguards too,
But single men in barricks, most remarkable like you;
An' if sometimes our conduck isn't all your fancy paints,
Why, single men in barricks don't grow into plaster saints;
   While it's Tommy this, an' Tommy that, an' "Tommy, fall be'ind,"
   But it's "Please to walk in front, sir," when there's trouble in the wind,
   There's trouble in the wind, my boys, there's trouble in the wind,
   O it's "Please to walk in front, sir," when there's trouble in the wind.

You talk o' better food for us, an' schools, an' fires, an' all:
We'll wait for extry rations if you treat us rational.
Don't mess about the cook-room slops, but prove it to our face
The Widow's Uniform is not the soldier-man's disgrace.
   For it's Tommy this, an' Tommy that, an' "Chuck him out, the brute!"
   But it's "Saviour of 'is country" when the guns begin to shoot;
   An' it's Tommy this, an' Tommy that, an' anything you please;
   An' Tommy ain't a bloomin' fool – you bet that Tommy sees!

JUDE THE OBSCURE
THOMAS HARDY
LONDON

1896

THE history of this novel (whose birth in its present shape has been much retarded by the necessities of periodical publication) is briefly as follows. The scheme was jotted down in 1890, from notes made in 1887 and onwards, some of the circumstances being suggested by the death of a woman in the former year. The scenes were revisited in October 1892; the narrative was written in outline in 1892 and the spring of 1893 onwards into the next year; the whole, with the exception of a few

The chronology accompanying Jude the Obscure describes Hardy's father as "a builder in a small but slowly developing way of business, thus setting the family apart socially from the 'work-folk' whom they clearly resembled in financial circumstances." Hardy

trained as an architect & later, on being appointed a Justice of the Peace, received invitations from the aristocracy. The oppressive effects of class, & its rigours, form a significant theme in his fiction.

Perhaps Hardy expresses his concerns most clearly in Chapter 2, Part 2 of *Jude the Obscure*: "For a moment there fell on Jude a true illumination: that here in the stone yard was a centre of effort as worthy as that dignified by the name of scholarly study within the noblest of the colleges." Hardy was neither Marxist nor "know your station" reactionary. The dignity of all effort was of equal value to him, & the right of each individual to choose his – or her – station in life.

His characters are, unfortunately, also subject to the forces (usually malign) of inexorable Fate. Religion, about which he was a regretful sceptic (see his poem *The Oxen*), always promises more than it can deliver: Jude aspires to a career in theology, but is rejected. Hardy was also much preoccupied with the fickle streams of desire, carrying often contradictory currents, which

chapters, being in the hands of the publisher by the end of 1894. It was begun as a serial story in *Harper's Magazine* at the end of November 1894, and was continued in monthly parts.

But, as in the case of *Tess of the D'Urbervilles*, the magazine version was for various reasons an abridged and modified one, the present edition being the first in which the whole appears as originally written. And in the difficulty of coming to an early decision in the matter of a title, the tale was issued under a provisional name, two such titles having, in fact, been successively adopted. The present and final title, deemed on the whole the best, was one of the earliest thought of.

For a novel addressed by a man to men and women of full age; which attempts to deal unaffectedly with the fret and fever, derision and disaster, that may press in the wake of the strongest passion known to humanity; to tell, without a mincing of words, of a deadly war waged between flesh and spirit; and to point the tragedy of unfulfilled aims, I am not aware that there is anything in the handling to which exception can be taken.

Like former productions of this pen, *Jude the Obscure* is simply an endeavour to give shape and coherence to a series of seemings, or personal impressions, the question of their consistency or their discordance, of their permanence or their transitoriness, being regarded as not of the first moment.   August 1895

[POSTSCRIPT]

The issue of this book sixteen years ago, with the explanatory Preface given above, was followed by unexpected incidents, and one can now look back for a moment at what happened. Within a day or two of its publication the reviewers pronounced upon it in tones to which the reception of *Tess of the D'Urbervilles* bore no comparison, though there were two or three dissentients from the chorus. This salutation of the story in England was instantly cabled to America, and the music was reinforced on that side of the Atlantic in a shrill crescendo.

In my own eyes the sad feature of the attack was that the greater part of the story – that which presented the shattered ideals of the two chief characters, and had been more especially, and indeed almost exclusively, the part of interest to myself – was practically ignored by the adverse press of the two countries; the while that some twenty or thirty pages of sorry detail deemed necessary to complete the narrative, and show the antitheses in Jude's life, were almost the sole portions read and regarded. And curiously enough, a reprint the next year of a fantastic tale that had been published in a family paper some time before, drew down upon my head a continuation of the same sort of invective from several quarters.

So much for the unhappy beginning of *Jude's* career as a book. After these verdicts from the press its next misfortune was to be burnt by a bishop – probably in his despair at not being able to burn me.

Then somebody discovered that *Jude* was a moral work – austere in its treatment of a difficult subject – as if the writer had not all the time said in the Preface that it was meant to be so. Thereupon many uncursed me, and the matter ended, the only effect of it on human conduct that I could discover being its effect on myself – the experience completely curing me of further interest in novel-writing.

One incident among many arising from the storm of words was that an American man of letters, who did not whitewash his own morals, informed me that, having bought a copy of the book on the strength of the shocked criticisms, he read on and on, wondering when the harmfulness was going to begin, and at last flung it across the room with execrations at having been induced by the rascally reviewers to waste a dollar-and-half on what he was pleased to call "a religious and ethical treatise."

I sympathized with him, and assured him honestly that the misrepresentations had been no collusive trick of mine to increase my circulation among the subscribers to the papers in question.

Then there was the case of the lady who having shuddered at the book in an influential article bearing intermediate headlines of horror, and printed in a world-read journal, wrote to me shortly afterwards that it was her desire to make my acquaintance.

To return, however, to the book itself. The marriage laws being used in great part as the tragic machinery of the tale, and its general drift on the domestic side tending to show that, in Diderot's words, the civil law should be only the enunciation of the law of nature (a statement that requires some qualification, by the way), I have been charged since 1895 with a large responsibility in this country for the present "shop-soiled" condition of the marriage theme (as a learned writer characterized it the other day). I do not know. My opinion at that time, if I remember rightly, was what it is now, that a marriage should be dissolvable as soon as it becomes a cruelty to either of the parties – being then essentially and morally no marriage – and it seemed a good foundation for the fable of a tragedy, told for its own sake as a presentation of particulars containing a good deal that was universal, and not without a hope that certain cathartic, Aristotelian qualities might be found therein.

The difficulties down to twenty or thirty years back of acquiring knowledge in letters without pecuniary means were used in the same way; though I was informed that some readers thought these episodes an attack on venerable institutions, and that when Ruskin College was subsequently founded it should have been called the College of Jude the Obscure.

Artistic effort always pays heavily for finding its tragedies in the forced adaptations of human instincts to rusty and irksome moulds that do not fit them. To do Bludyer and the conflagratory bishop justice, what they meant seems to have been only this: "We Britons hate ideas, and we are going to live up to that privilege of our native country. Your picture may not show the untrue, or the uncommon, or even be contrary to the canons of art; but it is not the view of life that we who thrive on conventions can permit to be painted."

But what did it matter. As for the matrimonial scenes, in spite of their "touching the spot," and the screaming of a poor lady in *Blackwood* that there was an unholy anti-marriage league afoot, the famous contract – sacrament I mean – is doing fairly well still, and people marry and give in what may or may not be true marriage as light-heartedly as ever. The author has even been reproached by some earnest correspondents that he has left the question where he found it, and has not pointed the way to a much-needed reform.

After the issue of *Jude the Obscure* as a serial story in Germany, an experienced reviewer of that country informed the writer that Sue Bridehead, the heroine, was the first delineation in fiction of the woman who was coming into notice in her thousands every year – the woman of the feminist movement – the slight, pale "bachelor" girl – the intellectualized, emancipated bundle of nerves that modern conditions were producing, mainly in cities as yet; who does not recognize the necessity for most of her sex to follow marriage as a profession, and boast themselves as superior people because they are licensed to be loved on the premises. The regret of this critic was that the portrait of the newcomer had been left to be drawn by a man, and was not done by one of her own sex, who would never have allowed her to break down at the end.

define sexual relations. There are, as Jude, Sue, Phillotson & Arabella discover, more victims than winners on the sexual wheel of fortune.

Whether this assurance is borne out by dates I cannot say. Nor am I able, across the gap of years since the production of the novel, to exercise more criticism upon it of a general kind than extends to a few verbal corrections, whatever, good or bad, it may contain. And no doubt there can be more in a book than the author consciously puts there, which will help either to its profit or to its disadvantage as the case may be.

*In **Jude the Obscure**, Hardy confronted, as explicitly as the times permitted, issues which had preoccupied him in every previous novel. His reward was to have the book declared "the most indecent novel ever written", then for it to be "burnt by a bishop – probably in his despair at not being able to burn me". For the remaining 33 years of his life he wrote no fiction, only poetry & dramatisations of earlier novels.*

T.H. April 1912

THE NIGGER OF THE *"NARCISSUS"*
JOSEPH CONRAD
LONDON

1897

[PREFACE]

A WORK that aspires, however humbly, to the condition of art should carry its justification in every line. And art itself may be defined as a single-minded attempt to render the highest kind of justice to the visible universe, by bringing to light the truth, manifold and one, underlying its every

Born 1857 in part of Poland ruled by the Russians, C's father was exiled by them for nationalist politics. C became a seaman in France, joined the

British merchant navy when 31; was master of ships in seas around China, India, Africa; wrote his experiences into novels showing how societies hold together or collapse in a hostile universe. The society is a small nation in Nostromo, his greatest book. In this, his 1st mature novel, it is a ship's crew with a black & a white member who refuse their share of work; the 1st because TB is killing him, the 2nd because he is a lazy scrounger. After a terrible storm wonderfully described, sympathy for the dying man & the scrounger's Socialist rhetoric nearly cause a mutiny. Discipline prevails, brings the ship to port. In C's bleak vision of the universe work is the only salvation & needs efficient officers: a conservative but not stupid idea that Kipling shared. But Kipling had a romantic faith in the white officer class. C's novels set in states which will not sink if badly run (because on dry African, English or Russian land) show upper classes more wrong-headed, greedy, corrupt or mad than any under them.

aspect. It is an attempt to find in its forms, in its colours, in its light, in its shadows, in the aspects of matter and in the facts of life what of each is fundamental, what is enduring and essential – their one illuminating and convincing quality – the very truth of their existence. The artist, then, like the thinker or the scientist, seeks the truth and makes his appeal. Impressed by the aspect of the world the thinker plunges into ideas, the scientist into facts – whence, presently, emerging they make their appeal to those qualities of our being that fit us best for the hazardous enterprise of living. They speak authoritatively to our common-sense, to our intelligence, to our desire of peace or to our desire of unrest; not seldom to our prejudices, sometimes to our fears, often to our egoism – but always to our credulity. And their words are heard with reverence, for their concern is with weighty matters: with the cultivation of our minds and the proper care of our bodies, with the attainment of our ambitions, with the perfection of the means and the glorification of our precious aims.

It is otherwise with the artist.

Confronted by the same enigmatical spectacle the artist descends within himself, and in that lonely region of stress and strife, if he be deserving and fortunate, he finds the terms of his appeal. His appeal is made to our less obvious capacities: to that part of our nature which, because of the warlike conditions of existence, is necessarily kept out of sight within the more resisting and hard qualities – like the vulnerable body within a steel armour. His appeal is less loud, more profound, less distinct, more stirring – and sooner forgotten. Yet its effect endures forever. The changing wisdom of successive generations discards ideas, questions facts, demolishes theories. But the artist appeals to that part of our being which is not dependent on wisdom;

to that in us which is a gift and not an acquisition – and, therefore, more permanently enduring. He speaks to our capacity for delight and wonder, to the sense of mystery surrounding our lives; to our sense of pity, and beauty, and pain; to the latent feeling of fellowship with all creation – and to the subtle but invincible conviction of solidarity that knits together the loneliness of innumerable hearts, to the solidarity in dreams, in joy, in sorrow, in aspirations, in illusions, in hope, in fear, which binds men to each other, which binds together all humanity – the dead to the living and the living to the unborn.

It is only some such train of thought, or rather of feeling, that can in a measure explain the aim of the attempt, made in the tale which follows, to present an unrestful episode in the obscure lives of a few individuals out of all the disregarded multitude of the bewildered, the simple and the voiceless. For, if any part of truth dwells in the belief confessed above, it becomes evident that there is not a place of splendour or a dark corner of the earth that does not deserve, if only a passing glance of wonder and pity. The motive then, may be held to justify the matter of the work; but this preface, which is simply an avowal of endeavour, cannot end here – for the avowal is not yet complete.

Fiction – if it at all aspires to be art – appeals to temperament. And in truth it must be, like painting, like music, like all art, the appeal of one temperament to all the other innumerable temperaments whose subtle and resistless power endows passing events with their true meaning, and creates the moral, the emotional atmosphere of the place and time. Such an appeal to be effective must be an impression conveyed through the senses; and, in fact, it cannot be made in any other way, because temperament, whether individual or collective, is not amenable to persuasion. All art, therefore, appeals primarily to the senses, and the artistic aim when expressing itself in written words must also make its appeal through the senses, if its high desire is to reach the secret spring of responsive emotions. It must strenuously aspire to the plasticity of sculpture, to the colour of painting, and to the magic suggestiveness of music – which is the art of arts. And it is only through complete, unswerving devotion to the perfect blending of form and substance; it is only through an unremitting never-discouraged care for the shape and ring of sentences that an approach can be made to plasticity, to colour, and that the light of magic suggestiveness may be brought to play for an evanescent instant over the commonplace surface of words: of the old, old words, worn thin, defaced by ages of careless usage.

The sincere endeavour to accomplish that creative task, to go as far on that road as his strength will carry him, to go undeterred by faltering, weariness or reproach, is the only valid justification for the worker in prose. And if his conscience is clear, his answer to those who in the fulness of a wisdom which looks for immediate profit, demand specifically to be edified, consoled, amused; who demand to be promptly improved, or encouraged, or frightened, or shocked, or charmed, must run thus:– My task which I am trying to achieve is, by the power of the written word to make you hear, to make you feel – it is, before all, to make you see. That – and no more, and it is everything. If I succeed, you shall find there according to your deserts: encouragement, consolation, fear, charm – all you demand – and, perhaps, also that glimpse of truth for which you have forgotten to ask.

To snatch in a moment of courage, from the remorseless rush of time, a passing phase of life, is only the beginning of the task. The task approached in tenderness and faith is to hold up unquestioningly, without choice and without fear, the rescued fragment before all eyes in the light of a sincere mood. It is to show its vibration, its colour, its form; and through its movement, its form, and its colour reveal the substance of its truth – disclose its inspiring secret: the stress and passion within the core of each convincing moment. In a single-minded attempt of that kind, if one be deserving and fortunate, one may perchance attain to such clearness of sincerity that at last the presented vision of regret or pity, of terror or mirth, shall awaken in the hearts of the beholders that feeling of unavoidable solidarity; of the solidarity in mysterious origin, in toil, in joy, in hope, in uncertain fate, which binds men to each other and all mankind to the visible world.

It is evident that he who, rightly or wrongly, holds by the convictions expresed above cannot be faithful to any one of the temporary formulas of his craft. The enduring part of them – the truth which each only imperfectly veils – should abide with him as the most precious of his possessions, but they all: Realism, Romanticism, Naturalism, even the unofficial sentimentalism (which like the poor, is exceedingly difficult to get rid of,) all these gods must, after a short period of fellowship, abandon him – even on the very threshold of the temple – to the stammerings of his conscience and to the outspoken consciousness of the difficulties of his work. In that uneasy solitude the supreme cry of Art for Art, itself, loses the exciting ring of its apparent immorality. It sounds far off. It has ceased to be a cry, and is heard only as a whisper, often incomprehensible, but at times and faintly encouraging.

Sometimes, stretched at ease in the shade of a roadside tree, we watch the motions of a labourer in a distant field, and after a time, begin to wonder languidly as to what the fellow may be at. We watch the movements of his body, the waving of his arms, we see him bend down, stand up, hesitate, begin again. It may add to the charm of an idle hour to be told the purpose of his exertions. If we know he is trying to lift a stone, to dig a ditch, to uproot a stump, we look with a more real interest at his efforts; we are disposed to condone the jar of his agitation upon the restfulness of the landscape; and even, if in a brotherly frame of mind, we may bring ourselves to forgive his failure. We understood his object; and, after all, the fellow has tried, and perhaps he had not the strength – and perhaps he had not the knowledge. We forgive, go on our way – and forget.

And so it is with the workman of art. Art is long and life is short, and success is very far off. And thus, doubtful of strength to travel so far, we talk a little about the aim – the aim of art, which, like life itself, is inspiring, difficult – obscured by mists. It is not in the clear logic of a triumphant conclusion; it is not in the unveiling of one of those heartless secrets which are called the Laws of Nature. It is not less great, but only more difficult.

To arrest, for the space of a breath, the hands busy about the work of the earth, and compel men entranced by the sight of distant goals to glance for a moment at the surrounding vision of form and colour, of sunshine and shadows; to make them pause for a look, for a sigh, for a smile – such is the aim, difficult and evanescent, and reserved only for a very few to achieve. But sometimes, by the deserving and the fortunate, even that task is accomplished. And when it is accomplished – behold! – all the truth of life is there: a moment of vision, a sigh a
smile – and the return to
an eternal
rest.

1898

*Born 1834, **P** aided his dad (the US's greatest mathematician & astronomer) in mapping the shape of our galaxy &, for the US government, exacter measurements of our planet & North America. Geographers in Europe adopted son **P**'s use of light waves to fix metre lengths, but he took more care to be exact than his bosses understood. He was made to resign & lived as a consulting chemist & inventor in frequent poverty. His discoveries in linear algebra, psychology, logic, semiotics & the pronunciation of Shakespeare's English were only valued by specialists ignorant of each other. He was not seen as **the most original & versatile intellect the Americas have so far produced** (a 1995 Encyclopaedia Britannica says) till long after his death in 1914, though late in **P**'s life William James advertised what **P** called **pragmatism** as a new philosophy, gave it an optimistic twist to help it reconcile scientific proof with religious faith, & in the USA made it very popular for a while. **P** at once renamed it*

PREFACE TO AN UNWRITTEN BOOK
CHARLES SANDERS PEIRCE: A FARM ON THE DELAWARE: PENNSYLVANIA

[PREFACE]

TO erect a philosophical edifice that shall outcast the vicissitudes of time, my care must be, not so much to set each brick with nicest accuracy, as to lay the foundations deep and massive. Aristotle built upon a few deliberately chosen concepts – such as matter and form, act and power – very broad, and in their outlines vague and rough, but solid, unshakable, and not easily undermined; and thence it has come to pass that Aristotelianism is babbled in every nursery, that "English Common Sense," for example, is thoroughly peripatetic, and that ordinary men live so completely within the house of the Stagyrite that whatever they see out of the windows appears to them incomprehensible and metaphysical. Long it has been only too manifest that, fondly habituated though we be to it, the old structure will not do for modern needs; and accordingly, under Descartes, Hobbes, Kant, and others, repairs, alterations, and partial demolitions have been carried on for the last three centuries. One system, also, stands upon its own ground; I mean the new Schelling-Hegel mansion, lately run up in the German taste, but with such oversights in its construction that, although brand new, it is already pronounced uninhabitable. The undertaking this volume inaugurates is to make a philosophy like that of Aristotle, that is to say, to outline a theory so comprehensive that, for a long time to come, the entire work of human reason, in philosophy of every school and kind, in mathematics, in psychology, in physical science, in history, in sociology, and in whatever other department there may be, shall appear as the filling up of its details. The first step toward this is to find simple concepts applicable to every subject.

But before all else, let me make the acquaintance

of my reader, and express my sincere esteem for him and the deep pleasure it is to me to address one so wise and so patient. I know his character pretty well, for both the subject and the style of this book ensure his being one out of millions. He will comprehend that it has not been written for the purpose of confirming him in his preconceived opinions, and he would not take the trouble to read it if it had. He is prepared to meet with propositions that he is inclined at first to dissent from; and he looks to being convinced that some of them are true, after all. He will reflect, too, that the thinking and writing of this book has taken, I won't say how long, quite certainly more than a quarter of an hour, and consequently fundamental objections of so obvious a nature that they must strike everyone instantaneously will have occurred to the author, although the replies to them may not be of that kind whose full force can be instantly apprehended.

The reader has a right to know how the author's opinions were formed. Not, of course, that he is expected to accept any conclusions that are not borne out by argument. But in discussions of extreme difficulty, like these, when good judgment is a factor, and pure ratiocination is not everything, it is prudent to take every element into consideration. From the moment when I could think at all, until now, about forty years, I have been diligently and incessantly occupied with the study of methods of inquiry, both those that have been and are pursued and those that ought to be pursued. For ten years before this study began, I had been in training in the chemical laboratory. I was thoroughly grounded not only in all that was then known of physics and chemistry, but also in the way in which those who were successfully advancing knowledge proceeded. I have paid the most attention to the methods of the most exact sciences, have intimately communed with some of the greatest minds of our times in physical science, and have myself made

PRAGMATICISM, a word ugly enough to save it (he said) from babysnatchers. Former philosophers had tried to answer some of the questions on page 21 by building a great new verbal system to explain everything (like Plato, Aristotle, Descartes, Locke, Hegel) or worked to knock such systems down (like Socrates, Voltaire, Hume, Nietzsche) & thus restore conventional, sensible or emotional answers most of us rely upon anyway. But to finally accept a system, or to finally reject every system, is to end enquiry. As a scientist P would not do that. He also knew common sense can only answer hard questions by stating them in an exact speech meaning the same to all who, by sharing discussion & experiment, unite to seek replies. He did not believe a final reply to any question was possible in our evolving universe, but thought everyone who wisely sought answers could get nearer the truth. His own wisdom appears in the clear sentences, erudition & wit of this preface. His Catholic breadth of vision recognised mediaeval schoolmen as contributors to modern thought.

positive contributions – none of them of any very great importance, perhaps – in mathematics, gravitation, optics, chemistry, astronomy, etc. I am saturated, through and through, with the spirit of the physical sciences. I have been a great student of logic, having read everything of any importance on the subject, devoting a great deal of time to medieval thought, without neglecting the works of the Greeks, the English, the Germans, the French, etc., and have produced systems of my own both in deductive and in inductive logic. In metaphysics, my training has been less systematic; yet I have read and deeply pondered upon all the main systems, never being satisfied until I was able to think about them as their own adovcates thought.

The first strictly philosophical books that I read were of the classical German schools: and I became so deeply imbued with many of their ways of thinking that I have never been able to disabuse myself of them. Yet my attitude was always that of a dweller in a laboratory, eager only to learn what I did not yet know, and not that of philosophers bred in theological seminaries, whose ruling impulse is to teach what they hold to be infallibly true. I devoted two hours a day to the study of Kant's *Critic of the Pure Reason* for more than three years, until I almost knew the whole book by heart, and had critically examined every section of it. For about two years, I had long and almost daily discussions with Chauncey Wright, one of the most acute of the followers of J.S.Mill.

The effect of these studies was that I came to hold the classical German philosophy to be, upon its argumentative side, of little weight; although I esteem it, perhaps am too partial to it, as a rich mine of philosophical suggestions. The English philosophy, meager and crude, as it is, in its conceptions, proceeds by surer methods and more accurate logic. The doctrine of the association of ideas is, to my thinking, the finest piece of philosophical work of the prescientific ages. Yet I can but pronounce English sensationalism to be entirely destitute of any solid bottom. From the evolutionary philosophers I have learned little; although I admit that, however hurriedly their theories have been knocked together, and however antiquated and ignorant Spencer's *First Principles* and general doctrines, yet they are under the guidance of a great and true idea, and are developing it by methods that are in their main features sound and scientific.

The works of Duns Scotus have strongly influenced me. If his logic and metaphysics, not slavishly worshipped, but torn away from its medievalism, be adapted to modern culture, under continual wholesome reminders of nominalistic criticisms, I am convinced that it will go far toward supplying the philosophy that is best to harmonize with physical science. But other conceptions have to be drawn from the history of science and from mathematics.

Thus, in brief, my philosophy may be described as the attempt of a physicist to make such conjecture as to the constitution of the universe as the methods of science may permit, with the aid of all that has been done by previous philosophers. I shall support my propositions by such arguments as I can. Demonstrative proof is not to be thought of. The demonstrations of the metaphysicians are all moonshine. The best that can be done is to supply a hypothesis, not devoid of all likelihood, in the general line of growth of scientific ideas, and capable of being verified or refuted by future observers.

Religious infallibilism, caught in the current of the times, shows symptoms of declaring itself to be only practically speaking infallible; and when it has thus once confessed itself subject to gradations, there will remain over no relic of the good old tenth-century infallibilism, except that of the infallible scientists, under which head I include, not merely the kind of characters that manufacture scientific catechisms and homilies, churches and creeds, and who are indeed "born missionaries," but all those respectable and cultivated persons who, having acquired their notions of science from reading, and not from research, have the idea that "science" means knowledge, while the truth is, it is a misnomer applied to the pursuit of those who are devoured by a desire to find things out.

Though infallibility in scientific matters seems to me irresistibly comical, I should be in a sad way if I could not retain a high respect for those who lay claim to it, for they comprise the greater part of the people who have any conversation at all. When I say they lay claim to it, I mean they assume the functions of it quite naturally and unconsciously. The full meaning of the adage *Humanum est errare*, they have never waked up to. In those sciences of measurement that are the least subject to error – metrology, geodesy, and metrical astronomy – no man of self-respect ever now states his result, without affixing to it its *probable error*; and if this practice is not followed in other sciences it is because in those the *probable errors* are too vast to be estimated.

I am a man of whom critics have never found anything good to say. When they could see no opportunity to injure me, they have held their peace. The little laudation I have had has come from such sources, that only the satisfaction I have derived from it, has been from such slices of bread and butter as it might waft my way. Only once, as far as I remember, in all my lifetime have I experienced the pleasure of praise – not for what it might bring but in itself. That pleasure was beatific; and the praise that conferred it was meant for blame. It was that a critic said of me that I did not seem to be *absolutely sure of my own conclusions*. Never, if I can help it, shall that critic's eye ever rest on what I am now writing; for I owe a great pleasure to him; and, such was his evident animus, that should he find that out, I fear the fires of hell would be fed with new fuel in his breast.

My book will have no instruction to impart to anybody. Like a mathematical treatise, it will suggest certain ideas and certain reasons for holding them true; but then, if you accept them, it must be because you like my reasons, and the responsibility lies with you. Man is essentially a social animal: but to be social is one thing, to be gregarious is another: I decline to serve as bellwether. My book is meant for people *who want to find out*; and people who want philosophy ladled out to them can go elsewhere. There are philosophical soup shops at every corner, thank God!

The development of my ideas has been the industry of thirty years. I did not know that I ever should get to publish them, their ripening seemed so slow. But the harvest time has come, as last, and to me that harvest seems a wild one, but of course it is not I who have to pass judgment. It is not quite you, either, individual reader; it is experience and history.

For years in the course of this ripening process. I used for myself to collect my ideas under the designation *fallibilism*; and indeed the first step toward *finding out* is to acknowledge you do not satisfactorily know already; so that no blight can so surely arrest all intellectual growth as the blight of cocksureness; and ninety-nine out of every hundred good heads are reduced to impotence by that malady – of whose inroads they are most strangely unaware! Indeed, out of a contrite fallibilism, combined with a high faith in the reality of knowledge, and an intense desire to find things out, all my philosophy has always seemed to me to grow.

THE IRRATIONAL KNOT
GEORGE BERNARD SHAW
LONDON

1905

[PREFACE]

THIS novel was written in the year 1880, only a few years after I had exported myself from Dublin to London in a condition of extreme rawness and inexperience concerning the specifically English side of the life with which the book pretends to deal. Everybody wrote novels then. It was my second attempt; and it shared the fate of my first. That is to say, nobody would publish it, though I tried all the London publishers and some American ones. And I should not greatly blame them if I could feel sure that it was the book's faults and not its qualities that repelled them.

I have narrated elsewhere how in the course of time the rejected MS. became Mrs. Annie Besant's excuse for lending me her ever helping hand by publishing it as a serial in a little propandist magazine of hers. That was how it got loose beyond all possibility of recapture. It is out of my power now to stand between it and the American public: all I can do is to rescue it from unauthorized mutilations and make the best of a jejune job.

At present, of course, I am not the author of *The Irrational Knot*. Physiologists inform us that the substance of our bodies (and consequently of our souls) is shed and renewed at such a rate that no part of us lasts longer then eight years: I am therefore not now in any atom of me the person who wrote *The Irrational Knot* in 1880. The last of that author perished in 1888; and two of his successors have since joined the majority. Fourth of his line, I cannot be expected to take any very lively interest in the novels of my literary greatgrand-father. Even my personal recollections of him are becoming vague and overlaid with those

*Intense public hunger for exotic plays grew with the huge growth of 19th-century cities. Theatres & music halls got built as fast as railway stations, the grandest with as many kinds of foyer, stair & seat as classes of customer, from proles packed into a steeply raked upper circle to toffs lounging at ease in boxes like small plush drawing rooms. Such theatres were as profitable to holding companies as super-cinemas in the 1930s & television networks in 2000. Yet between 1779 & 1930 – between Sheridan's **The Critic** & **Private Lives** by Noël Coward – hardly 1 play by an English writer was produced that is played or read after it. Throughout that time the office of Lord Chancellor not only banned plays about politics, but plays that might upset polite taste in other ways. In melodrama & comedy sex was still accepted as the main motive, but only when it cast no doubt on the ideal marriage in which all good middle-class folk were meant to find fulfilment. Marital strife could be*

shown in gaudy aristoc-
racies or the working
class, but no play could
show any present-day
urgencies without a
cosy moral or patriotic
message. Reference to
the main sex act was
banned also, as polite
folk never mentioned it.
From a multitude of
British playwrights only
3 were devious enough
to outwit the Lord
Chancellor & make
lasting works: Barrie (a
Scot) & 2 Irishmen, the
best of them being
Shaw. He learned his
craft in the 1st place
from Ibsen, & after him
from Wilde.

Ibsen is the best
poet-playwright since
Shakespeare. Between
1864 & 1900 he wrote
plays usually set in
middle-class homes of a
kind where folk in his
audience lived, & where
frigidity, fraud, greed,
lust, venereal disease,
corrupt local govern-
ment & the need to look
respectable cause as
much mayhem as the
remarriage of Hamlet's
mother. These plays
stirred Europe's thinkers
like depth charges:
Hauptmann in Berlin,
Chekhov in Moscow,
James Joyce in Dublin,
& in London, Shaw. He
loathed the idiocy of the
British theatre &
attacked it in his
reviews. Ibsen's plays
could only be acted
privately there & the

most misleading of all traditions, the traditions founded on the lies a man tells, and at last comes to believe, about himself *to* himself. Certain things, however, I remember very well. For instance, I am significantly clear as to the price of the paper on which I wrote *The Irrational Knot*. It was cheap – a white demy of unpretentious quality – so that sixpennorth lasted a long time. My daily allowance of composition was five pages of this demy in quarto; and I held my natural laziness sternly to that task day in, day out, to the end. I remember also that Bizet's Carmen being then new in London, I used it as a safety-valve for my romantic impulses. When I was tired of the sordid realism of Whatshisname (I have sent my only copy of *The Irrational Knot* to the printers, and cannot remember the name of my hero) I went to the piano and forgot him in the glamorous society of Carmen and her crimson toreador and yellow dragoon. Not that Bizet's music could infatuate me as it infatuated Nietzsche. Nursed on greater masters, I thought less of him than he deserved; but the Carmen music was – in places – exquisite of its kind, and could enchant a man like me, romantic enough to have come to the end of romance before I began to create in art for myself.

When I say that *I* did and felt these things, I mean, of course, that the predecessor whose name I bear did and felt them. The I of to-day is (? am) cool towards Carmen; and Carmen, I regret to say, does not take the slightest interest in him (? me). And now enough of this juggling with past and present Shaws. The grammatical complications of being a first person and several extinct third persons at the same moment are so frightful that I must return to the ordinary misusage, and ask the reader to make the necessary corrections in his or her own mind.

This book is not wholly a compound of intuition and ignorance. Take for example the profession of my hero, an Irish-American electrical engineer. That was by no means a flight of fancy. For you must not suppose, because I am a man of letters, that I never tried to earn an honest living. I began trying to commit that sin against my nature when I was fifteen, and persevered, from youthful timidity and diffidence, until I was twenty-three. My last attempt was in 1879, when a company was formed in London to exploit an ingenious invention by Mr. Thomas Alva Edison – a much too ingenious invention as it proved, being nothing less than a telephone of such stentorian efficiency that it bellowed your most private communications all over the house instead of whispering them with some sort of discretion. This was not what the British stockbroker wanted; so the company was soon merged in the National Telephone Company, after making a place for itself in the history of literature, quite unintentionally, by providing me with a job. Whilst the Edison Telephone Company lasted, it crowded the basement of a huge pile of offices in Queen Victoria Street with American artificers. These deluded and romantic men gave me a glimpse of the skilled proletariat of the United States. They sang obsolete sentimental songs with genuine emotion; and their language was frightful even to an Irishman. They worked with a ferocious energy which was out of all proportion to the actual result achieved. Indomitably resolved to assert their republican manhood by taking no orders from a tall-hatted Englishman whose stiff politeness covered his conviction that they were, relatively to himself, inferior and common persons, they insisted on being slave-driven with genuine American oaths by a genuine free and equal American foreman. They utterly despised the

*critics who saw them reacted with reviews which now read like a victim's account of a rape. Shaw's reaction was to write 2 plays of which Ibsen might have been proud: **Mrs Warren's Profession** & **Widowers' Houses**. They deal with the monetary foundation of polite society in brothels & rent from bad housing, yet show no impolite deeds, use no impolite words. They are bitter yet exciting plays. The Chancellor's office, of course, banned British public performance of them. They were acted 1st in the USA, France & Germany. But Shaw (who would have been a fine novelist if a publisher had printed his novels) now knew that, if a way through the Lord Chancellor's office were found, he could talk to Britain in plays – Wilde showed him the way. The plots of Wilde's plays about an unmarried mother & blackmailed minister of state depend upon Victorian conventions but are kept alive by speech that subverts them: **Oh I love London Society! It is entirely composed now of beautiful idiots & brilliant lunatics**. Shaw got the state censor to allow his bitter criticisms by making them comic.*

artfully slow British workman who did as little for his wages as he possibly could; never hurried himself; and had a deep reverence for any one whose pocket could be tapped by respectful behaviour. Need I add that they were contemptuously wondered at by this same British workman as a parcel of outlandish adult boys, who sweated themselves for their employer's benefit instead of looking after their own interests? They adored Mr. Edison as the greatest man of all time in every possible department of science, art and philosophy, and execrated Mr. Graham Bell, the inventor of the rival telephone, as his Satanic adversary; but each of them had (or pretended to have) on the brink of completion, an improvement on the telephone, usually a new transmitter. They were free-souled creatures, excellent company: sensitive, cheerful, and profane; liars, braggarts, and hustlers; with an air of making slow old England hum which never left them even when, as often happened, they were wrestling with difficulties of their own making, or struggling in no-thoroughfares from which they had to be retrieved like strayed sheep by Englishmen without imagination enough to go wrong.

In this environment I remained for some months. As I was interested in physics and had read Tyndall and Helmholtz, besides having learnt something in Ireland through a fortunate friendship with a cousin of Mr. Graham Bell, who was also a chemist and physicist, I was, I believe, the only person in the entire establishment who knew the current scientific explanation of telephony; and as I soon struck up a friendship with our official lecturer, a Colchester man whose strong point was pre-scientific agriculture. I often discharged his duties for him in a manner which, I am persuaded, laid the foundation of Mr. Edison's London reputation: my sole reward being my boyish delight in the half-concealed incredulity of our visitors (who were convinced by the hoarsely startling utterances of the telephone that the speaker, alleged by me to be twenty miles away, was really using a speaking-trumpet in the next room), and their obvious uncertainty, when the demonstration was over, as to whether they ought to tip me or not: a question they either decided in the negative or never decided at all; for I never got anything.

So much for my electrical engineer! To get him into contact with fashionable society before he became famous was also a problem easily solved. I knew of three English peers who actually preferred physical laboratories to stables, and scientific experts to gamekeepers: in fact, one of the experts was a friend of mine. And I knew from personal experience that if science brings men of all ranks into contact, art, especially music, does the same for men and women. An electrician who can play an accompaniment can go anywhere and know anybody. As far as mere access and acquaintance go there are no class barriers for him. My difficulty was not to get my hero into society, but to give any sort of plausibility to my picture of society when I got him into it. I lacked the touch of the literary diner-out; and I had, as the reader will probably find to his cost, the classical tradition which makes all the persons in a novel, except the comically vernacular ones, or the speakers of phonetically spelt dialect, utter themselves in the formal phrases and studied syntax of eighteenth-century rhetoric. In short I wrote in the style of Scott and Dickens; and as fashionable society then spoke and behaved, as it still does, in no style at all, my transcriptions of Oxford and Mayfair may nowadays suggest an unaccountable and ludicrous ignorance of a very superficial and accessible code of manners. I was not, however, so ignorant as might have been inferred at that time from my somewhat desperate financial condition.

I had, to begin with, a sort of backstairs knowledge; for in my teens I struggled for life in the office of an Irish gentleman who acted as land agent and private banker for many persons of distinction. Now it is possible for a London author to dine out in the highest circles for twenty years without learning as much about the human frailties of his hosts as the family solicitor or (in Ireland) the family land agent learns in twenty days; and some of this knowledge inevitably reaches his clerks, especially the clerk who keeps the cash, which was my particular department. He learns, if capable of the lesson, that the aristocratic profession has as few geniuses as any other profession; so that if you want a peerage of more than, say, half a dozen members, you must fill it up with many common persons, and even with some deplorably mean ones. For "service is no inheritance" either in the kitchen or the House of Lords; and the case presented by Mr. Barrie in his play of The Admirable Crichton, where the butler is the man of quality, and his master, the Earl, the man of rank, is no fantasy, but a quite common occurrence, and indeed to some extent an inevitable one, because the English are extremely particular in selecting their butlers, whilst they do not select their barons at all, taking them as the accident of birth sends them. The consequences include much ironic comedy. For instance, we have in England a curious belief in first rate people, meaning all the people we do not know; and this consoles us for the undeniable second-rateness of the people we do know, besides saving the credit of aristocracy as an institution. The unmet aristocrat is devoutly believed in; but he is always round the corner, never at hand. That the smart set exists; that there is above and beyond that smart set a class so blue of blood and exquisite in nature that it looks down even on the King with haughty condescension; that scepticism on these points is one of stigmata of plebeian baseness: all these imaginings are so common here that they constitute the real popular sociology of England as much as an unlimited credulity as to vaccination constitutes the real popular science of England. It is, of course, a timid superstition. A British peer or peeress who happens by chance to be genuinely noble is just as isolated at court as Goethe would have been among all the other grandsons of publicans, if they had formed a distinct class in Frankfurt or Weimar. This I knew very well when I wrote my novels; and if, as I suspect, I failed to create a convincingly verisimilar atmosphere of aristocracy, it was not because I had any illusions or ignorances as to the common humanity of the peerage, and not because I gave literary style to its conversation, but because, as I had never had any money, I was foolishly indifferent, to it, and so, having blinded myself to its enormous importance, necessarily missed the point of view, and with it the whole moral basis, of the class which rightly values money, and plenty of it, as the first condition of a bearable life.

Money is indeed the most important thing in the world; and all sound and successful personal and national morality should have this fact for its basis. Every teacher or twaddler who denies it or suppresses it, is an enemy of life. Money controls morality; and what makes the United States of America look so foolish even in foolish Europe is that they are always in a state of flurried concern and violent interference with morality, whereas they throw their money into the street to be scrambled for, and presently find that their cash reserves are not in their own hands, but in the pockets of a few millionaires who, bewildered by their luck, and unspeakably incapable of making any truly economic use of it, endeavour to "do good" with it by letting themselves be fleeced by philanthropic committee men, building contractors, librarians, and professors, in the name of education, science, art and what not; so that sensible people exhale relievedly when the pious millionaire dies, and his heirs, demoralized by being brought up on his outrageous income, begin the socially beneficent work of scattering his fortune through the channels of the trades that flourish by riotous living.

This, as I have said, I did not then understand; for I knew money only by the want of it. Ireland is a poor country; and my father was a poor man in a poor country. By this I do not mean that he was hungry and homeless, a hewer of wood and a drawer of water. My friend Mr. James Huneker, a man of gorgeous imagination and incorrigible romantisicm, has described me to the American public as a peasant lad who has raised himself, as all American presidents are assumed to have raised themselves, from the humblest departments of manual labour to the loftiest eminence. James flatters me. Had I been born a peasant, I should now be a tramp. My notion of my father's income is even vaguer than his own was – and that is saying a good deal – but he always had an income of at least three figures (four, if you count in dollars instead of pounds); and what made him poor was that he conceived himself as born to a social position which even in Ireland could have been maintained in dignified comfort only on twice or thrice what he had. And he married on that assumption. Fortunately for me, social opportunity is not always to be measured by income. There is an important economic factor, first analysed by an American economist (General Walker), and called rent of ability. Now this rent, when the ability is of the artistic or political sort, is often paid in kind. For example, a London possessor of such ability may, with barely enough money to maintain a furnished bedroom and a single presentable suit of clothes, see everything worth seeing that a millionare can see, and know everybody worth knowing that he can know. Long before I reached this point myself, a very trifling accomplishment gave me glimpses of the sort of fashionable life a peasant never sees. Thus I remember one evening during the novel-writing period when nobody would pay a farthing for a stroke of my pen, walking along Sloane Street in that blessed shield of literary shabbiness, evening dress. A man accosted me with an eloquent appeal for help, ending with the assurance that he had not a penny in the world. I replied, with exact truth, "Neither have I." He thanked me civilly, and went away, apparently not in the least surprised, leaving me to ask myself why I did not turn beggar too, since I felt sure that a man who did it as well as he, must be in comfortable circumstances.

Another reminiscence. A little past midnight, in the same costume, I was turning from Piccadilly into Bond Street, when a lady of the pavement, out of luck that evening so far, confided to me that the last bus for Brompton had passed, and that she should be grateful to any gentleman who would give her a lift in a hansom. My old-fashioned Irish gallantry had not then been worn off by age and England: besides, as a novelist who could find no publisher, I was touched by the similarity of our trades and predicaments. I excused myself very politely on the ground that my wife (invented for the occasion) was waiting for me at home, and that I felt sure so attractive a lady would have no difficulty in finding another escort. Unfortunately this speech made so favourable an impression on her that she immediately took my arm and declared her willingness to go anywhere with me, on the flattering ground that I was a perfect gentleman. In vain did I try to persuade her that in coming up Bond Street and deserting Piccadilly, she was throwing away her last chance of a hansom: she attached herself so devotedly to me that I could not without actual violence shake her off. At last I made a stand at the end of Old Bond Street. I took out my purse; opened it; and held it upside down. Her countenance fell, poor girl! She turned on her heel with a melancholy flirt of her skirt, and vanished.

Now on both these occasions I had been in the company of people who spent at least as much in a week as I did in a year. Why was I, a penniless and unknown young man, admitted there? Simply because, though I was an execrable pianist, and never improved until the happy invention of the pianola made a Paderewski of me, I could play a simple accompaniment at sight more congenially to a singer than most amateurs. It is true that the musical side of London society, with its streak of Bohemianism, and its necessary toleration of foreign ways and professional manners, is far less typically English than the sporting side or the political side or the Philistine side; so much so, indeed, that people may and do pass their lives in it without ever discovering what English plutocracy in the mass is really like: still, if you wander in it nocturnally for a fitful year or so as I did, with empty pockets and an utter impossibility of approaching it by daylight (owing to the deplorable decay of the morning wardrobe), you have something more actual to go on than the hallucinations of a peasant lad setting his foot manfully on the lowest rung of the social ladder. I never climbed any ladder: I have achieved eminence by sheer gravitation; and I hereby warn all peasant lads not to be duped by my pretended example into regarding their present servitude as a practicable first step to a celebrity so dazzling that its subject cannot even suppress his own bad novels.

Conceive me then at the writing of *The Irrational Knot* as a person neither belonging to the world I describe nor wholly ignorant of it, and on certain points quite incapable of conceiving it intuitively. A whole world of art which did not exist for it lay open to me. I was familiar with the greatest in that world: mighty poets, painters, and musicians were my intimates. I found the world of artificial greatness founded on convention and money so repugnant and contemptible by comparison that I had no sympathetic understanding of it. People are fond of blaming valets because no man is a hero to his valet. But it is equally true that no man is a valet to his hero; and the hero, consequently, is apt to blunder very ludicrously about valets, through judging them from an irrelevant standard of heroism: heroism, remember, having its faults as well as its qualities. I, always on the heroic plane imaginatively, had two disgusting faults which I did not recognize as faults because I could not help them. I was poor and (by day) shabby. I therefore tolerated the gross error that poverty, though an inconvenience and a trial, is not a sin and a disgrace; and I stood for my self-respect on the things I had: probity, ability, knowledge of art, laboriousness, and whatever else came cheaply to me. Because I could walk into Hampton Court Palace and the National Gallery (on free days) and enjoy Mantegna and Michael Angelo whilst millionaires were yawning miserably over inept gluttonies; because I could suffer more by hearing a movement of Beethoven's Ninth Symphony taken at a wrong tempo than a duchess by losing a diamond necklace, I was indifferent to the repulsive fact that if I had fallen in love with the duchess I did not possess a morning suit in which I could reasonable have expected her to touch me with the furthest protended pair of tongs; and I did not see that to remedy this I should have been prepared to wade through seas of other people's blood. Indeed it is this perception which constitutes an aristocracy nowadays. It is the secret of all our governing classes, which consist finally of people who, though perfectly prepared to be generous, humane, cultured, philanthropic, public spirited and personally charming in the second instance, are unalterably resolved, in the first, to have money enough for a handsome and delicate life, and will, in pursuit of that money, batter in the doors of their fellow men, sell them up, sweat them in fetid dens, shoot, stab, hang, imprison, sink, burn and destroy them in the name of law and order. And this shows their fundamental sanity and rightmindedness; for a sufficient income is indispensable to the practice of virtue; and the man who will let any unselfish consideration stand between him and its attainment is a weakling, a dupe and a predestined slave. If I could convince our impecunious mobs of this, the world would be reformed before the end of the week; for the sluggards who are content to be wealthy without working and the dastards who are content to work without being wealthy, together with all the pseudo-moralists and ethicists and cowardice mongers generally, would be exterminated without shrift, to the unutterable enlargement of life and ennoblement of humanity. We might even make some beginnings of civilization under such happy circumstances.

In the days of *The Irrational Knot* I had not learnt this lesson; consequently I did not understand the British peerage, just as I did not understand that glorious and beautiful phenomenon, the "heartless" rich American woman, who so thoroughly and admirably understands that conscience is a luxury, and should be indulged in only when the vital needs of life have been abundantly satisfied. The instinct which has led the British peerage to fortify itself by American alliances is healthy and well inspired. Thanks to it, we shall still have a few people to maintain the tradition of a handsome, free, proud, costly life, whilst the craven mass of us are keeping up our starveling pretence that it is more important to be good than to be rich, and piously cheating, robbing, and murdering one another by doing our duty as policemen, soldiers, bailiffs, jurymen, turnkeys, hangmen, tradesmen, and curates, at the command of those who know that the golden grapes are *not* sour. Why, good heavens! we shall all pretend that this straightforward truth of mine is mere Swiftian satire, because it would require a little courage to take it seriously and either act on it or make me drink the hemlock for uttering it.

There was the less excuse for my blindness because I was at that very moment laying the foundations of my high fortune by the most ruthless disrgard of all the quack duties which lead the peasant lad of fiction to the White House, and harness the real peasant boy to the plough until he is finally swept, as rubbish, into the workhouse. I was an ablebodied and ableminded young man in the strength of my youth; and my family, then heavily embarrassed, needed my help urgently. That I should have chosen to be a burden to them instead was, according to all the conventions of peasant lad fiction, monstrous. Well, without a blush I embraced the monstrosity. I did not throw myself into the struggle of life: I threw my mother into it. I was not a staff to my father's old age: I hung on to his coat tails. His reward was to live just long enough to read a review of one of these silly novels written in an obscure journal by a personal friend of my own (now eminent in literature as Mr. John Mackinnon Robertson) prefiguring me to some extent as a considerable author. I think, myself, that this was a handsome reward, far better worth having than a nice pension from a dutiful son struggling slavishly for his parent's bread in some sordid trade. Handsome or not, it was the only return he ever had for the little pension he contrived to export from Ireland for his family. My mother reinforced it by drudging in her elder years at the art of music which she had followed in her prime freely for love. I only helped to spend it. People wondered at my heartlessness: one young and romantic lady had the courage to remonstrate openly and indignantly with me, "for the which," as Pepys said of the shipwright's wife who refused his advances, "I did respect her." Callous as Comus to moral babble, I steadily wrote my five pages a day and made a man of myself (at my mother's expense) instead of a slave. And I protest that I will not suffer James Huneker or any romanticist to pass me off as a peasant boy qualifying for a chapter in Smiles's *Self Help*, or a good son supporting a helpless mother, instead of a stupendously selfish artist leaning with the full weight of his hungry body on an energetic and capable woman. No, James: such lies are not only unnecessary, but fearfully depressing and fundamentally immoral, besides being hardly fair to the supposed peasant lad's parents. My mother worked for my living instead of preaching that it was my duty to work for hers: therefore take off your hat to her, and blush.

It is now open to any one who pleases to read *The Irrational Knot*. I do not recommend him to; but it is possible that the same mysterious force which drove me through the labour of writing it may have had some purpose which will sustain others through the labour of reading

Shaw was a founder of the Fabian Society. The members were Marxist enough to believe a world ruled by competing finance corporations was bound for disaster, but did not think revolution would cure it. Many were civil servants who saved industrial Britain from chaos & epidemic by providing public lighting, water, transport & sewage systems. They believed democratic government could gradually take over all big business & manage it to profit everyone instead of a shareholding minority. A trade union-Fabian alliance created the British Labour Party.

it, and even reward them with some ghastly enjoyment of it. For my own part I cannot stand it. It is to me only one of the heaps of spoiled material that all apprenticeship involves. I consent to its publication because I remember that British colonel who called on Beethoven when the elderly composer was working at his posthumous quartets, and offered him a commission for a work in the style of his jejune septet. Beethoven drove the Colonel out of the house with objurgation. I think that was uncivil. There is a time for the septet, and a time for the posthumous quartets. It is true that if a man called on me now and asked me to write something like *The Irrational Knot* I should have to exercise great self-control. But there are people who read *Man and Superman*, and then tell me (actually to my face) that I have never done anything so good as *Cashel Byron's Profession*. After this, there may be a public for even *The Irrational Knot*; so let it go.

LONDON, May 26, 1905.

1907

In the 19th century England's best poets wrote poetic plays in blank verse as much like Shakespeare's as stuffed birds are like live ones. But S aimed, despite a prim board school education, to write like Dante. Born near Dublin he went to Trinity College, the Royal Irish College of Music, then headed for Europe. In Paris among Irish émigrés he studied writing & met Yeats, who wanted

THE PLAYBOY OF THE WESTERN WORLD
JOHN MILLINGTON SYNGE
LONDON

[PREFACE]

IN WRITING "The Playboy of the Western World", as in my other plays, I have used one or two words only that I have not heard among the country people of Ireland, or spoken in my own nursery before I could read the newspapers. A certain number of the phrases I employ I have heard also from herds and fishermen along the coast from Kerry to Mayo or from beggar-women and ballad-singers nearer Dublin; and I am glad to acknowledge how much I owe to the folk-imagination of these fine people. Any one who has lived in real intimacy with the Irish peasantry will know that the wildest saying and ideas in this play are tame indeed, compared with the fancies one may hear in any little hillside cabin in Geesala, or Carraroe, or Dingle Bay. All art is a collaboration; and there is little doubt that in the happy ages of literature, striking and beautiful phrases were as ready to the story-teller's or the playwright's hand, as the rich cloaks and dresses of his time. It is probably that when the Elizabethan dramatist took his ink-horn and sat down to his work he used many phrases that he had just heard, as he sat at dinner, from his mother or his children. In Ireland, those of us who know the people have the same privilege. When I was writing "The Shadow of the Glen", some years ago, I got more aid than any learning could have given me from a chink in the floor of the old Wicklow house where I was staying, that let me hear what was being said by the servant girls in the kitchen. This matter, I think, is of importance, for in countries where the imagination of the people, and the language they use, is rich and living, it is possible for a writer to be rich and copious in his words, and at the same time to give the reality, which is the root of all poetry, in a comprehensive and natural form. In the modern literature of towns, however, richness is found only in sonnets, or prose poems, or in one or two elaborate books that are far away from the profound and common interests of life. One has, on one side, Mallarmé and Huysmans producing this literature; and on the other, Ibsen and Zola dealing with the reality of life in joyless and pallid words. On the stage one must have reality, and one must have joy; and that is why the intellectual modern drama has failed, and people have grown sick of the false joy of the musical comedy, that has been given them in place of the rich joy found only in what is superb and wild in reality. In a good play every speech should be as fully flavoured as

to renew Irish literature. Like Tolstoy in Russia Yeats thought his nation would be revived if the upper classes learned from the peasants. He urged S to go back & learn Gaelic in Ireland & see how peasants who spoke it on the west coast lived. S did. It inspired his plays. He founded with Yeats & Lady Gregory the 1st Irish National Theatre, The Abbey. **The Playboy** *was 1st performed on January 16th 1907 & the audience rioted. S showed Irish peasants with sexual passions, & at times cowardly & cruel – so had betrayed his country! "Whatever will they think of us across the water?" The language also annoyed many Dubliners. Like MacDiarmid's Scots it was synthetic – in this case English but with Gaelic grammar, & enhanced into poetry by idioms of the folk it was written about. In the working world of West Ireland vivid sayings got invented &, like ballads, passed on. To be eavesdropped eventually by Synge. I love his hint that Mrs Shakespeare may have clipped her son around the ear & told him his head was full of scorpions. George Moore, then Ireland's* *most famous fiction writer, was sure S did not learn **through a crack** to spring **out of board school English into a beautiful style** & construct a play. He said a short story of his own, **The Untilled Field**, had inspired S to write **The Playboy of the Western World**.*

a nut or apple, and such speeches cannot be written by any one who works among people who have shut their lips on poetry. In Ireland, for a few years more, we have a popular imagination that is fiery, and magnificent, and tender; so that those of us who wish to write start with a chance that is not given to writers in places where the springtime of the local life has been forgotten, and the harvest is a memory only, and the straw has been turned into bricks.

J.M.S. 21st January 1907.

1920

POEMS
WILFRED OWEN
LONDON

For 60 years Europe's expanding empires had prepared for a mighty war by competitive arming with always deadlier weapons & by networks of secret treaties. Most folk in these empires cheered when it began. Owen, a clever young officer, thought it a valuable but dangerous test of manhood in 1914.

Written in June 1918, 5 months before his death, this Preface only exists as a scrawled draft, & yet it is the most famous 20th-century literary manifesto in English. It constitutes one of the earliest cathartic turns against the horror of the 1st World War, a stylized return of the repressed against the anxiety neurosis created in the minds of combatants by the conflict.

[PREFACE (unfinished)]

THIS BOOK is not about heroes. English Poetry is not yet fit to speak of them. Nor is it about deeds or lands, nor anything about glory, honour, dominion or power, except War. Above all, this book is not concerned with Poetry. The subject of it is War, and the pity of War. The Poetry is in the pity. Yet these elegies are not to this generation. This is in no sense consolatory.

They may be to the next. All the poet can do to-day is to warn. That is why the true Poets must be truthful. If I thought the letter of this book would last, I might have used proper names; but if the spirit of it survives Prussia, – my ambition and those names will be content; for they will have achieved themselves fresher fields than Flanders.

STRANGE MEETING

It seemed that out of the battle I escaped
Down some profound dull tunnel, long since scooped
Through granites which Titanic wars had groined.
Yet also there encumbered sleepers groaned,
Too fast in thought or death to be bestirred.
Then, as I probed them, one sprang up, and stared
With piteous recognition in fixed eyes,

Owen knew about neurosis – he had attended the War Hospital at Craiglockhart & had his nerves regenerated by the psychiatrist W.H.R. Rivers. 1 of Rivers's patients was haunted in dreams by a dead fellow-soldier: the mutilated or leprous officer would come nearer and nearer until the patient suddenly awoke pouring with sweat & in a state of the utmost terror. Owen's late poems are designed to have the same effect on civilian readers, bringing them nearer & nearer to the real circumstances of war – to the madness, inhumanity, bestiality of war.

The war purged Owen of bogus romantic dictions & attitudes. In the lethal landscape of the trenches, Georgian postures of rural nostalgia, upper-class syntax & swooning jingoism were killed. What survived was a new rhythm & language, close to the talk of common soldiery. This war had stripped elegy of its heroes, of its panoply of consolations, dominions & powers, leaving a poetry of true feeling, without the bullshit of a bankrupt officer class.

Lifting distressful hands as if to bless.
And by his smile, I knew that sullen hall;
Yet no blood reached there from the upper ground,
And no guns thumped, or down the flues made moan.
"Strange, friend," I said, "here is no cause to mourn."
"None," said the other, "save the undone years,
The hopelessness. Whatever hope is yours,
Was my life also; I went hunting wild
After the wildest beauty in the world,
Which lies not calm in eyes, or braided hair,
But mocks the steady running of the hour,
And if it grieves, grieves richlier than here.
For by my glee might many men have laughed,
And of my weeping something has been left,
Which must die now. I mean the truth untold,
The pity of war, the pity war distilled.
Now men will go content with what we spoiled,
Or, discontent, boil bloody, and be spilled.
They will be swift with swiftness of the tigress,
None will break ranks,
        though nations trek from progress.
Courage was mine, and I had mystery;
Wisdom was mine, and I had mastery;
To miss the march of this retreating world
Into vain citadels that are not walled.
Then, when much blood
        had clogged their chariot-wheels
I would go up and wash them from sweet wells,
Even with truths that lie too deep for taint.
I would have poured my spirit without stint
But not through wounds; not on the cess of war.
Foreheads of men have bled where no wounds were.
I am the enemy you killed, my friend.
I knew you in this dark; for so you frowned
Yesterday through me as you jabbed and killed.
I parried; but my hands were loath and cold.
Let us sleep now . . ."

POSTSCRIPT

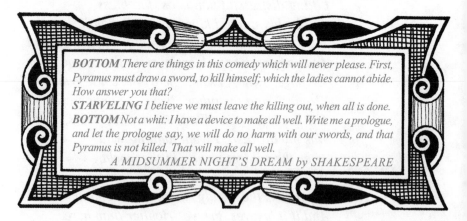

> **BOTTOM** *There are things in this comedy which will never please. First, Pyramus must draw a sword, to kill himself; which the ladies cannot abide. How answer you that?*
> **STARVELING** *I believe we must leave the killing out, when all is done.*
> **BOTTOM** *Not a whit: I have a device to make all well. Write me a prologue, and let the prologue say, we will do no harm with our swords, and that Pyramus is not killed. That will make all well.*
> *A MIDSUMMER NIGHT'S DREAM by SHAKESPEARE*

I**T IS DONE. ENDED. FINISHED. COMPLETE. THANK GOODNESS,** for I think goodness is god's kindest name. He, She or It (choose your favourite pronoun: just now I feel inclined to worship god the tree) has sterner names, like Reality, Nature, and Eternal Truth, compared with which each of us is a poor wee frail body – even such mighty truth-tellers as Moses, Jesus, Mahomet, Shakespeare, Jefferson, Robert Burns and Jane Austin. I apologise to any Christian I offend by naming Jesus as a human being, but his last words upon the cross persuade me that, whatever he did later, he too is one of us. So I thank GOODNESS for letting me live to the end of this book, for though stern Reality, Nature, Truth & Co generate and allow goodness they do not let us depend upon it, as a multitude of hungry, homeless, voteless people know in every nation except, maybe, some Scandinavian ones.

I need do nothing now but give, as I promised in my opening advert, the motives and circumstances that led me to make this book, then apologise for the result.

In the early 80s I borrowed from Campbell Semple *The Philosophy of Natural History* by his remote ancestor, William Smellie, whose preface suggested the plan of this book. I saw at once it was a book I would want if someone else made it, but nobody had. Desire for a non-existent thing is the best motive for making it, even if a wish for fame and cash drives the maker too. When relaxing from other work I began to take note of good prefaces from Chaucer's *Canterbury Tales* to Vonnegut's *Breakfast of*

Champions, which was how I first imagined this book starting and ending. I soon saw that most readers would, like myself, enjoy it more if they were given more information than Smellie's plan suggested. The ancient device of a marginal commentary or gloss seemed the best way to add this without breaking the flow of the most essential part.

So when a literary agent (Fiona Morrison) asked if I had ideas for a work of NON fiction (meaning a historical or biographical or critical work too speculative to be called factual) I suggested this one. When she asked for an introduction and specimen commentaries to show to publishers I quickly wrote the advert starting on page 7 and glosses on prefaces to *The Cloud of Unknowing*, Hobbes' *Leviathan* and *The Lyrical Ballads*. They were mainly, though not exactly, as printed here. Each gloss began with the sentence *This was written in an age of great revolutions* because I believed then, and believe still, that every generation sees an amazing change of social circumstances. The advert was cheekier. It wondered why university professors had not undertaken this anthology long before, and suggested they were unable to see the value of a book which could be made so easily – for I then thought it could be easily made. In the six centuries between Geoffrey Chaucer and Kurt Vonnegut literacy, I believed, had steadily grown with expanding populations, so the number of important books must also have steadily increased. I already knew many of the books and it would not be hard to find others that university professors agreed were best. I would photocopy their prefaces from reprints in public libraries, arrange these chronologically, then crib commentaries from the *Encyclopaedia Britannica* which Smellie had also pioneered. Anyone with a Scottish Higher Leaving Certificate in English and Lower Leaving Certificate in History can do *that*, especially if they were educated at Whitehill Senior Secondary School, east Glasgow.

From this you may deduce, dear reader, that although I was then over fifty I still believed in the progressive view of history – believed that each generation had added good new social and scientific and artistic works to those of the past, thus giving more people comfort, security and freedom for the future. Any honest news report about life in most Asian, African and South American lands proved that view was not inevitable, that it was being horribly disproved in many places, but my own family history showed such progress *had* occurred in Britain, and would enable me to make this book.

For my grandparents had been born in the middle of Victoria's reign. My mum's dad was a foreman shoemaker who brought his wife from Northampton to Glasgow when English employers blacklisted him for trade union activities. He also brought his daughters to tears by reading them Hardy's *Tess of the D'Urbervilles*. They did not regard Dickens and Hardy as English literary classics but as entertainingly truthful describers of the world they knew, Dickens showing the mainly comic aspects, Hardy the mainly tragic. My dad's dad was an industrial blacksmith and elder of a Congregational kirk: the kirk Cromwell worshipped in because the congregation chose its own priests. His political heroes were William Gladstone and Keir Hardie, both of whom wanted Scotland and Ireland to have independent governments, and British manual labourers to be as healthily and comfortably housed as their bosses, if not quite as spaciously. Like most of the literate working class my grandparents thought themselves middle class, though my dad's parents lived with five children, my mother's parents with three, in small one-room-and-kitchen rented flats without inside lavatories and baths, where water and food was heated by the kitchen fire. Most of the wealthy depended on such primitive heating and cooking before 1900, though their servants saved them from the sight of it. My dad, born 1897, left school at twelve, worked a weigh bridge in a Clydeside dock, and joined the army in 1914. He survived Flanders, lost his parents' Christian Liberal faith and became a Fabian Socialist, earning money between 1918 and 1939 by operating a machine in a cardboard box factory. In his spare time he worked without pay for co-operative out-door holiday organisations: The Camping Club of Great Britain, Scottish Youth Hostel Association and others.

That Trade Union shoemaker, Liberal blacksmith and Co-operative Fabian box-cutter were three types who created the first British Labour government: a party of MPs who preferred Ruskin to Marx and in 1924 passed parliamentary acts enabling town & rural councils to build the kind of housing scheme where I was born in 1934. Though my parents had only two children our flat had three rooms beside a lavatory – bathroom with hot tap water, a kitchen with that also and an electric cooker. Like most of the British working class we were further enriched by the second World War and its aftermath. My parents then paid for my health treatment and excellent education through their income tax, which I took for granted as the fair and democratic way of doing it. In their small book collection was Burns' *Poems,* Carlyle's *French Revolution,* Dickens' *Bleak House,* all Ibsen's plays in Archer's translation and the plays of Bernard Shaw. My dad was also a member of the Readers Union Book Club which brought into our house in the late 1940's the works of James Joyce, Hemingway, Orwell and Arthur Waley's translation of the Chinese *Monkey* epic and poetic anthology. Meanwhile Whitehill School was trying and failing to teach me Latin and Greek, but did introduce me to English literature from Chaucer to Conrad; and in Riddrie public library I discovered exciting translations of Heine's *Reisbilder* and Sartre's *Nausea.* I would be ungrateful if I did not mention the BBC Third Programme. This broadcasting network was set up with the help of émigré intellectuals of a Socialist sort driven out of mainland Europe by Fascism, but their outlook was, in the broadest sense of the word, catholic. It only broadcast in the evening between the hours of six and eleven, and broadcast nothing but music and plays and lectures which were labelled (in the slang of the forties and fifties) *highbrow,* but which contained no erudite jargon, so I hugely enjoyed it.

Like many others in those days I believed Britain had attained a high new state of civilisation from which it would never descend. For over a century folk had striven against corporate greed to make this a land where everyone's health care and education would be decided by their needs and abilities, not their parents' wealth. This state lasted for nearly forty years. It helped millions of working class children join the professional classes. It let a grocer's daughter become Britain's prime minister, let me become an artist and author who would turn Smellie's idea into a book.

In 1987 Fiona Morrison got a publisher's advance to let me work steadily on the book. I began by arranging prefaces I had chosen in chronological order, which gave my progressive view of history its first hard knock. Dates of the earliest works were not exact, but exact enough to show Chaucer did not lead a procession of great writers, he walked in a crowd of them – Langland, Barbour, the *Gawain* poet and others. After Chaucer's death in 1400 the crowd shrank to a widely spaced line of pedestrians. Two centuries passed before such a good crowd of vernacular English authors jostled again, apart from a wee flurry of them in Lowland Scotland around James IV's time. Why?

I took so long to find out why that I used up the advance of my first publisher (Canongate of Edinburgh) though I also added the long introduction on Hebrew, Greek, Roman and Christian writing and prefaces to Anglo-Saxon works. In 1990 I tackled the effects of the Norman Conquest, and later discharged my debt to Canongate by giving it a science-fiction novel. I then raised money by writing more fiction and in 1995 resumed work on this book for Bloomsbury of London. It has now been announced so confidently for so many years that respected guides to modern first editions began saying it was published in 1989. (Joseph Connolly suggests £20 or less is a good second hand price, R.B.Russell puts it at £10.) Only now, on Tuesday 21st of December 1999, as I sit in bed recovering from flu, is the book being finally completed.

Copyright costs have forced me to abandon my plan for a section of prefaces by great 20th-century authors, including those who now write Australian, Asian, African and Caribbean kinds of English. The book is only completed for the third millennium through help from nearly every writer I know well, and four in Glasgow University English Literature Department contacted through my friend Philip Hobsbaum. I admit to having tampered a little with some of their contributions (Janice Galloway says her commentaries on Brontë and George Eliot have Gray fingermarks all over them) but have nowhere contradicted their opinions. My main sorrow is that Chris Boyce, who gave notes for the commentary on Cowley's preface to the *History of the Royal Society*, and Iain Crichton Smith who glossed Keats' and Conrad's prefaces, can neither receive a copy of this book now, nor thanks for their help with it.

I have slighter regrets. Like most who have worked for years on a job I see how much better it could be made if begun over again. I would include prefaces by William Morris and Henry James, and commentaries on all the twentieth century prefaces I cannot afford to print, and many notes at the end to support my glib assertions in earlier pages. I would redraw the illustrations on pages 175 and

267 to enhance their clarity, and find something better than Dicky Doyle's old *Punch* cover to introduce the Liberal English section, which should have been called Liberal English, Irish, Scots and American. But I sympathise with Bloomsbury for stopping me continuing to revise for another year or two.

These sixteen years of intermittent work have seen the dismantling of a Russian military empire established with USA and British aid in 1944. It has seen the world-wide triumph of international capitalism with United States and British armed forces as its most militant powers, so there has been no reduction of world warfare. Britain is entering a new constitutional period after a gigantic reduction of local government democracy, also the biggest sale of public property to private businesses since the dissolution of the monasteries in 1540, the abolition of common land in the 1820s. Even Britain's public water supply, the greatest achievement of Victorian socialism, has been privatised, so a French company now owns a British reservoir. Despite protests by librarians the best of branch library stock have been sold and replaced by the kind of cheap paperback most newsagents sell. Despite protests by teachers our local school buildings are sold to private property developers, and schools in poor areas cannot supply their pupils with proper books, though deals with local businesses will equip them with continually replaceable word processors at the tax-payers' expense.

I consider this anthology a memorial to the kind of education British governments now think useless, especially for British working class children. But it has been my education, so I am bound to believe it one of the best in the world.

I no longer think social improvement inevitable anywhere, but still believe (as my dad and grandads did) that good co-operative 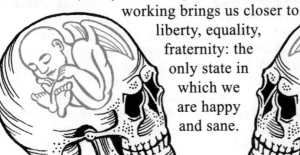 working brings us closer to liberty, equality, fraternity: the only state in which we are happy and sane.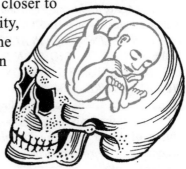

INDEX OF in principio

ANON: who generously supplied initiative, room, typist and typesetter to forward the making of this book from 1988 to 1990.

BEATTIE, Colin: publican, who generously funded the making of this book from December 1998 to July 1999.

BOYCE, Christopher: 1944–99: science writer, novelist and librarian; author of *Extraterrestrial Encounters* (science speculation), many short stories, *Catchworld, Brainfix* (science fiction), *Blooding Mr. Naylor* (crime), gloss on SPRAT and COWLEY'S *HISTORY OF THE ROYAL SOCIETY.*

CALDER, Angus: historian and literary critic, contributor to *Scotsman, Herald, Scotland on Sunday, Chapman.*, author of *The People's War, Revolutionary Empire, The Myth of the Blitz, Revolving Culture,* glosses on POPE'S *ILIAD,* COOK'S *VOYAGE TOWARD THE SOUTH POLE* and TENNYSON'S *PRINCESS.*

CALDER, Liz: director of Bloomsbury Publishing who funded the making of this book from August 1995 to August 1998.

CAMERON, Allan: journalist who writes for *Renaissance Studies, Reset, L'Unità,* translator into English of (among other work) Camporesi's *Anatomy of the Senses,* Bobbio's *Age of Rights* and *Right and Left,* author of glosses on WINSTANLEY'S *LAW OF FREEDOM ON A PLATFORM,* POPE'S *THE DUNCIAD & AN ESSAY ON MAN* and HUME'S *TREATISE ON HUMAN NATURE.*

CASTILLO, Susan: lecturer in English Literature at the University of Glasgow, author of *Notes from the Periphery: Marginality in North American Literature and Culture, Engendering Identities, Native American Women in Literature and Culture, Pós-Colonialismo e Identidade,* also poetry, essays, book reviews published in USA, Portugal, Italy and Japan and glosses on HAWTHORNE'S *TWICE-TOLD TALES,* STOWE'S *UNCLE TOM'S CABIN* and LONGFELLOW'S *SONG OF HIAWATHA.*

CHARLTON, Bruce: After gaining honours in Medicine from the Newcastle Medical School he trained in psychiatry, researched a doctorate on hormonal and brain changes in depression, then at Durham completed an MA thesis upon the literature of Alasdair Gray. He has since held a wide range of academic positions including lectureships in Psychology, Anatomy and Epidemiology. He is lecturer in psychology at Newcastle University and a Visiting Professor at St Bartholomew's Hospital, London. He has published over 100 research papers, a considerable quantity of journalism, an experimental radio drama, and has recently (this is planned to come out in early 2000) completed a book called *Psychiatry and the Human Condition.* Gloss on MALTHUS (etc.)

CRAWFORD, Robert: Professor of Modern Scottish Literature at the University of St Andrews, author of *A Scottish Assembly, Talkies, Masculinity, Spirit Machines* (poetry), *The Savage and the City in the Work of T.S. Eliot, Devolving English Literature, Identifying Poets: Self and Territory in 20th-century Poetry* (criticism), glosses on RAMSAY'S *THE EVER GREEN* and BURNS' *POEMS.*

CUZENS, Julie: secretary and typist who

HELPERS

patiently put a hundred and eighty prefaces on disk, not all of them finally used.

DONNELLY, Michael: conserver and historian, author of *Banner Bright* (on British trade union banners), *Thomas Muir of Huntershill* (biography), *People's Pictures – The Story of Tiles in Glasgow*, *Making the Colours Sing* (study of Scottish stained glass), many publications for Glasgow museum service, gloss on PAINE'S *RIGHTS OF MAN*.

EVARISTI, Marcella: playwright and journalist; author of *Scotia's Darlings*, *Dorothy and the Bitch*, *Hard to Get*, *Wedding Belles and Green Grasses*, *Eve Sets the Balls of Corruption Rolling*, *The Works*, *Commedia*, *Terrestrial Extras*, *The Hat*, *Troilus and Cressida and Di-Da Di-Da Di-Da*, *Trio for Strings*, *Thankyou for Not*, *Theory and Practice of Rings*, *The Offski Variations* (plays), glosses on AUSTEN'S *NORTHANGER ABBEY* and WILDE'S *THE PICTURE OF DORIAN GRAY*.

GALLOWAY, Janice: author of *Clara*, *Monster* (song cycles with composer Sally Beamish), *The Trick is to Keep Breathing*, *Blood*, *Foreign Parts*, *Where You Find It* (fiction), gloss on BRONTË'S *SHIRLEY* and ELIOT'S *FELIX HOLT* and *MIDDLEMARCH*.

GRANT, Robert: reader in English Literature at the University of Glasgow, author of articles, reviews and essays in the *Times Literary Supplement*, *Times Educational Supplement*, *Salisbury Review*, *Philosophic Quarterly*, *Cambridge Quarterly*, *Shakespeare Studies*, *National Review*; entries in *Encyclopaedia of Philosophy*, *A Dictionary of Conservative and Libertarian Thought*, *The Blackwell Dictionary of Twentieth-Century Social Thought*, *History of European Ideas*; introductions to Shakespeare's *The Tempest* and *Richard II*, gloss on MANDEVILLE'S *FABLE OF THE BEES*.

HIND, Archie: author of *The Dear Green Place* (novel), *The Sugarolly Story*, *Shoulder to Shoulder* (plays), *Hind Sight*, *Through with a Flourish*, *Ragtime*, *St. Valentine's Day* (revues), *Babes in the Broo* (pantomime), gloss on JEFFERSON'S *DECLARATION OF INDEPENDENCE*.

KELMAN, James: author of *Not Not While the Giro*, *Greyhound for Breakfast*, *The Burn* (stories), *Hardie and Baird & Other Plays* (plays), *The Busconductor Hines*, *A Chancer*, *A Disaffection*, *How Late It Was, How Late*, *The Good Times* (novels), glosses on BERKELEY'S *PRINCIPLES OF HUMAN KNOWLEDGE* and DICKENS' *BLEAK HOUSE*.

KENNEDY, A.L.: author of *The Life and Death of Colonel Blimp* (non fiction), *The Audition*, *Totally Out of It*, *The Year of the Prince*, *Just to Say*, *Stella does Tricks*, *Ghostdancing* (drama), *Night Geometry and the Garscadden Trains*, *Now that You're Back*, *Tea and Biscuits*, *Original Bliss* (short stories), *Looking for the Possible Dance*, *Everything You Need* (novels), gloss on STERNE'S *TRISTRAM SHANDY* and part of that on DARWIN'S *THE ORIGIN OF SPECIES*.

KING, Elspeth: curator and conserver of Scottish culture and working-class history; designer of many exhibitions and

Dunfermline Abbots House Museum, editor of *Blind Harry's Wallace* by Hamilton of Gilbertfield, *Stirling Letters* by Isabella Murray Wright, author of articles, catalogues and papers published by historical journals, Glasgow and other museum services, *William Wallace, Scotland's Liberator* (biography), *The Thenew Factor* (history of Glasgow women), gloss on OWEN'S *NEW VIEW OF SOCIETY*.

KUPPNER, Frank: author of *A Bad Day for the Sung Dynasty, The Intelligent Observation of Naked Women, Second Best Moments in Chinese History* (poems), *A Very Quiet Street, Something Very Like Murder* (unclassifiable studies of Scottish private life), *A Concussed History of Scotland, Life on a Dead Planet* (novels), *Ridiculous! Absurd! Disgusting!* (an unclassifiable mingling of novel and verse), glosses on CARROLL'S *THE HUNTING OF THE SNARK* and HOPKINS' *WRECK OF THE DEUTSCHLAND*.

LEEMING, Bruce: author of *An Anger Bequeathed, Now You Must Dance* (novels), *Engraving the Sky, Scots Haiku* (poetry), glosses on BENTHAM'S *FRAGMENT ON GOVERNMENT* and MILL'S *THE SUBJECTION OF WOMEN*.

LEONARD, Tom: poet and critic; author of *If Only Bunty Was Here* (play), *A Priest Came on at Merkland Street, Bunnit Hustlin, Ghostie Men* (poetry), *Intimate Voices* (selection of poetry and other writing 1965–83), *Satires and Profanities, The Mass Bombing of Iraq and Kuwait commonly known as "the Gulf War" with Leonard's Shorter Catechism* (political pieces), *Reports from the Present* (writing 1984–94), *Radical Renfrew* (poetry from the French Revolution to the First World War), *Places of the Mind: The Life and Work of James Thomson* (biography), gloss on *MIDSUMMER CUSHION*.

LOCHHEAD, Liz: author of *Memo for Spring, Islands, Grimm Sisters, Dreaming Frankenstein, Bagpipe Muzak* (poetry), *True Confessions and New Clichés* (lyrics and monologues), *Tartuffe* (Scots adaptation-translation), *Blood and Ice, Dracula, Same Difference, Sweet Nothings, Now and Then, True Confessions, Mary Queen of Scots Got Her Head Chopped Off, The Big Picture, Disgusting Objects, Shanghaied, Perfect Days* (plays), gloss on MARY SHELLEY'S *FRANKENSTEIN*.

LOTHIAN, Andrew: lawyer; regular contributor to *Plays and Players, Times Educational Supplement, Books in Scotland, Journal of the Law Society of Scotland*; author of *So Many Kinds of Yes, Petronius the Book, Lawful Occasions*, glosses on COKE'S *INSTITUTES*, BLACKSTONE on *LAWS OF ENGLAND*, STAIR on *LAWS OF SCOTLAND*, FRANKLIN'S *AUTOBIOGRAPHY*, THACKERAY'S *BOOK OF SNOBS* and MAYHEW'S *LONDON LABOUR AND THE LONDON POOR*.

MacDOUGALL, Carl: Publications: Stories: *The One-Legged Tap-Dancer, Elvis is Dead*. Novels: *Stone Over Water, The Lights Below, The Casanova Papers*. Anthologies: *The Devil and The Giro – Two Hundred Years of Scottish Short Stories*. History: *Glasgow's Glasgow*. To be published in 2000: *Early Days of A Better Nation – A Search for Scottish Identity, Into a Room – Selected Poems of William Soutar, Relative Strangers – A Childhood Memoir*. Has written a number of plays and adaptations for theatre and television. Stories, essays, journalism, and the glosses on SWIFT'S *TALE OF A TUB*, WEBSTER'S *AMERICAN ENGLISH DICTIONARY*, MACAULAY'S *HISTORY*

OF ENGLAND and RUSKIN'S *UNTO THIS LAST*.

MacLAVERTY, Bernard: author of *Cal, Lamb, Gracenotes* (novels), *Time to Dance, Secrets, Great Profundo, Walking the Dog* (short stories), also versions of these as radio, television and cinema plays, and the gloss on SYNGE'S *PLAYBOY OF THE WESTERN WORLD*.

MacNEACAIL, Aonghas: Gaelic poet and journalist, author of *Imaginary Wounds, Sireadh Bradain Sicur (Seeking the Wise Salmon), Cathadh Mor (The Great Snow Battle), An Seachnadh (The Avoiding), Rock and Water, Oideachadh Ceart (Proper Schooling)* (poetry), *Warrior Queen* (myth and legend), gloss on HARDY'S *JUDE THE OBSCURE*.

McALPINE, Morag: bookseller and unpaid editorial assistant from November 1998 to the end.

MALEY, Willy: reader in English Literature at the University of Glasgow, author of *A Spenser Chronology, Salvaging Spenser: Colonialism, Culture and Identity* (criticism), *From the Calton to Catalonia, No Mean Fighter, The Lions of Lisbon* (plays), glosses on WYCHERLEY'S *THE COUNTRY WIFE* and CONGREVE'S *THE WAY OF THE WORLD*.

MONTGOMERY, Catriona: Gaelic poet. Her first book *A'Choille Chiar*, was shared with her sister Morag, the second *Re Na H-Oidhche (The Length of the Night)* is in Gaelic and English. She wrote the gloss on HERRICK'S *HESPERIDES*.

MORGAN, Edwin: poet and critic; author of *The Charcoal-Burner, Columba* (opera librettos), *Nothing Not Giving Messages* (interview), *Essays, Crossing the Border* (criticism), *Beowulf, Sovpoems, Mayakovsky: Wi the Haill Voice*, Rostand's *Cyrano de Bergerac, Collected Translations* (translations), *The Second Life, From Glasgow to Saturn, The New Divan, Sonnets from Scotland, Selected Poems, From the Video Box, Themes on a Variation, Collected Poems, Hold Hands Among the Atoms, Sweeping Out the Dark, Virtual and Other Realities* (poetry), glosses on DRYDEN'S *THE HIND AND THE PANTHER, DON SEBASTIAN & AENEIS,* WORDSWORTH'S *PRELUDE,* POE'S *POEMS* and WHITMAN'S *LEAVES OF GRASS*.

MULRINE, Stephen: translator of plays by Gogol, Gorky, Chekhov, author of plays about Chekhov and Tolstoy, anthologised verse and gloss on URQUHART'S *TRANSLATION OF RABELAIS*.

MURRAY, Joe: Editor of *West Coast Magazine* and *Tales from the Coast* (short stories), former editor of TARANIS BOOKS, poetry editor of MYTHIC HORSE PRESS, author of *Ruchazie Moon and Some Other Poems*, partner in EM-DEE PRODUCTIONS who finally typeset this book.

MORRISON, Fiona: former literary agent who, by suggesting in 1983 that she could get the editor money in advance for a work of NON fiction, prompted him to write the earliest versions of his advertisement and glosses on *The Cloud of Unknowing*, Hobbes' *Leviathan* and Wordsworth's *Lyrical Ballads*.

NATIONAL LIBRARY OF SCOTLAND: This grew from the Scottish Advocates' Library founded by Stair (see page 311) of which Hume (see page 371) was the most famous custodian. It has waived permission fees for reproduction of illustrations on section title pages 267 and 321. The Library bought for its Original Manuscripts archive the Anthology's pre-1998 material, paying money that let the editor complete the book from August 1999 to the end.

ORWELL, George: Gloss on SMOLLETT'S *HUMPHRY CLINKER* is based upon "Tobias Smollett: Scotland's Best Novelist" in *Tribune*, 22 September 1944.

PEARSON, Scott: word processor and researcher who worked with the editor upon this book from 1985 to 1998. Most glosses by the editor are based on his notes.

PETRIE, David: He has taught at the universities of Berghazt, Edinburgh and Verona, and is currently best known in Italy for his struggle to get Italian universities to obey the European Supreme Court law that lecturers of all nationalities in European universities be paid equal wages for equal work. His gloss is on MARX'S *COMMUNIST MANIFESTO*.

PIETTE, Adam: is the author of *Remembering and the Sound of Words: Mallarmé, Proust, Joyce, Beckett* and *Imagination at War: British Fiction and Poetry, 1939-45*. He is currently lecturer at the University of Glasgow. He worked in Swiss universities for ten years previously. He also helps run the Edwin Morgan Centre for Creative Writing (Glasgow/Strathclyde), and he wrote the glosses on STEVENSON'S *MASTER OF BALLANTRAE* and OWEN'S *POEMS*.

SAUNDERS, Donald Goodbrand: Poet, author of *Findrinny*, and *Sour Gas and Crude*, editor and main author of *The Glasgow Diary*; typesetter and research helper from 1998 to 1990.

SOCIETY OF AUTHORS: who gave the author money to work on this book in 1991.

SCOTT, Paul Henderson: President of the *Saltire Society*, editor of *The Age of MacDiarmid* (with A. C. Davis), *A Scottish Postbag* (with George Bruce), *Scotland: A Concise Cultural History, Scotland: An Unwon Cause*, author of *1707: The Union of Scotland and England, Walter Scott and Scotland, John Galt, In Bed with an Elephant, Towards Independence: Essays on Scotland, Andrew Fletcher and the Treaty of Union, Scotland in Europe: A Dialogue with a Sceptical Friend, Defoe in Edinburgh and Other Papers, Still in Bed with an Elephant*, glosses on SMITH'S *WEALTH OF NATIONS*, SCOTT'S *WAVERLEY* and GALT'S *THE MEMBER*.

SCRUTON, Roger: philosopher, editor of *The Salisbury Review*, journalist, author of *A Fortnight's Anger, Francesca, A Dove Descending and other stories* (fiction), *Art and Imagination, The Aesthetics of Architecture, The Meaning of Conservatism, The Politics of Culture and other essays, A Short History of Modern Philosophy, A Dictionary of Political Thought, The Aesthetic Understanding, Kant, Untimely Tracts, Thinkers of the New Left, Sexual Desire, Spinoza, A Land Held Hostage, The Philosopher on Dover Beach and other essays, Xanthippic Dialogues, Modern Philosophy, The Classical Vernacular, Animal Rights and Wrongs, An Intelligent Person's Guide to Philosophy, The Aesthetics of Music, On Hunting*, gloss on BURKE'S *REFLECTIONS ON THE REVOLUTION IN FRANCE*.

SMITH, Iain Crichton: **1928-98:** poet and novelist, author of *The Law and the Grace, Selected Poems, The Exiles, A Life, Collected Poems, Ends and Beginnings* (poems), *Consider the Lilies, The Last Summer, My Last Duchess, In the Middle of the Wood* (novels), glosses on KEATS' *ENDYMION* and CONRAD'S *THE NIGGER OF THE "NARCISSUS"*.

SPENCE, Alan: author of *Plop, Ah!, Glasgow Zen* (poetry), *It's Colours They Are Fine, Stone Garden, The Magic Flute, Way to Go* (fiction), *Sailmaker, Space*

Invaders, *Changed Days*, *The Banyan Tree*, *On the Line* (plays), glosses on VAUGHAN'S *POEMS*, TRAHERNE'S *POEMS*.

THE TIMES LITERARY SUPPLEMENT: If any of the editor's introductions and glosses indicate an awareness of modern scholarship it is because he steadily read this journal from 1985 to 1999 inclusive, extracting useful facts and quotations from the reviews. He hopes the T.L.S. will repay this handsome acknowledgment (and advertisement) with a free subscription for life. (He is 65 at the time of this book's first edition.)

WOLFE-MURRAY, Stephanie: former director of Canongate Publishing who financed work on this book from 1984 to 1988.

WOOLF, Virginia: the gloss on BEHN'S *THE ROVER* and *OROONOKO* is taken from *A Room of One's Own*.

WU, Duncan: reader in English Literature at the University of Glasgow, editor of the *Charles Lamb Bulletin, Wordsworth: Selected Poems* (with Stephen Gill), *Romanticism: An Anthology, Romanticism: A Critical Reader, Women Romantic Poets: An Anthology, A Companion to Romanticism, Selected Writings of William Hazlitt*, author of *Wordsworth's Reading 1770–1799, Wordsworth's Reading 1800–1815, Six Contemporary Dramatists*, articles, reviews and essays in *New Statesman and Society, Daily Telegraph, Literary Review, Fiction Magazine, Review of English Studies, Notes and Queries, The Library*, glosses on PALEY'S *EVIDENCES*, COLERIDGE'S *KUBLA KHAN* and SHELLEY'S *PROMETHEUS UNBOUND*, ARNOLD'S *MIXED ESSAYS* and BROWNING'S *FERISHTAH'S FANCIES*.

PORTRAITS OF CONTRIBUTORS

Chris Boyce

Angus Calder

Allan Cameron

Susan Castillo

Bruce Charlton

Robert Crawford

Michael Donnelly

Marcella Evaristi

Janice Galloway

Robert Grant

Archie Hind around 1970

Archie Hind

James Kelman 1985

James Kelman

Allison Kennedy

Elspeth King

Frank Kuppner

Bruce Leeming

Tom Leonard

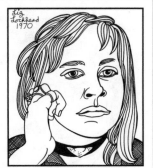

Liz Lochhead

Andrew Lothian

Carl MacDougall

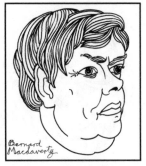

Bernard MacLaverty

Aonghas MacNeacail

Willy Maley

Catriona Montgomery

Edwin Morgan

Stephen Mulrine

David Petrie

Adam Piette **Paul H Scott** **Roger Scruton**

Iain Crichton Smith **Alan Spence** **Duncan Wu**